Comparative Politics

SECOND EDITION

Comparative Politics
An Institutional and Cross-National Approach

GREGORY S. MAHLER

University of Mississippi

PRENTICE HALL, Englewood Cliffs, New Jersey   07632

Library of Congress Cataloging-in-Publication Data

Mahler, Gregory S.
    Comparative politics : an institutional and cross-national
approach / Gregory S. Mahler.—2nd ed.
        p. cm

    Includes bibliographical references and index.
    1. Comparative government.   I. Title.
JF51.M423   1995
320.2—dc20   94-21377
ISBN 0-13-176611-2   CIP

Assistant editor: Jennie Katsaros
Editorial/production supervision and interior design: Barbara Reilly
Cover design: Deluca Design
Production coodinator: Robert Anderson
Copy editor: Eleanor Walter
Editorial assistant: Nicole Signoretti

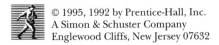 © 1995, 1992 by Prentice-Hall, Inc.
A Simon & Schuster Company
Englewood Cliffs, New Jersey 07632

Printed in the United States of America
10   9   8   7   6   5   4   3   2   1

ISBN 0-13-176611-2

Prentice-Hall International (UK) Limited, *London*
Prentice-Hall of Australia Pty. Limited, *Sydney*
Prentice-Hall Canada Inc., *Toronto*
Prentice-Hall Hispanoamericana, S.A., *Mexico*
Prentice-Hall of India Private Limited, *New Delhi*
Prentice-Hall of Japan, Inc., *Tokyo*
Simon & Schuster Asia Pte. Ltd., *Singapore*
Editora Prentice-Hall do Brasil, Ltda., *Rio de Janeiro*

*For
Marjorie,
Alden,
and
Darcy*

Contents

CHAPTER 15
The Mexican Political System   327

CHAPTER 16
The Nigerian Political System   349

Preface

It is a real pleasure to be able to work on the second edition of a project such as this. It affords the author the opportunity to correct errors that inadvertently slipped into the first edition, as well as making possible the updating of the material included in the book.

As the first edition of this volume was going to press, Germany was evolving from two states to one. While this process still has a long way to go before the German state can be referred to as economically and culturally homogeneous, many significant changes have been made in German political institutions since the first edition appeared.

More dramatic, of course, was the devolution and the ultimate demise of the Union of Soviet Socialist Republics (USSR). The chapter on the USSR that appeared in the first edition, while anticipating substantial changes—because Mikhail Gorbachev had already come to power, and significant changes were appearing in the Soviet Union on a regular basis—was not able to do justice to the extent of change that resulted from Gorbachev's reforms. I do not believe that *anyone* would have predicted at that time the degree of change that has taken place over the last couple of years. In fact, the chapter on Russia in this volume bears very little resemblance to the chapter on the Union of Soviet Socialist Republics in the first edition.

I am very pleased to be able to add to this edition two new "area studies" chapters, one on Canada and one on Nigeria. Both of these additions represent a real improvement. Canada is the largest trading partner of the United States; Canada and the United States share the largest open border in the world, which sees more transborder traffic and commerce than any other. Canada is, despite most Americans' benign ignorance of it, the most important country in the world to the United States, and it is important that American students become aware of that fact.

The addition of Nigeria represents an admission that the first edition of this work was inadequate in its treatment of the Third World. This edition now has an expanded and updated chapter on a Latin American nation (Mexico), and a new chapter on one of Africa's most important, if politically unstable, nations. A good deal of what has happened in Nigeria in the last two decades is characteristic of other African (and Asian, and Latin American) nations, so the Nigerian case study is of some value to us and to our students in our comparative undertaking.

This volume places an emphasis on political institutions—as indicated by the title—for the same reasons as were indicated in the first edition: their *ease of comparison,* their *facility of identification and classification,* and the extent to which they *lend themselves to analysis.* This emphasis on political institutions, combined with the cross-national perspective of this volume, gives students both the tools and the perspective to undertake a meaningful cross-national introduction to the political world in which they must operate.

ACKNOWLEDGMENTS

Once again I would like to acknowledge the assistance and encouragement of the outstanding professionals at Prentice Hall who have been associated with this undertaking. Jennie Katsaros began thinking about a second edition remarkably soon after the first edition appeared. Barbara Reilly oversaw the production process at Prentice Hall. Eleanor Walter was also extremely important in the editing and proofreading process.

I also want to thank the scholars who were contacted by Prentice Hall to review the first edition of the book and make suggestions for the second edition. Margaret C. Gonzalez (Louisiana State University), Jeffrey L. Jackson (State University of New York at Buffalo), Peggy Ann James (University of Wisconsin, Parkside), and Mohsen M. Milani (University of South Florida, Tampa) each made a number of very helpful suggestions. Much of the book's improved comprehensiveness is because of these individuals' suggestions and advice, which were much appreciated.

I also want to acknowledge the assistance of several students who have helped me gather specific material for this new edition. Josh Brown, Jerry Cooper, and Laura Hebert provided invaluable assistance in the revision process.

Finally, I want to once again acknowledge the role of my own students in the production of this book. It was my students' comments that initially convinced me to try my hand at writing a better text, and their subsequent comments have helped me a great deal in deciding what should be included in this type of work and the best way of presenting the material.

Comparative Politics

1

Comparative Political Analysis: An Introduction

WHY DO WE STUDY POLITICS?

Politics. The word conjures up visions of campaigns, elections, and speeches. For the student who is a bit more politically experienced, the word may suggest other images, images such as legislatures, executives, courts, political parties, and interest groups. The more advanced student may also associate concepts such as policy-making, power, influence, socialization, or recruitment with the concept of politics.

One point that is clear to all students is that the term "politics" is an extremely broad one. It means all of the things indicated above, and more. Political science as a discipline can be traced back to the time of Plato (c. 427–c. 347 B.C.) and Aristotle (384–322 B.C.). Aristotle is often referred to as the first "real" political scientist—and we could add "first comparativist" to his credits, as well—because of his study of the many political systems that he found in the political world of his time. His comparisons of constitutions and power structures contributed many words to today's political vocabulary, words such as "politics," "democracy," "oligarchy," and "aristocracy."[1]

The study of politics can be characterized as the study of patterns of systematic interactions between and among individuals and groups in a community or society. This study does not involve random interactions, but rather focuses upon those interactions that involve power or authority. Aristotle saw many different types of relationships involved in the "political" association, but central to the concept was the idea of *rule* or *authority*. In fact, one of the central criteria by which Aristotle classified constitutions in his study involved *where* power or authority to rule was located in the *polis*, the political system.[2] Much more recently, David Easton referred to politics as dealing with the "authoritative allocation of values for a society"[3]—the process by which social goals and standards are set, these standards being binding upon members of society. Harold Lasswell put the question succinctly in the title of his classic work, *Politics: Who Gets What, When, How?*[4] Thus, the study of politics may involve the study of legislatures, the study of voting, the study of political parties, the study of the role of a minority group in a political system, the study of power, more generally the study of how public policy is made, or all of these, and more.

Why do we study politics at all? It could be argued that political scientists since the time of Aristotle have been studying the same things—constitutions, rulers, the ruled, and so on—and we have not yet managed to come up with anything that could be called a perfect society. Why do we continue to study politics, then? If we have not found what we are looking for by now, are we likely to? What *are* we looking for? These are all good questions, and they are hard questions to answer, too.

What are we looking for? The range of subjects of our inquiry is extraordinarily broad. Some political scientists are trying to learn about justice, what it is, and how to get it. Others are concerned with how social policy is made; they may study political structures that are involved in the policy-making process. Others seek to understand why a given election is won by one political party rather than another. Others may seek to understand why people vote for anyone in an election. Still others study politics simply because political relationships seem to be important to our daily lives.

In short, there are as many different reasons for studying political behavior as there are different aspects of political behavior to study. One thing, however, is clear: We cannot charge solely the discipline of political science with the duty of finding the "good life"; political science is only *one* of the social sciences concerned with helping us to understand the complex world around us. The others, including economics, sociology, and anthropology, also study the same general types of social phenomena that we study.

The same type of question can also be asked in relation to comparative politics. Why should we study that field? What can we hope to learn? Before we can answer these questions, we have to decide what "comparative politics" is, and how it can be said to differ from the more generic "politics." Many American political scientists tend to label as comparative politics anything that does not fit into one of the subdisciplines of politics: international relations, methodology, political theory, or American politics. For them, the subdiscipline of comparative politics would include "politics in England," "politics in France," "politics in Russia," "politics in Zimbabwe," and so on. (The general formula is "politics in *X*," where any nation other than the United States could be substituted for the "*X*.")

It should be quickly added that American political scientists are not the only ones to have this perspective. In France, the study of American politics is found within the subdiscipline of comparative politics; there, any area studies other than French politics would fall in the comparative basket. The same could be said for anything other than German politics in Germany, or anything other than Canadian politics in Canada, and so on.

But comparative politics should be more than that. Studying "politics in *X*" more properly can be referred to as "area studies." Area studies, involving a detailed examination of politics within a specific geographical setting, certainly is a legitimate kind of inquiry, but not one that necessarily involves any explicit *comparison*. In fact, Macridis and Brown many years ago criticized comparative politics at the time for not being *truly* comparative, for being almost completely concerned with single cases (for example, "Politics in Egypt") and area studies (for example, "Politics in the Middle East").[5] Comparative politics is—or should be—*more* than area studies.

When we speak of comparative politics in this book, we are talking about the actual method of *comparison*. We all know what comparison is: It involves terms of relativity, terms such as "bigger," "stronger," "freer," "more stable," "less democratic," and so on. Comparative politics, then, involves no more and no less than *a comparative study of politics*—a search for similarities and differences between and among political phenomena, including political institutions (such as legislatures, political parties, or political interest groups), political behavior (such as voting, demonstrating, or reading political pamphlets), or political ideas (such as liberalism, conservatism, or Marxism). Everything that politics studies, comparative politics studies; the latter simply undertakes the study with an explicitly comparative *methodology* in mind.

We could make the argument, in fact, that *all* of political science is comparative. The study of international relations compares diplomatic relations and strategies over time and between nations. The study of political behavior compares and contrasts types of activity in different political contexts. The study of political philosophy compares different perspectives of what ought to be and what is. Even the study of American politics is implicitly comparative: We study the power of the president as compared to the power of the Supreme Court, or why one interest group is more powerful than another, or the change in the relationship between Congress and the president over time, and so on.

Returning to the question of why we should study comparative politics, then, an answer now may be suggested. Doggan and Pelassy have observed that

> Nothing is more natural than to study people, ideas, or institutions in relation to other people, ideas, or institutions. We gain knowledge through reference. . . . We compare to evaluate more objectively our situation as individuals, a community, or a nation.[6]

The study of comparative politics is useful because it gives us a broader perspective of political phenomena and political behavior, and this broader perspective can contribute a great deal to both our understanding and our appreciation of the phenomena we are studying. We compare to escape from our ethnocentrism, our assumptions that everyone behaves the same way we do; we seek to broaden our field of perspective. We compare to discover broader rules of behavior than we might find in more narrow studies.

For example, the simplicity and brevity of the Constitution of the United

States is even more impressive when it is examined alongside the much longer constitutions of other nations.[7] We can better understand the significance of presidential government when we know about alternatives to presidential government. We can learn something about those factors contributing to political stability by studying a country that is regarded as being politically stable. We can learn even more by including an *unstable* country in our study, and looking for similarities and differences between the two countries.

How Do We Study Politics?

There are two broad lanes on the road of inquiry; one is called the *normative* approach, and the other is called the *empirical* approach. The normative approach focuses upon philosophies, norms, or "shoulds." The empirical approach relies on measurement and observation rather than theory or norm. Normativists might investigate exactly the same questions as empiricists, but they go about their investigations differently. Normativists might study justice, equality, the "good society," and so on, and so might empiricists. The difference between the two groups is simply in how these questions would be approached.

Let us take an example to highlight differences in approach. Let us suppose that we have two political scientists interested in studying the concept of "justice." The normative approach might focus on the concept of justice itself: What is justice? What is a just society? How do we decide what is just and what is unjust? Does the concept of justice ever change or vary? *Should* it do so? *Should* all citizens in a society have equal resources? *Should* there be free education? Health care? What policy would principles of justice demand?

The empirical approach would not ask many of these questions. The job of the empiricist is not to ask what is better, or what *should* be, but simply to ask what *is*. The empirical approach might involve interviewing policymakers or justices and ascertaining what *they* feel justice is, and how they use that feeling in their work. It might involve studying capital punishment laws and their enforcement. It might involve examining economic distribution in a variety of settings in order to observe patterns of material distribution. *Do* all people in a society have roughly equivalent resources? *Do* all people in a society have equal access to education? To medical care? In brief, although both approaches would study the same general subject, the approaches would be different.

In fact, the empirical approach does not use only one method of gathering information. Arend Lijphart has suggested that there are *four* basic methods of discovering and establishing general empirical propositions. One of these methods is experimental; the three nonexperimental methods are the case study method, the statistical method, and the comparative method.[8]

The *case study method*[9] involves "the intensive study of individual cases. Case studies run the gamut from the most microcosmic to the most macrocosmic levels of political phenomena."[10] Micro-level work might focus on individuals; macro-level work might focus on political interest groups, regional groups, or institutional groups. An area study, as described above, *might* be a case study (such as voting behavior in Lesotho), but clearly not all case studies involve area studies. In this method, the investigator picks one case—whether that case be a single nation, a single voter, a single election, or a single political structure (such as a legislature, for example)—and studies it. Through the case study method one develops a certain amount of expertise in whatever one is studying, but the scope of one's study may be quite limited.

The *statistical method* involves more sophisticated forms of measurement and observation. Public opinion polls, survey research,[11] and various other forms of quantitative measurement are used to help make the measurement and observation that is characteristic of the empirical approach even more accurate.[12]

The *comparative method* may be likened to two or more case studies put together. We focus upon a particular political structure or behavior, and examine it in a comparative perspective. We look for similarities and differences in different settings. We may do our comparison in one setting, but compare across time—this is called *diachronic comparison*. For example, we may compare a given legislature in 1994 with the same legislature in 1934 and 1894 in order to observe differences in the relative power and structures of that legislature. Or we may compare institutions or behavior at one point in time—*synchronic comparison*—but compare across national borders: for example, examining the role of the legislature in Great Britain with the role of the legislature in Thailand or Jordan.[13]

These three *non*experimental methods are based exclusively upon observation and measurement. The *experimental* approach involves manipulation of variables. That is, whereas in the case study method one simply *observes* something, in the experimental method (as we observed above), one *manipulates* one variable in order to observe its effect upon another variable. This is difficult to do in most aspects of political research, because we are asking questions of extremely broad scope and cannot absolutely control the environment within which we are operating. We cannot, for example, set up two identical presidential elections—one with two candidates and one with three candidates—in order to see the relationship between the number of candidates and voting turnout. Society is too complex to enable us to manipulate and experiment with many political structures and institutions.

Each of the methods in the empirical approach has its own advantages and disadvantages for the researcher. The chief advantage of the comparative approach is the broad perspective that was mentioned earlier. For example, studying the British Parliament in 1994 may tell us a great deal about that institution. We will learn more about the *significance* of what we are observing, however, if we *compare* our observations—either compare the British Parliament of 1994 with those of 1794 and 1894, or compare the British Parliament of 1994 with the Indian Lok Sabha, the Japanese Diet, or the Israeli Knesset in the same year.

The study of comparative politics—or more properly, the comparative approach to the study of politics—is more and more common in the discipline of political science today. We find comparative studies of legislatures,[14] political elites,[15] ideologies,[16] women in politics,[17] constitutions,[18] legal cultures,[19] revolutionary movements,[20] political executives,[21] and political parties.[22] We also find comparative studies of the role of the military in government,[23] of democracies,[24] of *new* democracies,[25] of political development,[26] of political culture,[27] and of political behavior.[28]

THE NATURE OF COMPARATIVE POLITICAL ANALYSIS

How do we go about using the comparative method? If we start indiscriminately comparing every object on the political landscape, in a very short time we will find ourselves inundated with similarities and differences, most of which will turn out to be trivial distinctions either in scope or in significance. Suppose, for example, that we examine the political institution of the legislature. One of the first things that we will note once we start our measurement and observation is that legislatures are *not physically* the same. One legislature may have 100 seats, another may have 75 seats, and a third may have 500 seats. One building may be five stories high, another only two. One legislature may have its seats arranged in straight rows, while another may have its seats arranged in semicircles; indeed, one legislature may give its members individual desks, while another may only have long benches upon which many legislators must crowd.[29]

So what? Before we get bogged down in inconsequential detail (and of course detail *need* not be inconsequential, but such may be the case if proper planning does not precede study), we need to plot a course of inquiry. We need to decide what questions we are interested in investigating, and why, and we need to understand the relationships between and among the objects of our scrutiny.

In this book we are interested in presenting an introduction to the comparative study of politics. What does this mean? It means that we want to show *how* comparative analysis is undertaken, and *why* it is undertaken, and we want to provide examples of the types of things that one might look at while engaging in this kind of study.

In one very useful analysis of the values of comparative inquiry, Adam Przeworski and Henry Teune discussed two general approaches to the comparative method that they called the "most similar systems" design and the "most different systems" design. They argued that most comparativists use the "most similar systems" design: Investigators take two systems that are, for the most part, similar, and subsequently study differences that exist between the two basically similar systems. They may, then, observe the impact of these differences on some other social or political phenomenon. These studies are based on the belief that "systems as similar as possible with respect to as many features as possible constitute the optimal samples for comparative inquiry."[30] If some important differences are found between two essentially similar countries, "then the number of factors attributable to these differences will be sufficiently small to warrant explanation in terms of those differences alone."[31]

An example may help to make this clear. Let us begin by taking two essentially similar nations, say Canada and Australia. These two nations have similar political histories, similar political structures, and essentially similar political cultures.

If we notice that in Australia public policy appears to be made easily and efficiently, while in Canada it appears to be very difficult to enact public policy, we can conclude that the cause of this difficulty is probably *not* the structures, historical factors, and cultural factors that they share. It must be something else that accounts for the difference, and we will be able to look at a relatively small list of possible factors for explanation.

There is, however, a different approach to comparative inquiry that Przeworski and Teune call the "most different systems" approach. This approach allows us to select two or more systems to compare that may *not* be essentially similar. Instead of looking for differences between two or more essentially similar nations, we look for similarities between two or more essentially different nations.[32]

Let us take as an example of this approach the cases of Britain and the United Arab Emirates, two essentially very different nations in terms of their political structures and political behavior. If we find a political behavior that is similar in the two systems and we are interested in knowing why that behavior is the way that it is, we know that the explanation *cannot* lie in the many political structures and patterns of behavior that differ in the two nations; we must look elsewhere.

The point of all of this is to indicate that a number of different approaches are possible within the broad framework that we call the "comparative method." The important consideration in all cases is a theoretical rationale: *Why* are we undertaking the comparison that we are undertaking? What kind of objects do we want to study? As we indicated earlier, the subjects of comparative political inquiry are as disparate and varied as one might imagine. Generally, it can be suggested that there are three broad *categories* of subjects of examination in the comparative study of politics: public policy, political behavior, and governmental structures.

In studies of comparative public policy,[33] the focus of attention is upon *what governments do.* Comparisons may be made between governments of different nations, governments in various stages of development (for instance, "developed" nations vs. "underdeveloped" nations) or governments and policy over time (for instance, the government of Poland in 1974 and the government of Poland in 1994). Although the focus of attention is upon what governments *do*, these studies will invariably pay some attention to the related questions of how governments act, how it is that they do what they do, why governments act, and what stimuli help the governments in question to decide to act in the direction that they do at the time that they do.

A second general thrust of study is oriented to *political behavior.* Studies of this type may focus upon voting behavior, political stability, political elites, leaders in politics, party behavior, and so on.[34] The central ideas of this approach involve the assumption that if one understands how people behave in a political system—and this includes all people, both the leaders and the led—then one will develop an understanding about the political systems within which that behavior takes place. This approach will include some discussion of comparative public policy, primarily as an example of the behavior that is the primary object of study, and also may include some study of the governmental institutions within which the behavior takes place.

The third general approach focuses upon the *governmental institutions* themselves. This type of study may focus upon legislatures, executives, courts, constitutions, legal systems, bureaucracies, and perhaps even political parties.[35] By studying the *institutions* of a regime, it is argued, we are in a better position to understand how the regime operates than we would be with either the behavioral approach alone or the policy approach alone. This approach, as with the others, may well include some secondary subjects of scrutiny. It is entirely possible that a study of governmental institutions might include a subject of policy output as an example of what it is that governmental institutions produce. In addition, a study of governmental institutions might include discussion of political behavior—behavior of governmental officials as well as behavior of the public that may influence the government to act.

Often in comparative analysis we focus our attention on countries. Countries are important to study for a number of reasons, not the least of which is that they happen to be the units into which the contemporary world is divided. That is to say, it would be difficult to engage in comparative research without touching upon the political structure that we call the *nation-state*. Beyond this, however, nation-states often are useful bases for analysis because of what they represent.

A nation, a state, and a nation-state are not, strictly speaking, the same thing.[36] The concept of "nation" has been used in an anthropological way to denote a group of people with shared characteristics, perhaps a shared language, history, or culture. A "state," on the other hand, is a political entity, created by men and women, based upon accepted boundaries, and alterable by men and women. A "nation-state" involves instances in which the nation and the state overlap, where the unit that is found on the map corresponds to a meaningful use of the term "nation."

Political borders can (and do) change, either as a result of war, as a result of agreement between parties involved, or, perhaps, as a result of both. For example, the United States and Mexico have reached agreement over a method of having periodic meetings between the two countries to "correct" the mapping of their border because of the gradual movement of the Rio Grande![37]

It is possible to find self-proclaimed "nations" that are not "states" as the term was used above. For example, many Canadian citizens today who are living in the province of Quebec argue that there is a French "nation" in Canada that should be recognized as a state and should be given independence. They are not content with being a self-perceived nation within a state, having an identifiably different language, culture, and heritage, and having the powers that the Canadian federal balance gives to Quebec alone; many citizens of Quebec want to formalize their perceived differences with the rest of Canada and become an independent nation-state.[38] Similarly, the notion of Zionism at the turn of the twentieth century was based upon the idea that there was a "nation" of Jewish people that were "stateless" in a number of nation-states around the world, and a Jewish state was needed for them to call their home. This Zionist concept subsequently gave birth to the state of Israel.[39] It is indeed ironic that in a very similar manner today Palestinians are claiming the need for a state of their own, independent of Israel, Jordan, Egypt, Saudi Arabia, and other Middle Eastern states.

In any type of comparative political inquiry there are certain analytical problems of which we should be aware that could make our work more difficult than it otherwise might be. The first of these problems involves what we call the *levels of analysis*, and relates to the types of observations and measurements we are using and the types of conclusions that we can draw from those observations and measurements.[40] Generally, we can speak of two levels of data, or observation: an *individual* level, and an *aggregate* or *ecological* level. As the names suggest, the former focuses on individuals, the latter on groups.

We have all met what can be called problems of "over-generalization" in our lives. This is the case when an individual takes an observation made at the general level, over a large population, and assumes that it can be validly applied to *every* individual within that population. For example, to take a nonpolitical case, let us suppose that an individual has had some negative experiences with fast-food restaurants in the past and has decided that she really does not like the food served in these establishments. One day she finds herself travelling and looking for a place to have lunch; the only places available are fast-food restaurants. She enters, expecting to hate the food, and finds to her surprise that the food in *this* establishment is much better than her past experiences would have led her to expect. What we have here is an instance in which she has made a general observation (that is, food in a certain kind of restaurant is not very good), and she has encountered an individual case for which her general rule simply is not valid, or correct.

In political science we refer to this type of error as an "ecological fallacy." That is, we take data, a measurement or an observation from the broad, "ecological" level, and apply it (incorrectly) to an individual case. The observation may be quite correct over a large population, on the general level as a generalization, but that does not mean that it will be correct in *every* individual case within that population, and we need to be aware that when we make generalizations of this kind we may be making an error of this type.

More broadly, we have here a problem of two different levels of analysis—the individual level and the ecological, or aggregate, level. To take a political example, if we find on a national (aggregate) level that Republicans tend to vote more frequently than Democrats, that does not guarantee that every individual Republican that we might meet is going to vote and every individual Democrat that we might meet is not going to vote. It means that, on the whole, over the large population, Republicans *as a group* are more likely to vote than Democrats *as a group*.

To take another example, if we find in our cross-national research that the population of the Ivory Coast has overall a lower level of education than does the population of the United States (two aggregate-level observations), that does not mean that *every* citizen of the Ivory Coast is less educated than *every* citizen of the United States. It might in fact be the case that if we took a random sample from each nation we might select an American with a sixth grade education and a citizen of the Ivory Coast with a Ph.D. from Oxford University. In short, then, an "ecological fallacy" involves (incorrectly) taking what may be a perfectly valid observation or generalization on the aggregate level and assuming that it will *always* apply to *every* case on the individual level. It may apply in *most* cases, which may be why it is a general observation, but we may be leaving ourselves in a vulnerable position if we assume that it will *always* apply in *every* case.

We must also be aware of the reverse of the ecological fallacy, which is called the "individualistic fallacy." This occurs when we make an individual-level observation and incorrectly generalize from it to the aggregate level. For example, to stay with the example we just introduced, it would clearly be incorrect to conclude from meeting one Oxford-educated Ph.D. from the Ivory Coast that all citizens of the Ivory Coast have Ph.D. degrees from Oxford, or that all Ph.D. recipients from Oxford come from the Ivory Coast. To be sure, there may be several individuals in this category, but we would be incorrect to generalize from this individual case to the entire population.

The importance of the "levels of analysis" problem can be summed up, then, by stating that observations made on one level of analysis, either the individual level or the aggregate (or ecological) level, are safely used only on that level. It does regularly happen, of course, that we will undertake study in a situation in which we are forced to use data from one level to learn about another level. We may not be able to afford to question every individual in the Ivory Coast about his or her level of education, and we may *have* to rely on ecological or aggregate data. If all we have available to us is aggregate-level data about education (for example, average number of years of education), or health care (for example, number of hospital beds per population unit), or some similar characteristic, then we have to do our best with the data that we have. We simply must keep reminding ourselves that conclusions we draw from one level of data must be used *carefully* on another level.

Another major pitfall in comparative analysis that we want to try to avoid involves making assumptions about the functions performed by political structures. It is entirely possible that we will find in our research two institutions, or patterns of behavior, that look alike in two different settings, but which perform entirely different functions in their respective settings. We might study, for example, the House of Commons in Britain, and see that the legislature in that setting is most important in the process of selecting government leaders and in establishing governmental legitimacy. In another setting, however, a similarly structured legislature may not be at all significant in the creation of a government or in the establishment of legitimacy, and to assume that because the British House of Commons is significant in this regard, then *all* legislatures are significant in this regard, would be an example of an individualistic fallacy: incorrectly generalizing from the individual (British) level to the aggregate (all legislatures) level.

Although the major role of the U.S. legislature may be that of passing laws, the major function of legislatures such as those that existed in East Germany prior to German unification in 1989 and 1990 was *not* passing laws; in the case of East Germany, the legislature met for only about two days a year and simply rubber-stamped everything suggested to it by the Communist party organization there. The primary function of the legislature in East Germany was that of being a showcase, to demonstrate that East Germany had a "democratically elected" legislature.

The converse of this is also true. Whereas we might find one structure (for instance, a legislature) that performs two entirely different functions in two different nations, we might also find two entirely different structures in two different nations that perform similar or identical functions. Let's use the same general example we just used: Although the Congress performs the legislative function in the United States, the real designing of legislation in East Germany was done by the Central Committee of the Communist party, not the legislature (although the legislature did subsequently give its approval to the measure prior to its becoming "official").

This type of error—of "over-assuming"—can be especially troubling when students from stable, established Western democracies turn their attentions to non-Western systems. The problem of *political ethnocentrism*—of assuming that because political institutions or relationships work one way in stable Western democracies they must work the same way in *all* political systems—is a real one, and we must be continuously on guard against making these types of assumptions, or falling victim to cultural bias, especially when we turn our attention to political systems that are not stable, not "developed," or not Western.[41] Indeed, this paragraph would represent an example of Western ethnocentrism in its own right if we did not observe that in many settings the very institutions or patterns of behavior that we take for granted in the West—such as legislatures or elections—may simply be alien, or irrelevant, to other political cultures. This is a subject to which we shall return in some detail later in this text.

When we undertake comparative political analysis, then, we need to keep our eyes open for errors that we can make by simply assuming too much. We must take the political environment into consideration before drawing conclusions or making broad generalizations; we must make sure to "scout out the landscape" to make sure that we have included in our analysis all of the factors that may be of significance *in that particular political system*. In some systems the list of significant factors may be very long; in others it might be very short.

THE POLITICAL SYSTEM

We have been discussing comparative political analysis, and problems that may ensue in the research process, but we have not as yet laid out any framework for establishing the ground upon which we will base our research. The central concept in discussions of political analysis is that of *the political system*. Generally speaking, not confining ourselves only to the political, there are two types of systems that we can discuss: *analytic* systems and *concrete* systems.

We are all familiar with the concept of a system. Such terms as "nervous system," "electrical system," "stereo system," or even "solar system" are all examples of instances in which we use the word "system" in our daily lives. When we speak of a system such as one of these, we are speaking of a *set of related objects*. With a "concrete" or "real" system we can actually see (or touch, or feel, or measure) the system itself. For example, we could actually touch the components of a skeletal system if we wanted to. In an electrical system we can touch the wires involved and follow them along from one object to another. In the stereo system we can feel the parts of the system, the speakers, the amplifier, the turntable or compact disc player, the tape deck, and so on, and can follow the connecting links (wires) from one component to another. The solar system is a bit more difficult, since we cannot directly *touch* the force connecting the member units, but we can measure it with sophisticated instruments and observations. These, then, are concrete or real systems.

Much more interesting for us as political scientists, however, are "analytic" systems. We can define analytic systems as groups of objects that are connected with one another in an *analytic* way. That is, it is our theories and perceptions that provide the links between the objects in question. The political system that we refer to as American government is not "real" or "concrete" in the same manner that the plumbing system of a house is. We cannot actually touch or feel the links between and among the House of Representatives and the Senate and the Supreme Court and the White House and the governmental bureaucracy. (Literally, of course, we probably could make the argument that one could touch a telephone wire and trace it to a central switchboard where all Washington telephones are connected, and thereby claim that these institutions are, in fact, physically connected, but that would be stretching the point.) The important and meaningful connection among these institutions is *power*, and the power relationship that is to be found in the Constitution of the United States and in American political tradition.[42]

When we talk about "developing nations" or "the political left" or "legislatures" or "interest groups" or "the Middle East," we are using analytic concepts to bring together groups of objects—in many cases individuals, in other cases regions, nations, or institutions—that we perceive to have something in common. These are *political systems*, sets of political objects or political concepts that are theoretically related to each other in some analytic way. These systems of objects—analytic systems—are the basis of comparative political research.

We cannot stop at the level of the system, however. Systems can be broken down into *subsystems*. A subsystem is an analytical component of a political system that is a system in its own right. The American political system has many subsystems, each of which could be studied on its own. To begin, of course, there are fifty subsystems that we call states. If we wanted to, we could study the political system of one state on its own; if our focus is on the United States, however, the state would be perceived as a subsystem, not a system. Other subsystems of the American political system might be "the bureaucracy," "the legislature," "political parties," "men," "women," and so on. We can also talk about sub-subsystems, sub-sub-subsystems, and on and on.

Similarly, we can use the term "supersystem" to refer to that collection of objects of which our focus is only a part. If our focus is (still) on the American political system, then a supersystem might be "Western governments," or "democracies," or "presidential systems"—all groups of objects of which our focus is simply an example. Table 1.1 provides an illustration of the way in which we can use these terms.

We can shift our point of focus, too. If our focus is the American political system, then the Congress is a subsystem, and the House of Representatives is a sub-subsystem, and the Foreign Affairs Committee of the House of Representatives is a sub-sub-subsystem, and Republicans on the Foreign Affairs Committee are a sub-sub-sub-subsystem. If our focus were the House of Representatives, the Congress would

TABLE 1.1
Using Systems as Frames of Reference

Level	Set 1	Set 2
Super-supersystem	World governments	Constitutional systems
Supersystem	Democracies	Presidencies
System	(focus) **The American Political System**	
Subsystem	A state	The Congress
Sub-subsystem	A county	The Senate

be a supersystem, the American political system would be a super-supersystem, and the Foreign Affairs Committee would be a subsystem, and so on.

Although these terms may seem confusing at first, they can be extremely valuable in our analysis of politics. Unlike chemists or physicists, who may use sophisticated physical instruments to help them in their measurement and analysis, we political scientists have to rely on concepts and theoretical frameworks to help us with our measurement, observation, and analysis. Terminology, then, is important for us.

Just as with many of the other terms we have introduced in this chapter, the concept of a "system" is not as simple as it first appears. There have been a number of different approaches to political systems in the discipline over the years, each approach developing its own vocabulary and literature. Probably the two biggest contributions to "systems theories," in terms of their subsequent generation of literature in the discipline, have been made by David Easton and Gabriel Almond.

Easton's variation on the political system first introduced in the mid-1960s has been referred to as "Input-Output" analysis.[43] Although many political scientists today feel that Easton's variation never realized its potential as a theoretical framework capable of explaining the operation of the political system, it did give rise to a great deal of literature on "systems theory," and it can still be cited as an example of one way of looking at the political system, even if it does not provide all of the answers that earlier theorists had hoped it might.

Easton's analytic framework viewed the political system as a continuously operating mechanism, with "demands" and "supports" going in ("inputs"), and authoritative decisions and actions coming out ("outputs"). Demands are defined as "an expression of opinion that an authoritative allocation with regard to a particular subject matter should or should not be made by those responsible for doing so."[44] Supports are those inputs between the political system and its environment that remain after demands have been subtracted.[45] The framework includes very elaborate regulatory mechanisms for preventing demand overloads and for maintaining the smooth operation of the system.

One of the major criticisms of Easton's framework involved its ethnocentrism, a concept we introduced earlier. Many of the assumptions of Easton's model suggest that there will inevitably be the types of political structures and political behaviors commonly found in stable Western democracies (for example, legislatures, elections, bureaucracies, and so on), assumptions that are clearly not always valid. Further, the model was criticized by many because of what they suggested was an implied goal of "system maintenance" that put too much emphasis on political stability and that was inherently conservative.

The other major variation on systems theory was suggested by Gabriel Almond, and is referred to as "structural-functional" analysis.[46] This kind of analysis focuses upon what Almond refers to as political "structures," by which he means either political institutions or political behavior, and political "functions," by which he means the consequences of the institutions or the behavior. This kind of analysis asks the basic question, "What structures perform what functions and under what conditions in a political system?" While "function" may be interpreted to mean "consequence," the framework introduces a new term as well, "dysfunction." Simply put, a function (or "eufunction") is a *good* consequence, and a dysfunction is a *bad* consequence.

Both of these approaches, it should be explicitly noted, are quite sophisticated and quite substantial—far beyond our ability to discuss them adequately in this context. In addition, they are not the *only* variations on what is referred to as "systems theory." They are, however, the major variations, and the test of time has indicated their impact on the discipline of political science. The concept of the political system, whether we use Easton's input-output framework, or Almond's structure-function framework, or any of a number of other variations on the theme, is another tool we have at our disposal to help in our cross-national comparison.

It is important that we explicitly note that a political system need not be the same thing as a nation or a state. It may be convenient to use a nation or state as a point of departure in comparative analysis, but a "system" may be something else, as well. As we indicated above, we may want to study a "legislative system"; that is, a collection of objects that are in some analytic way related and whose relationship is based upon legislation or the legislature. We may want to study the OECS—the Organization of Eastern Caribbean States. We may want to study electoral systems. We may want to focus our attention on the individual level and study the systems of political thought that give rise to political actions. In short, although nation-states are convenient to study because we can find them on a map and their borders are (relatively) clearly defined, many of the subjects of comparative political analysis do not lie clearly within one set of national borders.

POLITICAL CULTURE

The concept of *political culture* is terribly important in the study of comparative politics. As Gabriel Almond has noted, "something like a notion of political culture has been around as long as men have spoken and written about politics,"[47] and related terms, terms such as "subculture," "elite political culture," "political socialization," and "cultural change," have also been used in a variety of settings since time immemorial. Indeed, Almond argues that the concept of political culture played a very important role in Plato's *Republic* when Plato observed that governments vary as the dispositions of men vary, and that there must be as many of the one as there are of the other. For we cannot suppose that States are made of "oak and rock" and not out of the human natures which are in them.[48]

The concept of a political culture can be traced from Plato through Aristotle, Machiavelli, Montesquieu, Rousseau, Tocqueville, and up to modern times.[49]

Political culture, Almond tells us, "is not a theory; it refers to a set of variables that may be used in the construction of theories."[50] It consists of "the system of empirical beliefs, expressive symbols, and values which defines the situation in which political action takes place."[51] It "is concerned with 'psychological orientation toward social objects . . . the political system as internalized in the cognitions, feelings, and evaluations of citizens.'"[52] The major dimensions of political culture include a sense of national identity, attitudes one holds toward oneself as a member of a polity, attitudes one holds toward one's fellow citizens, attitudes and expectations about governmental performance, and knowledge of and attitudes about the political decision-making processes.

In fact, scholars tell us, we can refer to three different directions in which political culture runs: a "system" culture, a "process" culture, and a "policy" culture.[53] The system dimension of political culture is made up of attitudes toward the nation, the regime, and the authorities who control power at any given time. This includes values related to national identity, regime legitimacy, institutional legitimacy, and the effectiveness of individuals who hold significant political positions. The process dimension of political culture is made up of attitudes toward the role that the individual him- or herself plays in the political arena, and attitudes about other political actors. The policy dimension of political culture focuses upon the results of politics, the "outputs" of the political system.

As we suggested above, the political culture is important because it refers to a number of political variables that we may use in our analysis of the political world and in our construction of political theories. Political culture has been argued to be significant in the process of political development (something to which we shall turn our attention in just a moment), in the development of regime legitimacy, in economic and industrial development, and in social integration and regime stability. It is a concept that we shall use on a number of occasions in this study, especially in the second half of this text when we turn our attention to some area studies to illustrate the importance of the political institutions and political behaviors that we shall examine in the first part of this book.

As we noted previously, however, when we consider political culture we must be aware of the danger of an *ethnocentric* approach to our study. We should not make the assumption that the way social relationships and institutions exist in our culture and society is necessarily the same way that they exist in all other societies; nor is it the standard for institutions and behavior that other cultures strive to develop. There are *many* characteristics of what can be called "Western culture" that are definitely not sought by non-Western societies. Indeed, there are many characteristics of contemporary Western society that we ourselves do not like, such as crime rates, drug problems, the weakening of the nuclear family unit, and so on. We must keep in mind that Western capitalist democracies are not always the model chosen by others in the world, and whether we agree with this or not, we must be careful not to assume that our way is the only way.

THE CONCEPT OF POLITICAL DEVELOPMENT

At the same time that we state that one of the primary objects of comparative political inquiry is the nation-state, or the country, we should be sure to add a temporal dimension to our analysis. That is, we do not want to fall victim to the (often implicit) assumption that the political world always stays the same. Just as times change in relation to fashions and fads, so too do political eras change, and what may be acceptable behavior or thought in one era may not be acceptable in another. Throughout political history we can see the development, or popularization, of many different ideas over time: Tyrannicide (the killing of unjust kings) was argued to be "just" at one point in time; revolutions and democratic institutions flourished in the eighteenth century, and so on.

In addition to being able to trace the development of political ideas across time, we can take a different temporal approach and look at the *development* across time of nation-states.[54] Individual nation-states do not spring fully blossomed and mature into the contemporary political world. *Political development* and *modernization* are processes; sometimes these processes happen speedily while at other times they take longer. Sometimes the evolution involved is gradual; other times it is abrupt, violent, and painful.

Often the terms "modernization" and "development" are used interchangeably to refer to the movement of a nation-state from one evolutionary stage to another. Some scholars, however, distinguish between the two terms:

> [Development is] an evolutionary process in which indigenous institutions adapt and control change and are not simply caught up in imitating and reacting to outside forces. Modernization is often contemporary, imported, and creates a dependency on the technologically advanced urban-industrial centers without helping local political and social institutions to grow and adapt. Development means that a system has some ability to be selective in the type and pace of changes, often imported, that occur in a country.[55]

In 1963 a long-term study of political modernization and political development was initiated by the Committee on Comparative Politics of the Social Science Research Center at the Center for Advanced Study in the Behavioral Studies at Palo Alto, California. This series of research projects yielded several studies that were published by the Princeton University Press in a series called Studies on Political Development.[56] Although a number of different subjects are covered in these studies, they all are based on the premise that political development—nation building—involves a number of "crises," and *all* nations, modern or not, go through these crises.[57] Each of these five crises will be briefly described here.

The Crisis of Identity

How do individuals in a political regime describe themselves politically? This crisis was faced in the United States in the late eighteenth century, when individuals had to learn to identify themselves first as Americans, rather than as Virginians or New Yorkers, for example. Again in 1860, large numbers of Americans started to think of their primary political identities as something other than American (for instance, "Southerner").

In the contemporary political world, one of the major hurdles faced by new and developing nations is the need to help citizens develop a national identity. Failure to do so can result in national stress and possibly civil war: The situation in Lebanon in which citizens identified themselves less as "Lebanese" than as Christians, Moslems, or Palestinians led to a civil war there; Ibo tribesmen in Nigeria did not want to think of themselves as Nigerians, and attempted (unsuccessfully) to break away from Nigeria and form a new nation, Biafra. The problem, however, is not restricted to new or "underdeveloped" nations: Recent civil war and genocide in what was Yugoslavia is a further illustration of the quest by ethnic groups to develop their own national identities.[58] Many French-Canadians today identify themselves as "Quebecois," not Canadians, and this continues to place stress on the Canadian political system. Similar situations exist for the Sikh population in India's Punjab region, the Eritreans in Somalia, and the Tamil population in Sri Lanka, among others.

The Crisis of Legitimacy

The concept of "legitimacy" suggests a sense on the part of the public that the government in power has a right to exist, or is acting "appropriately." People may disagree with specific governmental decisions or actions without necessarily denying the legitimacy of the regime. When governments lose their appearance of legitimacy to a major proportion of the populace, they have great difficulty staying in power and do so usually only with the coercive support of the military. Recent regimes that were dissolved as a result of a crucial loss of perceived legitimacy were in Iran (with the downfall of the government of the Shah in 1979), the Philippines (with the downfall of the Marcos regime from 1984 to 1986), and Nicaragua (with the downfall of the Somoza regime in 1979).

In other cases, regimes were not toppled but significant instances of social disruption occurred when groups in society ceased to recognize the legitimacy of government. A good case in point is the role of the Parti Québecois in Canada in advocating Quebec's secession from the Canadian federation. Similarly, the behavior of the Sikhs in India's Punjab state resulted in many deaths and much social disruption. Perhaps most notably in recent years, many governments in Eastern Europe—including those of East Germany, Poland, and Czechoslovakia—fell when substantial segments of their populations concluded that the governments of these states were no longer legitimate.

To a large degree the concept of legitimacy refers to the same general phenomenon that was called "institutionalization" by Samuel Huntington in his classic work *Political Order in Changing Societies*. There he defined institutionalization as the "process by which organizations and procedures acquire value and stability. The level of institutionalization of any political system can be defined by the adaptability, complexity, autonomy, and coherence of its organizations and procedures."[59]

It is often difficult to define precisely the point at which a loss of legitimacy may become critical. Clearly, there will always be some people in any regime who do not feel that the regime is constructed in, or is acting in, a legitimate manner. Established regimes can tolerate some of this thought; newer regimes can tolerate less, since they have less of a reserve of past legitimacy upon which to draw. At some point, one that depends upon the regime and the political system involved, a loss of legitimacy may become critical and the system may suffer irreparable harm.

The Crisis of Penetration

Are laws enforced? Do the policy decisions of the government "trickle down" to all levels of society, or are there areas of the nation in which the laws and policy decisions of the regime simply do not apply? To the extent that a geographic district may exist in which the laws of the regime are simply ignored, or to the extent that certain specific laws or administrative guidelines from the government are ignored throughout the nation (for instance, legislation prohibiting the consumption of alcohol), we can speak about problems of penetration. Examples of this might include American national civil rights policies in the early 1960s, when federal guidelines were not respected in Southern states (for example, the Mississippi National Guard had to be nationalized to enforce federal civil rights laws), or government encouragement of birth control in some Latin American or African nations.

The crisis of penetration, then, refers to the government's ability to follow through on, and to enforce, its decisions. Governments that are not able to do this, those that are not taken seriously by their publics, are less stable than others.

The Crisis of Participation

A system may suffer stress in both quantitative and qualitative dimensions of participation. Quantitatively, too little participation may result in a lack of legitimacy (for example, an election in which only 15 percent of the population participated), and too much participation—perhaps too many demands being made—may put too great a burden on the structures of the regime that are designed to respond to such communications. Qualitatively, relatively few demands that are in themselves extreme may put stress on the system. What should the role of the "mass" public be in relation to the "elite" of the regime? Examples of this type of question, which may create a dimension of crisis in a political regime, would be: (a) a racial majority demanding political opportunity in a regime that has been racially discriminatory, such as existed for many years in Rhodesia (now Zimbabwe) or such as exists today in South Africa; (b) a mass demonstration bringing hundreds of thousands of protesters together to criticize a regime, such as the kinds of demonstrations that were crucial in the downfall of Ferdinand Marcos in the Philippines in 1986 or the Shah of

Iran in 1979; or (c) individuals refusing to pay their income taxes as an act of political protest.

The Crisis of Distribution

One of the most visible problems of developing nations today is a *material* one: Food, medical supplies, housing, water, electricity, and so forth either are not being equitably distributed in a society, or, if they are equitably distributed, are not sufficient. (We should note, of course, that these problems are not restricted to developing nations. Some areas of the United States contain shocking examples of these same problems.) New nations have an incredible set of demands made upon them, and among the most visible of these demands are those related to distributive goods. Long food lines in Ethiopia, which resulted in food riots, led to the eventual overthrow of Emperor Haile Selassie in 1974. A lack of consumer goods in the Soviet Union was credited with motivating former Soviet President Mikhail Gorbachev to push for greater reforms in the economic sector there, reforms that eventually contributed to a dissolution of the political regime. A society in which a group feels that it is not receiving its fair share of the material benefits of government is a society ready for revolution.

These five dimensions of crisis in relation to problems of political development start to tell the story of the concerns confronting many of the developing nations today, not to mention the older and more established industrial democracies. These crises are exacerbated in the developing world, however, by more readily apparent problems such as low levels of literacy, poor general health care, high infant mortality, and an inability to control rapidly rising populations. To the extent that these and other problems remain and worsen, new nations will continue to experience great instability and turmoil.

The study of political development and political modernization involves considerably more than has been presented in this section. This text devotes a full chapter—Chapter 3—to an examination of political development and political modernization, and how these processes relate to a number of other subjects such as political economics.

THE INSTITUTIONAL APPROACH

The approach to comparative politics that is used in this volume is an *institutional* one. Although there is no doubt that an emphasis on either public policy or political behavior would be a vehicle that would work in an introduction to comparative politics, the institutional approach has been selected here for several reasons. First, it *lends itself to generalization* more readily than do the other approaches. When we learn how a "Westminster model" parliamentary system works in Britain, and we subsequently learn that Grenada, Tuvalu, and India have essentially Westminster-model parliamentary systems, we can relatively easily, and relatively accurately, transfer a good deal of what we learned about one system to another. An emphasis on public policy (for instance, British housing policy) or political behavior (for instance, British voting patterns) would not permit this transferability.

Second, the institutional approach *is more enduring*. Although it is true that individual nation-states do change their basic political institutions on occasion, it is much more often the case that political institutions do not change as radically or as frequently as either individual policies or aggregate behavior. The French electoral system changed in 1985, and changed again shortly thereafter, but this was a true deviation from the French norm and from the norm we shall see in other settings. On the other hand, housing policy, health policy, foreign policy, and environmental policy are subject to political change as the corresponding political climate changes.

Third, the institutional approach *lends itself to observation and measurement* more readily than do other approaches. Although polities such as Britain, France, or Germany have been the subject of a great deal of policy analysis and examination of political behavior, there are many polities in the world in which sophisticated policy analysis is simply not done, nor is detailed analysis of political behavior undertaken. We *can*, on the other hand, undertake an examination of those systems' political institutions.

To be sure, the institutional approach does not work all of the time; thus we will not use that approach exclusively here. We shall discuss aspects of public policy and political behavior in our analysis here, but the *primary* vehicle for analysis will be that of political institutions. In the case of our description of Russia, for example, we shall begin by observing that it is a polity in which an institutional approach has not appeared to work very well in recent history, and there we shall focus our efforts in alternative directions. However, on balance, we believe that the institutional approach is the best vehicle for an introduction to comparative politics.

THE COMPARATIVE METHOD IN PERSPECTIVE

Throughout the remainder of this text we shall endeavor to follow the guidelines that we have set down thus far as to the comparative method of inquiry. The value of the comparative method is in the broad perspective that it offers the student of political science; we will focus upon this broad perspective as we continue.

In the next several chapters we will develop a base for further inquiry. We will present a number of different political structures and behaviors comparatively, looking first at the existence of a structure in one setting and then at the same structure elsewhere. We will also search for similarities and differences in the structures under examination, in an effort to understand how the political environments within which the structures exist have influenced them. Subsequently, we will turn our attention to a number of brief area studies "portraits," which will give us the opportunity to better understand the political contexts within which the various political structures operate.

Notes

1. See Ernest Barker, ed. and trans., *The Politics of Aristotle* (New York: Oxford University Press, 1970), pp. xi–xix.
2. Ibid., p. 111.
3. David Easton, *A Framework for Political Analysis* (Englewood Cliffs, N.J.: Prentice Hall, 1965), p. 50.
4. Harold Lasswell, *Politics: Who Gets What, When, How?* (New York: McGraw-Hill, 1936).
5. See Roy C. Macridis and Bernard E. Brown, eds., *Comparative Politics: Notes and Readings* (Homewood, Ill.: Dorsey Press, 1977), pp. 2–4.
6. Mattei Dogan and Dominique Pelassy, *How to Compare Nations: Strategies in Comparative Politics* (Chatham, N.J.: Chatham House, 1984), p. 3.
7. See, for example, the historical work by George Billias, *American Constitutionalism Abroad: Selected Essays in Comparative Constitutional History* (New York: Greenwood Press, 1990), or Gary Jacobsohn, *Apple of Gold: Constitutionalism in Israel and the United States* (Princeton, N.J.: Princeton University Press, 1993).
8. Arend Lijphart, "The Comparable Cases Strategy in Comparative Research," *Comparative Political Studies* 8 (1975): 159. See also Arend Lijphart, "Comparative Politics and the Comparative Method," *American Political Science Review* 65 (1971): 682–693, and Theodore Meckstroth, "'Most Different Systems' and 'Most Similar Systems': A Study in the Logic of Comparative Inquiry," *Comparative Political Studies* 8 (1975): 132. Mattei Dogan's book, *How to Compare Nations: Strategies in Comparative Politics* (Chatham, N.J.: Chatham House, 1990), does a very good job of discussing these issues at greater length, as does the book by Louis Cantori and Andrew Ziegler, *Comparative Politics in the Post-Behavioral Era* (Boulder, Colo.: Lynne Rienner, 1988). A more recent study is by Charles Ragin and Howard Becker, eds., *What Is a Case? Exploring the Foundations of Social Inquiry* (New York: Cambridge University Press, 1992).
9. See James B. Christoph and Bernard F. Brown, *Cases in Comparative Politics* (Boston: Little, Brown, 1976) for a good example of this approach.
10. See Harry Eckstein, "Case Study and Theory in Political Science," in Fred Greenstein and Nelson Polsby, eds., *Handbook of Political Science: Strategies of Inquiry* (Reading, Mass.: Addison-Wesley, 1975), p. 79.
11. A very good essay on this can be found in the essay by Richard Boyd and Herbert Hyman, "Survey Research," in Greenstein and Polsby, eds., *Handbook of Political Science: Strategies of Inquiry*, pp. 265–350.
12. For a good introductory-level example of this approach, see Neil Agnew and Sandra Pyke, *The Science Game* (Englewood Cliffs, N.J.: Prentice Hall, 1978).
13. A good essay on the comparative method may be found in Michael Curtis, *Comparative Government and Politics: An Introductory Essay in Political Science* (New York: Harper and Row, 1978).
14. For example, Allan Kornberg, ed., *Legislatures in Comparative Perspective* (New York: David McKay, 1973), Jean Blondel, *Comparative Legislatures* (Englewood Cliffs, N.J.: Prentice Hall, 1973), or Gerhard Loewenberg and Samuel Patterson, *Comparing Legislatures* (Boston: Little, Brown, 1979). More recent studies include David Olson and Michael Mezey, *Legislatures in the Policy Process: The Dilemmas of Economic Policy* (New York: Cambridge University Press, 1991), and Philip Norton, *Legislatures* (Oxford: Oxford University Press, 1990).
15. For example, Andreas Kappeler, *The Formation of National Elites* (New York: New York University Press, 1992), or Neil Nevitte and Roger Gibbins, *New Elites in Old States: Ideologies in the Anglo-American Democracies* (New York: Oxford University Press, 1990).
16. For example, Lyman Sargent, *Contemporary Political Ideologies* (Fremont, Calif.: Wadsworth Publishing Co., 1993), Roy Macridis, *Contemporary Political Ideologies: Movements and Regimes* (New York: HarperCollins, 1992), or Mostafa Rejai, *Political Ideologies: A Comparative Approach* (Armonk, N.Y.: M.E. Sharpe, 1991).
17. For example, Michael Genovese, ed., *Women as National Leaders* (Newbury Park, Calif.: Sage Publications, 1993), Lois Lovelace Duke, ed., *Women in Politics: Outsiders or Insiders?* (En-

glewood Cliffs, N.J.: Prentice Hall, 1993), or Joanne Rajoppi, *Women in Office: Getting There and Staying There* (Westport, Conn.: Bergin and Garvey, 1993).

18. For example, Ivo Duchacek, *Power Maps: Comparative Politics of Constitutions* (Santa Barbara, Calif.: Clio Press, 1973), or C. Preston King and Andrea Bosco, *A Constitution for Europe: A Comparative Study of Federal Constitutions and Plans for the United States of Europe* (London: University of London Press, 1991).

19. For example, Csaba Varga, ed., *Comparative Legal Cultures* (New York: New York University Press, 1992).

20. See, for example, Thomas H. Greene, *Comparative Revolutionary Movements: Search for Theory and Justice* (Englewood Cliffs, N.J.: Prentice Hall, 1990).

21. For example, Richard Rose and Ezra Suleiman, eds., *Presidents and Prime Ministers* (Washington, D.C.: American Enterprise Institute, 1980), or Taketsugu Tsurutani and Jack Gabbert, eds., *Chief Executives: National Political Leadership in the United States, Mexico, Great Britain, Germany, and Japan* (Pullman: Washington State University Press, 1992).

22. For example, L. Hamon Zeigler, *Political Parties in Industrial Democracies* (Itasca, Ill.: F.E. Peacock Publishers, 1993), or Bruce Graham, *Representation and Party Politics* (Cambridge, Mass.: Basil Blackwell, 1993).

23. For example, Eric Nordlinger, *Soldiers in Politics: Military Coups and Governments* (Englewood Cliffs, N.J.: Prentice Hall, 1977). Two more specific examples of this research would include Avner Yaniv, *National Security and Democracy in Israel* (Boulder, Colo.: Lynne Rienner Publishers, 1993), and Joseph Keddell, Jr., *The Politics of Defense in Japan: Managing Internal and External Pressures* (Armonk, N.Y.: M.E. Sharpe, 1993).

24. Arend Lijphart, *Democracies: Patterns of Majoritarian and Consensus Government in Twenty-One Countries* (New Haven, Conn.: Yale University Press, 1984), T. J. Pempel, ed., *Uncommon Democracies: The One-Party Dominant Regimes* (Ithaca, N.Y.: Cornell University Press, 1990), or Arend Lijphart, *Electoral Systems and Party Systems: A Study of Twenty-Seven Democracies, 1945–1990* (New York: Oxford University Press, 1994).

25. Enrique A. Baloyra, ed., *Comparing New Democracies: Transition and Consolidation in Mediterranean Europe and the Southern Cone* (Boulder, Colo.: Westview Press, 1987), or Francisco Weffort, *New Democracies, Which Democracies?* (Washington, D.C.: Woodrow Wilson Center, 1992).

26. For example, Dirk Berg-Schlosser, *Political Stability and Development: A Comparative Study of Kenya, Tanzania, and Uganda* (Boulder, Colo.: Lynne Rienner, 1990).

27. For example, the classic in this area is Gabriel Almond and Sidney Verba, eds., *The Civic Culture Revisited* (Boston: Little, Brown, 1980). See also Daniel H. Levine, ed., *Constructing Culture and Power in Latin America* (Ann Arbor: University of Michigan Press, 1993).

28. For example, Richard Niemi and Herbert Weisberg, eds., *Controversies in Voting Behavior* (Washington, D.C.: Congressional Quarterly Press, 1993), or William Crotty, ed., *Political Science: Looking to the Future* (Evanston, Ill.: Northwestern University Press, 1991).

29. For an incredible collection of comparative data dealing with legislatures, see Valerie Herman, ed., *Parliaments of the World* (London: Macmillan, 1976). There is an entire section of this 985-page book dealing with seating arrangements in legislatures, and make sure to note Table 21 on seating arrangements, which is itself seven pages long!

30. Adam Przeworski and Henry Teune, *The Logic of Comparative Social Inquiry* (New York: Wiley, 1970), p. 32.

31. Ibid. See also Dogan and Pelassy, *How to Compare Nations*, chap. 16, "Comparing Similar Countries," pp. 117–126.

32. See Dogan and Pelassy, *How to Compare Nations*, chap. 17, "Comparing Contrasting Nations," pp. 127–132.

33. For example, see Stuart Nagel, ed., *Global Policy Studies: International Interaction Toward Improving Public Policy* (New York: St. Martin's Press, 1991), or Thomas Lynch and Lawrence Martin, eds., *Handbook of Comparative Public Budgeting and Financial Management* (New York: Marcel Dekker, 1993).

34. For example, Lewis Bowman and G. R. Boynton, eds., *Political Behavior and Public Opinion: Comparative Analysis* (Englewood Cliffs, N.J.: Prentice Hall, 1974).

35. There are few integrated and structural comparative studies. One is left to rely on more specific comparative studies, such as comparative studies of legislatures (see note 14), or comparative studies of executives (see note 21), for example.

36. See, for example, Leslie Pal and Rainer-Olaf Schultz, eds., *The Nation-State Versus Continental Integration: Canada in North America, Germany in Europe* (Bochum: Universitatsverlag Dr. N. Brockmeyer, 1991), or Alan Milward, *The European Rescue of the Nation-State* (Berkeley: University of California Press, 1992).

37. See the article by Douglas Littlefield, "The Rio Grande Compact of 1929: A Truce in an Interstate River War," *Pacific Historical Review* 60:4 (November 1991): 497–516.

38. See Kenneth McRoberts, *English Canada and Quebec: Avoiding the Issue* (North York, Ont.: York University Press, 1991), or Scott Adams, *Quebec, Meech Lake, and Canada: Two Languages, Two Cultures, Two Nations!* (Vancouver, B.C.: Habitat Canada Publishing, 1990).

39. A very good discussion of the concept of Zionism as a nationalist movement can be found in the study by Shlomo Avineri, *The Making of Modern Zionism* (New York: Basic Books, 1981).

40. Good discussions of problems of levels of analysis and other methodological difficulties can be found in Robert Bernstein and James A. Dyer, *An Introduction to Political Science Methods* (Englewood Cliffs, N.J.: Prentice-Hall, 1992), David Bositis, *Research Designs for Political Science: Contrivance and Demonstration in Theory and Practice* (Carbondale: Southern Illinois University Press, 1990), or Ronald Kinder and Thomas Palfrey, eds., *Experimental Foundations of Political Science* (Ann Arbor: University of Michigan Press, 1992).

41. Two very good—but different—illustrations of this concept can be found in Hugh D. Forbes, *Nationalism, Ethnocentrism, and Personality* (Chicago: University of Chicago Press, 1985), and Howard J. Wiarda, *Ethnocentrism in Foreign Policy: Can We Understand the Third World?* (Washington, D.C.: American Enterprise Institute for Public Policy Research, 1985). A different perspective can be found in Molefi K. Asante, *The Afrocentric Idea* (Philadelphia: Temple University Press, 1987).

42. A good recent example of the use of this perspective in a non-American context can be found in the article by Ada W. Finifter and Ellen Mickiewicz, "Redefining the Political System of the USSR: Mass Support for Political Change," *American Political Science Review* 86:4 (1992): 857–875.

43. David Easton, *A Systems Analysis of Political Life* (New York: Wiley, 1965).

44. Ibid., p. 38.

45. Ibid., p. 159.

46. Gabriel Almond, "Introduction," in Gabriel Almond and James Coleman, eds., *The Politics of the Developing Areas* (Princeton, N.J.: Princeton University Press, 1960).

47. Gabriel Almond, "The Intellectual History of the Civic Culture Concept," in Gabriel Almond and Sidney Verba, *The Civic Culture Revisited* (Boston: Little, Brown, 1980), p. 1.

48. Ibid., p. 2.

49. Ibid.

50. Ibid., p. 26.

51. Sidney Verba, "Comparative Political Culture," in Lucian Pye and Sidney Verba, eds., *Political Culture and Political Development* (Princeton, N.J.: Princeton University Press, 1965), p. 513.

52. Carole Pateman, "The Civic Culture: A Philosophic Critique," in Almond and Verba, *The Civic Culture Revisited*, p. 66.

53. This is a summation of a much more detailed discussion in Almond, "Intellectual History," pp. 27–29.

54. A very good recent work in this area is by Harry Eckstein, *Regarding Politics: Essays on Political Theory, Stability, and Change* (Berkeley: University of California Press, 1992).

55. Herbert Winter and Thomas Bellows, *People and Politics* (New York: Wiley, 1977), pp. 352–353.

56. Among the many volumes published in the series (Princeton, N.J.: Princeton University Press) were the following: Lucian Pye, ed., *Communications and Political Development* (1963),

Joseph LaPalombara, ed., *Bureaucracy and Political Development* (1963), Robert E. Ward and Dankwart Rustow, eds., *Political Modernization in Japan and Turkey* (1964), James S. Coleman, ed., *Education and Political Development* (1965), Lucian Pye and Sidney Verba, eds., *Political Culture and Political Development* (1965), Joseph LaPalombara and Myron Weiner, eds., *Political Parties and Political Development* (1966), Leonard Binder et al., *Crises and Sequences in Political Development* (1971), and Charles Tilly, ed., *The Formation of National States in Western Europe* (1975).

57. See especially Leonard Binder et al., *Crises and Sequences in Political Development.*

58. While there is a massive amount of writing on this subject, two very good recent essays are Radmila Nakarada, "The Mystery of Nationalism: The Paramount Case of Yugoslavia," *Millennium: Journal of International Studies* 20:3 (1991): 369–382, and Ivo Banac, "The Fearful Asymmetry of War: The Causes and Consequences of Yugoslavia's Demise," *Daedalus* 121:2 (1992) 141–174. A very good broader study is by Sabrina Ramet, *Nationalism and Federalism in Yugoslavia, 1962–1991* (Bloomington, Ind.: Indiana University Press, 1992).

59. Samuel P. Huntington, *Political Order in Changing Societies* (New Haven, Conn.: Yale University Press, 1968), p. 12.

2

Constitutions and Ideologies

CONSTITUTIONS AS POLITICAL STRUCTURES

One of the first things that an interested student of comparative politics will find as he or she peruses the literature is the heavy emphasis that is placed on the *state* or the *nation* as the unit of analysis. This is not to say that all comparative research takes place on this level; certainly a good deal of research has focused upon individuals, or policy, or developing and developed societies, and so on, but the state is a common subject of study.

Many characteristics of the state can be taken as the focus for a comparative study—and we will examine a number of them in this text—including *structural* characteristics (such as constitutions, legislatures, executives, judiciaries, political parties, and interest groups) and *behavioral* characteristics (such as ideology, political participation, and political socialization and recruitment). The initial area of our study should logically focus upon the structures that describe the parameters of the system, the boundaries and definitions of the component structures found within the political system. In this way we turn our attention first to a brief examination of constitutions and subsequently to a brief discussion of ideology and its place in political regimes.

It may be useful to think of constitutions as "power maps"[1] for political systems. That is, it is often the constitution of a nation that shows us the political lay of the land and that describes the manner in which power is distributed among the many actors in the political environment. We look to the constitution for an explanation of who has the power to do what, what the limitations on power are in a given state, and what the relationships are between and among the many political actors we may find in a given state. The idea of a constitution as a fundamental expression of the power relationships in a political regime dates back to the time of the Greek and Roman republics; constitutions were the focus for comparison in Aristotle's major studies of political systems.

WRITTEN AND UNWRITTEN CONSTITUTIONS

Studies of constitutional governments often rely on the structure or form of those written documents that we call constitutions. Yet, government with a written constitution is not the same thing as a constitutional government. A *written constitution* is essentially a basic expression of the ideas and organization of a government, formally presented in one document. Some constitutions are quite short—the U.S. Constitution, for example—while others are much longer, such as the constitution of India, the (now nonexistent) constitution of the former Soviet Union, or the constitution of Switzerland.[2] Some written constitutions are contained in one document, such as the Swiss Constitution, while others are found in several documents, such as the Canadian Constitution, which includes a "Constitution Act" as well as several other pieces of legislation and historical documents.

On the other hand, *constitutional government* can best be described as limited government. That is, there are certain things that the government may not do, whether it wants to or not; there are certain parameters beyond which the government may not go. The First Amendment to the U.S. Constitution is a clear example of this principle: It states in part that "Congress shall make *no law* . . . abridging the freedom of speech. . . ." (italics added). This is an *explicit* limitation upon the powers of government to act in a specific field of interest.

The fact of the matter is that we can find governments without written constitutions that can properly be called constitutional regimes, and conversely we can find governments that do have written constitutions but do not properly fit within the behavioral parameters we have set for a regime to be called a constitutional government. Several examples may help to make this clear.

Britain does not possess a document called "The Royal Constitution," or some such name, that might serve as the basic and central document for the political structures of the British political system. British political history points to a number of different documents that are part of the body of what is referred to as British constitutional law. These documents include the Magna Carta (1215), the Bill of Rights (1689), the Act of Settlement (1701), and certain special acts of the British Parliament. On the other hand, scholars agree that Britain *does* possess a constitutional government. There are limits beyond which the British government may not go. Yet Britain does *not* have a single, written document that can be called a written constitution.

The same thing can be said for constitutionalism in Israel. Although there was no single document called a constitution when the state of Israel came into existence in 1949, Israel has been writing a constitution one chapter at a time over the last forty-plus years. Today Israel's constitution is almost complete, but Israelis have been living without a formal, written constitution and an entrenched bill of rights until this time.[3]

Although the Soviet Union had until its recent demise a relatively new (1977) constitution that was highly detailed and specific,[4] many argued that the Soviet regime should not have been called a constitutional government. Why? There were, until the very final days of the regime (and it could be argued that even at that time this was a doubtful proposition), no effective limitations on Soviet governmental power. Rights were conditional: Article 39 of the Soviet Constitution stated that "the exercise of rights and liberties of citizens must not injure the interests of society and the state"[5]; Article 47 stated that "USSR citizens, in accordance with the goals of communist construction, are guaranteed freedom of scientific, technical, and artistic creation . . ."[6]; Article 51 stated that "in accordance with the goals of communist construction, USSR citizens have the right to unite in public organizations. . . ."[7] These few examples, which were typical of the document as a whole, show that expressions of rights did exist; however, they were always conditional, with the clear implication—which was shown to be the case in practice—that if the government believed that the "goals of communist construction" were not being served, the rights in question might be denied.

There is one other, more subtle distinction between these types of regimes that should be made explicit here. One type of constitution *gives* rights, and the other *recognizes* rights. This is not merely a semantic difference. The Soviet Constitution, in stating that the government gave citizens certain rights, implied that the government also had the power to *take away* these rights. If rights come from the state, the state can certainly take them away. In the (unwritten) British Constitution, or the (written) U.S. Constitution, rights are not *given;* they are *recognized,* by limiting what the government can do. The U.S. Constitution does not state that "citizens are given the right to free speech," although some people assume that it does. What is written in the Constitution is that "Congress shall make no law . . . abridging freedom of speech, or of the press . . ."; these rights and freedoms appear to *already* exist and belong to the people, and the Constitution recognizes this fact by forbidding the Congress to limit them. This is quite different from what was the case in the USSR.

It should be pointed out, however, that even the existence of a written constitution, in a constitutional culture of limited governmental power ("constitutional government"), does not absolutely guarantee either limited or unlimited individual rights. Freedom of speech is not absolute in either the United States or Britain, to take two examples; in both systems there is substantial judicial precedent documenting instances in which government can, in fact, restrict individuals' speech.[8]

Beyond this, even if we are examining a polity with a clear history of distinct constitutional protection of individual rights, short-term forces may occasionally motivate a polity to abrogate those rights: Japanese-Americans who lived in California shortly after Japan attacked Pearl Harbor were denied substantial "due process," lost their homes and most of their possessions, and were sent to "relocation camps" for the duration of World War II. The U.S. Supreme Court ruled at that time that this action on the part of the U.S. government was permissible because of the emergency situation posed by the war.[9] Only recently has the U.S. government officially apologized and made partial restitution.

When we discuss constitutional governments, thus, we are really not talking about whether there exists a single, specific document; rather, we are interested in a kind of political behavior, political culture, political tradition, or political history. The British Constitution is really a collection of documents and traditions, bound together in an abstract way. The U.S. Constitution is a single document, with subsequent judicial interpretation and expansion. The forms may vary, but the behavioral results are the same: Limits are imposed upon what governments may do.[10]

WHAT DO CONSTITUTIONS DO?

"Constitutions are codes of rules which aspire to regulate the allocation of functions, powers, and duties among the various agencies and officers of government, and define the relationship between these and the public."[11] Do constitutions make a difference? We have just argued that having a *written* constitution may not guarantee the behavior of a regime; does having *any* constitution matter? Today, more and more political scientists are putting *less* emphasis on a constitution as a significant structure in a political system. They argue that too often constitutions—whether written or unwritten—are not true reflections of the manner in which a political system operates, and therefore the constitution is of little use or value.[12]

Furthermore, in many instances constitutions omit discussions of political structures of the regime that are crucial to the operation of that regime. For example, political parties are nowhere mentioned in the (written) U.S. Constitution, yet it is difficult to conceive of government operating in the United States without political parties. To take another example, the (written) Canadian Constitution fails to mention the prime minister as a significant actor in the political system at all,[13] yet there is no doubt that this is the single most important office in the Canadian political arena. The (written) constitution of the former Soviet Union guaranteed certain rights, but practice indicated that these guarantees were hollow indeed. Given all of this, why is it that constitutions seem to be universally accepted as necessary to a political system? If a political structure is so pervasive, it must perform a very important function for the political systems in which it is found.

Several functions can be attributed to those political structures that we call constitutions, whether they are written or unwritten, whether they are followed or not, wherever they may be found. First, they serve as an expression of ideology and philosophy, a subject to which we shall return later in this chapter. Very often this kind of expression is found in a preamble to the constitution in question. For example, the preamble to Canada's Constitution Act of 1867 indicated that Canada would have a constitution "similar in principle" to that of Britain. This "similar in principle" clause was seen by scholars as incorporating—all by itself—all of the hundreds of years of British constitutional tradition into the Canadian political realm, and accordingly was regarded as being quite significant.[14]

Second, constitutions serve as an expression of the basic laws of the regime. These laws play a central role in the regime and are often so special that they can be modified or replaced only through extraordinary amendment procedures; sometimes they cannot be amended at all (for example, the clause in the German constitution guaranteeing human rights). Whereas an ordinary law can usually be passed with a "simple majority" approval of the legislature—a majority of those present and voting at the time—basic laws of the regime expressed in the constitution usually require special majorities of the legislature (two-thirds or three-quarters, for example) for approval. These special laws usually focus upon the rights of citizens; for instance, rights concerning language, speech, religion, assembly, the press, property, and so on.

Third, constitutions provide organizational frameworks for governments. Although they may not actually contain diagrams to explain how the various parts of the government interact with or relate to each other, these relationships are often explained in the text of the document. It is common for constitutions to contain several sections, and to devote a section each to the legislative branch of government, the executive branch of government, the judicial branch of government, and so on. Constitutions will discuss power relationships among the actors in the political system, covering the legislative process, the role of the executive in policy formation, and checks and balances among the actors. They may include impeachment of the executive and dissolution of the legislature, and perhaps discussion of succession as well.

Fourth, constitutions usually say something about the levels of government of the political system. They discuss how many levels of government there will be, and whether nations will be federal, confederal, or unitary. They often will describe what powers fall within the jurisdiction of the national government and what powers do not belong to the national government.

Finally, constitutions usually have an amendment clause. No matter how careful and insightful the authors of a constitution try to be, they usually recognize that they cannot foretell the future with a sufficiently high degree of accuracy. Accordingly, constitutions invariably need to be amended or altered at some point down the road. A constitution must contain directions for its own modifications; failure to do so might mean that when change becomes necessary, the entire system could collapse for want of a mechanism of change.

Constitutions, then, whether written or unwritten, play an important role in the regimes in which they are found. Some constitutions will be more important in one of the functions described above than in others. For example, the constitution of the Islamic Republic of Iran may be more important as an expression of ideology (and theology) than as a real organizational diagram of the government.[15] Similarly, the U.S. Constitution is more important as an expression of governmental organization and as a guideline for the power relationships of the regime than as an expression of the philosophy of the regime; the latter is usually said to be better expressed in the Declaration of Independence and the *Federalist Papers* than in the Constitution.

CONSTITUTIONALISM AND FEDERAL GOVERNMENT

An important dimension of our comparative study of politics involves how political systems are organized. In this respect we can identify several major options, including unitary, confederal, and federal political systems. It is important for us to understand the distinctions among these three organizational forms so as to appreciate fully some of the differences between governmental systems.

A *unitary system* is one that has only one level of government above the local level. In Great Britain, for example, although there are city and county governments, true *sovereignty*—the real power to make political decisions—resides with Parliament, and Parliament has the right to control whatever powers the cities or counties might exercise. Parliament has the power to grant the cities and counties more influence, or to take away policy jurisdiction they may already control.

The chief advantage of this type of system lies in its simplicity—there is only one responsible government with which to deal. Unitary governments, however, have proven to be less effective for large nations than for small nations, and they do not allow for ethnic and regional groups to exercise some degree of autonomy for themselves. Britain's unitary government has been the subject of tension in the past because some citizens in Wales, Scotland, and Northern Ireland have argued that it does not give regional and ethnic groups as much power as they might like. France, Italy, and Japan are other contemporary examples of unitary nations.

A *confederal* system—sometimes called a confederation—is a union of sovereign states that retain their sovereignty and powers, but coordinate their activities in certain respects. For example, a group of sovereign states may agree to coordinate their trade barriers, or their fishing activities in certain waters, or their oil production. The degree to which the units coordinate their behavior can vary greatly, as can the range of areas in which this coordination takes place. There are no true confederal states today; some have argued that the closest approximation to such an organization would be an international organization such as the European Economic Community.

The major advantage of confederations is their loose structure, which leaves a tremendous degree of flexibility and autonomy to member units. This structure allows the units to retain their individual characteristics and, to varying degrees, their own sovereignty to chart the policy directions they would most like to pursue. This same characteristic can be seen to be the main drawback of confederations as well: the inability to reconcile the varied interests of various member units. A confederation's citizens tend to identify most strongly with the member units, not the "national" unit, and priorities tend to be sectional, not broad. Often, action is taken only when all member units agree, which may mean that often no action is taken at all because unanimity is notoriously hard to achieve among large political units. Notable experiments in confederation that failed—the United States (1781–1787), Germany (1815–1866), and Switzerland (1815–1874)—were all reorganized as federations after it became clear that the confederal system would not further necessary common objectives.[16]

The European Community (EC)—often referred to today simply as "Europe"—began as an organization regulating tariffs among a small number of European nations. It has grown so much in power over the last several decades that it has become a real political entity in the region. European nations elect not only their own national legislators but also Members of the European Parliament (MEPs), who represent their region and nation in the European Parliament. The European Parliament has the ability to pass legislation regulating a wide range of economic issues in Europe.[17]

In a *federal* system there are two levels of government above the local level, each enjoying sovereignty in certain specific areas. For example, the central government may have the sole authority to coin money, raise an army, or declare war; the intermediate level of government (such as states, provinces, cantons, or Länder) may have sole authority to regulate education, criminal law, or civil law. Citizens deal with both levels of government.

Federal governments have been shown to have numerous advantages over other types of governments.[18] Federalism allows for both the expression of regional goals and a coordinated expression of national goals. One of the advantages of a federal system for member states is that the national level of government can absorb, through economic redistribution among member units, some of the costs of new technology or programs that would have to be absorbed completely by member units in a unitary or confederal system.[19]

The concept of federalism can be seen to have its roots early in political history—as far back as the historic Greek city-states, in fact. These early federations, for the most part, were not very stable or long-lived.[20] Modern federalism is usually dated from the American Constitutional Convention in Philadelphia in 1787.[21]

The number of federal states in the contemporary world is not great. Of the approximately 178[22] nation-states today, only twenty-one claim to be federal.[23] These twenty-one nations, however, cover more than half of the land surface of the globe, and include almost half of the world's population.[24] Federalism has proven to be a significant element "in situations in which sheer size, involving the separation and divergence of communities, has been the dominating feature."[25]

> Some authors argue that there is a direct correlation between large size and the advisability of federalism, and they quote Thomas Jefferson in support of their argument: "Our country is too large to have all its affairs directed by a single government."[26]

Of the six largest nations in the world, only China is unitary, and even China has some characteristics of federal government.[27] (The five other largest nations are Russia, Canada, the United States, Brazil, and Australia.)

There are many smaller federations, as well, including Mexico, Venezuela, and Argentina in Latin America; Nigeria in Africa; Switzerland in Europe; and India in Asia. Many of these nations opted for federalism not because of their large land area, but because of regional, ethnic, or linguistic characteristics of component groups that made a federal type of organization necessary. In general, federalism allows countries involved to maximize economic growth and political strength, while at the same time allowing for the expression of regional characteristics.[28]

Switzerland, for example, chose the federal system because it was best suited to the needs of that country's three language groups, German, French, and Italian. The Swiss Constitution, in fact, recognizes three official languages. Of the twenty-two Swiss cantons, there are eighteen unilingual cantons, three bilingual cantons, and one trilingual canton. The Swiss Constitution guarantees each citizen the right to communicate with the central government in any one of the three official languages.[29]

The federal system has been adapted in Germany. Rather than establishing clear divisions between areas of jurisdiction of the Bund (the central parliament) and the Länder (the member units), the German Constitution allows for a broad area of concurrent jurisdiction. The upper house of the national legislature, the Bundesrat, is chosen by the Länder governments; it has an absolute veto over matters affecting the Länder, but only a "suspensory" veto over matters of "national" concern.[30]

There does not appear to be a universally accepted theory of federalism, nor, for that matter, a clear definition of precisely what behavioral attributes are characteristic of federal government. Ivo Duchacek has suggested that:

> the term itself is unclear and controversial. It is often used to describe a *process* of combining territorial communities that had previously not been directly joined. . . . In addition, federalism is also a term used to describe the result or the tools of the federalizing process—a constitutional federal system and its institutions.[31]

The most common characterization of a federal government is that it is organized on two levels above the local level, one national unit and a number of intermediate-member units. Both levels of government rule over the same constituents, and both levels of government have the power to make certain decisions independently of the other.[32]

William Riker has suggested a useful framework within which the many federal governments of the world may be measured. He has suggested that federations can be measured along a "centralized-decentralized" dimension. This dimension may be defined by the following minimum and maximum, as illustrated in Figure 2.1:

Minimum: The ruler(s) of the federation can make decisions in only one narrowly restricted category of action without obtaining the approval of the rulers of the constituent units. . . .

Maximum: The ruler(s) of the federation can make decisions without consulting the rulers of the member governments in all but one narrowly restricted category of action.[33]

The closer to the "minimum" end of the scale a federal government is, the more it can be described as a "peripheral federation." The closer to the "maximum" end of

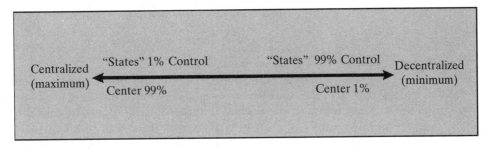

FIGURE 2.1   A Scale of Federalisms

the scale a federal government is, the more it can be described as a "centralized federation."

Although most modern federations have proven to be more stable and long-lived than their Hellenic ancestors, not all experiments with federation since the late eighteenth century have been successes. The more decentralized or peripheral a federation is, the weaker the center is as compared to the member units, the greater the centrifugal forces acting on a political system, and the greater the likelihood that the federation will not endure. Cases such as the United Arab Republic (1958–1961), the Federation of the West Indies, the Federation of Malaysia, and the Federation of Rhodesia and Nyasaland[34] are all illustrations of "premature federations"—unifications that took place before sufficient national integration and national development were attained—and are examples of unifications that did not last.

Federalism is significant as a political variable because the federal balance in a polity often influences the efficiency with which public policy is made.[35] To take one example, it is often difficult for the Canadian federal (national) government to set national policy because many substantial policy issues—such as health policy, education policy, much resource policy, and so on—fall within the policy jurisdiction of the provinces. Accordingly, if the federal government wants to enact a new health policy or a new job training program, it must frequently convene a meeting of the prime minister and the ten provincial premiers, or the federal education minister and the ten provincial education ministers (or comparable officials, depending upon the policy area involved), to "negotiate" a policy that will be acceptable to their respective governments. The provincial representatives will then return to their respective capitals and introduce the policy in their provincial legislatures.[36]

THE SEPARATION OF POWERS

The notion that centralized power is dangerous—that power must be a check on power—reached maturity in the eighteenth century, and its first full-scale application was to be found in the Constitutional Convention in Philadelphia in 1787. There, delegates to the federal convention continuously cited "the celebrated Montesquieu," John Locke, Thomas Hobbes, and others[37] in support of the idea that political power, in order to be safe, had to be divided. The legislature needed to have a check on the executive, the executive on the legislature, and so on. Many of John Locke's ideas were adopted and can be found in *The Federalist* (especially Number 47), among other places, and expressed the philosophy that the executive force had to be kept separate from the legislative force.[38]

Constitutions express the power relationships among the many actors in political regimes. The U.S. Constitution is explicit about the degree to which the president can take control of the work of the legislature (literally, he cannot), and the degree to which the Congress can take control of the work of the president (literally, it cannot). The situation, however, is one that *can* rapidly devolve into a stalemate: The president can veto work of the Congress, and Congress can refuse to pass legislative requests of the president, but neither can *force* the other to do anything. In other regimes the lines are much less clearly drawn. For example, in France the president can, under certain circumstances that we shall examine more closely later in this volume, simply issue decrees that have the force of legislation.

Hindsight tells us, as we shall see in a number of instances throughout this text, that the explicit lines drawn by the Founding Fathers to separate the executive and legislative branches of government were not absolutely necessary to ensure democratic government. There are other power relationships, which we will discuss in later chapters, that are used elsewhere that have proven to be just as democratic and just as stable.

In fact, it should be noted that while the idea that centralized power was inherently dangerous was popular at the time of the foundation of the American republic, in fact today many countries (some of them European) have had fairly successful experiences with centralized power structures. Thus the notion that centralized power must be a bad thing is not, in and of itself, one that is universally shared today.

THE IMPORTANCE OF CONSTITUTIONS

Constitutions can be examined on two levels. On one hand, we can look at a constitution on a "piece" level, and examine it section by section to see what structures and behaviors it prescribes for a given political system. Further, we can speculate as to the implications of these structures and behaviors for political life in that system. On the other hand, we can look at a constitution from the level of the political system and ask the same question: What does the constitution do? David Easton's framework of analysis is useful in examining this type of question.

In Chapter 1 we examined the concept of the political system, and we noted that Easton offered a variation of the general systems approach. This was referred to as "input-output analysis."[39] Demands and supports are fed into the political system as *inputs*. They are "processed" by the system itself; that is, the system is a giant conversion mechanism that is able to take demands and supports from the environment, digest them, and issue "authoritative allocations of values" in the forms of decisions and actions—*outputs*. These outputs filter through the environment as "feedback" and are subsequently reintroduced as new inputs, either demands or supports, and the cycle continues. The digesting and the processing phase of the system, what Easton labels "The Political System," is what government is all about: responding to demands and supports, making decisions, providing information, establishing legitimacy, and so on.

Instead of simply looking at a constitution from the perspective of what it says about the separation of powers, about the federal or unitary nature of the political system, about checks and balances, basic laws, amendments, and philosophy, we could ask the system-level question of how the constitution helps the political system to survive. To use Gabriel Almond's terms, introduced in Chapter 1, what are the functions (consequences) of the structures that we refer to as "constitutions"?

Ivo Duchacek has performed just such an analysis, and his work offers some answers to the question "What does the constitution do?" The answer that his study suggests is that a constitution helps a political system in the function of "system maintenance," or survival of the system, by helping the system to respond to the various demands and supports that are directed to it in the form of inputs. The constitution and the corresponding constitutional framework of powers help to process demands and supports and help to convert them into outputs, which subsequently are reintroduced as inputs. According to the framework suggested by Duchacek, constitutions play a crucial role in the system maintenance function suggested by Easton. Demands and supports are processed more smoothly because of (1) commitment to responsiveness; (2) specific institutions for rule-making, enforcement, and adjudicating; and (3) commitment to goals, all of which are found in a constitution.[40]

CONSTITUTIONS IN A COMPARATIVE PERSPECTIVE

The political structure that we call a constitution is a good place to begin our cross-national comparison, because it presents examples of some of the problems that we first discussed in Chapter 1. We cannot be analytically rigid when we are examining constitutional frameworks in comparative perspective. Sometimes we will find a piece of paper entitled "Constitution," and sometimes we will not. The mere existence of a piece of paper or parchment is no guarantee that a political system is constitutional, as we defined the term at the beginning of this chapter.

We have, then, the structures-and-functions problem that we mentioned in Chapter 1: The structure of a written constitution may perform different functions (have different consequences) in different political systems. Furthermore, different structures (in some places a written constitution, elsewhere tradition and custom) may perform the same function in different political systems. This is a scenario that we will see repeated in the next several chapters.

IDEOLOGIES

One of the functions that we ascribed to constitutions earlier in this chapter was to serve as an expression of ideology and philosophy for a regime. The term "ideology" is one that is often emotionally charged, and "ideologue" is often used as a description for an individual no longer approaching a situation from a rational perspective. Originally, ideologue referred to a student of how ideas are formed, and ideology was "a study of the process of forming ideas, a 'science of ideas.'"[41] The purpose behind the introduction of the concept of ideology was "to provide the new secular educators with a systematic educational theory. The unashamed view of the ideologues . . . was that the minds of the young should be bent to new, more healthy purposes."[42]

Actually, the term "ideology" has a number of meanings and connotations:

1. One meaning is that of "deception," "distortion," or "falseness." It conveys the notion of *subjectivism* as opposed to objectivity.
2. Ideology also conveys the notion of a *dream*, an impossible or unrealizable quest.
3. Ideology also means what may be called the *consciousness* of a society at any given moment, the values and beliefs and attitudes that hold it together.
4. Ideologies often correspond to *social criticism*, confronting existing beliefs and attempting through argument and persuasion to challenge and change them.
5. Ideology also provides a *set of concepts* through which people view the world and learn about it.
6. Ideologies can be a call for *committed action*.
7. Ideologies often become, under certain circumstances, a powerful *instrument of manipulation.*[43]

Ideologies, then, in a more expressly political context, involve a set of ideas that relate to the social/political world and that provide a general guideline for some action. One scholar has tersely indicated that "an ideology represents a practical attitude to the world"[44]; another has suggested that "ideologies are actually attempts to develop political accommodations to the economic and social conditions created by the Industrial Revolution."[45] Ideologies can serve many functions, as was indicated earlier. They can unite groups, serve as rallying cries, help to articulate philosophies, or serve as tools of political manipulation. In each of these areas, however, we can see the same two critical components: a relation to political ideas and a relation to political behavior.[46]

Ideologies give the regime its *raison d'être*, its sense of purpose, and serve as a philosophical point of reference for political behavior in the political system. Michael Curtis has suggested that all ideologies are amalgams of "facts, values, and mythology that provide some understanding of history and the supreme significance of or necessary leadership by a particular individual, group, class, or nation."[47]

Many different ideologies have existed in the modern political world. Some have come and gone in a brief period of time; others have long been in existence. Some ideologies have had a great deal of influence on major world events; others have not. What we could call "classical liberalism" was a very significant ideology at about the time of the American Revolution, and it continues to be significant today. Certainly Marxism is an example of an ideology that has had a very broad and profound influence in society, and an influence that has lasted for many years. Other "isms," including socialism, fascism, conservatism, and so on, have become part of our vocabulary over the years, as well.

Ideologies are often related to individually held attitudes toward political change, which are usually conceived as fitting along a "left-right" spectrum as illustrated in Figure 2.2. The "left-right" metaphor dates back to 1798, at which time the French Council of 500 was arranged in a semicircular hall of representatives according to their self-determined place in the political spectrum.[48] Those generally supporting the monarch's policies sat on his right, while those who proposed changes in his policies sat on his left; hence, "leftists" favored change and "rightists" preferred the status quo. These same general labels are used today. It should be kept in mind that the positions in Figure 2.2 and the descriptions that follow relate to *classical* political values: Those who consider themselves conservative in the United States in the 1990s do not hold the same values as would a classical conservative in the 1790s.

The "radical" position is often associated with violence, although that need not be the case.[49] Generally, the radical position is extremely dissatisfied with the way society (and politics) is organized and operating and is very impatient to undertake fundamental changes in society. Radicals favor drastic and immediate change. Of course, not all radicals are alike, and we could certainly distinguish among more or less "radical" radicals, depending upon the intensity of their beliefs, the strategies they might wish to employ (including more or less violence), the immediacy with which they want changes undertaken, and so on.

The classical liberal position is obviously more content with society as it exists than is the radical, but the liberal still believes that reform is possible, and indeed necessary, in society. Among the many differences between liberals and radicals are their views toward the law.

> Since radicals are basically opposed to the political system that governs them, they are apt to see the law as one way in which those who control the society maintain their control. Hence, radicals find it hard to respect the law. Liberals, on the other hand, generally respect the concept of the law, and although they may want to change certain specifics of the law, they usually will not violate it. Instead they try to change the law through legal procedures.[50]

Liberalism includes a belief in human potential, a belief in the ability of individuals to change social institutions for the better, a belief in human rationality, and a fundamental belief in human equality.

FIGURE 2.2 The Liberal-Conservative Spectrum

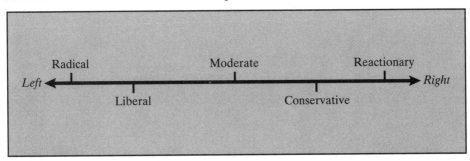

The moderate position is one that is basically satisfied with the way society is operating, and one that insists that any changes that might be made in society, social rules, and social values, should be made slowly, gradually, and in a way that will not be disruptive.

The classical conservative position can be described as being most satisfied with the way society is operating at the time, most satisfied with the status quo. The major difference between conservatives and liberals is that "conservatives support the status quo not so much because they like it but because they believe that it is the best that can be achieved at the moment."[51] Classical conservatives do not share the optimism of liberals that individuals have the capacity to improve society. They are more skeptical of human nature and believe that human nature may be selfish. They place more emphasis on respecting institutions and traditions because they are not sure that they (or others) are capable of devising a better system. They believe in elitism.

Finally, the classical reactionary position corresponds to that of the radical, only on the right end of the spectrum. The reactionary position proposes radical change backwards—that is, "retrogressive change," favoring "a policy that would return the society to a previous condition or even a former value system."[52]

It is important to note before we leave the left-right spectrum that it is *very much* a relative scale. Someone who is a "radical-liberal" may view a "moderate-liberal" as an "ultraconservative." Description may be to a large degree a matter of perspective. Indeed, in a classic study Louis Hartz essentially suggested that *all* American politics is "liberal" politics. "There has never been a 'liberal movement' or a real 'liberal party' in America: We have only had the American Way of Life, a nationalist articulation of Locke which usually does not know that Locke himself is involved."[53]

Thus, while the American left is part of the "classical liberal" tradition, so too is the American right, which Hartz suggests "exemplifies the tradition of big propertied liberalism in Europe."[54] Thus, America's entire left-right scale may be seen as existing within a small portion of the traditional left-right scale, as illustrated in Figure 2.3.

FIGURE 2.3   American Ideology on the Liberal-Conservative Spectrum

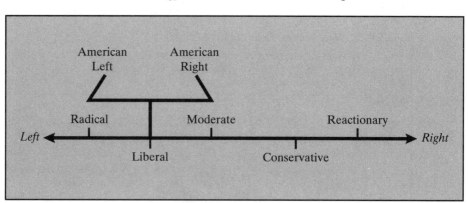

What is a radical policy today may be a moderate policy tomorrow; what is radical in one society may not be radical in another. To take but one example, it was not that long ago that talk of a Social Security system in the United States—in which the government became involved in a retirement pension scheme—was perceived as a radical socialist proposal, completely unthinkable. Yet, in 1994 no one in American society seriously advocates doing away with Social Security; individuals may propose ways of changing the way the system works, but they would not do away with the system completely. Another example could be found in proposals for socialized medical care. Socialized medicine may be seen today as a radical policy proposal in the United States—although clearly less radical than it was perceived fifteen or twenty years ago—but such may not always be the case. Socialized medicine is not seen as radical in virtually all industrialized countries outside of the United States, and it has been incorporated as part of the public sector.

CLASSIFICATION OF REGIMES

Care should be taken to avoid confusing ideologies—philosophies or values of political regimes—with the constitutional bases of regimes. The former concept asks the question "What does the regime stand for, and what does it want to accomplish?" The latter asks the question "Who governs, and how is power distributed in the political system?" As a general rule, "isms" refer to ideology, while the suffix "-cracy" refers to governance.[55] Calling the contemporary government of the Islamic Republic of Iran a "theocracy" tells us that its constitution is based upon religious precepts; it does not tell us about the values of the regime (other than those of Islam).

Apart from the "isms" that we have already met that are related to the classical liberal-conservative spectrum (that is, radicalism, liberalism, conservatism, reactionism), there are many other "isms." Some of these "isms" are related to purely ideological considerations; others are related to economic arguments. We will meet many of these "isms" later in this text, both in the chapter on economics and political development (Chapter 3) and in the area studies chapters. Among these "isms" could be included the following:

> *Anarchism*—a belief that all forms of government interfere with individual rights and freedoms and should, therefore, be abolished.[56]
>
> *Capitalism*—a belief in an economic system in which the major means of production are owned by individuals, not by the government of the state. The economic philosophy emphasizes *private ownership* and a *market economy*; that is, nonregulation of the marketplace by the government.[57]
>
> *Communism*—a theory evolved from *Marxism* (see below) with modifications from Lenin in the early twentieth century. A belief in government ownership of the major means of production, and of the general "primacy of politics over economics,"[58] that the government should actively regulate and control all sectors of the economy with little or no private property.[59]
>
> *Corporatism*—a belief that advocates a close degree of cooperation and coordination between the government and labor and business groups in the formation of economic policy.[60]

Fascism—a belief, which includes *national socialism,* that usually is said to include seven components: "irrationalism, social Darwinism, nationalism, glorification of the state, the leadership principle, racism (more important in national socialism than in fascism), and anticommunism."[61]

Feminism—a system of beliefs that has emerged primarily in the last twenty years, and primarily in the West. Developed in opposition to oppression of women, and in opposition to sexism in general. Feminism has developed many different schools, including liberal or reform feminism, Marxist feminism, socialist feminism, and radical feminism.[62]

Marxism—a complex framework describing the economic system and the inevitable conflict between the working class and the owners of the means of production. The theory suggested the inevitability of class conflict, and was subsequently adopted and modified by Lenin to create Soviet communism.[63]

Nationalism—includes identification with a national group and support for actions that will support and be to the benefit of the national group. This may or may not correspond to borders of a particular state as we defined the term in Chapter 1.[64]

Socialism—an ideology developed out of the industrial revolution that advocates governmental concern with individuals' quality of life, including concerns about education, medical care, and standard of living. Socialism may be found in democratic versions—such as Great Britain or Sweden—or in authoritarian versions—such as Nazi ("Nazi" was short for National Socialist") Germany or Fascist Italy.[65]

Totalitarianism—a system in which the government controls individual political behavior and individual political thought. This is distinguished from *authoritarianism* by its degree: The focus of authoritarian rule is individual behavior that affects the stability of the regime; the focus of totalitarian rule is virtually total.[66]

This cursory introduction to some of the major ideological frameworks is intended only to demonstrate the wide range of possible approaches to politics and conceptual frameworks that are available to the student. We shall see applied versions of many of these issues later in this volume as we examine specific problem areas (for example, Chapter 3: Political Development and Political Economics) or specific political systems (for example, the role of corporatism in Mexican economic policy).

Constitutions, Ideologies, and Classification

Aristotle provided us with terms that are still used today to discuss both *good* government and *bad* government. The Aristotelian forms of good government are the polity (rule by many in the general interest), the aristocracy (rule by a few in the general interest), and kingship (rule by one in the general interest). The divisions of bad government are tyranny (self-interested rule by one), the oligarchy (self-interested rule by a few), and the democracy (self-interested rule by many).

Aristotle provided what has come to be regarded as the "classical" division of systems of government, based upon two dimensions: the number of rulers in a system and in whose interest the rulers rule. This framework is summarized in Table 2.1.

If a constitution, written or not, is perceived as a framework establishing the

TABLE 2.1
The Aristotelian Classification of Regimes

Number of Rulers	Rule in General Interest ("Right" Type)	Self-Interested Rule ("Wrong" Type)
One	Kingship	Tyranny
Few	Aristocracy	Oligarchy
Many	Polity	Democracy

Source: Based on *The Politics of Aristotle,* ed. and trans. by Ernest Barker (New York: Oxford University Press, 1970), pp. 113–115.

skeleton of a political system, the manner in which it is constructed, and the means by which it will operate, then an ideology should be perceived as the *goals* of that framework. To what end does the regime exist? What is its reason for being? What does it offer, distinct from other regimes, to justify its existence? These are all questions that are addressed by ideologies. *What* the regime wants to do, in a very general philosophical sense, is included in an ideology; *how* the regime will operate to achieve these ends is addressed through the constitutional structure of the regime.

While a knowledge of the constitutional structure of a regime and its ideology does not tell us everything that is important to know about that system, it tells us a great deal. It gives us an indication of the type of public policy that we can expect to see in that setting, and how that public policy is likely to be enacted. It also indicates the range and amount of political behavior that we are likely to encounter. It is a good beginning. Before we turn our attention to more of the constitutional/ political structures of the regime, however, it is important to examine the *economic* dimension of the polity; there is a linkage between politics and economics, and that linkage can—and does—affect political behavior. It is to that task that we turn our attention in the next chapter.

Notes

1. Ivo Duchacek, *Power Maps: Comparative Politics of Constitutions* (Santa Barbara, Calif.: Clio Press, 1973).
2. "The Swiss Constitution of 1848 as amended in 1874 and in subsequent years is a written document like that of the U.S.A., although it is double in size to that of the American Constitution." See Vishnoo Bhagwan and Vidya Bhushan, *World Constitutions* (New Delhi: Sterling Publishers, 1984), p. 321.
3. This is discussed in a very good book by Daphna Sharfman, *Living Without a Constitution: Civil Rights in Israel* (Armonk, N.Y.: M. E. Sharpe, 1993).
4. See Robert Sharlet, *The New Soviet Constitution of 1977* (Brunswick, Ohio: King's Court Communications, 1978).
5. Ibid., p. 89.
6. Ibid., p. 92.
7. Ibid., p. 93.
8. This is a very important issue, and one that has received a great deal of attention in many societies. A recent article in the United Kingdom discussing this can be found in Salmon Rushdie, "Rushdie on Censorship," *Editor and Publisher* 126:13 (March 27, 1993), p. 6. A similar question in the American context is discussed in "Protecting 'Free Speech'," *The Christian Science Monitor* 85:88 (April 2, 1993), p. 20.

9. For discussion of this episode of American history, see Roger Daniels, *Prisoners Without Trial: Japanese Americans in World War II* (New York: Hill and Wang, 1993), David Takami, *Executive Order 9066: Fifty Years Before and Fifty Years After* (Seattle, Wash.: Wing Luke Asian Museum, 1992), or Roger Daniels, Sandra Taylor, and Harry Kitano, eds., *Japanese Americans: From Relocation to Redress* (Seattle: University of Washington Press, 1991).

10. Two good examples of recent comparative studies of constitutions are: Marian McKenna, ed., *The Canadian and American Constitutions in Comparative Perspective* (Calgary, Alberta: University of Calgary Press, 1993), and Preston King and Andrea Bosco, eds., *A Constitution for Europe: A Comparative Study of Federal Constitutions and Plans for the United States of Europe* (London: Lothian Foundation Press, 1991).

11. S. E. Finer, ed., *Five Constitutions* (Sussex: Harvester Press, 1979), p. 15.

12. Ibid.

13. The position of prime minister is mentioned in the Prime Minister's Residence Act—establishing an official residence for the prime minister—and the Prime Minister's Salary Act—authorizing the prime minister to receive a higher salary than other cabinet members—but the precise method of selection, powers, and similar important descriptions of the position are not included in constitutional documents.

14. Richard Van Loon and Michael Whittington, *The Canadian Political System* (Toronto: McGraw-Hill Ryerson, 1976), pp. 169–170.

15. See Samih Farsoun and Mehrdad Mashayekhi, eds., *Iran: Political Culture in the Islamic Republic* (New York: Routledge, 1992).

16. Thomas D. McGee, *Notes on Federal Governments: Past and Present* (Montreal: Dawson Brothers, 1865).

17. The literature on the European Parliament is rapidly increasing in size. A good recent article on the European Parliament and its political role can be found in Dick Leonard's "Parliament Prepares for Power," *International Management* 46:9 (November 1991): 76. An interesting parallel question on the role of British Members of the European Parliament can be found in Neasa MacErlean, "Non Honoured in Their Own Country," *Accountancy* 108 (August 1991): 68.

18. A very good recent study is that by Daniel Elazar, *Exploring Federalism* (Tuscaloosa: University of Alabama Press, 1987). See also Michael Burgess and Alain-G. Gagnon, *Comparative Federalism and Federation: Competing Traditions and Future Directions* (London: Harvester-Wheatsheaf, 1993), Mark Tushnet, ed., *Comparative Constitutional Federalism: Europe and America* (New York: Greenwood Press, 1990), or Harry Scheiber, ed., *North American and Comparative Federalism* (Berkeley: University of California Press, 1992).

19. Frank Trager, "On Federalism," in Thomas Frank, *Why Federations Fail* (New York: New York University Press, 1968), pp. x–xi.

20. See S. Rufus Davis, *The Federal Principle* (Los Angeles: University of California Press, 1978), p. 11, and William Riker, *Federalism: Origin, Operation, Significance* (Boston: Little, Brown, 1964), p. 5.

21. See Sobei Mogi, *The Problem of Federalism* (London: Allen and Unwin, 1931).

22. There are many different "firm" statements of the number of nation-states in the world today. One indicator is simply the number of members of the United Nations, which was 178 in 1993. See Mark Hoffman, ed., *The World Almanac and Book of Facts, 1993* (New York: Pharos Books, 1993).

23. Duchacek, *Power Maps*, p. 111.

24. Riker, *Federalism*, p. 1.

25. Arthur R. M. Lower, "Theories of Canadian Federalism—Yesterday and Today," in A.R.M. Lower, ed., *Evolving Canadian Federalism* (Durham, N.C.: Duke University Press, 1958), p. 3.

26. Ivo Duchacek, *Comparative Federalism: The Territorial Dimension of Politics* (New York: Holt, Rinehart, and Winston, 1970), p. 198.

27. Ibid.

28. Ronald Watts, *New Federations: Experiments in the Commonwealth* (Oxford: Clarendon Press, 1966).

29. See Ursula K. Hicks, *Federalism: Failure and Success* (New York: Oxford University Press, 1978), pp. 144–171.

30. Ibid.

31. Duchacek, *Comparative Federalism*, p. 189.

32. Ibid., p. 191. See also Edward McWhinney, *Comparative Federalism* (Toronto: University of Toronto Press, 1962). A very good collection of articles on this subject matter can be found in the volume by Herman Bakvis and William Chandler, *Federalism and the Role of the State* (Toronto: University of Toronto Press, 1987).

33. Riker, *Federalism*, p. 6.

34. See Amitai Etzioni, *Political Unification* (New York: Holt, Rinehart, and Winston, 1965), pp. 97–183, or William Livingston, ed., *Federalism in the Commonwealth* (London: Cassell, 1963).

35. A recent study of this problem is by Gregory Mahler, *New Dimensions of Canadian Federalism: Canada in a Comparative Perspective* (Rutherford, N.J.: Fairleigh Dickinson University Press, 1987).

36. A very good study of this method of policy-making is that by Richard Simeon, *Federal-Provincial Diplomacy: The Making of Recent Policy in Canada* (Toronto: University of Toronto Press, 1977). Simeon discusses pensions, financial reform, and constitutional amendment as three case studies.

37. See especially Paul Spurlin, *Montesquieu in America: 1760–1801* (Baton Rouge: Louisiana State University Press, 1940), John Loy, *Montesquieu* (New York: Twayne, 1968), Arthur Prescott, *Drafting the Federal Constitution* (Baton Rouge: Louisiana State University Press, 1941), and Clinton Rossiter, *1787: The Grand Convention* (New York: Macmillan, 1966).

38. See John Locke, *Second Treatise on Civil Government* (especially chap. 13, "Of the Subordination of the Powers of the Commonwealth," pp. 87–94), in Ernest Barker, *Social Contract: Essays by Locke, Hume & Rousseau* (New York: Oxford University Press, 1970).

39. See David Easton, *A Systems Analysis of Political Life* (New York: Wiley, 1965), esp. p. 32.

40. Duchacek, *Power Maps*, p. 236.

41. Leon Baradat, *Political Ideologies: Their Origins and Impact* (Englewood Cliffs, N.J.: Prentice Hall, 1988), p. 6.

42. Howard Williams, *Concepts of Ideology* (New York: St. Martin's Press, 1987), p. xi.

43. Roy C. Macridis, *Contemporary Political Ideologies* (Cambridge: Winthrop, 1980), pp. 3–4.

44. Williams, *Concepts of Ideology*, p. 122.

45. Baradat, *Political Ideologies*, p. 20.

46. Several very good new studies of comparative political ideology are: Roger Eatwell and Anthony Wright, eds., *Contemporary Political Ideologies* (New York: St. Martin's Press, 1993), Ian Adams, *Political Ideology Today* (New York: Manchester University Press, 1993), and Peter Collins, *Ideology After the Fall of Communism* (New York: Boyars and Bowerdean, 1993).

47. Michael Curtis, *Comparative Government and Politics* (New York: Harper and Row, 1978), p. 41.

48. Ibid., p. 158.

49. This discussion of the left-right spectrum and the five general attitudes to be found on it is based upon much more extensive discussion in Baradat, *Political Ideologies*, pp. 27–40.

50. Ibid., p. 30.

51. Ibid., p. 35.

52. Ibid., p. 39.

53. Louis Hartz, *The Liberal Tradition in America: An Interpretation of American Political Thought Since the Revolution* (New York: Harcourt, Brace and Company, 1955), p. 11.

54. Ibid., p. 15.

55. See William Ebenstein, *Today's ISMs* (Englewood Cliffs, N.J.: Prentice Hall, 1973).

56. See A. John Simmons, *On the Edge of Anarchy: Locke, Consent, and the Limits of Society* (Princeton, N.J.: Princeton University Press, 1993).

57. See Amir Ben-Porat, *The State and Capitalism in Israel* (Westport, Conn.: Greenwood Press, 1993), Samuel Bowles and Richard Edwards, *Understanding Capitalism: Competition, Com-*

mand, and Change in the U.S. Economy (New York: HarperCollins, 1993), Robert Heilbroner, *21st Century Capitalism* (New York: Norton, 1993), or Wil Hout, *Capitalism and the Third World: Development, Dependence, and the World System* (Brookfield, Vt.: E. Elgar, 1993).

58. William Ebenstein, *Today's ISMs: Communism, Fascism, Capitalism, Socialism* (Englewood Cliffs, N.J.: Prentice Hall, 1970), p. 31.

59. See Philippe van Parijs, *Marxism Recycled* (New York: Cambridge University Press, 1993), for a recent discussion of modern communism.

60. See Alan Cawson, *Corporatism and Political Theory* (New York: Basil Blackwell, 1986), or Colin Crouch and Ronald Dore, eds., *Corporatism and Accountability: Organized Interests in British Public Life* (Oxford: Clarendon, 1990).

61. Lyman Tower Sargent, *Contemporary Political Ideologies: A Comparative Analysis* (Chicago: Dorsey, 1987), p. 162. See also Richard J. Golsan, *Fascism, Aesthetics, and Culture* (Hanover, N.H.: University Press of New England, 1992), or Zeev Sternhell, *The Birth of Fascist Ideology: From Cultural Rebellion to Political Revolution* (Princeton, N.J.: Princeton University Press, 1994).

62. See Nancy Sorkin Rabinowitz and Amy Richlin, eds, *Feminist Theory and the Classics* (New York: Routledge, 1993), Glynis Carr, ed., *Turning the Century: Feminist Theory in the 1990s* (Lewisburg, Pa.: Bucknell University Press, 1992), or Marianne Hirsch and Evelyn Fox Keller, *Conflicts in Feminism* (New York: Routledge, 1990).

63. See van Parijs, *Marxism Recycled*, Keith Graham, *Karl Marx, Our Contemporary: Social Theory for a Post-Leninist World* (New York: Harvester-Wheatsheaf Press, 1992), or Kai Nielsen, *Marxism and the Moral Point of View: Morality, Ideology, and Historical Materialism* (Boulder, Colo.: Westview Press, 1989).

64. See John Breuilly, *Nationalism and the State* (New York: Manchester University Press, 1993), John R. Gillis, ed., *Commemorations: The Politics of National Identity* (Princeton, N.J.: Princeton University Press, 1994), or David Gordon, *Images of the West: Third World Perspectives* (Totowa, N.J.: Rowman and Littlefield, 1989).

65. For two examples of this literature, see David Schweickart, *Against Capitalism* (New York: Cambridge University Press, 1993), or Martin Hewitt, *Welfare, Ideology, and Need: Developing Perspectives on the Welfare State* (New York: Harvester Wheatsheaf Press, 1992).

66. The "classic" in this area is by Carl Friedrich, *Totalitarianism in Perspective* (New York: Praeger, 1969). See also Jay Taylor, *The Rise and Fall of Totalitarianism in the Twentieth Century* (New York: Paragon, 1993).

3

Political Development and Political Economics

POLITICS AND ECONOMICS

A clear link exists between the political and the economic world. Economic status and power, on a national level, are often perceived as being associated with political status and power.[1] Nations with resources have the ability to influence nations without resources, and this is true whether the resources are oil, wheat, or chromium. Thus is it important for us in this chapter to examine briefly the relationship between economic variables and political variables and to appreciate the very large differences in political and economic resources between the "developed" and the "developing" nations.

Developed and Developing Nations

In Chapter 1 we briefly discussed the concept of political development and the distinction between *development* and *modernization,* the latter having been described as "the process by which a society becomes 'modern.'"[2] One critic of the concept of modernization has suggested that modernization is not very helpful as an analytic tool because the term "modernization" is defined as "the equivalent of Westernization."[3] In a similar manner, one problem with the concept of "development" is, at least partially, that development implies a *normative* perspective.

> The starting-point is that we cannot avoid what the positivists disparagingly refer to as "value judgements." "Development" is inevitably a normative concept, almost a synonym for improvement. To pretend otherwise is just to hide one's value judgements.[4]

As a process, development is not only economic but is also "a multidimensional process involving the reorganization and reorientation of entire economic and social systems."[5]

Why is it that some countries are developed and others are not? That was the focus of much of the research in this field in the 1960s and 1970s. One of the classic works in the study of political development was Walt Rostow's 1962 book, *The States of Economic Growth: A Non-Communist Manifesto.*[6] Its emphasis was "on the psycho-cultural prerequisites of development,"[7] and it suggested that there were five stages of growth in the development process:

1. *Traditional society.* Prescientific, with a limit on how much economic development is possible.
2. *Preconditions for takeoff.* This involves the development of some science and expanded agricultural and industrial output, similar to that achieved in Western Europe by the eighteenth century.
3. *Take off.* This includes a rapid rise in the Gross Domestic Product, and expansion of economic and business institutions.
4. *The drive to technological maturity.* Here we include expansion of the investment base of the economy, and increased export markets with new products for the nation.
5. *High mass-consumption.* This economy is based upon consumer goods and services, typical of those of the industrialized Western democracies today.[8]

Many criticized Rostow's framework because it assumed that all countries followed the same (predetermined) pathway to development, and because it was culturally (Western) biased. Although it is clearly the case that this framework should not be taken as an iron law that is universally applicable to all societies—because all societies may not develop in the same stages, at the same time, and at the same speed—it is worth observing that there *are* some common patterns shared by many systems, as noted by Rostow. His work influenced many scholars but has not survived to the present day as a major influence in the discipline.

Another influence in thinking about development and modernization was the work of Samuel Huntington, who in 1965 suggested that urbanization, literacy, modern communication, and mass participation could be seen as instruments of political *decay* rather than as instruments of progress.[9] Later Huntington expanded upon this idea:

> Modernization in practice always involves change in and usually the disintegration of a traditional political system, but it does not necessarily involve significant movement toward a modern political system. . . . Yet the tendency is to think that because social modernization is taking place, political modernization also must be taking place."[10]

Between the 1970s and the present time, the concept of "political development" as a discrete, identifiable process has been used less and less frequently as the basis for the analysis of Third World politics. Basically, it was concluded that the concept of development itself was ethnocentric; it was based on an (often unstated) assumption that the Western democracies were developed and the countries of the Third World should aspire to become much the same as North America and Western Europe.

The distinction between the developed and the developing worlds sometimes is not as clear as we might like, although there is a general consensus upon which nations belong to the two groups. Objective indicators such as average gross national product and the gross domestic product (GNP and GDP*) are often used to distinguish between developed and developing nations.[11] For example, the 1993 World Bank *World Development Report* lists the "Low-Income Economies" as ranging from per capita gross national products of $80** in Mozambique to $610 in Egypt. "Middle-Income Economies" range from per capita gross national products of $650 in Bolivia to $7,800 in Saudi Arabia. The "High-Income Economies" range from per capita gross national products of $11,120 in Ireland to $33,610 in Switzerland.[12]

Frequently, the term "developing nations" is used interchangeably with the "Third World"; strictly speaking, they are *not* the same thing. The term "Third World" refers to nations that are not in the Western, capitalistic, industrial, and (generally) democratic states (including the United States, Britain, France, Japan, and so on), and also *not* in what used to be called the Eastern European Marxist-Leninist states (including the former Soviet Union and its satellites).

It is usually not a good idea to define a term only by what it is *not*, because there may be tremendous variation left in the category one is examining. This is certainly true of the concept of the Third World. Some Third World nations have tremendous financial problems: Brazil, for example, has a long-term foreign debt of $95 billion, the highest of any nation ranked by the World Bank, and a per capita gross national product of under $3,000 per year.[13] Others are extremely rich: Qatar has one of the highest per capita gross national products in the world—$14,770 in 1991.[14] To put Qatar and Brazil in the same category may make sense, but we have to be aware of what we are doing, and why.

There is a substantial literature devoted to the methodological question of how we should measure development. Often development is confused with economic growth; this can be a major problem in theory-building. If we believe that development is linked to poverty, unemployment, and inequality, for example, it is clear that a country's GNP can grow rapidly without our necessarily seeing any improvement in these three indicators of its "development."

---

*The gross national product (GNP) of a country is an estimation of the value of goods and services produced within a nation. It includes income sent into the country by citizens abroad and excludes income that foreigners in the country send overseas. The gross domestic product (GDP) is an estimation of the value of goods and services produced within a nation, *not* including income sent into the country by citizens abroad but including income that foreigners in the country send overseas.

**This figure is in 1991 U.S. dollars.

One author has suggested that the term "Third World" implies a number of characteristics, including a colonial history; a relatively underdeveloped economy and level of technological development, especially when compared to the United States or Europe; a lack of interest and/or success in developing "modern" (that is, European) social, cultural, and economic institutions; and a commitment to work for greater world equality in the realm of economic and social policy.[15] Elsewhere six common characteristics have been suggested as being typical of developing nations: (1) low levels of living standards; (2) low levels of productivity in work; (3) high rates of population growth; (4) high and rising levels of unemployment and underemployment; (5) dependence on agricultural production and "primary product exports"; and (6) dependence and vulnerability in international relations.[16]

> The "third world" is one result of the process by which, since the late fifteenth century, the previously scattered peoples of the globe have been brought together into what is in many respects a single society, economy, and political system. . . . What distinguishes the third world is its peripherality. Economic peripherality has meant separation from, and subordination to, the dominant industrial economies which have developed especially in Europe and North America. . . .[17]

Developing nations include the low- and middle-income nation-states. The World Bank defines as "low-income" those nations with a per capita GNP of $635 or less. The average per capita GNP in these nations was less than $350 in 1993. Middle income nations are in turn divided into two groups. Lower-middle-income nations were defined by the World Bank as those having $636 to $2,555 GNP per capita, and their average in 1993 was about $1,590; upper-middle-income nations were defined by the World Bank as those having $2,556 to $7,910 GNP per capita, and their average in 1993 was about $3,530. Overall the middle-income nations had an average per capita GNP of $2,480 in 1993.[18]

It is no coincidence, of course, that most members of what we call the Third World were the subjects of European colonialism, and most of the developed nations were the colonial powers themselves. Generally speaking, the significance of the system of colonialism can be found in "its lingering effects on the political and economic structures of Third World countries and on the psyche of colonized peoples, effects that have lingered because of the length and intensity of the experience."[19] European colonialism, among other things, created the "global political and economic order" that we know today.[20]

Although most of Latin America was independent by the middle of the nineteenth century, virtually the entire African continent was colonial until after World War II. We can find three interrelated sets of explanations for colonialism: socioeconomic, political, and romantic.[21] Patterns of colonialism that existed around the world were often primarily economic in nature; the colonial powers developed and exploited markets for their goods, as well as developing and exploiting sources of primary materials for their own industries. Thus the developing nations were sources of materials for industries in the colonial nations, and often did not develop any industries themselves.

Following the end of World War II most colonial empires began to be dismantled, and by the mid-1960s only a few colonial territories remained. By the 1980s there remained only a very few "microcolonies," as they were called, "virtually all of them islands."[22] We can point to Bermuda, Martinique, the Falkland Islands, and so on, as examples of remnants of colonial empires. These few examples are dwarfed by the long lists of new nations that have emerged from colonial domination.

The Distribution of Economic Resources

A tremendous difference exists in how economic resources are distributed around the world. As described by one author,[23] an "average nuclear family" household in North America would consist of a family of four with an annual income of about $25,000 to $30,000, who live in an apartment or a suburban house with separate bedrooms for each of the children and the parents, with many consumer goods and adequate food, and with the members of the family receiving adequate health care. The children would be able to attend college, if they so desired, and would live to an average age of 72 to 75 years.

On the other hand, a "typical extended family" household in Asia would consist of ten or more people, including parents, five to seven children, grandparents, and some aunts and uncles. The combined annual income of the household, both in money and "in kind" (including the food they grow), would be between $150 and $200 per year, on the average. They would probably live in a single room, and the parents and the older children would be agricultural workers. Typically, there would not be enough food to eat, the children would not attend school beyond a few years of elementary school, and there would be inadequate health care.[24]

As many observers have noted, the process of development in recent years has given reasons for both optimism and pessimism. On one hand, a number of developing nations appear to have made real and substantial economic progress over the last two decades or so. According to the World Bank, the increase in the gross *domestic* product of the low-income economies between 1980 and 1990 averaged about 6 percent.[25] Comparable progress included an increase in life expectancy (from an average of 42 years in 1960 to 62 years in 1991), a decline in infant mortality (cut from 109 deaths per 1,000 live births in 1970 to 71 deaths per 1,000 live births in 1991), and an increase in primary school enrollment (rising from 74 percent in 1970 to virtually 100 percent of the appropriate age group in 1990).[26]

These figures are *averages*, however, and as such they indicate that although some groups of individuals and/or nations have enjoyed improvements in their lot in life, others have not enjoyed the same improvements. It is clear that most of the items measured by these figures—such as wealth, income, job opportunities, education, medical care, housing, and agricultural production—are not evenly distributed between and among nations. We can take as an example of this a comparison of the per capita GNP of the United Arab Emirates of $20,140 annually in 1993—based on oil production—with the per capita GNP of Tanzania of $100 annually in 1993—based on not much of a developed economy at all.[27] Similarly, the infant mortality rates per 1,000 live births that we mentioned above vary dramatically: 149 for Mozambique, 42 for El Salvador, 5 for Japan.[28]

According to one observer, the "average per capita real incomes in the large majority of developing countries, especially in African and Asian low income ones, are no higher than they were in the late 1960s, and many seem to have retrogressed."[29] There is tremendous range of progress, even among the broad categories of nations. For example, among the "low-income economy" nations, India saw a 6.3 percent average annual growth rate in industry between 1980 and 1991; Tanzania saw a 2.4 percent decline. The agricultural sector of Togo's economy grew at an average rate of 5.3 percent; Rwanda's declined at an average annual rate of 1.5 percent. The manufacturing sector of Lesotho's economy grew at an average annual rate of 12.8 percent; that of Sierra Leone declined at a rate of 1.4 percent.[30] Although some Third World nations have substantial oil or mineral resources—such as the members of OPEC (Organization of Petroleum Exporting Countries); or Chile, Peru, Zaire, and Zambia, which control the world's copper supply; or Guinea, Guyana, Jamaica, and Sierra Leone, which control much of the planet's bauxite trade—"the vast majority of Third World countries are not so well endowed, being dependent on agricultural production."[31]

The "basic needs" approach to the study of development focuses on the question of the distribution of income and the distribution of "certain standards" of nutrition, health, and education services. It advocates "making the meeting of certain fundamental human needs a development priority," and is a widely shared approach to the study of the process of political development.[32] Not only are there dramatic differences *among* nations in terms of many of the basic needs of life, but it is often the case that *within* nations in which there has been a net increase in the standard of living, this increase is not evenly distributed.

In fact, the national increase is usually a product of a significant rise for a small minority of the population, while the majority of the population continues to exist with traditional standards of living. This phenomenon is illustrated in Table 3.1. In the case of Sri Lanka, for example, the poorest 40 percent of the population re-

TABLE 3.1
Distribution of Income in Seven Nations

	GNP Ranking Per Capita	Percent of National Income or Consumption Received by Top 10% of Population	Percent of National Income or Consumption Received by Bottom 40% of Population
Sweden	3	20.8	20.2
United States	8	25.0	15.7
France	10	25.5	18.4
Mexico	36	39.5	11.9
Poland	58	21.6	23.0
Sri Lanka	97	43.0	13.3
Ethiopia	125	27.5	20.7

Source: Rankings from World Bank, *World Development Report, 1993* (New York: Oxford University Press, 1993), pp. 238, 296.

ceives less than 14 percent of the national income or consumption, while the richest 10 percent of the population receives over 43 percent!

International Financial Relations and Debt

The inequality between and among nations in their wealth and economic viability has led to a growing system of *international dependence*, in which the "have-not" nations have come to rely more and more upon the aid programs of the "have" nations in order to survive. In many respects "the history of the Third World is to a large extent the history of its incorporation into a global economy dominated by the 'core' industrialized countries of Western Europe and the United States."[33] The programs of these core nations include grants, loans, and in-kind assistance (such as wheat or tractors).

The economic dependence of the developing nations upon the developed nations has grown into a major international problem in recent years as the international debts of some of the have-not nations have skyrocketed, and the likelihood that they will ever be able to repay their loans has decreased. It is easy to see that Mozambique, a country with an annual gross domestic product of $1.2 billion and a long-term debt of $4.1 billion, is going to have serious problems repaying its debts. Jamaica ($3.5 billion GDP and $3.8 billion in debt) has similar problems. Even countries with a slightly positive debt-to-GDP ratio (for example, Syria, with a GDP of $17.2 billion and a debt of $14.9 billion) have impossibly high burdens, since they cannot afford to pay 25 to 30 percent of their GDP in interest on loans every year. This is a point to which we shall return below.[34]

The foreign-debt problem is especially troubling to some because it often carries with it the specter of foreign intervention.[35] One recent study has suggested that over the next few years "Latin America will have to appropriate as much as about 30 percent of its export earnings for payment of interest on its external debt."[36]

Indeed, in July 1989 Brazil missed making a payment of $812 million owed to foreign governments, primarily because its trade surplus* with foreign countries had decreased in recent years and Brazil's government was concerned that a payment of that size could adversely affect the national economy. Brazil's inability to keep up payments on its present debts in turn affects the ease with which it will receive future loans. At the time of that missed payment, action had just been taken to freeze several loans to Brazil, including $900 million in fund loans, $600 million in commercial bank loans, and about $1.5 billion in Japanese assistance. Recently the World Bank tabled plans for two loans to Brazil totaling $725 million.[37]

One scholar has argued that:

> it is high time for the foreign aid community to take a hard look at costs and benefits of its work in general systems terms. How much has been spent and how much has been gained in overall results? How much have taxpayers in advanced countries contributed, and to what benefit, to those who live in poverty? . . . Development or-

*The trade surplus is the amount of the excess of value of sales of domestic (in this case, Brazilian) goods over the value of imported goods.

ganizations would be well advised to undertake self-evaluations to determine (1) to what extent they have helped the developing world; (2) to what extent they have caused or contributed to Third-World problems; and (3) who in the final analysis has benefited the most from the total amount of aid—the poor or the privileged of the Third World, Western commercial firms, or development bureaucrats, experts, and specialists?[38]

Many Third World nations are in the unfortunate position of having *single-product economies*, or nearly single-product economies; when their single crop (or industrial product) loses its value on the world market, the economy of the nation is severely hurt. Recent examples of this type of problem include the economy of the small Caribbean island of St. Vincent when the price of sugar fell sharply; the economy of Nigeria, Trinidad, or Mexico when the world price of oil declined; or the economy of Chile when the price of copper plummeted. A virtually single-product economy can also leave a nation vulnerable if it sells most of its product to only one other nation: One of the reasons that Brazil's economy took a downward turn had to do with its dependency upon world agricultural markets and the failure in the world market of some of its cash crops.[39]

Some of the problems faced by Third World countries can be attributed to the lack of economic independence that we suggested previously. It has generally been accepted that the economic success of Third World nations is very dependent upon the economic growth and expansion of the large industrialized nations.[40]

In practice economic development often means *industrialization*, because economies entirely dependent upon agriculture do not have high GNPs. The world's poorest nations are primarily agricultural and rural, whereas the richest nations tend to be industrial and urban. Associated with industrialization we can find such characteristics as higher literacy, higher GNPs, lower infant mortality, better health care, and a generally higher standard of living.

Economic Nationalism

There appears to be no clear-cut definition of exactly what economic nationalism is, or what set of domestic and international policies are mandated by it. According to Peter J. Burnell, however, "economic nationalism" as a term, "often carries, and is intended to carry, considerable normative weight, favourable or pejorative, depending on who is stating the claim."[41] The general idea implied by the term usually involves a strong feeling that the interests of the nation, as defined in a certain way (for example, social, political, economic, cultural), should take priority in economic policy-making, regardless of past practices, long-term goals, or short-run economic hurdles.

Economic nationalism does not necessarily mean opposition to all foreign interests, for what is in the interests of one's own nation may also be in the interests of others. Similarly, the primary targets of economic nationalism may not be a specific country or group of countries, but could be a type of multinational corporation (for example, mining companies)—or all foreign multinational corporations, for that matter.

Typically, the economic goals of nationalists involve developing industry in one's own country, broadening markets in international trade, decreasing economic dependence upon one or a few other countries, and regaining (or gaining for the first time) domestic economic control of important sectors of the economy. Examples include regaining control of the copper mines from foreign multinationals in Chile, nationalizing the asbestos mines in Quebec, or developing a domestic soft-drink market in India. The overall goal, then, is "a desire for greater national economic in dependence."[42] Additionally, there have been regional variations on the theme of economic nationalism, such as "pan-Arabism," "pan-Islam," "pan-Africanism," "Asian cooperation," and "pan-Americanism," to name some of the more visible examples.[43]

Foreign investment is often a target of economic nationalism. This type of investment is often sought by developing nations because it brings to a nation much-needed capital, thus helping to create industries and jobs. This in turn helps to create other industries and jobs. Problems may develop, however, when specific foreign industries become too large and powerful, or when a government suddenly perceives that it is not able to control the direction of its own economy because substantial economic actors—often the multinational corporations—have their own goals and strategies. According to Burnell, "Experience has shown . . . that foreign direct investment . . . will not necessarily bring to an LDC (less developed country) many, let alone all, of the possible benefits" sought by the promotion of foreign investment.[44]

INSTITUTIONS AND ECONOMIC DEVELOPMENT

Because our stress in this book is on political institutions, a word should be said about how the institutions on which we will be focusing our attention affect political development and economic policy. As one source notes: "Given the difficult task of creating political order in Third World countries, the processes of selecting and implementing constitutional processes are important. If constitutional processes fail to take hold, as is the case in many Third World countries, political development is greatly retarded."[45] Specifically, do institutions help shape the distribution process of economic values? Do institutions affect economic stability? Do some structures enhance economic development or detract from it, and why?

In recent years, more attention has been paid to "institutional" development in the Third World. The main reason for this is that "national economic management capacity is critically dependent on the efficient functioning of a few key national institutional processes such as budgeting and personnel management."[46] Moreover, as one author has noted:

> To shorten a long and complicated story, the failure of development efforts is assumed to be due basically to the weaknesses of the political systems of the LDCs. Given the paramount importance of the political system in providing leadership and direction for all other systems—economic, social, and administrative—the political system's inability to fulfill its role adversely affects the performance of all other sectors.[47]

Economic development is dependent on the capacity of a number of institutions to respond to project and policy initiatives.[48]

The purpose of economic policy in both developing and developed nations is the same: to guide or control the economy in such a way as to influence the size, growth, and distribution of its gross national product.[49] There is, obviously, an extremely wide range of policies that might be available to any government to use to influence the economy, including government expenditures, the level and composition of taxes, the role of local governments and other organizations in making and administering policy, monetary policy and institutions, trade policy, protectionism, and tariffs and exchange rates. These activities, and others, may be used in four broad areas of policy intervention: (1) altering the distribution of income through policies designed to change prices; (2) redistributing ownership of assets; (3) redistributing income through progressive income and wealth taxes; and (4) direct transfer payments and public provision of goods and services (such as public health programs or school lunch programs).[50]

Centralization and Decentralization

The concept of the political centralization of economic planning has been shown to have a direct relevance for the process of economic and political development.[51] During the years after 1970 many governments in the Third World tried new approaches to economic and social policy-making that included "decentralized authority for planning and administration to state, regional, district, and local agencies, field units of central ministries, local governments, and special-purpose organizations."[52]

As used here, the term "decentralization" suggests transferring planning and administrative authority from the central government in a political system to local units, field organizations, local governments, or special nongovernmental organizations.[53] Several good reasons exist for decentralizing policy and administration in the Third World. Specifically, decentralization:

1. Allows planners and managers to be closer to the problems they are trying to solve;
2. Minimizes "red tape," which results from a centralization of services;
3. Helps to increase officials' awareness of local problems;
4. Encourages penetration of policies into hinterlands—that is, areas far removed from the nation's capital—where governmental policies may be viewed as irrelevant;
5. Allows for greater representation for ethnic, religious, and other social groups in the policy-making process;
6. Encourages the development of leadership and administrative experience among people who might never have that option were all decisions to be made at the center;
7. Increases the efficiency of government at the center by freeing officials at the center from having to spend a great deal of time making decisions that could be made by individuals at the field or local level;
8. Increases communication and coordination between the center and the more remote areas of the nation;

9. Encourages more citizen participation in planning and administration;
10. Decreases the domination of the policy-making process by "entrenched local elites who are often unsympathetic to national development policies and insensitive to the needs of the poorer groups in rural communities";
11. Encourages greater flexibility and innovation;
12. Allows leaders to locate facilities and services in communities where they will be more useful than communities that might be selected by centralized leadership;
13. Increases stability and national unity by encouraging participation; and
14. Increases the efficiency with which public goods and services are delivered to the people of a nation.[54]

In Asia many of the best examples of conflicts over decentralization can be found in India, where despite a centralized federal system established by the British colonial government, there has been a fairly consistent movement to encourage local government and local administration:

> It seems that local government exists as a form of bureaucracy, but the constant revival of the concept of local elections reflects either a form of collective conscience that reminds leaders of the positive values in self-government, or a pragmatic approach that recognizes the value of local participation for achieving central goals.[55]

Pakistan, Thailand, Malaysia, and the Philippines are some other Asian nations that have undertaken experiments in decentralization in the last two decades.

Not only can government structures be slightly decentralized through a federal organization, but administration can be decentralized, too. Between 1967 and 1981 Thailand's government decentralized the administrative process to make it both more flexible and more responsive to local needs. Actions undertaken by the government included decentralizing industrial management, basic economic services, and social services, so as to increase the number of people who could benefit from governmental services and increase production opportunities for business. This included giving local authorities power over how some development funds would be spent and seeking local input on how villages should be organized and planned.[56]

In Africa, an example of this movement toward decentralization can be found in the case of Kenya, where the government began to decentralize planning and administration responsibilities in the early 1970s. This move to decentralization was prompted by a dissatisfaction with the results of planning undertaken by the central government and by a desire on the part of local leaders and administrators to play a more active role in the overall planning process.[57]

In Latin America the process of decentralization has met with great institutional opposition, primarily because "concentration of decision making within central government ministries, often referred to as overcentralization, is a fundamental characteristic of Latin American governments."[58] Much of the push toward decentralization in Latin America has resulted in the creation of "autonomous" government agencies; in a sense it is a curious form of decentralization because power still resides at the center, but it is placed with a different structure at the center.

For example, there are over 500 decentralized organizations and what have been called "parastatal enterprises" that have been established by the Mexican government. These include Petroleos Mexicanos (the state petroleum corporation, PEMEX) and the state coffee marketing board, which are decentralized organizations, and numerous banks, hotels, sugar mills, and food industries, which are parastatal enterprises. Additionally, over 800 independent commissions and councils, including the National Council on Agriculture and the Federal Commission on Electricity Rates, are significant public organizations involved in the creation and administration of public policy.

These parastatal enterprises operate legally, much as would private corporations. The greatest significant difference is that the parastatal enterprises have representatives of the government on their boards of directors, and their activities are generally subject to the oversight of the government. The centralized organizations are legally distinct, they own their own property, and they have their own governing boards. Unlike parastatal enterprises, however, they fall under provisions of administrative law rather than commercial law.[59]

Other attempts at decentralization in Latin America have resulted in regionalization. For instance, Venezuela has sought "to establish a new level of government between the center and the states and municipalities that can plan and coordinate the activities of all government units within each region."[60]

It is interesting to note that while we can identify movements toward decentralization of government in Third World countries around the world, the motivations for decentralizing planning and administration are not always the same. In some countries a desire for greater political legitimacy is the driving force; elsewhere the motivation comes from demands from regional, ethnic, tribal, or religious groups for greater participation in the policy-making process. In most instances, however, decentralization is seen as a way to make government more responsive, more efficient, and more effective.

Legislatures and Development

The link between elected assemblies and political development is a very significant one, because legislative institutions help to provide the legitimacy for the change and dynamism that are inherent in the term "development."[61] Very often the legislature as an institution is especially vulnerable to attack in a developing system because it is one of the few institutions specifically oriented to promote discussion and interest articulation, and thereby directly affects the legitimacy of the regime:

> The legislature is the political institution most likely to define political issues, and policies to resolve those issues, in sectional terms. The legislature is also perceived by executive decisionmakers as a body which lacks the expertise necessary to properly consider complex issues, and as a threat.[62]

As an institution, the legislature is especially concerned with the development of linkages between the political center of the nation and the more peripheral regions of the nation.[63] Legislators are often concerned with such issues as political representation, resource allocation, and public support for the legislature and, thereby, the regime.[64]

Bureaucracy and Development

One of the major problems faced by developing nations, to which we alluded earlier, is that they do not possess enough individuals with a sufficient level of bureaucratic skill to keep their new governments running relatively smoothly. Some new nations, such as India, were left with a reasonably large pool of trained talent when their colonizing powers left; elsewhere—in Africa, for example—colonial powers pulled out of nations without leaving behind an adequate cadre of trained and experienced administrative talent.[65]

The implications of this shortfall are immediately clear. Although the term "bureaucracy" may have negative connotations in many parts of the world, all nations need a body of individuals to administer programs, oversee the development of policy, and participate in the day-to-day operation of the government. Developing nations are, in respect of this need, no different from developed nations; their problem usually lies in not having an adequate supply of bureaucratic talent. As one observer noted, "African administrators whose responsibilities until recently were characterized by routine are catapulted to the top of the hierarchy, where they are expected to advise ministers and politicians regarding major programs of economic and social development.[66]

We shall return to a discussion of the role of the bureaucracy in Chapter 5, which examines the political executive.

Political Parties and Development

Other political institutions, apart from those described in a constitution, may have an impact on political and economic development. Such development-related issues as political participation, political legitimacy, national integration, and the management of conflict can be affected by political parties as well as by constitutional structures such as legislatures, for example.

Political parties clearly have an impact on types and levels of political participation, especially movements and demands for political participation, which "are a characteristic feature of political development."[67] Although the existence of political parties "does not in itself guarantee that governing elites . . . will welcome expanded political participation,"[68] parties are associated with the kind of debate, discussion, and interest-group activity conducive to expanded participation.

Political parties are a vehicle to mobilize the populace, and thus are an almost absolutely necessary structure for a system involved in political development. Even a one-party government can be democratic and mobilizing and thereby helpful in the developmental process.

Parties also can be significant in the process of the legitimation of political authority, which is important in the development process. Parties assist in the processes of political recruitment and political socialization, and help to pass on the political culture of the regime from one generation to another.

Although parties are not absolutely essential to the process of national integration (because we can identify a number of nations that resolved their "crises of national integration" before the advent of political parties), they can be very important in this function for contemporary developing nations. According to one view, "in most new nations of Asia and Africa, governing political parties are concerned with two elements of national integration—the issue of control over the nation's territory and the issue of subjective loyalties."[69]

Finally, political parties can be important vehicles for the resolution of conflict in developing systems. Parties often serve as "brokerage" mechanisms helping to facilitate conflict between and among groups in societies, especially in societies in which democratic elections are the vehicle for the selection of leaders.

Other Influences on Development

These three structures—legislatures, bureaucracy, and political parties—by no means make up an exhaustive list of the political structures and institutions that can influence the process of political development. Rather, they are indicated here simply as *illustrations* of the kinds of linkages that can exist between political institutions and the development process. Indeed, substantial research has focused on the impact on political development of communications,[70] education,[71] and the political culture,[72] to name only a few of the behavior and institutional subjects of inquiry in this regard.

POLITICAL ECONOMICS AND POLITICAL DEVELOPMENT

The problems suggested by the interaction of political economics and political development are faced everywhere in the contemporary world. Economic development requires political leadership and "control, integration, and coordination of financial and personnel management at the national level with conventional development efforts."[73] One useful indicator of the importance of political control for economic policy "lies in the priority which economic development has as a political goal of government."[74] As one observer has noted:

> All societies (developed and developing, rich and poor, high, middle, or low income) are faced with decisions concerning production, consumption, resource allocation, distribution, and growth. How these decisions are made, as well as their outcomes, depends on the interplay of a variety of general and specific factors. The general factors are those over which countries have very little or no control, for example, natural resource endowments, economic size, and international economic forces. Specific factors include a given country's unique history, the sociocultural environment, and the government's political ideology as is normally reflected in specific programs and policies it is willing to pursue.[75]

Theories of Development

The problem with much of what has been called "development theory" is that it has not adequately explained the phenomenon of development and evolution of political systems. "Dependency theory" became popular in the 1960s, and suggested solutions to the problem of a lack of economic development. The most common explanation of the theory was that underdevelopment was not simply a temporary condition leading, eventually, to development; rather, it was directly related to—and some said caused by—the expansion of capitalism and industrialism elsewhere in the world.[76] "The tendency to use the formula of *dependencia* to explain everything that seems wrong in the Third World has been at once understandable and quite damaging. . . ."[77]

Dependency theory made some important contributions to an understanding of the political world, however.[78] It showed us that modern developing nations differ in significant ways from the industrializing Western nations of the past; that world economic conditions inflict constraints on today's developing nations; and that there is an interaction between political, social, and economic factors in the process of development.[79]

Generally speaking, four broad schools of development theory can be said to exist, or to have existed,[80] although as we noted earlier they are no longer widely used. These are the liberal model, the historicist approach, the managerial approach, and the neo-Marxist approach.[81] We shall briefly describe each of these approaches here.

The *liberal model* of development suggested, most simply, that the process of development is a linear one, that stages or developmental phases are passed in the same order, and that all countries go through the development process. The "advanced" nations, the assumption went, started the process of development earlier; the developing countries were simply at an earlier stage of the process, and they would follow the evolution of the developed nations.

The *historicist approach* objected to the assumption of the liberal model that all countries would follow the same process. These social scientists suggested that not all societies started their evolution at the same point, and further suggested that because many Western characteristics were missing in a great number of developing societies, "many of the institutional configurations that characterized the transformation of Western societies were unlikely to be duplicated in subsequent modernization of other societies."[82] In other words, not all systems would follow the same pattern of political evolution, but rather would mature as a con sequence of particular national characteristics.

The *managerial approach* focused, as its name suggests, less on the broader questions of how political structures and behavior evolved, and more on questions of how problems are solved in society and how policy is made and evaluated. One of the most influential voices in this school moved his emphasis from having the goal of development be democracy to having the goal of development be stability and institutional order.[83]

Finally, the *neo-Marxist approach* focused not on the stages of development, or on the specific factors that influence development, or on how problems are solved in the development process, but rather on the "pathology of development, namely underdevelopment."

> The central idea of the neo-Marxist is that far from being independent occurrences, the development of the industrial countries and the underdevelopment of poor countries are opposite phases of the same historical process. . . .The historical process of the expansion and development of capitalism throughout the world simultaneously generated and continues to generate both economic development and structural underdevelopment.[84]

Problems of Development

It has been concluded, generally speaking, that "the cumulative benefits of economic growth have not 'trickled down,' or have not otherwise been sufficiently 'diffused' to the masses of the population in the developing world."[85] Indeed, whatever scholars' differences in theoretical approaches to problems of development, there is some general consensus on practical problems: "Those on the Left and on the Right as well as those in the middle tend to agree that the rate of growth achieved by most less developed countries (LDCs) after four decades of foreign assistance is less than satisfactory, if not disappointing."[86] There are a vast number of general problem areas that are significant across these LDCs, a few of which we shall briefly discuss here.

Population.   At the end of the 1980s the world's population was estimated to be nearly 5.5 billion. United Nations projections predict a world population of over 6.1 billion by the year 2000, and over 8.3 billion by the year 2025.[87] Population is a significant issue in the study of development for two distinct but interrelated reasons. First among these, of course, is the argument suggested by Thomas Malthus in 1798 (*An Essay on the Principle of Population*[88]) that the increase in population in a society will outstrip any increases in production or economic growth to be found in the economy, and that the only way for societies to avoid a "condition of chronic low levels of living" was for people to enage in "moral restraint" and limit the growth of their families.[89] Second, it has been argued that population increases often have favorable or unfavorable effects on the growth rates of economies.

At the beginning of the eighteenth century the world population doubling time was 240 years; at the beginning of the twentieth century it was 115 years, and in the period from 1930 to 1950 it was 70 years. As illustrated in Table 3.2, the world's population has increased the *rate* at which it is increasing, and today the world's population doubles approximately every 35 to 40 years.[90] Furthermore, as shown in Table 3.3, the proportion of the world's population living in the "underdeveloped" world is increasing: In 1950 approximately 67 percent of the world's population lived in underdeveloped nations; by the year 2000 it is expected that this figure will rise to almost 80 percent.

Although the size of one's family may be a matter of personal concern, it also has national and societal implications: If a nation's population grows at a rate

TABLE 3.2
World Population Increase

Year	Population (in millions)
1750	731
1800	890
1850	1,171
1900	1,668
1950	2,525
1980	4,432
2000	6,121 (projected)

Source: Adapted from J. Faaland and J. R. Parkinson, *The Political Economy of Development* (New York: St. Martin's Press, 1986), p. 168.

faster than the increase of its economy, to take a simple illustration, the increase in the amount of available food will not be adequate for the increase in mouths seeking that food. Conversely, of course, a population that is too *small* may limit the potential expansion of an economy; a nation cannot increase its factories if there are no people to work in those factories.

Not only is the *growth* of population a problem, but so too is its *distribution*. Increasingly, populations are moving out of the rural areas of nations into urban centers, often in search of jobs and a better life. Ironically, with this movement comes an increase in slums and overcrowded and unhealthy living environments. In 1970, 59 percent of Mexico's population lived in cities; by 1991 that figure had climbed to 73 percent. Similarly, in 1970 27 percent of the population of the Ivory Coast lived in urban areas, and twenty years later this had risen to 41 percent. Sometimes this urbanization is focused on a single city, often the national capital. While approximately 3 percent of the population of Canada lives in its capital city of Ottawa, 34 percent of the population of Costa Rica, 24 percent of the population of the Central African Republic, and 39 percent of the population of Uruguay live in their respective capital cities.[91]

India was the first developing country in the world to officially adopt a

TABLE 3.3
The Concentration of the World Population

	1950		1980		2000 (PROJECTED)	
	Number (in millions)	%	Number (in millions)	%	Number (in millions)	%
World, total	2,525		4,432		6,121	
Developed	832	33.0%	1,131	25.5%	1,271	20.8%
Underdeveloped	1,693	67.0%	3,301	74.5%	4,849	79.2%

Source: Based on data provided in J. Faaland and J. R. Parkinson, *The Political Economy of Development* (New York: St. Martin's Press, 1986), p. 169.

family-planning program: In the 1970s it was hoped that the government would be able to reach 90 million couples and convince half of them to limit the size of their families. To do this the government set up over 5,000 family-welfare planning centers in rural settings across the country. The program was criticized for a number of reasons, among which was that it overestimated the effectiveness of its "motivators," individuals who were charged with advocating smaller families.

> What . . . can you hope to accomplish in preaching family planning to a mass of starving illiterates living in dilapidated huts and unsanitary conditions, suffering from diseases and disabilities, and for whom life is an unending chain of misery, degradation and deprivation?[92]

One critical study estimated that in the period from 1968 to 1969 fewer than twenty-one sterilizations and fewer than eight IUD insertions were done for every technical staff person in the Indian program—not a very impressive rate of results.

In 1976 the Indian government started a new program that in effect included compulsory sterilization; over 7 million individuals were sterilized as part of this effort. This type of public policy raises significant philosophical warning flags for many observers: How much do we want governments to regulate personal behavior? This program may have been more effective than its predecessors in terms of results, but politically "the revulsion against this contributed to the downfall of Mrs. Gandhi's government in 1977."[93]

One study has suggested that there are six general policy options available to governments in their efforts to "control" population:

1. Through media and educational efforts to try to persuade people to have smaller families;
2. To establish family-planning programs to provide contraceptive services to encourage smaller families;
3. To provide economic incentives (and disincentives) to encourage smaller families;
4. To move families away from urban areas and toward rural areas to balance the distribution of the population (although this option does not limit growth);
5. To coerce people into having smaller families through laws and penalties;
6. To raise the social and economic status of women, thus encouraging delayed marriages and smaller families for the professional women.[94]

There are clear reasons why a government might want to establish population-planning policies. The problem is that population policy often runs squarely into questions of religious belief and issues affecting the most personal of family decisions, and governments have not been very effective in putting their policies into force. From an individual perspective, it may be a rational policy for a rural villager in Africa, for example, to have a large family: Without a social security system, this individual will be supported in his old age by his children. The best way to make sure that he has many children to help support him when he is old is to have many (more) children when he can, since he must allow for some level of infant mortality. From the national perspective, of course, this is *not* an optimal policy, since if a single family has, say, ten children, and each of those ten children marries and has ten children, and so on, the population growth will rapidly become an intolerable burden on society.

Quality of Life.   Many people in Third World nations are constantly struggling against malnutrition and disease. Life expectancy in 1991 averaged about 62 years in the low-income economy countries, as compared with 68 years in middle-income economy countries, and 77 years in high-income economy nations.[95] In the mid-1970s, almost half of the population of the developing world (excluding China), over a *billion* people, lived on inadequate diets, and one-third of them were children under the age of 2.[96] Today, "approximately 40 percent of all 2-year-olds in developing countries are short for their age. . . .The prevalence of stunting may be as high as 65 percent in India; it is more than 50 percent in Asia other than India and China. . . ."[97]

Education.   In many Third World countries, the "education industry" is the largest consumer of public revenues.[98] Literacy rates remain quite low in developing nations, averaging only 34 percent of the population in the least developed countries, compared with 65 percent in other Third World nations and 99 percent in the developed world.[99] Overall, it has been argued that "educational systems largely reflect and reproduce, rather than alter, the economic and social structures of the societies in which they exist."[100]

Agriculture.   It is clear that agriculture-based economies are not associated with rapid economic development. As industry expands, agriculture's share of the overall economy declines. Among the poorest countries in the world, only Benin has less than half of its population working in the agricultural sector; in many of the poorest countries, more than 80 percent of the population is engaged in agriculture. In Bangladesh this figure exceeds 90 percent.[101] Although countries differ greatly in their agricultural resources (including the quality of the soil, irrigation, and so on), new varieties of grains and plants and technology can make a remarkable difference in the economic productivity of an agricultural economy.

The basic objective of international concern over agriculture, of course, is to guarantee that all people will have adequate food supplies. The goal of governmental policy-making in this area is not only to expand food supplies through increasing production, especially in low-income, food-deficit countries, but also to maximize the stability of supplies in the face of production fluctuations and to secure access to food supplies on the part of all, especially poor people and poor nations.[102]

Industry and Employment.   One of the most important questions that governments must face in this area has to do with the distinction between the public and private sectors of the economy. Often these questions are pre-empted by fundamental ideological positions of the policy. For example, Lenin would not have considered private enterprise as a tool of national economic policy; conversely, state-owned industries are not popular tools in systems based on free enterprise. It is often the case that "the net effect of these various influences, except where there is a total commitment to public ownership, is that a mixed industrial sector emerges, partitioned (but not always neatly) between public and private operation."[103] In most developing countries, in fact, state-owned enterprises, such as utilities, transportation companies, or major industries, are common.[104]

Trade, Debt, and Foreign Economic Relations.   The problem of international debt, and particularly debt owed by developing nations to developed nations, is one that is attracting more and more attention today. Debate focuses upon who is to blame for the developing nations not being able to pay their obligations, how the problem should be resolved, and what structures should be developed to prevent these problems from recurring in the future.

Many argue that the current debt problem reflects a gross financial irresponsibility on the part of the debtor nations, suggesting that they continued borrowing money to prop up their societies without any regard for the future. Others suggest that this simply isn't true, that the developed nations actually encouraged the developing nations to borrow money, which contributed to a higher growth rate of the world's economy. "As late as 1981 many of these nations were upheld by the international financial institutions as the very model of economic management, precisely at a time when they had already accumulated vast debts,"[105] according to one observer.

The question of long-term responses also has been discussed at some length. Even if the quite substantial debts of the developing nations could simply be erased, the problem would not be solved. This statement applies equally well to present-day debt renegotiations, in which the developed nations—and financial institutions in those nations—lend the developing nations more money to cover their present payments, or allow them to postpone payments on part of the principal and interest that they owe at the present time. These actions do not solve the problem; they simply postpone its resolution. The debts will still be there, and the developing nations are hardly likely to be able to make the payments any more easily in the future (when in fact their debts will be greater) than they can today. (See Table 3.4.)

Even if the debt were done away with, the more fundamental problems would remain. One developmental problem is that a substantial proportion of the

TABLE 3.4
Debt Figures for Six Developing Nations

Nation	Total External Debt (in billions of U.S. dollars)	Total External Debt as a Percent of GNP
Brazil	$116.5	28.8%
Mexico	101.7	36.9
Egypt	40.6	133.1
Thailand	35.8	39.0
Philippines	31.9	70.2
Kenya	7.1	89.6

Source: World Bank, *World Development Report, 1993* (New York: Oxford University Press, 1993), pp. 278, 284.

world's nations do not have sufficient resources, or sufficiently developed resources, to offer their populations what they consider the basic requirements of life. The solution to this dilemma will require a wide range of actions, including increasing trade with the developing world, increasing investments in the developing world, restructuring of tariff barriers affecting trade with the developing world, increasing the resources available to the developing world, and so on.[106]

THE FUTURE FOR DEVELOPING NATIONS

The more one studies the developing world, the more serious the perceived problems become. Often faced with shortages of food and raw materials and a lack of industrial development, as well as an excess of population, developing nations confront almost insurmountable odds in the contemporary world. Even if one or two of these crises could be resolved, there would still be other problems, equally difficult to resolve, that would need to be overcome.

One necessity for these countries is institutional development. That is, if we define development as "an increased capacity for problem solving,"[107] then the developing world desperately needs growth in governmental institutions to assist in this increased capacity for problem solving. "Institutional change is primarily an entrepreneurial activity depending very much on the ability of practitioners to gain and retain the interest and attention of top decision makers."[108]

The real challenge for the developing world will be whether the resource and institutional growth that are so necessary for political and economic stability can take place in time, before the nations involved are absolutely overwhelmed by the crushing burden of debt, poverty, and population.

Notes

1. Wilfred L. David, *Conflicting Paradigms in the Economics of Developing Nations* (New York: Praeger, 1986), p. 3.
2. John Kautsky, *The Political Consequences of Modernization* (New York: Wiley, 1972), pp. 19–20.
3. Jacqueline Braveboy-Wagner, *Interpreting the Third World: Politics, Economics, and Social Issues* (New York: Praeger, 1986), p. 165.
4. Dudley Seers, "What Are We Trying to Measure?" in Nancy Baster, ed., *Measuring Development: The Role and Adequacy of Development Indicators* (London: Frank Cass, 1972), p. 22.
5. Michael P. Todaro, *Economic Development in the Third World* (New York: Longman, 1989), p. 62.
6. W. W. Rostow, *The Stages of Economic Growth* (Cambridge: Cambridge University Press, 1962).
7. Vicky Randall and Robin Theobald, *Political Change and Underdevelopment: A Critical Introduction to Third World Politics* (Durham, N.C.: Duke University Press, 1985), p. 19.
8. This summation of Rostow's framework is found in J. Faaland and J.R. Parkinson, *The Political Economy of Development* (New York: St. Martin's Press, 1986), pp. 5–6.
9. Samuel P. Huntington, "Political Development and Political Decay," *World Politics* 17 (1965): 386–430.
10. Samuel P. Huntington, *Political Order in Changing Societies* (New Haven, Conn.: Yale University Press, 1968), p. 35.
11. It must be recognized, however, that there are problems with using GNP as an indicator. According to the World Bank, "GNP per capita does not, by itself, constitute or measure

welfare or success in development. It does not distinguish between the aims and ultimate uses of a given product, nor does it say whether it merely offsets some natural or other obstacle, or harms or contributes to welfare. For example, GNP is higher in colder countries, where people spend money on heating and warm clothes, than in balmy climates, where people are comfortable wearing light clothes in the open air. More generally, GNP does not deal adequately with environmental issues, particularly natural resource use. . . ." World Bank, *World Development Report, 1993* (New York: Oxford University Press, 1993), pp. 306–307.

12. The United States ranks 120 out of 127 nations in the World Bank, passed by (in order) Germany—West Germany prior to unification—Denmark, Finland, Norway, Sweden, Japan, and Switzerland. See World Bank, *World Development Report*, pp. 238–239.

13. Ibid., p. 279.

14. Ibid., p. 304.

15. Braveboy-Wagner, *Interpreting the Third World*, p. 2.

16. Todaro, *Economic Development*, p. 27.

17. Christopher Clapham, *Third World Politics: An Introduction* (Madison: University of Wisconsin Press, 1985), p. 3.

18. The "middle-income" group itself has an extremely broad range, and it is divided into a "lower-middle-income" group and an "upper-middle-income" group. The "lower-middle-income" group has an average income of $1,590 per capita, ranging from $650 (Bolivia) to $2,520 (Malaysia) per capita. The "upper-middle-income" group has an average income of $3,530 per capita, ranging from $2,530 (Botswana) to $7,820 (Saudi Arabia) per capita. World Bank, *World Development Report*, pp. 238–239.

19. Braveboy-Wagner, *Interpreting the Third World*, p. 19.

20. Clapham, *Third World Politics*, p. 12.

21. Braveboy-Wagner, *Interpreting the Third World*, pp. 21–22.

22. Clapham, *Third World Politics*, p. 25.

23. Todaro, *Economic Development*, pp. 3–4.

24. Ibid., pp. 3–4.

25. World Bank, *World Development Report*, pp. 240–241.

26. Ibid., pp. 238, 292, 294.

27. Gabriel Almond and G. Bingham Powell, eds., *Comparative Politics Today: A World View* (Glenview, Ill.: Scott, Foresman, 1988), p. 19. Data from World Bank, *World Development Report*, p. 304.

28. Data from World Bank, *World Development Report*, p. 292, Beverly May Carl, *Economic Integration Among Developing Nations: Law and Policy* (New York: Praeger, 1986), p. 1.

29. David, *Conflicting Paradigms*, p. x.

30. World Bank, *World Development Report*, p. 240.

31. Braveboy-Wagner, *Interpreting the Third World*, p. 227.

32. Frances Stewart, *Basic Needs in Developing Countries* (Baltimore: Johns Hopkins University Press, 1985), p. 1.

33. Paul Cammack, David Pool, and William Tordoff, *Third World Politics: A Comparative Introduction* (Baltimore: Johns Hopkins University Press, 1988), p. 250.

34. World Bank, *World Development Report*, pp. 242, 278.

35. Anne O. Krueger, "Problems of Liberalization," in Armeane M. Choksi and Demetris Papageorgiou, *Economic Liberalization in Developing Countries* (New York: Basil Blackwell, 1986), p. 19.

36. Carl, *Economic Integration*, p. 2.

37. James Brooke, "Brazil Says There Is No Moratorium," *The New York Times* (July 8, 1989), p. 17.

38. Tri Q. Nguyen, *Third-World Development: Aspects of Political Legitimacy and Viability* (Rutherford, N.J.: Fairleigh Dickinson University Press, 1989), p. 115.

39. Almond and Powell, *Comparative Politics Today*, p. 23, United Nations, *1983 International Trade Statistics Yearbook* (New York: United Nations, 1985).

40. Wilfred Beckerman, "Stagflation and the Third World," in Sanjaya Lall and Frances Stewart, eds., *Theory and Reality in Development* (New York: St. Martin's Press, 1986), p. 38.

41. Peter J. Burnell, *Economic Nationalism in the Third World* (Boulder, Colo.: Westview Press, 1986), p. 16.

42. Ibid., p. 41.

43. Braveboy-Wagner, *Interpreting the Third World*, pp. 52–70.

44. Burnell, *Economic Nationalism*, p. 150.

45. David Roth, Paul Warwick, and David Paul, *Comparative Politics: Diverse States in an Interdependent World* (New York: Harper and Row, 1989), p. 107.

46. Glynn Cochrane, *Reforming National Institutions for Economic Development* (Boulder, Colo.: Westview Press, 1986), p. 2.

47. Nguyen, *Third-World Development*, p. 30.

48. Cochrane, *Reforming National Institutions*, p. 57.

49. Faaland and Parkinson, *The Political Economy of Development*, p. 83.

50. Todaro, *Economic Development*, pp. 177–181.

51. G. Shabbir Cheema and Dennis A. Rondinelli, eds., *Decentralization and Development: Policy Implementation in Developing Countries* (Beverly Hills, Calif.: Sage Publications, 1983).

52. Hidehiko Sazanami, "Introduction," in Cheema and Rondinelli, eds., *Decentralization and Development*, p. 7.

53. Dennis Rondinelli and G. Shabbir Cheema, "Implementing Decentralization Policies: An Introduction," in Cheema and Rondinelli, eds., *Decentralization and Development*, p. 18.

54. Ibid., pp. 14–17.

55. Harry J. Friedman, "Decentral Development in Asia: Local Political Alternatives," in Cheema and Rondinelli, eds., *Decentralization and Development*, p. 36.

56. Kuldeep Mathur, "Administrative Decentralization in Asia," in Cheema and Rondinelli, eds., *Decentralization and Development*, p. 61–62.

57. See Dennis Rondinelli, "Decentralization of Development Administration in East Africa," in Cheema and Rondinelli, eds., *Decentralization and Development*, pp. 77–83. Discussion of North Africa in this context can be found in the article by John Nellis, "Decentralization in North Africa: Problems of Policy Implementation," in Cheema and Rondinelli, eds., *Decentralization and Development*, pp. 127–182.

58. Richard Harris, "Centralization and Decentralization in Latin America," in Cheema and Rondinelli, eds., *Decentralization and Development*, p. 183.

59. Ibid., pp. 186–187.

60. Ibid., p. 191.

61. Allan Kornberg and Lloyd Musolf, "On Legislatures in Developmental Perspective," in Allan Kornberg and Lloyd Musolf, eds., *Legislatures in Developmental Perspective* (Durham, N.C.: Duke University Press, 1970), p. 28.

62. Chong Lim Kim, Joel Barkan, Ilter Turan, and Malcolm Jewell, *The Legislative Connection: The Politics of Representation in Kenya, Korea, and Turkey* (Durham, N.C.: Duke University Press, 1984), pp. 5–6.

63. Joel Smith and Lloyd Musolf, "Some Observations on Legislatures and Development," in Joel Smith and Lloyd Musolf, eds., *Legislatures in Development: Dynamics of Change in New and Old States* (Durham, N.C.: Duke University Press, 1979), pp. 3–42, or W. St. Clair-Daniel, "Caribbean Concepts of Parliament," *Parliamentarian* 66:4 (1985):211.

64. Each of these is discussed in some detail in Kim, Barkan, Turan, and Jewell, *The Legislative Connection*.

65. For examples of comparative research on the impact of bureaucracies on development, see Malcolm A. H. Wallis, *Bureaucracy: Its Role in Third World Development* (London: Macmillan, 1989), Joseph G. Jabbra, ed., *Bureaucracy and Development in the Arab World* (New York: E.J. Brill, 1989), Monte Palmer et al., *The Egyptian Bureaucracy* (Cairo: The American University in Cairo Press, 1989), or Ahmad Dahlan, *Politics, Administration, and Development in Saudi Arabia* (Brentwood, Md.: Amana Press, 1990).

66. Joseph LaPalombara, "An Overview of Bureaucracy and Political Development," in Joseph LaPalombara, ed., *Bureaucracy and Political Development* (Princeton, N.J.: Princeton University Press, 1967), p. 17.

67. Myron Weiner and Joseph LaPalombara, "The Impact of Parties on Political Development," in Joseph LaPalombara and Myron Weiner, eds., *Political Parties and Political Development* (Princeton, N.J.: Princeton University Press, 1966), p. 400.

68. Ibid., p. 401.

69. Ibid., p. 414.

70. The classic work in this field is by Lucian Pye, ed., *Communications and Political Development* (Princeton, N.J.: Princeton University Press, 1968). More recent works include Sarah King and Donald Cushman, *Political Communication: Engineering Visions of Order in the Socialist World* (Albany: State University of New York Press, 1992), José Marques de Melo, *Communication and Democracy: Brazilian Perspectives* (Sao Paulo: Escola de comunicacao e Artes, 1991), and Brennon Martin, *Communication and Development: A Case Study of Village Reading Centers in Thailand* (Chapel Hill: University of North Carolina Press, 1991).

71. James S. Coleman, ed., *Education and Political Development* (Princeton, N.J.: Princeton University Press, 1968).

72. Lucian Pye and Sidney Verba, eds., *Political Culture and Political Development* (Princeton, N.J.: Princeton University Press, 1968). More recent works would include Stephen Chilton, *Grounding Political Development* (Boulder, Colo.: Lynne Rienner, 1991).

73. Cochrane, *Reforming National Institutions*, p. 85.

74. Clapham, *Third World Politics*, p. 91.

75. David, *Conflicting Paradigms*, p. 23.

76. Braveboy-Wagner, *Interpreting the Third World*, p. 265.

77. Elbaki Hermassi, *The Third World Reassessed* (Berkeley: University of California Press, 1980), p. 35.

78. A good example of this kind of scholarship is the article by J. Samuel Valenzuela and Arturo Valenzuela, "Modernization and Dependency: Alternative Perspectives in the Study of Latin American Underdevelopment," *Comparative Politics* (July 1978): 535–557. See also James Caporaso, "Dependence, Dependency, and Power in the Global System: A Structural and Behavioral Analysis," *International Organization* 32 (1978):13–43.

79. Atul Kohli, ed., *The State and Development in the Third World* (Princeton, N.J.: Princeton University Press, 1986), p. 15.

80. A very good review of political development theory can be found in Richard A. Higgott, *Political Development Theory: The Contemporary Debate* (New York: St. Martin's Press, 1983).

81. Discussion of these four approaches is based upon a much longer discussion in Hermassi, *The Third World Reassessed*, pp. 17–40.

82. Hermassi, *The Third World Reassessed*, p. 20.

83. See Samuel Huntington, "Political Development and Political Decay," *World Politics* 17 (1965):386–430.

84. Hermassi, *The Third World Reassessed*, pp. 30–31.

85. David, *Conflicting Paradigms*, p. 137.

86. Nguyen, *Third-World Development*, p. 19.

87. Todaro, *Economic Development*, p. 187.

88. Thomas Robert Malthus, *Essay on the Principle of Population* (Ann Arbor: University of Michigan Press, 1959).

89. Todaro, p. 217. Malthus' name keeps surfacing in relation to this concept. See, for example, the article by James W. Michaels, "Malthus at Rio," *Forbes* (June 22, 1992), p. 10, which discusses the dangers of population growth at the 1992 United Nations Conference on the Environment and Development.

90. Faaland and Parkinson, *The Political Economy of Development*, p. 168; Todaro, *Economic Development*, p. 191.

91. World Bank, *World Development Report*, pp. 298–299.

92. Faaland and Parkinson, *The Political Economy of Development*, p. 180.

93. Ibid., p. 181.

94. Todaro, *Economic Development*, p. 231.

95. World Bank, *World Development Report*, pp. 238–239.

96. Todaro, p. 33.

97. World Bank, *World Development Report*, p. 75.

98. Todaro, *Economic Development*, p. 332–333.

99. Ibid., p. 35.

100. Ibid., p. 354. See also World Bank, *World Development Report*, pp. 238–239.

101. Faaland and Parkinson, *The Political Economy of Development*, p. 123.

102. Nurul Islam, "World Food Security: National and International Measures for Stabilisation of Supplies," in Sanjaya Lall and Frances Stewart, eds., *Theory and Reality in Development* (New York: St. Martin's Press, 1986), p. 192.

103. Faaland and Parkinson, *The Political Economy of Development*, p. 152.

104. See Malcolm Gillis, Dwight Perkins, Michael Roemer, and Donald Snodgrass, *Economics of Development* (New York: Norton, 1987), pp. 568–586.

105. Mahbub Ul Haq, "Proposal for an IMF Debt Refinancing Subsidiary," in Lall and Stewart, eds., *Theory and Reality in Development*, p. 88.

106. A tentative solution to the problem can be found in ibid., pp. 91–94.

107. Kornberg and Musolf, "On Legislatures in Developmental Perspective," p. 26.

108. Cochrane, *Reforming National Institutions*, p. 87.

Legislatures and Legislative Structures

INTRODUCTION

In 1690 John Locke published his *Second Treatise on Government*, in which he discussed the "true original, extent, and end of civil government." In his discussion of *why* individuals would leave the "state of nature" and join society, Locke suggested that the prime motivation for people doing such a thing was the preservation of "their lives, liberty, and estates, which I call by the general name, property."[1] (This phrase was subsequently amended by Thomas Jefferson in the Declaration of Independence to read "life, liberty, and the pursuit of happiness.")

There are "many things wanting" (lacking) in the state of nature, Locke suggested, and it was these missing structures that would prompt individuals to join society:

> (Section 124) First, there wants an established, settled, known law. . .
>
> (Section 125) Secondly, in the state of nature there wants a known and indifferent judge, with authority to determine all differences according to the established law. . .
>
> (Section 126) Thirdly, in the state of nature there often wants power to back and support the sentence when right . . .
>
> (Section 127) Thus mankind notwithstanding all the privileges of the state of nature, being but in an ill condition while they remain in it, are quickly driven into so-

ciety. . . . And in this we have the original right and rise of both the legislature and executive power as well as of the governments and societies themselves.[2]

Legislatures have come to be among the most popular subjects of analysis by political scientists in recent years;[3] indeed, there is now a journal devoted entirely to the study of legislatures: *Legislative Studies Quarterly*. Among other reasons for this phenomenon is the fact that legislatures are usually important structures in their respective governmental systems.[4] In addition, legislatures are among the oldest political institutions known to society. As we will see throughout this text, although the functions and powers of legislatures within their respective political systems have varied, and continue to vary today on a country-by-country basis,[5] they continue to be almost universally regarded as significant institutions.[6]

There have been many reasons suggested for the study of legislatures, including the fact that the "function of a legislature is to make the values, goals, and attitudes of a social system authoritative in the form of legislative decisions"; the fact that the legislators serve as role models for the public and in this way serve an educative function for society generally; and the fact that legislatures can be useful to society "by allowing for the expression of grievances in a public forum."[7] As a very general rationale, we may assert that "the very prevalence of legislative institutions . . . may be construed as affording *prima facie* evidence of their relevance for inquiry."[8]

It has been suggested that legislatures may be more important in some contexts than in others, much as we suggested at the end of Chapter 2 in relation to constitutions. This can be seen in the central role parliaments play in promoting regime stability,[9] or their effectiveness—or lack of it—in developing nations.[10] Another example of such a context is the process of modernization: Legislatures are important to study in this regard "because of their affinity to aspects of modernization itself."[11] Although legislatures may have more direct impact upon some subjects or processes (such as regularizing group interaction in society)[12] than others (such as land reform), it is not difficult to imagine ways in which legislatures can affect wide areas of human concern. The almost universal acceptance of the existence of legislatures in contemporary politics should in itself afford a sufficient rationale for their study.

ONE HOUSE OR TWO?

One of the initial characteristics of the legislative institution that we note when we look at a given legislature is whether it is *unicameral* or *bicameral*—whether it has one house or two houses.[13] One recent cross-national study of legislatures indicated that the number of unicameral and bicameral legislatures around the world is about even. In one of the best cross-national studies of the legislative institution, Jean Blondel found that of 107 nations which he studied that had legislatures, 52 had bicameral legislatures and 55 had unicameral legislatures.[14] The distribution of unicameral and bicameral legislatures around the world is not random: Bicameral legislatures are much more prevalent in some areas than in others, as Table 4.1 indicates.

If we want to explain why some nations have bicameral legislatures while others have unicameral legislatures, we must be very careful about making broad and

TABLE 4.1
Houses in Legislatures

Area	Unicameral	Bicameral
Atlantic area	7	15
East Europe and North Asia	10	3
Middle East and North Africa	6	4
South and East Asia	8	9
Sub-Saharan Africa	17	8
Latin America	7	13

Source: Data from Jean Blondel, *Comparative Legislatures* (Englewood Cliffs, N.J.: Prentice Hall, 1973), pp. 144–153.

sweeping generalizations. Political structures, as we have already seen, are not always what they appear to be, and legislatures are not exceptions to this rule. We *cannot* say that "legislatures serve function *X*" in all political systems, because we cannot be sure that in *all* cases that is true. The "levels of analysis" problem that we introduced in Chapter 1 is relevant here.

Why are some legislatures bicameral while others are unicameral? What do the second chambers do, where they exist? Before we can answer these questions, we must introduce a very important distinction in conceptual terms, one that will be used again and again throughout our study. This is the distinction between that which exists by legal establishment, by law, and that which exists by actual fact, although not by legal establishment. We refer to the former situation—establishment in law— as a *de jure* case, and to the latter situation—establishment in fact—as a *de facto* case.

In a number of instances throughout this text we will see political structures that simply are not the same *in fact* as they are *in law*. We will see, for example, that *de jure*, in law, an upper house of a given national legislature may have the power to delay or veto a bill passed by the lower house. It may be the case, however, that although the power exists *de jure*, it does not exist *de facto*. That upper house has not used its power of veto in over 200 years, and in the "real world," *de facto*, no matter what the law says it may do, custom and tradition prohibit the upper house from exercising what may be its legitimate legal power. In many cases, the *de facto* rule of custom and tradition is stronger than any *de jure* rule.

It should be clear now that it will be almost impossible to answer the questions that we posed earlier with any kind of broad single answer without stepping into the twin traps of the "ecological fallacy" and the "individualistic fallacy," which were introduced in Chapter 1. Bicameral legislatures may exist in a number of political settings for reasons that are completely inappropriate to one or two other nations (the ecological fallacy); we might find an explanation for the existence (or absence) of a legislature in a political system that simply would not be true for other nations (the individualistic fallacy). In short, we must proceed with caution when we generalize.

Countries that are small in size are more likely to have one chamber than two, because "the problem of the balance of political power is less difficult to solve in them than it is in big countries."[15] Bicameral systems are often regarded in socialist countries as leading to complications and delays, and as contributing few advantages to offset these costs. With the exception of Norway, all of the Scandinavian countries have, in the twentieth century, replaced bicameral systems with unicameral ones.

According to a study undertaken by the Inter-Parliamentary Union, the earliest example of a bicameral system occurred in England toward the end of the thirteenth century:

> It began with the institution of a Chamber for the high aristocracy and brought together the feudal magnates, the Lords Spiritual and Temporal. This arrangement has been maintained to the present day, although the aristocratic characteristic of the House of Lords has been reduced by the appointment to it of Life Peers. [These appointments are good only for the life of the holder, and cannot be passed from one generation to another, as can be the traditional peerage.] Furthermore, the power of the House of Lords has been greatly restricted in favour of the popular House, the House of Commons.[16]

At present, the Inter-Parliamentary Union asserts, the bicameral system can no longer be explained by the need for a separate aristocratic representation. Bicameral systems are justified primarily by two arguments. First, in federal states (as we shall further develop shortly) bicameralism reflects the split-government nature of the state. Second, in unitary states, bicameralism provides a "revising" chamber for legislation.[17]

Why would a second house exist in a political system? There are a number of possible explanations. A second house might be critical to the general political framework of the regime. It might be necessary that a federal political system be established, for example, in order to meet the conditions set by various member units of the future nation. If this is the case, one condition for national unification may be a bicameral legislature. The American "Great Compromise" in Philadelphia in 1787 is certainly one example of this genesis of a bicameral legislature. The large states wanted a representative legislature based upon population, while the small states wanted a representative legislature based upon "equal representation" for the member units (that is, an equal number of representatives per state). The Great Compromise meant that there would be a bicameral legislature, with one house based on population and the other based on an equal number of representatives for each state.[18]

To take another example, what today is the Canadian province of Quebec refused to join the Canadian confederation in 1867 without a guarantee that the future Dominion would be federal; Quebec wanted assurances that it would continue to control certain areas of policy jurisdiction as only a federation would permit. Once this was decided, it was inevitable that the new national legislature would be bicameral, with one house (the House of Commons) based upon population, and the other house (the Senate) *not* based upon population, but instead based upon equal representation for the regional units of Canada.

Where we find federal states we will almost always find a bicameral legislature in which the "lower" house represents the national, popular jurisdiction, while the "upper" house represents the intermediate political structures or territories.[19] The United States, Canada, and Germany are all examples of federal states with bicameral legislatures in which the lower houses are "national" and the upper houses are "regional."[20] (See Table 4.2.)

Although federal regimes are virtually always bicameral (the sole exception is Swaziland),[21] the association does not work in the other direction: Not all bicameral systems are federal. There are other reasons for bicameral structure than federal status. A new nation might adopt a bicameral legislative structure because that is the structure its colonial parent had, and that structure simply seemed the most normal alternative after independence was achieved. We will see that this "imitation" procedure is not at all uncommon for a variety of political structures, including executives and legal systems, when we start to examine political structures in a number of settings around the world.

Furthermore, sheer size of a nation may suggest a bicameral legislative structure to a political system. In addition, there may be such diversity in a political system that a second legislative house is felt to be needed, regardless of the fact that the political system is unitary and not federal.

The fact that virtually all federal systems are bicameral, but not all bicameral systems are federal, is illustrated in Table 4.3. We can see in this table that (1) federal systems are in a clear minority, and (2) unicameral and bicameral systems are just about evenly divided.

Where upper houses exist, the representational bases of the legislative chambers vary. They may represent assorted territorial units. In Canada, for example, the provinces of Ontario and Quebec each receive twenty-four senators, while all of the four western provinces together receive twenty-four senators. All of the maritime provinces together receive twenty-four senators, with the exception of Newfoundland, which joined the confederation last and therefore received six senators

TABLE 4.2
Some Bicameral Systems

Nation	Lower House	Represents	Upper House	Represents
United States	House of Representatives	Districts (people)	Senate	States
Canada	House of Commons	Districts (people)	Senate	Regions
India	Lok Sabha	Districts (people)	Rajya Sabha	States
Australia	House of Representatives	Districts (people)	Senate	States
Bahamas	House of Commons	Districts (people)	Senate	Appointed
Britain	House of Commons	Districts (people)	House of Lords	Appointed

TABLE 4.3
Systems and Houses

Area	Unicameral	Bicameral	Total
Unitary			
Atlantic area	7	9	
East Europe and North Asia	10	—	
Middle East and North Africa	6	4	
South and East Asia	8	7	
Sub-Saharan Africa	16	8	
Latin America	7	10	
Total	54	38	92
Federal			
Atlantic area	—	6	
East Europe and North Asia	—	3	
Middle East and North Africa	—	—	
South and East Asia	—	2	
Sub-Saharan Africa	1	—	
Latin America	—	3	
Total	1	14	15
Total	**55**	**52**	**107**

Source: Data from Jean Blondel, *Comparative Legislatures* (Englewood Cliffs, N.J.: Prentice Hall, 1973), pp. 144–153.

of its own. Upper houses may provide equal representation for member units of a federation (for example, two senators each for American states), or weighted representation for member units of a federation (for example, in the German system, some Länder have three deputies in the Bundesrat, some have four, some have five, and some have six, depending upon their size). Upper houses may simply provide an extra house in the legislature for a "sober second thought" on legislation, a house that is elected in the same manner as the lower house. In the case of Italy, for example, both houses are elected to represent the same constituency—the national population—with no geographic districts. Finally, they may provide several jurisdictions at once; the upper house in Japan represents *both* local and national units, and the British House of Lords represents hereditary positions, new political positions, judicial positions, and ecclesiastical positions.[22]

The terms "upper" and "lower" as adjectives for legislative houses are today strictly a product of convention. The terms date from early in British parliamentary history, when the House of Lords was felt to be superior to the House of Commons, even though (or perhaps because) it was not elected by the people. It was felt that the aristocratic nature of the House of Lords, the fact that it was *not* chosen by the public, made it the superior or upper house. Today, we use the term lower house to describe that house in a bicameral system (most) directly elected by the people, and upper house to describe that house farther from direct public control, although today many upper houses are elected directly by the public as well.

RELATIONS BETWEEN HOUSES

Where we find a unicameral legislature, for obvious reasons we do not have to inquire into the nature of the power relationship between legislative houses; whatever power may reside in the legislature in that particular system resides in the single house.

In bicameral settings the situation is not so simple. We may find instances in which the two houses act as equal partners in a cooperative venture; or the two houses have equal powers but are constantly feuding so that little is ever accomplished; or power is not balanced, and one house dominates the other. All of this confusion is exacerbated by the *de facto–de jure* distinction mentioned earlier. In many instances the real (*de facto*) relationship between the two houses is not the same as that written in law (*de jure*).

When we speak of a power relationship between any two actors (we can call them *A* and *B*), three possibilities emerge. *A* can have more power than *B*, *A* can have the same power as *B*, or *A* can have less power than *B*. The same options can be said to exist if *A* and *B* are two houses of a national legislative body. Let us briefly examine each of these possibilities, where bicameral legislatures exist. Table 4.4 shows us the frequencies with which these alternatives exist in the "real world" today.

The first relationship, in which the lower house is stronger than the upper house, is the most common relationship both in theory and in practice. Because many second chambers are not elected by the mass electorate, but are either appointed or hereditary bodies, many theorists argue that in principle upper houses *should* be weaker than lower houses; they are in essence "undemocratic" institutions. As Table 4.4 shows, Blondel's study of legislatures around the world found many instances in which the upper houses were *legally*, as well as behaviorally, weaker than lower houses.

It must be noted, however, that many of the political settings described in Table 4.4, in which the upper houses are indicated as being legally equal to the lower houses, do not practice this relationship. For example, although the Canadian Senate is in most respects "legally" equal to the House of Commons, and must approve all bills before they become laws, it has been described as having "retained a full set

TABLE 4.4
Powers of Second Chambers

Category	Number of Countries
Upper house weaker than lower house	26
Upper house equal to lower house	22
Upper house stronger than lower house	0
Upper house only advisory	1
No upper house	58

Source: Data from Jean Blondel, *Comparative Legislatures* (Englewood Cliffs, N.J.: Prentice Hall, 1973), pp. 144–153.

of legislative muscles, but consistently has refused to make real use of them."[23] Thus it should not be considered the *de facto* equal of the House of Commons.

In 1988, when the Canadian Senate (controlled by the Liberal Party) refused to pass a Free Trade Bill (introduced by the Conservative Government and approved by a Conservative majority in the House of Commons) that would affect Canadian and U.S. trade, the (Conservative) prime minister protested that the Senate's action was unacceptable because senators were not elected and thus they had no legitimate basis of power to block the will of the elected House of Commons. (It is worth noting that the senators held their ground. They insisted that they would not pass the bill unless the prime minister resigned, called for a new election, and received a new "national mandate." Prime Minister Brian Mulroney did just this. He was reelected with a substantial majority in November 1988, after which the Liberal-dominated Senate passed the bill re-introduced in the House of Commons by Mulroney's new Conservative government.) This situation has evolved to the point where the Canadian Senate almost never exercises its power, and when it does it is accused of being undemocratic. Thus, in Canada at least, the legal (*de jure*) status of the upper house does not reflect correctly the real (*de facto*) status of the upper house—that of being a rubber stamp.

In these legislative bodies, then, either the upper chamber legally has fewer powers than the lower house—as is the case in France, Turkey, India, and Norway—or it consistently chooses to exercise fewer powers than does the lower house, owing to political tradition or political culture (as we saw to be the case with the Canadian Senate).[24]

In other legislatures, the upper house is both legally and behaviorally an equal partner in the legislative process (although even if it is behaviorally equal, it may not have *identical* powers). Certainly among the best examples of this type of relationship is the U.S. Senate. Although the Senate is legally prohibited from certain legislative acts (according to the Constitution, for example, it cannot introduce tax bills), overall it is an equal partner in the legislative process. A bill simply cannot become a law without the Senate's approval. Similar situations, both *de jure* and *de facto*, may be found in Italy, Switzerland, Liberia, Mexico, and Jordan.

Although in theory we might find a legislature in which the upper house is actually stronger than the lower house—and we can find historical instances of this—in practice this is not common today. In some cases people might argue that the U.S. Senate is stronger and more important than the U.S. House of Representatives. The focus of attention, however, must be the question "Can the Senate pass laws without the approval of the House?" The answer is clearly "no." Blondel found *no* contemporary cases in which the power relationship was dominated by the upper house (remember that if we go back far enough in history, at one time the House of Lords dominated the House of Commons in Great Britain, for example[25]).

Finally, there are a few "variable" cases. Germany is a good example of a country with this type of structure. When legislation affects the German Länder, or states, the upper house has an absolute veto over legislation. Members of the upper house, the Bundesrat, are not directly elected by the public, but are chosen by the governments of the German states. Accordingly, if a bill that will affect the states (such as a bill on transportation policy, for example) is not approved by a majority of the representatives of the states in the upper house, it cannot become law. When legislation does *not* affect the states, such as bills focusing on foreign policy, the negative vote of the upper house may be overridden by the lower house. We shall further examine this process later in this volume.

Some upper houses, then, can be seen to have an *absolute veto* in the legislative process (for instance, the U.S. Senate); in which their refusal to approve legislation results in failure of the legislation in question. Other upper houses can be said to have *suspensory vetoes*; their refusal to approve legislation is only guaranteed to slow the legislative process a bit. Subsequent repassage by the lower house either with a regular majority (as in Great Britain) or a special majority (as in Germany) can create laws without the approval of the upper house. Still other upper houses may be said to have *rubber stamp* power only; in Canada, as we saw, the upper house legally has power to affect legislation but traditionally and culturally it is prohibited from using that power.

SIZES OF LEGISLATURES

Legislatures vary in terms of the number of houses they have, and they vary even more in terms of the number of members they have. Recent studies have found that houses of legislatures range in size from lows of 16 in the Caribbean island nation of St. Vincent and 24 in Barbados to a high of about 3,000 in China; upper chambers ranged in membership size from 6 (in Equatorial Guinea) to 1,174 (in Great Britain).[26]

Size of a legislative body may be determined by a number of factors, some philosophical and intentional, others accidental. Some legislative bodies continue to grow until it is clear that there simply is no *room* for them to grow more, and their size (number of members) is then "frozen." The U.S. House of Representatives is a good example of this. The representative-to-population ratio was one for every 30,000 people in 1787; by 1970 it was approximately one for every 500,000 people. The ratio has changed because the size of the House was frozen. In 1787 there were 66 members in the House; there were 242 in 1833. In 1921 a reapportionment based on the 1920 Census would have pushed the size of the House to 483. The House decided at that time to keep its membership at 435, arguing that "the great size of the membership had already resulted in serious limitations on the right of debate and an overconcentration of power in the hands of the leadership."[27] It took eight years before this view was incorporated in law, but in 1929 a law was passed and signed by President Herbert Hoover establishing the maximum size of the House of Representatives at 435 members.

The size of Canada's House of Commons has grown over the years, following this pattern of having a census every ten years and adding seats in the legislature to accommodate new population. In the last two decades the size of the House of Commons has grown from 263 to 295. Some voices in Canada are now calling for a freezing of the membership of the House of Commons, as was done to the U.S. House of Representatives in 1929. It seems likely that this will eventually happen, but it must be recalled that the British House of Commons grew to 630 members before its size was frozen.[28]

In other settings, the size of a legislative body may be symbolic. The size of the unicameral Israeli Knesset was determined by historic precedent: The Great Assembly—the first supreme legislative authority elected by the Jews in the fourth and fifth centuries B.C.—had 120 members, ten representatives for each of the twelve tribes of Israel. When the modern State of Israel was created in 1949 it was determined that the new national assembly should also have 120 members.[29] Size may also be decided by a formula; in the case of Germany's upper house, states have three, four, five, or six representatives each, depending upon their population.

POLITICAL PARTIES IN LEGISLATURES

One of the legislative structures about which we *can* generalize is the political party. Parties are, as a rule, highly significant structures in legislative systems, in terms of both their organizational influence and their influence over individual legislative behavior.[30] Each of these aspects of party influence merits some discussion here.

Although legislative bodies vary in both the nature and the degree of their internal organization, all legislatures have some organization. One of the major tools for the process of this organization is the political party. Parties provide candidates for formal legislative positions, such as the speaker, deputy speakers, committee chairs, and the like. Parties provide the basis around which formal organization of legislatures takes place.[31]

Parties also affect individual legislative behavior. In this context the concept of *party discipline* is central. Party discipline relates to the cohesion of the body of party members within the legislature. In a legislature with high party discipline, we can expect legislators to act (and this can include voting, debating, making speeches outside the legislature, introducing bills, or a number of other possible activities as well) in concert with their party leader's directions.[32] In legislatures with low party discipline, the concept of party label is less significant in terms of its usefulness in helping us to predict legislative behavior; individuals will act as they see fit, with little regard for directions from party leaders.

We can cite two examples to illustrate the idea of party discipline. In the British House of Commons, party discipline is very great. Members of the House of Commons invariably vote exactly as their leaders tell them to vote.[33] We would expect, for example, all members of the majority Conservative party to vote as a bloc, all the time. Any member who votes against his or her party may be subject to (party) sanctions, including withdrawal of campaign funds, being given poor committee assignments in the legislature (or no assignment at all, for that matter), and the like.[34] On occasion "free votes" take place in the House of Commons, during which time the Member of Parliament (MP) may vote as he or she wants.[35] This, however, is the only time the MP is expected to follow his or her own will in voting.

The United States offers a good example of a legislature with considerably weaker party discipline. This is not to say that there is *no* party discipline in the Congress. As a general rule, if we know legislators' party identifications, and if we know the position of the party leaders on a bill, we will be correct more often than we will be incorrect in predicting how legislators will behave. It is not at all uncommon, however, to find a group of Southern Democrats voting with Republicans, or a group of liberal Republicans voting with Democrats.

The concept of party discipline is very important to any discussion of legislative behavior, and even more important in some settings than in others, as we shall see later in this book. We shall return to this concept when we discuss political executives and their relationships to legislatures.

LEGISLATIVE COMMITTEES

Another of the major structures that we find in legislative bodies is that of the *committee*.[36] Committees exist to meet a real need in legislatures: Legislative bodies as a whole are generally too large and unwieldy to enable serious and complex discussion on highly specialized matters to take place. Additionally, the aspect of specialization is important in its own right. *No* legislator can be an expert on *every* subject. If, however, the entire legislative body is divided into groups, with each group specializing in a different aspect of the legislature's business, the work of the legislature can be performed more efficiently and more accurately. The idea of a division of labor and specialization serves as the primary justification for the legislative committee's existence.[37]

Let us imagine a legislature with 200 members. Each of those 200 legislators could not possibly develop and maintain sufficient expertise in all of the disparate business of the legislature (everything from defense weapons systems to tax legislation to national parks policy to agriculture subsidies) to enable the legislature to function at peak capacity. Accordingly, the 200 members will establish, say, twenty committees dealing with the various issues that the legislature must address. Each member may serve on two committees, and each committee will have twenty members. It is usually the case, as well, that the individual committees engage further in the "division of labor–specialization" behavior, too, forming a number of subcommittees so that committee members can specialize in very narrow aspects of the committee's work.

Thus our imaginary legislature might have an Agriculture Committee, a Defense Committee, and a Finance Committee, to take three examples. These committees, as we noted, will have subcommittees. Thus, members of the Agriculture Committee, who will all be generally well informed about all aspects of agriculture, will each be very well informed about some specific aspect of the Agriculture Committee's work (such as the wheat crop or price subsidies, for example).

Legislatures tend to have a number of different types of committees. *Standing* or *permanent* committees are committees that are established at the opening of the legislative term and last for the life of the legislature. *Select* committees are committees that tend to be given specific scopes of inquiry or special problems to address, as well as specific durations. Some bicameral systems have *joint committees*, which are made up of members from both houses. The *Committee of the Whole*, often found in legislatures, is a technical device used to establish a different set of procedural rules; a legislative body can "dissolve itself" into a Committee of the Whole, and without anything physically changing (the same legislators are still sitting in the same seats), there is a different set of rules governing debate time, how motions may be introduced, and so on, that applies to their proceedings.

The relative importance of committees varies on a legislature-by-legislature basis. In some systems (such as the U.S. legislature, for example), legislative committees are very important and have a significant role in the legislative process. In other systems (such as that of Great Britain, for example), the role of committees is quite weak; they are not as active in the "oversight" function as are American committees, and they do not play as significant a role in the legislative process as their American counterparts.[38] The ability of committees to examine, modify, delay, or even "kill" legislative proposals can be very significant and can be quite important in determining the amount of power the executive branch can exercise over the legislative branch of government.

HOW LEGISLATORS ARE SELECTED

There are a number of different "pathways to parliament."[39] Legislators may ultimately arrive at their legislative positions in any of a number of ways. Some legislators, of course, are not elected by the public at all, but are appointed by some individual or political body. Others *are* elected. In this section we want to examine how legislators come to play their roles.[40]

There are two major methods by which the public elects legislators, whether the legislators involved are in the upper house or the lower house of the legislature. One method we can refer to as "district-based" elections; the other method can be called "proportional representation" elections. Each of these methods affects the political system in which it is found.[41] There are a number of variations for each of these general methods (which vary on a country-by-country basis, as we will see in the next section of this book), but the broad principles are the same.

Single-Member-District Voting

Among the most common forms of district-based representation is the system that is referred to as a "single-member-district, plurality voting" system. In this kind of system, the entire nation is divided into a number of electoral boxes, or districts. Each district corresponds to a seat in the legislative house. Within each district, an electoral contest is held to determine the representative for that district, with the individual receiving the most votes (a *plurality*) being elected. Usually all of the districts in the nation hold their elections on the same day, although special elections may be held to replace a representative who has resigned or died.

The single-member-district, plurality (SMD-P) voting system, which exists in the United States, Canada, Great Britain, Mexico, Russia, and most nations, does not usually require that any of the candidates win a *majority* of the vote. (A majority is defined as one vote more than 50 percent of the total votes cast.) All that is required for an individual to win is that he or she wins *more* than anyone else (a plurality); this is why it is sometimes called a "first past the post" system. So, in a given contest with four candidates, it would be possible for an individual to be elected with only 32 percent of the vote, if the other three candidates each received less (for instance, 25, 23, and 20 percent, respectively).

Like every other political structure we might examine, the single-member-district system has both advantages and disadvantages. A major advantage is that representatives have specific districts that are "theirs" to represent, and people know who "their" representatives are.[42] A major disadvantage is that the SMD-P system overrepresents majorities, hides minorities, and promotes a two-party system at the expense of third and minor parties. Three examples will help to make this clear.

In the first illustration, let us take four imaginary electoral districts, each with 100 voters, as illustrated in Table 4.5. Let us suppose that in *each* of these districts, in which for simplicity's sake there are two political parties, Party *A* wins 51 votes and Party *B* wins 49 votes. When we total up the results in the four districts, Party *A* will have won 204 votes to 196 for Party B, a 51–49 percent margin; but Party *A* will have won 4 seats in the legislature to 0 seats for Party *B*, a very slight majority in popular votes turning into an overwhelming majority in legislative seats. In short, the votes for Party *B* will be "unrepresented." This is an extreme mathematical example, yet the principles it demonstrates are not at all uncommon.

The second example, shown in Table 4.6, illustrates how in a multiparty system (in this case, three parties, but the same principles would apply to four, five, or more parties) a very small margin—in this case, bare pluralities in place of bare majorities—in a number of districts can make a party *appear* very strong, when, in fact, that is not the case at all. Here, although the plurality party wins only 34 percent of the popular vote, that 34 percent will yield 100 percent of the seats in the legislature.

The third example, illustrated in Table 4.7, uses the same setting as Table 4.6: four districts of 100 voters, and three parties. We can see that in the most mathematically extreme case, a shift of only *two votes* (or one-half of 1 percent, in this case!) from Party *A* to Party *B* results in Party *B* winning two seats—that is, 50 per-

TABLE 4.5
A Two-Party, Single-Member-District System

District	Party A	Party B	Total
District 1	51	49	100
District 2	51	49	100
District 3	51	49	100
District 4	51	49	100
Total votes	204	196	400
Total seats	4	0	4

TABLE 4.6
A Three-Party, Single-Member-District System

District	Party A	Party B	Party C	Total
District 1	34	33	33	100
District 2	34	33	33	100
District 3	34	33	33	100
District 4	34	33	33	100
Total votes	136	132	132	400
Total seats	4	0	0	4

cent—in the legislature where it previously had none. In other words, a shift in popular support of as little as one-half of 1 percent of the "popular vote" has the potential to change the composition of the legislature by 50 percent. Party *C* is still shut out of the legislature, despite the fact that it received 33 percent of the vote—one vote out of three—and only one-half percent less than either Party *A* or Party *B*! Clearly this is the most extreme example we could design in a 100-person district, but the principles it illustrates would apply just as forcefully in an electoral district with 100,000 voters.

    Although these examples clearly are far simpler than the reality of electoral politics, the patterns of bias that they demonstrate *are* real. In the 1992 British general election the Conservative Party won 42 percent of the popular vote, yet received 51.6 percent of the seats in the House of Commons. The bias most severely affected the smaller parties, however, as demonstrated in Table 4.8. The Liberal Democrats received 3.1 percent of the seats in exchange for 18 percent of the votes, while other small parties received 3.7 percent of the seats in exchange for six percent of the votes. This was because, as we noted above, the other small parties were regionally concentrated (for instance, the Scottish Nationalist Party), and *where they ran candidates* they won significantly more frequently than did the Liberal Democrats.

    The problem with the SMD-P system is that if a party can't get more votes than all of the other parties in a district it might as well not run there, because it will get no representation at all, as illustrated in Table 4.8 by the British Liberal Demo-

TABLE 4.7
A Three-Party, Single-Member-District System

District	Party A	Party B	Party C	Total
District 1	34	33	33	100
District 2	34	33	33	100
District 3	33	34	33	100
District 4	33	34	33	100
Total votes	134	134	132	400
Total seats	2	2	0	4

TABLE 4.8
The 1992 British General Election

Party	Percent of Votes Won	Number of Seats Won	Percent of Seats
Conservative	42%	336	51.6%
Labour	34	271	41.6
Liberal Democrat	18	20	3.1
Other	6	24	3.7

Source: Facts on File 52:2682 (April 16, 1992): 261.

crats. This happened because although they could count on some votes from many districts, in most districts they did not have *more* votes than their competitors, so they ended up with no representation. One by-product of the SMD system is a two-party system; generally speaking it is extremely hard for third parties to win seats in SMD systems, so two major parties tend to dominate the political landscape.[43]

Proportional Representation Voting

There is an alternative electoral system to the SMD system, which is called the *proportional representation* (PR) system. The PR system is not based on geographical districts at all. Rather, the members of the electorate vote for the single *party* they prefer, not for candidates. The proportion of votes that a party receives in the election (for instance, 23 percent of the total votes cast) determines the proportion of seats it will receive in the legislature (for instance, 23 percent of the legislative seats).

An example may help to clarify this. The Israeli system has a "pure" PR electoral framework. At election time, voters cast their ballots for the political party they support. After the election, if the Labour Party has received 25 percent of the votes, it receives 25 percent of the 120 seats (that is, 30 seats) in the Israeli parliament, the Knesset. How are the individual winners determined? The process is simple. Prior to the election, all parties deposit lists of their candidates with a national election board, and these lists are made public. The parties usually submit lists of 120 names—one for each possible seat in the Knesset—even though they can be sure that they will not win 100 percent of the vote. After the election, if Labour has won 30 seats (25 percent of 120 seats), it simply counts down the top 30 names on its electoral list: Positions 1 through 30 are declared elected, positions 31 through 120 are not elected. This system has an added advantage: If a Member of Knesset dies during the term, or if someone resigns for any reason, a special election is not necessary; the next name on the party list enters the Knesset.[44]

The PR system, like the SMD system, has its advantages and disadvantages.[45] Its advantages center around the fact that it is highly representative. Parties in Israel need to win only 1.5 percent of the vote to win a seat in the legislature. This means that groups that are not pluralities can still be represented in the legislature. To take our example in Table 4.5, if all districts in a 100-seat legislature voted in the same 51–49 manner as the four districts we have drawn, in a PR system Party A would receive 51 seats, and Party B would receive 49 seats. In a comparable SMD system, Party A would receive 100 seats, and Party B would receive none.

The disadvantage of the PR system is that PR legislatures tend to be multi-party legislatures—since it is so easy for smaller parties to win representation—which means that they tend to be more unstable and to contain more radical and extreme groups than SMD, two-party legislatures.[46] To use our example from Table 4.6, in a PR system Party A would win 34 of 100 seats in the legislature; Party B, 33 seats; and Party C, 33 seats. This would require the formation of a coalition government, something we shall discuss later in this chapter, since no single party would control a majority of the legislative seats on its own. On the other hand, we might want to argue that this is not really a disadvantage at all—in fact, it is a real advantage, since groups that exist *should* be represented in the legislature.

There are variations on both the SMD and PR models described above. One variation on the SMD-plurality requires a *majority* for election. The single-member-district, majority (SMD-M) system invariably involves runoff elections; given the many political parties that might exist, few districts give a majority to a candidate on the first round of voting. Voting might be scheduled on two consecutive Sundays (we will see later in this text that this is the case in France), with the top two vote-getters from the first round having a runoff election on the second Sunday. Generally, few districts would elect candidates on the first round (that is, have candidates that can win majority margins); the other 85 to 90 percent of the districts have runoff elections.

Another variation on the district-based model involves the number of representatives per district. In a number of legislatures we can find "multiple-member districts" (MMD), in which the top vote-getters are elected. In elections for the lower house in Japan (the House of Representatives), each district elects from three to five representatives, depending on the size of the district. Voters vote for one candidate, and the top three (or four, or five, depending on the population living in the district) vote-getters are elected. Japan uses an even more complex multiple-member-district scheme for its upper house, the House of Councillors. We will look at this system in more detail later in this text.

Technically, American states fall in this "multiple-member" category, since each state is represented in the U.S. Senate by two senators and is, therefore, not a single-member district but rather a multiple-member district. The method of selection of U.S. senators is the SMD method rather than the MMD method, however, since election of senators is "staggered," and we elect only one senator at a time.[47]

We will see in the second part of this text—where we shall look at some of these cases and others in much greater detail—that there are a number of variations on the common themes when we study electoral processes. The complication is made even worse when we remember that many legislatures are bicameral, and the method of selecting the second house is rarely the same as the method of selecting the first house. Some nations have second chambers that are elected by the people (for instance, the United States, Italy, Australia, and Japan). Some second chambers are appointed by the head of state, usually on the "advice" of the chief executive (for instance, Canada). Some second chambers are elected by some other body (for instance, France and Norway). Some second chambers have members chosen by more than one method (for instance, Great Britain). In short, the electoral process is a complex subject, but one that will become clearer as we examine case studies later in this text.

LEGISLATIVE FUNCTIONS

There is a great deal of consensus in the discipline as to the structures and functions of legislatures, as well as their common attributes:

> Manifestations of parliament do share at least two identifying structural characteristics: . . . (1) their members are formally equal to one another in status, distinguishing parliaments from hierarchically organized organizations; and (2) the authority of their members depends upon their claim to be representing the rest of the community.[48]

In general, five broad functions that legislatures perform for political systems may be sifted from the many lists suggested in the literature. These are, not necessarily in order of importance:

1. criticism and control of the other branches of government, most notably the executive;
2. debate;
3. lawmaking or legislation;
4. communication with the public, representation, and legitimation; and
5. recruitment, education, and socialization.

It is, of course, true that not all legislatures can be said to perform all of these functions. Nor, if they do, can it be said that they perform them all equally well. On the other hand, some legislatures, because of idiosyncratic characteristics of the systems in which they can be found, may be said to perform functions in addition to the five outlined here. Because a legislature fails to perform *all* of these functions does not mean that it performs *none* of them. As has been suggested, "if an assembly exists, it must serve some function in its policy, or it would not be able to survive."[49]

Much research on legislatures mentions the *criticism and control* function as being necessary for the maintenance of a stable political system.[50] Such phrases as "criticizing and checking executive powers"[51] may frequently be found in the literature. This function of the legislative branch of government has its roots in seventeenth-and eighteenth-century democratic political theory; at that time the role of the legislature as a check on the arbitrary powers of monarchs was first really practiced. An outgrowth of this function has been the recent "decline of legislatures" literature.[52] This suggests that legislatures have, in modern times, been less and less able to perform this very important function satisfactorily.[53] Similarly, some have examined the relationship between the parliament and courts.[54] The question of parliament's relation with the executive is a subject to which we shall return later.

A second function ascribed to legislatures is that of *debate*, or discussion of values and rules for the political system. This has been variously described in the literature as "proposing, deliberating, and deciding about public policy,"[55] or as "providing a forum for discussion and criticism of government policies,"[56] to cite but two examples. While this function is closely related to both the lawmaking/legislating and the criticizing functions, it is easy to imagine situations in which it would *not* fit within those functional categories. For example, in many nations the legislature's role in the legislative process is rather modest. It might discuss a bill proposed by the executive or the bureaucracy, but the bill may become law even if it is never actually voted on and passed by the legislature. Alternatively, a legislature might have the power to vote on a bill *in toto*, but not to amend it, or it may vote to reject a bill and the bill may still become law by executive decree. In such instances, a legislature may appear to be performing both a debating and a legislating function, but *de facto* its function is limited to debate.

The function most frequently ascribed to legislatures in Western countries is that of *lawmaking*. As Jean Blondel observed: "From the theorists of the 17th Century to those of the contemporary world, it has been held as axiomatic . . . that the function of legislatures was to make laws."[57] This legislative function is one that is almost universally attributed to legislative bodies—even if they only ratify or "rubber-stamp" legislation introduced from outside the legislature. Increasingly, however, the lawmaking function is no longer being considered the litmus test by which a legislature is judged. One student of legislatures has observed that "in formal terms, the principal function of the Parliament . . . is to pass legislation. But, legislation is only a part of the Parliament's business."[58] Ultimately, the question of *how much* of a legislative function a legislature plays in a given political system is an empirical question, and one that varies on a country-by-country basis.

The fourth function suggested is that of *communication with the public, representation, and legitimation*. Included in this function are actions such as appraising and explaining to constituents actions taken within the legislature; answering mail and performing other forms of communication; interceding with members of a bureaucratic agency on behalf of individuals or groups;[59] having resources allocated to a constituency, and so forth. Many have argued that the relationship between legislatures and "big business," lobbies, and pressure groups is just as important for democratic government as is the representation of individual views and opinions.[60] Much of the legislator's individual authority derives from his or her ability to undertake these activities[61] and to perform them successfully. The collective actions of legislators in these matters, it has been argued, help build support not only for the legislature as an institution but also for the regime itself. By doing so, the legislature also helps clothe the actions of a regime's leaders with legitimacy.[62]

There is a chain of three interconnected concepts at work here. First, legislators are necessarily aware of communications, both supportive and demanding, from their constituents. Second, by performing actions in response to these communications, the legislators can be said to be acting in a representative manner. Third, by acting in a representative manner, the legislator can contribute significantly to the legitimacy of the governmental structure. We shall return to the theme of representativeness shortly.

The fifth function that has been attributed to legislatures is that of *recruitment, education, and socialization*. Through the process of attracting individuals to politics, giving them political experience, and enabling them to attain higher office, legislatures engage in the recruitment process—they draw people into the political arena.[63] By engaging in open and publicized debates, undertaking investigations, and participating in well-reported discussions, legislators help to educate the public both about issues that are important and about the possible positions to take on such issues. By serving as role models and by developing and maintaining political norms, legislatures actively participate in the process of political socialization, the transmission of political values.[64]

In some circumstances, legislatures are invested with special functions as a result of a particular constitutional framework or historical background. For example, in addition to the other functions it performs, the British Parliament (and many parliaments like it) also has an elective function—choosing the prime minister. The U.S. House of Representatives has a similar elective function (choosing the president), but because of the nature of the electoral college and the historical situations faced by the United States, the House rarely has been called upon to perform this task.

In addition to a consensus related to the functions just described, there is also some degree of consensus as to structures and other common attributes of legislatures. Legislatures are assemblies—assemblages of individuals, elected or appointed, who come together to perform some or all of the functions discussed above. These assemblies are governed by rules—either written or unwritten, perhaps encoded in a national constitution or perhaps encoded elsewhere—regarding the method of selection of legislators, their rights and duties, their roles in the political system, and their relationship with other branches of government. These assemblies may have many or few officers, and may have greater or lesser degrees of individual opportunities for action (such as introducing legislation, for example).

LEGISLATURES AND REPRESENTATION

It was indicated earlier that one of the most important functions usually ascribed to the legislature as an institution is that of *representation*.[65] Whether or not legislatures are truly representative in a demographic sense, the need for legislatures to *appear* representative is central to their mission.

Crucial to this issue, however, is the very idea of being a "representative." In the late eighteenth century the British Member of Parliament Edmund Burke introduced the idea of "virtual representation," in which he claimed that he could represent the views of the American colonies in the "no taxation without representation" controversy without actually *being* from the colonies. After all, he claimed, he knew what their view was, and he was capable of presenting it to the British Parliament.[66]

The question of how much representation is "enough" is central in a discussion of how "representative" a national legislature is.

For example, must a legislature be demographically representative? Must the distribution of population groups in the legislature accurately reflect their distribution in the general population? It is clear wherever we look that legislatures do not accurately reflect the demographic makeup of their settings.[67] To take the most obvious example, women are grossly underrepresented in their national legislatures.[68] In one recent cross-national study, nowhere did women exceed 10 percent of the membership of national legislatures[69] (although today women in both Norway and Sweden make up more than 10 percent of the total membership of parliament), and in most of the parliaments studied they numbered under 5 percent of the total membership.[70]

Similarly, ethnic, religious, and racial minorities also tend to be significantly underrepresented in national parliaments. Even in settings in which there are no legal barriers to representation, this is a function of educational, financial, career, and other sociological patterns of bias reflected in the electoral machinery of the nation.

Many argue that the important point is not the gender, ethnic identity, age, religion, or racial characteristic of the representative, but the degree to which he or she understands the views of his or her constituency.[71] The true role of the representative, some would argue, is to represent the interests of his or her constituency, since obviously one representative cannot actually belong to all of the many demographic groups he or she represents.

LEGISLATIVE ROLES

Legislative behavior is important to study because of the nature of the legislature itself, and because of the functions that the legislature serves in the political system of which it is a part. The nature of the legislature in virtually all political systems dictates that the output of the legislative body will be a function, to greater and lesser degrees, of the interaction between and among individual legislators, as well as between and among individual legislators and bureaucracies, societal needs and demands, and other extra-legislative factors.[72]

The role that legislators play in the generation of legislative output varies in different political systems. According to many theorists, the manner in which legislators perceive roles in different subsystems of the political world will influence the way they behave politically. A political role, as the term is used here, consists of "a pattern of expected behavior for individuals holding particular positions in a system."[73]

> Legislative role orientation, and hence behavior, is thus a product of both initial expectations held by an individual for the legislative position, and attitudes and perspectives subsequently developed in response to the expectations and requirements of significant others' interaction with him in the legislative system.[74]

Research indicates that when legislators perceive their role in the legislative process to be of minimal importance or significance for the political system, they will behave accordingly and are much more likely to become alienated, apathetic, or cynical than legislators who feel highly efficacious. Studies of the legislatures of Israel and Thailand, both of which afford "minimal legislative roles," illustrate this.[75]

Various lists, typologies, and frameworks of legislative roles have appeared in the literature. One author listed seventeen possible roles that legislators can play; others listed twenty-three.[76] Rather than debate the exact number of roles that a political actor, in this case a legislator, could assume (if, indeed, such an exhaustive list is even possible), we shall simply state that the possibilities are numerous. The literature seems to be in agreement that variations in role perceptions can affect role behavior, which in turn can affect legislative behavior.

Certainly one of the major distinctions in legislative roles comes in the description of a legislator as a "frontbencher" or a "backbencher." The names derive from positions in the British House of Commons, in which seats were, and still are, arranged in two sets of rows facing each other. Party leaders sit on the front benches of their respective sides; nonleaders, or followers, sit on the back benches—hence, "frontbenchers" for leaders and "backbenchers" for followers.

The prime minister and members of the cabinet sit on the front bench of the Government side of the House. Members who sit on the front bench of the Opposition side of the House are party leaders who *would* be in the cabinet if their party were in power. (See Figure 4.1.)

Although the words "frontbencher" and "backbencher" originated as positional terms, designating only where one sits, they are also terms of power.[77] This is true because as legislators' seniority and power increase, they tend to move to their party's front bench. Those seated on the front bench tend to have more power and influence than those not on the front benches.

Although the British model of legislature places an emphasis—because of its physical organization—on the "Government versus the Opposition" conflict in the legislature, not all legislatures are organized in this way. We noted in our discussion of ideology that "left" and "right" were simply holdovers from 1798, at which time the French Council of 500 was arranged in a semicircular hall of representatives according to their self-determined place in the political spectrum.[78] Those generally supporting the monarch's policies sat on his right, while those who proposed changes in his policies sat on his left—hence, we noted that "leftists" today tend to favor change and "rightists" tend to prefer the status quo. Like the French Council of 500, American legislative bodies also sit in a semicircular pattern.

All legislative behavior, and thus all legislative output, is influenced by many factors in the legislative system.[79] These factors include the constitutional system in which the legislator acts[80]; substructures within the legislative system, including committees[81]; legislative staff and services[82]; legislative buildings and facilities, including office space[83]; party organization and leadership inside the legislature[84]; legislators' backgrounds and socialization[85]; legislative recruitment[86]; constituency and interest group pressures[87]; and party organization outside of the legislature.[88]

All of these structures and subsystems of the legislative system influence leg-

FIGURE 4.1 Interior of the British House of Commons. General view from the Opposition benches looking toward the Speaker's Chair (rear center) and the Government benches (left). The Clerk's table is in the center. (*British Official Photograph: Crown Copyright Reserved. Issued by the Central Office of Information, London.*)

islative action, which in turn affects the larger political system. These structures and subsystems are of two types: those included within or related to the legislative assembly itself, and those found outside of the legislative assembly itself.

THE LEGISLATIVE PROCESS

As David Olson has argued, the most common pattern among parliaments in the process of handling legislation is to alternate the focus of activity between the *plenum*— the floor of the legislative house—and committee stages of legislation.[89] Table 4.9 shows the procedures for handling legislation in a typical legislative body; the description is generalized from actual procedures in a number of legislative bodies.[90]

Certainly one of the most important ingredients in the legislative process has to do with the sponsor of a bill. In systems with a high degree of party discipline, bills sponsored by the majority party are almost certain to pass, and bills sponsored

TABLE 4.9
Steps in Legislative Procedure in Selected Countries

Introduction

First reading: presentation of bill and discussion of its contents

Debate

Vote

To committee(s)

When (and if) bill emerges from committee(s):

Second reading: often presented by members of committee(s) that held hearings on the bill

Debate

Vote

Third reading

Debate

Final vote

In a bicameral system, the bill would then go to the second house, and usually go through the same procedure there.

by the minority party are correspondingly destined to fail. In parliamentary systems in which the leader of the executive branch (for instance, the prime minister) is also the leader of the legislative branch (a theme we will develop and explain in the next chapter), Government bills invariably become law, and Opposition bills invariably do not.[91]

When we speak of legislation, we do not only distinguish between frontbenchers and backbenchers, because this would group the Government frontbench with the Opposition frontbench, and the Government backbench with the Opposition backbench. Instead, we leave the Government frontbench standing alone, and group the Government backbench with the Opposition frontbench and backbench. Bills originating in the Government frontbench—where the members of the cabinet sit—are called Government bills. Bills originating from any other member of parliament, either in the Government backbenches or the Opposition frontbenches or backbenches, are called private members' bills.[92]

In a now-classic study of the relative difference in efficacy between Government bills and private members' bills, Sheva Weiss and Avraham Brichta found a marked, though predictable, difference in legislative effectiveness between the chances of passage of Government bills and private members' bills.[93] Bills introduced by the Government invariably pass and become law; bills introduced by private members do not usually enjoy the same fate.

The reason that bills suggested by Government backbenchers do not have the same success rate as Government bills has to do with party discipline, a concept we have already met. Because of party discipline, all Government bills will receive the support of all members of the Government side of the House, a majority. An individual backbencher on the Government side might have an idea for a bill that the Government does not support, but may not oppose. In this case, the Government might not invoke "tight party discipline" to have the bill passed. The Government, however, would invoke party discipline to defeat most proposals coming from the Opposition side of the house.

The same thing can be said for *parliamentary questions* that might be generated by private members. Most parliaments reserve some time every legislative day for questions to be asked by individual members. Very often questions asked by members of the Opposition are not treated with the same degree of care and seriousness as are questions from the Government side of the house.[94]

LEGISLATURES AND EXECUTIVES

Much has been made in recent years about the "decline of the legislature" as a viable political structure,[95] effectively able to counterbalance the growing structure of the political executive. The argument is made that in the modern political world the executive structure has grown at an alarming rate in terms of the increase in and centralization of its power, and the legislative structure has correspondingly lost power. This means that the legislature is less able today to provide a meaningful check on the power of the executive.[96]

Some have argued that there is nothing wrong with this scenario at all, and have gone so far as to suggest that the legislature *ought* to expedite this process by voluntarily ceding to the executive many of its own powers. The legislature can remain as an institution, according to these advocates, but it should permit the executive to lead, with the legislature's proper role being to follow.[97]

The question of the relationship between the legislature and the executive is one that can be addressed on two levels. On the normative level, we can ask about what the relationship *should* be. More precisely, which alternative best promotes democratic, representative government? On the empirical level, we can ask about the validity of the observations that legislatures are declining in significance while executives are on the ascent. Is that true? What happens to the executive structure when the legislature loses its power?

Evidence seems to show without fail that the executive institution is winning the battle for power with the legislative branch, generally speaking. There simply is no way that a legislative body can keep up with a rapidly expanding executive bureaucracy in terms of information, personnel, and ability to formulate policy. To take the example of foreign policy, it simply is not possible for the British House of Commons Committee on Foreign Affairs (with a staff of less than a dozen) to oversee successfully the Ministry of External Affairs (with a staff of literally thousands); the same could be said of the Israeli Knesset's Foreign Affairs and Security Committee's ability to oversee its Ministry of External Affairs, or the ability of the U.S. Senate's Foreign Relations Committee to oversee the policy of the U.S. State Department (although the U.S. Senate committees have *far* more in the way of committee staff than do committees of other national legislatures). In fact, what often ends up happening is that legislative committees become dependent on executive agencies— whether they be ministries of External Affairs, Defense, or Agriculture—to supply them with information, and the ability to control the information to which the legislature will have access gives the executive branch of government a permanent and overwhelming advantage in the legislative-executive power competition.

LEGISLATIVE REFORM

Although legislatures are generally regarded as having lost the battle for expanded power to executives, that does not mean that they have surrendered completely.[98] Indeed, in recent years we have seen a number of calls for reform, and in many instances some substantial changes have been made in the legislative process that have been designed to strengthen the legislature in relation to the executive and to regain some of the traditional powers of the legislature, although there have been some very clear limitations to this reform.[99]

We should note that the subject of legislative reform is not a new one; it has been discussed by legislatures for well over a hundred years.[100] The problem has been, of course, that parliamentary reform—that is, an increase in the *de facto* power of parliament in relation to the executive—is seen as being in a zero-sum game with the executive: Any gains on the part of parliament must come at the expense of the executive. It has been demonstrated in recent years[101] that it is possible to make some reforms without undermining the basic pillars of the parliamentary establishment,[102] and that members of parliament may be given the opportunity to contribute to the legislative process without fear that this may cause the collapse of parliamentary government.[103]

It is to an examination of the executive structure that we next turn our attention.

Notes

1. In Sir Ernest Barker, ed., *Social Contract: Essays by Locke, Hume, & Rousseau* (New York: Oxford University Press, 1970), p. 73.
2. Ibid., pp. 73–77.
3. What has become a definitive resource in the field appeared in 1985 and reviewed the state of the art of legislative studies until that time. See Gerhard Loewenberg, Samuel Patterson, and Malcolm Jewell, eds., *Handbook of Legislative Research* (Cambridge: Harvard University Press, 1985).
4. Jean Blondel once wrote that ". . . of the 138 countries which exist in the world today, only five, all in the Middle East, have never had a legislature." In Jean Blondel, *Comparative Legislatures* (Englewood Cliffs, N.J.: Prentice Hall, 1973), p. 7. See also A. Paul Pross, "Parliamentary Influence and the Diffusion of Power," *Canadian Journal of Political Science* 18:2 (1985):235–266.
5. The national legislature has been the most common level of study in recent years. Recent examples of such studies include: C. E. Franks, *Parliament of Canada* (Toronto: University of Toronto Press, 1987), Abdo Baaklini, *The Brazilian Legislature and Political System* (Westport, Conn.: Greenwood Press, 1992), Revesz Tumas, *The Hungarian Parliament* (Budapest: State Mutual Book and Periodical Service, 1985), Michael Metcalf, ed., *The Riksdag: A History of the Swedish Parliament* (New York: St. Martin's Press, 1988), and Gregory Mahler, *The Knesset: Parliament in the Israeli Political System* (Rutherford, N.J.: Fairleigh Dickinson University Press, 1982).
6. A very good recent study is that by Ezra Suleiman, *Parliaments and Parliamentarians in Democratic Politics* (New York: Holmes and Meier, 1986). Interesting variations are described in Graham White, "Westminster in the Arctic: The Adaptation of British Parliamentarism in

the Northwest Territories," *Canadian Journal of Political Science* 24:3 (September 1991): 499–523, and Burama Sagnia, *Historical Development of the Gambian Legislature* (Lawrenceville, Va.: Brunswick Publishing, 1990).

7. Allan Kornberg, *Canadian Legislative Behavior* (New York: Holt, Rinehart and Winston, 1967), p. 2. See also Frank Baumgartner, "Parliament's Capacity to Expand Political Controversy in France," *Legislative Studies Quarterly* 12 (1987):33–54.

8. Allan Kornberg, Harold Clarke, and George Watson, "Toward a Model of Parliamentary Recruitment in Canada," in *Legislatures in Comparative Perspective*, ed. Allan Kornberg (New York: David McKay, 1973), p. 271.

9. Joseph LaPalombara, *Politics Within Nations* (Englewood Cliffs, N.J.: Prentice Hall, 1974), p. 177. See also Philip S. Marmo, "A One-Party State—The Role of Parliament in Tanzania," *Parliamentarian* 70:2 (1989): 57–68, or Kevin J. O'Brien, "Is China's National People's Congress a `Conservative Legislature'?" *Asian Survey* 30:8 (1990):782–94.

10. See Michael Mezey's essay "The Functions of Legislatures in the Third World," in Loewenberg, Patterson, and Jewell, *Handbook*, pp. 733–772, Joel Smith and Lloyd Musolf, "Some Observations on Legislatures and Development," in Joel Smith and Lloyd Musolf, eds., *Legislatures in Development: Dynamics of Change in New and Old States* (Durham, N.C.: Duke University Press, 1979), pp. 3–42, or W. St. Clair-Daniel, "Caribbean Concepts of Parliament," *Parliamentarian* 66:4 (1985):211.

11. Kornberg, Clarke, and Watson, "Toward a Model," p. 276. See also Melissa Collie, "The Legislature and Distributive Policy Making in Formal Perspective," *Legislative Studies Quarterly* 13:4 (1988):427–458.

12. See, for examples of the range of issues that can be affected by legislatures, David Judge, *Parliament and Industry* (Brookfield, Vt.: Ashgate Publishing, 1990), Hugh M. Bochel, *Parliament and Welfare Policy* (Brookfield, Vt.: Ashgate Publishing, 1992), Stephen Ingle and Philip Tether, *Parliament and Health Policy* (Brookfield, Vt.: Ashgate Publishing, 1981), Charles Carstairs and Richard Ware, eds., *Parliament and International Relations* (Bristol, Pa.: Taylor and Francis, 1991), or V. V. Ramanadham and Yash Ghai, *Parliament and Public Enterprise* (West Hartfort, Conn.: Kumarian Press, 1982).

13. For those who enjoy exceptions to general rules, there are, in fact, *tri*cameral legislatures, too! To offer one example, the national legislature of the Isle of Man—the oldest continuously operating legislative body in the world—operates in three different situations: a lower house, an upper house, and both houses sitting together as a distinct third house.

14. Data come from Jean Blondel, *Comparative Legislatures*, pp. 144–153. To illustrate different nation-counts, note that Michael Curtis says that 47 out of 144 nations in the world are bicameral. See Michael Curtis, *Comparative Government and Politics* (New York: Harper and Row, 1978), p. 195.

15. Valerie Herman, ed., *Parliaments of the World* (London: Macmillan, 1976), p. 3.

16. Ibid.

17. See Donald Shell and David Beamish, *The House of Lords at Work: A Study with Particular Reference to the 1988–1989 Session* (New York: Oxford University Press, 1993).

18. See James Madison, *Notes of Debates in the Federal Convention of 1787*, introduction by Adrienne Koch (Athens: Ohio State University Press, 1966), pp. vii–xxiii.

19. See the data in Table 3.2.

20. See Joan Rydon, *The Federal Legislature: The Austrian Federal Parliament, 1901–1980* (New York: Oxford University Press, 1986).

21. Data come from Blondel, *Comparative Legislatures*, p. 152.

22. See E. A. Smith, *The House of Lords in British Politics and Society, 1815–1911* (London: Longman, 1992).

23. Kornberg, *Canadian Legislative Behavior*, p. 19. See Colin Campbell, *The Canadian Senate: A Lobby from Within* (Toronto: Macmillan of Canada, 1978).

24. Another example of this can be found in N. K. Trikha's volume *Second Chamber of India Parliament* (Columbia, Mo.: South Asia Books, 1984).

25. See Andrew Adonis, "The House of Lords in the 1980s," *Parliamentary Affairs* 41 (1988): 380. See also E. A. Smith, *The House of Lords.*

26. Blondel, *Comparative Legislatures*, pp. 144–153. Blondel's data are out of date, and also a bit inaccurate. Caribbean data come from my own research there in 1985; for the British upper house, a publication by the House of Lords itself gives its total membership as 1,174. See Nicholas Baldwin, *The House of Lords: Its Constitution and Functions* (Exeter: Exeter University, Teaching Services Centre, 1982), p. 7.

27. Robert Diamond, ed., *Origins and Development of Congress* (Washington, D.C.: Congressional Quarterly, 1976), pp. 127–128.

28. See Andrew Sancton, "Eroding Representation-by-Population in the Canadian House of Commons: The Representation Act, 1985," *Canadian Journal of Political Science* 23:3 (1990): 441–457.

29. Asher Zidon, *The Knesset* (New York: Herzl Press, 1967), p. 27.

30. A very good review essay is that by David Brady and Charles Bullock III, "Party and Factions Within Legislatures," in Loewenberg, Patterson, and Jewell, *Handbook*, pp. 135–189. See also Joseph A. Schlesinger and Mildred Schlesinger, "The Reaffirmation of a Multiparty System in France," *American Political Science Review* 84:4 (1990): 1077–1102, or Lieven De Winter, "Parties and Policy in Belgium," *European Journal of Political Research* 17:6 (1989): 707–730.

31. Jonathan Lemco, "The Fusion of Powers, Party Discipline, and the Canadian Parliament: A Critical Assessment," *Presidential Studies Quarterly* 18:2 (1988): 283–302, or E. Gene Frankland, "Parliamentary Politics and the Development of the Green Party in West Germany," *The Review of Politics* 51:3 (1989):386–411.

32. See Richard Rose, "British MPs: More Bark Than Bite," in Suleiman, *Parliaments*, pp. 8–40.

33. See J. Richard Piper, "British Backbench Rebellion and Government Appointments, 1945–1987," *Legislative Studies Quarterly* 16:2 (1991):219–238.

34. Mark Franklin, Alison Baxter, and Margaret Jordan, "Who Were the Rebels? Dissent in the House of Commons, 1970–1974," *Legislative Studies Quarterly* 11:2 (1986):143–160, and Edward Crowe, "The Web of Authority: Party Loyalty and Social Control in the British House of Commons," *Legislative Studies Quarterly* 11:2 (1986):161–186.

35. John R. Hibbing and David Marsh, "Accounting for the Voting Patterns of British MPs on Free Votes," *Legislative Studies Quarterly* 12:2 (1987):275–298.

36. A good review of the literature in this area can be found in the essays by Heinz Eulau, "Committee Selection," in Loewenberg, Patterson, and Jewell, *Handbook*, pp. 191–238, and Heinz Eulau and Vera McCluggage, "Standing Committees in Legislatures," in ibid., pp. 395–470.

37. See David Judge, *Backbench Specialization in the House of Commons* (Brookfield, Vt.: Ashgate Publishing, 1982).

38. Michael Jogerst, "Backbenchers and Select Committees in the British House of Commons: Can Parliament Offer Useful Roles for the Frustrated?" *European Journal of Political Research* 20:1 (1991):21–38. See also his fuller study: Michael Jogerst, *Reform in the House of Commons: The Select Committee System* (Lexington: University Press of Kentucky, 1992).

39. See Austin Ranney, *Pathways to Parliament* (Madison: University of Wisconsin Press, 1965).

40. A very good review essay dealing with elections is by Lyn Ragsdale, "Legislative Elections and Electoral Responsiveness," in Loewenberg, Patterson, and Jewell, *Handbook*, pp. 57–96. See also Andre Blais, "The Classification of Electoral Systems," *European Journal of Political Research* 16:1 (1988):99–110.

41. Arend Lijphart, "The Political Consequences of Electoral Laws, 1945–1985," *American Political Science Review* 84:2 (1990):481–496.

42. An example of this is John R. Hibbing, "Representing a Territory: Constituency Boundaries for the British House of Commons of the 1980s," *Journal of Politics* 48:4 (1986): 992–1005.

43. For discussions of recent British general elections, see David Butler and Dennis Kavanagh, *The British General Election of Nineteen Eighty-Three* (New York: St. Martin's Press, 1984), William Biller, et al., *How Voters Change: The Nineteen Eighty-Seven British Election Campaign in Perspective* (New York: Oxford University Press, 1990), and David Butler and Dennis Kavanagh, *The British General Election of 1992* (New York: St. Martin's Press, 1992).

44. See Gregory Mahler, *The Knesset: Parliament in the Israeli Political System* (Rutherford, N.J.: Fairleigh Dickinson University Press, 1981), especially chap. 2.

45. Rein Taagepera and Bernard Grofman, "Rethinking Duverger's Law: Predicting the Effective Number of Parties in Plurality and PR Systems—Parties Minus Issues Equals One," *European Journal of Political Research* 13:4 (1985):341–352. See also Andre Blais and R.K. Carty, "Does Proportional Representation Foster Voter Turnout?" *European Journal of Political Research* 18:2 (1990):167–181.

46. This was a major concern when the French changed from an SMD system to a PR system in 1985, but the concerns did not come to pass. Andrew Knapp, "Proportional but Bipolar: France's Electoral System in 1986," *West European Politics* 10:1 (1987): 89–114.

47. An interesting comparative study of this subject is Susan Welch and Donley Studlar, "Multi-Member Districts and the Representation of Women: Evidence from Britain and the United States," *Journal of Politics* 52:2 (1990):391–412.

48. Gerhard Loewenberg, *Modern Parliaments: Change or Decline* (Chicago: Atherton, 1971), p. 3.

49. Fred Riggs, "Legislative Structures: Some Thoughts on Elected National Assemblies," in Allan Kornberg, ed., *Legislatures in Comparative Perspective*, p. 74.

50. Lord Ponsonby of Shulbrede, "The House of Lords: An Effective Restraint on the Executive," *Parliamentarian* 69:2 (1988):83–86.

51. Kornberg, *Canadian Legislative Behavior*, p. 1. For a different illustration of this topic, see Jaako Nousianinen, "Bureaucratic Tradition, Semi-Presidential Rule, and Parliamentary Government: The Case of Finland," *European Journal of Political Research* 16:2 (1988): 229–249.

52. See, among others, Loewenberg, *Modern Parliaments*.

53. See Rudy Andeweg, "Executive-Legislative Relations in the Netherlands: Consecutive and Coexisting Patterns," *Legislative Studies Quarterly* 17:2 (1992):161–182.

54. See *Parliament, the Constitution, and the High Court* (Canberra: Australian Government Publishing Service, 1987).

55. John Wahlke et al., *The Legislative System* (New York: John Wiley, 1962).

56. Michael Mezey, "The Functions of a Minimal Legislature: Role Perceptions of Thai Legislators," *Western Political Quarterly* 25:4 (1972):686–701.

57. Blondel, *Comparative Legislatures*, p. 4.

58. Laxmi Singhvi, "Parliament in the Indian Political System," in Allan Kornberg, ed., *Legislatures in Developmental Perspective* (Durham, N.C.: Duke University Press, 1970), p. 217.

59. John Halligan et al., "Constituency Service Among Sub-National Legislators in Australia and Canada," *Legislative Studies Quarterly* 13:1 (1988):49–64. See also Philip Norton and David Wood, *Back from Westminster: Constituency Service by British Members of Parliament* (Lexington: University Press of Kentucky, 1993).

60. See Michael Rush, ed., *Parliament and Pressure Politics* (New York: Oxford University Press, 1990), or Mark Hollingsworth, *MPs for Hire: The Secret World of Political Lobbying* (London: Trafalgar Square, 1992).

61. Loewenberg, *Modern Parliaments*, p. 3. See also Eric Uslaner, "Casework and Institutional Design: Redeeming Promises in the Promised Land," *Legislative Studies Quarterly* 10:1 (1985):35–52.

62. David Easton, "A Re-Assessment of the Concept of Political Support," *British Journal of Political Science* 5:4 (1975):435–457.

63. Donley Studlar and Ian McAllister, "Political Recruitment to the Australian Legislature: Toward an Explanation of Women's Electoral Disadvantages," *Western Political Quarterly* 49:2 (1991):467–485.

64. Donley Studlar, Ian McAllister, and Alvaro Ascui, "Electing Women to the British Commons: Breakout from the Beleaguered Beachhead?" *Legislative Studies Quarterly* 13:4 (1988): 515.

65. Malcolm Jewell covers the literature in this area in his essay "Legislators and Constituents in the Representative Process," in Loewenberg, Patterson, and Jewell, *Handbook*, pp. 97–134.

66. For discussion of Burke's views, see George H. Sabine, *A History of Political Theory* (New York: Holt, Rinehart and Winston, 1961), p. 610.

67. A good example of such an issue is the discussion found in Augie Fleras, "From Social Control Towards Political Self-Determination? Maori Seats and the Politics of Separate Maori Representation in New Zealand," *Canadian Journal of Political Science* 18:3 (1985):599–608.

68. Wilma Rule, "Electoral Systems, Contextual Factors, and Women's Opportunity for Election to Parliament in Twenty-Three Democracies," *Western Political Quarterly* 40:3 (1987): 477–498. See also Donley Studlar and Susan Welch, "Understanding the Iron Law of Andrarchy: Effects of Candidate Gender on Voting in Scotland," *Comparative Political Studies* 20:2 (1987):174-191.

69. Walter S. G. Kohn, *Women in National Legislatures: A Comparative Study of Six Countries* (New York: Praeger, 1980), p. 234.

70. See Elizabeth Vallance and Elizabeth Davies, *Women of Europe: Women Members of the European Parliament and Equality Policy* (New York: Cambridge University Press, 1986).

71. In 1987 an entire issue of *Legislative Studies Quarterly* was devoted to this issue, including the following: Heinz Eulau, "Converse and Pierce on Representation in France: The Congruence Model Revisited," *Legislative Studies Quarterly* 12:2 (1987):171–214, John C. Wahlke, "Converse and Pierce on Representation in France: Legislative Behavior, 1967–1968," *Legislative Studies Quarterly* 12:2 (1987):215–226, Mark Franklin and Thomas Mackie, "Converse and Pierce on Representation in France: Electoral Behavior," *Legislative Studies Quarterly* 12:2 (1987):227–236, and Jean Charlot, "Converse and Pierce on Representation in France: The Responsible Party Model," *Legislative Studies Quarterly* 12:2 (1987):237–242. See also Chan Wook Park, "Constituency Representation in Korea: Sources and Consequences," *Legislative Studies Quarterly* 13:2 (1988):225–242, David Wood, "The Conservative Member of Parliament as Lobbyist for Constituency Economic Interests," *Political Studies* 35:3 (1987):393–409. See also Robert MacLennan, "Parliamentary Representation: What Is Wrong with the British Model?" *Parliamentary Affairs* 40:3 (1987):325, or J. Vincent Buck and Bruce Cain, "British MPs in Their Constituencies," *Legislative Studies Quarterly* 15:1 (1990): 127–144.

72. This is discussed by many contributors in Norman Ornstein, ed., *Role of the Legislature in Western Democracies* (Washington, D.C.: American Enterprise Institute for Public Policy Research, 1981).

73. Raymond Hopkins, "The Role of the M.P. in Tanzania," *American Political Science Review* 64:3 (1970):754.

74. Kornberg, *Canadian Legislative Behavior*, p. 8. For an example of a diagrammatic depiction of role orientations, see Malcolm Jewell and Samuel Patterson, *The Legislative Process in the United States* (New York: Random House, 1973), p. 408.

75. Mezey, "Thai Legislators," and Mahler, *The Knesset*, especially chap. 8.

76. LaPalombara, *Politics Within Nations*, pp. 180–182, and Jewell and Patterson, *Legislative Process*, respectively.

77. This is discussed in Jack Brand, *Power in Parliament: Back-Bench Parties and Policy* (New York: Oxford University Press, 1992).

78. Curtis, *Comparative Government and Politics*, p. 158.

79. See Ronald Hedlund, "Organizational Attributes of Legislative Institutions: Structure, Rules, Norms, Resources," in Loewenberg, Patterson, and Jewell, *Handbook*, pp. 321–394.

80. See M. Cormack, "The Australian Senate," *Parliamentarian* 53:3 (1972):175–185, J. Lynsky, "The Role of the British Backbencher in the Modification of Government Policy," *Western Political Quarterly* 23:2 (1970):333–347; and Sheva Weiss and Avraham Brichta, "Private Members' Bills in Israel's Parliament," *Parliamentary Affairs* 23:1 (1969):21–33.

81. See J. Pettifer, "Privilege in the Parliament of the Commonwealth of Australia," *Parliamentarian* 53:4 (1972):288.

82. See Susan Webb Hammond, "Legislative Staffs," in Loewenberg, Patterson, and Jewell, *Handbook*, pp. 273–320, M. Limaye, "On Private Members' Bills," *Journal of Constitutional and Parliamentary Studies* 3:1 (1969):110-113, J. Ley, "Strengthening the Position of the Backbencher in Papua, New Guinea," *Parliamentarian* 53 (1972):303–308, or J. Robinson, "Staffing the Legislature," in Kornberg, *Legislatures in Developmental Perspective*, pp. 367–390.

83. See A. McMullin, "Proposed New and Permanent Parliament Houses for the Australian Parliament," *Parliamentarian* 51:4 (1970):263–269.

84. See Robert Peabody, "Leadership in Legislatures: Evolution, Selection, and Functions," in Loewenberg, Patterson, and Jewell, *Handbook*, pp. 239–272.

85. Kornberg, *Canadian Legislative Behavior*, pp. 49–51.

86. See Donald R. Matthews, "Legislative Recruitment and Legislative Careers," in Loewenberg, Patterson, and Jewell, *Handbook*, pp. 17–56.

87. Singhvi, "Parliament in the Indian Political System," pp. 207–213.

88. Jewell, "Legislators and Constituents," p. 118.

89. See David Olson, *The Legislative Process: A Comparative Approach* (New York: Harper and Row, 1980), p. 346, for a discussion of specific procedures in a number of nations.

90. A good theoretical essay is that by William Panning, "Formal Models of Legislative Processes," in Loewenberg, Patterson, and Jewell, *Handbook*, pp. 669–700.

91. See Melissa P. Collie, "Voting Behavior in Legislatures," in Loewenberg, Patterson, and Jewell, *Handbook*, pp. 471–518.

92. See David Marsh and Melvyn Read, *Private Members' Bills* (New York: Cambridge University Press, 1988).

93. See Weiss and Brichta, "Private Members' Bills," p. 25.

94. See Mark Franklin and Philip Norton, eds., *Parliamentary Questions* (New York: Oxford University Press, 1993).

95. See Bert Rockman, "Legislative-Executive Relations and Legislative Oversight," in Loewenberg, Patterson, and Jewell, *Handbook*, pp. 519–572, Keith Hamm, "Legislative Committees, Executive Agencies, and Interest Groups," in ibid., pp. 573–620, and Bruce Oppenheimer, "Legislative Influence on Policy and Budgets," in ibid., pp. 621–668.

96. See, for an example of this argument, Bruce Lenman, *The Eclipse of Parliament: British Government and Politics Since 1914* (New York: Routledge, Chapman, and Hall, 1992).

97. See especially the classic argument of Samuel P. Huntington, "Congressional Responses to the Twentieth Century," in *Congress and the President*, ed. Ronald Moe (Pacific Palisades, Calif.: Goodyear Publishing Co., 1971), pp. 7–31.

98. See John Garrett, *Westminster: Does Parliament Work?* (London: Trafalgar Square, 1993).

99. See, for example, Andrew Cox and Stephen Kirby, *Congress, Parliament, and Defence: The Impact of Legislative Reform on Defence Accountability in Britain and America* (New York: St. Martin's Press, 1986), or Kevin J. O'Brien, "China's National People's Congress: Reform and Its Limits," *Legislative Studies Quarterly* 13:3 (1988): 343–374.

100. On this note see David Judge, "Why Reform? Parliamentary Reform Since 1832: An Interpretation," in David Judge, ed., *The Politics of Parliamentary Reform* (Rutherford, N.J.: Fairleigh Dickinson University Press, 1984), pp. 9–36.

101. Here I would recommend several essays, including the following: Philip Norton, "Behavioural Changes: Backbench Independence in the 1980s," in Philip Norton, ed., *Parliament in the 1980s* (Oxford: Basil Blackwell, 1985), pp. 22–47, Stephen Downs, "Structural Changes: Select Committees: Experiment and Establishment," in ibid., pp. 48–68, or Michael Rush, "Parliamentary Reform: The Canadian Experience," in Judge, *Parliamentary Reform*, pp. 147–164.

102. A. N. R. Robinson, "Parliamentary Reform: The Case of the Republic of Trinidad and Tobago," *Parliamentarian* 68:3 (1987): 113.

103. One example of this type of reform can be found in an article by Audrey O'Brien, "Parliamentary Task Forces in the Canadian House of Commons: A New Approach to Committee Activity," *Parliamentarian* 66:1 (1985): 28–32.

5

The Executive

INTRODUCTION

When John Locke wrote that the state of nature was wanting power to back and support the sentence of a national judiciary,[1] he was speaking of an executive power. There is a great deal of difference, however, between the kind of executive power that Locke had in mind and the kind of political executive that we find in contemporary political systems. What are the power situations in which contemporary political executives find themselves? How do they get where they are? What kind of relationships do they have with the legislatures of their respective political settings? It is to these questions that we shall try to respond in this chapter.

THE EXECUTIVE ROLES

What does an executive do in a political system? In his classic study of the American presidency, Clinton Rossiter listed ten distinct, identifiable roles that the president is expected to play in the American political arena:

1. Chief of State
2. Chief Executive
3. Commander-in-Chief
4. Chief Diplomat
5. Chief Legislator
6. Chief of Party

7. Voice of the People
8. Protector of Peace

9. Manager of Prosperity
10. World Leader[2]

When we look at this list of duties that the president must perform, we must marvel that anyone is able to handle the demands of the office. Indeed, this was one of the major themes of Rossiter's study. Wouldn't a political system be more efficiently run if it hired a *crew* of executives to handle all of these jobs, one job to a person? Actually, the concept of a *multiple executive* is not new at all, and in a number of different political contexts in the history of political systems the multiple executive has been tried out. At the Federal Convention in Philadelphia in 1787, where the U.S. Constitution was created, the idea of a multiple executive was suggested. It was rejected, however, because history had shown that it might tend to (1) cause divisiveness when a difficult decision needed to be made, and (2) obscure responsibility, or culpability, in that blame for a bad decision might be difficult to attribute to a single individual.[3]

In point of fact, Rossiter's list of ten roles for the president may be more detailed than is necessary. Political history has shown that we only need to separate the executive role into two components: a symbolic role and a political role.[4] In the symbolic role, the executive represents the dignity of the state. The chief executive lays wreaths on tombs, attends funerals, sponsors Easter egg hunts, lights the national Christmas tree, makes national proclamations, and generally serves a ceremonial function. In the political role, the chief executive "manages the national business" and makes the hard political decisions that need to be made. In this context the chief executive can be seen to be chief of the executive branch of government, the ultimate decision-maker in a huge pyramid of decision-makers, the owner of the desk where "the buck stops."

There are, generally speaking, four approaches to the executive institution found in political systems around the world, two of which we shall examine at this time. This is not to suggest that all political systems correspond precisely to one or the other of these four models; rather, it suggests that virtually all political systems are modelled after one or the other of the four general plans. We will see in the second part of this text that all political systems have their idiosyncratic differences, but at this stage of our study we are concerned with explaining the general models.

One general type of political executive can be referred to as the *presidential* model of executive, and the other type of political executive can be referred to as the *"Westminster" parliamentary-cabinet* form of executive. Later in this text we will add discussion of the *French parliamentary-cabinet* model and the *Soviet collective executive* model (although the Soviet model has become virtually extinct within the last few years); these really are variations on the two models we shall discuss here. As we did with our discussion of legislatures, we will preface our descriptions of executives by saying that what we are about to describe will vary in specific detail from country to country.

THE PRESIDENTIAL EXECUTIVE

The type of political executive with which American students are most familiar is the presidential executive. American students are often surprised to learn, however, that the presidential model of executive behavior is in a minority once we look beyond the borders of the United States. Developed in the United States, the model has been copied by a number of other political systems, primarily in Central and South America but also in Africa and Asia.

The presidential model centralizes both political power and symbolic authority in one individual, the president. The president is the individual presiding at ceremonial functions, and it is the president who symbolizes the nation in the eyes of the rest of the world. The president is the head of state. Foreign diplomats present their credentials to him. (Although a number of countries have had women presidents, we will use the masculine pronoun here.) He presents the State of the Union message to the Congress each year. He throws out the first ball to open the baseball season.[5]

Presidential systems do not separate the dignity and the business functions of the office, although such a separation has been suggested. For example, some have suggested that since the American government has the institution of the vice presidency, which has few constitutional duties and the primary significance of which is not in what it is but in what it might become,[6] a good use of the vice president might be to assign to him the ceremonial duties of office and give the president the important decision-making duties. The problem is that vice presidents do not jump at the idea of spending all of their time at funerals and ceremonies. Moreover, the public does not accept the idea either; the vice president is, after all, the second officer of American government, not the first, and the public wants to see the president.[7]

The strength of the presidency is in its independence. In the American presidential system, which is the model for presidential systems elsewhere, the chief executive is elected independently from the legislature. Presidential elections in the United States are held every four years, no more frequently and no less frequently. It is the fixed term of the president and the corresponding security in office that contribute to the president's base of power.[8]

As indicated in Figure 5.1, the president is independently elected on the basis of popular election. The American political system has an additional structure inserted between the populace and the president: the electoral college, which officially elects the president. The genesis of the electoral college is based on the Founding Fathers' distrust of the popular will. The founders were suspicious of popular opinion, and they felt that by having voters choose electors, who would subsequently cast ballots for the presidency, their concern could be resolved.[9] Recent American political history has shown the electoral college to be an anachronistic institution, and efforts are regularly made to do away with it and have the president directly elected by the public.

The fact that the American public votes in several different electoral contests—once for the president and vice president, once for the House of Represen-

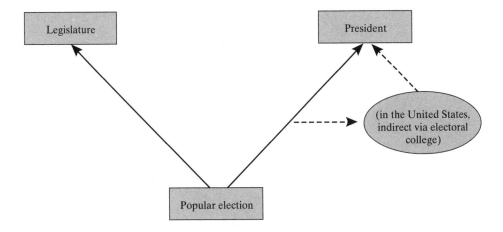

FIGURE 5.1   Presidential Systems' Bases of Power

tatives (all seats in the House come up for reelection every two years), and, where a contest is held, once for the Senate (Senate seats have six-year terms and are staggered so that both seats in any given state are not up for election at the same time)— is quite significant for a number of reasons. First, it gives the president an independent power base. Short of the process of impeachment (which history has shown can be instituted only for high crimes and treason, not simply for reasons of political opposition), the president does not depend on either the legislature or public opinion for continuation of his four-year term. Once he is in office, he remains there until the term is completed. This allows the president to take actions that may be unpopular with both the public and the legislature in the short term, but that the president feels, nonetheless, are the right actions to take.

A second significant point is that this relationship works in the other direction. That is, American legislators are chosen by the people, not by the president; as long as they keep their constituencies happy they can act independently of the president, and there is virtually nothing that the president can do to them. As already indicated, members of the House of Representatives are elected for two-year terms, and although the president may threaten not to campaign for them in the next election (or even may threaten to campaign against them) if they don't do what he wants, the president cannot directly affect their time in office; he cannot "fire" them. Senators are elected to six-year terms, and they, in a similar manner, are secure in their office.[10] A president might be angry when a senator from his or her party fails to support his legislation in the Senate, but there is little the president can do to directly punish a recalcitrant senator, short of threatening to withhold future support.[11]

A third significant point to note is that this structural independence of the branches of government (depicted in Figure 5.1) can have negative consequences. By virtue of the fact that both the executive and legislative branches of government have secure tenure in office, they can frustrate each other, but that is all they can do. The president can veto acts of Congress, but Congress can override the presidential veto. (The president of the United States does *not* have an "absolute" veto that is impossible to override, although presidents in some other systems do possess such absolute vetoes.) Congress can refuse to pass a legislative request of the president, but the president can try to accomplish his goals through executive decrees, executive agreements, and similar unilateral executive actions.

It is important to recall that the president is *not* part of the legislative branch of government, and cannot, literally, take part in the legislative process. Only senators can introduce bills in the Senate, and only representatives can introduce bills in the House. If the president is unable to find a legislative "sponsor" for a bill (something that, realistically, is unimaginable), he would be unable to introduce new legislation. The situation can thus deteriorate to a point of *immobilism*; each actor has enough power to frustrate and block the other, but not enough to achieve its own objectives, which means that it is possible that nothing will get done.

This situation is most evident in the United States when the executive and legislative branches of government are controlled by the two major political parties. When Richard Nixon (a Republican) was president he faced a Senate and House controlled by Democrats; the relationship between the two branches of government was frequently tense, with presidential vetoes and legislative defeats of presidential proposals flying back and forth.[12] This situation was repeated during the term of (Republican) Ronald Reagan in the 1980s. For some of that time Congress was partly controlled by Democrats (a Republican-controlled Senate and a Democrat-controlled House), and for some of that time it was fully controlled by a Democratic majority in both houses. This situation continued through the presidency of George Bush. Although Nixon, Reagan, and Bush were able to get the support of some Southern (and other conservative) Democrats, as a general rule much tension existed between the two branches.

Party difference is not a *requirement* for this kind of tension, however. The four years of Jimmy Carter (a Democratic president with a Democratic Congress) were not terribly productive, either, and often witnessed the same tension. After his inauguration, Carter proposed a national energy program, which he labelled as "the moral equivalent of war." By the time Congress acted (over two years later), Carter's original legislative proposals bore little resemblance to the legislation produced by the Congress.[13] More recently the presidency of Bill Clinton, a Democratic president with a Democrat-controlled Congress, has displayed the same lack of clear legislative success.

In brief, although the executive and legislative branches of government *may* pull in tandem, they do not *necessarily* do so, and the structure of the independently selected presidency and legislature does enable the state of immobilism to develop.

THE PARLIAMENTARY EXECUTIVE

The parliamentary executive is more complex than its presidential alternative, if for no other reason than that it is in reality a *multiple executive*.[14] The ceremonial function and the decision-making function are performed by two separate individuals, whose titles vary by political system (see Table 5.1), and to whom we can generically refer as the *head of state* and the *chief executive*.

The function of the head of state is to symbolize the state and the dignity of the political regime. The head of state will receive ambassadors, host receptions, lay wreaths at tombs, and perform many of the ceremonial tasks government requires. Heads of state, generally speaking, are chosen in one of three ways. First, in a number of political systems—about a third of all parliamentary systems—the head of state is a hereditary position, one that "belongs" to a royal family. Certainly among the best-known examples of this manner of selection is the British monarchy, which has a clearly delineated line of succession.

A second pattern of selection is one in which the head of state is selected by a governmental body, often the legislature. The president of Israel is elected by the Israeli parliament—the Knesset—and the president of India is elected by the combined membership of the Indian parliament—the Lok Sabha and the Rajya Sabha. Finally, a third method of selection has been referred to as "self-selection." It is characteristic of political systems in which power has been seized, such as the position of Fidel Castro in Cuba, or the former position of Idi Amin as president-for-life in Uganda.[15]

The chief executive, on the other hand, is precisely what the title implies: the chief of the executive branch of government.[16] The chief executive is a full-time politician, devoting little time to ceremonial duties of office. Generally speaking, the chief executive in a parliamentary regime performs the same tasks as the chief executive in a presidential regime, but not the symbolic activities. Both executives coordinate government policy-making. Both executives are assisted by cabinets of individuals heading separate departments or ministries of government. Both executives are responsible for the day-to-day operation of government.

In many political systems the position of chief executive is totally without legal basis, but instead is founded on years of political custom and tradition—which

TABLE 5.1
Executive Titles

Nation	Model of Government	Head of State	Chief Executive
Australia	Parliamentary	Governor-general[a]	Prime minister
Canada	Parliamentary	Governor-general[a]	Prime minister
India	Parliamentary	President	Prime minister
Israel	Parliamentary	President	Prime minister
Italy	Parliamentary	President	Prime minister
Japan	Parliamentary	Emperor	Prime minister
Mexico	Presidential	President	President
United Kingdom	Parliamentary	Queen	Prime minister
United States	Presidential	President	President
Germany	Parliamentary	President	Chancellor

[a]Serving on behalf of the monarch in his or her absence.

we have already noted can be just as important as written constitutional measures. In other systems the position is legally entrenched and described in great detail in constitutional documents.[17] The manner in which the office of the chief executive in parliamentary systems was created is significant in that it tells us a great deal about both the position of the chief executive and the manner in which that position relates to the position of the head of state.

The Changing Role of the Monarchy

Even though we will not focus on British politics until later in this volume, the fact is that when we discuss the development of parliamentary government we *are*, in fact, discussing British political history (just as we are discussing American political history when we speak of the development of the presidential model of government). Although many parliamentary systems today differ to varying degrees from the contemporary British system, the parliamentary system of government as we know it was born in England, and is generally regarded as starting with Robert Walpole as prime minister in 1741. An exceedingly brief survey of nine centuries of political history is in order here to help to understand and appreciate the role of the monarchy today.[18]

When William, Duke of Normandy, took the English throne in 1066 there already existed a political structure called the *witenagemot,* a legislative assembly of sorts, which formally elected him king. William the Conqueror (as he became known) extended and formalized the continental feudal system during his tenure and institutionalized the *Curia Regis* (the King's Court) as a political body. At this time there was no distinction among the legislative, executive, and judicial functions of government (John Locke was not to come onto the scene for another 600 years): All government was the king. The king used both the Curia Regis and the witenagemot as sources of funds, and in return for members' financial support he listened to their counsel and advice, although he was clearly not bound to accept it.

In 1215 the group of barons of the realm that had made up the Curia Regis drew up a document that was called the *Magna Carta.* This document described what the barons considered to be the proper relationship between the king and themselves. It is important to note that this was not a declaration of *new* rights and privileges; rather, it was an expression of what the barons asserted to have been the relationship for some time. Contrary to popular misconceptions, the Magna Carta dealt with the barons, not the common people. They argued that the king had been forgetting some of the powers and rights that kings had already given to barons and the public. This "Great Charter" was a significant constitutional document. It expounded upon political obligations of the time: people's obligations to the king, the king's obligations to the people, and how law and justice should be administered.

During the thirteenth century the financial resources of the barons of the Curia Regis were not sufficient for the needs of government, and the Curia Regis called upon representatives of towns and counties for "aids"—financial help. In exchange for their financial contributions, the representatives of the towns and counties were admitted to the Curia Regis alongside the barons, thus giving the Curia Regis two classes of members: the earlier baronial membership, which became the

House of Lords, and its new (and often elected) membership, which became the House of Commons. The term "parliament" was first used during the thirteenth century to refer to the debating function of these bodies.

Because the king was receiving financial assistance from both groups, he was now obligated to discuss public affairs not only with the baronial nobility but also with the representatives of the commoners. The public's representatives had an important weapon in their hands to ensure that they were listened to: the right to assent, or refuse to assent, to the king's proposals for raising and spending money. Parliament, especially the House of Commons, used this power as a condition with the king: its approval of royal financial proposals in exchange for the king's attention to public grievances. By about the year 1500 the Commons had grown in political strength to the point at which it could introduce proposals on its own to change laws and could offer amendments to bills that had originated in the House of Lords, the superior house of the legislature.

The seventeenth century saw the legislature's power grow in relation to the monarch's, and it was a period of much stress. King James I, who reigned from 1603 to 1625, was an advocate of the "divine right of kings" theory,[19] which argued that the monarch derived his power directly from God and not from the people. James had little need for Parliament as an institution, and he argued that any privileges of Parliament were gifts from the King, not rights of Parliament. During James's twenty-two-year reign, Parliament sat for only eight years. On a number of occasions he "dissolved" the House of Commons, declared that they were not "truly" elected, and sent them home—in effect, he fired them.

Charles I succeeded his father, James I, in 1625, and continued his father's practice of imprisoning members of Parliament (especially, of course, members of the House of Commons) who opposed him. When Charles could not control a Parliament, he dissolved it and called for new elections after a period of time. By 1640 Charles was in need of funds and convened Parliament to authorize new taxes. The Commons refused; only three weeks later Charles again dissolved Parliament. This became known as the "Short Parliament."

Six months later another Parliament assembled; it became known as the "Long Parliament." The issue upon which the election for the House of Commons had been held was the question of whether the king should rule Parliament or Parliament should rule the king. Within two years an armed struggle ensued (referred to as the English Civil War, 1642–1648) between supporters of the king and supporters of the Parliament. Eventually the royal army was defeated and Charles was captured and sentenced to death following a trial in 1649 as "a tyrant, traitor, murderer, and public enemy." The Commons dissolved the monarchy and established a republic, led by Oliver Cromwell. In 1660 the Long Parliament dissolved itself, and the Convention that was elected to take its place restored the royal family to the throne. Charles II, the son of Charles I, became king of England.

Through the reigns of Charles II (1660–1685) and his brother James II (1685–1688), the tensions between the Parliament and the monarch grew again, and in 1688 James II was pressured into abdicating—resigning his position as monarch. Parliament then invited William, Prince of Orange and grandson of Charles I, to rule, and William and his wife, Mary, were proclaimed king and queen by Parliament in 1688.

During the reign of William and Mary the English constitutional system became much more stable; indeed, it laid much of the groundwork for stable constitutional government to come. In 1689 the British *Bill of Rights* became law. It asserted that taxes could be raised only with the assent of Parliament, guaranteed the people the right to petition the king, limited the use of the army without the consent of Parliament, guaranteed free elections and freedom of speech and debate in Parliament, limited excessive bail, prohibited "cruel and unusual punishment," and asserted that Parliament ought to meet frequently. Parliament became institutionalized as a significant political actor in the English system of government.

Constitutional Monarchy

Over nearly the last three centuries, the relationship between the king and the Parliament has evolved to a point that not even William and Mary would recognize it. *De jure*, under law, most powers of the British government (and, in a parallel fashion, parliamentary governments generally) are still exercised in the name of the king or queen, but today they are invariably exercised "on the advice" of the chief executive.

In the eighteenth and nineteenth centuries, the king relied more and more on his *cabinet*, a group of advisors, for guidance. In the early eighteenth century the role of the cabinet was only that of providing advice; the king still could do as he pleased. As ideas of democratic and republican government grew over the next two centuries, the power relationship changed so that the king was now *obligated*, although not *legally required*, to accept the advice of his cabinet. The cabinet by now was primarily chosen from that house of Parliament elected by the public, the House of Commons. Now the cabinet was in reality governing in the name of the king, and without consulting him.

Among the most striking characteristics of parliamentary government today, wherever we find it, is the duality of its executive leadership that we referred to earlier. The monarch is the official (*de jure*) head of state, but the active (*de facto*) head of government is the prime minister. Appointments are made, acts of Parliament or the legislature are proclaimed, and all government is carried on in the name of the monarch, although it is the prime minister and his or her cabinet who make all of the selections for appointments, who author or sponsor legislative proposals, and who make the administrative decisions that keep government running.

Legal bases for the prime minister and the cabinet are rare, as we noted earlier, and in many political systems both the prime minister and the cabinet are constitutionally nonexistent institutions. In the case of Great Britain (and many Commonwealth nations), the cabinet's legal claim to power rests in the fact that ever since the seventeenth century the monarch has had a Privy Council to advise him or her—a kind of present-day cabinet. Today, although the Privy Council is no longer active, cabinet members are first made members of the Privy Council and then are appointed to the cabinet. The cabinet meets as a "subcommittee" of the (inactive)

Privy Council and acts in the name of the Privy Council, a body that *does* have constitutional and legal status. Discussing the relationship between the Canadian cabinet and the Queen's Privy Council for Canada, R. MacGregor Dawson noted:

> Those appointed to the Privy Council remain members for life, and hence will include not only ministers from the present Cabinet, but also all surviving ministers of past Cabinets as well. The Privy Council would therefore, if active, be a large and politically cumbersome body with members continually at cross-purposes with one another; but it has saved itself from this embarrassment by the simple device of holding no meetings.
>
> The Cabinet, lacking any legal status of its own, masquerades as the Privy Council when it desires to assume formal power; it speaks and acts in the name of the entire Council.[20]

The Selection of the Chief Executive

Although the British monarch may have felt free to choose whomever he or she wanted as advisors in the seventeenth and eighteenth centuries, that is no longer the case today. The process by which the head of state in a parliamentary political system selects the chief executive is another one of those patterns of behavior that may legally (*de jure*) be entirely up to the head of state; practically and politically (*de facto*), however, the head of state usually has little or no choice in the matter at all.

In parliamentary systems of government, unlike their presidential counterparts, there is no special election for the chief executive. The chief executive is elected as a member of the legislature, just as all of the other members of the legislature are elected. Elections for the legislature are held on a regular basis, which varies with the political system. In Britain, the term of the House of Commons is limited to five years. (Keep in mind, of course, that the upper house, the House of Lords, is appointed, not elected, and hence has nothing to do with the selection of the executive.) In Israel, to take another example, elections must be held at least every four years.

After the elections for legislative seats have taken place (a process that we described in Chapter 4), it is the duty of the head of state to invite someone to create a Government. (It should be noted at this point that the term "Government" with a capital *G* has a specific meaning in this volume, namely the prime minister and the cabinet; "government" with a small *g* refers to the general structures of the political system.) Although the head of state in most systems is technically free to select whomever he or she wants for the Government, in practice and custom (*de facto*) heads of state are required to invite the leader of the largest political party in the legislature—a recognition of the will of the people—as indicated in Figure 5.2.[21]

Once the head of state designates an individual to create a Government, that individual will subsequently advise the head of state as to whom to appoint to the cabinet. After the new Government (the new prime minister and the new cabinet) has been assembled, in most political systems that Government must first receive a *vote of confidence* from the legislature before it assumes power. The vote of confidence is simply a vote by a majority of the legislative house indicating its confidence in, or

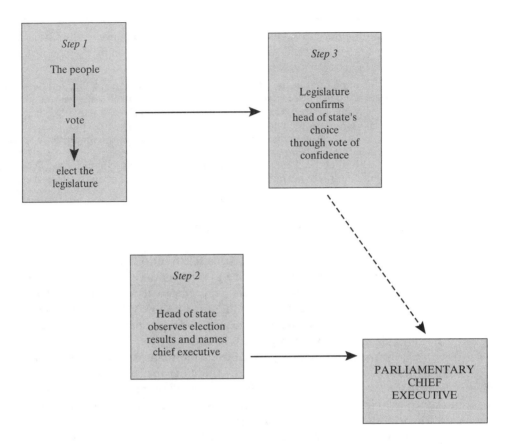

FIGURE 5.2   The Selection of the Parliamentary Chief Executive

support for, the prime minister and his or her cabinet. (Keep in mind that the vote of confidence will typically involve only the lower house of the legislature—the House of Commons in Britain, for instance—and will generally not involve the upper house at all.)

In most political systems if the Government does not receive a vote of confidence—if it receives the support of less than a majority of the legislature in a vote—it cannot take office, and another Government must be designated by the head of state. Britain represents an exception to the general rule that newly designated Governments need votes of confidence. In Britain, and in many other Commonwealth nations, the designation by the head of state *assumes* legislative confidence (that is, the head of state wouldn't make the appointment without making sure of legislative support first), and the Government assumes power immediately, without first needing an expression of confidence from the legislature.

The institution of the vote of confidence is an indication of *legislative su-*

premacy in the political system. That is, the legislature "hires" the executive (although the head of state may nominate him or her) or invests him or her with power. The chancellor in Germany, as well as the prime minister in Israel or Japan or India, to cite just a few examples, assumes power only after receiving a majority vote of support in the legislature.

This legislative power works in the other direction, too. Just as the legislature "hires" the executive, by expressing support for one of its members forming a Government, it can "fire" the executive by expressing a lack of support or confidence in the Government. Whenever the chief executive loses the confidence of the legislature, whenever the legislature passes a resolution of *no confidence* (or, conversely, fails to pass an expression of confidence), the chief executive is in fact fired. Even if the legislature expresses a lack of confidence in the chief executive only a week after that person has assumed office, he or she must resign. In some systems this resignation is a legal requirement; elsewhere it is simply a custom that has the force of law.[22] In some political systems a specific vote of no confidence is not even required to fire a chief executive: If the Government is defeated on any major piece of legislation, that is considered an expression of a lack of confidence in the Government. It should be added that in most parliamentary systems, with their strong tradition of party discipline and the ability of the prime minister to muster a majority, votes of no confidence are very rare. They do, however, happen from time to time.

When the prime minister resigns, we say that the *Government has fallen.* A Government falls when either of two things happens: It loses on a question of confidence or a major piece of legislation, leading the prime minister to resign, or the prime minister resigns for some other reason. The resignation of an individual minister does not cause a Government to fall, but the resignation of the prime minister does cause the Government to fall.[23]

The prime minister in a parliamentary system, then, does not have the job security of a president in a presidential system. The prime minister is selected by the head of state to be chief executive precisely because he or she is the leader of the largest party in the legislature. If this individual's party controls a majority of the legislative seats, and if the prime minister can maintain that majority through party discipline, this person should be able to remain prime minister for the entire term of the legislature (and perhaps several terms of the legislature). If, however, the prime minister does not control a majority, or if the prime minister is not able to retain the support of a majority of the legislature, his or her tenure might be brief.

Of course, if there is a party with a majority, the head of state will appoint its leader to be prime minister. (Obviously, if the head of state appointed anyone else, the majority party would make sure that the new Government failed to receive a vote of confidence.) If there is no majority party, one of three situations is possible. First, the head of state may appoint someone to head a *minority government*, one in which the prime minister does not control over 50 percent of the seats in the legislature. Minority governments tend to be short-lived. They usually obtain an initial vote of confidence through a temporary understanding among a number of parties who do not want to have to contest another election right away, and who see a minority government as the least of several evils. These initial understandings usually break down after a short while and result in a no-confidence vote and the fall of the Government.[24]

An example of such a government occurred in 1979 in Canada. The Conservative Party, headed by Joe Clark, won slightly less than half of the seats in the House of Commons; it captured 48.2 percent of the House seats (136 of 282 seats) based on 35.8 percent of the popular vote. (Based on our discussion of electoral systems in Chapter 4, it should be clear how in a single-member-district system such as Canada's, 35.8 percent of the popular vote could yield 48.2 percent of the seats in the legislature.) The two left-of-center parties, the Liberals (114) and the (socialist) New Democratic Party (26) combined, controlled 49.6 percent of the seats in Parliament, with a small conservative faction, the Social Credit Party, controlling about 2 percent (6 seats). Clark vowed to run the government "as if he had a majority," believing that the (conservative) Social Credit Party would prefer his (Conservative Party) leadership to that of the Liberal and socialist opposition. This gave him a practical working arrangement of 142 seats out of 282 in any parliamentary vote, a clear (but bare) majority. The Conservative and Social Credit parties never entered into a formal coalition, however.

Approximately six months after the election, Clark introduced his first budget in the House of Commons, and the Social Credit Party announced that it found some of the tax measures in the budget so objectionable that it intended to abstain on the budget vote. This left a 136-member Conservative Party to face a 140-member opposition. A motion of no confidence was introduced by the opposition parties, and the Clark Government fell.

A second alternative when there is no majority party is for the head of state to appoint someone to form a *coalition government*. A coalition government is one in which two or more nonmajority parties pool their legislative seats to form a majority parliamentary bloc. There may well be a formal agreement drawn up among the participants in the coalition, in which they agree to team up and create a majority in the legislature to support a Government. We will discuss coalition governments shortly.

The third alternative, and one usually not taken right away, is for the head of state to not form *any* Government, but instead to *dissolve the legislature*—fire the newly elected legislators—and call for new elections in the hope that the next elections will result in one party winning a clear mandate. This usually is not taken as a first resort, but if the head of state appoints a minority government, which falls within a short period of time, it may be clear to him or her that political stability is simply not possible with the legislature constituted in its current form. If such is the case, the head of state may dissolve the legislature and call for new elections.[25]

The chief executive, then, is selected by the head of state *from* the legislature. The chief executive retains his or her position as long as the legislature continues to express support for the Government by approving the proposals of the Government. The concept of party discipline is very important in this regard, for it is party discipline that enables the prime minister to control the legislature. There is a circular relationship at work here: The prime minister is selected to be prime minister precisely because he or she is the chosen leader of the largest party in the legislature. This person will remain prime minister as long as he or she can control a majority of the legislature. When a majority *cannot* be controlled, a motion of no confidence will be passed, and the prime minister will be forced (through either law or custom) to resign.

At this point it is *not* necessary that new elections be held. The head of state must now reassess the situation and may invite someone else (or perhaps even the same person who last failed) to try to form a new Government and receive an expression of legislative confidence. This process—a Government being designated, receiving a vote of confidence, surviving for a period of time, receiving a vote of no confidence and falling, a new Government being designated, and so on—can go on, over and over again, until the head of state decides that there is no point in trying again. At that point the head of state will issue a *writ of dissolution,* "dissolving" the legislature (much as Charles I did in 1640), and will call for new elections. Thus the entire process starts again, as indicated in Figure 5.3.

It occasionally happens that a chief executive will *cause* his or her own Government to fall, for what we can call reasons of electoral advantage. Let us suppose that in a hypothetical political system the constitution requires that elections be held at least every five years (as is the case in Great Britain). Elections held in January 1994 result in the Liberal Party winning 56 of the 100 seats in the legislature, and the Conservative Party winning the remaining 44 seats. The leader of the Liberal Party, I. Maginary, becomes prime minister. As time goes by, Maginary's popularity, and correspondingly the popularity of his Liberal Party, fluctuates up and down, depending on economic factors, world events, and so on.

Prime Minister Maginary knows that if the present Government can keep the majority in the legislature satisfied, the constitution will require that elections be held *by* January 1999 (five years after the last election). In late 1997, three years into the term of the legislature but almost two years before elections *must* be held, Maginary's popularity is at an all-time high, as depicted in Figure 5.4. After some discussion with political advisors, the Maginary Government resigns and asks the head of state to dissolve the legislature and to call for new elections. They do this because they feel that if the elections are held now, they may win control of the legislature by an *even bigger* margin than they did in 1994. The head of state has no real choice in the matter: Maginary's Liberal Party controls a majority in the legislature, and supports Maginary's decision to call for early elections. If the head of state were to refuse to dissolve the legislature, and tried to name some other leader (such as the leader of the opposition Conservative Party) to form a Government, the Maginary-Liberal group would vote the new Government down by a 56–44 vote. The head of state, then, grants Prime Minister Maginary a dissolution and calls for new elections to be held, typically in eight to ten weeks. During the interim period, the Maginary Government continues in office as the "Acting Government," and Maginary's title is "Acting Prime Minister" until the next election is held and a new Prime Minister is designated by the head of state.

Although the example just presented is hypothetical, the situation it depicts happens *regularly* in parliamentary systems. In recent years, dissolutions of this type

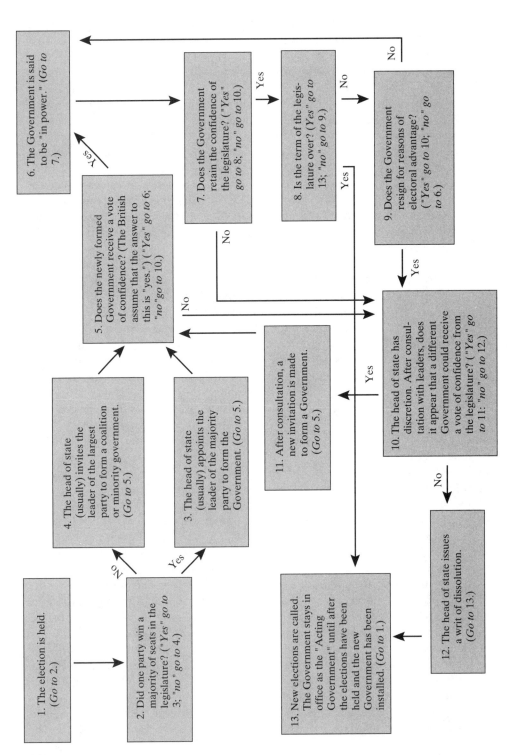

FIGURE 5.3   The Government-Formation Process: A Flow Chart Presentation

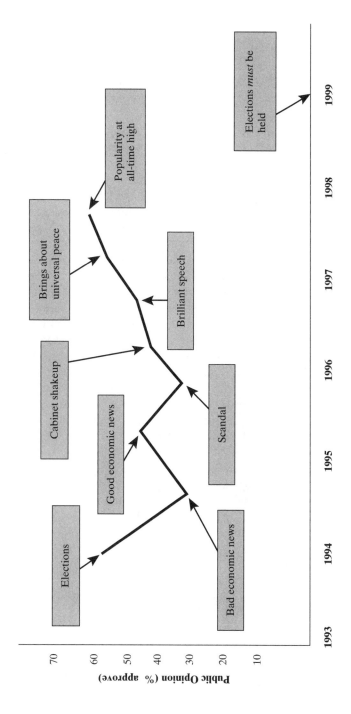

FIGURE 5.4   Government Falling as a Result of Fluctuations in Public Opinion

have taken place in Japan, France, Great Britain, Israel, Belgium, and India, among other nations.

COALITION GOVERNMENTS

In political systems that have more than two major political parties it regularly is the case that no single party controls a majority in the legislature. (Clearly, in a two-party system we don't have this problem. Unless there is a tie—which is quite rare—one of the two parties must, by definition, have more than half of the legislative seats.) Where no party has a majority, as was indicated previously, several options are available to the head of state in the creation of a Government. The most commonly used option is the creation of a *coalition government.*

Let us take a hypothetical newly elected legislature to use as an example as we discuss the process of coalition formation. Imagine a 100-seat legislature with five political parties, as described in Table 5.2. In this instance, the head of state would most likely invite the leader of Party *A* to form a Government, since Leader *A* has the largest popular mandate. We should note, however, that in most systems the head of state is not *required* to invite Leader *A*; the head of state can invite anyone that he or she feels has the best chance to form a coalition successfully. Leader *A* needs to find an additional 18 seats in order to form a majority of 51 to support her Government in the legislature. In this case, Leader *A* could go to either the leader of Party *B*, or the leader of Party *C*, to find a partner. Of course, Leader *A* could go to *more* than one other party, to try to form an *ABC* coalition, for example.

Usually, Leader *A* will have to promise the leader(s) of other parties involved in the coalition some reward for joining the coalition. In most instances, this reward is a cabinet position (or several cabinet positions). Sometimes the payoff is a promise that a certain piece of legislation that the prospective coalition partner has drafted will be passed as part of the Government's program.[26] Sometimes both types of payoff are required.

If Leader *A* can reach an agreement with one or more partners to form a coalition that will control a majority of the seats in the legislature, then Leader *A* will receive her vote of confidence, and the Government can be said to be installed. If, however, Leader *A* *cannot* find sufficient coalition partnership within a constitutionally mandated period of time, usually two to three weeks, then Leader *A* must return

TABLE 5.2
A Hypothetical Legislative Composition

Party A	33 seats
Party B	20 seats
Party C	18 seats
Party D	16 seats
Party E	13 seats

her "mandate" to the head of state and inform the head of state of her inability to form a coalition.

At this point, as indicated earlier, the head of state makes a decision. The head of state could either dissolve the legislature and call for new elections, with the hope that in another election a party seeking seats in the next legislature might win a majority, or at least a large enough plurality to be able to form a coalition easily; or the head of state could invite some other party leader to try to form a government. In our hypothetical example, the head of state at this point might turn to Leader *B* to see whether he could form a coalition.

The process then goes on and on in this fashion. At each occasion that a Government fails to retain the confidence, or support, of a majority in the legislature—that is, a motion of no confidence introduced by the opposition passes, or a motion of confidence introduced by a Government supporter fails—the head of state must decide whether *another* leader might be able to succeed. Elections, after all, are expensive, and usually divisive, and one doesn't want to have a national election every six months.

Coalition majority governments *tend* to be less stable than single-party majority governments in parliamentary systems.[27] In a single-party majority system, the prime minister must be concerned with party discipline keeping party followers in line. In a coalition system, the flow of power is more diffuse. The prime minister exercises party discipline over his or her party followers, and counts on the leader(s)

TABLE 5.3
The Complexity of the Coalition-Formation Process

Party	Seats	Majority Possibilities
Situation I: Simplest		
Party A	44 seats	AB,AC,BC,ABC
Party B	42 seats	
Party C	14 seats	
Situation II: More Complex		
Party A	38 seats	AB,AC,AD,ABC,ABD,
Party B	20 seats	ABE, ACD, ACE, etc.
Party C	17 seats	
Party D	15 seats	
Party E	10 seats	
Situation III: Most Complex		
Party A	30 seats	ABC,ABD,ABE,ABF,ABG
Party B	19 seats	BCDE,CDEFGH, etc.
Party C	12 seats	
Party D	9 seats	
Party E	8 seats	
Party F	8 seats	
Party G	7 seats	
Party H	7 seats	

of the partner coalition party or parties to do the same. Coalitions usually fail because of differences between party leaders—in our example above, because Leader *B* has a disagreement with Leader *A* and pulls the support of Party *B* out of the *AB* coalition—*not* because of a failure of party discipline within either Party *A* or Party *B*.[28]

As might be expected, the complexity of the coalition-formation process is a direct function of the number of political parties in a legislature.[29] In the example in Table 5.3, it is clear that Situation I is most simple, Situation II more complex, and Situation III even more complex. The more parties there are, the more possibilities there are for a winning coalition to form; the more partners there are in a coalition, the more possibilities there are for intra-coalition conflict to cause a coalition to fall apart.

The study of coalitions has been interesting to many in recent years because of cabinet instability in many political systems.[30] Coalition governments in Italy, Israel, Japan, Belgium, and related minority government problems in France, Britain, and Canada, among other nations, have stimulated an interest in many political scientists in how and why coalitions are created.[31]

As we indicated in Chapter 4, coalition governments often become necessary as a result of a nation's electoral system: Where proportional representation elections exist, there almost inevitably results a multiparty system in the legislature, which *often* means that no single party will control a majority of the seats in the legislative assembly. This necessitates, as we have indicated here, that a coalition be formed. The motivations involved in the selection of coalition partners vary as a result of ideology and political culture.[32] Often economic issues provide the central concerns upon which parties coalesce.[33] In any event, the existence of coalitions adds a note of uncertainty and instability to a political equation *in addition to* whatever uncertainty or instability may have already existed.

THE EXECUTIVE FUNCTION: PUBLIC ADMINISTRATION AND THE BUREAUCRACY

Apart from the creation of a cabinet, the other manifest function of the political executive is to administer policy. In this respect, this volume would be seriously remiss if we did not discuss, albeit briefly, the comparative study of public administration and a comparative analysis of the structure that has come to be called "the bureaucracy." Public bureaucracies are perhaps the *most common* political structures in the world today; they exist in all political systems, whether they are democratic or authoritarian, "presidential" or "parliamentary," "developed" or "underdeveloped." They are as nearly a universal political structure as one can find: As a specialized structure, "bureaucracy is common to all contemporary nation-states."[34]

The term "bureaucracy" itself is something of a problem because it has a number of definitions, some value-free and some quite judgmental. The scholar whose work is most closely associated with the term, and who contributed most to its development, is Max Weber (1864–1920). Weber's concern was "less with organizational efficiency than with the expansion of bureaucratic power, and with the implications of that expansion for fundamental liberal values."[35]

Weber saw "modern officialdom" as having six characteristic patterns of behavior:

1. It has "fixed and official jurisdictional areas," which are "generally ordered by rules or administrative regulations";
2. The authority to give orders is also limited by rules, and officials have "coercive means" that they may use to enforce those rules;
3. The management of the office "is based upon written documents ('the files')," which requires a substantial staff to keep records;
4. Management "presupposes thorough and expert training";
5. Office activity requires the full attention of the official; and
6. "The management of the office follows general rules."[36]

Generally, bureaucracies have been studied from several different perspectives.[37] First, they can be studied from an *organizational* perspective, focusing upon structures, organizational charts, lines of communication, hierarchical organization, its formal rules, and how it operates.[38] Second, bureaucracies can be studied from a *behavioral* perspective, seeking to understand what bureaucracies do, how they behave, and what behavioral characteristics distinguish bureaucracies from other hierarchically organized structures.[39] A third approach focuses on how well bureaucracies *achieve their goals*, and discusses their efficiency, specialization, rational activity, and role in the framework of democratic government.[40]

Bureaucracies (and here we speak of *public* bureaucracies, although most of what we say about public bureaucracies applies to private bureaucracies as well) are typically complex systems of personnel, usually organized in a hierarchical fashion. That is, bureaucracies are usually *pyramidally* shaped, with the number of employees in higher positions being fewer than those in lower positions.

The nature of a bureaucracy is usually that specialized jobs are performed by different divisions of the organization, and the organization is divided into *functional* categories. Bureaucracies are also well known for having well-institutionalized sets of *rules*, or *procedures*, and a relatively rigid set of *precedents* that govern their behavior.[41]

Bureaucracies often claim to be based on some kind of merit system, in which one takes an examination to receive a position, or receives a position based on some perceived objective skills. This is characteristic of more developed nations[42] and is a reaction to practices dating back to the early years of the American Republic. President Andrew Jackson coined the term "the spoils system," referring to a chief executive's right to appoint public personnel as one of the "spoils" of an electoral victory.

It is often the case in political bureaucracies that some type of *civil service* system exists that protects the lower-level bureaucrats from political interference in their jobs; if they have been working for several years under the direction of one political party, they need not fear that they will lose their jobs should the opposition party gain control of the government. The other side of this coin, of course, is that a party that is new to government does not have the ability to put an unlimited number of its followers into positions of power when it wins an election. They must compete for positions through the established civil service system that exists at the time. Parties that have been out of power for a long time often claim that the bureaucracy "represents" the interests of the "old order," and that it is "resisting" their proposed changes. Often this is actually the case.

Top-level positions in the bureaucracy often are *political appointments*; there *is* an expectation that after an election is held all officials at this level will submit their resignations and permit a new cohort of political appointees to direct the administration of policy. Thus in a typical government ministry the minister and the deputy ministers will clearly be political appointments, with the minister being an MP and the deputy ministers being party loyalists, but the director-general (or an official with a similar title) will be a civil servant who remains in office even with a change of administrations.

The function of the bureaucracy is theoretically to *administer* the policy of the executive and to *offer specialized advice* to the executive,[43] not to make policy of its own. As we indicated earlier, however, one of the frequent complaints about bureaucracies is that they *do*, in fact, make policy in an "irresponsible" way—"irresponsible" because nobody elected them.[44] As society has grown more and more complex, resulting in the gradual expansion of the executive branch of government over the legislative branch of government—something we discussed in Chapter 4—this administration has required more and more personnel, leading to a rapid growth of public bureaucracies.[45] Often the growth of bureaucracy in modern society is decried, but it has been demonstrated to be *necessary* to administer more and more complex social policy.

PRESIDENTIAL AND PARLIAMENTARY SYSTEMS: SOME COMPARISONS

Clearly there are a number of major and significant differences in structure between the presidential and the parliamentary-cabinet system. A question for us to ask at this time is this: What are the *behavioral* implications of the differences between the two systems, and how will the two systems differ in terms of policy output and day-to-day operation? Several significant dimensions of difference are mentioned here.

The first distinction has to do with the idea of *responsible government*. Responsible government in this context does not mean trustworthy or rational government, but instead refers to the Government's ability to *deliver* on its promises. Responsible government comes about in parliamentary systems through some of the structural characteristics we have already met. The idea of party discipline suggests that legislators will vote (and speak and act) in the manner that their party leader suggests. The selection of the prime minister as leader of the largest party in the legislature and the notion of the vote of confidence ensure that the prime minister will always have the support of (and therefore because of party discipline be able to control) a majority of the legislature. Consequently, whatever the prime minister wants will have the approval of a majority of the legislature. If the prime minister's proposals do *not* receive a parliamentary majority, of course, the prime minister will have to resign.

This means that when the prime minister promises the public that his or her Government will act in a certain way, that person is in a position to follow through on that promise. In addition to being the leader of the executive branch of government, the prime minister is *also* (by definition) the leader of the legislative branch of government.

Contrast this with the presidential system, in which the notion of separation of powers and checks and balances—something that explicitly does *not* apply in a parliamentary system—is so important. One of the central principles of presidential government is that the legislature is free to deny requests of the president. Consequently, although a presidential candidate may run for office on the basis of his or her position on a single issue or a number of issues, in most cases the candidate cannot guarantee delivery of campaign promises. To enact policy, the legislature *must* be convinced that the president's policy preferences are the right ones.

Which system is "best"? It is hard to say, and the answer depends on certain value judgments, since each system has its own strengths and weaknesses. On one hand, the parliamentary system does have a real advantage in rapid policy delivery, through the notions of party discipline and cabinet leadership. On the other hand, if *good* policy can be passed quickly, so can *bad* policy. Many in parliamentary systems bemoan the overwhelming influence of party discipline and corresponding "prime ministerial dictatorship," however, and some have even suggested that respective systems consider changes to the presidential model.[46]

The corresponding weakness/strength of the presidential system is precisely its slower, more deliberative legislative process. The argument that is suggested is that whereas it may (and almost always does) take longer to pass policy, groups that are in a minority in an issue area have more opportunity to protect their interests, and the policy that is ultimately passed is more likely to be a good one. Put slightly more cynically, the policy that is ultimately passed is likely to offend as few as possible. On the other hand, a policy decision that is *urgently needed* may go unanswered for a long time while the legislature deliberates and argues with the president.

Another major area of difference between the two systems has to do with stability and tenure of office. In the presidential system, both the president and the legislature have fixed terms of office. They can be secure in their knowledge of their fixed terms in these positions, barring extraordinary occurrences (such as impeachment and conviction of the president in the United States, for example). This security permits both the president and the legislature to take either an unpopular position or an antagonistic position in relation to the other branch of government if it is believed that such a position is the proper one to take.

The parliamentary system offers no such job security. The chief executive can lose this position at any time, depending on the mood of the legislature. A chief executive worried about keeping his or her job, then, would be less likely to take a position that is clearly disapproved of by the legislature than would a president, although an individual out of step with the legislature would not be likely to be chief executive in a parliamentary system. Moreover, the legislature would be less likely to rebel against executive leadership: Party discipline would tend to force party members to follow the instructions of their leader (and the leader of the majority party, of course, would be the chief executive). If the legislature became too contentious, the chief executive could request a writ of dissolution from the head of state, effectively "firing" the legislature and calling for new elections.

As we indicated earlier, it is easy to see that each of these systems has advantages and disadvantages in terms of stability, policy output, protection of minority rights, ability to deliver on campaign promises, responsiveness to public opinion, and so on.[47] Some of these values are simply inverses of others: Responsiveness to majority public opinion may infringe on minority rights, for example. What is seen as an advantage to one observer may be a distinct disadvantage to another.

Both the presidential and the parliamentary models of executive structure are conducive to democratic government. Both models can be responsive to public opinion, both can provide effective leadership, and both can provide for the general welfare of the political system. The differences between the two types of systems are differences of structure and process, not ideology. As such, it is difficult to argue that one type of system is, overall, *better* than the other; they are simply *different.*

Notes

1. See Locke's Section 126 in Sir Ernest Barker, ed., *Social Contract: Essays by Locke, Hume & Rousseau* (New York: Oxford University Press, 1970).

2. Clinton Rossiter, *The American Presidency* (New York: Mentor, 1960), pp. 14–40 passim.

3. See James Madison, *Notes on Debates in the Federal Convention of 1787* (Athens: Ohio University Press, 1966), passim.

4. See Joseph LaPalombara, *Politics Within Nations* (Englewood Cliffs, N.J.: Prentice Hall, 1974), pp. 190–196.

5. For descriptions of the American presidency, see Amos Kiewe, ed., *The Modern Presidency and Crisis Rhetoric* (Westport, Conn: Greenwood Publishing, 1993), Congressional Quarterly Staff, *The Presidency A to Z: A Ready Reference Encyclopedia* (Washington, D.C.: Congressional Quarterly, 1992), or Robert Shogan, *The Riddle of Power: Presidential Leadership from Truman to Bush* (New York: New American Library, 1992). Classic studies of the presidency can be found in Rossiter, *American Presidency*, or Richard Neustadt, *Presidential Power* (New York: New American Library, 1964). One example of recent work on the president and Congress is Calvin Mouw and Michael MacKuen, "The Strategic Configuration, Personal Influence, and Presidential Power in Congress," *Western Political Quarterly* 45:3 (1992): pp. 579–609.

6. The famous quote by John Adams, the first vice president of the United States, is as follows: "I am possessed of two separate powers, the one *in esse* and the other *in posse*. I am Vice President. In this I am nothing, but I may be everything." Rossiter, *The American Presidency*, p. 131.

7. On the powers of the vice president, see Rossiter, *American Presidency*, pp. 129–135.

8. On presidential elections, see Diana Reische, *Electing a U.S. President* (New York: Franklin Watts, 1992), Myron Levine, *Presidential Campaigns and Elections: Issues, Images, and Partisanship* (Itasca, Ill: F. E. Peacock, 1992), Herb Asher, *Presidential Elections and American Politics: Voters, Candidates, and Campaigns Since 1952* (Belmont, Calif.: Wadsworth Publishing,

1992), James David Barber, *The Pulse of Politics: Electing Presidents in the Media Age* (New Brunswick, N.J.: Transaction, 1992), or Martin Wattenberg, *The Rise of Candidate-Centered Politics: Presidential Elections of the 1980s* (Cambridge: Harvard University Press, 1991).

9. *Federalist* Number 68 by Alexander Hamilton discusses the rationalization of this structure. See *The Federalist Papers* (New York: New American Library, 1961), pp. 411–415.

10. See Ronald Moe, ed., *Congress and the President* (Pacific Palisades, Calif.: Goodyear, 1971).

11. See Mark A. Peterson, *Legislating Together: The White House and Capitol Hill from Eisenhower to Reagan* (Cambridge: Harvard University Press, 1990), Martin L. Fausold and Alan Shank, eds., *The Constitution and the American Presidency* (Albany: State University of New York Press, 1991), or Louis Fisher, *Constitutional Conflicts Between Congress and the President* (Lawrence: University Press of Kansas, 1991).

12. This constant tension is discussed in William Safire, *Before the Fall: An Inside View of the Pre-Watergate White House* (Da Capo Press, 1988), and John R. Greene, *The Limits of Power: The Nixon and Ford Administrations* (Bloomington: Indiana University Press, 1992).

13. See Charles O. Jones, *The Trusteeship Presidency: Jimmy Carter and the United States Congress* (Baton Rouge: Louisiana State University Press, 1988), Garland Haas, *Jimmy Carter and the Politics of Frustration* (Jefferson, N.C.: McFarland and Company, 1992), or Burton I. Kaufman, *The Presidency of James Earl Carter, Jr.* (Lawrence: University Press of Kansas, 1993).

14. Some good comparative works include Richard Rose and Ezra Suleiman, eds., *Presidents and Prime Ministers* (Washington, D.C.: American Enterprise Institute, 1980), Arend Lijphart, *Parliamentary vs. Presidential Government* (New York: Oxford University Press, 1992), and, with a different perspective, Michael Foley, *The Rise of the British Presidency* (New York: St. Martin's Press, 1993).

15. LaPalombara, pp. 192–194. See also the data in Jean Blondel, *Comparative Legislatures*, pp. 144-153, column 39.

16. See G. W. Jones, ed., *West European Prime Ministers* (Portland, Ore.: International Specialized Book Services, 1991).

17. See, for example, *The Saint Vincent Constitution Order, 1979*, establishing a constitution for the new nation of St. Vincent. Sections 50 and 51 outline the Executive Power: Section 50 states that "The executive authority of Saint Vincent is vested in Her Majesty [and] . . . may be exercised on behalf of Her Majesty by the Governor-General. . . ." Section 51 notes that "(1) There shall be a Prime Minister of Saint Vincent who shall be appointed by the Governor-General. (2) Whenever the Governor-General has occasion to appoint a Prime Minister he shall appoint a Representative who appears to him likely to command the support of the majority of Representatives. . . . (6) The Governor-General shall remove the Prime Minister from office if a resolution of no confidence in the Government is passed by the House and the Prime Minister does not within three days either resign from his office or advise the Governor-General to dissolve Parliament." *Saint Vincent Constitution Order, 1979* (Kingstown, St. Vincent: Government Printing Office, 1979), pp. 38–39.

18. This section is based on a much longer discussion of the same subject in the now-classic study by Sydney Bailey, *British Parliamentary Democracy* (Boston: Houghton Mifflin, 1958), pp. 12–20.

19. This argument was expounded on at length in his *True Law of Free Monarchies* in 1603.

20. R. M. Dawson, *The Government of Canada* (Toronto: University of Toronto Press, 1965), pp. 184-185.

21. In fact, most cabinet members come from the legislative body. See Blondel, *Comparative Legislatures*, pp. 144-153, column 40.

22. One system with a legal requirement is Barbados. See the *Barbados Independence Order, 1966*: [Section 66 (1)] "The Office of Prime Minister shall become vacant. . . . [(2)] If the House of Assembly by a resolution which has received the affirmative vote of a majority of all the members thereof resolves that the appointment of the Prime Minister ought to be revoked . . ," pp. 62–63.

23. Blondel, *Comparative Legislatures*, pp. 144-153, column 42.

24. See Kaare Strom, "Deferred Gratification and Minority Governments in Scandinavia," *Legislative Studies Quarterly* 11:4 (1986): 583–606.

25. Blondel, *Comparative Legislatures*, pp. 144-153, column 41.

26. Ian Budge and Michael Laver, "Office Seeking and Policy Pursuit in Coalition Theory," *Legislative Studies Quarterly* 11:4 (1986): 485–506; Robert L. Peterson and Martine M. DeRidder, "Government Formation as a Policy-Making Arena," *Legislative Studies Quarterly* 11:4 (1986): 565–582; Michael Laver and Norman Schofield, *Multiparty Government: The Politics of Coalition in Europe* (New York: Oxford University Press, 1990).

27. John Frendreis, Dennis Gleiber, and Eric Browne, "The Study of Cabinet Dissolutions in Parliamentary Democracies," *Legislative Studies Quarterly* 11:4 (1986): 619–628. See also Ian Budge and Hans Keman, *Parties and Democracy: Coalition Formation and Government Functioning in Twenty States* (New York: Oxford University Press, 1990).

28. A very good comparative study is by Lawrence C. Dodd, *Coalitions in Parliamentary Government* (Princeton, N.J.: Princeton University Press, 1976).

29. Hans Daalder, "Changing Procedures and Changing Strategies in Dutch Coalition Building," *Legislative Studies Quarterly* 11:4 (1986): 507–532.

30. Eric C. Browne and Mark N. Franklin, "New Directions in Coalition Research," *Legislative Studies Quarterly* 11:4 (1986): 469–484. In the same issue of *Legislative Studies Quarterly* see also Ian Budge and Michael Laver, "Office Seeking and Political Pursuit in Coalition Theory," pp. 485–506, and Robert L. Peterson and Martine DeRidder, "Government Formation as a Policy-Making Arena," pp. 565–582.

31. See, for further reading on coalitions, A. DeSwann, *Coalition Theories and Cabinet Formations* (San Francisco: Jossey-Bass, 1973), William Gamson, "A Theory of Coalition Formation," *American Sociological Review* 26 (1961): 373–382, or Gregory Mahler and Richard Trilling, "Coalition Behavior and Cabinet Formation: The Case of Israel," *Comparative Political Studies* 8 (1975): 200–233.

32. William Reisinger, "Situational and Motivational Assumptions in Theories of Coalition Formation," *Legislative Studies Quarterly* 11:4 (1986): 551–564.

33. John Robertson, "Economic Polarization and Cabinet Formation in Western Europe," *Legislative Studies Quarterly* 11:4 (1986): 533–550.

34. Ferrel Heady, *Public Administration: A Comparative Perspective* (New York: Marcel Dekker, 1984), p. 59.

35. David Beetham, *Bureaucracy* (Minneapolis: University of Minnesota Press, 1987), p. 58.

36. Max Weber, "Bureaucracy," in H. H. Gerth and C. Wright Mills, eds., *From Max Weber: Essays in Sociology* (New York: Oxford University Press, 1978), p. 196. See also Claude Lefort, *The Political Forms of Modern Society: Bureaucracy, Democracy, Totalitarianism* (Cambridge: M.I.T. Press, 1986): 96.

37. This section is based on much more detailed analysis in Heady, *Public Administration*, pp. 61–64.

38. This is the approach of B. Guy Peters, *The Politics of Bureaucracy: A Comparative Perspective* (New York: Longman, 1978).

39. To a substantial degree this approach is illustrated by Eva Etzioni-Halevy, *Bureaucracy and Democracy: A Political Dilemma* (London: Routledge and Kegan Paul, 1983).

40. An example of this kind of study might be John Burke, *Bureaucratic Responsibility* (Baltimore: Johns Hopkins University Press, 1986).

41. See Bogdan Mieczkowski, *Dysfunctional Bureaucracy: A Comparative and Historical Perspective* (Lanham, Md.: University Press of America, 1991), and Metin Heper, ed., *The State and Public Bureaucracies: A Comparative Perspective* (Westport, Conn.: Greenwood Press, 1987).

42. See the discussion by Heady, "Relating Bureaucratic and Political Development" in his *Public Administration*, pp. 409–417.

43. A very good study of the *advising* function is edited by William Plowden, *Advising the Rulers* (Oxford: Basil Blackwell, 1987).

44. A very good discussion of some of the philosophical dimensions of this problem, and how democratic control can coexist with bureaucracy can be found in Judith Gruber, *Controlling Bureaucracies: Dilemmas in Democratic Governance* (Los Angeles: University of California Press, 1987).

45. This point is discussed at some length in Peters, *The Politics of Bureaucracy*. Peters's second chapter is entitled "The Growth of Government and Administration," and he discusses the

growth of administration not only in the executive branch, but also in the legislature and in other areas of the government.

46. See, for example, Avraham Brichta and Yair Zalmanovitch, "The Proposals for Presidential Government in Israel: A Case Study in the Possibility of Institutional Transference," *Comparative Politics* 19:1 (1986): 57–68.

47. Some discussion of this may be found in Jaakko Nousiainen, "Bureaucratic Tradition, Semi-Presidential Rule and Parliamentary Government: The Case of Finland," *European Journal of Political Research* 16:2 (1988): 229–249.

6

Judiciaries and the Legal Order

ON THE COMPARATIVE STUDY OF JUDICIARIES

After our discussion of legislative and executive structures, the structure of government suggested by John Locke in 1690 that remains to be discussed is "a known and indifferent judge, with authority to determine all differences according to the established law."[1] One of the functions that was ascribed to constitutions in our discussion in Chapter 2 was that they serve as an expression of the basic laws of the regime. At this point of our inquiry we should say something about the function of legal systems in political processes and the importance of legal culture in general, and something about the role of judges and courts in political systems.

Of the three major Lockean governmental structures—the legislature, the executive, and the judiciary—that can be observed on a cross-national basis, courts and legal systems generally continually receive the least attention in introductory texts and comparative studies,[2] unless, of course, the study in question explicitly focuses on the judiciary or the law.[3] Why is this the case? Two possible suggestions can be offered here.

First, as far as systemic characteristics and political institutions go, legal systems and courts may be the most *system-specific.* That is, although both executives and legislatures have structural idiosyncrasies, and have behavior that varies on a country-by-country basis, we can still make a number of useful generalizations about both their structures (for instance, "presidential" systems as compared with "parlia-

mentary" systems) and their behavior (for instance, a system with high party discipline compared with a system with low party discipline). This level of generalization
is hard to achieve with legal systems and courts. Although we can speak of constitutional regimes—governments of laws, not ruled by individual whim—we very quickly
get to the point at which individual system–level characteristics of judiciaries must
be discussed; consequently, generalizability is low.

Second, while executives and legislatures are undoubtedly part of the political process, in many political systems the courts are explicitly *excluded from* the political arena.[4] This is not a refutation of Locke's argument that courts (judges) are
necessary to society; it simply limits the role of the judges and the courts to one of
arbitration or mediation. They are not part of the law-making or policy-making
process, specifically, or the political arena, generally. (It should be noted, in fact, that
Locke suggested the function of the judge was to "determine all differences according to the *established* law," [emphasis added] *not* to make the law or public policy.) Accordingly, many political scientists have left the judiciary out of their studies
of the political arena and the policy-making process generally.

In explaining the almost-nonpolitical role of the courts, one recent study
pointed out that courts, "logically and historically, have been undemocratic institutions. An increased role for the courts, then, could render a political order less democratic."[5] Thus, although the courts have often been significant in maintaining
individual rights, they have often kept a low profile in their respective polities,
thereby generating relatively little scholarship on their *comparative* political impact.

Although courts are often "nonpolitical" in nature, they *do* play a significant
role in political systems. As we shall see, in many systems courts play a role in shaping the law through *judicial review*. In other systems the role of the courts may be
more circumscribed, but they still interpret statutes, hear cases involving government
leaders, and generally participate in official government action.

> Courts are, in sum, part of every political system, and the politics of none can be un-
> derstood without an appreciation of their role. Yet modern political science has
> tended to downplay or even ignore judicial institutions, and to the extent that it has
> done this, its analyses of politics remain incomplete. As we more fully comprehend
> the roles of courts in each modern democracy, we will be in a better position to con-
> struct genuine comparative theories both about courts themselves and modern po-
> litical development.[6]

THE IDEA OF LAW

The idea of law tends to be assumed whenever we think of politics. That is, there is
an implicit (Western, ethnocentric) assumption that political systems are based, to
varying degrees, on the rule of law. This assumption is made because so many of our
contacts with government come in relation to governmental rules, regulations, and
administrative guidelines. It is almost impossible to think of government existing
without laws; the "authoritative allocation of values" with which politics is concerned
deals with laws.

Law is generally regarded as one of the greatest achievements of civilization.[7] It is concerned with basic rules of conduct that reflect to some degree the concept of justice. These rules concern the relationships of the individual with government and with other individuals. An ideal of justice frequently expressed is that the government should be a government of laws and not of men.[8] Whether this goal can be achieved is questionable, as laws are made and administered by human beings. But in practice this ideal is generally interpreted to mean a legal system that treats everyone equally and that is not subject to change through the arbitrary acts of a dictator, or even the whim of transient majorities.[9] Hence, even in the seventeenth century, John Locke saw *law* as being the principal attraction of society: "Thus mankind, notwithstanding all the privileges of the state of nature, being but in an ill condition while they remain in it, are quickly driven into society. . . . [They] take sanctuary under the established laws of government."[10]

There are a number of different *kinds* of law to which the interested student can find reference, including positive law, divine law, moral law, natural law, and scientific law,[11] among others. *Scientific laws* refer to observations and measurements that have been empirically determined and that focus on physical, biological, and chemical concepts, not social questions. *Moral laws* refer to precepts or guidelines that are based on subjective values, beliefs, and attitudes, focusing on behavior: the proper way of doing things. We must note, however, that moral laws, unlike scientific laws, will vary depending on the value system used to construct them. *Divine law*, as well, will be seen to vary depending on the religious or theological conceptual framework from which it is said to be derived.

The two major approaches to law with which we as social scientists are concerned are natural law and positive law. *Natural law* refers to a body of precepts governing human behavior that is "more basic than man-made law, and one that is based on fundamental principles of justice."[12] The type of law with which governments are most concerned is *positive law*, which can be said to have three major identifiable characteristics: (1) it is man-made law, (2) it is designed to govern human behavior, and (3) it is enforceable by appropriate governmental action.

Conflict has erupted throughout human history when natural law and positive law appear to conflict. Political philosophers from the time of Cicero (106–43 B.C.), including John of Salisbury, Thomas Aquinas, Thomas Hobbes, John Locke, Jean-Jacques Rousseau, David Hume, Jeremy Bentham, and Karl Marx, through philosophers of the present day have dealt with this thorny issue.[13] What is the individual to do when the law of the state tells one to do one thing, but one's perception of natural law, of the *fundamental* standard of "rightness," says to do something else? Many have argued that human laws (positive laws) that conflict with natural laws (or religious laws) are null and void. St. Augustine's "two sword" theory in the early fifth century was one attempt to resolve this conflict.[14] Augustine argued that natural law and divine law were the same thing: The laws of nature are God's laws. Individuals are required to obey earthly (positive) law only insofar as it does not conflict with natural law. When natural law and positive law conflict, it is the law of God that must be obeyed, according to Augustine.

LEGAL CULTURES

The concept of a "culture" is one that has been developed primarily by sociologists and anthropologists. A legal culture can be considered to be:

> a set of deeply rooted, historically conditioned attitudes about the nature of law, about the role of law in the society and the polity, about the proper organization and operation of a legal system, and about the way law is, or should be made, applied, studied, perfected, and taught. The legal tradition relates the legal system to the culture of which it is a partial expression.[15]

The concept of a legal culture, then, focuses on the beliefs, attitudes, and values of society *relative to the law and politics*.[16]

These values have to do with the nature and process of justice in the political system, the concept of equality, and, more basically, the nature of law in the regime itself. The latter includes the very fundamental question of law and its influence on government policy.

We mentioned earlier the idea that political systems should be "governments of law and not of men." This reflects one of the most central questions of any political regime: Is the government bound to obey its own laws, or is it permitted to go beyond the laws in its execution of public policy? The reader will recall that in our discussion of constitutions and constitutional government one of the dividing lines between (behaviorally) constitutional and unconstitutional regimes was the degree to which the behavior of regimes was *limited*, controlled by law. Are there limits beyond which the government absolutely may not go? Or, conversely, is the function of law perceived to be primarily that of controlling individual behavior, keeping individuals "under control," while the government may do whatever it wishes?

It is precisely this type of normative, philosophical question that is addressed by the concept of the legal culture. This explains why legal cultures are so difficult to study: They are blends of philosophy, sometimes quite complex, and cannot readily be described in only a few words. To appreciate fully the legal culture of a political system, we must understand its political and social history, its political structures, and the political values and attitudes dominant in that political system at any given time.

A nation's legal culture will shape the role that the law and legal institutions play in the political realm. For example, the fact that the United States is "the most litigious country in the world"[17] suggests that Americans are more likely to look to the courts than might citizens of other polities. On the other hand, "the Japanese legal culture puts a premium on informal settlement of legal disputes based on informal controls and social sanction without legal procedure." Japanese citizens thus are hesitant to resort to the courts to resolve political issues, although "when the traditional means of conciliation and mediation fail, the Japanese become very determined to exhaust all avenues of legal device and remedy."[18]

Although political cultures do vary on a nation-by-nation basis, there are certain "families" or groupings of legal cultures that may be suggested here for purposes of generalization. These are (1) the Romano-Germanic family, (2) the family of the common law, (3) the family of socialist law, and (4) the non-Western legal families.[19]

The *Romano-Germanic* approach to law, sometimes referred to as "code" law, has developed from the basis of Roman law at the time of Emperor Justinian (A.D. 533).[20] This type of law, as contrasted with common law, is based on comprehensively written legislative statutes, often bound together as "codes." The *Code Napoleon* was just such a bound collection; the Emperor Napoleon (reigned 1804–1815) decided that law throughout his empire needed to be standardized, and he had a single, comprehensive set of laws assembled and disseminated. The *Code Napoleon* influenced legal structures from Europe to North America to Asia. The French legal system is characteristic of a code law system, and in North America today the legal systems of Louisiana and Quebec have similar characteristics, evidence of their (French) colonial heritage.

The *common law* system, found in England and countries modeled on English law (including the United States), is sometimes called "Anglo-American" law,[21] and has been referred to as "judge-made law."[22] This is not to suggest that today's laws in these political systems are not made by the legislatures of those systems or, conversely, that today's laws are made by judges in those systems. Rather, the term suggests that when the science of the law was being developed in England in the twelfth century, it was the judges who made decisions. Today *judicial precedent* plays a major role in common law nations—the process is referred to as *stare decisis* (to stand by things decided).[23] A judge may use a previously adjudicated case as a guide for his or her decision, but the judge may decide that there are new characteristics involved in the case that require deviation from earlier decisions. Of course, today the legislature plays a highly significant role in designing the laws the judge is applying to the specific situation.

The differences between the code law systems and the common law systems can easily be overstated, but two main characteristics should be pointed out. First, judges play a slightly less significant role in decision making in the code law systems, with correspondingly greater influence exercised by the legislature. Second, the common law system, characteristic of Anglo-American nations, tries to minimize the likelihood of an innocent person being convicted by setting up various procedural and substantive safeguards. The code law system, characterized by the system found in France, "lays more stress on preventing a guilty person from escaping punishment."[24]

Socialist law derives from a different philosophical root.[25] Karl Marx and his philosophy assumed that law was a tool of the state in capitalist societies, and it was used to oppress the working class. Marx argued that in a perfect socialist state there would be no need for law at all, once the economic ills of society were cured. In fact, of course, things have not turned out to be quite as simple as Marx expected. Law in the former Soviet Union, perhaps the best example of a socialist system, played if anything a *greater* role than in Western democracies.[26]

Recent Soviet Marxists saw law as a tool of the state, to be used to work toward a socialist society. The state could (and should) *use* law to further its ends. This resulted in a kind of twisted logical circle: Law exists to further the interests of citizens. The state knows better than any individuals what the interests of the citizens are. Anything the state does, therefore, must be legal. Thus law becomes simply another instrument of state policy. When we discussed the former Soviet constitutional system in Chapter 2, we indicated the difference in approaches to civil and political rights in the former Soviet Union and Western democracies.

In *non-Western legal systems*, such as those of some developing nations, legal cultures are quite different and depend on (1) local traditions and customs, (2) the legal culture of the colonizing power (if any) that controlled the political infrastructure prior to independence, and (3) the degree to which the colonizing power permitted autonomy and development during the colonial era. In some non-Western systems religious law, especially Islamic law, has a major role in the general legal framework of the regime. In others, religious and tribal laws are blended with colonial legal values. Elsewhere, developing nations have completely forsaken their traditional legal cultures and have opted instead for modern legal structures and processes.[27] To take just one example, the legal culture found in Israel today is a blend of Turkish law and British law (former colonial powers in the Middle East), religious law (including Jewish, Moslem, and Christian components), as well as contemporary legal and judicial values.[28]

SOURCES OF LAW

For as long as political systems have been based on the rule of law, there have been a variety of sources for the laws that have existed. In the Middle Ages, the sole source of law might have been the monarch in power, or perhaps the monarch in combination with religious guidelines. A number of different sources may be singled out and mentioned here.

Prior to the creation of society, with its rules and regulations and formal legal structures, patterns of behavior were governed by *religious* or *moral values*. This kind of law generally comes in entire bodies, often in a specifically delineated set. Thus the Mosaic Law—the Ten Commandments brought down from Mount Sinai by Moses—was a *body* of law. Similarly, the Koran, the sacred book of the Moslem religion, contains a *body* of laws. This religious law often is interpreted to be natural law, as we distinguished the terms earlier, although some might want to argue that religious law may contain elements much more specific than natural law. For example, religious laws may prohibit the consumption of certain foods, or working on a certain day of the week, when there is no immediately apparent reason why this should be considered to be part of a "law of nature." Depending on the nature of a society, this type of religious or moral value may become entrenched in the legal framework of a political system.[29]

Some monarchs, notably James I of England (reigned 1603–1625), used religion as a basis of their power. In his *True Law of Free Monarchies*,[30] James I developed his theory of the "divine right of kings," arguing that rulers derived their powers from God, and what they wanted was law. James I was not the only monarch to believe this, and *the will of the monarch* became a major source of law for a long time.

Another source of law is *tradition* or *custom*. We made the distinction in our discussion of legislatures and executives between *de jure* (in law) and *de facto* (in fact) political power, and argued that tradition may develop the force of law, even if it never becomes law. The tradition in England, for example, that the monarch selects the leader of the largest party in the House of Commons to be prime minister has become so established that it is taken as part of the "Westminster model" constitutional regime there. Similarly, the tradition that the prime minister must resign if he or she receives a vote of no confidence may take on the force of law, even if it hasn't become actual law.

Sometimes traditions are left unwritten, as the case of the head of state acting "on the advice" of the chief executive illustrates. On other occasions, however, traditions are actually formalized and made part of the constitutional or legal framework of a political system. For example, the tradition of American presidents serving only two terms of office was firmly entrenched in American politics prior to World War II. George Washington started the tradition, and if a president did not bow out of politics at the end of his first term of office, he inevitably did so at the end of his second term. When Franklin Delano Roosevelt violated this tradition and ran for a third term, and then a fourth term, some reacted quite strongly. This reaction led to the Twenty-second Amendment to the Constitution, limiting presidential terms of office.[31]

Certainly a major source of law in contemporary regimes is the constitution of the regime. Some national constitutions include specific legal proscriptions that must be followed in the political system, as well as more general descriptions of the structures and institutions to be found in the regime. The U.S. Constitution, for example, contains a number of specific limitations and guidelines that are not only laws in their own right (for instance, "Congress shall make no law . . . abridging the freedom of speech . . ."), but have also generated an entire body of supplementary law.

This happens through yet another source of law, *the judiciary*. Judicial decision making, including the interpretation of constitutional dogma and legislative statutes and the application of judicial precedents to new circumstances, has resulted in a great deal of "judge-made" law. Judge-made law is derived from, based on, what is in the constitution, supplementing constitutional parameters and helping the court to be more "relevant" to contemporary times.

Another governmental structure directly concerned with the creation of law is, of course, *the legislature*. The legislature as an institution derives its name from the law (*legis*), and certainly one of the functions most commonly attributed to the legislature is the lawmaking function. We have already seen that this may not, in fact, be the case in every political regime. Often the legislature is more important in a specific political system in some other capacity—its legislative function may be primarily that of a rubber stamp.

More and more often today we see arguments that legislatures are in a decline as far as their legitimate legislative powers are concerned. The argument suggests that, in both presidential and parliamentary systems of government, legislatures are surrendering their legislative powers to the executive branch in exchange for the rubber stamp function. The question important to ask is, Why is this so?[32]

Theodore Lowi has argued that part of this problem stems from the complexity of modern society and government. It was easy for legislatures in 1690 to perform their legislative tasks; for example, to pass laws forbidding poaching on the king's land. It is much harder for legislatures to address the complex social problems of the 1990s. For example, how can a legislature fight poverty? It could pass a law making it illegal to be poor, but that would not solve the problem. Lowi suggests in his book *The End of Liberalism* that problems such as these may be beyond the competence of legislatures. Often the only response to these complex problems that is available to a legislature is to pass the buck to an executive agency, appropriate some money, and give the executive agency authority to set rules and policy by itself.[33]

This has led to yet another source of law—*administrative decisions*. A legislature may decide, for example, that it does not have either the time or the capacity to make highly specialized policy decisions regarding food and drugs. Its response to this quandary, given a feeling that some regulation in this area is clearly necessary, might be to establish, say, a National Food and Drugs Agency, giving commissioners of the agency authority to set standards and regulations ensuring a constant quality of both food and drugs. The actions of a majority of commissioners, then, may have the force of law (violations of their decisions and rules could result in fines or imprisonment) and could have the same *effect* as legislated laws, even though the legislature really was not responsible for specific policy set by the agency.[34]

We can see, then, that although positive laws may derive from a number of sources, their effects can be the same. Whether these laws stem from religious or moral values, tradition or custom, a constitution, judicial interpretation, legislation, or administrative actions and decisions, all serve the functions of regulating behavior in society.

STRUCTURES IN LEGAL SYSTEMS

The heart of a judicial system's structure is to be found in its network of *courts*. Theodore Becker, a significant contributor to the cross-national literature on judiciaries, has characterized courts as having seven components. A court is:

1. An individual or group of individuals
2. With power to make decisions in disputes
3. Before whom the parties or their advocates present the facts involved in the dispute and cite principles (in statutes, or other forms) that
4. Are applied by that individual or those individuals
5. Who *believe* that they should listen to the facts and apply cited principles impartially, and
6. That they may so decide, and
7. As an independent body.[35]

The main service of modern courts, then, is to serve as an arena in which *controlled* conflict may take place. The controls exercised on this conflict are very rigid, emphasizing verbal, conceptual, legal, and philosophical strengths rather than physical strength. (Let us not forget that at the time of King Arthur, conflicts were often resolved by "champions" in physical combat!)

Martin Shapiro has suggested that the basic concept explaining the role of courts in the resolution of conflict is that of the "triad."

Cutting quite across cultural lines, it appears that whenever two persons come into a conflict that they cannot themselves solve, one solution appealing to common sense is to call upon a third for assistance in achieving a resolution. . . . [F]rom its overwhelming appeal to common sense stems the basic political legitimacy of courts everywhere. . . . [This is] a logic so compelling that courts have become a universal political phenomenon.[36]

To process the disputes as smoothly and efficiently as possible, judicial structures are established in political systems. These frameworks include not only the body of laws of a political regime but also a series of courts to make decisions based on these laws. The actual structures of these courts vary tremendously on a system-by-system basis. Federal political systems may have legal infrastructures that reflect their federal makeup; unitary systems may be more simple. Some systems may have very specialized courts as part of their judicial structure, while others may not.

Judiciaries *tend* to be organized in a pyramidal fashion, with a large number of courts of initial adjudication, fewer appeals courts, and a single, ultimate, supreme court. In many judicial systems, *all* cases must begin on the "ground floor" and work their way up through the judicial system. There are instances in some judicial systems, however, in which the appeals courts and supreme court may have some *original jurisdiction*—some cases may start at the intermediate or top level, and not have to work their way up to that point.

The question of jurisdiction, of which court (or level of court) has authority to adjudicate a specific question, can be quite complex.[37] For example, in the U.S. judicial system, jurisdiction is divided between federal courts and state courts, reflecting the federal nature of the polity. The initial determination that must be made in any exercise in litigation is where jurisdiction lies: Is the question a federal case or a state case? Sometimes jurisdiction might overlap: In the United States today, for example, it is not a federal crime to rob a bank, but a state crime. It is, however, a federal crime to rob a bank insured by the federal government (and, it turns out, virtually all banks today are federally insured).

So, the individual who robs a federally insured bank actually commits *two* crimes: robbing a bank (a state crime), and robbing a federally insured bank (a federal crime), and can, accordingly, face two trials. (Parenthetically, it should be noted that this liability to face two trials is not the same thing as "double jeopardy," against which the individual is protected under the Fifth Amendment to the U.S. Constitution. The Fifth Amendment says that no person shall "be subject for the same offense to be twice put in jeopardy of life or limb. . . . " If a person commits two offenses, even in the same act, he or she may be tried twice; he or she may not be tried twice for the same offense.)

The U.S. federal judicial structure, then, consists of a single federal judicial pyramid and fifty separate state judicial pyramids. This double-structured judicial framework was designed to accommodate the federal nature of the American political arena, although it does occasionally make determination of jurisdiction more difficult.

Other political systems manage to allow for reflection of their federal character in their judicial systems without this parallel structure. In Canada, for example, there is no "double-pyramid" structure.[38] Courts are "constituted, maintained, and organized" by the provinces in the areas of both civil and criminal law. At the same time, however, to balance the grant of exclusive power over civil *procedure* given to the provinces, the federal government has exclusive jurisdiction over criminal *procedure*, and it is the federal government that controls the appointment, salary, and tenure of the judges in the courts that are established by the provinces. Thus the Canadian federal judicial structure appears as ten separate provincial pyramids, designed by the provinces and staffed by federal appointments. Civil procedure is established by the provinces (so that, for example, civil procedures in Ontario might be different from civil procedures in British Columbia), but criminal procedure will be standardized through its control by the federal government. There is, moreover, a single Supreme Court of Canada that acts as an appeals court for the entire nation.[39]

Australia, similarly, has a federal political system reflected in its judicial structure. The High Court of Australia can hear appeals from the Federal Court of Appeal or Court of Criminal Appeal, and can also hear appeals from state and territory supreme courts. Federalism, it has been suggested, has been "largely responsible for [the] Australian profusion of legalism."[40]

It can be seen, then, that the actual structural design of judicial systems varies on a nation-by-nation basis. Questions of jurisdiction, appeals, and procedure are so tailored to individual national characteristics that even members of the same legal cultural "families" that we saw earlier—the common law family, for example, or the code law family—may differ significantly in terms of specific political structures. Not only do Canada and the United States differ significantly in the manner in which their judicial structures reflect their federal natures, but even within a nation judicial structures can vary. For example, the court structure in Massachusetts differs from courts in California, and courts in Alberta differ from courts in Newfoundland.

JUDICIAL FUNCTIONS

The judicial function has been characterized by one scholar of comparative politics as:

> the determination of the meaning of laws and rules, the imposition of penalties for violating those rules, the deciding on the relative rights and obligations of individuals and the community, the determination of the area of freedom to be allowed persons within the political system, and the arbitration of disputes between individuals and officials.[41]

With such a list of functions, it is no wonder that courts or judiciaries are important political structures! Given a focus on *functions*, it is easy to see that the *structure* of a judiciary can vary, as we have just indicated.

Some of these functions performed by the judiciary are not unique to the judiciary. The legislature may act to clarify its own laws and rules, or mandate specific penalties for violations of rules, thus limiting the freedom of the judiciary. Actions of the executive may serve to arbitrate disputes between individuals and officials. In many instances, however, the judiciary is uniquely qualified to provide services beyond the capabilities of other governmental structures.

Because the courts can be seen as *impartial* to conflicts that come before them, they can be especially influential in both establishing facts and interpreting law. They can mediate in disputes between and among executive agencies and legislative structures, and may be applied to by citizens with complaints that they feel are not being properly addressed by other governmental agencies.

Additionally, judges are often in an invaluable position to protect minority rights. Most judicial systems offer some degree of protection for judges, shielding them from political consequences of their actions. Judges not only can take a nonpolitical view of conflicts, but they are also free to act; in most systems judges cannot be fired for unpopular decisions. Judges have the power to hand down decisions that might be so unpopular, socially or politically, that legislators or executives might hesitate to act on them, and judges need not be worried about losing their positions. Short of treason or a major criminal offense, judges are often "irresponsible" to majority opinion.

An "irresponsible" judiciary, of course, can be seen as either good or bad, depending on one's view of the policy question under consideration. Some citizens might view a court decision giving individual women the right to decide whether or not to have an abortion as legal toleration of murder; others might see the same decision as a victory for individual rights and freedom of choice. One constituency might cry that a court's decision banning prayer in public school is an act of atheism, while others may argue that the decision has nothing to do with *religion* at all, simply with *religion in school,* and is, therefore, a protection of the rights of a minority in the school who don't want to follow the majority's religious preferences.

JUDICIARIES IN THE POLITICAL ARENA

The judiciary may, in many political systems, engage in a lawmaking function of a sort, by interpreting laws made elsewhere. As a general rule, however, the courts prefer to stay out of the political arena.

> In some political matters the judiciary is unable or unwilling to act. Courts may be excluded from jurisdiction in certain subjects, as in Switzerland where federal laws cannot be challenged in the courts, or in France where *actes de gouvernement* remain outside the province of the courts.[42]

Even in the United States, where the U.S. Supreme Court is among the most politically active high tribunals in the world, the Court is hesitant to inject itself into the political arena, often deciding controversial cases in the most narrow manner possible to avoid political controversy. In addition to making decisions in politically controversial cases, courts may be involved in the political process by issuing writs, court orders, or injunctions in politically sensitive matters.

Clearly, however, the most direct interaction between the courts and other political structures in a regime comes through the pattern of behavior that we refer to as *judicial review.* Judicial review is the process by which courts are in the position to rule on the propriety or legality of action of the legislative and executive branches of government.[43] More specifically,

> judicial review refers to the judicial power to decide on the constitutionality of activities undertaken by other governmental institutions, most notably those decisions, laws, and policies advanced by executives and legislatures.[44]

As is indicated in Table 6.1, the concept of judicial review exists only in a clear minority of the approximately 170 nations in the world, and where it does exist, the *extent* of its scope and ability to review the actions of other governmental structures varies. That is, not all of the courts listed in Table 6.1 are as powerful in their respective political systems as is the Supreme Court in the United States.

The idea of judicial review, although most strongly institutionalized today in the United States, was not, as some scholars have suggested, "invented" in American colonial days, or with the decision of Chief Justice John Marshall in the case of *Marbury v. Madison* in 1803.[45] We can go back to the time of Plato to find discussion of judicial review, in a primitive sense, when Plato discussed the establishment of a "nocturnal council of magistrates" to be the "guardians of our god-given constitution."[46] Charles G. Haines, a leading scholar of American constitutionalism, has argued that:

> the practice of English colonial administration agencies and of the assertion of authority by the Privy Council influenced the [American] colonists in that they realized the possibility of having their judgments reviewed and in certain instances their statutes invalidated by a superior tribunal.[47]

Although judicial review may not exist at the present time in all judicial systems, there clearly is an ingredient of *change* that we must keep in mind. For example, most studies take it as a given that there is no judicial review in Great Britain, and that the *fundamental* principle underlying the operation of British politics is that of parliamentary supremacy. While this is true, it also has recently been pointed out that the role of the courts in the British political culture has changed, and that this reflects "deep-seated changes occurring in the institutional fabric of British government," especially in the realm of administrative law. It has been shown that "until twenty years ago judges took an extremely restrained position vis-à-vis administrative agencies," but more recently scholars have noted "an embryonic move toward judicial activism."[48] Although this is not meant to suggest that British courts will soon be nullifying Acts of Parliament, it does illustrate the fact that all political institutions, courts included, can change over time.

Theodore Becker, in his comprehensive cross-national study of judicial pol-

TABLE 6.1
Some Countries Whose Political Systems Include Judicial Review

Western Europe and North America	Latin America	Asia and the Pacific	Other
Austria	Argentina	Australia	Ghana
Canada	Brazil	India	Israel
Denmark	Colombia	Japan	Nigeria
Ireland	Mexico	Pakistan	
Norway		Philippines	

Sources: Monte Palmer and William Thompson, *The Comparative Analysis of Politics* (Itasca, Ill.: F. E. Peacock, 1978), p. 136; Theodore Becker, *Comparative Judicial Politics* (Chicago: Rand McNally, 1970), pp. 137, 209, 213, 219–222.

itics, indicated three dimensions along which we can locate judicial systems. First, there are different types of "judicial reviewing organs." Second, there are differences in the processes by which questions of constitutionality can reach the courts. Third, there are differences in the type of proceedings and ranges of jurisdiction of the reviewing courts.[49]

There are two major types of judicial review mechanisms to be found today. One, in the American model, uses the *regular* courts to make decisions. Judicial review is simply added to the other duties performed by the courts in the political system. The other major type of judicial review structure comes from Europe and provides a *special* constitutional court or reviewing body to perform the judicial-review function. The Constitutional Court found today in France is a good example of this.[50]

Political systems vary as well in the question of *who* can initiate suit. In the United States, only someone "injured" by an act can initiate suit. The U.S. Supreme Court will not issue an advisory opinion, or permit an uninvolved party to commence litigation; the Supreme Court of Canada will. In some political systems, those affected by an act are specifically *not* permitted to initiate a suit. Rather, only specific governmental agencies may apply for judicial review. In still other systems, the access to the judicial review process is very liberal, and anyone can bring a case into the reviewing process. In Colombia, for example, "anyone could introduce a petition of unconstitutionality directly to the Supreme Court, without even having to prove a case or controversy existed, or that he had any real or personal interest in the constitutionality of the law in question."[51]

The third dimension of distinction, according to Becker, deals with the scope of jurisdiction of the courts. Americans are familiar with a judicial system that exercises a *very broad* range of judicial review. Elsewhere, this breadth is not necessarily the case. In Israel, for example, although the court may rule on local ordinances as well as actions by the executive branch of government, it will not review laws enacted by the Knesset, Israel's Parliament.[52] In Italy, it has been pointed out, although there is no direct judicial review, the strength of the system of administrative courts results in the "potential political impact" of the courts remaining strong.[53]

The justification of judicial review—a practice many condemn as undemocratic in that it permits an (often) unelected and therefore "irresponsible" judiciary to reverse or nullify actions of democratically elected legislators and executives—is basically that there is inevitably some degree of uncertainty about constitutional matters, whether they be powers of an executive or parameters of permissible legislation. As well as being structural blueprints of a regime, constitutions, as we indicated in Chapter 2, in effect provide limitations on what government may or may not do in a political environment. The authors of a constitution do not have unlimited foresight, and therefore it is inevitable that eventually even sincere, honest, ethical individuals of good will (not to mention dishonest and unethical individuals) will disagree over what is permissible governmental behavior and what is impermissible governmental behavior. At that time the court is the appropriate organ of government to step into the picture and help to resolve the conflict.

COURTS IN COMPARATIVE PERSPECTIVE

We began this chapter by observing that courts, as the third of the "standard" three branches of government, tend not to receive the same amount of attention in introductory cross-national studies as either legislatures or executives. It was suggested that this is so primarily because (1) legal systems and legal cultures are more system-specific, and hence more difficult to generalize about, and (2) in many political systems courts and judiciaries are specifically *excluded from* the political process, and, therefore, are not really of direct relevance to discussions of political behavior.

Throughout this chapter we have further developed both of these arguments. Once we have gone beyond general philosophical arguments about law, and about the various sources of law, we find it necessary to qualify virtually all of our observations with phrases such as "in some systems. . . , while in other systems. . . . " Descriptions of the actual structure of courts, as well as powers and jurisdictions of courts, are highly limited: They rarely go beyond national boundaries.

We have seen, however, that judiciaries as well as legal cultures are highly significant to the political systems of which they are a part. The legal culture sets the *tone*, at a minimum, for the operation of the political regime. Even if the legal culture does not describe specific political structures, it does include the essential philosophical and theoretical principles that will underlie the daily operation of the regime. The judiciary, as a governmental structure, may be more or less political in its operation. Even when it is at its *minimum* political dimension, however, it is important for the regime in terms of the services it provides in areas of mediation, conflict resolution, and the promotion of regime legitimacy and stability.

Notes

1. See Locke's Section 125 in Sir Ernest Barker, ed., *Social Contract: Essays by Locke, Hume, & Rousseau* (New York: Oxford University Press, 1970).

2. For example, Joseph LaPalombara's *Politics Within Nations* (Englewood Cliffs, N.J.: Prentice-Hall, 1974) had fourteen chapters, with chapters on legislatures, executives, bureaucracies, interest groups, political parties, participation, and so on, but judiciaries and courts were not discussed.

3. See, for example, Glendon Schubert and David J. Danelski, eds., *Comparative Judicial Behavior* (New York: Oxford University Press, 1969), or Theodore L. Becker, *Comparative Judicial Politics* (Chicago: Rand McNally, 1970).

4. See, for two different types of discussions of this issue, Frederick Lee Morton, *Law, Politics, and the Judicial Process in Canada* (Calgary: University of Calgary Press, 1992), or Thomas M. Franck, *Political Questions/Judicial Answers: Does the Rule of Law Apply to Foreign Affairs?* (Princeton, N.J.: Princeton University Press, 1992).

5. Jerold Waltman and Kenneth Holland, "Preface," in *The Political Role of Law Courts in Modern Democracies*, ed. Jerold Waltman and Kenneth Holland (New York: St. Martin's Press, 1988), p. vi.

6. Jerold Waltman, "Introduction," in Waltman and Holland, *The Political Role of Law Courts*, p. 5.

7. Discussion of "The Supremacy of Lex" and related issues is included in the volume edited by W. E. Butler, *Perestroika and the Rule of Law: Anglo-American and Soviet Perspectives* (New York: St. Martin's Press, 1991).

8. This passage became well known when it was used by John Adams in 1774 in the *Boston Gazette*, number 7. Adams credited this formulation to the philosopher James Harrington (1611–1677), the author of the work *The Commonwealth of Oceana* (1656). See *Bartlett's Fa-*

miliar Quotations (Boston: Little, Brown, 1980) as included in *Microsoft Bookshelf, 1991 Edition CD-ROM Data Base.*

9. Herbert Winter and Thomas Bellows, *People and Politics* (New York: John Wiley, 1977), p. 307.

10. See Locke's Section 127 in Barker, *Social Contract*, p. 74.

11. For an example of writing on natural law, see Alexander D'Entreves, *Natural Law: An Introduction to Legal Philosophy* (New Brunswick, N.J.: Transaction Publishers, 1993), or Yves Simon, *The Tradition of Natural Law* (New York: Fordham University Press, 1992); on moral law, see Robert George, *Making Men Moral: Civil Liberties and Public Morality* (New York: Oxford University Press, 1993); on divine law, see Milner Ball, *The Word and the Law* (Chicago: University of Chicago Press, 1993).

12. Winter and Bellows, *People and Politics*, p. 308.

13. See George Sabine, *A History of Political Theory* (New York: Holt, Rinehart and Winston, 1961), p. 942.

14. Sabine, *History of Political Thought*, pp. 194–196.

15. John Merryman, *The Civil Law Tradition*, quoted in Henry Ehrmann, *Comparative Legal Cultures* (Englewood Cliffs, N.J.: Prentice-Hall, 1976), p. 8.

16. See Csaba Varga, ed., *Comparative Legal Cultures* (New York: New York University Press, 1992), or John Merryman and David Clark, *Comparative Law: Western European and Latin American Legal Systems Cases and Materials* (Charlottesville,Va.: Michie Company, 1993).

17. Kenneth Holland, "The Courts in the United States," in Waltman and Holland, *The Political Role of Law Courts*, p. 7.

18. Hiroshi Itoh, "The Courts in Japan," in Waltman and Holland, *The Political Role of Law Courts*, p. 211.

19. Ehrmann, *Comparative Legal Cultures*, p. 13. This and the following several paragraphs are based on more extended material in Ehrmann, and Winter and Bellows, *People and Politics*, pp. 309–310 and 319–322.

20. A good discussion of this can be found in Martin Shapiro, *Courts: A Comparative and Political Analysis* (Chicago: University of Chicago Press, 1981), chap. 3: "The Civil Law System and Preexisting Legal Rules."

21. A thorough discussion of the assumptions of the Anglo-American legal process can be found in Mirjan R. Damaska, *The Faces of Justice and State Authority* (New Haven, Conn.: Yale University Press, 1986), or Edgar Bodenheimer, John Oakley, and Jean Love, *Anglo-American Legal System: Introduction, Readings, and Cases* (St. Paul, Minn.: West Publishing, 1988).

22. On common law more generally, see James Stoner, Jr., *Common Law and Liberal Theory: Locke, Hobbes, and the Origins of American Constitutionalism* (Lawrence: University Press of Kansas, 1992), or Gerald Postema, *Bentham and the Common Law Tradition* (New York: Oxford University Press, 1989).

23. See P. S. Atiyah and Robert Summers, *Form and Substance in Anglo-American Law: A Comparative Study in Legal Reasoning, Legal Theory, and Legal Institutions* (New York: Oxford University Press, 1991).

24. Winter and Bellows, *People and Politics*, p. 316.

25. See Christine Sypnowich, *The Concept of Socialist Law* (New York: Oxford University Press, 1990), for a full discussion.

26. For discussion of this relationship, see Maria Los, *Communist Ideology, Law, and Crime: A Comparative View of the U.S.S.R. and Poland* (New York: St. Martin's Press, 1988).

27. See Alan Watson, *Legal Transplants: An Approach to Comparative Law* (Athens: University of Georgia Press, 1993) for a full discussion of the wide range of legal systems in the world.

28. See Gregory Mahler, *Israel: Government and Politics in a Maturing State* (New York: Harcourt, Brace, Jovanovich, 1990), pp. 187–190.

29. On religion and law, see Edwin Firmage, Bernard Weiss, and John Welch, eds., *Religion and Law: Biblical-Judaic and Islamic Perspectives* (Winona Lake, Ind.: Eisenbraums, 1990), Samuel Hoenig, *The Essence of Talmudic Law and Thought* (Northvale, N.J.: Jason Aronson, 1993), or Chibli Mallat, *The Renewal of Islamic Law* (New York: Cambridge University Press, 1993).

30. Sydney Bailey, *British Parliamentary Democracy* (Boston: Houghton Mifflin, 1958), pp. 15-16.

31. See Kenneth Thompson, ed., *The Presidency and the Constitutional System* (Lanham, Md.: University Press of America, 1990), or Richard Neustadt, *Presidential Power and the Modern Presidents: The Politics of Leadership from Roosevelt to Reagan* (New York: Free Press, 1990).

32. See the references to the "decline of legislatures" literature discussed in Chapter 4 of this book.

33. Theodore Lowi, *The End of Liberalism* (New York: W.W. Norton, 1969), esp. chap. 5, pp. 128–156.

34. See Peter Cane, *An Introduction to Administrative Law* (New York: Oxford University Press, 1992), or Christopher Edley, Jr., *Administrative Law: Rethinking Judicial Control of Bureaucracy* (New Haven, Conn.: Yale University Press, 1992).

35. Becker, *Comparative Judicial Politics*, p. 13.

36. Martin Shapiro, *Courts: A Comparative and Political Analysis* (Chicago: The University of Chicago Press, 1981), p. 1.

37. Two very good discussions of this issue can be found in Martin Redish, *The Federal Courts in the Political Order: Judicial Jurisdiction and American Political Theory* (Durham, N.C.: Carolina Academic Press, 1991), and David Currie, *Federal Jurisdiction in a Nutshell* (St. Paul, Minn.: West Publishing, 1990).

38. See the British North America Act (Canada Act) of 1867, Section 92 (14) for provincial legislative jurisdictions, and Section 91 (27) for federal legislative jurisdiction. The interested student can find this in Robert Jackson and Doreen Jackson, *Politics in Canada: Culture, Institutions, Behaviour and Public Policy* (Scarborough, Ont.: Prentice-Hall Canada, 1990), pp. 673–755.

39. See Jackson and Jackson, *Politics in Canada*, pp. 197–201.

40. Roman Tomasic, "The Courts in Australia," in Waltman and Holland, *The Political Role of Law Courts*, p. 50.

41. Michael Curtis, *Comparative Government and Politics* (New York: Harper and Row, 1977), p. 102.

42. Curtis, *Comparative Government*, p. 107.

43. See Donald Jackson and Neal Tate, eds., *Comparative Judicial Review and Public Policy* (Westport, Conn.: Greenwood Publishing, 1992), Donald Lively, *Judicial Review and the Consent of the Governed: Activist Ways and Popular Ends* (Jefferson, N.C.: McFarland and Company, 1990), or Sylvia Snowiss, *Judicial Review and the Law of the Constitution* (New Haven, Conn.: Yale University Press, 1990).

44. Monte Palmer and William Thompson, *The Comparative Analysis of Politics* (Itasca, Ill.: F.E. Peacock, 1978), p. 136.

45. Three good references to this decision and its impact can be found in Bernard Schwartz, *A History of the Supreme Court* (New York: Oxford University Press, 1993), Edward White, *The Marshall Court and Cultural Change* (New York: Oxford University Press, 1991), and Maureen Harrison and Steve Gilbert, eds., *Landmark Decisions of the United States Supreme Court* (Beverly Hills, Cal.: Excellent Books, 1992).

46. Becker, *Comparative Judicial Politics*, p. 206.

47. C. G. Haines, *The American Doctrine of Judicial Review* (New York: Russell and Russell, 1959), p. 44, cited in Becker, *Comparative Judicial Politics*, p. 218.

48. Jerold Waltman, "The Courts in England," in Waltman and Holland, *The Political Role of Law Courts*, pp. 119–120.

49. Becker, *Comparative Judicial Politics*, p. 206.

50. This is discussed in Peter Hall, Jack Hayward, and Howard Machlin, eds., *Developments in French Politics* (New York: St. Martin's Press, 1990), and Ian Derbyshire, *Politics in France: From Giscard to Mitterand* (New York: Chambers, 1992).

51. Becker, *Comparative Judicial Politics*, p. 208.

52. A very good study of this is Yaacov Zemach, *Political Questions in the Courts* (Detroit: Wayne State University Press, 1976), p. 21. For a more general discussion of the role of the judiciary in Israeli politics, see Mahler, *Israel*, pp. 187–190.

53. Giuseppe Di Federico and Carlo Guarnieri, "The Courts in Italy," in Waltman and Holland, *The Political Role of Law Courts*, pp. 170–171.

7

Interest Groups and Political Parties

ELECTIONS AND VOTING

A number of variables should be considered in the process of political analysis before we can appreciate or understand a specific political system in its entirety. We
need to know something about the electoral system of a nation, because it is clear
that the electoral system can influence the pattern of selection of legislators and executives, as we indicated in chapters 4 and 5. Related to this, we need to understand
the party system of the political regime under consideration. Whether a polity has
one, two, three, or twenty-three political parties has great significance for the operation of constitutional structures in that system, as does the type of behavior exercised by adherents of the parties.

PLURALISM AND CORPORATISM

Among the most basic concepts in modern political science is the idea of "pluralism." The idea of pluralism suggests that "multiple, competing elites (including interest groups) determine public policy through bargaining and compromise."[1] This
same subject, although referred to as "factions" and not called "pluralism" at the
time, was present at the establishment of American political institutions, and was
the theme of one of James Madison's contributions to *The Federalist Papers*, No. 10.[2]

The center of the concept of pluralism includes the idea of individual rationality and individual choice, and the premise that a rational individual will act in his or her own self-interest.[3]

According to what is called "pluralist theory,"[4] interest groups could be called "advantage groups": People join them because they perceive that it is to their advantage to do so. Interest groups are the focus of pluralist theory; pluralist theorists believe that individuals join groups because they think that they will be better represented and have more political influence if they join a group than if they do not join a group. Policy outcomes, then, are simply perceived as a result of group competition, not necessarily a product of majority rule: A well-organized minority can defeat a less well-organized majority in the process of competition for policy outcomes.

The original group theorist was Arthur Bentley, whose 1908 work[5] was very popular in the 1950s; it was expanded upon by David Truman, whose book *The Governmental Process* became one of the classics of political science in 1951. Truman took the idea of interest groups further than had Bentley; he suggested that individuals belonged to several different interest groups, different group loyalties reflecting different aspects of their interests and personalities. This gave rise to Truman's idea of "overlapping" group affiliations. According to Truman:

> "Interest group" refers to any group that, on the basis of one or more shared attitudes, makes certain claims upon other groups in the society for the establishment, maintenance, or enhancement of forms of behavior that are implied by the shared attitudes.[6]

Not only did Truman consider organized interest groups as part of what he called "the governmental process," but he also considered *potential* interest groups part of the process.

The problem with Truman's theories was that they did not fare very well at the hands of empirical research. Political scientists seeking to test the role of interest groups in the (American) political process found that interest groups "were *not* invariably major actors in any policy dispute"(emphasis added).[7]

Mancur Olson's work *The Logic of Collective Action*[8] helped to explain the problems with Truman's theory, because Olson pointed out that it was not logical, or rational, for an individual to invest his or her time or effort in joining an organization if that organization was working for a *collective good*. He defined a "collective good" as "any good such that, if any person X in a group . . . consumes it, it cannot feasibly be withheld from the others in that group."[9] By this definition, it would not be "rational" for an individual to contribute funds to and work hard for a clean air fund, because if the goal was achieved it would also be available to individuals who had not contributed. Thus Olson's work demonstrated that if there already was an interest group to further a certain goal, it might *not* be the case that all individuals interested in that goal would join the group: They could enjoy the benefits of the group without contributing anything to the efforts of the group.

The idea of *corporatism* implies a "close interaction of groups and government."[10] For some, it further suggests "a situation where the interest organizations are integrated in the governmental decision-making process of a society."[11] Modern development of the idea of corporatism, called "neo-corporatism," "emphasizes the characteristics of the interest associations entering a relationship with the state apparatus, and the nature of this relationship, i.e., the ways in which they are recognized and granted a representational monopoly by the state."[12]

Thus, a theory of neo-corporatism takes up where the theory of pluralism leaves off. It suggests that groups *are*, in fact, of significance in the political system, although it accepts Olson's suggestion that not all individuals with shared interests will necessarily join those groups. There are a number of common elements in the several variations of neo-corporatist theory today:

1. Monopolies of interest representation exist and are important to explain political behaviour and policy outcomes.
2. Hierarchies emerge among associations and they may sub-ordinate and co-ordinate the activities of whole economic sectors and/or social classes.
3. Membership in associations is not always voluntary . . . arrangements exist both to bind members to "their" associations and to prevent the emergence of competing ones.
4. Interest associations are not just the passive recipients of already formed member interests, but may play an active role in identifying and forming those interests.
5. Interest associations do not merely transmit member preferences to authorities, but may actively and coercively govern the behaviour of their members, especially through devolved responsibility for the implementation of public policy.
6. The state may not be either an arena for which interests contend or another interest group with which they must compete, but a constitutive element engaged in defining...the activities of associations. . . .
7. Interest associations are not always autonomous entities pressuring the state from without and seeking access wherever they can find an opportunity. . . .[13]

The idea of *conflict*, then, is to be found at the center of neo-corporatist theory just as it is to be found at the center of pluralist theory.[14] In many respects pluralism and corporatism (or neo-corporatism) are at different ends of a continuum, because both argue for the significance of the *group* in the political process. Where they differ is on the relationship between government and groups; perhaps put another way, the degree to which the government establishes a patron-client relationship with specific interest groups.

INTEREST GROUPS

Although political systems may contain political structures, designed to ensure popular representation in the governmental policy-making process, most notably the legislature, it is entirely likely that the formal governmental (constitutional) structures of representation will not prove to be sufficient for representing all shades of public opinion.

Two additional structures are available in the political environment to supplement the formal (constitutional) representative structures, and they are quite effective in many political regimes. Both the *interest group* and the *political party* can play significant roles in political systems in assisting formal-legal structures in the processing of political demands and the communication of public beliefs, attitudes, and values.

Although interest groups and political parties have a number of characteristics and functions in common,[15] we should be very careful to distinguish between the two types of structures, for they really are quite different. As we indicated earlier, group theory suggests that *all* public opinion can be described in group terms and that individual opinion is essentially unimportant, save for the fact that individuals *make up* groups. All public opinion either originates with groups or is articulated by groups, so we do not really need to worry about individual representation as long as a mechanism for group representation exists.[16]

Interest groups are collections of individuals who share common beliefs, attitudes, values, or concerns.[17] The shared concern(s) may focus on serious issues, such as concern about nuclear weapons, concern about gun control, concern about air and/or water pollution, or concern about a minimum wage or work conditions. The shared concern(s) may also be a bit more frivolous, such as (with due apologies to any offended!) love of Angora cats or appreciation of Ford Edsels.

Interest groups come into existence because a collection of individuals sees something to be gained by such an association: either material gains (higher wages by joining a union, or free auto towing and maps by joining an automobile club); psychological gains (a feeling of "brotherhood" from joining a fraternity, or a sense of theological or eschatological satisfaction by joining a church); recreational gains (lower ski-lift fees by joining a ski association, or a sense of pastime well spent by joining an antique car club); humanitarian gains (helping to do away with nuclear proliferation by joining a sit-in group, or promoting civil rights by contributing to a civil rights organization), and so on.[18]

Interest groups may be highly organized, with weekly meetings, dues collection, a monthly newsletter, and membership cards. They may also be quite loosely organized, or not formally organized at all, for that matter.[19] Their scope of concern may be quite broad, or quite narrow. Groups might be open to anyone interested, or limited in membership. They may, in short, vary greatly.

Group theorists suggest that interest groups play a very important function in the political arena. They can be important as *linkage mechanisms*, some argue, because they are very effective communicators of segments of public opinion.[20] Because interest groups generally are of limited scope, they are able to communicate their collective opinion more effectively than can individuals. The National Rifle Association (NRA) and the American Medical Association (AMA) are two examples of interest groups that, although numerically not overwhelmingly large, are very effective in exerting political pressure in the areas of concern to their members.[21]

The argument for interest group utility suggests that political (formal, constitutional, legislative) representatives simply *cannot* represent all of their constituents. On any given issue in relation to which a legislator takes a position, it is almost inevitable that he or she will alienate some group. An American legislator voting in favor of gun control, for example, is going to irritate constituents who oppose gun control. What is more, once their representative has come out on the opposite side of an issue, the anti-gun-control constituents (to use the same example) are no longer—strictly speaking—represented by "their" representative in the legislature. The existence of an interest group, in this case the NRA, affords these individuals recourse to an *alternative* representational structure, one that will voice their concerns and act on their collective behalf.

Many political scientists use the terms "interest group" and "pressure group" interchangeably. Others, however, make a distinction between the two terms, and whether or not the student *chooses* to make this distinction, he or she should be aware of the distinctions that are drawn.[22] Pressure groups, simply put, are said to be a subset of interest groups that are organized exclusively for the purpose of political lobbying. Thus we can say that all pressure groups are interest groups, but not all interest groups are pressure groups.

There are clearly many interest groups ("collections of individuals who share a common belief, attitude, value, or concern") whose activities are oriented around unequivocally nonpolitical themes. For example, the Rocky Mountain Cavy Club is an interest group that meets once a month to have cavy (guinea pig) shows and competitions, give prizes and award ribbons, and which publishes a monthly newsletter, "Cavy Chatter." Theirs is obviously a nonpolitical concern! Other interest groups are *usually* nonpolitical. The American Automobile Association (AAA) has as its primary *raison d'être* auto safety, and provides its members with a number of benefits: maps, car insurance, tow service, and so on. On occasions, however, the AAA *has* become politically active, such as when Congress was considering an extra tax on gasoline. The AAA, acting on behalf of its members (drivers), lobbied effectively against such a tax.

Still other interest groups are *exclusively* political, having as their primary reason for being a policy objective: the Vietnam Veterans to End the War in Vietnam, Concerned Citizens for Proposition 13, the National Organization for Women lobbying for the Equal Rights Amendment, and so on. Pressure groups are almost invariably very narrow in scope—usually related to a single issue—and ostensibly temporary. Once their policy objective is achieved, they no longer have a reason for being. General interest groups, on the other hand, are much longer-lived, and their reason for being is not as transient.

POLITICAL PARTIES

This political dimension of interest group activity leads us to our next distinction, namely the difference between interest groups (and here the term includes our pressure-group subcategory) and political parties. A number of distinctions have been pointed out in detailed studies, including permanence of organization and levels of organization (political parties tend to be more permanent and institutionalized than interest groups), and breadth of issue concerns (parties almost invariably are concerned with a broad range of issues, while interest groups usually focus on a more narrow range of issues).

The single most important difference, however, relates to the ultimate *goals* of the organization. The goal of the interest group is to satisfy its members, either through the organization itself (for instance, the activities of the Cavy Club), or through political pressure resulting in a specific policy outcome (for instance, the NRA helping to defeat gun-control legislation). The goal of a political party is to win political office, gain political power, and thereby control the policy-making process.[23] The interest group does not care which party or which individual wins an election as long as its specific policy concern prevails. The political party is much broader in scope, and seeks to hold power (to the point of perhaps modifying some of its issue positions if that will help it to control power); the interest group is not concerned with power so much as with policy outcome.[24]

Parties have been said to derive from a number of different sources.[25] One source of party development is factions within a national legislature. American political parties can be seen to be examples of this; they originally formed as groups of legislative supporters of Thomas Jefferson and Alexander Hamilton, which subsequently established formal organizations leading to the creation of the Jeffersonian-Democrats and the Federalists.[26] A second source of party organization is labor movements. The British Labour Party is a good example of this type of party,[27] in which an already existing labor organization (itself an interest group) decides to develop an explicitly political identity, seeking not only to influence labor policy but also to control power. Still another point of origin of political parties is the national-liberation movement.[28] The Congress Party in India was not primarily a political party under British rule; rather, it was organized to help achieve Indian independence, and to help drive the British out of India. Once the British left, the conversion from liberation movement to political party was easily achieved.[29] Finally, parties may be created for ideological reasons, to represent a viewpoint not otherwise represented in the polity.[30]

As organizations, political parties vary greatly in a number of different respects, including membership, size, and structure of organization, not to mention variation in the number of parties active in the system itself.[31] One of the primary structural distinctions among parties is whether they are "mass" parties or "cadre" parties. Maurice Duverger, in his classic work *Political Parties*, suggested that "the difference involved is not one of size but of structure." For mass parties, the recruiting of members is a fundamental activity; "the members are therefore the very substance of the party, the stuff of its activity. Without members, the party would be like a teacher without pupils."[32] Also, mass parties are *financially* based on the mass; the party finances are, to a large extent, based on member dues. Thus Duverger suggested that:

> the mass-party technique in effect replaces the capitalist financing of electioneering by democratic financing. Instead of appealing to a few big private donors . . . to meet campaign expenses—which makes the candidate (and the person elected) dependent on them—the mass party spreads the burden over the largest possible number of members, each of whom contributes a modest sum.[33]

The cadre party is of a different sort. As Duverger suggested, "what the mass party secures by numbers, the cadre party achieves by selection; . . . it is dependent upon rigid and exclusive selection."[34] Sometimes the distinction between mass and cadre parties is made less clear because the cadre parties may admit numbers of the mass in imitation of a mass party; there are few *pure* cadre parties today. Contemporary American parties, for example, are disguised cadre parties. They have democratic constitutions and permit mass participation, but they are steered by a much smaller group of individuals. According to Duverger, in 1950 "the Turkish Democratic party claimed before the election that it had 'three or four million members'. Obviously it was referring to supporters; in actual fact it was a cadre party."[35] Generally, then, cadre parties correspond to more caucus-organized types of parties, usually decentralized, while mass parties tend to correspond to parties based on branches, more centrally organized and "firmly knit."[36]

The number of political parties in an electoral system is, as was suggested in Chapter 4, a function of several factors, including ideology, political culture, electoral laws, and methods of election.[37] Duverger noted that the relationship between the electoral regime and the number of political parties "can be expressed in the following formula: The simple-majority single-ballot system favours the two-party system."[38] There are a number of different-sized party systems: single-party systems, two-party systems, two-party-plus systems, and multiparty systems. Even this classification is too general, though, because a number of different variations of two-party systems may be discerned.[39]

Political parties are an important part of a theory of pluralism. If "political pluralism," as one author has put it, highlights the "existence of a 'plurality of groups that are both independent and non-inclusive,'" then parties are an important part of that pluralistic model.[40] As we saw in chapters 4 and 5, parties are absolutely crucial as a part of a "responsible government" model: Obviously, "party discipline" could not exist without political parties, and it is party discipline that is the vehicle for responsible government, a government able to "deliver" on its promises.[41]

Internal party organization, clearly, varies on a party-by-party basis.[42] Some parties are highly unified, while others are collections of factions that may not have a great deal in common except their commitment to share power. Some parties are very democratic organizations, not only permitting but indeed encouraging intra-party competition, while others permit no internal competition at all and are simply organizations dedicated to following and supporting a single individual's political advancement.

Political parties, much as interest groups, serve a number of important functions in the political regime. They are, among other things, rather elaborate personnel services, serving as a mechanism for assisting in the hiring of political leaders.[43] They help to organize political groups.[44] They help to articulate political demands.[45] They serve as a point of reference for bewildered voters who are overwhelmed by the political world: Party label is often the only clue available to voters to guide their behavior, and it is widely used as such.[46]

Another important function served by the political party as an organization is in the process of political development.[47] Parties are important vehicles in the process of political recruitment—we shall discuss this in more detail in Chapter 8—helping to bring individuals into the political arena by offering a convenient vehicle for participation to the masses.[48]

Parties also serve as structures that mobilize the electorate—"get out the vote" and invite participation—through competition between parties (or within a party, in one-party systems).[49] Through this action, we are told, they contribute to a sense of "national integration"—the "amalgamation of disparate social, economic, religious, ethnic, and geographic elements into a single nation-state,"[50] thus helping to develop a sense of political nationhood on the part of the masses.[51]

In short, research has shown that political parties can play significant roles in five important respects in the process of political development. First, parties encourage and facilitate political participation. Second, they help to stimulate a sense of governmental legitimacy through the campaign process and the debate that ensues. Third, they contribute to the development of a sense of national integration. They also play an important role in conflict management within the polity, providing a vehicle by which differences of opinion over policy preferences can be peacefully resolved. Finally, political parties play an important role in the political socialization function in society, helping to transmit attitudes and values from one generation to another.[52]

Much as the interest group was seen to be a political structure that assists in the representation function in the political world, so too the political party serves as a "linkage mechanism"[53] in passing along public opinions from various groups in the electorate to government officials. Of course, the degree to which parties serve these several functions depends upon the individual party organization and the political system within which it is found. Depending upon the number of political parties in a system, the degree of party discipline found in the political system, and the ideology and constituency of the party in question, the role of the party will vary.

Scholars have speculated about the future of political parties, and whether they can continue to be as central a political structure in their respective political systems as they have been in the past. The continual growth of executive power in political systems all over the world, combined with greater public attention to politics and increasingly aggressive media, means that traditional assumptions about political parties and political party behavior have to be rethought.[54]

ELECTORAL SYSTEMS

We saw in Chapter 4 that the system of representation found in a given nation can drastically affect the composition of its national legislature. Proportional representation elections lead to multipartyism and corresponding instability brought on by necessary coalition governments. Single-member-district elections tend to provide a much greater degree of stability because they lead to the existence of a two-party system (or sometimes what is called a two-party-plus system), but they have the distinct disadvantage of "hiding" minorities. We saw that groups constituting 20 to 30 percent of the population could end up with no representation in the national legislature. Thus, different systems of electoral representation can make a difference in how *effective* a system of representation is.[55]

In this section we shall discuss several aspects of electoral systems other than how (and whether) electoral districts are drawn, and whether representation is based on geographical districts or proportional representation. First, we shall briefly discuss some different classifications of electoral systems. Second, we shall discuss some other structures of electoral systems that can influence the outcomes of elections, such as electoral laws, campaigns, and the like. Third, we shall discuss the more philosophical question of the importance of elections themselves.

Political scientist Robert Dahl[56] has suggested a number of characteristics of an "ideal" election. Before the voting period, all voters would have the opportunity to make sure that their choices were included among the alternatives to be voted upon, and all voters would be equally (well) informed. During an election all eligible voters would vote, all their votes would be counted equally, and the candidate with the most votes would win. After the election the winning choice would be implemented.

Elections have been classified in a number of different ways, depending upon degree of choice between parties and degree of choice between candidates.[57] Some political systems are extremely open, and many parties are permitted to compete; examples of this type of system might include Italy or Australia. Others are less open, with a much narrower range of parties that can compete, as is the case in Singapore or Tanzania. Still others do not permit more than one party to compete in any election, as is the case in Kenya. Similarly, the degree of choice between candidates ranges from a highly competitive system, such as that which we described in Israel, to a system in which there is no choice between candidates for the voters: They vote for predetermined candidates chosen by the competing parties. These different characteristics have suggested four broad types of elections: competitive, dominant-party, candidate-choice, and acclamatory.

In "competitive" elections, voters are presented with a choice between competing parties, and the number of parties presenting alternatives to the voters may range from two to over a dozen. Voters may not have the ability to actually select *which* party candidates they most prefer; this is an option in Japan, but not in Great Britain.

In "dominant-party" elections, voters may have the legal right to vote for any party they want, but they do not, in fact, have a real choice, for a variety of reasons. Sometimes actual intimidation is involved, where even "secret" votes are checked. Voters not voting for the "correct" party can suffer injury, even death, as was the case in recent elections in Haiti.[58] Elsewhere it is not intimidation, but instead fraud or corruption, which keeps the single dominant party in power. This was the case in the Philippines under President Marcos,[59] and was claimed to be the case in the 1988 elections in Mexico.[60] Still elsewhere a single party stays dominant over a longer period of time simply as a result of its ability to claim that it is the only "real" possible governing party. Perhaps it wraps itself up in the national flag; perhaps it claims to be the heir of an independence movement—we could cite the Congress Party of India as an example of this type of party.[61] These dominant-party elections "are a surprisingly common and resilient type of election in the third world."[62]

"Candidate-choice" elections are also somewhat common in the developing world. In this type of election, voters are not offered a choice between political parties—there is only one "permissible" political party—but they are given a choice between or among several candidates from that one approved party in any given election. To take one example, in Kenya there may be several KANU (Kenyan African National Union) candidates competing for each race; the voters have a choice between candidates, but not between parties.[63]

Finally, in "acclamatory" elections voters have no choice either between parties or between candidates. The most frequently cited example of this style of election in recent years was in the Soviet Union, where virtually all of the more than 1,500 members of the Supreme Soviet "ran" for their positions without opposition. Although not all of these "candidates" were members of the Communist party, virtually all of them ran unopposed: A nominating body at the constituency level would nominate a single candidate to run for the office. With the dismantling of the Soviet Union and its Eastern European puppet regimes, this type of electoral system virtually disappeared as a common alternative in the world.

Whatever the general type of electoral system that exists, it is clear that there are many legal and behavioral characteristics of a political regime that can affect electoral behavior. In some of the cases just cited the regimes actually have statutes outlawing opposition parties: In these regimes it is clear that the legal behavior of the government affects the type and style of electoral behavior we can witness.

Electoral law can have a profound effect on the outcome of elections, whatever the basis of representation is.[64] There is a very wide range of electoral law that could be examined by an interested student, including regulations governing who can be a candidate, how campaigns are run, which parties can compete, and who the voters will be, among others.

Regulations governing *who can be a candidate* in an election vary widely.[65] All systems have some *age* criterion for candidacy, often simply legal majority but sometimes more than that. (For example, in the United States citizens may vote in federal elections at the age of 18 years; one cannot be a member of the House of Representatives until the age of 25, and one cannot be a member of the Senate until the age of 30. State requirements vary.) Some systems have a *residency* requirement (that one must live in the district one represents), while others do not. Some have *gender, race,* or *ethnic group* restrictions on candicacy, as well.

Some systems have quite stringent sets of laws governing *how the election campaigns are to be run*, which clearly are of great significance in a campaign.[66] Limitations on *fund-raising*, for example, can determine who can afford to run for office and who cannot.[67] This kind of limitation can certainly affect who is more likely to win the election, because it affects the amount of campaigning one can do and the amount of advertising one can buy.[68] Specifically, of course, *the media* are often crucial, and thus are regulated in campaigns.[69] During the last month of the 1988 Israeli election campaign, each party was given ten free minutes of prime time televison each evening, six nights a week; parties already having seats in the legislature received an additional four free minutes per seat they controlled.[70]

It is common to find legislation governing *which parties* can compete in elections. This kind of limitation ranges from the most rigid, which might indicate that only a single party was legally permitted to submit candidates in an election—the type of situation found in many one-party states—to a much more flexible situation. There may simply be requirements affecting (1) a minimum number of individuals who must sign a party petition before a party may submit a candidate, (2) monetary "deposits" that must be paid by political parties, which are returned if they receive a certain percentage of the vote (this is designed to discourage parties from submitting "unrealistic" candidates who will receive very little public support), or (3) deadlines by which parties must submit their candidates.

Finally, it is common to find governmental regulations affecting *who can vote* in an election.[71] These regulations usually include an *age* requirement, a *registration* requirement (for instance, one must register to vote 60 days before an election or one cannot vote), a *residency* requirement (for instance, one must live in the district in which one votes), or a *literacy* requirement, ranging from a minimal requirement that an individual be able to read a ballot (although many systems will provide readers if that is a problem) to a much more rigorous requirement that one be able to "pass an examination to demonstrate one's literacy" before one can vote. The latter type of test was used as a vehicle for preventing Southern blacks from voting for many years in the United States. In addition, it still happens in some systems that *gender, ethnic group,* or *racial* characteristics also are the subject of regulation in terms of who can vote in an election.

We have addressed some of the issues related to various structures affecting the operation of elections, but we have not yet answered the more general questions: What do elections do? Why bother to have them? What do elections decide?[72] Answers to these questions may seem so obvious that they are not worth asking, but the exercise is probably worth doing so that we can be sure about some of the assumptions we may be making.[73]

Probably the most common answer to the question "Why have elections?" involves *choosing representatives.* The idea of representation is a central one in democratic theory, and has been discussed by Thomas Hobbes (1651), John Locke (1690), Jean-Jacques Rousseau (1762), Edmund Burke (1790), and John Stuart Mill (1861), among many other great thinkers of modern history. Although representatives may be selected in any number of ways, clearly one of the most obvious ways—and most defensible in terms of democratic theory—is through election.

Another function of elections is to offer the (voting) public a *choice* among a variety of political parties, candidates, governments, or policy preferences. In democratic polities, the electorate chooses between two or more political parties, and these parties (often) represent different positions on controversial issues of the day. Thus elections may help to resolve some issues dividing society.

Elections also serve as a vehicle for *creating governments* in democratic systems. As we described earlier in this text, most systems in the world are parliamentary, not presidential, so most voters in the world do not actually have an opportunity to vote for a *government.* Rather, they vote for a representative (and, often, a political party), and dynamics within the legislature after the election will determine which government is formed. Although it may still be necessary to create a coalition (as we described earlier in this text) in order to establish a majority in a legislature, elections often serve the function of creating a government by giving an individual candidate a mandate, or giving a specific political party a mandate to govern.

Elections *influence policy* by choosing which politicians will be exercising power. By giving some politicians mandates to rule rather than others, voters in an indirect way can influence the types of public policy made by the governments that represent them.

Elections also *provide legitimacy* for the government. Governments derive legitimacy by appearing to be responsible and responsive to the public over which they rule, and by appearing to be ruling in a just manner; that is, the government that is in power *ought* to be in power. Elections vest legitimacy in governments by providing the mandates we mentioned above, and a government that is perceived as being legitimate can rule more easily than a government not viewed that way.

Elections also serve an *educative* function in that during the campaign period there is usually an increased level of discussion of the major issues of the day. Individuals who pay attention to campaign debates and speeches can learn a great deal about their political system, international affairs, domestic social or economic issues, or any of a number of other aspects of the political world.

Finally, elections can *influence political parties.* A party that regularly loses elections will receive a message: "Change the alternatives you are offering us." In the spring of 1989, the British Labour Party changed—after years and years of debate and argument—its unilateral nuclear disarmament policy, largely as a result of arguments that it would continue to lose to the Conservative Party as long as it held the extreme anti-nuclear position it had been advocating for the preceding decade. Political parties, as we defined them earlier, are committed to *winning* elections, and will usually try to do whatever is necessary to win. Elections can send messages to parties that will influence what they do and what they think.

Ultimately, of course, the study of elections involves more than the study of electoral *systems.* It focuses on the relationship between the mass public and the elite that make up the cadre of political leaders of a system. It focuses on voting behavior, public opinion, and individual political attitudes, as well as questions related to political stability and the process of political recruitment.

POLITICAL PARTICIPATION AND VOTING BEHAVIOR

The act of voting is clearly influenced by much more than only the types of structural electoral characteristics we have been discussing here. While it is clearly the case that if the law says one must be 21 years of age in order to vote, one simply *cannot* vote at age 19, it does not necessarily follow that if the law says one must be 21 years of age in order to vote one will *always* vote if one has the opportunity. Motivation, attitudes, values, and political opinions all affect participation, whether we are limiting our discussion of political participation to voting in an election, or whether we are including participating in a political demonstration, such as over a million students in Beijing lobbying for a greater democratization of Chinese politics in May 1989.[74]

Voting is a *kind* of political participation, but we certainly should not be so simplistic as to equate voting with all other types of participation.[75] In a stable Western democracy, we may automatically think of election campaigns when we think of "participation," but that is not the case everywhere. It is not hard to imagine situations in which wearing a certain style of clothing would be taken—legitimately—as a political gesture. Going to church in a society that is officially atheistic may have political implications. We certainly would accept making public speeches as political behavior, or burning draft cards, or participating in an organized boycott. In short, although we may use voting as a yardstick by which we measure political behavior in stable Western democracies, we must keep in mind that political behavior as a variable may be *culture-* or *system-dependent*, and what is one society's casual entertainment may be another society's politically significant act.

How have social scientists explained the variations in participation from country to country over the years? Several explanations have been offered, some on the macro-level, some on the micro-level. We shall briefly discuss each of these here.

Micro-level characteristics are those centered on the political individual and his or her beliefs, attitudes, and values. Such characteristics as *resources*—including income, education, and perhaps employment or transportation—and *psychological characteristics*, including political attitudes and orientations, are clearly of great significance in explaining why individuals behave as they do.

Macro-level characteristics affecting political participation include many of those factors suggested above, including electoral rules, opportunities (one cannot vote for a candidate for president, no matter how strongly one supports that candidate, if there is no election scheduled to be held for the next two years), and costs in time, money, and effort. (Participating in a demonstration tolerated by the government on a pleasant day requires a different amount of effort and degree of commitment from participants than does participating in a demonstration in a monsoon, or with temperatures at 20 degrees below zero, when you know that the government intends to jail—and/or shoot—all participants in the demonstration.)

GROUPS, PARTIES, ELECTIONS, AND VOTING

The terms "parties," "(interest) groups," and "elections" are central in any discussion of democratic politics. They are even central in discussion of political participation in systems that may not, at any given time, be democratic. After all, the existence of over a million Chinese students in Beijing in May 1989 showed the potential impact of an interest group: The "critical mass" that was present was so large that even the Chinese Army was not able to control students' behavior for quite a period of time. Political parties and interest groups—whatever the degree of organization of the latter—are the primary vehicles by which collective public opinion is communicated to the political elite in most political systems.[76]

Studying only the formal organizations of political parties and (organized) interest groups, however, is not adequate to ensure a thorough understanding of the operation of the political system. Analyses of public opinion and voting behavior show us that there are many micro-level—that is, varying on an individual-by-individual basis—factors equally important in helping us to understand how political systems operate. We turn our attention to many of these factors in the next chapter.

Notes

1. Harmon Zeigler, *Pluralism, Corporatism, and Confucianism: Political Association and Conflict Regulation in the United States, Europe, and Taiwan* (Philadelphia: Temple University Press, 1988), p. 3.

2. Alexander Hamilton, James Madison, and John Jay, *The Federalist Papers* (New York: New American Library, 1961), pp. 77–83.

3. Recent studies of pluralism include F. Clark Power and Daniel Lapsley, eds., *The Challenge of Pluralism: Education, Politics, and Values* (South Bend, Ind.: University of Notre Dame Press, 1993), Gale Stokes, *The New Pluralism: A History of Eastern Europe Since 1968* (New York: Oxford University Press, 1993), or Paul Schumaker, *Critical Pluralism, Democratic Performance, and Community Power* (Lawrence: University Press of Kansas, 1990).

4. This section is based on a much longer analysis in Zeigler, *Pluralism*, pp. 4–11.

5. Arthur F. Bentley, *The Process of Government: A Study of Social Pressures* (Chicago: University of Chicago Press, 1908).

6. David Truman, *The Governmental Process* (New York: Knopf, 1951), p. 33.

7. Ziegler, *Pluralism*, p. 7.

8. Mancur Olson, *The Logic of Collective Action: Public Goods and the Theory of Groups* (Cambridge: Harvard University Press, 1965).

9. Olson, *Logic*, p. 14.

10. Zeigler, *Pluralism*, p. 15. See also Peter Williamson, *Corporatism in Perspective: An Introductory Guide to Corporatist Theory* (Beverly Hills, Calif.: Sage Publications, 1989), and Marco Wilke, *Corporatism and the Stability of Capitalist Democracies* (New York: Peter Lang, 1991).

11. O. Ruin, "Participatory Democracy and Corporatism: The Case of Sweden," *Scandinavian Political Studies* 9 (1974): 171–186, as cited in Gerhard Lehmbruch and Philippe Schmitter, eds., *Patterns of Corporatist Policy-Making* (Beverly Hills, Calif.: Sage Publications, 1982), p. 4.

12. Marino Regini, "Changing Relationships Between Labour and the State in Italy: Towards a Neo-Corporatist System?" in Lehmbruch and Schmitter, *Patterns*, p. 112.

13. Philippe C. Schmitter, "Reflections on Where the Theory of Neo-Corporatism Has Gone and Where the Praxis of Neo-Corporatism May Be Going," in Lehmbruch and Schmitter, *Patterns*, pp. 260–261.

14. Four different examples of research dealing with corporatism and group conflict are Jeffrey Anderson, *The Territorial Imperative: Pluralism, Corporatism, and Economic Crisis* (New York: Cambridge University Press, 1992), Colin Crouch, ed., *Corporatism and Accountability: Organized Interests in British Public Life* (New York: Oxford University Press, 1990), Robert Bianchi, *Unruly Corporatism: Associational Life in Twentieth-Century Egypt* (New York: Oxford University Press, 1989), and M. Donald Hancock, *West Germany: The Politics of Democratic Corporatism* (Chatham, N.J.: Chatham House Publishers, 1989).

15. See *inter alia*, Norman Luttbeg, ed., *Public Opinion and Public Policy* (Homewood, Ill.: Dorsey Press, 1974), especially pp. 1–10, 109, and 187.

16. Truman, *The Governmental Process*, especially pp. 129–139, offers the classic articulation of this argument.

17. See Graham Wilson, *Interest Groups* (Cambridge, Mass.: Blackwell Publishers, 1990); Clive Thomas, *First World Interest Groups: A Comparative Perspective* (Westport, Conn.: Greenwood, 1993), or Philip Mundo, *Interest Groups: Cases and Characteristics* (Chicago, Ill.: Nelson-Hall, 1992).

18. See Michael Curtis, *Comparative Government and Politics* (New York: Harper and Row, 1978), pp. 141–143. An interesting listing of a range of groups can be found in *Guardian Directory of Pressure Groups in European Communities* (London: Gale Research, 1992).

19. One of the classic typologies developed for the study of interest groups was developed by Gabriel Almond and can be found in his introduction to G. Almond and J. S. Coleman, eds., *The Politics of the Developing Areas* (Princeton, N.J.: Princeton University Press, 1960), pp. 33ff.

20. There has been a great deal of work in this area. Among more recent work would be included the following: Lawrence Rothenberg, *Linking Citizens to Government: Interest Group Politics at Common Cause* (New York: Cambridge University Press, 1992), and Laura Woliver,

From Outrage to Action: The Politics of Grass-Roots Dissent (Urbana: University of Illinois Press, 1992).

21. See Luttbeg, pp. 187–188. The articles reprinted in this section of this reader that deal with the pressure groups model of political linkage are all very well done and provide illustrations of the linkage suggested by the theory.

22. This distinction is developed in Jeremy Richardson, ed., *Pressure Groups* (New York: Oxford University Press, 1993).

23. See Leon Epstein, *Political Parties in Western Democracies* (New Brunswick, N.J.: Transaction, 1992), Harmon Zeigler, *Political Parties in Industrial Democracies* (Itasca, Ill.: F. E. Peacock, 1993), Ferdinand Muller-Rommel and Geoffrey Pridham, eds., *Small Parties in Western Europe: Comparative and National Perspectives* (Beverly Hills, Calif.: Sage Publications, 1991), or Charles Ameringer, ed., *Political Parties of the Americas, 1980s to 1990s: Canada, Latin America, and the West Indies* (Westport, Conn.: Greenwood, 1992).

24. For further distinctions, see Curtis, pp. 143–144. A very well-written essay that develops this distinction is that by Dennis C. Beller and Frank B. Belloni, "Party and Faction: Modes of Political Competition," pp. 417–50 in Frank Belloni and Dennis Beller, eds., *Factional Politics: Political Parties and Factionalism in Comparative Perspective* (Santa Barbara, Calif.: ABC-Clio Press, 1978).

25. One of the classic essays in this area is that by J. LaPalombara and M. Weiner, "The Origin and Development of Political Parties," in J. LaPalombara and M. Weiner, eds., *Political Parties and Political Development* (Princeton, N.J.: Princeton University Press, 1966), pp. 3–6.

26. A good discussion of this is found in James Sterling Young, *The Washington Community: 1800–1828* (New York: Harcourt, Brace and World, 1966). See also Dean McSweeney and John Zvesper, *American Political Parties: The Formation, Decline, and Reform of the American Party System* (London: Routledge, 1991).

27. See Keith Laybourn, *Rise of Labour: The British Labour Party, 1890–1979* (London: Routledge, 1991). For a comparative perspective, see Francis F. Pixen, ed., *Labor Parties in Postindustrial Societies* (New York: Oxford University Press, 1992).

28. There is very substantial literature in this area, including *inter alia* the following: John Garang, *The Call for Democracy in Sudan* (London: Kegan Paul, 1992), Mary-Alice Waters, *The Rise and Fall of the Nicaraguan Revolution* (Ventura, Calif.: Pathfinder, 1992), Nigel Harris, *National Liberation* (Reno: University of Nevada Press, 1993), or H. E. Chehabi, *Iranian Politics and Religious Modernism: The Liberation Movement of Iran Under the Shah and Khomeini* (Ithaca, N.Y.: Cornell University Press, 1990).

29. This is discussed in Surdan Naidu, *The Congress Party in Transition* (Columbia, Mo.: South Asia Books, 1991).

30. One of the best illustrations of ideological parties, of course, involves communist and Marxist parties. See Charles Hobday, *Communist and Marxist Parties of the World* (Detroit, Mich.: St. James Press, 1990).

31. Probably the best single reference book is Alan Day and Henry Degenhardt, eds., *Political Parties of the World* (Detroit: Gale Research Company, 1980). This is an over-500-page compendium listing all political parties in the world (at the time) and their leadership structures, ideologies, electoral histories, and any other descriptive characteristics readily available.

32. Maurice Duverger, *Political Parties* (New York: John Wiley, 1963), p. 63.

33. Ibid.

34. Ibid., p. 64.

35. Ibid., p. 65.

36. Ibid., p. 67.

37. See Joseph Schlesinger, *Political Parties and the Winning of Office* (Ann Arbor: University of Michigan Press, 1991), Mark Franklin, Tom Mackie, and Henry Valen, eds., *Electoral Change: Responses to Evolving Social and Attitudinal Structures in Western Countries* (New York: Cambridge University Press, 1992), and Gerald Pomper, *Voters, Elections, and Parties: The Practice of Democratic Theory* (New Brunswick, N.J.: Transaction, 1992).

38. Duverger, *Political Parties*, p. 217.

39. One of the better theoretical essays in this area is by John G. Grumm, "Theories of Electoral Systems," in Andrew Milnor, ed., *Comparative Political Parties* (New York: Crowell, 1969), pp. 230–250.

40. Giovanni Sartori, *Parties and Party Systems: A Framework for Analysis* (Cambridge: Cambridge University Press, 1976), p. 15.

41. See Michael Jogerst, *Reform in the House of Commons: The Select Committee System* (Lexington: University Press of Kentucky, 1993), or John Kenneth White and Jerome Mileur, eds., *Challenges to Party Government* (Carbondale: Southern Illinois University Press, 1992).

42. One example of a study of internal party structure is by Ralph Goldman, *The National Party Chairmen and Committees: Factionalism at the Top* (Armonk, N.Y.: M.E. Sharpe, 1990).

43. One of the classics in this area is the work of Austin Ranney, *Pathways to Parliament: Candidate Selection in Britain* (Madison: University of Wisconsin Press, 1965). A classic American study would be that by Samuel Eldersveld, *Political Parties: A Behavioral Analysis* (Chicago: Rand McNally, 1964), chap. 22.

44. One of the best essays of this nature is by Samuel Barnes, "Party Democracy and the Logic of Collective Action," in W. J. Crotty, ed., *Approaches to the Study of Party Organization* (Boston: Allyn and Bacon, 1968), pp. 105–138. See also Sandy Maisel, *The Parties Respond: Changes in the American Party System* (Boulder, Colo.: Westview, 1990), or Gerald Pomper, *Passions and Interests: Political Party Concepts of American Democracy* (Lawrence: University Press of Kansas, 1992).

45. See Kay Lawson, *The Comparative Study of Political Parties* (New York: St. Martin's Press, 1976), pp. 136–161.

46. Two classic references for party voting are H. A. Scarrow, "Distinguishing Between Political Parties: The Case of Canada," *Midwest Journal of Political Science* 9 (1965): 61–76, and Leon Epstein, *Political Parties*, pp. 80ff. Epstein argues that "European voting is probably more highly structured than American."

47. A historical example is the study by Gale Stokes, *Politics as Development: The Emergence of Political Parties in Nineteenth-Century Serbia* (Durham, N.C.: Duke University Press, 1990). Studies with more recent points of focus include: Michael F. Holt, *Political Parties and American Political Development* (Baton Rouge: Louisiana State University Press, 1992), and Wolfgang Rudig, *Explaining Green Party Development: Reflections on a Theoretical Framework* (Glasgow: University of Strathclyde, 1990).

48. A very good study of this nature is by Leonard Binder, "Political Recruitment and Participation in Egypt," in LaPalombara and Weiner, *Political Parties*, pp. 217–240.

49. This is discussed at some length by M. Margaret Conway, *Political Participation in the United States* (Washington, D.C.: Congressional Quarterly, 1991), and William Crotty, ed., *Political Participation and American Democracy* (Westport, Conn.: Greenwood Publishing, 1991).

50. Myron Weiner and Joseph LaPalombara, "The Impact of Parties on Political Development," in LaPalombara and Weiner, *Political Parties*, p. 413.

51. See Stein Rokkan, "Electoral Mobilization, Party Competition, and National Integration," in LaPalombara and Weiner, *Political Parties*, pp. 241–266, and Rupert Emerson, "Parties and National Integration in Africa," in ibid., pp. 267–302.

52. Myron Weiner and Joseph LaPalombara, "The Impact of Parties on Political Development," in LaPalombara and Weiner, *Political Parties*, p. 413.

53. Luttbeg, *Public Opinion*, pp. 109–186. See also Kay Lawson, "When Linkage Fails," in Kay Lawson and Peter Merkl, eds., *When Parties Fail: Emerging Alternative Organizations* (Princeton, N.J.: Princeton University Press, 1988), pp. 13–40.

54. An example of this kind of study is the work by Louis Maisel and Paul Sacks, eds., *The Future of Political Parties* (Beverly Hills, Calif.: Sage, 1975).

55. See David Butler, "Electoral Systems," in David Butler, Howard Penniman, and Austin Ranney eds., *Democracy at the Polls: A Comparative Study of Competitive National Elections* (Washington, D.C.: American Enterprise Institute, 1981), pp. 7–25. A fairly sophisticated discussion of this is presented in the volume by Richard S. Katz, *A Theory of Parties and Electoral Systems* (Baltimore: Johns Hopkins University Press, 1980).

56. Robert Dahl, *A Preface to Democratic Theory* (Chicago: University of Chicago Press, 1956), pp. 67–71.

57. Much of the discussion that follows based upon this point is based upon more detailed discussion in Martin Harrop and William Miller, *Elections and Voters: A Comparative Introduction* (New York: Meredith Press, 1987), pp. 2–5.

58. The violence associated with the presidential election campaign was discussed in "Campaign of Violence," *Time* 136:26 (December 17, 1990): 43. Later coverage included the

piece by Howard French, "Haitian Townspeople Tell of New Fear of Violence," *The New York Times* 142 (March 1, 1993): A3.

59. This was discussed in Harry Anderson's piece, "Marcos and the Election Mess: Washington Rethinks Its Options After a Vote Marred by 'Wholesale Fraud'," *Newsweek* 107:7 (February 17, 1986): 14.

60. Stryker McGuire, "A Compromised Election: Despite Cries of Fraud, Mexico's Ruling Party Claims a Close Victory," *Newsweek* 112:3 (July 18, 1988): 36.

61. Two studies of the Congress Party include Rekha Chowdhary, *Ideology and Politcs of Ruling Parties in India* (New Delhi: Deep and Deep, 1991), and N. S. Gehlot, ed., *The Congress Party in India: Policies, Culture, Performance* (New Delhi: Deep and Deep, 1991).

62. Harrop and Miller, *Elections and Voters*, p. 4.

63. See Jennifer Widner, *The Rise of a Party-State in Kenya: From "Harambee" to "Nyayo!"* (Berkeley: University of California Press, 1992).

64. A wide range of electoral laws are discussed in the book published by the Inter-Parliamentary Union, *Chronicle of Parliamentary Elections and Developments* (Geneva: Inter-Parliamentary Union, 1991). See also Mark Franklin, Thomas Mackie, and Henry Valen, *Electoral Change: Responses to Evolving Social and Attitudinal Structures in Western Countries* (New York: Cambridge University Press, 1992), Andrew Reeve and Alan Ware, *Electoral Systems: A Comparative and Theoretical Introduction* (New York: Routledge, 1992), and Arend Lijphart, *Electoral Systems and Party Systems: A Study of Twenty-Seven Democracies, 1945–1990* (New York: Oxford University Press, 1994).

65. Many of these issues are discussed in Austin Ranney, "Candidate Selection," in Butler, Penniman, and Ranney, *Democracy at the Polls*, pp. 76–105.

66. See Howard Penniman, "Campaign Styles and Methods," in Butler, Penniman, and Ranney, eds., *Democracy at the Polls*, pp. 107–136. Similar issues are discussed in Leslie Seidle, ed., *Comparative Issues in Party and Election Finance* (Toronto: Dundurn Press, 1991), and Brooks Jackson, *Broken Promises: Why the Federal Election Commission Failed* (New York: Twentieth Century Fund, 1990).

67. A very good article on this subject is by Benjamin Ginsberg and John C. Green, "The Best Congress Money Can Buy: Campaign Contributions and Congressional Behavior," in Benjamin Ginsberg and Alan Stone, eds., *Do Elections Matter?* (Armonk, N.Y.: M.E. Sharpe, 1986), pp. 75–90.

68. This is discussed by K. Z. Paltiel, "Campaign Finance: Contrasting Practices and Reforms," in Butler, Penniman, and Ranney, *Democracy at the Polls*, pp. 138–172.

69. See Anthony Smith, "Mass Communications," in Butler, Penniman, and Ranney, *Democracy at the Polls*, pp. 173–195. See also J. Leonard Reinsch, *Getting Elected: From Radio and Roosevelt to Television and Reagan* (New York: Hippocrene Books, 1990).

70. Gregory Mahler, *Israel: Politics and Government in a Maturing State* (New York: Harcourt, Brace, Jovanovich, 1989), p. 132.

71. This is discussed in Ivor Crewe, "Electoral Participation," in Butler, Penniman, and Ranney, *Democracy at the Polls*, pp. 216–264. See also Karen Arlington and William Taylor, eds., *Voting Rights in America: Continuing the Quest for Full Participation* (Washington, D.C.: Joint Center for Political and Economic Studies, 1992).

72. This question is asked by Anthony King, "What Do Elections Decide?" in Butler, Penniman, and Ranney, *Democracy at the Polls*, pp. 293–325.

73. This is based upon much more extensive discussion and analysis in Harrop and Miller, *Elections and Voters*, pp. 245–268.

74. Roger DesForges, Luo Ning, and Wu Yen-bo, eds., *Chinese Democracy and the Crisis of 1989: Chinese and American Reflections* (Albany: State University of New York Press, 1993). See also Timothy Brook, *Quelling the People: The Military Supression of the Beijing Democracy Movement* (New York: Oxford University Press, 1992).

75. See Christian Potholm, Richard Morgan, and Erik Potholm, *Just Do It: Political Participation in the 1990s* (Lanham, Md.: University Press of America, 1993). See also the publication by the United Nations, *Equality in Political Participation* (New York: United Nations, 1991).

76. There is substantial comparative literature on parties and interest groups. Examples of the types of works now available include the following: Keith Archer, *Political Choices and Elec-*

toral Consequences: A Study of Organized Labour and the New Democratic Party (Toronto: University of Toronto Press, 1990), John Frears, *Parties and Voting in France* (New York: St. Martin's Press, 1991), Margaret Keck, *The Worker's Party and Democratization in Brazil* (New Haven, Conn.: Yale University Press, 1992), Louis Goodman, William Leogrande, and Johanna Forman, eds., *Political Parties and Democracy in Central America* (Boulder, Colo.: Westview Press, 1992), Robert Garner and Richard Kelly, *British Political Parties Today* (New York: St. Martin's Press, 1993), L. P. Misquitta, *Pressure Groups and Democracy in India* (New York: Sterling Publications, 1991), and Ronald Hrebenar, *The Japanese Party System* (Boulder, Colo.: Westview, 1992).

The Individual and the Political Environment

THE POLITICAL SYSTEM REVISITED

In Chapter 1 we introduced the concept of the political system, a set of related objects connected with one another in an analytic way. We indicated at the time that the relationships of these objects were to be *perceived* by the observer: Sometimes the links between objects are clear and distinct, and sometimes they are not. The links between the U.S. House of Representatives and the U.S. Senate are reasonably clear; the links between multinational corporations and a Third World nation's political stability may be less so.

Thus far in this comparative study we have focused our attention upon the central political structures of regimes: constitutional frameworks, legislatures, executives, bureaucracies, judiciaries, and political parties and interest groups. We must keep in mind, though, that these political structures, however similar or varied they may be and however they may be related to other constitutional structures in their political regimes, all operate within a political context or a political environment, and not in a vacuum. Thus, although it is possible for us to speak abstractly about constitutional structures in presidential systems or parliamentary systems, we cannot be content to end our cross-national political analysis at that point; the political environment introduces a broad range of variables into our examination.

Although we have now examined a very wide range of political structures that exist in the political system, there are still a number of other variables—some at the individual level, and some at the level of the political system—that should be considered to be part of the political environment within which an individual operates in the normal process of political participation.

On the individual level, it is appropriate for us to understand how individual political attitudes are developed and passed from generation to generation—the process of *political socialization*—so as to appreciate the political culture of the regime. Moreover, preliminary examination may indicate a need to understand the process of *political recruitment*. We should ask: How are political leaders and political elites selected from among the ranks of the masses?

At the level of the political system, we need to understand several other possible influences on political behavior. The subject of political recruitment introduces questions related to the relation of the *political elite* to the masses. We know that the recruitment process serves to separate the elite from the masses, but how "open" is the elite? In addition, although the *military* is not a significant political structure in stable democracies such as Great Britain, Canada, or the United States, in some political cultures (such as those in Latin America or Africa) it is taken very seriously as a political actor, and we shall briefly discuss its political role here. Finally, we shall briefly discuss the subject of *political violence*, since it is a type of political behavior that is of significance to the political system in the context of "systems maintenance," which we discussed in Chapter 1.

All of this is a weighty assignment for the beginning student. The solution to this quandary that is selected by many authors of introductory texts is to give short shrift to the constitutional structures and political institutions of any regime, and to focus instead in great detail upon the topics mentioned above. In this text we do the opposite, for reasons that were discussed in the Preface.

In the sections of this chapter that follow, we will *briefly* discuss the several individual and systemic structures and behaviors referred to above. We will undertake to discuss their potential impact upon the political systems of which they are a part. They will not, however, be the *primary* foci for our area studies chapters in the second part of this text. Our assumption here is that the student is better prepared for further cross-national study with an introduction emphasizing political structures and political institutions and placing less emphasis on the many variables in the political environment, rather than one that emphasizes the many variables in the political environment but gives short shrift to the decision-making processes of political regimes.[1]

After brief discussion of the several factors that may be of significance in the political environment within which a political system operates, we will turn our attention in the second part of this text to a number of area studies chapters. These chapters will focus primarily upon the structures and processes described in chapters 2 through 8. Where some of the environmental variables described here are of great significance, they will be discussed as well, but we will not undertake to comprehensively treat *all* of these factors in *all* chapters; time and space simply do not permit such a treatment.

THE STUDY OF POLITICAL SOCIALIZATION AND POLITICAL ATTITUDES

Contemporary studies focusing upon political actors are often based upon the assumption that *who the actors are* affect the product generated by the systems of which they are a part.[2] This includes the study of values, attitudes, beliefs, and skills that actors bring with them to the political arena, and leads us to a discussion of political socialization.[3] Although the concept of political socialization has not yet proven to be as valuable an explanatory tool as many had hoped when it became a popular subject of study in the 1960s, many people continue to believe that it still has value as a factor contributing to a greater understanding of how individual political behavior is motivated.[4]

Interest in political socialization is not a creation of contemporary political scientists. Plato dealt with the problem of political education in his *Republic*, as did Aristotle in his *Politics* and *Ethics*; the debate has continued from the time of Jean-Jacques Rousseau to that of B. F. Skinner:

> From time immemorial, social philosophers have thought that political education *should* have an early start. For Plato and Rousseau there was also little question about the feasibility of such early instruction; to them it was common sense that young children could be educated in fundamental political matters.[5]

Current interest in the study of political socialization was given a major impetus by the work of Herbert Hyman, who in 1959 was perhaps the first modern political scientist to urge the study of political socialization as a subfield of political science.

Political socialization has been conceptualized as the process by which "the individual acquires attitudes, beliefs, and values relating to the political system of which he is a member and to his own role as a citizen within that political system."[6] Elsewhere, socialization has been defined as "those developmental processes through which persons acquire political orientations and patterns of behavior."[7] The important thing to note in these and other conceptualizations is that socialization is conceived of as a *process*; that is, it is an ongoing action that is not finished as long as the individual is still able to perceive his or her environment and respond to it.

The process of political socialization may be either direct or indirect, formal or informal.

> Much of . . . civic education takes place informally. From an early age children learn about government and politics and begin to prepare for their adult political roles, through processes which neither they nor those who instruct them are especially conscious of, but which nevertheless provide the basis of democratic political participation.[8]

While the idea of direct, formal political socialization has negative connotations for many because of its similarity to the "indoctrination" of youth in more authoritarian political systems, it is nonetheless the case that there are many societal actions that are directly politically socializing which exist virtually unopposed even in "democratic" regimes—including civics courses and the Pledge of Allegiance, for example.

Many theoretical gaps still need to be filled in socialization research, and much attention needs to be given to several major questions yet outstanding. In the introductory essay to his now-classic book *Socialization to Politics,* Jack Dennis suggested "ten central problem dimensions" related to contemporary socialization research. These several problem dimensions of socialization research include the system relevance of political socialization; varieties of the content of political socialization; socialization across the life cycle and generations; cross-cultural and subcultural aspects and variations in socialization; the political learning process; the agents and agencies of political socialization; the extent and relative effects of political socialization upon different individuals; and, finally, problems related to specialized political socialization, especially socialization of political elites.[9]

Although researchers concerned with political socialization have been conscious of the need to theoretically relate their work to general theories of political behavior, this task has not yet been performed to the satisfaction of all. Jack Dennis suggested over two decades ago that "the question about what effects political socialization has upon political life" is "the most important aspect of political socialization research for the development of a theory of politics."[10] If one perceives political phenomena as existing and taking place within a political system, it becomes necessary to prove the relevance of any study of such political phenomena to a better knowledge of the system itself; if "system relevance" cannot be demonstrated, then the entire body of political socialization literature is of only dubious value, as many people claim.[11]

It has been argued that at a minimum, political socialization is important to the political system because it generates a general support for the political system in which it takes place. What is not known, however, is that proportion of whatever diffuse or general support for a political system exists that may be attributed to socialization. There are other factors that generate diffuse support in a political system—such as popular leaders, popular decisions or policies, and the like—and it has not yet been sufficiently illustrated that it is the process of political socialization itself that plays a meaningful and significant role in the creation of diffuse support. Quite clearly, to measure the effects of socialization upon diffuse support, all other factors would need to be held constant. Since this has not yet been accomplished, the positive effect of political socialization on diffuse support has not yet been proven, although it has been asserted and suggested.[12]

It is interesting to note that *negatively* the effect of socialization upon diffuse support has been illustrated to some degree. In one study, investigators have shown a relationship between the cynicism of parents to government and an increased occurrence of such cynicism in their children, with clear implications for diffuse support for government, generally. This work suggests several theoretical questions that have yet to be resolved or substantiated.[13]

Once it is established that the study of political socialization is relevant to the study of politics, generally, and once we have examined the gaps in the attempt to establish this fact, we can turn our attention to the "what" of the process: What is the object, the content, of political socialization that is supposed to be of significance for the political system? Many subjects are suggested as being taught in this process, including the general political culture, political roles, knowledge of how the political system operates, and the like.

Perhaps the best-known exposition on political culture and the passing of political cultures from one generation to another is to be found in Gabriel Almond and Sidney Verba's classic work *The Civic Culture.*

> When we speak of the political culture of a society, we refer to the political system as internalized in the cognitions, feelings, and evaluations of its population. People are induced into it just as they are socialized into non-political roles and social systems.[14]

Similarly, Gabriel Almond has written elsewhere that political socialization is "the process of induction into the political culture. Its end product is a set of attitudes—cognitions, value standards, and feelings—toward the political system."[15]

Political roles, as well as a political culture, are also suggested as being among the objects taught by political socialization. As the term is used here, a "political role" is "a pattern of expected behavior for individuals holding particular positions in a system."[16] Roles and role behavior are clearly not established from the time of birth, but are taught and learned phenomena. As such, they are a part of the content of political socialization.[17]

A general knowledge of the political system and the manner in which it operates is also included in the content of political socialization. Such subjects as how the system works, the functioning of different branches of the government, what the role of political parties is in the political system, and so on—all are introduced to individuals through the socialization process.[18]

It has also been suggested that the process of socialization may play a significant role in participation in politics itself.[19] That is, not only can socialization help the political system by promoting diffuse support, but it can also help the system by promoting participation within the structures of the political framework.

While many theorists have focused their attention on the "what" of the process of socialization—the content of what is learned—theoretical gaps exist in other areas of their work as well. Another area of study that has been given considerable attention in investigation, and that is by no means resolved, is the "when" of the process—a temporal dimension of socialization, including the individual's development across the life cycle and differences across generations. As indicated previously, political socialization is best conceived as a process, and as such it is not a phenomenon to be studied merely in individuals between the ages of, say, 6 and 16 years, with no consideration given to earlier and later years. Studies examining the temporal nature of political socialization have focused on such questions as when the process begins, which are the most important years for later political attitudes, and how long the political socialization process can be said to continue.

Research has shown that there is a strong relationship between the time of initial socialization to politics and the agents of initial political socialization. One study found that legislators could be placed along a bidimensional continuum:

> ranging from those who were socialized early (childhood or grammar school) by the family, through those socialized as adolescents by self (self starters), to those whose

socialization was delayed until the post-adolescent period and occurred because of external events and conditions.[20]

It has been difficult to show the consequences of this differential socialization, however. While we can say that different agents of socialization are most effective at different times of the age span, problems appear when we try to translate this fact into its effect on legislative behavior, for example.

Different points in the life cycle are significant in terms of *what* will be learned, as well as *by what agent* the socialization will be influenced. It has been clearly demonstrated[21] that children are first aware of executive positions in government, such as the president or a mayor, and not until they grow older do they perceive legislators—such as congressmen, for example—as anything but "the president's helpers." Jean Piaget has shown[22] that certain concepts are more difficult than others for a child to learn. For example, in one set of studies there was much confusion for young children as to whether they were citizens of Switzerland or citizens of Geneva; it was not until the children reached a higher level of cognitive development that they saw that these two possibilities were not mutually exclusive.

Still other studies have focused upon intergenerational differences in socialization. Although this area of socialization research has not received as much attention as others, it clearly suggests several theoretically interesting questions that are worth further investigation. To take one example, if aging seems to promote greater consistency in partisan orientation in politics,[23] what implications exist for those individuals investigating the agents of socialization? That is, if aging makes an individual more partisan, it seems likely that the individual would also become more sensitive, and responsive, to partisan political stimuli, and thereby tend to be further socialized to follow the party line. This is but one of the several hypotheses that could be investigated in this general area; much work has yet to be done.

What Jack Dennis called the "spatial"[24] dimension of political socialization research is yet another area among the ten "central problem dimensions" suggested as being keys to contemporary political socialization research. This spatial dimension includes cross-cultural as well as subcultural and group variations in the socialization process.

Cross-cultural differences and similarities may, in fact, be among the most valuable of the several types of socialization studies, because they have implications for several of the central problem dimensions discussed here.[25] By finding differences in the socialization processes in two different cultural settings, implications can be drawn relating not only to the effectiveness of various agents of socialization but also to system relevance of the study of political socialization.

Within a single national setting, studies of subcultural and group variations in political socialization may have the same value as cross-cultural research. One good example of this type of research is a 1968 study by Dean Jaros and others: Through a study of a specific American subculture, in this case the "Appalachian personality," Jaros attempted not only to theorize about the effectiveness of certain agents of socialization in Appalachia as compared with an earlier and comparable study in New Haven, Connecticut,[26] but also to make several theoretical suggestions pertaining to the effects of socialization on the development of political cynicism, and thereby its relevance for system maintenance. Similar studies have been undertaken investigating other subcultural or group characteristics, including race, gender, ethnic group membership, and social class.[27]

The actual question of how learning takes place—the "how" of the socialization question that asks "who learns what from whom, how, and when"—is certainly no less important than any other aspect of socialization that we have already mentioned. This "how" question encompasses several components, and can be seen to often include both the "when" and the "from whom" aspects of socialization theory.

Often when people ask how political learning takes place, what they are *in fact* asking is which agents are active in the political learning process, rather than really inquiring about learning theory:

> Q. "How did Alden come to believe that?"
> A. "Oh, it was a book she read."

In many cases this "from whom or what" response to our "how" question is the only response possible. That is, the questioner in this case is not *really* looking for an answer couched in terms of learning theory; the individual is interested in the active elements involved in the process of Alden coming to believe something that she does. In other instances, the "how" is answered in temporal terms, employing such implicit concepts as maturation, for example:

> Q. "How did Darcy come to believe that?"
> A. "She is at an age when she rebels against us."

Or an answer can come in terms of both the "when" and the "from whom":

> Q. "How did Alden come to believe that?"
> A. "Now that she is 16, she and her sister Darcy talk about politics a great deal."

Thus we can see that often in political socialization research the question being answered, which is ostensibly our "how" question, often is not answered in "how" (learning theory) terms at all. Rather, it is answered in terms of either the agents of socialization involved ("from whom or what"), or temporal-chronological factors ("when"), or both.[28]

By far the most attention in political socialization research has been given to the "by whom or what" question: The examination of those agents and factors that are most influential in the socialization process. Many different factors have been suggested by political scientists as being the most influential in the socialization process, including among the most visible sources of political socialization parents, teachers, neighbors, peers, the media, and members of the extended family.[29]

It has been almost traditionally accepted that the family is foremost among the many agents of socialization influential during childhood. Aristotle wrote of the overriding importance of the family in socialization. A more contemporary author suggests that "the most important source of children's conceptions of authority undoubtedly is the civic instruction which goes on incidental to normal activities in the family."[30]

The literature also shows us that one by-product of the impressionability of the socialization process is that the child is likely to form political impressions, images, and even opinions before he or she has any real political knowledge upon which to base those feelings. The child's first conception of political authority seems to have "more affective than cognitive content. . . . The prevailing adult theme of cynicism toward politics and politicians evidently develops at adolescence or later."[31] There is a tendency for children to develop party identification early, with no cognitive reason for preferring one party over another. Greenstein wrote that by the fourth grade, more than 60 percent of the children in one study[32] could give a party identification, even if they could not give a satisfactory reason for why they had chosen that party.

The ninth general set of issues suggested by Jack Dennis concerns the "extent" of political socialization; that is, to what degree one is politicized when one is socialized to politics. Does political socialization merely involve imparting a sensitivity or awareness of issues upon an individual, or does it imply a true politicization of the individual—not only is the individual aware of issues, but he or she also has opinions on all the issues involved. This has vital consequences for the political system—in a truly participatory democracy, in which a characteristic of the system is the encouragement of citizen participation in the governmental process, it is important to know those factors that are more and less influential in politicizing the electorate. This is yet another aspect of political socialization research that has received relatively little attention, but that certainly merits a great deal of investigation.

A final area of political socialization research involves specialized political socialization. This has especially focused upon elite socialization—specifically upon those who are politically active, including legislators.[33] In many ways this area of political socialization research has claimed to be the most relevant for the political system, generally, by arguing that "*who the legislators are* affects the product generated by the systems of which they are a part."[34] By studying the socialization of legislators or other political elites we know better what *kind* of individual attains formal office, for example, and thereby we have some basis for predicting *how* political elites will perform. As political socialization theory becomes more developed, we should be able to better predict how those political elites will behave once they are in office.

THE STUDY OF POLITICAL RECRUITMENT

The study of political recruitment has not been subjected to the same questions of "relevance for the political system" as has political socialization research. Potential critics and challengers have been satisfied with observations that the channels that are open for people to enter the political elite level, and subsequently to become officeholders, influence to a large extent *which* people become political elites and subsequent officeholders. This has *de facto* significance for the political system, and therefore is relevant for study, since potential critics accept the argument that who the political elite are makes a difference in terms of policy and action in the political system.[35]

Political recruitment research, however, suffers from several of the same theoretical problems as political socialization research. Significant among those problems is that theorists are not in agreement as to exactly *what* political recruitment is.[36] Although, as with socialization literature, theorists agree that political recruitment is a *process*, definitions suggested in the literature differ, and these differences are not always of an insignificant nature. One author, for example, suggested that:

> political recruitment refers to the processes that select from among the several million socially favored and politically motivated citizens comprising the political stratum those several thousand who reach positions of significant national influence.[37]

The definitional problem is not an insignificant one. Moshe Czudnowski clearly recognized this problem when he asked:

> Should [political recruitment] be defined with reference to a point of destination, a state of affairs which indicates the completion of the process and if so, what is this terminal point? Or should it be defined with reference to motivations or behavioral characteristics, and the conditions under which they occur?[38]

It seems that the more broadly applicable definition may be Gabriel Almond's: He defines recruitment as the function of the political system that draws upon members of the society, inducts them "into the specialized roles of the political system, trains them with political cognitive maps, values, expectations, and affects." Thereby, he writes, the recruitment function "takes up where the general political socialization function leaves off."[39]

Part of the definition problem is that the term "recruitment" is used to cover two actual processes: *initial recruitment* to politics, and *promotion* within the political infrastructure. Lester Milbrath broke down the overall recruitment process into several levels of participation.[40] He argued that there is a hierarchy of political involvement and participation in the United States, ranging from the individual who is merely a "spectator," to a "gladiator" who is actively involved in the political arena, and "transitionals" in the middle. The advantage of this kind of approach is that it allows us to break down the general process into its component parts, and thereby allows us to examine more closely each distinct segment of the overall recruitment process.

Although a number of studies of political recruitment have been undertaken, with a wide diversity of foci, several central areas of research may be singled out as a basis for an examination of this area (much as we did with the political socialization question). To take one example, Moshe Czudnowski suggested a sixfold framework for the study of political recruitment, including (1) social background characteristics; (2) political socialization and recruitment factors; (3) initial activity and apprenticeship, (4) occupations; (5) motivations; and (6) the selection process itself.[41]

Although this particular framework is made up of several components, a broader examination of the literature seems to indicate the existence of two *major* foci of study: (1) studies examining the characteristics or background of those who are recruited, and (2) studies focusing upon the recruitment process itself. It is interesting to note at this point that while most theorists do recognize political recruitment as a process, similar to political socialization, the bulk of the attention in the literature is not focused upon the process—the "how" aspect—of the question, but rather upon the "who" of the question, the social background studies of those who are recruited.

The rationale for gathering social background data, and therefore for this type of study, is based upon two assumptions. The first assumption is that "relationships exist between social background characteristics and opportunities to gain access to political offices"; the second assumption is that "the social background characteristics are related to variations in the attitudes and behavior of political elites."[42] Available data to support the latter hypothesis, that there is a link between social background characteristics and attitudes and behavior of political elites, do not appear consistent. Rather, the degree of association appears to vary from one political system to another.[43]

Generally speaking, the literature has tended to substantiate the first assumption underlying the study of social background data; there *does* appear to be a relationship between social background characteristics and the opportunity to gain access to political office. It *does* appear to be the case that individuals from the middle and upper classes of some societies tend to be disproportionately recruited in relation to their size in populations as a whole. This bias appears to exist not only in national political office but also in *all* aspects of the political system, including party work and local-level offices.[44]

One interesting finding of the social background research has been the discovery of the strong association between certain occupations and subsequent elective office. The relationship between legislators and the practice of law prior to election has frequently been cited; in the United States, "it is proverbial that U.S. congressmen are lawyers."[45] While the relationship may be "proverbial" in the United States, studies show that this affinity is not as universal as many believe. It has been demonstrated that whereas 58 percent of American legislators are lawyers, only about 2 percent of Swedish legislators are lawyers. In fact, of twenty-two nations examined in one study, the average percentage of legislators who previously were lawyers was 16 percent, a far cry from a universally "proverbial" relationship.[46]

In addition to the "who" of the recruitment process, considerable attention has been paid to the questions of how and why individuals are recruited; this attention is directed toward an examination of the recruitment process itself. A number of studies have focused on the role that parties and other groups play in the recruitment process. Still others are oriented toward psychological factors involved in the recruitment process, and the roles that the electoral system and opportunity in general play in the process. This focus upon the *process* of political recruitment, the channels of the selection process and gates and gatekeepers involved, has not received the same amount of attention as have studies of social background variables, although it has become a more popular area of research in recent years.

is, like several we have met in this text, a problematic one: It means different things to different people. On one hand, "elite" simply means "best," and there is very little that is objectionable in that. On the other hand, "elite" is sometimes interpreted more broadly to refer to "the power holders of a body politic."[54] In this sense:

> The concept of the elite is classificatory and descriptive, designating the holders of high positions in a given society. There are as many elites as there are values. Besides an elite of power (the political elite) there are elites of wealth, respect, and knowledge (to name but a few).[55]

The question is this: How does the existence of a political elite fit in with the idea of democratic government? We know that democracy places many requirements on citizens, including that they be informed, be knowledgeable, have principles, and be rational, and we know that not all voters are like that. Fortunately, we have been told that not *all* voters need to have these characteristics for a democratic system to survive.[56] If enough individuals are adequately motivated and informed, the system can continue to operate.

The key ingredient here is what are called "elite-mass linkages," the patterns of relationships existing between the elite and the masses that allow the elite to govern on behalf of the masses. The elite can govern by force, through coercion such as we find in military regimes (which we shall discuss in just a moment); in the contemporary world, military regimes are more and more common. The political system will be more stable, however, and will have to expend less of its resources on coercive measures, if it can govern through a sense of legitimacy on the part of the mass public, not through a sense of coercion. This will be based upon the degree to which the mass public shares the views of the political and socioeconomic elite.[57]

The existence of elites *can* be compatible with democratic government under some circumstances.[58] The most important single characteristic appears to be that an *open elite* exist: that it is possible for the masses to become part of the elite.[59] Again, this ties in with our discussion of recruitment processes in a regime. Where there are effective recruitment structures, a relatively open elite can exist; where sufficient opportunities do not exist, and where we find a relatively "closed" elite, we will invariably find a system of lower legitimacy and less stability.[60]

THE MILITARY

The military is another societal structure that is significant in both the socialization and recruitment processes. It is sometimes regarded as *the* "elite" in developing nations, and it is also a structure that can be significant on its own in shaping the type and style of political participation that is permitted in the political arena. Although the military is not perceived as a politically significant actor in most stable Western democracies, we should not let a pervasive Western ethnocentrism (and here we really mean an Anglo-American ethnocentrism, since the military has clearly played significant political roles in modern French and German history) blind us to the fact that the military, as an institution, is a *highly significant* political actor in many developing regimes.

Studies focusing on the role played by parties in the recruitment process have shown that the significance of parties in recruitment varies on a country-by-country basis. In the United States, for example, parties have lost much of the influence that they once had over the recruitment process, and they are currently struggling to maintain control over candidate selection. The loss of their influence can primarily be attributed to changes in the primary system and the increased openness of party conventions. As such, the loss of influence varies on a state-by-state basis, depending upon electoral laws in force.[47]

Outside of the United States, one need not look too far to see evidence of the importance of the party in the recruitment process, although it, too, varies on a country-by-country basis.[48] To take one example, it has been suggested that one of the more striking features of the preparliamentary political careers of legislators in the Canadian Parliament is the "large proportion of MPs, regardless of party, who had been party activists."[49] In Israel, to take another example, it would be almost unheard of for anyone to attain a political office *without* being a strong party worker.[50]

Other groups have been shown to have an impact on the recruitment process, sometimes through the political party itself. In two studies, Czudnowski[51] demonstrated the conditions under which political parties may become very group-oriented in their selection procedures for candidates for the national legislature, to the extent of permitting groups to dictate who "their" representatives on the party electoral list will be. It was suggested that group-oriented recruitment is positively associated with a proportional-representation electoral system. If this is correct, then groups other than political parties in a political system may take on explicitly political recruitment roles.

Yet another important factor that can influence the recruitment process is opportunity. Regardless of the size of the political stratum, or the number of "self-starters" ready to run for office, recruitment cannot take place if vacancies in office are not present.[52] Moreover, different recruitment rates exist for different offices; in the United States, recruitment to the presidency is more difficult than recruitment to the Senate, because turnover in the Senate is greater, and there are more opportunities there. Similarly, recruitment will be greater for the House of Representatives than the Senate, and greater for state legislative office than for national legislative office.

THE ROLE OF THE POLITICAL ELITE

Now that we have briefly examined *how* the political elite become the elite, it is important to understand the *role* of the political elite in the polity. Is "elitism" compatible with democratic government? How should the elite behave, and how should the masses relate to the elite? The use of the word "should" here warns us that we are leaving the empirical world and entering the normative world, our query more in the realm of philosophers than most questions we have addressed thus far in this volume. Because these are important questions, however, we will endeavor to highlight some of the most important issues raised by them.[53] The concept of a political elite

One need only look at military or military-supported coups[61] or attempted coups in very recent history—in Spain, Nigeria, Nicaragua, Bolivia, the Philippines, Fiji, and Sri Lanka, to take but a few examples—to see that in many instances political leaders are more concerned with what the military reaction will be to their decisions than they are with what the reactions of their respective legislatures or courts will be.[62] In fact, even in countries such as India or Guatemala, where civilian governments "are clearly in control," the armed forces have been shown to exert considerable political influence.[63]

> They are symbols of state sovereignty and the primary defenders against possible external or internal attack against the government. Given their prestige, responsibilities, and the material resources needed to fulfill these responsibilities, all military establishments exercise a significant degree of political influence. . . .[64]

The study of what has been called "praetorianism," or military coups, has been justified on many counts, including the fact that such events happen frequently; as Chairman Mao said in China, power "grows out of the barrel of a gun." Among twenty Latin American nations, only two—Costa Rica and Mexico—have not experienced at least one attempted coup since 1945. In one recent study, it was suggested that 57 percent of the Third World states examined had been under military rule for half or more than half of their respective periods of independence.[65] According to one observer, "Between 1945 and 1976, soldiers carried out successful coups in half of the eighteen Asian states," and, more generally, "it turns out that the military have intervened in approximately two-thirds of the more than one hundred non-Western states since 1945."[66]

Although coups may be ostensibly motivated "for public-spirited reasons on behalf of constitution and nation," research has shown that "almost all coups are at least partly, and usually primarily, inspired by the military's own interests."[67] One result of a military takeover is almost invariably a significant increase in the defense budget of the regime.[68] Examined more broadly, the result of recent research shows that "military rule was found to have negative or zero-order correlations with economic development." Moreover, "'politicians in uniform' invariably caused political decay."[69]

The issue of civilian control of the military is a very important one, especially in developing societies in which (civilian) governments may not yet have acquired the same degree of legitimacy and stability that one finds in the older Western democracies. The key issue involved in the maintenance of civilian control involves finding ways to set limits within which military leaders, and all members of the armed forces, "accept the government's definition of appropriate areas of responsibility."[70]

This does not mean in the final analysis that the military is prohibited from lobbying for policies it supports, but it does mean that the military agrees to do this in acceptable ways, and that the military agrees to accept the consequences of the policy-making process. Thus, the military accepts a subordinate role in the political system. Ironically, in military regimes the leaders face the same problems as previous civilian governments did: how to keep their military underlings loyal and prevent an overthrow of the (military) forces in power at the time.[71]

Remember that the military *is* a political institution in most countries. The role of the military in a political system is also significantly affected by that country's political culture, history, and tradition: In some Latin American systems the idea of a military coup, if not desirable, is certainly recognized as a statistical possibility—in fact, a probability—over the course of time.

POLITICAL PARTICIPATION AND POLITICAL VIOLENCE

The discussion of the role of the military in democratic politics shows that it is not only *participation* that is crucial for regimes, but also the *type* of participation that takes place. There is one kind of participation that we should mention briefly here which can be of great significance in the political arena: political violence.

"Violence" is one of those terms that means different things to different people.[72] We all might agree that throwing a brick through a window—or shooting someone—is an act of violence, but there are also other types of violence that we should keep in mind. Some would argue that there are certain social patterns of behavior—such as racism, for example—that can be referred to as "institutional violence," although others specifically reject "unjust social or political policies" as long as they do not involve physical force.[73] If we define violence as the infliction or threat of injury against persons or objects, we can see that a very wide range of behavior can be included in our discussion.

The range of actions that might be classified as political violence is so broad that systematic theory construction is terribly difficult. One recent attempt began with a framework focusing upon "who" did "what" to "whom," and subsequently tried to study the "symbolic addressee" of the violence, the claimed "social basis" of the act of violence, the size of the organization undertaking the violence, and "why" the action took place.[74]

Among the many types of behavior that we can consider to be examples of political violence might be a riot or a demonstration that turns violent, an assassination, a kidnapping, a mass revolution, a coup d'état, guerrilla warfare, terrorism, and, of course, conventional war. Motivations for these actions might be ideological (a Marxist revolution or Marxist-inspired coup), religious (the Islamic revolution in Iran, or the Sikh separatist battles in the Punjab in India), nationalistic (resistance of the Afghan guerrillas against Soviet military forces), or personal (an assassination ordered by a leader to remove a potential political competitor), or the motivation could come from some combination of these and other reasons.

Consistent with other warnings about ethnocentrism in this text, it is important to remember that American politics in recent years has not been completely confined to peaceful constitutional discourse. Political assassinations, such as the shootings of President John F. Kennedy, presidential candidate Robert F. Kennedy, or civil rights leader Rev. Martin Luther King, Jr., are acts of political violence. Ku Klux Klan violence in the American South is political violence.[75] Illegal activities by the Federal Bureau of Investigation in the 1960s and 1970s caused "violence" against American citizens. The Ohio National Guard fired on college students at Kent State

University who were participating in a demonstration against the Vietnam War in May 1970, resulting in the deaths of four students.[76] That was political violence. This is not meant to suggest that all American politics is violent, but it should serve as a reminder that political violence can exist even in stable, democratic societies.

Because our space is limited here, we shall confine our discussion to a limited number of types of violence. We shall briefly discuss two types of revolution: revolution from "above," the *coup d'état*, and revolution from "below," otherwise known as the *jacquerie*. We shall also briefly discuss guerrilla movements and terrorism, and attempt to point out similarities and differences between the two.[77]

Most simply, a revolution typically involves a changing of one government, or type of government, for another.[78] One relatively rigid definition that has been offered argues that a revolution involves a "relatively sudden violent and illegal attempt to change the regime of a state or other political organisation, in which large sections of the population are involved as participants."[79] Others might disagree with this view, however, claiming that revolutions often seek to restore legality against a regime that has voided the country's law, and thus they cannot be "illegal" actions. In brief, although there may not be universal agreement over exactly how we define "revolution," there is a general consensus that it involves a change of regimes.

A mass revolution is sometimes referred to as a *jacquerie*, and involves significant and radical changes in the ruling class. Four "great" revolutions of modern times are the American Revolution (1776), the French Revolution (1789), the Russian Revolution (1917–21), and the Chinese Revolution (1927–49).

Another type of revolutionary change, although not one directly involving "large sections of the population," is the *coup d'état*, a sudden seizure of power from above instead of using the masses from below. A coup "does not call on mass support to effect [leadership] changes, though it may seek legitimation of the changes by a plebiscite or mass demonstration."[80] Coups are usually carried out by individuals near the center of power who have access to resources and political support. The most common type of coup is called a *military coup*. The military coup, sometimes called a "colonel's" or a "general's coup," involves military leaders taking over a polity because of their dissatisfaction with civilian control. This has happened recently in Bolivia, Fiji, and Nigeria. A coup may also be led by nonmilitary individuals outside of the leadership structure who assassinate or depose the incumbent ruler to substitute themselves as rulers. This took place in Afghanistan several years ago when the Soviet-supported regime was established.

The distinction between *terrorism* and a *guerrilla* action can sometimes be unclear. Generally, we can define terrorism as "the use of violence or the threat of violence, to coerce governments, authorities, or populations by inducing fear."[81] There is often a symbolic dimension to the terrorist act, as well. The terrorist seeks to influence political behavior of a government through extranormal means, usually having tried and exhausted all conventional political options. "Terrorism" is a relatively recent political label in its common usage, although phrases such as "Reign of Terror" (in the French Revolution in 1794) demonstrate that the concept certainly existed long ago.[82]

If we look at groups generally labelled as "terrorists" today, we often find self-described "national liberation" groups (such as the Irish Republican Army fighting for independence against the British, or the Palestine Liberation Organization fighting for independence against the Israelis). This highlights one very problematic characteristic of the label "terrorist": It is strongly influenced by perspective, as the following example shows.

Menachem Begin, the prime minister of Israel from 1977 to 1984, was asked how he responded to charges that there was really no difference between his actions against the British in Palestine preceeding Israeli independence in 1948—the British referred to him at the time as a "terrorist" and offered a reward of 10,000 pounds sterling, dead or alive, for his capture—and the actions of Yassir Arafat and the Palestine Liberation Organization against Israel in recent years. Begin's response illustrated the issue of perspective perfectly. He said, "Of course there is a difference. He is a terrorist. I was a freedom fighter."[83]

"Terrorist" is also used as a label for more random acts of violence, such as one finds in the recent cases of the Japanese Red Army, the Italian Red Brigade, the West German Bader-Meinhof Gang, Saddam Hussein's act of "environmental terrorism" in dumping oil in the Persian Gulf as part of Iraq's war effort, and in the yet unused but often discussed context of "nuclear terrorism." In these cases, the terrorist motive is not nationalism, but is instead directed at some policy-related goal, such as the presence of foreign multinationals, environmental concerns, foreign policy issues, the release of "political prisoners," and the like.[84]

Guerrilla action, on the other hand, tends to be a bit different in terms of the targets sought by the participants. The usual distinction drawn suggests that guerrillas tend to focus their attention on *government* targets, usually military targets, rather than the often random *civilian* targets used by terrorists.[85] Using this distinction, the Afghan "freedom fighters" might be classified as guerrilla fighters because their targets were Soviet Army tanks, barracks, and supply depots; what distinguished them from a "conventional" army was that they weren't representing a conventional government, and they would strike and then retreat into the mountains to avoid Soviet retribution and to re-group. By contrast, an incident in which the Irish Republican Army left a bomb in front of Harrods' department store in London, killing and injuring innocent passersby, would be called an act of terrorism because the target was "random" and in no way strategic.

These and other types of political violence are of significance for the political system because they offer fundamental challenges to the institutions of the regime. They operate *outside* of the system, as it were, simply rejecting the ability of the institutions and behaviors of the political system to handle their demands.

THE POLITICAL ENVIRONMENT IN PERSPECTIVE

We have, in this chapter, briefly looked at a number of what might be called *environmental* characteristics of political regimes, in addition to the structural characteristics that we have been examining until this time. Although our discussion here has not been comprehensive, we have undertaken to introduce the student to many of the concepts currently discussed by comparativists engaged in cross-national research.

It is clear that political structures, like constitutions, cannot be examined in a vacuum. While constitutions might do a great deal to inform us about the behavior of a political regime and the relationships between and among the various actors and structures within that regime, we know from what we have already seen that there may well be a number of very significant details of the political regime that are *not* included in the constitution (such as customs, traditions, political culture, political parties, and the like). Similarly, just studying the constitutional structures of a regime may omit a number of significant political details, and to this extent other variables must be included in area studies to make them complete.

In some political regimes, an understanding of the political party system is absolutely essential for an accurate understanding of the way that the regime operates. In other systems, ideology is more important than parties. Elsewhere the political culture may be terribly significant, and so on. The fact of the matter is that the political environments within which we must study political regimes vary widely, and as we noted in Chapter 1, when we discussed the framework of a structural-functional approach to politics, significant structures in one environment will not necessarily be significant in another environment.

The remainder of this text focuses upon our area studies exercises, or "portraits." These are not full-scale studies of the political systems concerned; such an undertaking could not be expected in the amount of space allocated here. What these portraits do attempt is to provide the student with an *introduction* to the political structures and processes of *major significance* in that particular regime. Federalism is a major variable in the German political system, thus it is discussed; it is not relevant (except insofar as it does not exist) in Japan. The upper house of the legislature is significant in Germany and relatively insignificant in Great Britain; accordingly, it receives more attention in our discussion in relation to the former than the latter.

The comparative study of politics can be a fascinating and highly informative undertaking. In these days of a constantly shrinking world, where a "spaceship earth" conception of international relations is becoming more common, it is to be hoped that the student will take more of an interest in the political world outside of his or her national borders. The following mini-studies are meant to encourage the interested students to go further, to undertake more cross-national study, and to use a comparative approach in future activities of inquiry.

Notes

1. An example of the latter is G. Almond and G. Bingham Powell, eds., *Comparative Politics Today: A World View* (Boston: Little, Brown, 1980).

2. Allan Kornberg, *Canadian Legislative Behavior* (New York: Holt, Rinehart and Winston, 1967), p. 42.

3. Jean Blondel, *Comparative Legislatures* (Englewood Cliffs, N.J.: Prentice Hall, 1973), p. 76.

4. Recent work in the field of political socialization would include—but not be limited to—the following: Allan Kornberg and Harold Clarke, *Citizens and Community: Political Support in a Representative Democracy* (New York: Cambridge University Press, 1992), Roberta Sigel, ed., *Political Learning in Adulthood: A Sourcebook of Theory and Research* (Chicago: University

of Chicago Press, 1989), Bernhard Claussen and Horst Mueller, eds., *Political Socialization of the Young in East and West* (New York: Peter Land Publishing, 1990), Albert Hughes, *Political Socialization of Soviet Youth* (New York: Edwin Mellen Press, 1992), or Tawfic Farah and Yasumasa Kuroda, eds., *Political Socialization in the Arab States* (Boulder, Colo.: Lynne Rienner, 1986).

5. David Easton and Jack Dennis, *Children in the Political System* (New York: McGraw-Hill, 1969), p. 76. For other discussions of the classical heritage of the debate over socialization, see the following: Kenneth Langton, *Political Socialization* (New York: Oxford University Press, 1969), p. 3, Richard Dawson and Kenneth Prewitt, *Political Socialization* (Boston: Little, Brown, 1969), p. 6, Fred Greenstein, *Children and Politics* (New Haven, Conn.: Yale University Press, 1965), pp. 2–3, and Roberta Sigel, "Assumptions About the Learning of Political Values," *The Annals of the American Academy of Political and Social Science* 361 (1965): 1–9.

6. Edward Greenberg, *Political Socialization* (New York: Atherton, 1970), p. 3. See also Herbert Hyman, *Political Socialization* (Glencoe, Ill.: The Free Press, 1959), p. 18.

7. Easton and Dennis, *Children*, p. 7.

8. Greenstein, *Children and Politics*, p. 5.

9. Jack Dennis, ed., *Socialization to Politics* (New York: John Wiley, 1973), p. 4.

10. Ibid., p. 5.

11. Study continues to be undertaken based upon the pioneering work of Jack Dennis, including M. Chey and K. W. Kim, "Cultural Origins of Public Support for Democracy in Korea: An Empirical Test of the Douglas-Wildavsky Theory of Culture," *Comparative Political Studies* 22:2 (1989): 217–238, P. Dekker, "Ideological Identification and (de)Pillarisation in the Netherlands," *Netherlands Journal of Sociology* 26:2 (1990): 168–185, Y. Bilu, "The Other as a Nightmare: The Israeli-Arab Encounter as Reflected in Children's Dreams in Israel and the West Bank," *Political Psychology* 10:3 (1989): 365–389, and G. L. Allen, "Children's Political Socialization and Cognition," *Human Development* 32:1 (1989): 1–4.

12. See David Easton, *A Framework for Political Analysis* (Englewood Cliffs, N.J.: Prentice Hall, 1965): 124–125.

13. Dean Jaros and others, "The Malevolent Leader: Political Socialization in an American Subculture," *American Political Science Review* 62 (1968): 564–575; see also David Easton and Jack Dennis, "The Child's Image of Government," *The Annals* 361 (1965): 40–57, Robert Hess and David Easton, "The Child's Changing Image of the President," *Public Opinion Quarterly* 24 (1960): 632–644, David Easton and Robert Hess, "The Child's Political World," *Midwest Journal of Political Science* 6 (1962): 229–246, and Fred Greenstein, "The Benevolent Leader: Children's Images of Political Authority," *American Political Science Review* 54 (1960): 934–943.

14. Gabriel Almond and Sidney Verba, *The Civic Culture* (Boston: Little, Brown, 1965), p. 14.

15. Almond, "Introduction," in Gabriel Almond and James Coleman, *The Politics of the Developing Areas* (Princeton, N.J.: Princeton University Press, 1960), p. 27.

16. Raymond Hopkins, "The Role of the MP in Tanzania," *American Political Science Review* 64 (1970): 754–771.

17. Kenneth Prewitt, Heinz Eulau, and Betty Zisk, "Political Socialization and Political Roles," *Public Opinion Quarterly* 30 (1966–67): 569–583.

18. Lewis Froman and James Skipper, "An Approach to the Learning of Party Identification," *Public Opinion Quarterly* 27 (1963): 473–480.

19. Norman Nie, G. Bingham Powell, and Kenneth Prewitt, "Social Structure and Political Participation," *American Political Science Review* 63 (1969): 361–378; and Lester Milbrath, *Political Participation* (Chicago: Rand McNally, 1965).

20. Allan Kornberg and Norman Thomas, "The Political Socialization of National Legislative Elites in the United States and Canada," *Journal of Politics* 27 (1965): 761–775.

21. See, for example, Greenstein, *Children and Politics*, pp. 60–61.

22. Jean Piaget and Anne-Marie Weil, "The Development in Children of the Idea of the Homeland," *International Social Science Bulletin* 3 (1951): 561–578.

23. John Crittendon, "Aging and Political Participation," *Western Political Quarterly* 16 (1962): 648–657.

24. Dennis, *Socialization*, p. 16.

25. An example of such a study would be Allan Kornberg and Joel Smith, "Self-Concepts of American and Canadian Party Officials," *Polity* 3:1 (1970): 70–99.

26. Jaros and others, "The Malevolent Leader," pp. 564–575, and Greenstein, "The Benevolent Leader," pp. 934–943.

27. Other studies would include Dwayne Marvick, "Political Socialization of the American Negro," *The Annals* 361 (1965): 112–127; Michael Parenti, "Ethnic Politics and the Persistence of Ethnic Identification," *American Political Science Review* 61 (1967): 717–726, and Martin Levin, "Social Climates and Political Socialization," *Public Opinion Quarterly* 25 (1961): 596–606.

28. Lewis Froman, "Learning Political Attitudes," *Western Political Quarterly* 15 (1962): 304–313.

29. Greenstein, *Children and Politics*, p. 12.

30. Ibid., p. 44.

31. Ibid., p. 154.

32. Ibid., p. 71.

33. For illustrations of this type of literature, see Subrata K. Mitra, *Power, Protest, and Participation: Local Elites and Development in India* (London: Routledge, 1992), Fatima Mernissi, *The Veil and the Male Elite: A Feminist Interpretation of Women's Rights in Islam* (Reading, Mass.: Addison-Wesley, 1992), or Joseph Esherick and Mary Rankin, eds., *Chinese Local Elites and Patterns of Dominance* (Berkeley: University of California Press, 1990).

34. See Kornberg, *Canadian Legislative Behavior*, p. 42, for an example.

35. See Jean Blondel, *World Leaders: Heads of Government in the Postwar Period* (Beverly Hills, Calif.: Sage Publications, 1980), p. 115.

36. There is much discussion of this debate in the volume by Joel Silbey, ed., *The Congress of the United States: Patterns of Recruitment, Leadership, and Internal Structure, 1789–1989* (Los Alamitos, Calif.: Carlson Publishing, 1991).

37. Robert Putnam, *The Comparative Study of Political Elites* (Englewood Cliffs, N.J.: Prentice Hall, 1976), p. 46.

38. Moshe Czudnowski, "Political Recruitment," in Fred Greenstein and Nelson Polsby, eds., *Handbook of Political Science* (Reading, Mass.: Addison-Wesley, 1975), p. 159. For a European perspective, see H. Derlien, "Continuity and Change in the West German Federal Executive Elite," *European Journal of Political Research* 18:3 (1990): 349–372, or J. Wasilewski, "The Patterns of Bureaucratic Elite Recruitment in Poland in the 1970s and 1980s," *Soviet Studies* 42:4 (1990): 743–757.

39. Almond, "Introduction," p. 31.

40. Milbrath, *Political Participation*.

41. Czudnowski, "Political Recruitment," pp. 178–229.

42. Harold Clarke and Richard Price, "Political Recruitment: Theoretical Overview and Review of the Literature," in Harold Clarke and Richard Price, eds., *Recruitment and Leadership Selection in Canada* (Toronto: Holt, Rinehart, and Winston, 1976), p. 7.

43. As reported in Louis Edinger and Donald Searing, "Social Background in Elite Analysis: A Methodological Inquiry," *American Political Science Review* 59 (1967): 428–445.

44. See, for examples of such studies, the following: Donald Matthews, *U.S. Senators and Their World* (New York: Vintage Books, 1960), or Frederick Frey, *The Turkish Political Elite* (Cambridge, Mass.: M.I.T. Press, 1965).

45. M. Pederson, "Lawyers in Politics: The Danish Folketing and United States Legislatures," in Samuel Patterson and John Wahlke, eds., *Comparative Legislative Behavior: Frontiers of Research* (New York: Wiley, 1972), p. 25.

46. Ibid.

47. See Leo Snowiss, "Congressional Recruitment and Representation," *American Political Science Review* 60 (1966): 627–639.

48. A very good review of the literature on political parties can be found in Frank Belloni and Dennis Beller, eds., *Faction Politics: Political Parties and Factionalism in Comparative Perspective* (Santa Barbara, Calif.: A.B.C. Clio, 1987).

49. Kornberg, *Canadian Legislative Behavior*, p. 54.

50. Gregory Mahler, *The Knesset: Parliament in the Israeli Political System* (Rutherford, N.J.: Fairleigh Dickinson University Press, 1981), especially chap. 6.

51. Moshe Czudnowski, "Sociocultural Variables and Legislative Recruitment," *Comparative Politics* 4 (1972): 561–587, and Moshe Czudnowski, "Legislative Recruitment Under Proportional Representation in Israel: A Model and a Case Study," *Midwest Journal of Political Science* 14 (1970): 216–248.

52. Malcolm Jewell and Samuel Patterson, *The Legislative Process in the United States* (New York: Random House, 1973), p. 88.

53. See, for examples of recent work in this area, John Higley and Richard Gunther, eds., *Elites and Democratic Consolidation in Latin America and Southern Europe* (New York: Cambridge University Press, 1991), Suzanne Keller, *Beyond the Ruling Class: Strategic Elites in Modern Society* (New Brunswick, N.J.: Transaction, 1991), Jeffrey Bell, *Populism and Elitism: Politics in the Age of Equality* (Washington, D.C.: Regnery Gateway, 1992), or Eva Etzioni-Halevy, *The Elite Connection: Problems and Potential of Western Democracy* (Cambridge, Mass.: Blackwell, 1993).

54. Harold Lasswell, Daniel Lerner, and C. Easton Rothwell, *The Comparative Study of Elites* (Cambridge, Mass.: M.I.T. Press, 1965), p. 13.

55. Ibid., p. 4.

56. Bernard Berelson, Paul Lazarsfeld, and William McPhee, *Voting* (Chicago: University of Chicago Press, 1954), pp. 305–323.

57. Putnam, *Political Elites*, p. 138–139.

58. A very good discussion of these issues can be found in Peter Bachrach, ed., *Political Elites in a Democracy* (New York: Atherton, 1973).

59. Peter Y. Medding, "Patterns of Elite Consensus and Elite Competition: A Model and a Case Study," in Harold Clarke and Moshe Czudnowski, eds., *Political Elites in Anglo-American Democracies* (DeKalb: Northern Illinois University Press, 1987), pp. 17–43.

60. See Peter McDonough, "'Let Us Make the Revolution, Before the People Do': Elite-Mass Relations in Brazil," in Moshe Czudnowski, ed., *Political Elites and Social Change: Studies of Elite Roles and Attitudes* (DeKalb: Northern Illinois University Press, 1983), pp. 188–218.

61. See, for example, Samuel Decalo, *Coups and Army Rule in Africa: Motivations and Constraints* (New Haven, Conn.: Yale University Press, 1990), Francis Deng and I. William Zartman, eds., *Conflict Resolution in Africa* (Washington, D.C.: Brookings Institution, 1991), Michael Radu, *Latin American Revolutionaries: Groups, Goals, Methods* (Washington, D.C.: Pergamon-Brassey's International Defense Publishers, 1990), or Karen Remmer, *Military Rule in Latin America* (Boulder, Colo.: Westview Press, 1991).

62. See, for example, Anita Isaacs, *The Politics of Military Rule and Transition in Ecuador: Dancing with the People* (Pittsburgh: University of Pittsburgh Press, 1992), or Paul Drake and Ivan Jansic, eds., *The Struggle for Democracy in Chile, 1982–1990* (Lincoln: University of Nebraska Press, 1991).

63. Louis Goodman, Johanna Mendelson, and Juan Rial, eds., *The Military and Democracy: The Future of Civil-Military Relations in Latin America* (Lexington, Mass.: Lexington Books, 1990).

64. Eric Nordlinger, *Soldiers in Politics: Military Coups and Governments* (Englewood Cliffs, N.J.: Prentice Hall, 1977), p. 3.

65. Talukder Maniruzzaman, *Military Withdrawal from Politics: A Comparative Study* (Cambridge, Mass.: Ballinger Publishing, 1987), p. 18.

66. Nordlinger, *Soldiers*, pp. 5–6. For examples of this kind of literature see the following: William Gutteridge, *The Military in African Politics* (London: Methuen, 1969), J. Stephen Hoadley, *Soldiers and Politics in Southeast Asia: Civil-Military Relations in Comparative Perspective* (Cambridge, Mass.: Schenkman, 1975), John J. Johnson, *The Military and Society in Latin America* (Stanford, Calif.: Stanford University Press, 1964), Claude E. Welch, ed., *Soldier and State in Africa* (Evanston, Ill.: Northwestern University Press, 1970).

67. Nordlinger, *Soldiers*, p. 192.

68. Maniruzzaman, *Military Withdrawal*, p. 3.

69. Ibid., p. 205.

70. Claude E. Welch, Jr., *Civilian Control of the Military: Theory and Cases from Developing Countries* (Albany: State University of New York Press, 1976), p. 2.

71. Christopher Clapham and George Philip, *The Political Dilemmas of Military Regimes* (Totowa, N.J.: Barnes and Noble Books, 1985).

72. For examples of recent discussions of this nature, see John E. Finn, *Constitutions in Crisis: Political Violence and the Rule of Law* (New York: Oxford University Press, 1991), Christopher Hewitt, *Consequences of Political Violence* (Brookfield, Vt.: Gower, 1993), Michael Smith, *Rural Development in the Crossfire: The Role of Grassroots Support Organizations in Situations of Political Violence in Peru* (Ottawa: International Development Research Center, 1991), or Philip Schlesinger, *Media, State, and Nation: Political Violence and Collective Identities* (Beverly Hills, Calif.: Sage Publications, 1991).

73. Peter Merkl, ed., *Political Violence and Terror: Motifs and Motivations* (Berkeley: University of California Press, 1986), p. 20.

74. Ibid., pp. 32–33.

75. Two interesting sources on this topic are by Bill Stanton, *Klanwatch: Bringing the Ku Klux Klan to Justice* (New York: Dutton, 1992), and James Ridgeway, *Blood in the Face: The Ku Klux Klan, Aryan Nations, Nazi Skinheads, and the Rise of a New White Culture* (New York: Thunder's Mouth Press, 1991).

76. See Kim Sorvig, *To Heal Kent State: A Memorial Meditation* (Orlando, Fla.: World View Press, 1990).

77. These distinctions are discussed in Finn, *Constitutions in Crisis.*

78. See Yeager Hudson and Creighton Peden, *Revolution, Violence, and Equality* (Lewiston, N.Y.: Edwin Mellen Press, 1990).

79. John R. Thackrah, *Encyclopedia of Terrorism and Political Violence* (London: Routledge and Kegan Paul, 1987), p. 215.

80. Ibid., p. 42.

81. Richard Clutterbuck, *Guerrillas and Terrorists* (London: Faber and Faber, 1977), p. 21.

82. Edgar O'Ballance, *Language of Violence: The Blood Politics of Terrorism* (San Rafael, Calif.: Presidio Press, 1979), pp. 1–8.

83. Interview with the author in the Knesset, April 3, 1975.

84. See Henry Han, *Terrorism and Political Violence* (New York: Oceana Publications, 1993), or R. G. Rey and Christopher Morris, *Violence, Terrorism, and Justice* (New York: Cambridge University Press, 1991).

85. This distinction is discussed in Cynthia Brown, *In Desperate Straits: Human Rights in Peru After a Decade of Democracy and Insurgency* (New York: Human Rights Watch, 1990).

9

The British Political System

The British political system is regarded by many as the "mother" of modern democratic political systems. The institution of Parliament developed in Great Britain, and the role of the monarchy in Britain devolved to a point at which it could exist in harmony with democratic political norms. The Westminster model of parliamentary government to which we have referred again and again in this text is derived, of course, from the parliamentary system that evolved in Britain at Westminster. It seems logical, therefore, that the subject of our first area studies chapter should be Great Britain.

Many students are confused as to the distinctions that should be drawn between the names England, (Great) Britain, and the United Kingdom. These three names are, strictly speaking, not interchangeable; they refer to different political systems. The United Kingdom is a country in Western Europe with a population of nearly 60 million people and a national capital in London. The formal name of the United Kingdom (usually abbreviated U.K.) is the United Kingdom of Great Britain and Northern Ireland. (Prior to 1922, the year when Ireland was divided into Northern Ireland and the Republic of Ireland, the formal name of the U.K. was the United Kingdom of Great Britain and Ireland.) Great Britain is the principal island of the United Kingdom, and it comprises England, Scotland, and Wales. England is an administrative unit of the United Kingdom of Great Britain and Northern Ireland; it occupies most of the southern half of the island of Great Britain. Having said all of this, we should note that today the term "Britain" is generally used interchangeably with "United Kingdom" or "England," even though they do not refer to precisely the same thing.

THE BRITISH CONSTITUTION

In Chapter 2 we discussed the distinction between governments with written constitutions and those with "constitutional government," and pointed out that a political system need not have a written document entitled "Ye Olde Constitution" in order to be referred to as a constitutional regime. Indeed, the example that we used at that time was Great Britain. Students of British politics agree that for all intents and purposes there is a British Constitution, in the sense that there is a body of fundamental precepts underlying the British political regime. The fact that Britain does not have a specific document called a constitution has led some to say that Britain has no constitution. This error "confuses the constitution with what is usually only one of its sources."[1]

Britain's lack of a written constitution is certainly not a result of British inexperience with constitution writing. The British Parliament has written constitutions for a number of former territories and possessions that are today independent nations, most in the Commonwealth of Nations. In 1867 the British North America Act was passed by Parliament. It united Canada (today Ontario and Quebec) with Nova Scotia and New Brunswick to form the Dominion of Canada (we shall return to a study of Canada's political system later in this text). Australia received its constitution in 1901. The Union of South Africa Constitution was passed in 1909. New Zealand was granted responsible government in 1852.[2] Many, many constitutions have been written for newly independent countries—formerly members of the British Empire—since that time.

Constitutions of political regimes can frequently be said to have several components: (1) written charters or collections of historic documents, (2) legislative statutes of "constitutional" significance, (3) judicial interpretation, and (4) customs and precedents.

> If the core of the constitution consists of a written document adopted or promulgated at a particular time, the state is said to have a written constitution. If, on the other hand, there is no such single document, the state is usually considered to possess an unwritten constitution. The importance of such a classification may be easily exaggerated. The "written" constitutions acquire many unwritten parts and through the years they become overlaid with legislative amplifications, judicial interpretations, and customary provisions. The "unwritten" ones usually have important parts committed to paper as charters or broad constitutional statutes. In the course of time the two types come more and more to resemble one another.[3]

One scholar of the British constitutional system suggests that there are essentially three sources from which the British Constitution emanates: statutory law (Acts of Parliament), common law and judicial decisions, and "the customs of the Constitution."[4] Although there is no single document that can be called "the" British

Constitution, scholars agree that fundamentally this is not significant; whether or not there is a single document, Britain has a constitution.

Statutory law is law that derives from Acts of Parliament. These acts result from a prescribed legislative process in the British Parliament—the House of Commons and the House of Lords. We should note that while not all Acts of Parliament can or should be regarded as constitutional acts, "there is scarcely a session of Parliament that does not contribute to the constitutional structure statutes that add to or alter the basic law of the land."[5] As indicated above, constitutional acts are those that address broad or fundamental questions of major significance to the regime—questions relating to the monarchy, the Parliament, rights and freedoms of citizens, elections, and the like. Acts that are usually considered to be part of the "unwritten" British Constitution include the Magna Carta (1215), the Petition of Right (1626), the Habeas Corpus Act (1679), the Bill of Rights (1689), the Act of Settlement (1701), the Acts of Union with Scotland (1707) and Ireland (1800), the Great Reform Act (1832), the Parliament Act (1911), and the Statute of Westminster (1931), among many others.[6]

Common-law sources of constitutional doctrines are a bit harder to pin down, for they are by nature less precise. Common law, by definition, is concerned with customs; according to Blackstone, they are "not set down in any written statute or ordinance, but depending on immemorial usage for their support."[7] Many judicial decisions eventually become part of the body of common law in a political system, and acquire "constitutional" status over time. Generally speaking, judicial interpretation is of less significance in the British Constitution than in the U.S. Constitution. Because Britain operates under a system of legislative supremacy, with no judicial review of legislative statutes, the British judiciary has a lower profile than its American counterpart. As one observer has noted: "The British courts, however, in interpreting and clarifying the law frequently declare what the constitution is. The civil liberties of British subjects are largely embedded in the common law and thus have been defined and protected by the courts."[8]

The third source of British constitutional doctrine has been referred to as "customs of the Constitution." A number of these customs may be highlighted here:

1. The Cabinet consists of members of, and is responsible to, Parliament.
2. The Sovereign does not attend Cabinet meetings.
3. The Sovereign does not withhold assent from (veto) Bills which have passed the two Houses of Parliament.
4. The Speaker (presiding officer) of the House of Commons takes no part in political controversy.[9]

These four points are illustrative of the many customs of behavior that have evolved over the years in the British political system to the point that they can be referred to as being "constitutional" in nature today. Although the monarch today may *legally* retain the right to veto or withhold assent from an act of the British Parliament, it would be regarded as *unconstitutional* for her to do so.[10] This distinction may strike many students as being quite curious, that an action may be at the same time both *legal* and *unconstitutional.* The law may permit an action that has, through custom over time, become impermissible. This is a valid distinction, and an important one to recall.

It has been suggested that it is important to distinguish "between the Constitution and the principles which underlie it. The Principles are in one sense more important than the Constitution itself." Constitutions may change, through statutory acts, common law, judicial decisions, or custom—but principles remain.[11] Two fundamental principles underlie the British Constitution. The first principle involves the *rule of law.* Citizens are entitled to the protection of law, and both individuals and the government of the state are to be limited in what they can do by the law of the regime. The second principle is that *Parliament is sovereign,* a principle that we suggested earlier in this chapter. This point can be elaborated on as follows: (1) There is no law of an earlier Parliament that the current Parliament cannot change if it wishes to do so; (2) there is no clear distinction between "constitutional" Acts of Parliament and Acts of Parliament that are not "constitutional"; and (3) no person or body (for instance, the courts) can nullify an Act of Parliament on the grounds that the act is opposed to the Constitution.[12] Thus anything the British Parliament does, is by definition constitutional.

A number of structural characteristics of the British political system can be regarded as almost "constitutional" in their significance for, and centrality in, the regime.[13] First, the United Kingdom is a unitary political system, not a federal system. There is no "sharing" of power between the national government and some intermediate level of government; there is no intermediate level of government in the United Kingdom to correspond to states in the United States or provinces in Canada or Länder in Germany. This is significant in that Parliament thereby becomes more relevant to the daily routine of life in Britain because it influences many aspects of life affected by intermediate levels of government in other political systems.

Second, as we noted earlier in this text, the Westminster model generally is composed of four parts. First, the chief executive is not the same as the head of state. Second, the executive powers of government are exercised by the chief executive and his or her cabinet. Third, the chief executive and the cabinet all come from and are part of the legislature. Fourth, the chief executive and the cabinet are responsible to, and can be fired by, the legislature. This Westminster model differs significantly from the American system in that there is no clear separation of powers, which is so important to the American political culture. The concern of the American Founding Fathers over "checks and balances" simply is not to be found in the Westminster political structure. The political executive is actually part of the legislature, and the courts do not have the power to limit what the legislature does.

A third political structure identified with the British constitutional regime, and which was implied in the preceding paragraph, is that the prime minister and cabinet are drawn from, and are responsible to, the national legislature. Although occasionally some cabinet members may not be from the legislature, the prime minister and the bulk of the cabinet will invariably be from the House of Commons (or whatever the name of the lower, elected, house of the national legislature is in other systems modelled after the British Parliament). They will remain in office only as long as they continue to be supported by a majority of the lower house of the national legislature.

A fourth major significant political structure in the British system is that of political parties. Political parties are so much a part of the British political system that it is almost impossible to imagine British politics operating in their absence.

THE BRITISH EXECUTIVE

The British system, as we have made clear, is the model for the "split executive" parliamentary model that we described and discussed earlier in this text. The role of the monarch is one that has evolved over a long period of time; its function is one of both substance and style. George Orwell, the noted English author, observed in 1944 that:

> in a dictatorship the power and the glory belong to the same person. In England the real power belongs to unprepossessing men in bowler hats: the creature who rides in a gilded coach behind soldiers in steel breastplates is really a waxwork. It is at any rate possible that while this division of functions exists a Hitler or a Stalin cannot come to power.[14]

The Monarch

In our earlier discussion of the political executive, a brief outline of the evolution—perhaps *devolution* is a more appropriate term—of the power of the British monarchy was presented, tracing the many changes in the influence of the British monarch in the political system. We saw at that time that while at one point the monarch had absolute power to promulgate laws, fire the legislature, and imprison political opponents, the situation changed radically (but gradually) over time. As democratic institutions became more popular they also became more powerful, and the ability of the reigning monarch to resist reform diminished. Monarchs more sympathetic to liberal ideas, such as William and Mary (who were proclaimed king and queen by Parliament in 1688), helped the process to maintain, and in fact to increase, its momentum.

Today, not even William and Mary would recognize the relationship between the monarch and the Parliament. *De jure*, under law, most powers of British government are still exercised in the name of the king or queen, but today they are exercised "on the advice" of the chief executive. In the eighteenth and nineteenth centuries, the king relied more and more on his cabinet—a group of advisors—for guidance. In the early eighteenth century, the role of the cabinet was only that of providing *advice*; the king still did as he pleased.

As ideas of democratic and republican government took hold over the next two centuries, the power relationship changed so that the king was now *obligated* (although not *legally* required) to accept the advice of his cabinet. Cabinet members now were exclusively drawn from the chamber of Parliament that was chosen by the public, namely the House of Commons. Now the cabinet was in reality governing in the name of the king without consulting him.

The monarch has the constitutional right, as Bagehot put it, to be consulted, to advise, and to warn. When Anthony Eden resigned as Foreign Secretary in 1938, King George VI protested to Neville Chamberlain, the Prime Minister, that he had not been kept properly informed. It is clearly a valuable safeguard that Prime Ministers should be under such an obligation, and should have to bear it in mind when they may be tempted to arbitrary action. Cabinet papers, Foreign Office dispatches from overseas posts, and major departmental memoranda are sent to the Monarch.[15]

"The elaborate pretense that the Queen is still the real ruler of Britain still decorates the machinery of British government," has noted one observer. Two examples of this pretence can be offered here by way of illustration. All Royal Commissions begin with a message from the monarch: "Greeting! Now Know Ye That We, reposing great trust and confidence in your knowledge and ability. . . ." Legislative acts begin with the words "Be it enacted by the Queen most Excellent Majesty, by and with the advice and consent of the Lords Spiritual and Temporal, and Commons, in this present Parliament assembled. . . ."[16]

The most visible example of the "royal pretence," though, occurs on an annual basis when the queen opens the session of Parliament, seated on her throne in the House of Lords. She "summons the Commons" to the chamber of the House of Lords and reads her "speech from the throne," in which she outlines the plans she has for "her" government. The fraud here, of course, is that the speech that she reads is written by the prime minister and cabinet; like a puppet, she says whatever she is told to say.[17]

The Selection of the Chief Executive

Among the most striking characteristics of British parliamentary government today is the duality of its executive leadership, as we mentioned earlier. The monarch is the official (*de jure*) head of state, but the active (*de facto*) head of government is the prime minister. Appointments are made, acts of Parliament are proclaimed, and all government is carried on in the name of the monarch. It is the prime minister and his or her cabinet, however, who make all the selections for appointments, who author or sponsor legislative proposals, and who make the administrative decisions that keep government running. The legal claim to power of the cabinet rests in the fact that, since the seventeenth century, the monarch has had a *Privy Council* to advise him or her—a kind of present-day cabinet. Today, although the Privy Council is no longer active, cabinet members must *first* be made members of the Privy Council, and *then* are appointed to the cabinet.[18] The cabinet meets as a subcommittee of the (inactive) Privy Council and acts in the name of the Privy Council.

> The Privy Council has survived as the formal machinery through which the monarch exercises her prerogative powers when necessary. Although membership of the Privy Council is extensive, comprising all past and present cabinet ministers and a number of other public figures to a total of about three hundred in all, its working character is that of a small number of ministers who are called together to witness the signature by the monarch of some formal document.[19]

Although the British monarch was free to choose whomever he or she wanted as advisors in the seventeenth and eighteenth centuries, such is no longer the case today. As soon as election returns are in, if an incumbent prime minister's party has lost its majority, this person submits his or her resignation to the queen, and subsequently the new majority leader in the House of Commons is "invited" to form a government. Symbolically the act is described as "the queen has invited Mrs. Thatcher to form a Government," or "the queen has invited Mr. Major to form a Government." But this is not a realistic description of the process today; there really is no alternative for the Queen to the invitation that is issued.

"In theory, the Queen has the right both to dissolve parliament and to choose the prime minister"—the first power has not really been exercised in the past hundred years; the second power "only recently has become a fiction."[20] This lack of real power in the selection of a prime minister is, to a very large degree, the result of clear majorities existing in the House of Commons with "obvious" prime ministerial choices. Should some future election produce an inconclusive result, with no clear majority present in the House of Commons, the monarch may again be called upon to take part in the selection process.

The Cabinet and the Prime Minister

In his classic work on the British cabinet, Sir Ivor Jennings wrote in 1951 that "it is a peculiarity of our Constitution that the principles governing the formation and working of the Cabinet and its relations with Parliament can be stated with hardly any reference to the law."[21] In the twentieth century, the British Parliament finally took statutory notice of the cabinet when it passed the Ministers of the Crown Act (1937), naming a number of "cabinet rank" positions and fixing appropriate salaries for the positions.[22]

The development of the position of prime minister is generally regarded as following the evolution of the cabinet itself. The earliest of cabinets, it will be recalled, were simply collections of advisors to powerful monarchs. Cabinet members held little power, and none was first among the group of equals. George I (who ruled from 1714 to 1727) started the practice of having his cabinet meet in his absence. The result of this:

> was to transform what had been a mere inner group of royal advisors into a board of government with an independent existence of its own. Having lost its natural president, it was inevitable that it should find one of its own, a "prime minister" in fact, upon whom would fall the task of coordinating policy, which before had been the King's.[23]

The first "modern" prime minister is usually cited as being Sir Robert Walpole, who held office from 1721 to 1742.

Ever since World War II the style and power of prime ministers have varied, and the range of roles played by the prime minister "has prompted a long-running debate about the power of the Prime Minister between 'the presidential school' and 'the chairmanship school.'"[24] One student of the office has observed that "prime ministers do not have to be exceptional individuals in order to dominate their ministries." There are devices by which even less exceptional individuals can keep their colleagues under control, such as assignments to cabinet committees, the frequency with which cabinet meetings are held, and even periodic reconstruction of the cabinet.[25]

The prime minister is first minister of the cabinet, but the power exercised by the incumbent of that position varies widely depending upon the political environment of the time. Some British prime ministers have had a tremendous amount of power; others have simply been in the role of "chairman of the board." "Viewed from the top, British government looks more like a mountain range than a single pyramid of power. The Prime Minister is preeminent among these peaks, but the political significance of this preeminence is ambiguous."[26]

Although the prime minister has traditionally received the bulk of the attention of scholarship related to the executive branch of government in Britain, there has been some scholarship in recent years that focuses upon the cabinet itself and upon individual ministers. As one scholar has noted, it is ministries that "are responsible for converting public resources into the programme outputs of the mixed economy welfare state, such as defence, health, agriculture, and education."[27] It is the ministers, after all, who are responsible for maintaining some degree of continuity in the various ministries, and who are responsible for gathering resources for public programs. It is the ministers who are in a position to oversee and—to some degree—direct the vast civil service, a subject to which we shall return shortly.

The individual ministries are also important to some degree because they may serve as a step to the prime ministership for a given individual. Some ministries (such as Treasury or Defence) have more status than others (such as Agriculture or the Welsh Office).[28]

Individual ministers have several different constituencies that must be kept in mind, simultaneously, as they perform their jobs. First, they must direct their own ministries, thus being in a position of responsibility for a vast network of civil service employees. Second, they must be aware of and responsible to Parliament, for the Government as a whole is responsible to Parliament for what it does. Third, they must respond to the needs and desires of the public outside of Westminster, including their own political parties, trade unions, chambers of commerce, professional organizations and interest groups, as well as international factors.[29]

The cabinet has varied in size in this century, ranging from 16 to 23 members; at the present time it has 21 members.[30] This size is a function of both the preferences of the prime minister and the political situation of the time. Although the prime minister may have a free hand in the selection of his or her cabinet—in that the monarch will appoint to the cabinet whomever the prime minister requests—this "free hand" is not *totally* free. The prime minister is guided by a number of factors:

1) the need to include as many of the leading members of his party as possible and to represent the various groups and shades of opinion;

2) the convenience of having a reasonable number of reliable friends and close supporters;

3) the need to achieve adequate co-ordination between departments;

4) the desirability of avoiding friction and jealousy between the "ins" and the "outs" as well as to silence potential critics.[31]

The role of the prime minister in the British political system can be analytically broken down into seven different components.[32] First, the prime minister is concerned with *party management.* The prime minister holds that office precisely because the individual is head of his or her party in the House of Commons, and prime ministers must be careful during their tenure in that office to maintain party support. Certainly one way to do this is through party patronage; much of the prime minister's influence is said to stem from the exercise of patronage—appointments to either cabinet-level or subcabinet-level positions. This patronage ensures a good deal of the necessary support for a prime minister. A majority of the 635 members of the House of Commons is 318; by the time a prime minister appoints about twenty MPs to cabinet positions, and another sixty to subcabinet-rank positions, and yet another two to three dozen to positions of parliamentary private secretary, this individual has a bloc of almost one-third of the votes necessary for remaining in office.

The Government exists strictly because it controls a majority in the House of Commons. "In theory, the House of Commons controls the Government, the latter is responsible to the former. . . . In practice, through the party system the Government controls the House." The ultimate weapon of the Government to keep its party members in control is the power of dissolution, but this is too severe a threat to bandy about lightly. "The majority must be treated with respect and given reasonably full information in response to questions. . . . Even the strongest Governments have been known to bow to 'the sense of the House'."[33]

The relationship between the House of Commons and the prime minister and cabinet is one that has traditionally received a good deal of attention. A modern classic in this area is Bernard Crick's *The Reform of Parliament.*[34] Crick argued that there has been a decline in the power of Parliament to the extent that British government is no longer really parliamentary government, but is really simply cabinet government.

> Experience between 1976 and 1979 showed that it is for the Government itself to decide when its majority must be considered as lost. So long as the [Labour] Callaghan Government could rely on the Liberal Party's support in any vote of confidence, it was prepared to accept a number of defeats which might have prompted another Government to dissolve Parliament.
>
> In other words, the vital votes, other than those of no confidence, are those the Government chooses to regard as such; then the possibility of calling a second vote normally allows any intra-party rebellions to be contained by permitting the rebels to return to the party fold on the crucial question of confidence after voting against the leadership on the substantive issue.[35]

The second major job of a prime minister involves the *timing and winning of a general election.* Although six of the ten individuals who have become prime minister since World War II assumed their office in the middle of a Parliament—including the current prime minister, John Major, who was chosen by the Conservatives in

Parliament to succeed Margaret Thatcher when she retired in November 1990—"winning" a national election is necessary for a prime minister to retain his or her power. Assuming that a Parliament does not die simply by the "efflux of time"—that is, the legally set maximum term of Parliament has been reached and elections must be called—only the prime minister has the power to choose a date for a national election (and to advise the monarch to dissolve Parliament and call for an election on a given day). Prime ministers want to set election dates such that balloting day coincides with their parties' popular periods, not with inevitable slippages in popularity.

Winning an election in his own right was very important to John Major to establish his own power base and legitimacy. Major indicated on the morning after the April 9, 1992, national general election that "I can now accept that the country have elected me in my own right. . . . I am immensely proud of that."[36] More than just pride was at stake, because Major needed an election to demonstrate to his party in Parliament that he could, in fact, receive the level of public support necessary to rule.

A third dimension of activity for the prime minister involves his or her *image in Parliament.* Contacts in both the majority and opposition parties must be nurtured. Until World War II, the prime minister was personally "Leader of the House of Commons." Since that time other requirements have prevented the prime minister from holding this position personally, but the prime minister must still be aware of, and concerned with, happenings in the House of Commons.

Related to this is a fourth facet of the prime minister's role: participating in *parliamentary question time.* Twice a week the prime minister appears in the House of Commons to answer parliamentary questions, primarily from the members of the Opposition. Prime ministers take this activity seriously, as a poor performance can affect both their image in Parliament and their image with the public. Accordingly, prime ministers devote a significant amount of time to preparation for this encounter. One student of this phenomenon indicated that "on two nights a week the Prime Minister receives up to three boxes of files in preparation for the next day's ordeal, reading these ahead of Cabinet papers or Foreign Office telegrams."[37]

Yet another dimension of the prime minister's activity involves *debating policy.* The prime minister does not devote a great deal of his or her time to general debate; this individual's energies are focused elsewhere. Research has shown that in a typical year the prime minister will participate in only six major debates, which are usually on only three issues: international affairs, the economy, and the business of the Government.[38] As far as general debate is concerned, the prime minister usually has ministers in charge of relevant departments articulate the Government's position in a debate.

Prime ministers are also concerned with *press publicity.* The prime minister, after all, must worry about the general image of his or her Government, and there is continuous activity on the part of prime ministers to convince the public that their party merits public support. Generally speaking, the press is happy to oblige the prime minister with media attention; this is an example of a symbiotic relationship in which both the prime minister and the press profit from media coverage of the prime minister.

The seventh and final component of behavior of the prime minister is one to which we have already alluded: *chairing the cabinet.* The one or two times a week that the prime minister sits down with the heads of the various departments of government allows for crucial policy discussion to take place, as well as for communication of problems from ministers to the prime minister. All cabinet members are affected by the principle of "collective responsibility." This means that the cabinet as a whole is responsible for acts of the Government, and no member of the cabinet may attack or criticize actions of the Government after a collective policy decision has been made.

The cabinet meeting provides an opportunity for recalcitrant ministers to air their views; beyond this their only recourse is to resign from the cabinet. The rule of collective responsibility applies to the prime minister and departmental ministers, so it is important for the prime minister to use the cabinet meeting to find out what his or her Government is doing. "Constitutionally, a Cabinet decision takes precedence over the wishes of an individual Minister, including the Prime Minister."[39] Because a prime minister does not want to be in a position in which he or she is fighting with a majority of his or her own party leaders, the prime minister will often lead by following the decisions of the cabinet.

Margaret Thatcher and "Thatcherism"

The arrival of Margaret Thatcher as prime minister in May 1979 affected British politics significantly and "changed the nature of contemporary Conservatism,"[40] notwithstanding her sudden and unexpected departure from the public arena in 1990. Thatcher's strong anti-socialist and anti-union style was not an example of a consensual style of leadership: She knew what she wanted to accomplish, and she worked in a determined manner to accomplish it. She introduced a style to contemporary British politics that came to be known first as "conviction politics," and subsequently as "Thatcherism."

> "Thatcherism" is more usefully regarded as a style than as an ideology: an ideology is a consistent system of ideas whereas what she called her conviction politics were largely instinctive and very much the product of her own experience. These instincts were narrow in range, dogmatically voiced; that she came to be credited with an "ism," a most un-Tory achievement, is a tribute to the force of her beliefs rather than to their coherence.[41]

If conviction politics meant engaging in an ideological battle within her own party, she was quite willing to do so.[42] Indeed, many observers of British politics have indicated that "the main feature of the first Thatcher administration was the Prime Minister's near total dominance over economic policy formation."[43]

When Thatcher moved into 10 Downing Street the British economy was weak, and she had a goal of "reshaping the public sector."[44] She sought to turn the economy around, to a substantial degree through legislation nullifying many of the socialist policies that had been directing the economy for years, and engaging in direct conflict with the powerful labor unions.[45] In the 1979 campaign, Thatcher had called for "a radical 'counter revolution' to set the people free," declaring that:

the last two decades had seen an inexorable rise in government spending, accounting for 33 percent of the nation's GDP in 1959 and 41 percent in 1978; a dangerous growth in trade union power; a diminution in freedom of choice; and a decline in moral standards and law and order. [She] saw the ratchet shifting slowly but surely leftwards, with the country on the verge of becoming an Eastern European–style socialist state. The 1979 election was thus depicted as the "last chance" to halt this movement and to restore the proper balance between the individual and the state.[46]

The Thatcher government "privatized" a number of government-owned industries (for instance, overseeing the conversion of British Telecom from a government-run business to a private corporation with stockholders).[47] The government cut subsidies, reduced services, and fought with local governments, which—often still controlled by the Labour opposition party—sought to move into policy areas vacated by the central government. After her 1983 reelection, Margaret Thatcher continued in the same directions: "Inflation would be brought lower, public expenditure and borrowing firmly controlled, taxes cut. This time there was a list of industries to be privatised. . . . "[48]

Ultimately, Thatcher's "conviction style" of politics—specifically her insistence on new taxes and her opposition to further integrating Britain into the European economy—alienated even most of her supporters in the Conservative Party. In November 1990, Margaret Thatcher's leadership of the Conservative Party was challenged by former (Conservative) Defence Minister Michael Heseltine. Heseltine received enough votes on the first ballot of the party leadership vote to convince Thatcher that she would not win, and she indicated that she would resign as leader and prime minister once the party selected a new leader. On the next ballot, it was not Heseltine, but Thatcher's hand-picked successor, John Major, who was elected leader of the Conservative Party. The day after that vote Margaret Thatcher visited the queen to submit her resignation, and the queen "invited" Major to form a Government.

Since that time John Major has steered a more moderate Conservative line, and the Conservative Party was re-elected under Major's leadership in April 1992. During his first year-and-a-half as prime minister, Major did away with some of the taxes created by Thatcher's government that were especially unpopular, played a significant role in the Persian Gulf war, and actively worked with other European leaders to negotiate the Maastricht Treaty for European unity. His re-election in 1992—the fourth straight win for the Conservative Party—showed that a substantial proportion of the British public supported his record.

THE CIVIL SERVICE

It was suggested previously that the civil service is an integral part of British government and politics.[49] When cabinet ministers seek to have policy implemented, it is through the civil service that they operate. The civil service is, ostensibly, nonpolitical, and its function is to administer the policies of the government of the day.

The issue of the political role of the civil service came to the fore on several highly visible and politically controversial issues in the 1980s. One case involved the

Official Secrets Act (1911) and the leaking of certain documents to the House of Commons, documents critical of government policy in the 1982 Falklands war against Argentina. Another case involved whether the testimony of civil servants could be required by the Defence Committee of the House of Commons in its investigation into a scandal involving military contracts to manufacture helicopters. Still another case involved a former intelligence agent and dealt with the degree to which he was free to publish his memoirs.[50]

All of these cases were significant in helping to define the role of the civil servant as an apolitical employee of the government. Recent studies have indicated that today nearly 600,000 civil servants work for the British government (down from a high of 732,000 in 1979), about one-sixth of them working in the Inner London area.[51] Only a very small proportion of the civil servants are high-ranking policymakers; the vast majority are individuals working in offices of the many government agencies around the nation. Recent governments have been concerned with the higher ranks of the civil service because "civil service and administrative reforms have been seen as intimately linked to the 'sharp end' of the Government's policy outputs."[52]

The high-ranking civil servants, sometimes referred to as "Mandarins," play an important role in government. The Permanent Secretaries, the highest nonpolitical appointments in the civil service, provide the continuity and expertise that link one government to the next. "The relationship between ministers and permanent secretaries has been described as 'the vital joint in Whitehall—the elbow of government, between decision and execution'."[53] One study of this relationship has concluded that "civil servants have more influence, and ministers less, than constitutional theory suggests."[54]

The British civil service has been modified in several ways since the arrival of Margaret Thatcher as prime minister. Management structures, financial organization, privatization, and reorganization have all contributed to a decrease in the cost of running the central government bureaucracy. Some observers have noted, however, that most of these modifications have been at the edges of the bureaucracy, in one case "concentrated on the 2 percent of the Department's budget which it spends on running itself," and that essentially little of substance has been accomplished in the way of reform.[55]

LOCAL GOVERNMENT

Another area of government in Great Britain that cannot be ignored is the local level. Although we earlier referred to Britain as a unitary, and not a federal, government because all sovereignty was based at Westminster, it is the case that although ultimate sovereignty resides at Westminster, the central government has decentralized many governmental functions, and local government is often significant in Britain.

This became especially true after Thatcherism began to reshape many fundamental domestic policies of the central government. In regions of Britain where Thatcher's Conservative Party was very unpopular, local governments sought to continue many of the programs that Thatcher was discontinuing or cutting back at the national level.[56] This resulted, ultimately, in Thatcher's pushing a bill through Parliament that did away with some local governments (such as the Greater London Council, for example). She also put a number of different systems into operation that sought to establish limits on the financial resources of the local governments.[57] Similarly, the Thatcher government sought to regulate and limit the powers of the QUANGOs (Quasi-Autonomous Non-Government Organisations), which were so much a part of the British state that had developed through the late 1970s.[58]

The theme that permeated the Thatcher years more than any other, according to one student of the period, was the search by the central government "for more effective instruments of control (not influence) over the expenditures of sub-central government. . . . The government has also sought to restrict the size of the public sector by privatization."[59]

THE BRITISH PARLIAMENT

We have already discussed the manner in which the British political system came to be bicameral: The House of Lords evolved as a political structure prior to the creation of the House of Commons. In Britain, a bicameral national legislature is not a function of a federal regime as is the case in the United States, Germany, or Canada. Instead, it is a result of a class-conscious society and political evolution.

For a brief period of time, from 1649 to 1660, the House of Commons declared that the House of Lords "was useless and dangerous" and was accordingly "wholly abolished and taken away."[60] The House of Lords was revived in 1660, and since that time the relationship between the two houses has passed through three distinct phases. The first phase, from 1660 to 1810, saw a period of general predominance of the House of Lords, although the House of Commons was not without influence.

Between 1811 and 1911, a number of changes took place that affected the relationship between the two houses. The Reform Acts of 1832, 1867, and 1884 strengthened the House of Commons in relation to the House of Lords. The increased acceptance of the idea that the cabinet should be responsible to the House of Commons (and should, therefore, resign if the House of Commons should fail to support its policies) clearly limited the future role of the House of Lords. When the House of Lords rejected a number of Government bills that had passed the House of Commons in 1910, the Government pushed through The Parliament Act of 1911, which limited the power of the Lords in two aspects: (1) Money bills could only be delayed for one month after being approved by the House of Commons, and then they became law even without the approval of the Lords; and (2) other public bills could be delayed for up to two years, after which time they would become law with only the approval of the Commons. (This period was shortened to one year by The Parliament Act of 1949.) The Parliament Act of 1911, which institutionalized these two radical limitations on the power of the House of Lords, was passed by the Lords only after it became clear that if they failed to do so, the king was prepared to appoint enough new peers sympathetic to the bill to guarantee its passage.[61]

The third phase, from 1911 to the present time, has seen the House of Commons as the clearly dominant power in the relationship. The House of Lords no longer challenges major legislative policy of the Government. It occasionally revises or amends bills, and has been known to oppose outright acts of the Commons; under the Parliament Act of 1911, however, its power to influence the policy of the Government is severely limited.[62]

The House of Lords

One of the major roles of the House of Lords is not legislative at all, but judicial. The House of Lords inherited a number of judicial functions from the *Curia Regis*, and is now the supreme judicial tribunal of the United Kingdom. Originally, the entire House of Lords acted as an appeals court; in 1876 an act was passed allowing for the appointment to the House of Lords of "Lords of Appeal in Ordinary," who held peerage for life only. (That is, their membership in the House of Lords was only for those individuals, and would not be hereditary and thereby passed to their children.) Today there is a special Appellate Committee of the House of Lords, specially appointed Lords who sit on an Appellate Court for Britain.

The House of Lords may not act as a "constitutional court" as is the case with the U.S. Supreme Court, however. Since there is no single "written" British Constitution, all legislation in Britain that is properly passed is constitutional and cannot be voided.

The nonjudicial function of the House of Lords has been said to have four components:

1. The examination and revision of Bills brought from the House of Commons. . . .
2. The initiation of Bills dealing with subjects of a comparatively non-controversial character. . . .
3. The interposition of so much delay (and no more) in the passing of a Bill into law as may be needed to enable the opinion of the nation to be adequately expressed upon it...
4. Full and free discussion of large and important questions. . . . [63]

Early in its existence, prior to the seventeenth century, "there were usually between seventy and one hundred persons who sat in the House of Lords in response to the King's writ of summons."[64] Today there are almost 800 hereditary peers and peeresses and 350 life peers and peeresses. Additionally, membership of the House of Lords includes twenty Law Lords and twenty-six Lords Spiritual (bishops and archbishops in the Church of England). One source has calculated that among the regular attendees in the House of Lords, 49 percent support the Conservative Party, 16 percent support the Labour Party, 10 percent support the Liberal-Social Democratic Alliance, and 25 percent are "independent 'crossbenchers'."[65]

A number of efforts have been undertaken to "reform" the House of Lords, but none has been effective. Some argue that the House of Lords should be replaced by an elected second chamber. Others have argued that the second chamber should simply be abolished. Still others have argued that if the House of Lords is retained, at least its members should be elected, and not appointed, with their positions not to be inherited by their children.

One response to the demand for reform has been the introduction of life peerages. Since the late nineteenth century, more and more members of the House of Lords have been appointed as life peers. They serve as members of the House of Lords as long as they live, but their titles are not on passed to their heirs, as is the case with normal peerages. The life peerages Act (1958) has resulted in a great increase in the number of life peers in the House of Lords, and since 1964 few new hereditary peerages have been created.[66]

One idea proposed in 1948 was that women should be permitted to serve in the House of Lords, but the tradition-conscious House of Lords opposed the idea. peeresses, women who inherited a seat in the House of Lords from their fathers in the absence of a male heir, were forbidden from sitting and voting in the House of Lords. This policy has since been changed, and today there are a number of peeresses in the House of Lords.[67]

Only since 1963 has it been possible for individuals to resign from the House of Lords—to renounce their peerages. Traditionally, one could not renounce one's title; since the law forbade individuals from serving in both Houses of Parliament, if a member of the House of Commons had a father who was a peer in the House of Lords, and his father died, that Commons member had to resign his seat in the Commons and take his father's seat in the Lords. He could not simply renounce his new peerage and stay in the Commons. In 1963, party leaders in Parliament agreed to allow peers to renounce their positions, thus allowing members of the House of Commons who "accidentally" became peers to retain their elected positions.[68]

The House of Commons

We saw earlier that the original *raison d'être* of the House of Commons was fundraising; the king needed to raise more money than the House of Lords could provide, and politically he could do so only by summoning representatives of the public. Early Parliaments were primarily concerned with two tasks: First, they agreed to requests from the king for money; second, as a *quid pro quo* for giving the king money, they presented the king with petitions of grievances.

The nineteenth century was a period of reform for the House of Commons, during which time the franchise was expanded and direct representation was improved. The Reform Act of 1867 allowed all householders to vote, as well as all persons occupying lodgings of an annual value of £10 or more. Similar measures were enacted for Scotland and Ireland in 1868. The Ballot Act of 1872 brought secret voting, and the Reform Act of 1884 further expanded suffrage. (Women over 30 were first allowed to vote in 1918; in 1928, requirements for women to vote were made the same as those for men.)[69]

The development of the cabinet in the eighteenth century greatly changed the role of the House of Commons.[70] The position of the Speaker became very important for the behavior of the House. The Speaker was originally perceived as the king's representative in the House; by 1640, the Speaker was the representative of the House of Commons to the king. Today, the Speaker has great power to control debate and legislation. Speakers are elected by a new House of Commons immediately after a general election. The majority party nominates a candidate who invariably wins on a party-line vote. The Speaker will maintain his or her (and at this writing it is "her," with the 1992 election of Betty Boothroyd as Britain's first "Madame Speaker" of the House of Commons) position for the life of the Parliament. He or she can suspend a member from the House should the member's behavior be perceived as sufficiently disruptive to merit such a punishment.

Although it was not always thus, a filibuster—unlimited debate to block legislative action—is no longer possible in the House of Commons. Members of Parliament whose speech is repetitious or irrelevant, or who are clearly attempting to procrastinate, may be ruled out of order by the Speaker. Debate may be limited by the Speaker, and ever since 1968 the Speaker has not even been required to give reasons for not accepting motion for debate.[71] Moreover, debate can be controlled by the Government through use of a number of technical devices so as to have its legislative program passed.

One of the most important functions of the House is to serve as a link between the people and the government. There is a wide range of pressure groups in Britain, and these groups regularly focus their efforts upon the House of Commons. In the Thatcher era, however, the pressure groups were not as successful as they had been in earlier years.[72] "The experience of the first two years of the 1979 Conservative government shows that Governments can, in the medium term at any rate, ignore a wide range of political pressures if they want to."[73]

Legislation

There are a number of different types of legislation in the British House of Commons. We can initially distinguish between *Government bills* and *private members' bills.* Government bills are bills that are introduced and sponsored by the cabinet, and to which strong party discipline is applied. These bills are virtually assured of passage and account for an overwhelming share of the legislation in the House of Commons. Private members' bills are proposals for legislation that are introduced by noncabinet members (including members of the majority party who are not in the cabinet, as well as by members of all of the opposition parties).

When the Parliament that had been elected in October 1974 adjourned in August 1978, in its almost four-year session it had passed 48 private members' bills into law, only 11.5 percent of the 417 private members' bills that had been introduced over that period. In comparison, nearly 93 percent of the Government bills introduced during the same period were passed into law.[74] Private members' bills are legally restricted in only one way: they may not deal with money, either raising it or spending it. Moreover, private members' bills are placed on a separate calendar, usually handled only on Friday afternoons, and few members of Parliament have the opportunity to introduce their own proposals over the course of a legislative session because of the limitation of time.[75]

Since there would not be time in a legislative session for all members of Parliament who wanted to submit private members' bills of their own to do so, a "ballot," or drawing, is held at the beginning of each new legislative session in the fall to determine which members of Parliament will have the opportunity to introduce their own pieces of legislation. One recent recommendation made by members of Parliament for a change in House rules involved this "ballot":

> The ballot for private members' bills should be held before the summer adjournment of the House instead of the autumn at the beginning of the new session. This would give the lucky members who come high in the ballot much more time to decide their topic of legislation and to prepare the content of the bill.[76]

Besides distinguishing between bills on the basis of who introduces them in the House of Commons, we can also distinguish between bills in terms of their scope: What do the proposed pieces of legislation intend to do? *Public bills* are drafts of new laws that would affect the country as a whole, such as tax law, criminal law, and so on. *Private bills* have individual application only, such as a special act of citizenship, for instance.[77]

The legislative process in the House of Commons involves the "standard" parliamentary procedure that we covered earlier in this text.

> When a Bill, thrashed out in the Cabinet or in its Legislation Committee and drawn up by the parliamentary counsel in due legal form...is presented to the Commons (or in some cases first to the Lords) its First Reading is generally formal. Second Reading Debate, normally in the full House (though in 1965 it was agreed that certain Second Readings of "uncontroversial Bills" might go to Committee) provides an opportunity for the discussion of general principles but it also lays down the basic framework of the Bill which cannot be altered at the Committee stage. This stage is concerned with the details of the Bill and amendments are confined within the aforementioned principles. . . . It is usually taken "upstairs" in one of the Standing Committees of about fifty members unless the Bill is of great constitutional significance, is likely to go through quickly, or a Government with a small majority fears too frequent defeat. There follows the Report Stage, usually brief, and a final Third Reading at which the major parties once more deploy their general arguments of principle, though the result, with the Whips on, is normally a foregone conclusion. Governments, of course, during all this process, may accept amendments which do not go to the heart of the Bill. Any other proposed change is discussed as a matter of "confidence" and defeat would normally lead to the Government's resignation or, more usually now, to a dissolution and a General election.[78]

After bills are passed in the House of Commons they are sent to the House of Lords, where they follow a similiar three-reading procedure prior to passage. As was indicated above, if the House of Lords does not approve a bill, it can no longer kill the bill, but can only delay its eventual passage.

A final, special, procedure should be mentioned here that relates to the "royal pretence" that was mentioned earlier. Bills approved by both Houses of Parliament must be given the Royal Assent (approval by the queen) before they become law. Never since 1707 this Royal Assent been refused to a bill that has passed both Houses of Parliament. The monarch has not given the Royal Assent in person since 1854; today it is done by a Commission.

For the giving of the Royal Assent, the Commons are summoned to the Lords' Chamber by the Gentlemen Usher of the Black Rod. Three Commissioners are seated between the Woolsack and the Throne. The title of each Bill which is to receive the Assent is read, and the Assent is signified by the Clerk of the Parliaments. The assenting formula is still given in Norman French. For Public Bills, and Private Bills of a local character, is it "La reine le veult" (the Queen wishes it). For Private Bills of a personal character the formula is "Soit fait comme il est desire" (let what is desired be done). The formula for Bills granting supply or imposing taxation is "La reine remercie ses bons sujets, accepte leur benevolence, et ainsi le veult" (the Queen thanks her good subjects, accepts their benevolence, and so wishes it). The formula for refusing the assent was formerly "La reine s'avisera" (the Queen will consider the matter).[79]

POLITICAL PARTIES AND VOTING

It has been suggested by a noted scholar that "British government is party government."[80] Parties organize electoral activity, including the selection of candidates in elections, the construction of programs, and the operation of election campaigns. In the general elections, citizens vote not so much for the individual candidates whose names appear on the ballot papers, but rather for the party team with which the candidate is affiliated.

Politics in Britain has often been referred to as "the politics of class,"[81] so it should come as no surprise that support for political parties in Britain has frequently been explained in terms of class allegiances. Today the allegiances have been described as "Labour, representing the working community, versus the Conservatives, representing capital."[82]

An interesting aspect of the ubiquity of parties in the British political system, though, is that they are "unknown to the constitutional law."[83] Parties originally developed in Britain over the issue of royal power, with the Tories (later to be called the Conservatives) favoring the royalty, and the Whigs (later to become the Liberals) opposing the royalists. Around the time of their development, in 1688 or so, neither the Tories nor the Whigs could have been called political parties in the contemporary sense of the word.[84] Neither group was mass-based or electoral in nature; both were groups of elite politicians acting as factions.

One of the early developmental problems of political parties involved the question of opposition to the monarch.[85] The concept of a "loyal opposition" developed slowly, and not without a great deal of friction, because early on it was difficult for many to accept the notion that it was possible to be *against* a government in power without being against the regime *itself.*

> So long as government was the task of the King and his friends at court, to be opposed to the acts of the government was to be opposed to the King, and it was no doubt difficult to distinguish between the King as a person and the monarchy as an institution. This attitude reached its logical conclusion in the Civil War. The majority of parliamentary leaders did not see how they could oppose Charles I without opposing the monarchial system, so having beheaded Charles, they abolished Kingship.[86]

By the middle of the eighteenth century, the concept of a "loyal opposition" was accepted. Edmund Burke, a great British politician of the time, argued that to combine to oppose or topple the government was not treason: "When bad men combine, the good must associate; else they will fall, one by one. . . . "[87]

Generally, the British party system is an integral part of the British political system. "The most obvious virtue of the party system," one student of British politics has written, "is that it ensures stable government and that it always presents the possibility of an alternative government." Parties contribute a great deal of stability to the political system, by providing the basis for the formation of Governments and by "enabling the Government, as leaders of the most powerful party in the House of Commons, to secure the passage of their programme of legislation."[88]

Britain is usually regarded as a two-party political system. Strictly speaking, this is not true. Britain can be said to have a two-party system by one measure only: The number of political parties that have formed a Government since 1945 is two—Conservative and Labour. By any other measure, however, Britain has a multiparty system.

> FACT: In 1987, on the average, there were 3.6 candidates contesting each seat in the British House of Commons, not two, as we would expect in a two-party system.
>
> FACT: The two major parties—Labour and Conservative—have together received *at most* 75 percent of the vote in recent national elections; put another way, at least one voter in four has voted for a party other than the "big two" in all recent elections.
>
> FACT: Outside of England (in Northern Ireland, Scotland, and Wales), the "minor" parties win significant proportions of votes in electoral competitions.
>
> FACT: The two major parties do not control all of the seats in the House of Commons today.[89]

This misperception about the British party system is largely a result of the relationship between electoral systems and party systems, which we discussed earlier. Britain has a single-member-district, plurality voting electoral system—what we earlier called a "first past the post" system. It doesn't matter whether a given candidate receives a *majority* of votes in a constituency as long as he or she has a *plurality*—more votes than any other candidate. From 1945 through 1970, about three-fourths of the

TABLE 9.1
Results of the 1992 and 1987 British General Elections

Party	PERCENT OF VOTES WON		NUMBER OF SEATS WON		PERCENT OF SEATS WON	
	1992	1987	1992	1987	1992	1987
Conservative	42%	42%	336	375	51.6%	57.7%
Labour	34	31	271	229	41.6	35.2
Liberal Democrat	18	23	20	22	3.1	3.4
Other	6	4	24	24	3.7	3.7

Source: Facts on File 52:2682 (April 16, 1992): 261.

members of Parliament were elected with more than one-half of the votes of their constituencies. "But the proportion of MPs elected with an absolute majority fell to 36 percent elected in February, 1974, rising again to 40 percent in October, 1974."[90]

One development in the political system in recent years that has proven to be significant was the appearance of the Alliance, a partnership of the Liberal Party with the new Social Democratic Party.[91] The Liberals, led by David Steel, and the Social Democrats, led by David Owen, garnered over 25 percent of the vote in 1983, approximately 23 percent of the vote in 1987, and approximately 18 percent of the vote in 1992.[92]

In the British political system one consequence of the single-member-district, plurality voting system is that the nonmajor parties are systematically and continuously underrepresented in the House of Commons. As one scholar has noted, "there is probably no facet of British government more in need of reform than the electoral system by which the nation chooses its representatives at Westminster."[93] If the Liberal Party (today part of the Liberal Democratic Party) were contesting elections in a system of proportional representation, "it would be a major party with approximately 100 seats or more."[94]

The fact is that the British electoral system usually "manufactures a majority party in Parliament from a minority of votes."[95] There has not been a single political party that has won over half of the votes in a parliamentary election since 1935. The closest that any party has come to a majority of the votes was in 1955, when the Conservative Party won 49.7 percent of the vote. The extreme bias of the single-member-district, plurality system can be illustrated by the October 1974 election, in which the Labour Party won a bare majority in the House of Commons of 319 seats (out of 635, a *bare* majority), with 39.2 percent of the vote. The Liberal Party had 18.3 percent of the vote (almost half of the Labour vote), and yet received only 13 seats in the House of Commons (4 percent of the Labour total).[96]

This situation was repeated, only more vividly, in the elections of 1983, 1987, and 1992. The Conservative government of Margaret Thatcher was returned to power, winning 397, 375, and 336 of 650 seats in the House of Commons (61, 57.7, and 51.7 percent of the seats, respectively) in return for 42 percent of the votes in each election. That is, nearly 60 percent of the voters did *not* choose the Conservative Party, but the Conservative Party was elected with a parliamentary majority. In the three elections, the Labour Party won 209, 229, and 271 seats (32, 35.2, and 41.7 percent of the seats, respectively) in return for 28, 31, and 34 percent of the votes. The Liberal-Social Democratic Alliance won 23, 22, and 20 seats (3.5, 3.4, and 3.1 percent of the seats, respectively) in return for 25, 23, and 18 percent of the total vote. In 1983 Labour got 3 percent more votes than did the Liberal-Social Democratic Alliance, and won 186 more seats; in 1987 it received 8 percent more votes and won 207 more seats, a difference of 31.8 percent of the seats; and in 1992 it received 16 percent more votes and won 251 more seats, a difference of 38.6 percent of the seats. Post-election analysis suggested that:

> A lasting controversy is expected to arise because of the failure of the Alliance to win anything approaching the number of seats that their share of the vote would seem

to have justified, and which they would have received under the proportional representation system used in most European countries. The British winner-take-all system, on which the American system is based, has survived unchanged for 700 years of parliamentary history.[97]

Although Britain is erroneously referred to as a two-party system, it traditionally has been dominated by three parties—the Conservative Party, the Labour Party, and the Liberal Party. The traditional competition for power through the early twentieth century took place between the Liberals and the Conservatives, which evolved from the Whigs and the Tories, respectively. During the latter part of the nineteenth century, the rivalry between these two parties increased as electoral reforms were undertaken and more people began to participate in politics.

The Labour Party arrived on the political scene around the turn of the twentieth century. Toward the end of the 1800s in Britain there were several movements mobilizing for working-class representation in the House of Commons. In 1900 they met in London and formed the Labour Representation Committee.[98] Two candidates from this group were elected to the House of Commons in 1900, and twenty-seven were elected in 1906. In 1918 the Labour Party was formally organized.

The decline of the Liberals and the ascent of Labour as the second of two "major" parties took place in relatively rapid order.

> In 1906 the Liberals dominated the political scene. They had won the largest majority in the House of Commons since the Reform Bill; even without their parliamentary allies, the new Labour Party, they secured over 50 percent of the popular vote. Less than two decades later, although they were still getting 30 percent of the vote, they were struggling desperately for survival. In 1929, their last serious challenge for governmental power won them 23 percent of the vote. Until 1974 they never again rose above 12 percent, and in 1951 and 1955, when they contested barely a sixth of the seats in Commons, they sank to a mere 2.5 percent of the vote.[99]

Constitutionally, elections for the House of Commons must be held at least every five years. As we have seen, however, since the British Constitution is "unwritten," the constitutional parameters relating to elections are whatever the House of Commons says they should be. In 1694, the Commons passed the Triennial Act, setting the maximum term of the House at three years; in 1716, the maximum term was extended to seven years by the Septennial Act. It wasn't until 1911 that the present five-year constitutional limitation was set. Since 1911 it has usually been the case that elections have been called before the five-year limit on the life of a Parliament. There have been two noteworthy exceptions to this rule, however. During both World War I and World War II, Parliament decided—and legislated accordingly—to postpone elections because of the feeling that electoral uncertainty would not help the war efforts. Consequently, "the Parliament chosen in 1910 was not dissolved until the end of 1918, and there was no general election in Britain between 1935 and 1945."[100]

Essentially it can be argued that one person, the prime minister, decides when a national election will take place. Although since 1911 the constitution has required (with the two exceptions noted) that elections be held at least every five years, in point of fact the prime minister has felt free over the years to request that the monarch dissolve Parliament and call for new elections at a time earlier than required that is an advantage to the Government in power. Tradition requires (although technically the law does not) that the monarch grant a dissolution when one is requested by the prime minister.

One of the most remarkable differences between the British electoral process and many other electoral processes is the relative brevity of the campaign period in Britain. In the American system, for example, primaries sometimes start as much as eleven months before elections, and informal campaigning may begin long before that. In Britain, the Government's ability to call a "surprise" election may be a real strategic advantage; "approximately three weeks after a dissolution, the entire electorate of Britain goes to the polls."[101]

One of the reasons that such a short campaign period is possible is that there are no required party primaries to select nominees to stand for election. Party candidates are selected by local party organizations (although the precise method of the selection process differs among the parties). Nomination to run for office requires only ten signatures on a petition, in addition to a deposit of £150, which is forfeited if a candidate does not receive at least one-eighth of the vote in a constituency.[102] This is intended to discourage "frivolous" candidacies, although the decline of the value of the pound makes that threat less effective today.

SUMMARY

This chapter presented few major deviations from what we learned in earlier chapters. The British political system *is* the "Westminister model" that we met earlier. In this presentation of the major structures of the British political system, we have briefly shown the manner in which it is possible to look at a political system using the general approach we introduced at the beginning of this text.

We have seen in this chapter that in a nation's constitutional makeup, custom and tradition may be just as important as written statutes, if not more so. The fact that it is even possible to imagine actions in the British political system that might be *legal* yet *unconstitutional* attests to the relative importance of the unwritten law of tradition. Britain offers a clear example of a political system in which one must be familiar with the political environment and political history of a nation before one can seriously attempt to understand how public policy is made there.

Notes

1. Max Beloff and Gillian Peele, *The Government of the United Kingdom* (New York: W.W. Norton, 1980), p. 10.
2. George W. Keeton, *Government in Action in the United Kingdom* (London: Ernest Benn, Ltd., 1970), pp. 29–30.
3. Hiram Stout, *British Government* (New York: Oxford University Press, 1953), p. 19.
4. Sydney D. Bailey, *British Parliamentary Democracy* (Boston: Houghton Mifflin, 1958), p. 2.
5. Stout, *Government*, pp. 20–21.
6. Ibid., p. 20. See also Bailey, *Parliamentary Democracy*, p. 3.
7. Beloff and Peele, *Government*, pp. 10–11; Bailey, *Parliamentary Democracy*, p. 3.

8. Stout, *Government*, p. 21.

9. Bailey, *Parliamentary Democracy*, p. 4.

10. See *The Monarchy in Britain* (London: Her Majesty's Stationery Office, 1981), pp. 8–11.

11. Bailey, *Parliamentary Democracy*, p. 5.

12. Ibid., p. 6.

13. Stout, *Government*, pp. 26–27.

14. Anthony Sampson, *The New Anatomy of Britain* (New York: Stein and Day, 1972), p. 215.

15. Max Nicholson, *The System* (New York: McGraw-Hill, 1967), p. 158.

16. Sampson, *New Anatomy*, p. 215.

17. Ibid.

18. Stout, *Government*, pp. 70–71.

19. Beloff and Peele, *Government*, p. 67.

20. Sampson, *New Anatomy*, pp. 217–218.

21. Sir Ivor Jennings, *Cabinet Government* (Cambridge: Cambridge University Press, 1951), p. 79.

22. Stout, *Government*, p. 77.

23. K.R. MacKenzie, *The English Parliament* (New York: Penguin Books, 1950), p. 81.

24. James Barber, "The Power of the Prime Minister," in R.L. Borthwick and J.E. Spence, *British Politics in Perspective* (New York: St. Martin's Press, 1984), p. 73. See also Michael Foley, *The Rise of the British Presidency* (New York: St. Martin's Press, 1993).

25. John P. Mackintosh, "The Position of the Prime Minister," in Anthony King, ed., *The British Prime Minister* (London: Macmillan, 1969), p. 33. See also Martin Burch, "The Demise of Cabinet Government?" in Lynton Robins, ed., *Political Institutions in Britain: Development and Change* (New York: Longman, 1987), pp. 19–37.

26. Richard Rose, "British Government: The Job at the Top," in Richard Rose and Ezra Suleiman, eds., *Presidents and Prime Ministers* (Washington, D.C.: American Enterprise Institute, 1980), p. 1.

27. Richard Rose, *Ministers and Ministries: A Functional Analysis* (Oxford: Clarendon Press, 1987), p. 4.

28. A table ranking the political status of the many cabinet portfolios can be found in Rose, *Ministers and Ministries*, p. 86.

29. Peter Hennessy, *Cabinet* (Oxford: Basil Blackwell, 1986), pp. 1–15.

30. *Facts on File* 52:2682 (April 16, 1992): 262.

31. H. Victor Wiseman, *Politics in Everyday Life* (Oxford: Basil Blackwell, 1966), pp. 167–169.

32. Rose, "The Job at the Top," pp. 3–26.

33. Wiseman, *Politics*, p. 159.

34. Bernard Crick, *The Reform of Parliament* (New York: Anchor Books, 1964).

35. Beloff and Peele, *Government*, p. 102.

36. *Facts on File* 52:2682 (April 16, 1992): 261.

37. Rose, "The Job at the Top," pp. 12–13.

38. Ibid.

39. Ibid., p.25.

40. Martin Holmes, *The First Thatcher Government, 1979–1983: Contemporary Conservatism and Economic Change* (Boulder, Colo.: Westview Press, 1985), p. 1.

41. Peter Jenkins, *Mrs. Thatcher's Revolution: The Ending of the Socialist Era* (Cambridge: Harvard University Press, 1988), p. 81. See also Dennis Kavanagh, "Margaret Thatcher: A Case of Prime Ministerial Power?" in Robins, *Political Institutions*, pp. 9–18.

42. Indeed, the Thatcher government's goal of lowering inflation at almost any cost "brought about a fundamental division of opinion within the Conservative Cabinet, backbench MPs and the party itself. The conflict between the political monetarists, or dries, and the left-wing Conservatives, or wets, was a marked feature of the whole of the period from 1979 to 1983." Holmes, *Thatcher Government*, p. 74.

43. Holmes, *Thatcher Government*, p. 199.

44. Anthony Harrison and John Gretton, eds., *Reshaping Central Government* (New Brunswick, N.J.: Transaction Books, 1987), p. 1.

45. A good description of this relationship is in Dave Marsh and Jeff King, "The Unions Under Thatcher," in Robins, *Political Institutions*, pp. 213–229. See also David Marsh, *The New Politics of British Trade Unionism: Union Power and the Thatcher Legacy* (Basingstoke: Macmillan, 1992), and David Powell, *British Politics and the Labour Question, 1868–1990* (Basingstoke: Macmillan, 1992).

46. Ian Derbyshire, *Politics in Britain: From Callaghan to Thatcher* (Oxford: W & R Chambers, 1988), p. 73.

47. On recent directions of policy, see Bony Baldry and Jane Ewart-Biggs, *Social Policy* (London: Wroxton Papers in Politics, 1990), and Brian W. Hogwood, *Trends in British Public Policy: Do Governments Make Any Difference?* (Philadelphia: Open University Press, 1992).

48. Jenkins, *Mrs. Thatcher's Revolution*, pp. 173–174. See also a description of her goals and plans in Derbyshire, *Politics in Britain*, pp. 109–113.

49. A good general treatment of this is in the volume by Andrew Gray and William Jenkins, *Administrative Politics in British Government* (New York: St. Martin's Press, 1985).

50. See the discussion of the cases of Clive Ponting, Westland Helicopters, and Peter Wright in Gavin Drewry and Tony Butcher, *The Civil Service Today* (Oxford: Basil Blackwell, 1988), pp. 1–8.

51. See Harrison and Gretton, *Reshaping Central Government*, p. 2. See also Drewry and Butcher, *The Civil Service Today*, p. 10.

52. John R. Greenaway, "The Higher Civil Service at the Crossroads: The Impact of the Thatcher Government," in Robins, *Political Institutions*, p. 49.

53. Anthony Sampson, as quoted in Drewry and Butcher, *The Civil Service Today*, p. 151.

54. John Greenwood and David Wilson, *Public Administration in Britain* (London: Allen and Unwin, 1984), p. 84.

55. Harrison and Gretton, *Reshaping Central Government*, pp. 192–193.

56. A very good essay discussing this problem is that by Mike Goldsmith and Ken Newton, "Central-Local Government Relations: The Irresistible Rise of Centralised Power," in Hugh Berrington, ed., *Change in British Politics* (London: Frank Cass, 1984), pp. 216–233. See also R. A. W. Rhodes, "Mrs. Thatcher and Local Government: Intentions and Achievements," in Robins, *Political Institutions*, pp. 98–120.

57. A good discussion of this problem can be found in George Jones and John Stewart, *The Case for Local Government* (London: Allen and Unwin, 1985).

58. See Andrew Gamble, *Britain in Decline: Economic Policy, Political Strategy, and the British State* (New York: St. Martin's Press, 1990).

59. R.A.W. Rhodes, *Beyond Westminster and Whitehall: The Sub-Central Governments of Britain* (London: Allen and Unwin, 1988), p. 381.

60. Bailey, *Parliamentary Democracy*, p. 35. See also Stout, *Government*, pp. 89–92.

61. Frank Stacey, *British Government* (London: Oxford University Press, 1975), p. 72.

62. Bailey, *Parliamentary Democracy*, pp. 36–37, 41.

63. Ibid., p. 38.

64. Ibid., p. 42.

65. Ian Derbyshire, *Politics in Britain*, p. 4.

66. Nicholson, *The System*, p. 153.

67. Keeton, *Government in Action*, p. 63.

68. Nicholson, *The System*, p. 153.

69. Bailey, *Parliamentary Democracy*, pp. 65–69.

70. A very good description of the development of parliamentary government and the role of the Parliament can be found in Michael Rush, *Parliamentary Government in Britain* (New York: Holmes and Meier, 1981), pp. 19–47.

71. Stacey, *British Government*, pp. 38–39.

72. See Michael Moran, "The Changing World of British Pressure Groups," in Robins, *Political Institutions*, pp. 179–187.

73. Wyn Grant, "The Role and Power of Pressure Groups," in Borthwick and Spence, *British Politics in Perspective*, p. 142.

74. Beloff and Peele, *Government*, p. 107.

75. Wiseman, *Politics*, p. 147.

76. Stacey, *British Government*, p. 56.

77. Stout, *British Government*, pp. 128–137.

78. Wiseman, *Politics*, p. 148. See also, for a very good cross-national treatment of this subject, David Olson, *The Legislative Process: A Comparative Approach* (New York: Harper and Row, 1980), p. 346.

79. Bailey, *Parliamentary Democracy*, p. 108.

80. Richard Rose, *Politics in England* (Boston: Little, Brown, 1980), p. 249. See also Jack Brand, *British Parliamentary Parties: Policy and Power* (New York: Oxford University Press, 1992).

81. Derbyshire, *Politics in Britain*, p. 5.

82. Ibid. There is a much longer discussion of the nature of the interparty differences in economic and social policy here, pp. 6–14.

83. Keeton, *Government in Action*, p. 90.

84. Stout, *British Government*, p. 163.

85. A very good discussion of the evolution of British parties can be found in H.M. Crucker, "The Evolution of the Political Parties," in Borthwick and Spence, *British Politics in Perspective*, pp. 104–21.

86. Bailey, *Parliamentary Democracy*, p. 138.

87. Ibid.

88. Keeton, *Government in Action*, p. 93.

89. Rose, *Politics*, p. 257.

90. Ibid., p. 255.

91. A discussion of the creation of the Alliance can be found in David Denver, "The S.D.P.-Liberal Alliance: The End of the Two-Party System?" in Berrington, *Change in British Politics*, pp. 75–102. A very good description of recent Alliance strategy can be found in David Butler and Paul Jowett, *Party Strategies in Britain: A Study of the 1984 European Elections* (New York: St. Martin's Press, 1985), chap. 8: "The Alliance and Others." In 1989 the Liberal Party formally merged with the Social-Democratic Alliance and formed the Liberal Democrats.

92. Derbyshire, *Politics in Britain*, pp. 146–147; *Facts on File* 52:2682 (April 16, 1992): 261.

93. Geoffrey Alderman, "The Electoral System," in Borthwick and Spence, *British Politics in Perspective*, p. 19.

94. Rose, *Politics*, p. 258.

95. Ibid., p. 256.

96. Ibid.

97. See *The New York Times*, June 10, 1983, p. 14, col. 3; June 11, 1983, p. 4, col. 1.

98. Stout, *British Government*, p. 200.

99. David Butler and Donald Stokes, *Political Change in Britain* (New York: St. Martin's Press, 1976), p. 117.

100. Stout, *British Government*, p. 200.

101. Ibid., p. 211.

102. Rose, *Politics*, p. 251.

10

The French Political System

We saw in Chapter 9 that the constitutional system of Great Britain is the product of a gradual evolutionary process that has taken place over a period of several hundred years; the same cannot be said of the constitutional system of France. In the case of Britain, we can point to specific dates of constitutional significance—for instance, the signing of the Magna Carta in 1215—but the general constitutional *system*, broadly interpreted, has remained intact and has changed only slowly over a long period of time. The French system is more properly characterized as experiencing a number of (more or less) sudden and severe alterations of the entire political regime, not merely evolutionary modifications of aspects of the system.

A Constitutional History of France

The fact that we refer to the current system of government in France as the "Fifth Republic" suggests, and properly so, that earlier republics have come and gone. Many of these arrivals and departures have been not slow and moderate, but abrupt and violent substitutions of one system of government for another—revolutions in fact if not in name.

It behooves us at this point to examine briefly the recent constitutional history of France that has led to the establishment of the Fifth Republic. This is an appropriate inquiry for us to undertake because it will become clear, as we continue our examination of significant French political structures later in this chapter, that many contemporary political institutions in the French system were so designed precisely because of earlier experiences in France's political and constitutional history.

The Third Republic

We will begin our discussion of modern French political structures with the Third Republic,[1] which has been referred to by some as a "republic by default."

> The National Assembly that was hurriedly elected in 1871 to provide a government capable of negotiating peace with Bismarck's Germany did not want a republic at all: more than 400 of its 650 deputies were monarchists. But since the Assembly could not agree on which of the three dynasties (Bourbon, Orleans, Bonaparte) should be called upon to provide a King, the precise nature of the regime was left unsettled.[2]

Although the Third Republic dates from 1870, its constitution was not assembled until 1875. The structures of the Third Republic were fairly basic: The bicameral parliament was composed of a Chamber of Deputies and a Senate, the deputies elected by the people and the senators elected indirectly and over-representing rural areas.[3] The combined legislature, called the National Assembly, elected a president for a seven-year term. Ministers were responsible to the legislature, and with the consent of the Senate the president could dissolve the Chamber of Deputies before its four-year term expired.

The fact that the Third Republic lasted as long as it did—seventy years, from 1870 until 1940—is an anomaly of French political history. One should not deduce from the relative longevity of the Third Republic that its life was placid and stable; such was not the case. A number of crises arose during the Republic that caused many people to fear that the Republic was in danger of extinction.[4]

Interestingly, World War I did not appear to have a deleterious effect upon the regime. Rather, the economic depression that rampaged through Europe after that war severely affected the Government. In 1935 a temporary electoral alliance of a number of political parties helped elect Leon Blum premier. The Spanish Civil War in 1936 affected the stability of the Blum regime, as did a number of other social issues, and the Government resigned after a year.

From 1936 through 1940 several governments were created and dissolved. The Spanish Civil War, the Munich Agreement of 1938 between Neville Chamberlain (the British prime minister) and Adolph Hitler over the annexation of Czechoslovakia by Germany, the Nazi-Soviet Nonaggression Pact of 1939, and the German invasion of Norway and the Low Countries left French governments powerless to act.

The phenomenon that most people associate with French politics under the Third and Fourth Republics is no doubt ministerial instability, the frequent turnovers of cabinets. This aspect can be illustrated by comparing the number of French and British cabinets and premiers (or prime ministers) during similar periods, as indicated in Table 10.1.

The major explanation for the frequency of new cabinets in France during the Third Republic can be found in the Chamber of Deputies. There were usually

TABLE 10.1
Ministerial Instability in France: A Comparative Perspective

	3rd Republic France, 1879–1940	Britain, 1880–1940	4th Republic France, 1947–1958	Britain, 1945–1963
Number of cabinets	94	21	18	5
Average cabinet life	8 mos.	36 mos.	8 mos.	43 mos.
Number of premiers	44	11	15	4
Average tenure of premier	16 mos.	60 mos.	9 mos.	54 mos.

Source: Adapted from material in Roy Pierce, *French Politics and Political Institutions* (New York: Harper & Row, 1968), pp. 19–21.

eight to ten parties to be found in the legislature, which invariably meant that coalitions were necessary to form government majorities. These coalitions (as we have seen is often the case with coalitions) were not durable enough to withstand the short-term pressures brought about by rapidly evolving political events, which resulted in the collapse of government after government.

In June 1940 a new cabinet was formed, which was led by the World War I hero Marshal Henri Petain. The hope was that Petain, as a military hero, would be able to provide strong leadership in the face of powerful external pressure from Hitler's Nazi Germany. He *did* provide leadership, but in an unexpected direction. Immediately after taking power on June 16, 1940, Petain opened negotiations with the Nazis, and less than a week later (on June 22, 1940) he signed an armistice with Germany dividing France into an occupied northern half and an unoccupied southern half, the latter governed from the city of Vichy. From this time until November 1942, when Germany occupied all of France, the Vichy regime governed the southern half of France without a constitution, a legislature, or presidential elections. The Third Republic was dead.[5]

The Fourth Republic

When France was liberated in 1944, General Charles de Gaulle, who had led a National Council of Resistance from London during the war, became head of the new Government.

> An assembly existed, but it was purely consultative. The cabinet was chosen by de Gaulle and was responsible to him alone. Thus the regime in the first fourteen months following the Liberation was rightly called a "dictatorship by consent."[6]

In October 1945, "French voters by an overwhelming majority of 18,600,000 to 700,777 decided to leave the Third Republic in its grave."[7] The first postwar legislature was subsequently elected, and one of its first tasks was to construct a new constitution; this combination legislature–constitutional convention was called the Constituent Assembly. There was no agreement, however, on the direction that should be followed in France's constitutional future.[8]

The first draft of the constitution was presented to the voters in May 1946 for ratification and was rejected by a narrow margin: 10,584,539 to 9,454,034. This plan proposed abolition of the Senate as an essentially "undemocratic" institution (since it was not directly elected by the public), and proposed a weak executive, with virtually all powers vested in a unicameral National Assembly. The draft had the support of the left parties, the Communists and the Socialists, but was opposed by moderate parties and a new political organization, the Popular Republican Movement (MRP).

The second Constituent Assembly, which was elected in June 1946, produced a modified draft constitution that resembled the first proposal in many respects. It placed almost complete authority in the elected National Assembly, a term previously used to designate the entire two-house parliament, with a weak Council of the Republic as a second legislative house.[9]

Members of the National Assembly were to be elected from multimember districts, averaging five deputies per district, by proportional representation. The executive was to remain weak. In October 1946 this plan was presented to the French public, and it received a singularly unenthusiastic approval: 9,297,470 votes in favor, 8,165,459 against, and 7,775,893 eligible voters not voting. General de Gaulle and his supporters, who had argued for a stronger executive and opposed the plan, claimed that the new constitution would never last since it was supported by only slightly more than a third of the electorate.[10]

A number of constitutional devices were subsequently included in the constitution to promote governmental stability, such as the 1954 change making the investiture of a prime minister easier by requiring a relative, or simple, majority (a majority of those present and voting) rather than an absolute majority (a majority of all members of the legislature). Despite this, however, the multiparty system encouraged by the proportional representation electoral framework led to an *absence* of stable parliamentary majorities and produced a change in cabinets averaging once every six months.

Although domestic issues were the primary source of political conflict in the early postwar years, by the mid-1950s it was international events that consumed governmental attention. The Government was able to handle almost all of the crises it faced. The war in Indochina (Vietnam) was ended in 1954. France accepted West Germany into the North Atlantic Treaty Organization (NATO) in 1957, and joined the European Economic Community (the Common Market). Both Morocco and Tunisia were granted independence in 1956. Also in 1956 the French government passed legislation to "set France's African colonies south of the Sahara on the road to real, and not sham, self-government."[11] The question of Algeria, however, proved to be too much for the Government.

In April 1958 the French army stationed in Algeria supported a revolt launched by European settlers in Algiers and called for the formation of a "Government of Public Safety" in Paris. They demanded that the present Government resign, and that General de Gaulle be called out of political retirement to take power.[12] The Government in power accepted General de Gaulle as "the only possible savior-assassin of the regime. One June 1, 1958, by a vote of 329 to 224, the Assembly accepted de Gaulle as Prime Minister, and the next day empowered him to supervise the drafting of a new constitution."[13] The Fourth Republic was dead.

THE CONSTITUTIONAL SYSTEM OF THE FIFTH REPUBLIC

When on June 1, 1958, the National Assembly invested de Gaulle as prime minister, there were many deputies in the Assembly who were suspicious of de Gaulle and feared that his selection would lead to the creation of another Napoleon-like emperor. De Gaulle himself had done a good deal to foster this kind of fear during the years he was out of government by regularly calling for strong executive leadership and a new constitutional regime. In June 1946 de Gaulle had delivered in the town of Bayeux what would prove to be one of his most famous speeches. He set forth his notion of the type of strong, vigorous executive leadership that he thought France needed.[14]

In spite of de Gaulle's protestations that at the age of 67 he did not pose a Napoleon-like threat to French liberty, when the legislature authorized him to draft a new constitution it attached two highly significant conditions: First, the constitution of the new Fifth Republic had to retain the two distinct offices of the president and the premier. Second, the new constitution would have to retain the characteristic of having the premier "responsible to" the legislature. The latter requirement was included on the assumption that de Gaulle himself would seek the premier's office, and thus the legislature would still have some degree of control over any future acts of de Gaulle.[15]

It is interesting to note that although de Gaulle was given authority by the legislature of the Fourth Republic to draft a new constitution that he would subsequently submit to the public in a referendum for approval, many have argued since 1958 that this grant of power was illegal. The constitution of the Fourth Republic, still in effect when de Gaulle was working on his draft constitution, provided that constitutional amendments could be initiated *only* in parliament. Thus it has been argued by anti-Gaullists that the de Gaulle constitution of the Fifth Republic was simply a "coup d'état that had only a thin veneer of legality."[16]

The de Gaulle constitution does not fit neatly into one or the other of the two major models of executive leadership (presidential or parliamentary) that we introduced earlier in this text. The presidential model has a single individual playing the roles of both head of state and chief executive, elected independently of the legislature and having a base of power independent of the legislature. The parliamentary model separates the two executive roles: the weak figurehead chosen by one of a number of different mechanisms (such as heredity or election) and the powerful chief executive coming from, being a part of, and being responsible to the legislature. The de Gaulle constitution bridges the two systems, and is accordingly sometimes referred to as either a "quasi-presidential" or a "quasi-parliamentary" system.

The de Gaulle constitution of 1958 brought together elements of both the Bonaparte era and the Republican era. "The Constitution established a strong Executive in the form of a President with independent power to govern and a cabinet headed by a Prime Minister responsible to a popularly elected assembly."[17] To put the institution of the French president in a comparative perspective, the president of France had both in theory and in practice the power that the British prime minister had in practice but not in theory. The French model, unlike the standard Westminster model power relationship, produced a politically significant head of state and a weak chief executive. This is a significant departure from other parliamentary regimes that we have met and will meet later, and it warrants more attention here.

The so-called de Gaulle constitution of 1958 was drafted by a small group of individuals led by Michel Debré, the future prime minister.[18] No person other than de Gaulle had more influence on the 1958 constitution than Debré. The new constitution was submitted to a Constitutional Advisory Committee, primarily made up of legislators, and subsequently presented to the public for approval in a national referendum.

A strong presidency, coupled with some structural changes in the powers of the legislature, was the major thrust of changes that the Fifth Republic would make to the political system of the Fourth Republic. This was clearly in response to what were seen as the fundamental weaknesses of the Fourth Republic: a lack of leadership and parliamentary instability. We now turn our attention to an examination of the organization of the Fifth Republic, and to some of the prominent political structures to be found therein.

UNITARY GOVERNMENT IN FRANCE

"The political framework within which French cities deal with the changing needs and demands of their populations is built on three levels of government: the commune, the department, and the national government."[19] Just as French parliamentary government is a variation of the "normal" parliamentary model, so too the French style of unitary government appears to be different from other unitary governments.

Remember that while unitary governments and federal governments both have local as well as national levels, they differ in the existence of an intermediate level of government. The United States, Canada, and Germany are examples of federal governments in which power is shared (to different degrees) between the "central" or "national" governments and the intermediate governments—states, provinces, or Länder. The primary alternative to the federal system is the unitary regime, in which there is no intermediate level of government. The "typical" unitary government (if such can be said to exist) is found in Great Britain, in which a national level of government and a local level of government divide functions that would be of concern to the intermediate level of government in a federal regime.

The French system is an odd form of unitary government, because although there is much sharing of power between the national and local levels of government, there are intermediate levels of government designed to assist in the *administration* of policy.[20] Locally, the mayor and municipal council deal with two kinds of decisions: decisions on how to carry out and finance state-mandated services, and priority-setting decisions in areas not controlled by the state. The *commune*, the lowest-level political organization of the state, is the central administrative unit of the state.

The second level of French government is the *department*. The *prefect* is the representative of national government in the department. This individual has "wide-ranging powers over local government, . . . control of the legality of local governmental decisions and review of the substance of the commune's decisions in policy areas where the commune is not bound by national legislation."[21] A good deal of the commune's legislation cannot go into effect without the prefect's approval. There are ninety-five departments in France, most of which today have the same borders they did at the time of the French Revolution in 1789.

Departments are governed by a departmental council (*conseil général*); for purposes of administration, departments are divided into subunits called *cantons*, and each canton elects one member to the departmental council. Like the commune, the department "is both a self-governing body and an administrative level of the state."[22] The chief executive of government at the departmental level is not an elected official at all, but an appointed prefect.

It can be seen, then, that although France is invariably—and correctly—classified as a unitary regime, it is a unitary regime with many characteristics that might seem to be more appropriate for a federal system than a unitary system. Departments and cantons both exist above the local (commune) level, and we will see later, particularly in regard to the Senate, that they play a significant role in the French political system.

EXECUTIVE STRUCTURES

The Presidency

"When General de Gaulle returned to power in 1958, it was generally expected that the presidency of the Republic would be invested with a novel significance in the policy processes of the new Republic."[23] The "keystone" of the Fifth Republic's constitutional makeup is the presidency.[24] It was by making the president (usually the weak figurehead actor in split-executive parliamentary systems) the keystone of the system, rather than the prime minister (usually the dominant figure in parliamentary systems), that de Gaulle and his coauthors of the new constitution were able to put so much power in the hands of a single political actor and yet were still able to stay within the conditions set down by the Fourth Republic legislators permitting a new constitution to be written and submitted to the public for approval.

The system of executive power in the Fifth Republic is similar in many respects to those found today in Austria, Finland, Ireland, and Iceland, in which the president is popularly elected. In those systems, however, the president is significantly weaker than in the French system, "because his role is circumscribed by his being subject to ouster by Parliament (as in Iceland), by strong legislative powers that Parliament possesses (as in Finland), or by the role of strong, disciplined parties (as in Austria). The French president, in contrast, suffers from none of these limitations."[25]

We suggested earlier that constitutions are often written in response to political regimes of the past. "The Constitution of the Fifth Republic was written in reaction against the constitutional pattern of the parliamentary system,"[26] and the new institution of the French president was a reaction against the weak, impotent prime ministers of the Fourth Republic. The Fifth Republic president had powers that could be exercised without the consent of either the Government (the prime minister and the cabinet) or the legislature, and it was these powers that placed the president in the paramount position of leadership in the French political system.

De Gaulle's goal in designing the constitution the way he did was "to free the executive from legislative domination and so to make possible greater governmental stability."[27] The president was given absolute power, without needing the consent of either the Government or the Parliament, to:

1. Appoint the Prime Minister;
2. Dissolve Parliament;
3. Assume Emergency Powers under Article 16;
4. Ask Parliament to reconsider a law just passed;
5. Refer a law to the Constitutional Council for judgment on its constitutionality;
6. Preside over the Council of Ministers (the Cabinet);
7. Serve as Commander in Chief;
8. Exercise the right of Pardon;
9. Decide whether or not to submit a bill to popular referendum when the Parliament or the Prime Minister suggest it.[28]

We should note the presidential power to dissolve the National Assembly (the lower house of the bicameral legislature) at any time the president wished, except while exercising emergency powers under Article 16 (see below) or if the National Assembly had already been dissolved once within a year. It is not unusual to find this power in the hands of the head of state in other political systems; the British monarch has the same power. The difference, a significant one, is that although *de jure* (in law) the British monarch may use this power at any time, *de facto* (in fact) she will use it *only* "on the advice" of the prime minister. The French president possessed this power both *de jure* and *de facto*. French presidents since the time of de Gaulle have used the power on their own initiative, without consulting or seeking approval of or acting on request of the prime minister and cabinet.

To take one example, in October 1962, angered by de Gaulle's use of the referendum to secure an amendment to the constitution providing for direct popular election of the president, the National Assembly took its anger out on de Gaulle's prime minister, Georges Pompidou, and voted to censure the Government. De Gaulle responded to this action by activating Article 12 of the constitution and dissolving the National Assembly, and elections took place the following month.[29] The act of dissolution worked to the advantage of both de Gaulle and Pompidou, because the newly elected National Assembly had significantly more Gaullists than had the legislature that was dissolved.

A major set of presidential powers included in the de Gaulle constitution of the Fifth Republic dealt with emergency powers of the president. Article 16 of the constitution stated that "when the institutions of the Republic, national independence, the integrity of national territory, or the application of international commitments are threatened in a serious and immediate fashion, and the normal functioning of public institutions is interrupted," the president is authorized to "take the measures required by these circumstances."[30]

The measures that the president could take were virtually unlimited. The only checks on his (or her) power (and they are really not checks at all) were that (1) the president must consult with the prime minister, the presidents of the two houses of legislature, and the Constitutional Council, and (2) the legislature must remain in session during the period of the declared emergency. It should be noted that the first item required the president only to *consult* with others, not to seek their approval or permission, so these "checks" really did nothing to limit what the president did.

Article 16 has been used only once during the Fifth Republic. In April 1961 a group of French generals who opposed governmental policy leading to Algerian independence from France threatened to invade the French mainland and take over the Government. De Gaulle acted under Article 16, announced that "the institutions of the Republic" were threatened, and declared a state of emergency. The attempted coup was put down within a very few days, but de Gaulle let his Article 16 powers remain in force for over five months; only the president decides when to deactivate the Article 16 powers.[31]

It can be seen, then, that there really are no "checks and balances" in the traditional sense over the president's use of the broad emergency powers in Article 16. The president needs no countersignature, no "advice and consent," no one's permission to declare the state of emergency, and the state of emergency remains until the president, and only the president, decides to declare the emergency over. A president who wished to assume dictatorial powers could constitutionally do so.

Yet another set of powers exclusively reserved for the president had to do with justice-related issues. Again, without the permission or countersignature of either the Government or the legislature, the president had the power to appoint three of the nine members of the Constitutional Council, which will be further discussed later. Moreover, the president had the right of pardon.

Beyond these powers, anything the president wanted to do in the French political system could only be done in collaboration with others. For example, only the president has the power to call for a referendum, to submit a political issue to the voters, but theoretically he may call for a referendum only if asked to do so by either the Government or the legislature.

In practice, however, the president, and not the Government or the legislature, has decided whether or not to hold a referendum. A communiqué issued by the Council of Ministers on November 16, 1960, stated: "General de Gaulle indicated his intention of submitting . . . by means of the referendum, a Government bill relating to the organization of the public powers in Algeria, pending self-determination." The president has usually made known his desire for a referendum, and the prime minister has accordingly requested the referendum, thus observing the con-

stitutional requirements. The French legislature has never to date used its constitutional right to request the president to submit a question to referendum.[32]

This theoretical control over the referendum was in direct response to the
history of its use (or rather, abuse) in French politics. Napoleon frequently resorted
to the referendum, often as a means of achieving a goal that the legislature would
not permit, and the public at the time did not prove to be terribly discriminating in
its approval of Napoleon's ideas. The founders of the Fifth Republic, while giving
the president great emergency powers, did not want to give a charismatic president
license to regularly go around the duly elected legislators in the policy-making
process.

> The device of the referendum allows the President to present an issue to the public
> in terms that often simplify complex matters by demanding a yes or no answer from
> the voter. By [threatening to resign if he lost and] staking his office on the outcome
> of the referendum and threatening the public that without him the political system
> would return to the disorders of the Fourth Republic, de Gaulle was able to win mas-
> sive public approvals in the referendum.[33]

The idea of the referendum was "essential" to de Gaulle's constitutional
scheme because it provided "an alternative to Parliament as the agency for legitimizing public policy." De Gaulle perceived that in the French political system the
political parties were a "screen rather than a transmission belt" between the government and the public, and "as Parliament is the arena of partisan representation,
it was important that the executive be able to bypass Parliament in the policy-making
process in cases where it believed that it could win popular, but not parliamentary,
support."[34]

Given that the president has only the above-mentioned powers (even though
they *are* significant powers), which he can perform independently of all others, what
has caused the French political leadership system to evolve to a point at which it has
been argued to resemble the American presidency as much as, if not more than, the
Westminster model of parliamentary government?

The answer can only partially be attributed to the constitutional grant of special powers to the president. There is in French politics a "fundamental difference
between the role which the constitution and those who actually drafted it assigned
to the presidency and the actual significance which the office has taken on in the
process of decision making." This divergence of reality from intent demonstrates
how a "conjunction of circumstances of personality can thoroughly transform constitutional institutions and their underlying ideas."[35]

Certainly a major reason for the evolution of the presidency as a significant
political institution must be the first holder of the office, Charles de Gaulle.[36] De
Gaulle was a charismatic leader who favored strong executive leadership, and in the
same way that initial incumbents of many political offices leave lasting impressions
on the institutions they helped to create, de Gaulle's role in the development of the
French presidency cannot be overstated. De Gaulle was a hero of World War II, leader
of the Resistance, and leader of the transition team of 1958 that guided the Fourth
Republic into the Fifth Republic. His perception of the presidency, which we have

seen he first expressed in 1946 in his Bayeux speech calling for strong, vigorous executive leadership, was almost bound to become embedded in the political system.

A second reason for the growth of the relative power of the French presidency can be found in the constitutional amendment of October 1962, which established the direct popular election of the president for a seven-year term of office.[37] In the 1958 constitution, the president was to be elected by an electoral college made up of local and provincial officials and national legislators. By having the president directly elected by the people, and therefore responsible to them and not to the legislators, de Gaulle gave the presidency a tremendous infusion of power and legitimacy.

Direct popular election "endowed the presidency with the legitimacy of a direct popular vote which, it was hoped, would accrue to the office when it was occupied by a less charismatic personality than General de Gaulle."[38] The result of this was "a mixed system of authority in which, as long as the President and government are of the same party, the presidential elements are likely to dominate." As President Georges Pompidou described the system in 1964:

> France has now chosen a system midway between the American presidential regime and the British parliamentary regime, where the chief of state, who formulates general policy, has the basis of his authority in universal suffrage but can only exercise his functions with a government that he may have chosen and named, but which in order to survive must maintain the confidence of the Assembly.[39]

The apparent similarity to the American system can be overstated, however. Apart from the strong head of state, which is a single deviation from "normal" parliamentary systems, the French system is still much closer to the parliamentary model than to the American presidential model. This is so for a number of reasons:

1. By holding the power of dissolution (Article 12) over parliament, the French President can "interfere directly" with parliamentary organization and activity. The American President, of course, cannot.
2. By dissolving parliament the French President can, like the British Prime Minister, create a plebiscitory situation to receive popular support for his actions. The American President, of course, cannot dissolve the legislature.
3. The President has vast emergency powers under Article 16, with no judicial oversight as exists in the United States with the judicial review of the Supreme Court.[40]

The Prime Minister

Given the dominant role of the president in the French political system, it should be fairly clear that the role of the prime minister in the Fifth Republic will be of considerably *less* significance than it is in most parliamentary systems, although this has been less true in recent years than it was in the first two decades or so of the Fifth Republic. (It should be noted that the formal title of the chief executive in France is "prime minister," not "premier." "Premier" was used in the Third and Fourth Republics, and is still often used today as an incorrect holdover from former regimes.)

In the French system, the role of the prime minister "has been limited to a joint formulation of policy with the President (in which the premier has played an increasingly subordinate role) and to manage the legislature so that it will accept the government's program."[41] One student of the French political system has suggested that in the Fifth Republic the prime minister is "merely the 'head of government,' while the president is the actual decision-maker. He leaves to the premier the role of being a link between the president and Parliament, particularly on matters the president is not interested in."[42]

Having said that the prime minister is the very junior partner of the "dual executive," in terms of the division of executive power, it should be pointed out that "the premier and his government have become a great deal stronger than ever before in their relations with the Assembly."

> Among the new rights accorded to the government by the Fifth Republic . . . are the right to the priority of government bills in the parliamentary timetable, the right to propose amendments to bills, and the right to open a general debate on a measure in either chamber. Thus deputies now hear the government's case on a bill before the *rapporteur* of the relevant committee can present his criticisms, and the debate takes place on the government's text, not the text that emerges from committee. Moreover, the government has the right to reject amendments proposed from the floor after the committee stage and also to force the chamber to vote either on particular clauses of the bill or on the bill as a whole. The government can also spur a decision on a bill over which there is disagreement between the Senate and the Assembly. What the government cannot do, however, is to secure the passage of a bill (unless it is on finance) that the Assembly refuses to approve.[43]

The President, the Prime Minister, and Cohabitation

The model of French politics described above seemed to operate reasonably well until the election of 1986. To understand the significance of the 1986 election it is necessary to go back to April and May of 1981, at which time François Mitterand was elected president (the first time a Socialist had been elected president of France). One of his first actions was to dissolve the (at that time conservative-dominated) National Assembly and call for new elections, producing a Socialist-dominated legislature. At that time he appointed a Socialist prime minister, Pierre Mauroy, and everything continued normally until the next elections.

By the time of the next elections for the National Assembly—something we shall discuss in more detail later—the Socialists had lost much of their glamour, however, and captured only 216 out of 577 seats in the Assembly. President Mitterand invited Jacques Chirac, leader of the largest party within the majority (conservative) coalition to become prime minister. He and Chirac agreed to a new power-sharing arrangement between the (Socialist) president and the (conservative) prime minister, something that came to be called *cohabitation*.[44] For the duration of Mitterand's term, his powers were considerably reduced from their pre-1986 level, and the powers of the prime minister were considerably greater than they had been previously.[45]

This practice has continued in recent years, and the current situation in France can be more accurately characterized as one with two almost-equally powerful actors rather than one dominated by the president, as was the case during the first two decades of the Fifth Republic.[46] After the July 1993 election for the National Assembly, Edouard Balladur—the conservative candidate of the Rassemblement pour la République—indicated that he would continue to be a strong leader of the right-of-center as the new prime minister.[47]

THE LEGISLATURE

The Legislature and the Government

The executive branch dominates the legislative process in a number of ways in the Fifth Republic. Two of these forms of domination are functions of direct limitation on the power of the legislature. First, the legislature cannot propose "increasing expenditures or lowering revenue in relation to the details of and total range of government budgetary proposals."[48] Second, the legislature can only pass laws dealing with matters that are specifically delegated to it in the constitution. Each of these points is of sufficient significance to warrant further discussion here.

The budgetary process in any political system is a point of vulnerability for the Government. Governments that are unable to have their budgets passed find themselves at the mercy of their respective legislatures, literally unable to carry on the business of governing. The Fifth Republic's constitution places strong restrictions on the legislature's ability to obstruct or delay the Government in the budgetary arena.

> The Fifth Republic has streamlined budgetary procedures by giving the Assembly only forty days in which to vote on the government's proposals, thereafter the budget goes automatically to the Senate for two weeks. Differences are debated in conference committee. But if parliament does not vote the budget within seventy days, the government may bring it into effect by ordinance. Under any circumstances, the six-sevenths of the budget for "continuing services" must become law without change, and under Article 40 no deputy can propose increasing expenditures or lowering revenue in relation to the details of and total range of government budgetary proposals.[49]

The knowledge that the essence of the Government's budget will become law in any case, and the limitations imposed upon the legislature in terms of changes it can and cannot propose to the Government's budget, place the legislature at a severe disadvantage in relation to the Government.

In addition, the 1958 constitution departed from "the traditional French republican principle of unrestricted parliamentary sovereignty" by specifically listing the legislative powers of parliament (Article 34), indicating those areas in which parliament could legislate; fields not specifically reserved for the legislature were left to the Government "to decide by decree."

> This arrangement, which might seem like a serious encroachment on the power of Parliament, is not highly restrictive for two reasons. First, no subject of central importance is omitted from the list. Second, the list can be extended by Parliament

through the adoption of an organic law (a law implementing provisions of the Constitution).[50]

There are a number of other ways in which the executive is able to influence the legislative process. First, the Government controls the agenda of the National Assembly, and "by means of its power to determine the agenda the government can insure that its bills have priority over 'private members'." The Government has the power to stipulate which portions of its legislative proposals can be amended, and how much time can be spent on each section of the bill.

Moreover, the Government can call for a "blocked vote" requiring the legislative chambers to vote on a bill in its original text "incorporating only those amendments proposed or accepted by the government."[51] As a more severe action, the Government can announce that it is making the passage of a bill into a question of confidence. If it does this, the bill automatically passes "unless a censure motion is filed by one-tenth of the deputies within 24 hours and an absolute majority of the deputies vote in support of censure."[52]

The question of the relation between the Government and the National Assembly over the concept of "censure" or "confidence" is interesting, because it is another area in which the usual vulnerability of the executive branch to the will of the legislature has been modified from the "standard" model. Although some texts declare that "if a motion of censure is adopted by the National Assembly, the Government must resign,"[53] history has shown that this rule of thumb has not always been followed.

The French president has the right to dissolve the National Assembly virtually at will, and Charles de Gaulle on more than one occasion dissolved the National Assembly when it censured his prime minister and Government. He then immediately reappointed the same prime minister and cabinet without their having resigned.

The censure process is more difficult to operate in France than it is in many parliamentary systems, although it is not as difficult as we shall see is the case with the German "positive vote of no confidence." Opposition members can introduce motions of censure if the motion is signed by one-tenth of the deputies of the National Assembly (totalling 491). After the motion is introduced, 48 hours must pass before it can be debated and voted on; in order for it to pass, the motion must receive an absolute majority of deputies' support (half plus one of the 491 deputies), not just a majority of deputies present and voting. Opposition members who sign a motion of censure are enjoined from being cosignatories of another such motion during the same legislative session; this is designed to prevent a constant stream of motions that are sure to be defeated.[54]

Although the National Assembly may pass motions censuring the Government, or withdrawing its support from the Government, it may not "pass resolutions or otherwise express its views on policy unless the government asks it to do so." The reason for this is that "the framers of the constitution of the Fifth Republic wanted to maintain the ultimate control of the National Assembly over the Government without permitting either the National Assembly or the Senate to become policymaking agencies."[55]

The Senate

In 1947 the founders of the Fourth Republic decided to do away with the Senate as the second half of the legislative body in the (then) new regime. Their argument was that the Senate was (1) undemocratically selected, since it was not directly elected by the people; (2) overrepresentative of rural areas; and (3) either redundant or antidemocratic—if it agreed with the lower house it was redundant and therefore unnecessary, and if it disagreed with the popularly elected lower house it was antidemocratic, since the lower house *was* popularly elected and the Senate was not. After some discussion, a weak "Council of the Republic" was substituted for the Senate in the Fourth Republic. In 1958 Charles de Gaulle brought back the second house to the French legislative system.

The Senate is sometimes referred to as the "agricultural" chamber of the legislature, because it tends to overrepresent rural areas of France. The unit of representation in the Senate is the *department*; the number of senators representing a given department varies from one or two to over five, depending upon the size and population of the department. The precise manner by which senators are selected will be discussed further; here we are interested in the Senate's role in the French legislative system.

Generally speaking, the Senate is the inferior of the two legislative bodies in France today. Although its resuscitators in 1958 sought to restore the Senate to the position of legislative equality it had enjoyed in the Third Republic, today its position falls far short of that target. This inferior position can be measured in a number of ways. For instance, the Senate meets less frequently than does the Assembly. As another indicator, in the period from 1959 to 1977, only 245 bills introduced by legislators became laws (as compared with 1,617 bills introduced by the Government); of these, only 23 percent originated in the Senate.[56]

We do not want to overstate the argument for the Senate's inferior position, however.[57] The Senate sometimes can be an effective legislative body in terms of its ability to provide a "sober second thought" to legislative proposals, especially to Government proposals. This is true for very much the same reason as it is for the House of Lords in Great Britain. Because the Government is responsible to the lower house, and can be fired by the lower house, party discipline will keep criticism in that body to a minimum. The upper house, to which the Government is *not* responsible, often has more freedom to inquire and criticize than does the lower house. An additional basis of power for the Senate in France is more parallel to the upper house in Germany (the Bundesrat) than to the House of Lords in Great Britain; although France is not a federal regime, senators represent geographical districts, or departments, and when Government bills deal with regional issues, agriculture, or similar questions, the Senate is likely to play a more significant role in the legislative process than it otherwise would.

The Legislative Process

This having been said, it must be noted again that the Senate of the Fifth Republic is not an equal partner in the legislative process. The legislative process in the Fifth

Republic is clearly dominated by the Government in the National Assembly, with the Senate often not much more than an afterthought in the process.

> As in the Fourth Republic, and in Britain, West Germany, and Italy, a distinction is made between government bills (*projets de loi*) and private members' bills (*propositions de loi*), with the former accounting for most of the bills introduced in the Assembly. When a bill is introduced, it is sent first to the *bureau*; and the speaker, who heads that unit, transmits the bill directly to a legislative committee. When the committee has done its work, the *rapporteur* formally reports the bill to the floor for what is technically the initial "reading" of it. The ensuing debate, which provides an opportunity for the introduction of amendments, is followed by a vote. After its passage by the Assembly, the bill is transmitted to the Senate. If that chamber accepts the original version of the bill, it is sent to the government for signature. If the Senate rejects the bill, the subsequent procedure varies. There can be a resort to the shuttle (*navette*)—the sending of a bill back and forth between the two chambers until a common version is achieved; second, the government may request the establishment of a conference committee (*commission mixte paritaire*); third, the government may ask each chamber for a "second reading" (i.e., a reconsideration and new vote on the original bill); and fourth, if disagreement persists, the government may ask the Assembly to determine the final version of the bill by simple majority vote.[58]

The Government's ability to select among these several options when inter-chamber disagreement arises in the legislative process gives it a great deal of power. Ultimately, the Government can choose to simply ignore the Senate and ask the National Assembly to determine the final version of a bill. If the National Assembly wants to pass a bill that the Government does not want, it can simply let the *navette* go on endlessly, or keep the bill off the agenda. Finally, of course, if the Government finds both chambers noncompliant, it has the ultimate power to couple a "blocked vote" with a question of confidence to force its proposals through the legislative process.

THE CONSTITUTIONAL COUNCIL

As is the case in most parliamentary systems of government, France has no active tradition of judicial review in politics.[59] "The sovereignty of parliament means that the legislature has the last word and that a law enacted in constitutionally prescribed form is not subject to further scrutiny."[60] In spite of this, the Constitutional Council of the Fifth Republic was designed (Articles 56 through 63 of the Constitution) "to ensure that constitutional provisions would possess a certain superiority over ordinary laws." Its function is to rule on the standing orders of the legislature and, on request of the Government majority (but not a legislative minority), to determine the boundaries of executive and legislative competence and "whether laws . . . or treaties are in conformity with the constitution."[61] It also is required to supervise presidential and parliamentary elections, as well as referenda.

Many people in 1958 feared the creation of a Constitutional Council as it was described at the time because it sounded very much like the U.S. Supreme Court; the powers of the U.S. Supreme Court were thought to be too sweeping to transplant to the French system. The fears of an activist judiciary have not been realized, however, primarily because the members of the Constitutional Council were generally sympathetic to Government policy. Three of the nine regular judges are appointed by the president, three by the president of the National Assembly, and three by the president of the Senate. The nine judges serve nine-year terms. Former presidents of the Republic are on the Constitutional Council for life terms.

The bulk of the Constitutional Council's work has been in adjudicating jurisdictional disputes between the presidency and the legislature "over boundaries of law and regulation." The Constitutional Council so consistently ruled on behalf of the president's point of view that it became perceived as an "auxiliary of executive authority."[62]

> By the end of 1963, the Constitutional Council had decided 31 disputes over the respective rule-making powers of the Parliament and the Government. In 22 cases it decided that the rule-making power in question was properly the Government's; in four it decided that the proper jurisdiction was parliamentary, and in the others there was either no decision or a decision dividing the rule-making power between the Government and Parliament.[63]

PARTY POLITICS AND THE ELECTORAL PROCESS

There have traditionally been a number of political parties active in the French political system. In modern times, it was not until the Fifth Republic that a true majority party existed in France, the UNR-UDR (Union for a New Republic-Democratic Union for the Republic).[64] Throughout French history, the political party systems that existed failed to provide a basis for stable elections; the parties failed to govern. "In a fragmented multi-party system elections never conferred the right to govern upon a majority, no party saw as its role support for the government of the day and the defense of its record before the electorate."[65] Henry Ehrmann has written:

> The inconveniences of the French multiparty system were compounded by the constitutional arrangements and parliamentary practices of the Third and Fourth Republics. To survive and to govern effectively, a government needed more than just the absence of a majority willing to overthrow it; it needed a positive majority in favor of the government's policy and its legislative proposals. This, however, was difficult to obtain where majorities consisted not of disciplined parties or of parliamentary groups kept in line by an effective whip, but to a large extent of ephemeral coalitions. Their cohesion or disruption depended on whatever problem was under consideration. As different problems came up, governments toppled or were condemned to immobility.[66]

General Charles de Gaulle, in his criticisms of the Government in the Fourth Republic, described this anarchic situation of no responsible government and no responsible opposition as "*le regime des partis.*"[67] It was strictly speaking, a regime *with* parties, not a regime *of* parties. Party *control* (in the sense of stable party government) of the regime did not come until de Gaulle's supporters won parliamentary majorities in the Fifth Republic.

Gaullism and Presidential Leadership

Certainly among the most significant modern phenomena in the French party system was the rise of the Gaullist "nonparty" that became institutionalized as the significant political organization of the regime. Originally, "Gaullism" was a movement of support for Charles de Gaulle that claimed to be an alternative to divisive political parties; both organizationally and ideologically it insisted upon being regarded simply as a following for de Gaulle. Its ideology was the ideology of de Gaulle; its organization was designed to further the interests and goals of de Gaulle. It "pretended not to be a party at all, but rather a national *movement*, an alternative to parties."[68]

The Gaullist ideology was perceived as a rightist ideology because of de Gaulle's pro-business attitudes and his frequent indifference to socioeconomic political issues. The Gaullist party was able to draw from the political left as well as the right, however, because of de Gaulle's antiparliamentary attitudes, shared with the Communist party (the PCF); his positive view of the Church, which was shared with the Popular Republican Movement (MRP); and his commitment to plebiscitory democracy and frequent referenda, generally a left-wing attitude. In 1962 the Union for a New Republic (UNR), in fact the Gaullist party of its day, combined with a generally conservative working-class party called the Democratic Union of Labor to form the Democratic Union for the Republic (UDR).

When de Gaulle left the political scene and Georges Pompidou, his former prime minister, became president, the Gaullist movement weakened somewhat, but not as much or as rapidly as many had predicted it would. Pompidou's presidency "was no period of dramatic social and economic change. By now the broad lines of French development were clearly fixed and Pompidou continued the course set in the 1960s."[69] Many had claimed that the UDR—the Democratic Union for the Republic, the descendent of the UNR—and Gaullism in general were simply personalistic followings for de Gaulle; as soon as de Gaulle left politics, the critics said, the Gaullists as a political bloc would fall apart.

Pompidou reigned over the demise of the UDR between 1970 and 1974. By the time of the parliamentary elections in 1973, the UDR had so weakened that it joined with the Independent Republicans and the Center of Democracy and Progress (CDP) in an electoral alliance called the Union of Republicans for Progress (URP). But even with that its parliamentary representation fell from 273 seats in 1968 to 185 in 1973.

With the election of Valéry Giscard d'Estaing as president in 1974, the UDR became an "also-ran." Giscard, an Independent Republican, drew a good deal of what was left in the UDR to his party. The Giscard years were associated with an economic liberalism, a theme of national unity, and a "more liberal functioning of institutions,"[70] the latter including a slight increase of the power of the parliament compared to earlier regimes.

In 1981 the Socialist party rose to prominence under President François Mitterand. In the 1981 campaign many of the principal issues were economic, and Mitterand was able to convince a majority of the French voters that they should give the political left a chance to lead France. Mitterand became the first Socialist to be elected president, and as was indicated earlier, he immediately dissolved the National Assembly and called for new elections so that he could have a Socialist-dominated Assembly to help enact his program. The Socialists, riding on the coattails of the newly elected president, won a clear majority (262 of the 491 seats), and with their non-Communist allies controlled 285 seats in the National Assembly. With a clear majority in the legislature, Mitterand was able to implement a number of socialist policies.[71]

The perception at the time was that the "intention of the French Socialist administration, presided over by Mitterand, was 'to give the state back to the people'."[72] Mitterand believed that while centralization had been necessary in the creation of France, at the time of his election decentralization was necessary for the future of France. Mitterand was a political realist, recognizing that the forces that elected him were as much a response to the economic climate of the time as they were indications of fundamental agreement with his ideology.[73] However:

> the euphoria which surrounded the Socialists' victory became short-lived. Despite commitments to a substantially higher rate of economic growth and to a sharp decline in unemployment, the reality of their first years in government proved very different. Stimulating demand failed to revive a sluggish economy and unemployment continued its inexorable rise.[74]

Public reaction against the Mitterand Government and some of its policies led to a decline in public support for the Socialists. In local elections in 1982 and 1983, many of the supporters who had worked so hard for Mitterand in 1981 supported conservative candidates, and the conservative parties made great progress. In the long view, "the years of socialist government did not produce the revolution of which many of its supporters dreamed." Social inequality and injustice did not disappear; the economy did not expand as promised. "Instead economic growth proved sluggish and many of the basic divisive features of society showed themselves highly resilient to change."[75]

In March 1986 the "French socialist experience"[76] came to an end with a conservative victory in the elections for the National Assembly, resulting in the *cohabitation* arrangement between Socialist President Mitterand and conservative Prime Minister Chirac discussed earlier. The conservatives thought that this was a foreshadowing of a presidential victory in 1988, but such was not the case: President Mitterand, with a much more economically moderate and ideologically toned-down campaign than he had run in 1981, defeated his opponent Chirac and won re-election to the presidency.

French Political Parties

The political party system of contemporary France presents a broad spectrum of ideologies to the observer; parties represent a variety of shades of public opinion from the far left to the far right. Most contemporary texts dealing with French politics[77] discuss the party system in terms of component parties, and move from left to right (or right to left) along the political spectrum, describing the respective ideologies and policy positions of the many contemporary French parties.[78]

The number of political parties has varied over the years, with various temporary and permanent alliances and coalitions affecting the number and structures of political organizations active at any given time. Moreover, a number of political parties have changed their names over the years, so at first glance it is often difficult to follow the evolution of the parties.

This point of temporary electoral alliances between parties is worth noting. Because of the nature of the electoral system—a point to which we shall turn shortly—many parties have decided that although they are not going to *merge* permanently with one another, their views are similar enough that they should not compete *against* each other in elections.

This kind of attitude gave rise to the Union of Republicans for Progress (URP) in 1973, leading to a coordination of candidacies around France among the Independent Republican Party, the Democratic Union for the Republic (UDR), and the Center for Democracy and Progress (CDP). The same thing happened in the elections of 1978 and 1981, with the French Democratic Union (UDF) resulting from coordination between the Republican Party (PR, formed by Giscard from the Independent Republican Party in 1977), the Center for Social Democrats (CDS, a new party organized from the earlier CDP), and some others. In both 1988 and 1993, the Union for French Democracy and the Rally for the Republic contested the elections jointly as the Union of the Rally and of the Center (URC). Subsequently, many of the various right-wing parties joined the URC prior to the second ballot.

Another more recent phenomenon involves the development of the National Front (FN), led by Jean-Marie Le Pen.[79] The National Front has been variously labelled as "extreme right" and neo-Nazi, and has campaigned strongly in favor of statism and against foreigners. Despite the continued high profile of LePen, and the fact that it had candidates in 100 districts at the time of the second ballot in the 1993 election, the party lost its single seat in the National Assembly in the 1993 elections.[80]

Elections to the National Assembly

If France were a "typical" parliamentary system, we would have only elections to the national legislature to study at this point. The selection of the head of state would not be politically significant, and the selection of the chief executive would automatically follow the leader of the majority in the lower house of the national legislature. However, because of de Gaulle's 1962 referendum—to have the president directly elected by the citizenry rather than indirectly elected by a complex electoral college, as had been the case previously—any discussion of French elections must include both presidential and parliamentary elections. We will begin our brief discussion with the National Assembly, move to the presidency, and conclude with a discussion of selection of senators.

French elections for the National Assembly are for terms of five years (or less, if the Assembly is dissolved early) and for the most part have been based upon a *majority* approach to voting rather than a *plurality* approach, as is the case in Great

Britain (or the United States).[81] That is, in electoral contests for the National Assembly the initial question asked on election day after the polls close is *not* "Who received the most votes?" Recall that in single-member-district, plurality voting systems, the candidate who receives the most votes is the winner; if there are six candidates and the candidate with the most votes receives only 25 percent of the total vote, that candidate is elected even though 75 percent of the public did not vote for him or her. In majority-based elections, unlike plurality-based elections, to win a race on the first ballot one must receive a majority of the vote.

We said earlier that French elections for the National Assembly have "for the most part been based upon a majority approach" because for about one year—from March 1986 until June 1987—the electoral system was changed from universal direct election (as described further below) to a proportional representation electoral system. (That is, proportional representation within departments, not nationally, with a 5 percent threshold necessary for election.)[82] Proportional representation replaced the single-member-district model when it became clear to President Mitterand that his Socialist party faced an overwhelming rejection by the voters in the election of March 1986.

With the majority voting system and a level of public opinion support at only 30 percent, the Socialists would very likely have become a tiny minority in the Assembly. With proportional representation voting, the Socialists won 206 out of 577 seats in the National Assembly, but the parties of the right controlled a majority in the Assembly and a conservative government was formed. This resulted in the period of *cohabitation* we referred to earlier. The system of proportional representation elections "generated a storm from political elites, indifference from the public, and a commitment by the new government to get rid of it again."[83] Within a year of the election the new conservative-dominated government restored the former electoral system.[84]

When the presidential elections were held in April and May of 1988 and President Mitterand was reelected, he again—much as he did immediately after his first electoral victory seven years earlier—dissolved the National Assembly and called for new elections. Again, as in 1981, the French public gave the left a majority in the Assembly, although the Socialist party alone did not receive the outright majority in 1988 that it did in 1981, and it had to make arrangements with the Communists[85] to maintain a majority.

Given the number of political parties in the French electoral system, it is clear that few candidates will win majorities outright. This has led to France's unique two-ballot "simple majority" system of voting.[86] To be a candidate for the National Assembly, an individual must post a deposit of 1,000 francs (about $200), which is refunded if the candidate receives at least 5 percent of the vote. The first election is held on a Sunday, and a candidate who receives an absolute majority (50 percent of the vote plus one vote) of the total votes cast in his district is elected on the first round of voting.[87] If no candidate wins a majority on the first ballot, a second ballot is held on the following Sunday. At that time, the candidate who receives a *plurality* of the votes is declared the winner. (See Table 10.2.)

Elections to the National Assembly on the first ballot are the exception

TABLE 10.2
The French Parliamentary Election of 1993

Parties	After the First Round	After the Second Round	Change Total	from 1988
PC (Communist Party)	0	24	24	- 2
PS (Socialist Party)	0	53	53	- 205
MRG (Radical Left Movement)	0	6	6	- 4
Maj. p. (Presidential Majority)	0	8	8	- 6
Divers (Various Left Parties)	0	1	1	+ 1
UDF (Union for French Democracy)*	5	21	26	+ 9
UDF-CDS (Center of Social Democrats)	12	47	59	+ 10
UDF-PR (Republican Party)	19	85	104	+ 44
UDF-Rad. (Radical Party)	0	13	13	+ 10
UDF-PSD (Social-Democratic Party)	0	7	7	+ 5
RPR (Rally for the Republic)	42	200	242	+115
Div. d (Various Right Parties)	2	33	35	+ 25
CNI (National Center of Independents)	0	1	1	—
FN (National Front)	0	0	0	- 1
Total	80	497	577	

* The UDF was formed in 1978 as an alignment of non-Gaullist right-of-center candidates. It is affiliated with several other parties.

Source:: Le Monde: Edition internationale no. 2317, 25–31 March, 1993, p. 7; Press and Information Office, Embassy of France, Washington, D.C.

rather than the rule. In the June 1988 parliamentary elections, only 122 of 577 races (21.1 percent) were decided on the first ballot; this figure was even lower—80 of the 577 races (13.9 percent)—in the election of July, 1993.[88]

When the second round of elections are held, no new candidate for office may register. In order to contest the second ballot, a candidate must have received 12.5 percent of the vote on the first round. (This was 10 percent in the 1978 election.) Although this means that technically several candidates could compete in the second round of voting (since more than two candidates could receive 12.5 percent of the vote on the first round), most second ballots turn out to be duels between two parties because of the alliances that we mentioned earlier.

For example, the Republican party and the Center of Social Democrats may sign a preelection agreement within the framework of the UDF that they would both compete in the first round, but that the second-place party of the two would bow out in the second round and throw its support to the other in order to help defeat the Socialist party or Communist party candidate in the district.

This kind of preelectoral alliance/agreement has had the effect in many cases of turning the first ballot into a type of primary election, in which a number of candidates from the left may compete, and a number of candidates from the right may compete, with the understanding that the top vote-getter from the left will "represent" the left, and the top vote-getter from the right will "represent" the right. "The parties of the left have agreed at every election since 1962 . . . that only one candidate of the left shall remain at the second ballot and that it shall be he who scored most votes at the first."[89]

Presidential Elections

The electoral system for the presidency is essentially the same. Anyone can be a candidate for president, providing he or she deposits 10,000 francs ($2,000, which is forfeited if the candidate fails to receive at least 5 percent of the vote) and obtains nomination petitions signed by 100 "notables" (National Assembly deputies, senators, mayors, or departmental councillors). Candidates are given free TV and radio time by the state.

A candidate must receive an absolute majority of the public votes in order to win on the first ballot. This has never happened in Fifth Republic France; the most votes that Charles de Gaulle ever received on the first ballot was 44 percent of the total votes cast. The second ballot is limited to the top two vote-getters from the first round, and takes place two weeks after the first round of voting.

As the data in Table 10.3 show, it is possible to win (receive a plurality) on the first ballot and lose on the second ballot. In the first-round voting for the presidency on April 26, 1981, the incumbent, Valéry Giscard d'Estaing, won a plurality with 28.3 percent of the vote. François Mitterand came in second with 25.9 percent of the vote. On the second ballot, Republican Giscard received the votes of the rightist voters, and Socialist Mitterand received the support of the leftist voters. The combined leftist vote defeated the combined rightist vote, 51.75 percent to 48.24 percent.

TABLE 10.3
The French Presidential Election of 1981

	FIRST ROUND: APRIL 26, 1981		SECOND ROUND: MAY 10, 1981	
	Number of Votes Cast	**Percent of Votes Cast**	**Number of Votes Cast**	**Percent of Votes Cast**
V. Giscard D'Estaing[a]	8,222,432	28.3	14,642,306	48.24
F. Mitterand	7,505,960	25.9	15,708,262	51.75
J. Chirac	5,225,848	18.0		
G. Marchais	4,456,922	15.3		
B. LaLonde	1,126,254	3.9		
A. LaGuiller	668,057	2.3		
M. Crepeau	642,847	2.2		
M. Debré	481,821	1.7		
M.-F. Garaud	386,623	1.3		
H. Bouchardeau	321,353	1.1		

[a] incumbent

Source: Dominique and Michele Fremy, eds., *Quid* (Paris: Editions Robert Laffont, 1981), p. 755.

TABLE 10.4
The French Presidential Election of 1988

	FIRST ROUND: APRIL 24, 1988		SECOND ROUND: MAY 8, 1988	
	Number of Votes Cast	Percent of Votes Cast	Number of Votes Cast	Percent of Votes Cast
F. Mitterand[a]	10,381,332	34.1	16,704,279	54.02
J. Chirac	6,075,160	20.0	14,218,970	45.98
R. Barre	5,035,144	16.5		
J. M. Le Pen	4,376,742	14.4		
A. LaJoinie	2,056,261	6.8		
A. Waechter	1,149,897	3.8		
P. Juquin	639,133	2.1		
A. LaGuiller	606,201	2.0		
P. Boussel	116,874	0.4		

[a] incumbent

Source: Dominique and Michele Fremy, eds., *Quid* (Paris: Editions Robert Laffont, 1981), p. 755; *Quid, 1989,* p. 727.

On the other hand, in the 1988 presidential election (see Table 10.4) President Mitterand received a plurality on the first ballot with 34.1 percent of the vote, and went on to win on the second ballot with almost 54 percent of the vote.[90]

Election of Senators

The selection of senators differs from the single-member-district, majority voting selection of deputies to the National Assembly. Senators are intended to represent the administrative/territorial units of France, and the method of their selection reflects this.

Senators are elected for terms of nine years by "indirect universal suffrage."[91] The department is the unit of representation; senators are elected from departments by departmental electoral colleges. These electoral colleges range from 270 electors in smaller departments to over 6,000 electors in the larger departments, depending upon the population of the department.[92] Deputies in the National Assembly from districts in a given department, departmental councillors, and delegates chosen by municipal councils—all comprise these electoral colleges. Thus the Senate is elected by the 577 National Assembly deputies, about 3,000 *conseillers généraux,* and about 100,000 delegates from the municipal councils.[93] (See Table 10.5.)

The larger departments (seven in all) elect five or more senators; smaller departments choose fewer. In the departments that choose five or more senators, senators are chosen by proportional representation voting; electors vote for a party list; and parties receive a number of senatorial positions corresponding to the proportion of the vote they received. In the smaller departments, senators are elected on a two-ballot system very similar to elections for the National Assembly: A majority is required on the first ballot, and a plurality is required on the second ballot.

TABLE 10.5
The French Senate in 1992

Party	Number of Seats
PC (Communist Party)	15
PS (Socialist Party)	67
Various Left Parties	13
UDF (Union for French Democracy)*	15
UDF-CDS (Center of Social Democrat)	42
UDF-Rad (Radical Party)	12
UDF-PR (Republican Party)	44
UDF-PSD (Social-Democratic Party)	3
RPR (Rally for the Republic)	88
Various Right Parties	22

* The UDF was formed in 1978 as an alignment of non-Gaullist right-of-center candidates. It is affiliated with several other parties.

Source: Le Monde, September 29, 1992, p. 3.

The Senate is often referred to as an "agricultural chamber" because of its malrepresentation of the French population. "Rural France is overrepresented and urban France is underrepresented in the Senate." For example, "the eight departments of the Paris Region, plus five other departments which each had more than one million inhabitants . . . contain one-third of the French population, and while they have 32 percent of the . . . seats in the National Assembly, they have only 26 percent of such seats in the Senate."[94]

Although senators serve nine-year terms, Senate elections are held every three years. The Senate is divided into three equal groups, referred to as Series A (102), Series B (102), and Series C (117 seats, of which 115 are elected), determined by an alphabetical list of departments.[95] One group is elected every three years.

SUMMARY

We have seen in this chapter that the French political system can almost be seen as a variation of the Westminster model of government in several respects, many of them quite significant. The dual executive, although resembling the British model on paper, is quite different in its actual day-to-day behavior and power structure. The French president is virtually unique in the parliamentary world (except for political systems modelled after France), having both in theory and in practice all of the power that the British monarchy has only in theory.

The French Constitution is partially responsible for this. When Charles de Gaulle and his colleagues designed the constitutional structures in the Fifth Republic, they took pains to provide for strong executive leadership—to a large extent to compensate for years of weak executives and strong, and uncontrollable, legislatures. The fact that the legislatures in both the Third and Fourth Republics were unstable foundations upon which to base a government was not lost on the founders of the Fifth Republic.

The legislative bodies of the Fifth Republic are typical of other parliamentary legislatures in a number of respects. First, of course, they are inferior to the executive branch of government. The legislature is *not* expected to be a major policy-making body in the political system. Its function is to approve the policies of the executive, and, if the executive becomes too unpopular, to replace the Government. Second, the upper house of the legislature is inferior to the lower house of the legislature. Ultimately, the Senate can have only a suspensory veto over the actions of the National Assembly; it can slow down the actions of that house, but it cannot prevent National Assembly legislation from becoming law.

French elections differ from elections in other political systems because of the single-member-district, majority voting system used for the National Assembly, and the two-wave voting for the presidency. Again, we see that the structure of the electoral system can have an impact upon the political party system in a country. France has a number of political parties, not just one or two, and these parties do their best to operate within the rules of the Fifth Republic's electoral system.

In the case of France, then, we have been able to see a number of applications of the material we described in the first part of this text. Constitutions, executives, legislatures, electoral systems, and political parties all matter in the day-to-day operation of a political regime. We will continue to see in the following chapters that some of the idiosyncratic features of political regimes are of tremendous significance in the daily operation of government.

Notes

1. For discussion of French political history prior to the Third Republic, see Roy Pierce, *French Politics and Political Institutions* (New York: Harper and Row, 1968), p. 2, Gwendolen Carter, *The Government of France* (New York: Harcourt Brace Jovanovich, 1972), p. 20, William Safran, *The French Polity* (New York: David McKay, 1977), p. 6, or John Ambler, *The Government and Politics of France* (Boston: Houghton Mifflin, 1971), pp. 3–4.
2. William Safran, *The French Polity*, 2nd ed. (New York: Longman, 1985), p. 5.
3. Ambler, *The Government and Politics of France*, p. 7.
4. Further discussion of this period can be found in Carter, *The Government of France*, pp. 22–23, and Ambler, *The Government and Politics of France*, p. 7.
5. See Stanley Hoffman, "Aspects du Regime de Vichy," *Revue Francais de Science Politique* 6 (1956): 44–69.
6. Carter, *The Government of France*, p. 25.
7. Ambler, *The Government and Politics of France*, p. 10.
8. The best general discussions of problems and performances of the Fourth Republic are to be found in three sources: Philip Williams, *Crisis and Compromise: Politics in the Fourth Republic* (New York: Doubleday, 1966), Duncan MacRae, *Parliament, Parties, and Society in France: 1946–1958* (New York: St. Martin's Press, 1967), and François Goguel, *France Under the Fourth Republic* (Ithaca, N.Y.: Cornell University Press, 1952).
9. Ambler, *The Government and Politics of France*, p. 11.
10. Ibid., p. 11.
11. Pierce, *French Politics and Political Institutions*, p. 44.
12. Safran, *The French Polity*, p. 11.
13. Ambler, *The Government and Politics of France*, p. 13.
14. See the text of de Gaulle's Bayeux speech in Martin Harrison, ed., *French Politics* (Lexington, Mass.: D.C. Heath, 1969), pp. 24–28.
15. Safran, *The French Polity*, pp. 127–128.

16. Ibid., p. 59.

17. Roy C. Macridis, *French Politics in Transition* (Cambridge, Mass.: Winthrop, 1975), p. 6.

18. On the origins and drafting of the new constitution, see Nicholas Wahl and Stanley Hoffman, "The French Constitution of 1958," *American Political Science Review* 53 (1959): 332–382. See Michel Debré, "The New Constitution," in Harrison, *French Politics*, pp. 31–33.

19. Suzanne Berger, *The French Political System* (New York: Random House, 1974), p. 126. Much of the material in this section, and all quotes unless otherwise noted, derive from Berger, pp. 126–131.

20. See John A. Rohr, "French Constitutionalism and the Administrative State: A Comparative Textual Study," *Administration and Society* 24:2 (1992): pp. 224–240.

21. Berger, *The French Political System*, p. 127.

22. Ibid., p. 131.

23. Henry Ehrmann, *Politics in France* (Boston: Little, Brown, 1976), p. 267.

24. Ambler, *Government and Politics of France*, p. 125.

25. Safran, *The French Polity*, p. 128.

26. Berger, *The French Political System*, p. 40.

27. Leslie Derfler, *President and Parliament: A Short History of the French Presidency* (Boca Raton, Fla.: University Presses of Florida, 1983), p. 169.

28. Ambler, *The Government and Politics of France*, p. 126.

29. Pierce, *French Politics and Political Institutions*, pp. 62–63.

30. For the full text of the Constitution, see Pierce, *French Politics and Political Institutions*, pp. 227–254, or Ambler, *The Government and Politics of France*, pp. 237–248.

31. Berger, *The French Political System*, pp. 52–53.

32. Pierce, *French Politics and Political Institutions*, pp. 54–55.

33. Berger, *The French Political System*, p. 54.

34. Pierce, *French Politics and Political Institutions*, p. 54.

35. Ehrmann, *Politics in France*, p. 268.

36. See de Gaulle, "Charles de Gaulle and the Presidency," in Harrison, *French Politics*, pp. 48–54.

37. See Henry Ehrmann, "Direct Democracy in France," *American Political Science Review* 57 (1963): 883–901.

38. Ehrmann, *Politics in France*, p. 269.

39. Berger, *The French Political System*, p. 56.

40. Ehrmann, *Politics in France*, pp. 270–272.

41. Carter, *The Government of France*, p. 81. See also Michel Debré, "The Need for a Prime Minister" and Merry Bromberger's essays, "Georges Pompidou Becomes Prime Minister" and "President and Prime Minister: Two Conflicting Analyses," in Harrison, *French Politics*, pp. 65–78.

42. Safran, *The French Polity*, p. 130.

43. Carter, *The Government of France*, p. 83.

44. See John Frears, "Cohabitation," in Penniman, *France at the Polls*, pp. 228–236.

45. A good description of this period can be found in Ian Derbyshire, *Politics in France: From Giscard to Mitterand* (London: W & R Chambers, 1987), pp. 105–114.

46. See Alistair Cole, "President Mitterand and the French Political System," *Journal of Political Science* 20 (1992): 86–93.

47. He discusses these issues in the article "Edouard Balladur, le fils politique de Georges Pompidou," in *Le Monde: Edition internationale* no. 2317, 25–31 March 1993, p. 3.

48. Carter, *The Government of France*, p. 75.

49. Ibid. See also Pierce, *French Politics and Political Institutions*, p 87.

50. Pierce, *French Politics and Political Institutions*, p. 78–79.

51. Philip E. Converse and Roy Pierce, *Political Representation in France* (Cambridge: Harvard University Press, 1986), p. 533.

52. Carter, *The Government of France*, p. 72.

53. Pierce, *French Politics and Political Institutions*, p. 91.

54. Carter, *The Government of France*, p. 72.

55. Pierce, *French Politics and Political Institutions*, p. 91.

56. Safran, *The French Polity*, pp. 171–172.

57. See the essays by François Goguel, "The Role of the Senate," and Michel Debré, "The Future of the Senate," in Harrison, *French Politics*, pp. 114–118.

58. Safran, *The French Polity*, p. 165.

59. See Alec Stone, "Where Judicial Politics Are Legislative Politics: The French Constitutional Council," *West European Politics* 15:3 (1992): 29–43.

60. Carter, *The Government of France*, p. 324.

61. Ibid., pp. 32–33.

62. Berger, *The French Political System*, p. 57.

63. Pierce, *French Politics and Political Institutions*, p. 80.

64. Carter, *The Government of France*, p. 39.

65. J. R. Frears, *Political Parties and Elections in the French Fifth Republic* (New York: St. Martin's Press, 1977), p. 12.

66. Ehrmann, *Politics in France*, pp. 223–224.

67. Frears, *Political Parties*, p. 12.

68. Safran, *The French Polity*, p. 68.

69. D. L. Hanley, A. P. Kerr, and N. H. Waites, *Contemporary France: Politics and Society Since 1945* (Boston: Routledge and Kegan Paul, 1979), p. 41.

70. J. R. Frears, *France in the Giscard Presidency* (London: Allen and Unwin, 1981), p. 162. See also the volume edited by Vincent Wright, *Continuity and Change in France* (London: Allen and Unwin, 1984), for a collection of essays offering a general description of the Giscard years.

71. A very good book about François Mitterand written before his candidacy is that by C. L. Manceron and B. Pingaud, *François Mitterand: L'Homme, Les Idées, Le Programme* (Paris: Flammarion, 1981).

72. Michael Keating and Paul Hainsworth, *Decentralisation and Change in Contemporary France* (Brookfield, Vt.: Gower, 1986), p. 15.

73. Maurice Larkin, *France Since the Popular Front: Government and People, 1936–1986* (Oxford: Clarendon Press, 1988), p. 356.

74. John Tuppen, *France Under Recession: 1981–1986* (Albany: State University of New York Press, 1988), p. 1.

75. Ibid., p. 257.

76. Sonia Mazey and Michael Newman, eds., *Mitterand's France* (London: Croom Helm, 1987), p. 4. A very good analysis of Mitterand's success/failure in the first years can be found in the chapter by Michael Newman, "Conclusion—The Balance Sheet," pp. 218–234.

77. See Berger, *The French Political System*, pp. 78–97, Ehrmann, *Politics in France*, pp. 226–262, Pierce, *French Politics and Political Institutions*, pp. 100–128, Carter, *The Government of France*, pp. 40–49, Safran, *The French Polity*, pp. 74–97.

78. A very good survey of French parties is that edited by David S. Bell, *Contemporary French Political Parties* (New York: St. Martin's Press, 1981).

79. See N. Mayer and Pascal Perrimeau, "Why Do They Vote for Le Pen?" *European Journal of Political Research* 22:1 (1992): 123–137, Piero Ignazi and Colette Ysmal, "New and Old Extreme Right Parties: The French Front National and the Italian Movimento Sociale," *European Journal of Political Research* 22:1 (1992): 101–122, and Pierre Bréchon and Subrata Kumar Mitra, "The National Front in France: The Emergence of an Extreme Right Protest Movement," *Comparative Politics* 25:1 (1992): 63–80.

80. Olivier Biffaud, "Front national: accès interdit au Palais-Bourbon," *Le Monde: Edition internationale* no. 2317, 25–31 March 1993, p. 5.

81. An interesting consequence of the electoral system involves its effects on specific groups in the electorate. See Karen Beckwith, "Comparative Research and Electoral Systems: Lessons from France and Italy," *Women and Politics* 12:1 (1992): 1–23.

82. The exact operation of this proportional representation system can be found in John Frears, "The 1986 Parliamentary Elections," in Howard Penniman, ed., *France at the Polls, 1981 and 1986: Three National Elections* (Durham, N.C.: Duke University Press, 1988), pp. 211–214.

83. Ibid., p. 211.

84. See Dominique and Michele Fremy, *Quid, 1989* (Paris: Robert Laffont, 1988), pp. 686, 732.

85. A very good article on the French Communist party is that by George Ross, "Party Decline and Changing Party Systems: France and the French Communist Party," *Comparative Politics* 25:1 (1992): 43–62.

86. J. R. Frears and Jean-Luc Parodi, *War Will Not Take Place: The French Parliamentary Elections of March, 1978* (New York: Holmes and Meier, 1979), p. 11. Much of the couple of paragraphs that follow are based upon material from this source.

87. Unless turnout is very small and the candidate has received the votes of less than one-quarter of all of the registered electors.

88. The 1988 data come from *Quid, 1989*, p. 732–733; the 1993 data come from *Le Monde: Edition internationale* no. 2317, 25–31 March 1993, p. 7.

89. Frears and Parodi, *War Will Not Take Place*, p. 12.

90. *Quid, 1989*, p. 727.

91. *Quid, 1989*, p. 705.

92. Pierce, *French Politics and Political Institutions*, p. 75.

93. Frears, *Political Parties*, p. 224. Each department, has a council, called the *conseil général*, which consists of from about twenty to seventy members who are elected from subdivisions of the department, called *cantons*. Elections of departmental councillors (*conseillers généraux*) are called *elections cantonales*. Each city and town in France has a municipal council. Election of municipal councillors are called *elections municipales*. See Pierce, *French Politics and Political Institutions*, p. 75.

94. Pierce, *French Politics and Political Institutions*, p. 75.

95. *Quid, 1989*, p. 685.

11

The German Political System

THE GERMAN CONSTITUTIONAL FRAMEWORK

When World War II ended in 1945, the four Occupying Powers (the United States, the United Kingdom, France, and the Soviet Union) agreed to work toward an eventual reunification of the occupied German territories. By December 1947, however, at the London Conference of the Council of Foreign Ministers of the four Occupying Powers, it was becoming clear to the British, French, and American representatives that the Soviet Union was not prepared to move speedily to a "normalization" and reunification of Germany. Accordingly, the three Western powers decided to move forward and attempt to restore normal civilian government on their own.

Many of the German political leaders were concerned about this decision; they believed that such an action would result in a permanent division of Germany, with the Soviet Union controlling the eastern half of the country. On this ground, many West German leaders opposed the creation of a West German constitution until such time as Germany was reunified. After some discussion, a compromise was reached: The West Germans agreed to construct a "temporary" constitution that would serve as the basis of the political system until such time as Germany was reunified.

In September 1948 the Parliamentary Council met in Bonn and drafted a document called the *Basic Law* for the three Western Occupied Zones. According to its preamble, the Basic Law was designed to "give a new order to political life for a transitional period," and was constructed not only for the West Germans but also "on behalf of those Germans to whom participation was denied." Article 146 stated that the Basic Law "shall cease to be in force on the day on which a constitution adopted by a free decision of the German people comes into force."[1] The document was drafted by representatives of the three Western Occupying Powers and West German leaders acceptable to the Occupying Powers.

The construction of the Basic Law was finally completed in May 1949. To avoid the appearance of establishing a permanent political system, the Basic Law was never submitted to the West German people for ratification by popular approval. Rather, the Basic Law was submitted to the legislatures of the West German states (the Länder) and approved by that mechanism, winning the endorsement of all of the West German Länder except Bavaria.[2] The West German Basic Law was finally approved on May 23, 1949. And, just as so many of the West German leaders had feared, the German Democratic Republic (East Germany) came into existence less than a month later.

Just over forty-one years later, on October 2, 1990, East and West Germany reunited after four decades of partition and tension. The early years of the separation included a blockade of West Berlin; the most dramatic sign of the partition was a wall dividing the east and west parts of the city of Berlin. The reunited Germany, now the most populous and economically powerful nation in the European Community, adopted West Germany's constitutional system; the highly centralized political structures of communist East Germany disappeared. The period of reunification was a difficult one. Many Germans were excited about the prospect of reuniting East and West Germany, but at the same time they were concerned about both the costs of reunification[3] and the fear that their reunification and their new role as the largest and most economically powerful European nation might engender among other European nations.

Many details can be pointed out that distinguish the 1949 Basic Law from the Weimar Constitution of 1919 that preceded it. One of the major perceived shortcomings of the Weimar Constitution was that it actually promoted internal discord through a number of supposedly democratic structures, especially the power of the presidency and the mass plebiscites that were so frequently used. The Basic Law sought, through a number of political structures, to remedy the defect of "too much democracy"[4] in the earlier regime.

Essentially, the Basic Law sought to modify many of the structures of direct democracy that had existed earlier. Except in extraordinary circumstances, elections would be held every four years. Moreover, the public would vote *only* for representatives to the lower house of the legislature. The president, the chancellor, and members of the upper legislative house would all be chosen by indirect means. Additionally, structures were established to make it more difficult to overthrow chancellors—the title given to the chief executive in Germany—with votes of no confidence, something to which we shall return later in this chapter.

Although the Basic Law sought to "dampen" or "modify" many of the (perceived) "overly democratic" structures of the Weimar regime, it did *not* intend correspondingly to restrict individual freedoms or rights. To the contrary: Articles of the Basic Law that deal with civil and political rights (Articles 1–19) are given a "preferred position" in the Basic Law; as one scholar has noted, "for the first time in German history, there were no loopholes left in the protection of individual rights."[5] Neither Article 1, which focuses on human dignity, nor Article 20, which guarantees Germans the "right to resist any person or persons seeking to abolish [the German] constitutional order," *can* be amended. Other articles dealing with civil and political rights cannot be suspended except after a ruling by the Federal Constitutional Court (Article 18).[6] The Basic Law can be amended by a two-thirds majority vote of each house of the federal legislature (subject to the limitations mentioned above), and "has been altered more often in twenty-five years than the American in two hundred."[7]

FEDERALISM IN GERMANY

Federal Powers

Germany is the only major state of Western Europe that has a federal rather than a unitary political structure, and some have regarded this as "an unexpected state of affairs":

> The Federal Republic is no larger than Britain and more or less as densely populated. Socially the country is more homogeneous than at any time in the past. The economy is highly integrated on a nation-wide basis, and communications are very well developed. Culturally there are provincial variations, but these are probably less marked than in a number of other European countries of comparable size.[8]

After some reflection, however, German federalism should not be such a surprise. This is so for several reasons, including (1) a general fear of centralized government that developed during the Nazi period; (2) a history of federal and confederal relations in Germany, with the exception of the centralized Nazi era, going back to 1871 when the German Reich was formed and "composed of twenty-five 'historic' German states that 'voluntarily' entered into a federation,"[9] and (3) the pattern of administration of the Occupying Powers from 1945 to 1949 that led to the creation of seven of today's sixteen states or Länder (the singular of *Länder* is *Land*). Three of today's Länder existed as separate political entities prior to 1945.[10] Thus German federalism was "a device which perpetuated into the era of a single national state the particularist habits and traditions of the dynasties and estates which were dominant in the separate states of Germany."[11]

The federal nature of the German political system has resulted in wide disparities between and among the intermediate levels of political organization. The Länder vary greatly in size and in population, as illustrated in Table 11.1.

The German federal system, often referred to as an example of "cooperative federalism,"[12] gives the intermediate-level components of the regime, the Länder, a great deal of political power—far more power than is found in American states. There are a number of formal, constitutional mechanisms that help to institution-

TABLE 11.1
Länder in the German Federal System

Land	Area (Square Miles)	Population (in millions)	Bundesrat Seats
Baden-Württemberg	13,739	9.35	6
Bavaria	27,114	11.04	6
Berlin[a]	184	1.88	4
Brandenburg[a]	10,036	2.70	4
Bremen	155	0.65	3
Hamburg	287	1.57	3
Hesse	8,113	5.55	4
Lower Saxony	18,127	7.19	6
Mecklenburg-West Pomerania[a]	8,685	2.10	3
N. Rhine-Westphalia	13,084	16.67	6
Rhineland-Palatinate	7,621	3.61	4
Saarland	987	1.04	3
Saxony[a]	6,562	4.90	4
Saxony-Anhalt[a]	9,650	3.00	4
Schleswig-Holstein	6,018	2.61	4
Thüringia[a]	5,983	2.50	4

[a] Formerly part of the German Democratic Republic.
Source: Adapted from Guido Goldman, *The German Political System* (New York: Random House, 1974), pp. 155–156, M. Donald Hancock, *West Germany: The Politics of Democratic Corporatism* (Chatham, N. J.: Chatham House, 1989), p. 74, "Update Germany," InterNationes Press, Bonn, Report SO-7-1990, p. 2, *Europea World Yearbook, 1993*, p. 1227.

alize the power bases of the Länder. Article 28 of the Basic Law requires that the Länder "conform to the principles of republican, democratic, and social government based on the rule of law," but leaves questions of specific governmental structure, on the Länder level, up to the state governments. The state of Bavaria has a bicameral legislature; all others have unicameral legislatures. States are allowed to determine their own electoral structures.

It can be suggested that the Länder are as powerful as they are in the German political system largely because of the several different types of legislation discussed in the Basic Law. The Basic Law essentially balances centralized and decentralized powers by distinguishing among three different types of legislation.

Article 73 gives exclusive *federal jurisdiction* over legislation involving foreign affairs, citizenship, money, customs, immigration, federal railroads, post and telecommunications services, federal employees, copyrights, and cooperation of the central government and Länder in criminal matters. The Länder are given *residual* powers in Article 70: "The Länder shall have the right to legislate insofar as this Basic Law does not confer legislative power on the Federation." Finally, Articles 72 and 74 list twenty-three specific areas in which *jurisdiction is concurrent*; The Länder may legislate in these areas "as long as, and to the extent that, the Federation does not exercise its right to legislate." Among these areas of concurrent jurisdiction would be included civil and criminal law; registration of births, deaths, and marriages; issues related to public welfare; labor laws; regulation of education; road traffic and highways; and some health-related matters.

The Länder have maintained a great deal of influence in the German political system for several reasons. One is that there are many legislative powers left residually to them. Another is the constitutional provision that stimulates the "cooperative federalism" by requiring that the states administer most national policy, although this does not include foreign affairs and defense matters.[13]

Certainly another factor that must be considered is the role of the upper house of the federal parliament, the Bundesrat, in the political process. This is a structure that we will discuss further later in this chapter, but at this point we need to mention that all deputies in the upper house are chosen by the Länder legislatures, not the people, and are correspondingly perceived to represent the Länder governments.

Legislation within the federal jurisdiction that affects the Länder, even if the Länder themselves cannot legislate on the issue, must be approved by a majority of the Länders' representatives in the Bundesrat, or it does not become law. The Länder, therefore, have *sole* jurisdiction through the residual clause of Article 70 over any subject matter not given to the federal government. They have *concurrent* (shared) jurisdiction over a number of subject matters in areas specified by the Basic Law. Even in the areas that are described in the Basic Law as exclusively federal jurisdiction, the Länder are not without influence, because issues that might affect them must be approved by their representatives in the Bundesrat.

The Constitutional Court

Yet another structure in Germany that reinforces the federal nature of the polity is the Constitutional Court. Unlike the U.S. Supreme Court, the Constitutional Court of Germany is not a court of appeal for either criminal or civil cases. Rather, the Constitutional Court:

> is a watchdog for the Basic Law. Its mission is not only to defend individual liberty and civil rights but to protect the legislature from the courts applying laws incorrectly. The Court is the final arbiter of disputes between the federal executive and the Bundestag, between the federal government and the states, between the different states, and between other courts.[14]

Like the U.S. Supreme Court, the Constitutional Court is autonomous and has an extremely broad jurisdiction. On a number of occasions over the years the Constitutional Court has ruled against the federal government, supporting an interpretation of the Basic Law favoring expansion of the powers of the Länder.

EXECUTIVE STRUCTURES

We indicated earlier that the office of the president was seen by many in Germany to be one of the structural weaknesses of the Weimar regime. The Parliamentary

Council that drafted the Basic Law in 1948 felt that the institution of the presidency in the Weimar period was, to some degree, responsible for the weakness of the chancellor at that time, and consequently responsible for the use of "emergency rule" that led to the rise of Hitler and the corresponding abuse of law.

Consequently, when the members of the Parliamentary Council met in 1948 to construct a new set of political structures, there was little sense that a strong head of state was necessary for the political regime. Their primary goals with respect to executive powers were straightforward, and dealt with a "neutralized" presidency, a strengthened chancellorship, and controls on parliament.[15]

First, members of the Parliamentary Council believed that the president should be "neutralized," which meant that he or she should have few, if any, significant political powers, and should play the figurehead role in office that the constitutional monarchs of Britain or Scandinavia play. This also meant that the presidency should be an explicitly nonpolitical office.

Second, members felt that the position of the head of the government, the chancellor, should be strengthened. The chancellor should not be as vulnerable to short-term political pressures as he had been in the Weimar regime, and his base of power should be more secure.[16]

Third, members of the council wanted to design a structure in which there would be "penalties" imposed on the legislature if it started to use its power in relation to the chancellor "irresponsibly." "Irresponsibly" in this case refers to the type of behavior observed in the Weimar regime in which several small parties would get together to vote no confidence in a chancellor and subsequently not be able to agree on a replacement. The "penalty" structure designed was part of a "constructive" vote of no confidence, something that we shall describe below.

The Federal President

Articles 54 through 61 of the Basic Law deal with the office of the federal president. The president is to be elected, without debate, by a special Federal Convention made up of members of the Bundestag (the lower house of the federal legislature) and an equal number of members elected by the legislative assemblies of the states. The vote in the special convention must be by a majority of the delegates, on the first two ballots; if no one wins a majority on either of the first two ballots, the candidate receiving a plurality on the third ballot is elected.

The federal president has very few real powers. All orders and decrees of the federal president *must* be countersigned by the federal chancellor or an appropriate federal minister. This is significantly different from the relationship between most heads of state and their chief executives and cabinets: In most systems, legally (*de jure*) the head of state has a great deal of political power, although actually (*de facto*) it is recognized that the head of state will only act "on the advice" of his or her chief executive. In Germany, the head of state is *legally* restricted to the passive role. The fact that the head of state must have all orders and decrees countersigned is a legal acknowledgment of this individual's lack of power in the political system. The two exceptions to the countersignature rule are (1) the appointment and dismissal of the federal chancellor, and (2) the dissolution of the Bundestag, both of which we will address later.

The president appoints and dismisses ministers, federal judges, and federal civil servants; promulgates laws, represents the federation in its international relations, and concludes treaties, all "on the advice," of course, of the federal chancellor. Above all, the federal president is expected to be "above politics," to be nonpartisan, and to represent Germany to the world.

The Chancellor and the Cabinet

What is officially referred to as "the Federal Government" in Germany refers to the federal chancellor and his or her cabinet.[17] The present cabinet is composed of the chancellor and twenty ministers.[18] The chief executive in Germany is the chancellor, and as is usually the case with parliamentary systems of government, it is the chief executive, not the head of state, to whom we must turn to see the real locus of power in the political arena. The chancellor "has been seen as the keystone of the political system, the guarantee of stability and coherence in the democratic structure of German politics."[19] The chancellor is more powerful than most parliamentary chief executives, primarily because the chancellor has greater job security than most. This is, in fact, the single most significant difference between the German chief executive and chief executives in other political regimes, and it has led the German system to be referred to as "Chancellor Democracy."[20]

Elections are held for the Bundestag at least every four years. According to Article 39, "The Bundestag . . . term shall end four years after its first meeting or on its dissolution. The new election shall be held during the last three months of the term or within sixty days after dissolution." The Bundestag must assemble within thirty days after the election. The Bundestag determines the termination and resumption of its meetings, but may be called into special session by the federal president, the federal chancellor, or one-third of the Bundestag members.

After the elections of the members of the Bundestag, the president proposes a chancellor-designate, which in Germany has been either the leader of the majority party in the Bundestag (in 1957) or the leader of the apparent majority coalition. Article 63 of the Basic Law stipulates the procedure of the election of the federal chancellor, and states that "the Federal Chancellor shall be elected, without debate, by the Bundestag upon the proposal of the Federal President."

If the federal president makes a designation that is not supported by a majority in the Bundestag, the Bundestag has the power to reject his candidate: If the person proposed by the president is not supported by a majority, "the Bundestag may elect within fourteen days of the ballot a Federal Chancellor by more than one-half of its members."

If the Bundestag rejects the federal president's nominee, and cannot agree on majority support for its *own* candidate within fourteen days, a new vote in the Bundestag must be taken "without delay, in which the person obtaining the largest number of votes shall be elected." If this person has been elected by a majority of Bundestag members, the federal president *must* appoint him or her within seven days. If this newly elected person has *not* been elected by a majority, but only by a plurality, the federal president must *either* appoint him or her within seven days, or else dissolve the Bundestag and call for new elections within sixty days. (To date, all chancellors have been those approved as initial presidential designations, indicating the degree to which federal presidents make only "realistic" nominations.)

Once a chancellor has been confirmed by the Bundestag, it is extremely hard to fire that individual. One of the major distinctions between presidential and parliamentary systems that we observed earlier in this text was in respect to tenure: Presidents generally have fixed terms of office, whereas prime ministers can lose their positions at any time through votes of no confidence by the legislature. The Parliamentary Council of 1948 did not want the chancellor to be in an overly vulnerable position and, accordingly, developed a new political structure to help protect the chancellor's job security: the *positive* or *constructive vote of no confidence.*

The positive vote of no confidence is described in Article 67 of the Basic Law:

> The Bundestag can express its lack of confidence in the Federal Chancellor only by electing a successor with the majority of its members and by requesting the Federal President to dismiss the Federal Chancellor. The Federal President must comply with this request and appoint the person elected. . . . Forty-eight hours must elapse between the motion and the vote thereon.

In short, having a majority of members of the Bundestag express their lack of confidence in a chancellor is *not* sufficient to dismiss that chancellor; they must at the same time (actually, prior to that time) agree on a successor that a majority of the Bundestag can support. This is, as might be guessed, a very difficult task, and has helped the federal chancellor to weather strife and complaints that might have much more serious consequences—such as causing the Government to fall—in other political systems.

This positive vote of no confidence has led some to refer to the German political system as a "semiparliamentary system" rather than a parliamentary system, arguing that a "genuine parliamentary system, in the sense of enforceable responsibility of the executive to parliament, existed in Germany only as long as the Weimar Constitution functioned."[21] The difficulty of obtaining a positive vote of nonconfidence is so great that the Government is virtually no longer responsible to the Bundestag, except in truly extraordinary instances.

In September 1982, just such an unusual incident did arise for the first time. After constant feuding within the Social Democratic/Free Democratic party coalition, the Free Democratic Party (FDP) minor partner decided to withdraw its support for the Government of Helmut Schmidt.[22] In itself this guaranteed only a simple vote of no confidence, and not a positive, or constructive, vote of no confidence. After consultation, however, it became clear that the leader of the more conservative Christian Democratic/Christian Socialist Union (CDU/CSU) bloc—Helmut Kohl—was willing to make policy concessions to the Free Democrats that convinced the FDP deputies to join with the CDU/CSU deputies in a positive vote of no confidence, voting Helmut Schmidt out and Helmut Kohl in. This was, for reasons we have suggested above, an extremely rare occurrence in German politics.[23]

In addition to the unlikelihood that the chancellor will be thrown out of office, the chancellor has the added leverage of being able to *use* a vote of confidence as a weapon. Article 68 states that if the chancellor *asks* for a vote of confidence, and does not receive it, he or she can ask for a dissolution of the Bundestag and call for new elections. This has been used in the past by chancellors to either (1) push a piece of legislation through the Bundestag that might have difficulty otherwise by referring to the vote on the bill as a question of confidence, or (2) bring about an early dissolution for electoral gain. Newly selected Chancellor Kohl used this vehicle after his accession to the chancellorship in September 1982 to seek a popular mandate from the German people, since his party had not won a majority with him as leader. He received the mandate he sought in the March 1983 elections.

Unlike other political systems, in Germany the head of state does not possess the legal power to dissolve the Bundestag anytime he or she wants to do so. (We did point out, of course, that although most heads of state have this power legally, they really only exercise it "on the advice" of their chief executives. In Germany the head of state does not even possess the power legally.) The federal president can dissolve the Bundestag *only* under one of two circumstances: first, if his nominee for chancellor is not approved by the Bundestag, and the chancellor eventually chosen by the Bundestag does not have majority support and is not acceptable to the president, as we described above; and second, if the chancellor requests a vote of confidence in the Bundestag, and the Bundestag fails to give him one, *and* the chancellor subsequently requests a dissolution.

Chancellors who know that elections must be held within the next year or so, and who see their popularity as being very high, have been known to use the "confidence mechanism" to secure an early dissolution. They do this by asking for a vote of confidence *and instructing their own party supporters to vote against them,* thereby ensuring that they will lose the vote of confidence. (Note, however, that this is not the same as a positive vote of no confidence; the Bundestag has not agreed on a replacement for the chancellor.) The chancellor's supporters will go along with this, of course, since it is in their own interest to have elections held at a time when their party and their leader are both popular.

We can see, then, that the German chancellor is stronger in the political system than virtually any other parliamentary chief executive we can think of. The chancellor not only has the usual tool of party discipline at his disposal, but he also has the resources of (1) being extraordinarily difficult to dismiss, and (2) being able to threaten the legislature with dissolution if it is not cooperative.

Ministers in the Federal Republic share in collective responsibility, as do ministers in other parliamentary regimes, but they have more individual authority than do ministers in many other parliamentary systems because they tend to manage their individual departments "on their own responsibility," with less collective input than in many other parliamentary systems. The cabinet, as well, tends to be smaller than in many other nations, with recent cabinets consisting of fifteen or sixteen members. The major limitation on the cabinet as a collective policymaker has been the fact

that governments have involved coalitions, and in many instances the coalition partners have not been able to agree in cabinet; "many policy issues have to be prepared
outside the Government."[24]

THE LEGISLATIVE STRUCTURES

The Bundestag

Several aspects of the federal legislature have already been introduced. We saw in
earlier chapters of this text how the members of the Bundestag (the "federal diet,"
the lower house of the legislature) are elected. We have seen the relationship between the Bundestag and the federal chancellor; the chancellor is dominant and is
beyond the normal reach of the legislature in terms of the usual meaning of "responsible government." We saw in a very introductory manner that the Bundesrat
(the "federal council," the upper house of the legislature) is important in the federal structure of the regime. Some of these items deserve further consideration at
this point.

The Bundestag is clearly perceived in the Basic Law to be the center of legislative activity in the German political regime. To this should be added the qualifi-
cation that the German political system is essentially designed to be managed by the
chancellor and the cabinet. The job of the Bundestag is to choose its leader; once this
is accomplished, it is expected that the Bundestag will sit back and let itself be led by
the Government. The degree of difficulty of the positive vote of no confidence is an
indication that the framers of the Basic Law did not *intend* for the Bundestag to exercise its role as the ultimate authority in the regime very often; nor has it done so.

The Bundesrat

Article 50 of the Basic Law indicates that "the Länder shall participate through the
Bundesrat in the legislation and administration of the Federation." The Bundesrat,
the upper house in the political regime, is primarily important insofar as the federal
distribution of powers is concerned. As was seen in Table 11.1, the Länder each have
either three, four, five, or six deputies in the Bundesrat, depending upon their size.
Article 51 of the Basic Law indicates that every Land shall have at least three seats in
the Bundesrat; Länder with more than 2 million inhabitants shall have four, Länder
with more than 6 million inhabitants shall have five, and Länder with more than 7
million inhabitants shall have six votes.[25]

This difference in the size of Bundesrat delegations, however, does not al-
leviate disproportionate representation. To take two examples, the city-state of Bremen (with three delegates) has one Bundesrat representative for each 266,666
people, and the state of North Rhine-Westphalia (with six delegates) has one Bundesrat representative for each 2.8 million people.

The Land governments (the legislative assemblies of the Länder) choose
their three, four, five, or six delegates to the Bundesrat. Since the Bundesrat dele-

gates are chosen by the Land governments, they will all be of the political party that controls the majority in the Land legislature. Bundesrat delegates from a Land *must* cast their votes as a bloc; they may not divide their three, four, five, or six votes.

The role of the Bundesrat in the German legislative process varies, depending upon the specific piece of legislation involved. According to the Basic Law (Articles 77 and 78), bills intended to become federal laws require adoption by the Bundestag. Bills can be introduced in the Bundestag by either the Bundesrat, the Bundestag, or the federal Government (the chancellor and the cabinet).

The Legislative Process

The legislative process is relatively complex.[26] All bills begin their legislative journey in the Bundestag. Bills introduced by the Bundesrat (a small number) go first to the Government for comment before being introduced in the Bundestag.[27] Bills being introduced by the Government (more than half of the total)[28] go first to the Bundesrat for comment before being introduced in the Bundestag. In each of these cases, *scrutiny* is implied, not *veto* power; the goal is for government actors to let other government actors know what is happening. Bills starting in the Bundestag (almost half) are simply introduced there, and they do not go to either the Bundesrat or the Government for advance scrutiny and comment.

Once bills are introduced, they first go through the "Bundestag phase" of the legislative process, including a first reading, a vote in the Bundestag, assignment to committee followed by a committee report, a second reading and vote in the Bundestag covering specific details of the proposed legislation, followed by a third reading and vote.

If a bill passes the Bundestag phase of the legislative process—and it may not do so—it goes to the Bundesrat. This is the first opportunity for the Bundesrat to see bills that were initiated in the Bundestag (other bills either were initiated in the Bundesrat, or were initiated in the Government and were first sent to the Bundesrat for review and comment prior to going to the Bundestag). The Bundesrat can approve the bill, in which case it is sent on to the federal president to sign and to the chancellor or appropriate minister to countersign, or within two weeks the Bundesrat may ask for a meeting of the Bundestag-Bundesrat Mediation Committee to try to find a compromise.

At this point an important distinction must be made. Bills that "affect the Länder" *require the approval* of the Bundesrat: It has an *absolute veto* over this kind of legislation.[29] Bills that do not directly affect the Länder—for example, questions dealing with foreign policy—do not require Bundesrat approval; over these bills the Bundesrat has only a *suspensory veto*.

In cases over which the Bundesrat has an absolute veto, and in which it does not approve of the Bundestag bill, a compromise must be reached by the Mediation Committee and must be subsequently approved by both houses before it can be promulgated (handed down as law). Failing this, the bill does not become law. In cases over which the Bundesrat does not have an absolute veto, and in which the Bundesrat does not approve of the Bundestag bill, it may enter a suspensive veto, but only after an effort at compromise through the Mediation Committee has been made. In that case, it must act within one week of Bundestag action on the compromise, or, if no new compromise is proposed by the committee, within one week of the completion of its work. If the Bundesrat enters its objection by a vote of a majority of its members, then the Bundestag can override it by the same majority; if the Bundesrat has entered its objections by a vote of two-thirds of its members, it can only be overridden in the Bundestag by a vote of two-thirds of the Members present, but these two-thirds must also constitute at least a majority of the total membership. If the Bundesrat fails to act within the prescribed time limits, bills which do not specifically require its approval are ready for promulgation.[30]

The structure of the Mediation Committee is modeled after the conference committee of the U.S. Congress. Members are appointed from *each* house of the legislature. Unlike the American conference committee, however, which is only a temporary political structure and which is created *de novo* for each bill over which a compromise is necessary, the Mediation Committee is a standing committee—permanent for the life of the legislature. It is composed of Bundesrat members (one from each Land) and Bundestag members, divided proportionally to reflect party distribution in that house.

The Bundesrat, then, while not having an absolute veto in all cases as is the case with the U.S. Senate, is a reasonably powerful upper house as the data in Table 11.2 demonstrate. Over the years its veto power has expanded to include a substantial proportion of all federal legislation. To some degree this expansion occurred through judicial decisions. Article 84 of the Basic Law gave the states the task of administering much federal legislation; the states argued before the courts—successfully—that since they had to *administer* the law, they were *affected by* the law, and

TABLE 11.2
West German Legislative Productivity, 1983–1987

Productivity Measure	Number
Bills initiated by	
Federal government	280
Bundestag	183
Bundesrat	59
Total	522
Origins of ratified bills	
Federal government	273
Bundestag	42
Bundesrat	32
Joint	9
Total	356
Mediation committees created	6

Source: Statistisches Jahrbuch für die Bundesrepublik Deutschland 1988, p. 91, as cited in M. Donald Hancock, *West Germany: The Politics of Democratic Corporatism* (Chatham, N. J.: Chatham House, 1989), p. 60.

accordingly the Bundesrat should have absolute veto power. Accordingly, today states argue that even if a law affects them only because they must administer it, the entire law may be vetoed by the Bundesrat in the legislative process.

POLITICAL PARTIES AND THE ELECTORAL PROCESS

The Electoral Process

Germany's is a political system with many political parties, but one that has been dominated by just a few parties over the last thirty years; the system has evolved since the 1949 election to become a two-coalition, if not a two-party, system. In the elections of October 5, 1980, although twenty political parties appeared on West German ballots, the five major parties (CDU, CSU, FDP, SPD, Greens) won 99.5 percent of the votes; in the March 6, 1983, elections, the five major parties again won 99.5 percent of the votes; in the January 1987 elections, the five major parties won 98.7 percent of the votes; in the December 1990 elections—the first election after unification—these five parties won 92.2 percent of the votes.[31] The reasons for this are complex, and to explain the pattern of the parties' election returns over the years we must know something of the manner in which the German electoral system operates.

In 1949, at the time of the creation of the Federal Republic, each citizen voted only once in each election. This system was changed in 1953 when a second vote for each citizen in each election was added.[32] When Germans go to the polls they receive a ballot with two columns, as illustrated in Figure 11.1. In the left-hand column, the citizen votes directly for a candidate who has been nominated by a local political party organization (there are no primary elections in Germany), in a single-member-district, plurality voting electoral framework. Germany is now divided into 331 single-member districts[33] from which deputies are selected by simple plurality margins: Whichever candidate in a district receives the most votes wins. Interestingly, if two or more candidates receive the same number of votes, the returning officer (the official in charge of administering the election) for the electoral district draws lots to decide the winner.

In the right-hand column the citizen casts a "second vote" for a political party, not a candidate, in a proportional respresentation electoral competition. Parties receive seats on the basis of the percentage of votes they receive in the election. Another 331 deputies are elected to the Bundestag through this electoral route, bringing the total number of seats in the Bundestag to 662.

Some argue that the second ballot is in many ways more important than the first, "direct," ballot, because it is the second ballot that determines the final proportion of parliamentary seats that each party will receive in the Bundestag. The number of "district" seats is subtracted from the total number of seats due to the party on the basis of its performance in the proportional representation elections, determining the number of "at large" seats the party will receive. For example, if a party wins 25 percent of the vote on the proportional ballot—thus earning a total of 164 seats in the new Bundestag (25 percent of 656 total seats available yields 164

FIGURE 11.1   A Sample Ballot for Bundestag Elections
Source: Adapted from Rolf H. W. Theen and Frank L. Wilson, *Comparative Politics: An Introduction to Six Countries* (Englewood Cliffs, N. J.: Prentice Hall, 1986), p. 270. Reprinted with permission.

seats)—and it wins 80 district seats, it will be awarded 84 at large seats to bring its total to the percentage it earned in the election. Individual candidates will be selected, in order, from party lists that have already been filed with the government.

> The second ballot provision made the system basically proportional, with two important exceptions. A party had to secure at least five percent of the second ballot vote, or win three "direct" district (first ballot) contests in order to share in the pro-

portional distribution of parliamentary seats. Secondly, if a party won more district contests (first ballot) than it was entitled to according to its totals on the second ballot, it was allowed to keep the extra seats and the parliament was enlarged accordingly. In the last West German parliament, for example, there was one of these "excess mandates" and the Bundestag had 497 members in addition to 22 from West Berlin.[34]

Table 11.3 indicates the distribution of seats in the Bundestag among the several states in both the single-member-district races.

The rationale behind the two-vote electoral system is that it allows for the accuracy of proportional representation, while still allowing for the "personal representation" of the single-member-district electoral structure. Another function of the system has to do with interest groups and interest group representation. One study has suggested that for individual candidates who seek to enter the parliament from outside of political party organizations, it is "virtually impossible to gain nomination as a party candidate for a direct seat"[35]; that is, for a seat for which voters ballot directly for an individual candidate. Significant interest groups may have sufficient influence at the Länder level, however, to be able to influence the Länder political parties to include "their" candidates on the party's "proportional representation" part of the ballot.

Voting turnout is regularly high: 89 percent of the electorate voted in 1983;

TABLE 11.3
Bundestag Representation of German Länder

District	Number of Seats[a]
Bavaria	44
Baden-Württemberg	36
Berlin	13[b]
Brandenburg	12[b]
Bremen	3
Hamburg	8
Hesse	22
Lower Saxony	30
Mecklenburg-West Pomerania	9[b]
N. Rhine-Westphalia	73
Rhineland-Palatinate	16
Saarland	21[b]
Saxony-Anhalt	13[b]
Schleswig-Holstein	11
Thüringia	12[b]
Total district seats	328

[a]Unless otherwise noted, number of seats won in the 1987 federal election.

[b]Number of districts created in the former regions of East Germany and reunified Berlin for the 1990 elections.

Source: Adapted from Helmut Goebel and Herbert Blondiau, eds., *Procedures, Programmes, Profiles: The Federal Republic of Germany Elects the German Bundestag* (Bonn: Inter-Nationes, 1980), p. 31; and "Bulletin: Vertrag zur Vorbereitung und Durchführung der ersten gesamtdeutschen Wahl des Deutschen Bundestages," *Presse- und Informationsamt der Bundesregierung*, Nr. 97/S, Bonn, den 7. August 1990, pp. 831–32.

84.3 percent voted in 1987; and in the first election after unification 77.8 percent of the eligible voters participated.[36] Every citizen over the age of 18 years has a vote, and eligibility certificates are mailed by the Federal Board of Elections to lists of eligible voters prepared by the local census bureau. Overall, the German electorate "is both *stable* in the sense of supporting prosystem parties over time, and *in transition* in the sense of becoming more sophisticated about issues and policies and more willing to use the ballot to effect political change and secure the desired policy outputs."[37]

We might think that the proportional representation component of the electoral system would encourage a large number of political parties to flourish in the Federal Republic of Germany, as was the case in Weimar Germany. There was much discussion about this possible consequence when the authors of the Basic Law met in 1948; the structure that has evolved over the years to prevent the proliferation of minor parties in Germany is called the Five Percent Clause.

Proportional representation electoral systems, as we saw earlier in this text, can have the negative effect in a political system of providing *too much* representation. If every party that receives, say, 1 percent of the vote is given representation in the legislature, we may find a legislature with so many political parties that coalition governments are necessary, leading to what we saw can be less stable governments. Under the Weimar Constitution, which preceded World War II, a proportional representation system existed in Germany, which resulted in a large number of political parties. In fact, fourteen different parties successfully competed for the Reichstag election of September 14, 1930, and nine of them received between three and thirty seats. Many Germans thought that it was wrong that "although none of these nine parties had even five percent of the total vote, they still took part in deciding who was to form the government."[38]

There is a difficult trade-off involved in this policy, one that we discussed earlier. On one hand, single-member districts fail to represent minority blocs in electoral districts; on the other hand, proportional representation systems may result in unreasonable influence for minor parties and consequent system instability. To limit the danger of tiny parliamentary blocs gaining a disproportionate amount of political influence and resulting in political instability through resultant coalition governments, the Federal Election Law introduced the Five Percent Clause.[39]

The *Five Percent Clause* indicates that parties can win seats from the proportional representation "second votes" *only* if they poll at least 5 percent of the second votes, or (1) if they have won at least three constituency seats, or (2) if they represent an officially registered "national minority" (such as the party of the Danish minority in Schleswig-Holstein).[40]

The Five Percent Clause has been of tremendous significance for the political parties in Germany. In the first Bundestag in 1949 there were ten parties represented, but ever since the Five Percent Clause was introduced, there have been only four (until the 1983 election added a fifth). The 1990 post-unification election expanded this slightly. The Five Percent Clause serves as a real psychological barrier for new parties, as well as a legal or structural barrier; many voters feel that voting for a minor party amounts to "throwing away" their votes, since the minor parties will probably *not* win 5 percent of the vote. The major parties usually can be counted upon to remind the voters of this principle. This is undoubtedly why only one new party has emerged in the Bundestag since the Five Percent Clause came into force.

When East and West Germany were reunified in 1990, there was serious concern expressed on the part of many political parties in (what had been) East Germany that they would not be able to compete with the larger, better-organized parties in (what had been) West Germany in the 1990 elections. The Supreme Court, in fact, threw out the Five Percent Clause as unconstitutionally discriminating against the smaller (formerly) East German parties. On the advice of the Supreme Court the law was amended so that political parties in the former German Democratic Republic (East Germany) could form alliances and run on joint tickets, and so that votes for the proportional seats would be counted separately in the former East Germany and West Germany.[41] This allowed smaller East German parties to compete against smaller East German parties, and not have to compete against the larger, better-organized West German parties.

Political Parties

As is the case in most democratic systems, it is impossible to discuss the German political system without an explicit discussion of political parties. Unlike many democracies, however, in Germany parties are constitutionally included in the political system. The Basic Law specifically refers to political parties, and Article 21 "guarantees the legitimacy of parties and their right to exist—if they accept the principles of democratic government."[42] The Federal Republic has thoroughly institutionalized the structure of political parties, and we describe the working of the German politics as "party government," as we do in other parliamentary democracies.

Although a large number of political parties have consistently competed in German elections, various structures in the political system—most notably the Five Percent Clause we just discussed—have made it extremely difficult for minority or splinter parties to form and flourish. The Five Percent Clause "was designed to prevent a recurrence of the splintering of the parliament into numerous parties which drastically weakened the Weimar Republic."[43]

The Five Percent Clause has been successful in this goal. In the elections in West Germany since the Five Percent Clause came into effect, support for political parties other than the five large parties has decreased markedly, as indicated in Table 11.4. In the elections of October 1980, twenty parties appeared on the ballot; only four parties won seats. The Greens, the newest small party, which was supported by a coalition of "environmentalists, nuclear energy opponents, and people reacting against an industrial society,"[44] received only 1.5 percent of the vote at that time. Two other extremist parties of the left and right, the (left-wing) German Communist Party (DKP) and the (right-wing) National Democratic Party (NPD), each won less than 0.3 percent of the vote. In the March 1983 elections, the Greens finally broke the Five Percent Clause barrier (with 5.6 percent of the vote) and won 27 seats in the Bundestag[45]; they won 42 seats in the Bundestag in 1987.[46]

Four political parties have proven over time to play a significant political role

TABLE 11.4
Federal Election Results in Germany (in Percent of Votes Cast)

					PARTY				
Year	CDU/ CSU	SPD	FDP	Green	PDS	DSU	Alliance 90/ Greens	Other	Turnout
1949	31.6%	29.2%	11.9%					27.8%	78.5%
1953	45.2	28.8	9.5					16.5	86.0
1957	50.2	31.8	7.7					10.3	87.8
1961	45.3	36.2	12.8					5.7	87.7
1965	47.6	39.3	9.5					3.6	86.8
1969	46.1	42.7	5.8					5.4	86.7
1972	44.9	45.8	8.4					0.9	91.2
1976	48.6	42.6	7.9					0.9	91.0
1980	44.5	42.9	10.6	1.5%				0.5	88.7
1983	48.8	38.2	6.9	5.6				0.5	89.1
1987	44.3	37.0	9.1	8.4				1.2	84.3
1990	43.8	33.5	11.0	3.9	2.4%	0.2%	1.2%	4.0	77.8

Former West German Parties

CDU	Christian Democratic Union
CSU	Christian Socialist Union
SPD	Social Democratic Party
FDP	Free Democratic Party
Green	Green-Environmental Party

Former East German Parties

PDS	Party of Democratic Socialism
DSU	German Social Union
Alliance 90/Greens	East German Green Party

Source: Adapted from *The Week in Germany,* October 10, 1980, p. 2, and December 7, 1990, p. 1 (New York: German Information Center); and M. Donald Hancock, *West Germany: The Politics of Democratic Corporatism* (Chatham, N.J.: Chatham House, 1989), p. 79.

in the German political system, all participating in government coalitions at one point or another. From 1949 through 1956, and from 1961 through 1965, West Germany was governed by a coalition of the Christian Democratic Union (CDU) and Christian Socialist Union (CSU) parties (the CSU is the CDU in the state of Bavaria—they act as one party in the government), and the Free Democratic Party (FDP). In 1957 the CDU/CSU had an outright majority in the Bundestag—the only time an outright majority has been obtained by a political party—and formed a government without a coalition, which lasted until elections in 1961. From 1965 through 1969, a "grand coalition" existed, in which all the major parties, including the Social Democratic Party (SPD), participated in the Government. From 1969 until 1982, all governments were SPD and FDP coalitions.[47]

In September 1982, as we have already discussed, primarily as a result of economic pressure exerted on the Government, the FDP/SPD coalition came apart, and the FDP gave its support instead to the CDU/CSU bloc. Accordingly, Chancellor Schmidt of the Social Democratic Party resigned, and Helmut Kohl of the Christian Democratic Union/Christian Socialist Union bloc became chancellor. This coalition has stayed in power since that time.

The CDU is essentially a conservative party, and was founded in 1945 upon Christian, conservative, social principles.[48] The CSU was also founded in 1945 and appears on the ballot only in Bavaria, while the CDU is a more national party, appearing on all ballots *except* in Bavaria. The CDU and CSU are almost always in agreement on major issues, and are considered as one party in the Bundestag. From 1949 through the 1969 elections the CDU/CSU pair dominated West German elections, and it has continued to do so since the March 1983 elections.[49] In its early years the CDU had very little in the way of internal party organization, but this changed following its loss of power in 1969. The CDU party subsequently made a number of changes in its internal organization and party machinery to help mobilize and control its members and supporters.[50]

The Free Democratic Party (FDP) is the liberal-center party in Germany, and has proven to be much more active in the German political system than its relatively small size might suggest. It has been referred to as the "party of coalition,"[51] having served as a coalition partner with both the CDU/CSU and the SPD. The FDP is generally perceived as a centrist party, and thus has been the only acceptable partner for the more conservative CDU/CSU and for the more liberal SPD.[52]

Although the results of the election shown in Table 11.4 do not demonstrate it, many supporters of the FDP were seriously concerned at the time of the 1987 election campaign that the FDP might not meet the 5 percent threshold for legislature, given the gradual decline in the public level of support for the party and the increase in support for the Greens. Indeed, as one scholar has written, the FDP is "a part of electoral instability. Less than half its voters are loyal regulars,"[53] and that means that its electoral strength is seriously vulnerable to short-term political issues.

The Social Democratic Party (SPD) dates back to the 1860s, and was a traditional social democratic party, oriented to the working class.

> By 1912 it had become the strongest political party in Germany. After the First World War, during the Weimar period, it worked toward securing an orderly transition from the imperial state to the newly-formed republic. During the Nazi period, many SPD leaders fled into exile, or were imprisoned in concentration camps. At the end of World War II, the SPD reemerged as a major political party.[54]

The SPD is a left-of-center political party, although not perceived as a radically left organization. Its economic policies are a very moderate version of socialist thought, much more sympathetic to free-market economic policies than to Marxist thought. The SPD first participated in a cabinet in the Grand Coalition of 1965; in 1969 the SPD led the cabinet formation process for the first time, joining in a coalition with the FDP. This alliance continued through the elections of 1972, 1976, and 1980, dissolving in October 1982, as indicated above.[55]

As already stated, the Green Movement in Germany became a parliamentary political party only in recent years.[56] The Green Movement emerged in Germany in 1975, and for many years existed as a lobby in West Germany, applying pressure for changes in society which "did not pose an immediate threat to the established 'people's' or 'catch-all' parties."[57] Membership in the Greens rose from 3,000 in October 1979 to over 10,000 in January 1980; in March 1980 the Greens met to formulate a formal political party program.[58]

The Greens were especially important as a demonstration that views that were outside the mainstream of West German political thought could win representation in parliament. As some scholars have noted, "the acid test of any truly democratic legitimation of protest movements, however large their following, is their ability to achieve representation of their interests in parliament."[59] Although there had been several protest movements with various degrees of popular support in West Germany between the formation of the Federal Republic and 1983,[60] the Greens' victory in 1983 offered the first instance of parliamentary political victory for an organization that could be called a "protest movement."

The Greens have not been a typical German party, and their parliamentarians have not been typical legislators in either behavior or demeanor.[61] The average Green legislator was almost ten years younger than other legislators, and "six of the ten youngest deputies in Parliament were Greens."[62] The Green party has the lowest degree of organization of the major German parties. That is, the ratio of its voters to its formal members is higher than the other parties, as indicated in Table 11.5.

In the 1980 federal elections the Greens did not cross the threshold required for representation. In the 1983 federal election the Greens received 5.6 percent of the vote, and entered the federal parliament for the first time.[63] They increased this margin of voter support in 1987 with 8.4 percent of the vote.[64] The (former West German) Greens did not get enough votes in the 1990 election to win any seats in the new legislature. The (former East German) Alliance 90/Greens, however, did win sufficient votes to be represented, so the Green movement has continued to be represented in the federal legislature.

The reunification of Germany introduced several new political parties to the democratic arena. The largest of these, the former communist East German party—the Socialist Unity party—changed its name to the Party of Democratic Socialism in preparation for the first national elections, which were held in 1990.[65]

TABLE 11.5
West German Party Organization and Voter Support, 1983

Party	Voters	Members	Ratio
Greens	2,167,431	25,000	87:1
SPD	14,865,807	950,000	16:1
CDU	14,857,680	734,082	20:1
CSU	4,140,865	182,665	23:1
FDP	2,706,942	78,763	34:1

Source: Adapted from Werner Hulsberg, *The German Greens: A Social and Political Profile*, trans. Gus Fagan (London: Verso, 1988), p. 108.

THE GERMAN POLITICAL SYSTEM

We see in Germany, then, a political system that is *similar to* others that we have already seen and others that we will yet see, but that differs in a number of important aspects from those other systems. Although there are many idiosyncratic structural and procedural differences between Germany and other nations, the most significant differences that we have highlighted in this chapter number four.

First, Germany is federal, and the role of the states (Länder) in the German political system is quite significant. Through the veto power of the Bundesrat, the Länder exercise a great influence in the policy-making process generally, and in the legislative process specifically. The federal distribution of power in Germany makes Germany unlike any other European political system we will see here and will make for an interesting comparison with Canada, which we will see later.

Second, the "normal" responsibility of the chief executive to the (lower house of the) legislature is different in the German political system. The political structure of the "positive vote of no confidence" has many implications for the degree to which the chancellor must worry about the likelihood that he will be dismissed by the Bundestag.

Third, the German electoral structure offers a unique blend of methods of selection for a national legislature. By combining single-member-district with proportional-representation selection, the Germans have attempted to blend the advantages of each: the minority representation of proportional representation with the stability and orientation of district-based representation. Moreover, by establishing the "Five Percent Clause" the Germans have attempted to resolve the major drawback of proportional representation—namely a proliferation of political parties and the ensuing political instability of the regime. By all appearances, they have succeeded.

Fourth, from a legislative point of view the German case is quite interesting. In some political systems (such as that of the United States, for example) the upper house has, both in law (*de jure*) and in fact (*de facto*), an absolute veto. Laws cannot be made without the approval of the upper house, and the legislative process operates accordingly. In other political systems (such as those of Britain and France, for example) the upper house has only a suspensory veto, both in law and in fact. If both the Government and the lower house want a piece of proposed legislation passed, it will become law, and the most that the upper chamber can do is to slow down the process (of course, the technical details of how this is accomplished vary from country to country). In Germany, on the other hand, both in law and in fact, the upper house sometimes has an *absolute veto* and sometimes has a *suspensory veto*, depending on the focus of legislation under consideration.

This brief discussion of the German political system, then, although only covering a very small portion of all of the significant structures of the political regime, points out some of the interesting, significant, and, in some cases, unique characteristics of the German polity. We will see in the chapters that follow that many of the political structures that are so appropriate to the German political culture would *not* work elsewhere. Other regimes have developed their own mechanisms and structures for processing political demands and supports.

Notes

1. Guido Goldman, *The German Political System* (New York: Random House, 1974), pp. 157, 214. The full text of the Basic Law can be found here.

2. See M. Donald Hancock, *West Germany: The Politics of Democratic Corporatism* (Chatham, N.J.: Chatham House, 1989), pp. 29–30. According to Hancock, a majority of the members of Bavaria's parliament opposed the Basic Law "because it provided for a more centralized form of government than they would have wished. Nonetheless, the Bavarian Landtag endorsed the Basic Law as binding on the state."

3. For a brief discussion of the costs of unification and problems immediately following unification, see "Economic Affairs of Germany" in "Germany," *Europa World Yearbook 1993*, p. 1208.

4. On this note, an interesting study was published in 1966 by Karl Jasper, a well-known German philosopher, who argued that "the Federal Republic of Germany is well on its way to abolishing parliamentary democracy and may be drifting toward some kind of dictatorship. . . ." See Karl Jasper, *The Future of Germany* (trans. E. B. Ashton) (Chicago: University of Chicago Press, 1967), p. v.

5. Klaus von Beyme, *The Political System of the Federal Republic of Germany* (New York: St. Martin's Press, 1983), p. 12.

6. See Goldman, *The German Political System*, pp. 157–164. All quotes from the Basic Law are taken from the text in Goldman, and will not be given individual citations.

7. Lewis Edinger, *Politics in West Germany* (Boston: Little, Brown, 1977), p. 11.

8. Nevil Johnson, *State and Government in the Federal Republic of Germany: The Executive at Work* (New York: Pergamon, 1983), p. 3.

9. David Conradt, *The German Polity*, 3rd ed. (New York: Longman, 1986), p. 210.

10. The three were Bavaria, Hamburg, and Bremen. See Conradt, *The German Polity*, p. 212.

11. Johnson, *State and Government*, p. 7.

12. Hancock, *West Germany*, p. 49.

13. Ibid.

14. Peter Katzenstein, *Policy and Politics in West Germany: The Growth of a Semisovereign State* (Philadelphia: Temple University Press, 1987), pp. 17–18.

15. Johnson, *State and Government*, pp. 49–50.

16. See the discussion of "The Elevation of the Chancellor" in Gordon Smith, *Democracy in Western Germany: Parties and Politics in the Federal Republic* (New York: Holmes and Meier, 1986), p. 56.

17. Johnson, *State and Government*, p. 50.

18. See "The Government (February, 1993)" in "Germany," *Europa World Yearbook 1993*, p. 1226.

19. Johnson, *State and Government*, p. 54.

20. For example, see Conradt, *The German Polity*, p. 162.

21. John Herz, *The Government of Germany* (New York: Harcourt, Brace, Jovanovich, 1972), p. 123.

22. A good analysis of this period can be found in Ian Derbyshire, *Politics in West Germany: From Schmidt to Kohl* (London: W & R Chambers, 1987), pp. 35–39.

23. This is discussed in some detail in Hancock, *West Germany*, pp. 121–124.

24. Johnson, *State and Government*, pp. 68–69.

25. See "Germany," *Europa World Yearbook 1993*, p. 1227.

26. See Gerhardt Loewenberg, *Parliament in the German Political System* (Ithaca, N.Y.: Cornell University Press, 1967), p. 269.

27. Ibid.

28. Ibid., p. 270.

29. Loewenberg writes that about 60 percent of important measures require Bundesrat approval. The Basic Law sections that determine which subjects are subject to Bundesrat approval are "scattered over many sections of the document." Loewenberg, *Parliament*, pp. 365–366, n. 214.

30. Loewenberg, *Parliament*, p. 366.

31. "Germany: Elections, Parliament, and Political Parties" (New York: German Information Center, 1990), pp. 20–21. Results of the December 1990 election were published in *The Week in Germany*, December 7, 1990 (New York: German Information Center), p. 1.

32. Von Beyme, *The Political System*, p. 26.

33. A list of the new districts was published in a bulletin released by the German Information Office: "Bulletin: Vertrag zur Vorbereitung und Durchführung der ersten gesamtdeutschen Wahl des Deutschen Bundestages," Press- und Informationsamt der Bundesregierung, Nr. 97/S, Bonn, den 7 August, 1990, pp. 831–832.

34. David P. Conradt, *Unified Germany at the Polls: Political Parties and the 1990 Federal Election* (Baltimore: Johns Hopkins University Press, 1990), pp. 23–24.

35. Eva Kolinsky, *Parties, Opposition, and Society in West Germany* (New York: St. Martin's Press, 1984), p. 40.

36. "Germany: Elections, Parliament, and Political Parties," p. 21. The 1990 turnout data come from *The Week in Germany*, December 7, 1990, p. 1.

37. Conradt, *The German Polity*, p. 140.

38. Helmut Gobel and Herbert Blondiau, eds., *Procedures, Programmes, Profiles: The Federal Republic of Germany Elects the German Bundestag on 5 October, 1980* (Bonn: Inter-Nationes, 1980), p. 13.

39. For a discussion of the evolution of this point, see Karl H. Cerny, ed., *Germany at the Polls: The Bundestag Election of 1976* (Washington, D.C.: American Enterprise Institute, 1978), pp. 3–17.

40. Gobel and Blondiau, *Procedures*, p. 13.

41. "Germany: Elections, Parliament, and Political Parties," p. 8.

42. Russell J. Dalton, *Politics: West Germany* (Boston: Little, Brown, 1989), p. 246.

43. G. Merten, ed., *The Week in Germany* 11:35 (September 19, 1980) (New York: German Information Center, 1980), p. 2.

44. Ibid.

45. For 1980 election results see Merten, *The Week in Germany* 11:38 (October 10, 1980), p. 2.

46. For 1987 election results, see *Facts on File* 47:2410 (January 30, 1987), pp. 52–53.

47. There is much good discussion of the evolution of the party system in the chapter by Gerhard Loewenberg, "The Remaking of the German Party System," in Cerny, *Germany at the Polls*.

48. See Geoffrey Pridham, *Christian Democracy in Western Germany* (New York: St. Martin's Press, 1977).

49. A good description of West German politics under the CDU/CSU/FDP coalition can be found in Derbyshire, *Politics in West Germany*, pp. 46–56.

50. See Kolinsky, *Parties, Opposition, and Society*, pp. 122–149.

51. Merten, *The Week* 11:35, p. 3.

52. See Christian Soe, "The Free Democratic Party," in H. Peter Wallach and George Romoser, eds., *West German Politics in the Mid-Eighties* (New York: Praeger, 1985).

53. Kolinsky, *Parties, Opposition, and Society*, p. 101.

54. Merten, *The Week* 11:35, p. 3.

55. A very good study of the role of the Social Democrats while in power can be found in the work by Gerard Braunthal, *The West German Social Democrats, 1969–1982: Profile of a Party in Power* (Boulder, Colo.: Westview Press, 1983). He specifically discusses the series of coalition governments on pp. 224–232. See also Douglas Chalmers, *The Social Democratic Party of Germany* (New Haven, Conn.: Yale University Press, 1966).

56. See Gerd Langguth, *The Green Factor in German Politics: From Protest Movement to Political Party* (Boulder, Colo.: Westview Press, 1986).

57. Elim Papadakis, *The Green Movement in West Germany* (New York: St. Martin's Press, 1984), p. 13.

58. Ibid., pp. 159, 161.

59. Rob Burns and Wilfried van der Will, *Protest and Democracy in West Germany: Extra-Parliamentary Opposition and the Democratic Agenda* (New York: St. Martin's Press, 1988), p. 230.

60. Among these might be included the opposition to remilitarization and nuclear weapons (1950–1969), the movement of students against authoritarianism (1965–1969), the women's movement (1968–1985), environmentalism (1970s and 1980s), and mass opposition to nuclear arms (1980–1986). See Burns and van der Will, *Protest and Democracy*, who have chapters on each of these protest movements.

61. A good analysis of the Greens can be found in Werner Hulsberg, *The German Greens: A Social and Political Profile* (trans. Gus Fagan) (London: Verso, 1988), especially in chap. 7, "The Greens: A Preliminary Assessment," and chap. 8, "The Crisis of Orientation."

62. Dalton, *Politics: West Germany*, p. 293, n. 15.

63. Papadakis, *The Green Movement*, p. 196.

64. Hulsberg, *German Greens*, p. 247. In Appendix I of his study, Hulsberg provides election results for the Greens in Land and Federal elections between 1978 and 1987.

65. "Germany: Elections, Parliament, and Political Parties," p. 19.

12

The Japanese Political System

THE JAPANESE POLITICAL HERITAGE

Modern Japanese political history usually is said to have begun with a series of events in 1867 and 1868 known as the *Meiji Restoration*. During that period the emperor Meiji ended the history of rule of the Tokugawa Shogunate, which had lasted since 1603, and took power.[1] Between 1603 and 1867 the political regime of the Tokugawa Shogunate had "coordinated" Japanese government. The Shogunate system "was far from being a centralized government; some three-fourths of the national territory and considerable political power were still held by more than two hundred fifty feudal lords."[2]

The Meiji Restoration changed this and centralized Japanese politics considerably. This "restoration" in 1867 did not entail directly substituting a Meiji emperor for the Tokugawa rulers; the leaders of the movement to abolish the Tokugawa power system did not intend to support the 15-year-old Meiji in his claim to be heir to powers of his eighth-century ancestors, "who were vested by right of divine descent with absolute power over the state."[3] The Meiji claim, though, was a focal point for the various forces supporting the overthrow of the Tokugawa regime.

During the period from 1868, by which time Tokugawa rule was finished, until the 1889 establishment of the Meiji Constitution, a number of significant experiments in social and political thought were undertaken; some were successful, and some were not. Many social innovations were undertaken successfully, such as the abolition of the traditional land-tenure system and the rigid four-class system of merchant, artisan, peasant, and samurai. In the place of these archaic social institutions were substituted mass public education, equal protection under law, a merchant marine, modern industrial and technological development, and modern armed forces.

Politically, the interregnum was uncertain; leaders could agree on a dislike for the old Shogunate, but they could not agree on what they wanted in its place. Some leaders favored bringing Western ideas to Japan and studied Western political philosophers such as Rousseau, Montesquieu, Locke, and others. Finally, however, the traditional power bases were victorious; the Constitution of 1889 "reflected the natural desire of the oligarchs to perpetuate their own authority" under the Meiji emperor.

> Although scarcely ideal as a foundation for a liberal political system . . . it should not be forgotten that the Meiji Constitution and governmental system were not notably illiberal in terms of prevailing European practice in 1890. They did mark a major departure from earlier Japanese political institutions and processes.[4]

Modern Japanese politics has taken place in two significantly different constitutional regimes. The Meiji Constitution was drawn up in 1889 and put into effect in the name of the Emperor Meiji. The present-day constitution of Japan, sometimes referred to as the "MacArthur Constitution," was primarily authored by Americans operating out of the office of the Supreme Commander for the Allied Powers (SCAP) occupying Japan at the end of World War II, and it was put into effect by Emperor Hirohito in the name of the Japanese people.

> As late as January 30, 1946, General Douglas MacArthur assured visiting Allied representatives that constitutional reform was not within his powers. One month later, however, he had decided the best way to prod reform was to prepare a model constitution for the Japanese. Within another three weeks, an entirely new constitution was drafted by SCAP officials. Symbolically, on Washington's birthday, Japan accepted the basic principles of the constitution. By March 5, the Emperor had approved the "drastic revision." By late June, the Japanese had writhed through four drafts, which were but slight revisions of the original document. By October 7, the new constitution had passed both houses of the Diet, under tremendous pressure from SCAP, and had been approved by the defunct Privy Council. On November 3, 1946, the Emperor promulgated the new constitution of Japan, which went into effect May 3, 1947.[5]

The Meiji Constitution was based upon the emperor, granted by the emperor, and amendable only by the emperor. Its basic philosophy was that "the Emperor is sacred and inviolable." Although others acted in the name of the emperor, his ultimate authority was never questioned in theory. The MacArthur Constitution was "revolutionary" to the extent that its preamble began with the (American-style) phrase "We, the Japanese people, acting through our duly elected representatives . . . do proclaim that sovereign power resides with the people and do firmly establish this Constitution." One student of this subject concluded that "these are most explicit expressions of the doctrine of popular sovereignty, *a doctrine completely alien to Japanese thoughts*"[6] (emphasis added).

The new constitution also redirected the basic distribution of powers of the state.[7] The Meiji Constitution had placed the bulk of power in the hands of the emperor's ministers, who were responsible to the emperor. Over time, through World War II, this power was gradually eroded as the consent of the Imperial Diet (parliament) became necessary for the passage of laws: "thus the Diet could deliberate on laws; it could not determine them." Under the MacArthur Constitution, the Diet is "the highest organ of state power, and shall be the law-making organ of the state." (Chapter 4, Article 41)[8] This formula redistributed power away from the emperor and his ministers and directed it to the legislature. The MacArthur Constitution drafted by the Americans in 1946:

> patched together an almost ideally democratic constitution, one that could scarcely have gained serious consideration if advocated for adoption in the United States. It had even less relevance to the traditional and dominant political aspirations of practices of Japan.[9]

Certainly among the most interesting and unique features of the MacArthur Constitution was the "renunciation of war" clause (Article 9). In this clause of the constitution the Japanese "forever renounce war as a sovereign right of the nation and the threat or use of force as a means of settling international disputes." To achieve this goal, "land, sea, and air forces, as well as other war potential, *will never be maintained*"[10] (emphasis added). This last part of Article 9 has not survived, in practice, since 1946. Today, Japan does have an army and a navy, and (ironically) has been encouraged by the United States to further develop these forces as a strategic balance to political and military instability in that part of the world.[11]

Many critics of the Japanese Constitution argued not only that it was literally "imposed" on Japan by the Occupation forces, but that it was *conceptually* alien to Japan's political culture—that it had "foreign ideas which did not accord with Japanese character and tradition." It is worth noting, however, that in the almost forty years since the constitution was promulgated, "there has yet to be a formal motion in the Diet to amend the Constitution."[12]

EXECUTIVE STRUCTURES

The executive structure of the Japanese political system bears some resemblance to a Westminster-model executive, at least superficially. Upon initial inspection we can see a prime minister and an emperor. The former is apparently actively involved in the day-to-day operations of the Government, and the latter is evidently held in great esteem by the public, with primarily symbolic functions.

This first impression does not tell the full story, however. The assumption that the emperor plays a role in Japanese politics corresponding to the role of the monarch in British politics is an overstatement of the emperor's position. Similarly, because of some idiosyncratic characteristics of the Japanese political world that we will discuss shortly, the position of the prime minister in Tokyo is different from that in London.

The Emperor

The royal family in Japan has an impressive lineage. The late Emperor Hirohito was "officially held to be the 124th monarch of Japan descended in a direct line from the legendary Emperor Jimmu, who supposedly founded the dynasty in 660 B.C."[13] This date, traditionally held to be the founding date of the empire, is regarded by students of Japanese politics as being "mythological," but "there is reliable evidence that [the dynasty] existed by at least the early sixth century, A.D., and has been continuous since then."[14]

The name of former Emperor Hirohito was given to him by his grandfather, the Emperor Meiji. The current emperor, whose title is "His Imperial Majesty Akihito," was born in 1933 and succeeded to the throne in January 1989; he was given his name by his father. In present-day Japan it is not considered proper to use the emperor's name in public; it almost never appears in print or is heard in conversation. Hirohito chose "Showa" as the name of his regime.[15] The marriage of Crown Prince Naruhito in June 1993 was of great significance to the Japanese because of the symbolic importance of the monarchy.

The difference in the role of the emperor in the two modern Japanese constitutions cannot be overstated. The Meiji Constitution stated that "the Empire of Japan shall be reigned over and governed by a line of Emperors unbroken for ages eternal," and that "the Emperor is sacred and inviolable . . . the head of the Empire, combining in Himself the rights of sovereignty."[16] Even though the power of the emperor vis-à-vis the military eroded after 1932, allowing the military leaders to force the emperor into a war with the United States, the emperor remained a dominant figure in the constitutional system.

In the MacArthur Constitution, the status of the emperor was *radically* altered; "perhaps the most profound change brought about by the new constitution was the change in the status of the emperor."[17] The authors of the new constitution knew that the Japanese would strenuously object to their doing away with the institution of the imperial family, so they kept the institution but stripped it of all power. The emperor today has only a symbolic role in the political system. Not only does he not have any political or executive functions, but he is specifically enjoined (prohibited) from such tasks. Article I of the constitution states that "the Emperor shall be the symbol of the state and of the unity of the people, deriving his position from the will of the people with whom resides sovereign power." Article I goes on to be quite explicit: "the Emperor shall perform only such acts in matters of state as are provided for in this Constitution, and *he shall not have powers related to government*"[18] (emphasis added).

Under the constitution of Meiji, the emperor was supreme; today, the emperor "is no longer absolute monarch, and his activities in matters of state are strictly ceremonial . . . in both theory and practice he is powerless." To put his role in a comparative perspective, "he does not even have the traditional 'right to be consulted, the right to encourage, the right to warn' which Bagehot ascribed to British monarchs."

> In attending to ceremonial state functions, he acts under the direction of the Cabinet, and he does not have "powers related to government." He appoints the Prime Minister as designated by the Diet—in this act he does not retain even the theoretical discretion that the Queen of England still enjoys—and the Chief Justice of the Supreme Court as recommended by the Cabinet. Under instruction from the Cabinet, he promulgates all laws, convokes the Diet, dissolves the House of Representatives, proclaims elections, attests the appointment and dismissal of state ministers, awards honors, receives foreign ambassadors and dignitaries, and performs other ceremonial functions. In short, the constitutional role of the Emperor is to clothe the everyday acts of the government with the dignity and majesty of the throne.[19]

None of the many tasks of the emperor involve his own initiative, decisions, or choice; like the British monarch, he acts "on the advice" of government leaders; unlike the British monarch, he has been explicitly, *legally*, stripped of all political power. On rare occasions it is possible that the emperor may exert some influence, primarily in areas concerning the imperial family, or in a moment of grave national crisis. One such instance occurred at the end of World War II in August 1945, when the cabinet was unable to reach a decision on whether to surrender; the emperor apparently played a pivotal role in convincing the cabinet to accept Allied surrender terms. When the emperor does exert influence today, it is usually based purely upon his "personal and institutional prestige. He has no legal or theoretical right to do so, and thus his official position is far weaker than the British monarch."[20]

Technically, it is worth noting (and it is not merely an exercise in semantics to do so) that the emperor is not even a "chief of state" or "head of state," but is only the "symbol of the state." He does not possess powers that most chiefs of state or heads of state, such as the British monarch or the German president, possess, even only in theory. Thus, while the Meiji emperor was among the most powerful individuals in the world by virtue of his position in the Japanese political system, the Japanese emperor today has extremely little political significance, and is less powerful than most comparable political figures in other political systems.

The Prime Minister

As we would predict from our basic Westminster-model format, the real power in Japan lies in the hands of the Government—namely the prime minister and the cabinet—and not the emperor.[21] Because the emperor is explicitly prohibited from *all* political action, however, the Japanese Government in many respects has *more* power than its British counterpart.

In Britain, and British-model countries, although the head of state acts "on the advice of the Government"—when he or she dissolves the legislature and calls for new elections, for example—it is *still* the head of state who has the power of dissolution. Under extraordinary circumstances the head of state may choose *not* to follow the advice of his or her Government.[22] In Japan, those powers usually held by the head of state (even only formally) to be exercised "on the advice of the Government" are *not* held by the emperor; they are simply held by the Government both *de jure* (in law) and *de facto* (in fact).

As in many other parliamentary systems, the Japanese legislature, the Diet, is bicameral: It has two chambers, and as is usually the case in bicameral parliamentary systems, the Government is "responsible," or answerable, only to the lower house, the House of Representatives.

> The Constitution does not require that the Prime Minister be a Representative (merely that he be a member of the Diet), but as in England constitutional practice demands that he be nominated from the lower house. The reason is that in the event of a disagreement between Representatives and Councillors on the choice of a Prime Minister, the decision of the House of Representatives is final (Article 67 of the Constitution).[23]

To date, all of Japan's postwar prime ministers have been members of the House of Representatives.[24] In practice, virtually all of the cabinet come from the House of Representatives, with perhaps two or three members coming from the upper house, the House of Councillors.

Also typical of other parliamentary nations, cabinet members wear a number of different hats—they play several roles at the same time. They are members of the legislative branch of government, they are members of the cabinet and thereby the executive branch of government, and they are each responsible for vast government bureaucracies and thereby play administrative roles. In addition to these three roles, which are typical of all parliamentary systems, cabinet members in Japan may be said to "wear a fourth hat" characteristic of those countries in which cabinets are based upon coalitions of several political parties: Cabinet members in Japan are either leaders of political parties or leaders of factions of political parties.

"While the Emperor is the symbol of the state under the new Constitution, the Prime Minister is the head of the Government. Since World War Two the roles of the Prime Minister and Cabinet have grown vastly more important than they formerly were." Under the Meiji regime the executive power *de jure* belonged to the emperor, who was advised by his ministers. Article 65 of the 1947 constitution "provides that 'Executive power shall be vested in the Cabinet' so that the Cabinet exercises executive authority in its own right."[25]

The Japanese Cabinet is specifically given a large number of powers in the constitution. "It administers the affairs of state through a vast bureaucracy . . . in 53 primary ministries and agencies. . . . Above all, the Cabinet has the right to initiate both ordinary legislation and amendments to the Constitution."[26] Powers of the cabinet can be broken down into several categories—executive, legislative, and judicial—and are illustrated in Table 12.1.

Coalition Governments

Because Japan has a multiparty system, it would be predictable that coalition governments would form there. What makes the Japanese political system especially interesting is that for the most part, all of the coalitions that have formed have been

TABLE 12.1
Powers of the Japanese Cabinet as Found in the Constitution

Executive Powers
  1. Supervise the administration of the state (Section 72)
  2. Manage foreign affairs and treaties (Section 73)
  3. Control financial policy (Sections 83, 87)
  4. Enact cabinet orders (Section 73)

Legislative Powers
  1. Submit bills to the Diet (Section 72)
  2. Prepare the national budget (Sections 73, 86)
  3. Report to the Diet on state expenses (Section 90)
  4. "Advise" the emperor as to when to call sessions of the Diet (Section 7)
  5. Sign laws (Section 74)

Judicial Powers
  1. Name the chief justice of the Supreme Court (Section 6)
  2. Appoint justices to courts (Sections 79, 80)

Source: Based on text in Warren Tsuneishi, *Japanese Political Style* (New York: Harper & Row, 1966), pp. 42–43.

coalitions *within* one massive party, the Liberal-Democratic party (LDP). In 1955 the nonsocialist parties in Japan combined to form the LDP, which has always had a majority in the House of Representatives in combination with a number of smaller conservative offshoot parties. The components of the LDP coalition, however, have not completely disappeared, and the LDP party leader must always keep leaders of the party's various factions happy if he or she wants to stay in power.

In fact, some have suggested that the real core of Japanese party politics cannot be described by interparty competition. Rather, they argue, the most important single characteristic of Japanese politics is the elaborate factional infighting within the LDP, as well as the interaction between various interest groups and the LDP leadership (some of it clearly corrupt). In the past several years, as we shall describe later in this chapter, we have seen a number of political crises brought about by charges of corruption within the LDP, and even more recently a new political party has emerged from within the LDP as a response to this tradition of corruption and political crisis.

In a groundbreaking study over twenty years ago, Michael Leiserson was able to identify six levels of cabinet positions in Japan. He suggested that for the LDP leader to stay in power, the party needed to distribute enough "valuable" cabinet positions to each party faction to retain their support. Factions more valuable to the coalition would receive more valuable cabinet positions. Leiserson ranked the cabinet positions as follows:

    A. Prime Minister

    B. Finance Minister, Party Secretary-General

C. Trade and Industry Minister, Agriculture Minister, Transportation Minister, Construction Minister, Party Executive Board Chairman, Party Policy Board Chairman

D. Foreign Minister, Deputy Prime Minister, Party Vice President, Cabinet Minister without Portfolio

E. Education Minister, Welfare Minister, Labor Minister, Defense Minister, Justice Minister, Post Office Minister, Interior Minister

F. Administrative Management Agency Director, Science and Technology Minister.[27]

Ever since the establishment of the cabinet system in Japan in 1885, nearly seventy cabinets have come into existence under both the Meiji and the 1947 constitutions. Thus the average Japanese cabinet has lasted for about fourteen months.[28] In recent years the cabinet has usually had about twelve members, far smaller than many of its European counterparts.

The prime minister is head of the cabinet, and for reasons that we indicated earlier—because the emperor is unusually weak—the prime minister is unusually strong. This individual's powers include the following:

1. Power to appoint and dismiss other cabinet members without consulting the Diet;
2. Control over branches of administration;
3. Countersignature power on *all* laws and cabinet orders—they must be signed by the prime minister *as well as* the relevant minister;
4. Power to preside at cabinet meetings;
5. Power to decide jurisdictional disputes between cabinet officers;
6. Power to cause resignation of the entire cabinet by his own resignation.[29]

Under the Meiji Constitution, through 1932, the prime minister was chosen by the emperor from among leaders in the Diet (as is the case in most parliamentary systems); from 1932 until the end of World War II, prime ministers were not party leaders but generals. Under the 1947 constitution, it is not the emperor who selects the prime minister, even on a *pro forma* basis, but the Diet itself. At its first meeting after a new election, the Diet selects a prime minister from its own membership. If the House of Councillors does not concur with the House of Representatives within a ten-day period, the House of Representatives' choice becomes prime minister anyway. The emperor is then required to ratify the choice of the Diet (which he always has done).[30]

The prime minister has the right to choose his own cabinet, and will do so, as we indicated above, in a manner so as to strengthen his coalition and therefore his political power. As more than one scholar has noted, "The first job of the new prime minister is to distribute Diet, cabinet, and party positions, and finalize the lineup."[31] Unlike other parliamentary systems, in which a vote of confidence is needed before the prime minister and cabinet officially take office, the Japanese prime minister (since he is *chosen* by the legislature and not by the head of state) needs no subsequent vote of confidence. What is more, the Japanese prime minister may change the composition of the cabinet at any time; he does not need to go back to the legislature for a subsequent vote of confidence.[32]

The Cabinet

The cabinet is responsible to the House of Representatives in the same manner that we have seen in other nations. If the House of Representatives (the Government is responsible only to the lower house, not the upper house) passes a resolution of no confidence or fails to pass a resolution of confidence in the cabinet—and this is quite rare in Japanese politics—Article 69 of the constitution requires that "the Cabinet shall resign en masse, unless the House of Representatives is dissolved within ten days."[33]

Thus, the cabinet has a choice to make if it receives a vote of no confidence: Either it can resign immediately, or it can dissolve the House of Representatives and call for new elections. If it chooses the latter route, dissolution, it *still* must resign en masse (under Article 70) "upon the first convocation of the Diet after a general election of members of the lower house"—that is, as soon as the House of Representatives meets after the election—even if the party of the Government wins the election. This required resignation does not, of course, prevent the same prime minister from being renamed prime minister in the new Government.[34]

The cabinet is also constitutionally mandated to resign upon the resignation (or death) of the prime minister. Dissolution, of course, affects only the House of Representatives. "The House of Councillors, having a fixed term, cannot be dissolved. Its sessions are, however, suspended when the lower house has been dissolved and resume only with the convocation of the postelection Diet."[35]

Administrative Structures

The number of public employees in Japan increased dramatically between the end of World War II and the mid-1960s. In fact, there was such a growth of the governmental bureaucracy that a "capping" law was passed in 1969, limiting the increase of civil servants in the regular ministries and national government agencies. There is in effect a "zero-sum game" in government personnel: Any increase in one division must be matched by a comparable decrease in another.[36] In fact, a government task force recommended a 5 percent cut in the number of national employees between 1982 and 1986 in an attempt to reduce government expenditures.[37]

The administrative branch of Japanese government "plays an important role in the ongoing process of making decisions and setting national goals, as well as in the implementation of policies."[38] Cabinet officials oversee huge bureaucratic structures; the Japanese administrative bureaucracy contains a vast civil service, with a very small number of political appointments. The bureaucracy plays an active role in the "drafting and implementation of laws and the issuance of ministerial rules,"[39] which are often regarded as being just as important as laws passed by the Diet.[40]

THE DIET

The Japanese Diet is the oldest parliamentary body in Asia, having been in continuous existence since 1890.[41] Today, power in the Japanese political system, as we have seen, is not

> vested in the crown to be exercised by the cabinet, as in England. Nor has the power of the cabinet grown in an entirely extra-constitutional fashion, as in the United States. Indeed, in Japanese constitutional theory, the cabinet holds an inferior status, as compared with the Diet, the highest organ of state power.[42]

The constitution describes the Diet as "the highest organ of state power,"[43] and it sets forth in some detail the structure and power of the Diet in relation to other political bodies in the political system. The significance of this is most obvious:

> when compared with comparable clauses of the Meiji Constitution. Under the terms of that document, the emperor was more than the highest organ of state power; in a mystical way, he embodied the state and wielded its sovereign powers. Although laws were formally the product of the Imperial Diet, both the emperor and the Cabinet had the power to issue decrees that had the force of law. The present Constitution vests sovereignty in the people and makes the Diet both the highest organ of the people's sovereignty and the sole source of law. These changes are basic to both the legal and the power structure of the Japanese state. The government has thus been technically transformed from an emperor-centered to a parliament-centered system, and the elected representatives of the people have, in theory at least, become vastly more powerful.[44]

In the new constitution, then, "the Diet was transformed from an instrument for endorsing the Emperor's legislative authority to the highest organ of state power and the sole law-making organ of the state."[45] The Japanese legislature is called the "Diet" in English because it was modelled upon the German Diet that existed when the first Japanese Constitution was drawn up in the late 1880s. The British, French, and American systems were all used as models, in different eras, for Japanese political evolution.[46]

That the Japanese Diet today is a bicameral legislative body is a result of the insistence of the Japanese leaders during the time of MacArthur's occupation of Japan. The American constitutional authorities on MacArthur's staff wanted to abolish the House of Peers (the upper house in Japan during the Meiji era), and they argued that Japan did not need a second house in its new constitutional structure, since Japan had a unitary, not a federal, political system. The American authors of the "new" Japanese constitution, in fact, deleted the upper house from the first drafts of their proposed Japanese constitution.

Japanese officials insisted on the inclusion of a second house, however, not because it was justified by a federal political system (which Japan was clearly not), but primarily because it was necessary for a "sober second thought," a "check against hasty, ill-considered measures supported by a majority party in the lower house."[47] The American concession in this regard, "allowing" the Japanese to have a bicameral legislature, was "the only major concession to Japanese opinion made by MacArthur's staff in the new Japanese constitution."[48]

The Diet performs a number of significant political functions in the Japanese system today.[49] First, as with all parliamentary bodies, we must identify its primary function not as passing legislation, but as the selection of a Government, the "designation of a cabinet." Second, to a lesser degree that we will discuss shortly, the Diet does play a role in the making of governmental policy, primarily responding to proposals from the Government. Third, the Diet initiates constitutional amendments, "ratifies treaties, and oversees administration, all powers that previously belonged to the Emperor." Fourth, the Diet participates in the process of making foreign policy, by holding hearings and ratifying treaties undertaken by the Government. Fifth, the Diet participates in the normal functioning of Government operations by virtue of its "power to investigate government operations." Finally, and most important to many, the Diet "functions as a public forum where the great issues of the day are publicized, analyzed, debated, and then acted upon."[50]

Bicameralism

The upper house of the bicameral legislature—the House of Councillors—is the less important of the two. It was designed "to attract well-known people who were not necessarily professional politicians."[51] To help distinguish the role of the House of Councillors—supposedly existing to provide stability and a "sober second thought" to actions of the House of Representatives—from the role of the lower house, councillors were given six-year terms of office, with half of the 252 members being elected every three years. Members of the House of Representatives—511 in number[52]—serve up to four-year terms, subject to early dissolution.

The two houses of the Diet do not have equal power. The constitution notes that the lower house is superior to the upper house in several specific areas, including (1) the enactment of laws, (2) the passage of the budget, (3) the approval of treaties, and (4) the selection of the prime minister.[53]

As we noted above, the relationship is not the same between the Government and each of the two houses of the Diet. The Government is responsible to the House of Representatives, and must maintain the "confidence" of the House of Representatives. In a manner similar to that which we have noted elsewhere, although the Government is vulnerable to the House of Representatives—in that the House of Representatives can pass a motion of no confidence and in effect fire the Government—the House of Representatives is correspondingly vulnerable to the Government, since the Government has the power of dissolution—in effect, the power to fire the lower house of the Diet.

The Government is *not* correspondingly responsible to the House of Councillors, and in this respect we are reminded of the relationship between the British cabinet and the House of Commons and that between the British cabinet and the House of Lords. Accordingly, since the Government is not vulnerable to the councillors, the councillors are not vulnerable to the Government: "The House of Councillors may not be dissolved."[54]

The Legislative Process

The legislative powers of the House of Councillors appear to be very similar to those of the House of Representatives, with the three exceptions noted above: in the areas of treaties, budget bills, and the selection of the prime minister. If the two houses cannot agree, the will of a majority of the lower house prevails over the will of the upper house. In all other matters the approval of both houses is necessary, although the lower house can override the upper house with a two-thirds majority if the two houses cannot agree on a compromise over disputed legislation. This has not happened very frequently: only twenty-nine times since the end of World War II.[55]

Although the influence of the House of Councillors in the legislative process may thus be only that of a suspensory veto (since the lower house has the power to override the upper house), in specific political eras when the Government's majority in the House of Representatives does not approach a two-thirds share of the membership, and when the Government knows it does not have the votes to override the upper house, the House of Councillors' veto may in fact be more than merely suspensory. A Government that can count on only 55 or 60 percent of the House of Representatives' membership may feel compelled to reach a compromise with the House of Councillors rather than try to override the House of Councillors with a two-thirds vote that it knows it cannot obtain.

Most bills originate somewhere in the ministries, and after working their way through the bureaucratic network the bills appear in the cabinet for its approval for submission in the Diet as Government bills. Not all ministry proposals are endorsed by the cabinet, but those that are endorsed are submitted by the prime minister to the Diet. "Budget bills must go to the lower house first. Five days after submission of a bill to one house, the other must receive a copy for preliminary study."[56]

When a bill is submitted to either house of the Diet, either the Speaker of the House of Representatives or the President of the House of Councillors immediately channels the bill to the appropriate standing committee. There are sixteen standing committees in each house, and committees are the same in both houses. The committees are:

1. Foreign Affairs
2. Finance
3. Education
4. Welfare and Labor
5. Agriculture, Forestry, and Fisheries
6. Commerce and Industry
7. Transport
8. Communications
9. Construction
10. Local Administration
11. Budget
12. Accounting
13. House Management
14. Discipline
15. Cabinet
16. Judicial Affairs.[57]

The committee stage in the House of Representatives may be bypassed if a majority of the House concurs. This does not apply to the House of Councillors.

Comittees hold hearings on bills, calling as witnesses cabinet members, ministerial officials, concerned bureaucrats, interest group representatives, and members of the public. After the committee has finished its hearings, it reports to the full House. Unlike other parliamentary bodies that employ variations of the "three reading" model in their legislative process, the houses of the Japanese Diet have only a single reading and vote following the committee stage. Voting in the House of Representatives, as one might guess, "runs strictly along party lines."[58] If a bill passes, it goes to the other house of the Diet where the same procedure is followed.

> If the other house makes changes, the bill goes back to the first house. If there is still disagreement, then a conference committee tries to resolve it, or the lower house can try to override the upper by a two-thirds vote for passage. In the case of disagreement between the houses on budget bills or treaties, or in the absence of upper house action in thirty days, the lower house decision by ordinary majority is sufficient to pass the bill. The bill is signed into law by the sponsoring minister, the Emperor, and the Prime Minister: they do not possess a veto after Diet passage.[59]

The cabinet is not the only source of legislation in the Diet, although it is the largest source. Bills in both houses also originate in committees and from private members; regular private members' bills must have at least twenty co-sponsors, and bills dealing with budgetary matters need fifty co-sponsors.[60] One long-term study found that between 1947 and 1975, approximately 85 percent of all bills passed were bills introduced by the Government, whereas about 15 percent were introduced by private members.

Many of these private members' bills, of course, *really* originated in the bureaucracy and were introduced as private members' bills because of the unwillingness of the cabinet, or the relevant minister, or some bureaucrat in the chain of command below that, to approve the proposal as an official Government idea.

> The scheduling and flow of legislative business is controlled by the Committee on House Management, composed of senior and experienced representatives of each political party in numbers proportional to that party's strength in the lower house. Under normal circumstances—a term that applies to a large majority of the bills coming before the house—this system works quite effectively. On noncontroversial matters, the members of the Committee on House Management are briefed in advance by their parties' Diet Strategy Committee and are able to calendar bills and assign time quotas to each party for speaking on the issue involved. On controversial matters, however, the system sometimes breaks down completely, and the committee is unable to agree. In such cases the matter is usually referred to the secretaries-general of all the parties for negotiation and settlement. Protracted negotiations can ensue during which the normal functioning of the house may come to a complete halt.[61]

POLITICAL PARTIES AND ELECTIONS

The Japanese political party system has been variously described as a multiparty system,[62] a "one and one-half party system,"[63] and a "six quarter-parties system."[64] Japan has actually had a large number of political parties since the advent of the MacArthur

Constitution; at one point immediately after the war there were apparently in excess of 1,000 "registered groups" active in politics.

This fact notwithstanding, however, Japan has had a paucity of truly ideological political parties. "Even the three or four major ones offered a bewildering shift of names, symptomatic of the bland transfer of members' allegiance, and an almost total lack of true political principles."[65] Essentially, as we noted earlier, in modern times Japan has been led by a single party, the Liberal Democratic party (LDP), with opposition parties rising and falling in popularity while the LDP ruled.[66]

In November 1955 Japan's two major (ideologically) conservative parties, the (inappropriately named) Liberal party and the Democratic party, combined to offer a significant opposition force to the Socialist party, which was a major force in Japan at the time. This new party was called the Liberal Democratic party.[67] For a brief period thereafter, a two-party system prevailed in Japan. Soon, however, intra-party factionalism and competition led to splintering of the parties, and Japan reverted to a multiparty system.[68]

The System of Political Parties

The modern party structure of Japanese politics has been dominated by two major parties, the Liberal Democratic party and the Japan Socialist party. The party system has been characterized as "a dominant party that monopolizes power and alone knows how to govern, while opposed by a permanent minority group that at times seems 'positively afraid of power'."[69] This "traditional" pattern of party power changed somewhat in the summer of 1993 as several new parties were created in a wave of party reform that swept Japanese politics.

The Japan Socialist party (JSP) dates from November 1945, and has been characterized as a party "of permanent opposition."[70] For many years the Socialist party strongly advocated unarmed neutrality in foreign policy, and loudly criticized Japan's Self-Defense Forces as violating the "constitutional renunciation of 'land, sea, and air forces, as well as other war potential' (Article 9)."[71] In recent years the JSP has moderated its view and softened its traditional anti-American positions.

A third significant party—"Komeito," or Clean Government party—has sought to control the political center in electoral competitions. Komeito was originally created to be the political arm of a major Buddhist sect with over 16 million members.[72] Komeito's philosophy suggests that "centrism is a position in which it should be possible to overcome the confrontation between the left and the right and to create a third solution that can be a national consensus."[73]

> Considering the weakness of the Socialist Party and the fierce hostilities, suspicions, and rivalry that beset the five opposition parties collectively, some understanding of the basic immobilism of Japanese party politics begins to emerge. [The LDP survives as the basis of government] partly because of a lack of any credible alternative.[74]

As could be seen in the results of the 1990 elections for the House of Representatives (summarized in Table 12.2), there were a number of parties active in Japanese politics, even if the Liberal Democrats dominated the political scene. Many

TABLE 12.2
Results of 1990 and 1993 Elections for the Japanese House
of Representatives

Party	Number of Seats (1990)	Number of Seats (1993)	Difference
Liberal Democratic	275	223	− 52
Socialist	136	70	− 66
Komeito ("Clean")	45	51	+ 6
Independents	22	30	+ 8
Japan Renewal	a	55	+ 55
Japan New	a	35	+ 35
Harbinger	a	13	+ 13
Other	34	34	−
Total	512[b]	511[b]	− 1[b]

[a]Indicates party did not exist in 1990 election.
[b]The size of the House of Representatives was decreased by one seat prior to the 1993 election as a result of a reapportionment.
Source: The New York Times (July 19, 1993), p. A9; *Facts on File* 53:2747 (July 22, 1993), p. 552.

of these parties were the results of a number of evolutionary changes in party names, organizations, and ideology. Some of the contemporary political parties had very clearly delineated policy platforms differentiating them from other parties. Others of the several parties had a number of policy positions in common, and differed on minor points.[75] This situation of uncertainty about party ideology and behavior led one student of Japanese politics to posit two general characteristics of the political party situation in Japan:

> First, none of the parties—except perhaps the Clean Government and Communist parties—are truly mass membership organizations. They notably lack solid bases in popular involvement and support. They normally operate in Tokyo and among circles limited almost exclusively to professional politicians and administrators. They are essentially parliamentary parties. Their prime focus of interest is the lower house of the National Diet and what goes on there. Only during election campaigns do they engage in massive and sustained contact with the people.
>
> Second, the two largest parties are internally disunited. . . . The results of such a situation are constant instability and strife within each party.[76]

The party situation changed somewhat on June 18, 1993, when members of the majority Liberal Democratic Party joined with opposition legislators in the House of Representatives and passed a no-confidence vote that forced the resignation of Prime Minister Kiichi Miyazawa.[77] Only one other LDP prime minister had been defeated on a nonconfidence motion since 1955—Masayoshi Ohira in 1980—and as a result of the fall of the Miyazawa Government, the lower house of parliament was dissolved and new elections were scheduled for July 18.

Many of the LDP members who had voted against the Miyazawa Government joined together to create a new political party, the Renewal Party, which campaigned against the corruption and stagnation of the LDP during the period leading up to the election. In the final analysis, although the LDP won a plurality of the vote, it was deprived of an outright majority for the first time, and was forced to enter a coalition government with a non-LDP prime minister, Morihiro Hosokawa, although that government lasted only a brief time before it, too, fell for scandal-related reasons leading to the creation of a government headed by Tsutomu Hata.

Electoral Activity

Japan has a history of national elections dating back to 1889, although early elections had very small electorates because of rigid restrictions based upon tax and residency qualifications.[78] Today, elections are highly visible, and the public participation rate is correspondingly high, as indicated in Table 12.2.

Japan is a unitary, not a federal, state, and is divided into forty-seven administrative regions called *prefectures*. These include 655 cities, 2,000 towns, and 591 villages.[79] Each of these bodies has its own autonomous government with an elected assembly.[80]

Elections for both the lower house (the House of Representatives) and for part of the upper house (the House of Councillors) are based upon electoral districts that to varying degrees are themselves based upon these prefectural units. We will discuss each of the electoral frameworks separately here.

Elections for the House of Representatives are based upon multiple-member districts such as those we described earlier in this volume. Currently, there are 130 "medium-sized" districts that elect 511 members to the House of Representatives. The electoral districts are constructed "by dividing up the forty-six [now that Okinawa has been returned to Japanese jurisdiction, there are forty-seven] prefectures in such a way that the districts do not cross prefectural boundaries."[81]

Lightly populated prefectures such as Saga and Kochi are single constituencies in themselves; more heavily populated prefectures such as Tokyo may be divided into as many as seven constituencies.[82] The system "has no multiple voting or proportional representation. It is technically a multimember constituency, single-vote system."[83] The 130 districts each send from three to five members to the House of Representatives (with one exception of a one-member district). Each voter votes once, and the top three, four, or five vote-getters (whichever is appropriate to the district in question) are elected. Obviously, no majority is required. "Thus, for example, in the Shizuoka Prefecture third district, which is entitled to four seats in the House of Representatives, the four candidates receiving the highest number of votes win the four seats."[84]

How do would-be representatives become candidates for the House of Representatives election? It is done on a flexible basis; there are no nominating conventions or public primary elections. Hopefuls simply notify the chairmen of local election boards and pay deposits that are returned if the candidate wins a minimal percentage of the vote. (This is designed to discourage frivolous candidacies.) Nomination by parties is done by party election committees that are established for that purpose by the party organization.[85]

In the multiple-member-district races, each party can have several candidates competing for seats. This explains how the Liberal Democratic party was able to control 53.7 percent of the seats in the House of Representatives following the 1990 election, although it won only 46.1 percent of the vote. It is worth noting that the Democratic Socialist party won 14 seats (2.7 percent of the total) with 4.8 percent of the vote, whereas the Japan Communist party won almost the same number or seats—16 seats, or 3.1 percent of the total—with not quite 8 percent of the votes.

More dramatically, while 7.96 percent of the vote earned the Japan Communist party 16 seats in the House of Representatives, 7.98 percent of the vote earned the Komeito party 45 seats in the House of Representatives! This shows that there is a great value to effective candidacy planning.[86] "The secret of success lies in achieving an optimal relationship between the number of candidates a party runs in a given election district and the number of votes it controls in that area."[87]

These electoral competitions, it has been argued, "exacerbate intraparty factional rivalry" for the simple reason that:

> the candidate's most formidable rivals quite often are members of his own party and not of the opposition. Consider as an extreme case the sad fate of Representative Ozawa Taro, Liberal-Democratic incumbent who in 1963 faced the formidable task of running not only against his Socialist opponents but against two of the best-known politicians in the country, former Prime Minister Kishi Nobusuke and future Prime Minister Sato Eisaku. Seven candidates contested the five seats allotted to the First District of Yamaguchi Prefecture: 3 Liberal-Democrats, 2 Socialists, a Democratic Socialist, and a Communist. Altogether the conservatives polled 188,583 votes which, if distributed evenly among the three, would have ensured re-election for all. But Sato gained 94,785 votes, Kishi 49,877, and Ozawa only 43,841. Sato's great pulling power reduced Ozawa's total, with the result that his Socialist and Democratic Socialist opponents with 50,000–66,000 votes took the other three seats.[88]

Elections, as in many parliamentary systems, are required at least every four years, but usually are held more frequently than that for political reasons. In fact, until very recently no postwar Diet had lasted its full four-year term of office. When the House of Representatives is dissolved, "the Government must call a general election within 60 days. The actual date of the election must be announced at least 25 days in advance."[89] In 1993, the House of Representatives was dissolved on June 18 and elections were held one month later.

The upper house of the Diet, the House of Councillors, is not terribly significant in the operation of the Government, as we indicated earlier. Members of the House of Councillors are elected for six-year terms, half of the membership being elected every three years. Like many other parliamentary upper houses, the House of Councillors cannot be dissolved by the Government, because the Government is not responsible to the House of Councillors. Councillors all serve their full six-year terms.

Like the lower house of the German legislature, the House of Councillors in Japan has two separate electorates. Japanese voters each have two votes in elections for the upper house, the House of Councillors. The 252 members of the House of Councillors are divided into two groups, the "prefectural" or "local" representatives, and the national "proportional representation" representatives. Of the 252 members, 152 represent prefectural constituencies, and 100 represent the proportional representation, national constituency. Since half of the House of Councillors is elected every three years, this means that at each House of Councillors election 76 prefectural or local representatives will be elected and 50 national representatives will be elected.

The prefectural or local representatives are elected from multiple-member districts. "Each of the 47 prefectures is entitled to from two to eight seats in the House of Councillors, the more populous prefectures having more seats than the less populous."[90] Only the prefectures of Tokyo and Hokkaido are large enough to have eight seats in the House of Councillors.[91] Since 76 of the 152 prefectural representatives are elected every three years, half of each prefecture's seats are contested at every election as illustrated in Table 12.3. Much as with the elections for the House of Representatives, there will be many candidates competing for the one to four seats in each prefecture, and each voter casts one vote, with the top one to four (as appropriate) vote-getters being elected.

Until 1980 the 50 members of the national constituency of the House of Councillors elected every three years were elected from a single national multiple-member district (in this case, 50 members) in which there might have been as many as 200 to 250 candidates competing for the 50 seats; the top 50 vote-getters were the winners. In 1980 this system was changed so that the 50 national representatives would be elected by a system of proportional representation.

Recent Elections

In all Japanese elections in the last two decades the Liberal Democratic party has dominated seats in the Diet. As we noted above, however, this domination was weakened in the July 1993 election, which resulted for the first time in the LDP having to form a coalition with another party.[92] The December 1972 election for the House of Representatives had been relatively close for the LDP, but the LDP found the election of the House of Councillors in July 1974 especially alarming. In this election the

TABLE 12.3
**Composition of the Japanese House of Councillors Following the 1992
Elections**

Party	Seats Up for Election (Won)	Seats Not Up for Election	New Strength	Before Election
Liberal Democratic	75 (69)	39	108	114
Socialist	22 (22)	49	71	71
Komeito ("Clean")	10 (14)	10	24	20
Communist	9 (6)	5	11	14
Other	11 (16)	22	38	33
Total	127 (127)	125	252	252

Source: Asahi Evening News (July 27, 1992), p. 1.

LDP faced its most severe challenge to date; it ended up controlling 129 seats (along with its conservative allies) against 122 seats for the opposition, a majority of only seven seats.[93]

One of the major issues in the election was the close relationship between the LDP and what was called "big business." Many voters were concerned with what was referred to as the "money-dominated election"[94] in which many candidates spent fortunes (provided by business supporters) on their campaigns. The charge that interest groups exert a disproportionate influence in Japanese politics (for example, in the legislative process) has frequently—too frequently, many Japanese feel—been a major issue in elections;[95] accusations of corruption, bribery, or some other kind of undue influence have figured prominently as campaign issues in recent years.[96]

The next election, in 1976, followed the only full four-year term of the House of Representatives in postwar Japanese history. The election was held as late as possible because of the massive political scandal at the time dealing with payoffs to politicians by Lockheed Aircraft Company. The election was thus dubbed the "Lockheed election." In that election the LDP won only 249 seats; by co-opting a number of conservative independents after the election, the party was able to raise its results to 257—one seat above the "minimum majority" of 256, a figure that was subsequently raised to 260.[97]

The election of October 1979 was called over a year before it was necessary, because Prime Minister Ohira felt that his party was increasing its strength and would do well. The media were predicting an LDP landslide; however, the LDP performed very poorly, winning only 248 seats, far less than a majority. With some postelection co-optation of other conservative independents, the LDP was able to assemble a majority again, but the Ohira government was weakened by the election results.

The first simultaneous election for both houses of the Diet in Japanese history was scheduled for June 22, 1980. Although the opposition parties had hopes of significant gains, their plans were frustrated by the sudden death of Prime Minister Ohira ten days before the election; the major target of the opposition parties had disappeared. It was ironic—although perhaps predictable—that after the prime minister's death his party's performance in the election improved remarkably from the preceeding election, to a substantial degree because of a "sympathy vote." The LDP won a landslide victory, garnering 286 seats in the House of Representatives (its largest majority since 1969) and maintaining a solid majority in the House of Councillors.

Scandal again was the theme of the 1983 election; this time the general topic was the "Tanaka problem"—referring to the scandal involving former Prime Minister Tanaka, who had been found guilty of accepting bribes offered by Lockheed Aircraft in return for a Japan Air Lines purchase of its airplanes—as well as the issue of political ethics in the LDP. Prime Minister Yasuhiro Nakasone sought to distance himself from the guilty verdict, but he was not completely successful; the LDP's majority fell from 286 seats to 250 seats, a much smaller margin.

In June 1986 Nakasone dissolved the House of Representatives eighteen months before elections were required so that there could be another election for both houses of the Diet at the same time. It was believed that a double election encourages greater voter turnout, and would thereby favor the party that was in power. The election, held on July 6, gave the Liberal Democratic party "its most resounding election victory since it was formed" in 1955.[98]

Nakasone stepped down as prime minister and president of the Liberal Democratic party in October 1987, as required by the constitution of the LDP,[99] and his place was taken by Noboru Takeshita. As had some of his predecessors, Takeshita suffered the effects of a variety of political scandals. His party's candidate lost in a by-election race in February 1989 as a result "of public anger about a widening stock scandal and a recently enacted sales tax."[100] Takeshita resigned as a result of the scandal in the early summer, and was replaced by Soucuke Uno. He was forced to resign in less than a month as a result of a sex scandal, leaving new Prime Minister Toshiki Kaifu trying to rebuild the reeling Liberal Democratic party top leadership.

The February 1990 election for the House of Representatives returned the Liberal Democratic party to power, although with a smaller majority (275) than it had enjoyed following the 1986 election (300). Prime Minister Kaifu expressed satisfaction at his party's retaining control of the House of Representatives, and vowed to restore the credibility of the Liberal Democrats. The big winners in the 1990 election were the supporters of the Japan Socialist Party, whose representation in the House increased from 85 seats to 136 seats; the Komeito, Democratic Socialist party, and United Socialist Democratic party all declined in strength in the new legislature.

As was noted above, the tremendous popular discontent with scandals and corruption of the old-guard Liberal Democrats gave rise to a seven-party coalition government following the 1993 election. There was a significant decrease in support for the Socialist party (which lost nearly half its seats in the House of Representatives) and an increase in "reform" and "renewal" parties. Many suggested that the coalition, led by Morihiro Hosokawa of the new Japan New Party, would in the final analysis be too fragile to survive more than a short period of time, and that the long-term implications of the election were unclear.[101] The sudden demise of the Hosokawa government in the spring of 1994 demonstrated this to be true: the survivability of the government of Tsutomu Hata which succeeded Hosokawa's government was equally unclear.

SUMMARY

The Japanese political system is a hybrid. The modern political structure of Japan is a result of a highly artificial combination of Western constitutional ideas and Japanese political and cultural history. The authors of the MacArthur Constitution gave Japan a constitutional framework, which they thought would lead to stable and democratic government. So far, to the surprise of some, they appear to have succeeded.

Japan has taken a number of political cues from Western Europe and the United States, and, as we have seen in this chapter, has adapted many of these cues to be appropriate to the Japanese culture. The imperial family, although *de jure* of little significance, is still quite important in Japan. The legislature is typical of many of the Westminster-model bodies we have already met, with some extra authority given to the Government as a result of the emperor's unique lack of power. The electoral system is different from any we have met thus far, yet it seems to be consistent with ideas we have met dealing with democratic elections and popular representation.

The Japanese political system, then, presents some very interesting variations on the several themes common to the many political systems we have already encountered, and provides illustrations of the ways in which political structures may alter in order to be appropriate to the political culture in which they are found.

Notes

1. A good history of Japanese political institutions can be found in Ryosuke Ishii, *A History of Political Institutions in Japan* (Tokyo: University of Tokyo Press, 1980).
2. Robert E. Ward, *Japan's Political System* (Englewood Cliffs, N.J.: Prentice Hall, 1978), p. 8.
3. Ibid., p. 9.
4. Ibid., p. 11.
5. Ardath Burks, *The Government of Japan* (New York: Thomas Y. Crowell, 1964), p. 25.
6. See Kazuo Kawai, "Sovereignty and Democracy in the Japanese Constitution," *American Political Science Review* 49 (1955): 663. For a broader discussion of Japanese political culture and democratic values, see Takeshi Ishida and Ellis S. Krauss, eds., *Democracy in Japan* (Pittsburgh: University of Pittsburgh Press, 1989).
7. See Kent E. Calder, *Crisis and Compensation: Public Policy and Political Stability in Japan, 1949–1986* (Princeton, N.J.: Princeton University Press, 1988).
8. Burks, *The Government of Japan*, p. 19.
9. Robert E. Ward, "The Origins of the Present Japanese Constitution," *American Political Science Review* 50 (1956): 1001. (All future references to Ward are to his 1978 book, not this article.)
10. Burks, *The Government of Japan*, p. 21.
11. See Joseph P. Keddell, Jr., *The Politics of Defense in Japan: Managing Internal and External Pressures* (Armonk, N.Y.: M.E. Sharpe, 1993), K.V. Kesavan, ed., *Contemporary Japanese Politics and Foreign Policy* (London: Sangam Studies, 1989), or Mike Mochizuki et al., *Japan and the United States: Troubled Partners in a Changing World* (Washington, D.C.: Brassey's, 1991).
12. Charles F. Bingman, *Japanese Government, Leadership, and Management* (New York: St. Martin's Press, 1989), p. 5.
13. Warren Tsuneishi, *Japanese Political Style* (New York: Harper and Row, 1966), p. 55.
14. Ward, *Japan's Political System*, p. 147.
15. Tsuneishi, *Japanese Political Style*, p. 56.
16. Theodore McNelly, *Politics and Government in Japan* (Boston: Houghton Mifflin, 1972), p. 181.
17. Bradley Richardson and Scott Flanagan, *Politics: Japan* (Boston: Little, Brown, 1984), p. 36.
18. McNelly, *Politics and Government in Japan*, p. 181.
19. Tsuneishi, *Japanese Political Style*, p. 58.
20. Ward, *Japan's Political System*, p. 157.
21. See Kenyi Hayao, *The Japanese Prime Minister and Public Policy* (Pittsburgh: University of Pittsburgh Press, 1993).
22. In 1975 Australia faced a truly unprecedented constitutional crisis when its head of state—Governor General John Kerr—fired a popularly elected Prime Minister, Gough Whitlam, even though Whitlam still controlled a majority in the lower house of the legislature. This happened because of a conflict that had developed between the two houses of parliament,

one controlled by one party and the other controlled by another party. See Gough Whitlam, *The Truth of the Matter* (London: Penguin Books, 1979), and Garfield Barwick, *Sir John Did His Duty* (Wahroonga: Serendip Publications, 1983).

23. Tsuneishi, *Japanese Political Style*, p. 87.

24. *The Diet, Elections, and Political Parties* (Tokyo: Foreign Press Center, 1985), p. 17.

25. McNelly, *Politics and Government in Japan*, p. 156.

26. Tsuneishi, *Japanese Political Style*, p. 43.

27. Michael Leiserson, "Factions and Coalitions in One-Party Japan," *American Political Science Review* 62 (1968): 778.

28. McNelly, *Politics and Government in Japan*, p. 166.

29. Ibid., p. 159.

30. It is worth noting that the Constitution *requires* the emperor to ratify the choice of the House, so the fact that the emperor has consistently done so is not remarkable. It is interesting to speculate what the political results might be if the emperor were to *refuse* to ratify the choice of the House.

31. Jun-ichi Kyogoku, *The Political Dynamics of Japan*, trans. Nobutaka Ike (Tokyo: University of Tokyo Press, 1987), p. 193.

32. Tsuneishi, *Japanese Political Style*, p. 48.

33. Ward, *Japan's Political System*, p. 153.

34. McNelly, *Politics and Government in Japan*, p. 165.

35. Ward, *Japan's Political System*, p. 153.

36. Bingman, *Japanese Government*, pp. 26–27.

37. *Administrative Reform in Japan* (Tokyo: Foreign Press Center, 1984), p. 17.

38. Richardson and Flanagan, *Politics: Japan*, p. 48.

39. Ibid.

40. See Gary D. Allinson and Yasunori Sone, eds., *Political Dynamics in Contemporary Japan* (Ithaca, N.Y.: Cornell University Press, 1993).

41. McNelly, *Politics and Government in Japan*, p. 144.

42. Burks, *The Government of Japan*, p. 107. A very interesting comparative study of the Japanese Diet and the U.S. Congress can be found in Francis R. Valeo and Charles E. Morrison, eds., *The Japanese Diet and the U.S. Congress* (Boulder, Colo.: Westview Press, 1983).

43. See Hans Baerwald, *Japan's Parliament: An Introduction* (Cambridge: Cambridge University Press, 1974), p. 122.

44. Ward, *Japan's Political System*, p. 149.

45. *The Diet, Elections, and Political Parties*, pp. 9–10.

46. Frank Langdon, *Politics in Japan* (Boston: Little, Brown, 1967), p. 163.

47. McNelly, *Politics and Government in Japan*, p. 134.

48. Tsuneishi, *Japanese Political Style*, p. 87.

49. For a full discussion, see Daniel B. Ramsdell, *The Japanese Diet: Stability and Change in the Japanese House of Representatives, 1890–1990* (Lanham, Md.: University Press of America, 1992).

50. Tsuneishi, *Japanese Political Style*, p. 89.

51. Langdon, *Politics in Japan*, p. 164.

52. There had been 512 members of the House of Representatives until 1993, but a reapportionment led to the reduction of parliament by one seat for the 1993 elections. See "Slimmer Vote for a Ruling Party in Japan," *The New York Times* (July 19, 1993), p. A9.

53. *The Diet, Elections, and Political Parties*, p. 13.

54. McNelly, *Politics and Government in Japan*, p. 136.

55. *The Diet, Elections, and Political Parties*, p. 14.

56. Langdon, *Politics in Japan*, p. 168.

57. Tsuneishi, *Japanese Political Style*, p. 93; McNelly, *Politics and Government in Japan*, p. 137.

58. McNelly, *Politics and Government in Japan*, p. 139.

59. Langdon, *Politics in Japan*, p. 169.

60. Hattie Kawahara Colton, "The Working of the Japanese Diet," *Pacific Affairs* 28 (1955): 372.

61. Ward, *Japan's Political System*, p. 150.

62. Ibid., p. 110.

63. Tsuneishi, *Japanese Political Style*, p. 124.

64. Burks, *The Government of Japan*, p. 77.

65. Ibid., p. 75.

66. Several essays in Ronald J. Hrebenar, *The Japanese Party System*, 2nd ed. (Boulder, Colo.: Westview Press, 1991), discuss issues related to this.

67. A very good examination of the Liberal Democratic party can be found in the article by Nobuo Tomita, Akira Nakamura, and Ronald Hrebenar, "The Liberal Democratic Party: The Ruling Party of Japan," in Hrebenar, *The Japanese Party System*, pp. 235–282.

68. McNelly, *Politics and Government in Japan*, pp. 90, 120.

69. Tsuneishi, *Japanese Political Style*, p. 124.

70. Ronald Hrebenar, "The Changing Postwar Party System," in Ronald Hrebenar, ed., *The Japanese Party System: From One-Party Rule to Coalition Government* (Boulder, Colo.: Westview Press, 1986), p. 7. See also J.A.A. Stockwin, "The Japan Socialist Party: A Politics of Permanent Opposition," in Hrebenar, *The Japanese Party System*, p. 83.

71. *The Diet, Elections, and Political Parties*, p. 98.

72. Bingman, *Japanese Government*, p. 8.

73. *The Diet, Elections, and Political Parties*, p. 94.

74. Ward, *Japan's Political System*, p. 110.

75. For descriptions of the major issue positions of the large parties in Japan today, see Langdon, *Politics in Japan*, pp. 132–142.

76. Ward, *Japan's Political System*, p. 110.

77. David E. Sanger, "Japanese Party Crumbles Further as 44 Quit to Form a Rival Group," *The New York Times* (June 23, 1993), p. A1.

78. Ward, *Japan's Political System*, p. 113.

79. A good discussion of local government in Japan can be found in Bingman, *Japanese Government*, pp. 47–75. See also Ritsuo Akimoto, "Leadership and Power Structure in Local Politics," in Hiroshi Itoh, *Japanese Politics: An Inside View* (Ithaca, N.Y.: Cornell University Press, 1973), pp. 167–180.

80. As of April 1986, local governments had a total of 3,217,000 employees, of which teachers accounted for 31.3 percent and policemen 6.7 percent. See *Statistical Handbook of Japan* (Tokyo: Statistics Bureau, Management and Coordination Agency, 1988), pp. 145–146.

81. McNelly, *Politics and Government in Japan*, p. 131.

82. Tsuneishi, *Japanese Political Style*, p. 153.

83. Ward, *Japan's Political System*, p. 114.

84. McNelly, *Politics and Government in Japan*, p. 131.

85. Ibid., p. 132.

86. See Ronald Hrebenar, "Rules of the Game: The Impact of the Electoral System on Political Parties," in Hrebenar, *The Japanese Party System*, pp. 32–54.

87. Ward, *Japan's Political System*, p. 126.

88. Tsuneishi, *Japanese Political Style*, p. 154.

89. Ibid., pp. 150–151.

90. McNelly, *Politics and Government in Japan*, p. 135.

91. Tsuneishi, *Japanese Political Style*, p. 156.

92. Much of what follows in this section is based upon much more substantial discussion in *The Diet, Elections, and Political Parties*, pp. 51–62.

93. A good discussion of changes in party support as a function of economic variables can be found in Nobutaka Ike, *A Theory of Japanese Democracy* (Boulder, Colo.: Westview Press, 1978), pp. 115–120.

94. A saying circulating at the time was "'five you win and three you lose,' with 'five' standing for ¥500 million and 'three' for ¥300 million in campaign expenditures." *The Diet, Elections, and Political Parties*, p. 53.

95. The relationship between "big business" and politics is something that has been the focus of much scandal and political tension in Japan in recent years. See Harold Wilensky, *Democratic Corporatism and Policy Linkages: The Interdependence of Industrial, Labor-Market, Incomes, and Social Policies in Eight Countries* (Berkeley: University of California Press, 1987).

96. See the article by Naoki Kobayashi, "Interest Groups in the Legislative Process," in Itoh, *Japanese Politics: An Inside View*, pp. 68–87.

97. *The Diet, Elections, and Political Parties*, p. 53.

98. Takashi Oka, "Nakasone Wins Big, But Faces Party Leadership Struggle," *Christian Science Monitor*, July 8, 1986, p. 1, col. 3. See also Sam Jameson, "Japanese Ruling Party Wins Vote in Landslide," *Los Angeles Times*, July 7, 1986, p. 9, col. 3.

99. The LDP limits its leaders to two terms of two years each, and Nakasone's second term ended October 30, 1987. Andrew Horvat, "Nakasone Sets Stage for July 6 Double Election," *Los Angeles Times*, June 3, 1986, p. 4, col. 1. On the contest for the new leader, see Takashi Oka, "Race to Replace Nakasone in Full Swing; Math Gets Complicated as Japan's Contenders Tally Factions Support," *Christian Science Monitor*, July 20, 1987, p. 3, col. 1.

100. Susan Chira, "Japanese Ruling Party Suffers Setback in Upper House By-Election," *The New York Times*, February 13, 1989, p. A7.

101. "Japanese Parliament Elects Hosokawa Premier; Seven-Party Coalition Assumes Power," *Facts on File* 53:2750 (August 12, 1993), p. 585.

13

The Canadian Political System

INTRODUCTION

Although there are many respects in which the Canadian political system is similar to the British political system—such as being modelled after the British parliamentary form of government, having more than two political parties, and single-member-district voting for the lower house and an appointed upper house—it will become apparent in the course of this discussion that in spite of these similarities, many significant structural and behavioral differences exist between the two nations. In this chapter we shall discuss the nature of the Canadian political system, including its constitutional framework, its party system, its special federal and binational character, its political institutions, and the power relationships that exist between and among actors in the political system.

THE CONSTITUTIONAL SYSTEM

Canada became an independent and self-governing dominion as a result of the British North America Act (hereafter referred to as the BNA Act) of 1867. From 1867 until 1982, although Canada was technically independent (because the basis of its constitution was an act of the British Parliament) any amendment to the Canadian Constitution had to be enacted not by Canada, but by Britain. This was traditionally done by the British Parliament whenever Canada's Parliament so requested.[1] Thus, from 1867 until 1982 it was said that the BNA Act, as amended, formed the basis of the Canadian Constitution.

The BNA Act provided for the creation of a federal union in North America, and thereby dealt with such topics as language, the explicit powers of the provinces and the national government, the structure and composition of Parliament, and so on. One of the document's broadest but most important phrases was found in the preamble, in which it was written that Canada would have a government ". . . similar in principle to that of the United Kingdom."[2]

It has been suggested that the "similar in principle" clause was for many years the source of many Canadian civil liberties:

> The primary constitutional source of Canadian civil liberties is the preamble to the BNA Act, which states that we are to have a constitution similar in principle to that of the United Kingdom. Consequently, because the United Kingdom has no entrenched Bill of Rights, the actual extent of the rights and freedoms of Canadians is enshrined only in the many centuries of British legal tradition—a fact which, while not a restriction on our liberties, makes them difficult to define precisely.[3]

In other areas of constitutional evolution, the "similar in principle" clause may be seen as a basis for much of the broader Canadian political culture, including such characteristics as representative and parliamentary government, a powerful cabinet, majoritarianism, and so on.

There were, of course, other components of the Canadian Constitution, too. In the same manner that the BNA Act was considered to be part of the Canadian Constitution, so too were several other acts of the British Parliament that affected Canada. Most of these other acts were concerned with "the gradual process of withdrawal of British authority," and were more significant at the time of their passage than they are now.[4]

Additionally, several wholly Canadian statutes were seen as contributing to the Canadian Constitution. Among these statutes were included acts affecting the creation of the western provinces, for example. As well, several statutes that were called "organic laws"[5] were usually considered to be included in the constitution. These laws involved basic principles of the regime, and were simply acts of Parliament; as such they could be amended or altered by other acts of Parliament.

Since the federal nature of the Canadian government left a great deal of legislating to the individual provinces, many suggested that there was a large body of provincial legislation that also needed to be included when one referred to the Canadian Constitution. The Canadian Constitution, then, was until 1982 an amorphous document in that it drew upon acts of the British Parliament, the Canadian Parliament, and the several provincial parliaments, as well as British common law and political culture through the "similar in principle" clause.

In the spring of 1982, at the request of the Canadian Government, the British Parliament passed the Canada Act, which put the Canadian Constitution under Canadian control for the first time in Canada's history.[6] The Canada Act had a number of major consequences for Canadian constitutional evolution. First, by passing the Canada Act the British Parliament changed the name of the British North America Act to the Constitution Act. (Thus the British North America Act of 1867 is now referred to as the Constitution Act of 1867; the British North America Act of 1886 is now referred to as the Constitution Act of 1886, and so on.)

Second, included in the passage of the Canada Act was a new Bill of Rights that was to be added to the Canadian Constitution. Canada had never had a Bill of Rights before, relying for the basis of its citizens' civil rights as we noted earlier upon the "similar in principle" clause in the preamble of the BNA Act and the British constitutional heritage that this implied.

Third, in the Canada Act the British Parliament added an amending formula to the British North America Act. Previously, whenever Canada wanted to amend its constitution it had to ask the British Parliament to pass a new British North America Act; many Canadians felt that the time had come to stop this anachronistic practice.

Finally, by passing the Canada Act the British Parliament renounced the right to ever again legislate for Canada. Where previously Canada might have been *de facto* an independent nation, *de jure* (legally) it was dependent upon Britain for its constitutional structure. Henceforth, Canada was to be both *de facto* and *de jure* independent.[7]

Canada's British heritage comes not only from the fact that Britain administered Canada prior to Canadian independence, but also (if not more so) from the fact that much of Canadian political culture is rooted in British history. Indeed, the majority of Canada's population from 1763 to 1900 was of Anglo-Celtic stock, and Britain has since been an appropriate source of values, attitudes, and culture. Additionally, of course, Britain has since been a major source of immigrants for Canada, thus ensuring that a large proportion of the Canadian population would continually be aware of, and interested in, British cultural values.[8]

The "similar in principle" clause would not have been so important if the Canadian people were not oriented toward the British political culture to begin with; its vagueness certainly would have permitted greater deviation from the British model than exists today had Canada wanted it. The clause draws its real importance from the fact that Canadians are already oriented toward the "Westminster model," and willingly adopt the structures and culture implied by the clause.

FEDERALISM IN CANADA

Structurally, the BNA Act created a federal government; it gave most major legislative power to the national government, but reserved for the provincial governments several areas of sovereignty. Unlike some other federal systems, in Canada the provinces have not lost their powers over the years to the national government, partly because of the restraint exercised by successive national governments, and partly "because judicial interpretation of the provincial powers to regulate property and civil rights greatly expanded the scope of provincial authority."[9]

The Canadian political system has evolved over the last 125-plus years to the form in which it is found today. The concept of federalism existed in Canada prior to the creation of the British North America Act of 1867; it was used as the basis of the act, drawing upon experiences of Canada and of other nations.[10]

> The national purpose of the Fathers of Confederation is clearly evident in the British North America Act. In contrast to the Constitution of the United States, which had just endured the war between the States, the BNA Act assigns both the general and residual powers of government to the Dominion (national government), not the Provinces. . . . But it was not to be so. It is commonly known that the decisions of the Judicial Committee of the Privy Council (the highest judicial organ in Canada until the Supreme Court of Canada was made the final judicial body) abridged the general powers of the Dominion governments and enhanced the legislative powers of the Provinces.[11]

The relevant sections of the British North America Act (now the Constitution Act) are worth noting. Section 91 of the Act indicates that the national legislature will have the jurisdiction "to make Laws for the Peace, Order, and good Government of Canada" in relation to all matters not "assigned exclusively to the Legislatures of the Provinces." It then offers "for greater Certainty, but not so as to restrict the Generality of the foregoing Terms of this Section," a list of thirty-one powers (originally twenty-nine powers) of the federal government. Section 92 deals with the provinces: "In each Province the Legislature may exclusively make Laws in relation to Matters coming within the Classes of Subject next hereinafter enumerated," and lists sixteen specific areas of jurisdiction, one of which (Section 13) is "Property and Civil Rights."

The problem for Canadian government today is that many aspects of governmental responsibility that have developed since 1867 have been ruled first by the (British) Judicial Committee of the Privy Council—which acted as the ultimate judicial body for Canada in Canada's early years—and later by the Supreme Court of Canada, to fall under the "Property and Civil Rights" clause of Section 92 rather than the "Peace, Order, and good Government" clause of Section 91.

In apparent disregard of the passage of Section 91 stating "but not so as to restrict the generality of the foregoing Terms," the judicial bodies of Canada ruled that since the Founders put a list of powers for the Dominion into Section 91, those (and only those) must be the powers they intended for the Dominion government, and nothing more. In several instances, the Justices have denied that the "Peace, Order and good Government" clause gave the Dominion jurisdiction, and apparently doubted "that the Dominion could have any power at all except those specifically enumerated in Section 91."[12]

So, at the same time that the Supreme Court in the United States was making decisions that resulted in *greater* federal jurisdiction at the expense of the states, decisions in Canada were going in the other direction, ruling that jurisdiction belonged to the provinces, not the Dominion. What kept the Dominion government in a position of some influence was money. Specifically, the provinces could not *afford* all of the projects that the courts were ruling were their responsibility, so the Dominion government was able to regain much of its lost influence through its "power of the purse" and a variety of tax-renting, revenue sharing, and conditional grant schemes.[13]

Certainly one of the major underlying questions in modern Canadian politics has to do with where, on a central-peripheral scale similar to that which we observed in Chapter 2, Canada should orient its federal-provincial jurisdictions.[14] Many have argued that federalism has been the saving grace of the Canadian political arena for the last hundred years or so.[15] Others argue that "federalism has had a great deal to do with the problem of national unity that their country has experienced throughout its history."[16] One author has gone so far as to suggest that the separatist issue in Quebec is related to general problems of federalism, and has added that "to the extent that separatist opinion may be understood as a concern about the necessary conditions of political community, the question posed by separatism becomes for us a question about federalism."[17]

It may be that much of the indecision about the precise power distribution that should exist in the Canadian polity (that is, Should the Dominion or the provinces be dominant?) can be attributed to the fact that Canadian history has seen both of these power relationships exist.[18] Cairns has argued that:

> The evolution of Canadian federalism is frequently described in terms of alternations between periods of centralization and decentralization. . . . Periods of centralization are customarily considered to be the early post-Confederation years, both world wars, and the post–World War II period up to 1957. . . . The intervening periods . . . are variously described as periods of provincial ascendancy, or as periods in which both government levels handled important responsibilities with neither enjoying a clearly dominant position.[19]

This phenomenon has led, Cairns argued, to the "other crisis" in Canadian politics: "the crisis of a political system with a declining capacity for the effective use of the authority of government for the attainment of public goals."[20]

FRENCH CANADA AND QUEBEC

Since before Confederation in 1867, the question of the relation between Quebec and the rest of Canada has been one of the major points of contention—if not *the* major point of contention—in the Canadian political system. Whatever the policy issue in question—whether it involves health policy, energy policy, education policy, or labor policy, to take just a few examples—it seems to be more intensely debated in Quebec than in any other Canadian province. This is because, some have argued, Quebec approaches many debates not only as *federal-provincial* conflicts, but also as *nationalistic* conflicts involving a very real *nationalism* for French Canadians.[21]

We should note that the term "French Canadian" is not, strictly speaking, the same as *Québecois*, since there are French Canadians living outside of Quebec (primarily in Ontario and New Brunswick).[22] It is true, however, that the overwhelming majority of Canada's French-speaking population lives in the province of Quebec, and that Quebec is approximately as unilingual and French as the rest of Canada is unilingual and English.

At the time of Confederation, Quebec had significant concerns about joining the English-dominated union, but fear of attack from its neighbor to the south motivated it to act despite these concerns. Quebec insisted, however, on a decentralized federal system in which it would retain control over policies most important to its unique character, especially language and education.[23] Ever since Confederation, politics in Quebec have varied from more to less militantly nationalistic,[24] and at times over the last 125 years the situation has even become violent. While the issue of Quebec nationalism is too complex to adequately resolve here, we can highlight some of the issues that have figured prominently in debates over the years.[25]

Culture.   The government of Quebec has jealously guarded areas of policy that are especially important to French Canadian nationalism over the years, focusing especially on language, culture, education, and religion. Before the "Quiet Revolution" of the 1960s, the Quebec political culture was

> generally very traditional, conservative, patronage-oriented, authoritarian, backward, rural, corrupt, and heavily influenced by the Roman Catholic Church. Over the past 30 years or so, however, it has become progressive, if not radical, urban, democratic, modern, secularized, and bureaucratized. The only feature apparently common to the two periods, the importance of nationalism, has even changed in nature. Rather than nationalism of survival, it has become . . . one of expansion and growth, which is outward-looking and aggressive.[26]

During the "Quiet Revolution" the people of Quebec made it clear that they would no longer accept a "second-class" citizenship,[27] and that they wanted significant changes in their society. These changes took place with remarkable speed, and Quebec society today is significantly different from Quebec society of the 1950s and early 1960s.

"Special Status."   Quebec has argued that it is not simply one of ten provinces. Many Québecois support a "two nations" theory of Canadian federalism.[28] They suggest that Canada is a federation of two nations, one English and one French; the English nation can be subdivided into nine units that correspond to nine of Canada's provinces today, and the French nation corresponds to Quebec.

In recent constitutional discussions and debates, Quebec has insisted on a constitutional recognition that it has a "special status" in the federal system, although the precise meaning of that phrase has never been made clear. This has resulted in a wide range of responses from the other provinces to Quebec's demand, ranging from moderate support to furious opposition. In fact, Quebec has not yet ratified the present—1982—Constitution, and has said that it will not do so until its "special status" is recognized in that document through an appropriate amendment.[29]

Decentralized Federalism and Public Policy.   Quebec has consistently favored a decentralized federalism for Canada's national government. Quebec's government has traditionally argued that the provinces should have primary competence in virtually all policy areas, ranging from education to many foreign aid programs, and in many instances Quebec has refused conditional grant programs from the federal government[30] because of its desire to keep the federal government from expanding the range of programs it controls or influences in contemporary society.

This debate over the optimal balance of Canada's constitutional structures has been long and at times heated. Quebec has had a referendum on "sovereignty-association," and more than one study of the effects of secession has been undertaken.[31] Despite this fact, Quebec continues as a member of the federal system and continues to work with the rest of Canada to discover a new "balance" for Canadian federalism that feels best to all of Canada's components.

In the federal election of October 1993, the *Bloc Québecois*, a party ultimately dedicated to Quebec's sovereignty, won fifty-four of Quebec's seventy-five seats in the House of Commons, and became the "Official Opposition" in the federal House of Commons by virtue of being the second-largest political party there. The leader of the *Bloc*, Lucien Bouchard, indicated his commitment to work toward Quebec's sovereignty in future actions.

THE CANADIAN EXECUTIVE

Under the BNA Act the national legislature was to be bicameral, and the executive power of the government was to be maintained by the governor-general, the representative of the Crown in Canada. The power structure in the government has changed since the 1867 Act in the manner we described in Chapter 5, so that today the executive power is vested in the prime minister and the cabinet—nowhere mentioned in the act. The governor-general is primarily a figurehead.[32]

The cabinet is the repository of the true executive powers in Canadian government today. Although its formal (*de jure*, legal) function is to advise the sovereign or the sovereign's representative, over the years power has come to rest in the cabinet itself rather than of the governor-general.

> The constitutional authority of the Prime Minister and Cabinet derives from the fact that the Cabinet is a committee of the Queen's Privy Council for Canada and as such tenders advice to Her Majesty's representative, the Governor-General. When the Crown lost most of its political importance, the cabinet, though not mentioned in the BNA Act, remained the agent of executive authority.[33]

The cabinet provides a link between the legislative power of the nation and the executive power of the nation in that virtually all members of the cabinet are members of Parliament, and the cabinet itself is responsible to the House of Commons in the way we used the term in Chapter 4. The cabinet, therefore, ". . . is a legislative, executive, and administrative body,"[34] and is central in the Canadian governmental system. The crucial factor in this linkage between the executive and the legislative powers in the cabinet is the need for cabinet members to hold positions in the House of Commons or the Senate, because this overlap ensures that the cabinet will not forget its responsibility to the Parliament.

The leader of the cabinet is the prime minister, who is more than simply a first among equals. He or she appoints others to the cabinet (appointments are of course actually made by the governor-general "on the advice" of the prime minister), and may ask for their resignations if he or she wishes; although cabinet decisions are theoretically reached by a consensus of the cabinet, the prime minister may impose a policy upon his or her cabinet colleagues. It is the prime minister who decides how best to balance the cabinet, both geographically and ideologically, when he or she "suggests" cabinet appointments to the governor-general.

It has been suggested that the prime minister has certain built-in advantages over his or her cabinet colleagues. First, the size of the prime minister's staff has greatly increased over time, giving him or her an advantage over other cabinet members with smaller staffs. Second, through his or her power to assign colleagues to cabinet committees, the prime minister has a great deal of leverage as well as influence over the individual ministers. Third, cabinet members must spend a great deal of their time administering their various portfolios; thus they are more involved with detailed work than the prime minister, who has greater control over his or her own calendar and schedule. Finally, even though the cabinet is collectively responsible to the Parliament, each cabinet member is individually responsible to the prime minister, since the prime minister "suggested" his or her appointment to the governor-general; thus the prime minister has another source of influence or leverage over individual cabinet members.[35]

Excluding from consideration minority and coalition governments, which have been few in modern Canadian history, the Canadian prime minister has always been the leader of the majority party in the House of Commons, and thus has selected members of his or her cabinet from among his party colleagues. He or she is required to "balance" the cabinet according to many varied criteria, including regional, cultural, religious, ethnic, and economic criteria.[36]

Parliamentary government in Canada today could more realistically be called cabinet government; the true role of members of Parliament is to react to their leaders' ideas, to support or oppose cabinet proposals. Jackson and Atkinson wrote that responsibility and control of the legislative system ". . . rest in the hands of the government. The Canadian Parliament . . . does not make laws, it passes them."[37]

This situation has, as one might imagine, resulted in criticism of the cabinet and the prime minister as being dictatorial and domineering. In fact, however, this state of affairs is not at all unusual, as we have already seen in other instances. Defenders of the system contend that this situation is not unique to Canada, and that it is a normal by-product of a responsible-party, parliamentary system of government.[38]

The office of the governor-general is still the repository for most of the formal powers that were lodged there in 1867, the *de jure* executive powers that we referred to earlier in this book. The governor-general's loss of real or *de facto* power is as much a result of British parliamentary development as it is a result of Canadian parliamentary development; most major changes in the evolution of the office were made prior to Canadian independence in 1867. Today the governor-general plays a political role very similar to that of the heads of state in other parliamentary regimes. He or she "acts on the advice" of the cabinet and the prime minister, and may assent, or refuse to assent, to bills passed by both Houses of Parliament (although precedent has established that the power to refuse to assent to legislation is no longer a practicable option open to him or her).

LEGISLATIVE STRUCTURES

The BNA Act provided for a bicameral legislature—a Senate and a House of Commons. The Senate was to be appointed and to resemble other "upper" houses of the time (1867) in that it was to provide a check on the House of Commons, be more representative of property, and guarantee provincial and regional representation in the government's policy-making process.

Provinces are not represented in the Canadian Senate in the same manner as are states in the U.S. Senate; the Canadian Senate was constructed to equally represent the different geographical *regions*, not the provinces, thus providing that the membership of the upper house was not based upon population. (The provinces of Quebec and Ontario each have twenty-four senators. All of the western provinces together have twenty-four, giving six each to British Columbia, Alberta, Saskatchewan, and Manitoba. Prior to 1949, all of the maritime provinces, together had twenty-four, giving ten to New Brunswick, ten to Nova Scotia, and four to Prince Edward Island. When Newfoundland was admitted to the Confederation in 1949 it received six senators of its own, bringing the Senate total to 102.) The Constitution provides for extra senators to be appointed under special circumstances (for instance, to allow for the breaking of a deadlock within the Senate and the Commons).

The 102-member Senate has historically been hampered in its legislative task by two major factors. First, the Senate suffers from a type of personnel problem. Although senators must now retire at the age of seventy-five, many senators are inactive in the Senate's affairs because of either illness or old age. Additionally, because appointment to the Senate is a political honor, many senators see the position *only* as one of honor; they attend the work of the Senate very rarely, instead spending their time in business outside of the Senate. Senators need only attend once every two years in order to keep their seats. This situation results in a small core of senators having to do the work of the entire house, making it virtually impossible for the body to perform up to its potential.

A second major factor hampering the Senate's performance of its legislative task is that most legislation, and all financial legislation, originates in the House of Commons, and consequently the Senate has little work to do early in its session and a great deal of work to do later in each session when bills from the Commons are sent to the Senate for passage. This leaves the Senate little time for serious consideration of the bills themselves.

Many observers note that the strength of the present-day Senate lies in its committees. In the contemporary political setting, the Senate, through its committees, has become a major screening point for much private legislation in the Canadian political system, in part because similar opportunities are not readily available in the House of Commons. In committees the Senate not only acts in regard to private bills, but also provides whatever scrutiny of the executive is possible and attempts to review legislation passed in the Commons. Indeed, scrutiny of the executive in many respects can be better performed in the Senate than in the Commons; because of party discipline and the "responsibility" of the Government to the House of Commons, the Commons cannot feel as free to criticize the executive part of the government. Too much criticism of the Government in the Commons could embarrass the Government, since it must maintain the confidence of the Commons. That is not the case in the Senate.

Since the Senate "has retained a full set of legislative muscles, but consistently has refused to make real use of them,"[39] it has been subjected to much criticism in the Canadian political arena. The debate has long gone on as to whether the Senate should be left as it is, be reformed, or simply be abolished.[40] One result of the Senate's weak and secondary role in the Canadian legislative process is that it is not included in a good number of political studies about Canada, simply because it is so insignificant in the policy formation process.

In recent years, however, the movement for Senate reform has become increasingly popular in Canada. The movement took on its most formal power when the province of Alberta passed a law indicating that the citizens of Alberta would vote for nominees for the Senate; subsequently, the governor-general would be morally bound (the law suggested) to appoint the individual(s) who had been elected by the people of Alberta when an opening came about in the Senate. The cries for Senate reform continue to be heard across Canada, and most students of the institution agree that there *will* be significant reform of the Senate in the near future.[41]

Several topics related to the House of Commons and its role in the Canadian political system are important in our inquiry here inasmuch as they may affect legislative behavior in the Parliament. The legislative process itself has been discussed at length in several different places, and it is not necessary to repeat a description of the legislative process at this point.[42] Rather, we shall discuss some of the characteristics of Parliament that are relevant to our study, characteristics that include the role of political parties in the Commons; formal Commons structures and their impact upon legislative behavior; and the role of the backbencher in the House of Commons, generally.

The party's role vis-à-vis parliamentary action is significant in the Canadian political system. As elsewhere in parliamentary nations, party discipline exists in the House of Commons. That is, once parties have decided on their policy, party members are expected to support that policy in the House, through their speeches or their votes. If a member does not follow the party line, he or she can expect the party to react in an appropriate manner.

Research has shown, however, that "discipline" in the House of Commons may not mean the same thing as "discipline" in other legislative bodies. In a study of Canadian legislative behavior, Kornberg wrote that many MPs prefaced their comments on the subject with the statement "If by discipline you mean are we coerced, the answer is 'no.'"[43] The term "coerced" could be (and is) used in many other national legislative contexts, even those found in long-established democratic settings. Kornberg has suggested that the Canadian case is noteworthy because "not only is discipline in a responsible party legislature not overly stringent, but the parties allow their members almost unlimited latitude in conforming to a caucus decision."[44]

This is not to say, however, that the parties are insignificant in terms of what the House of Commons does. Whether individual MPs are coerced or encouraged, voting in the Commons does reflect the existence of a disciplined responsible-party system. Whether the party members in the House of Commons vote in line with their party's policy out of fear, out of pragmatism, or for normative reasons, the end result is the same: The political party is a significant factor in the House of Commons.

The House of Commons is the source of the authority of the executive power of the prime minister and his or her cabinet. The governor-general traditionally invites the leader of the largest party in the House of Commons to form a Government, which is responsible to the House of Commons. Should the House express a lack of confidence in the Government, or defeat a major piece of legislation proposed by the Government, the Government would fall.

The powers and structures of the Canadian House of Commons are very similar to those that we met in the British situation. What has been referred to as the "Parliamentary Life-Cycle"[45]—from the governor-general summoning both Houses of Parliament together for the Speech from the Throne, through normal business during the parliamentary session, through a vote of nonconfidence or the termination of Parliament because of the expiration of its term of office—follows the Westminster model very closely.

Parliamentary reform was undertaken in the 1980s to make the role of the individual MP more meaningful in the Canadian Parliament—specifically, in the Canadian House of Commons. Changes were introduced that would guarantee that a certain number of *private members' bills*—bills introduced not by members of the Cabinet or party leaders, but by individual "private" members of Parliament—would have an opportunity to be introduced each session. Other changes were introduced to adopt a new committee system in the House of Commons that was intended to give the individual MP more freedom from party discipline, and correspondingly more opportunity to voice his or her own opinion concerning legislation in Parliament.[46]

The stages of the legislative process in Canada follow the British model in a similar manner. Different calendars exist for Government business and private members' business, with a limit on the amount of time each day that can be spent on private members' business. *Government bills* typically begin in cabinet, where policy discussion leads to a recommendation for legislation. Legislation is drafted (typically by the Department of Justice) and approved by the appropriate minister and subsequently the entire cabinet before it is actually introduced in Parliament. Bills are introduced in either house of Parliament; Government bills, however, invariably are first introduced in the House of Commons. There they receive a first reading and brief discussion, and a second reading (with a debate and a vote on the principles of the bill); then they are referred to legislative committee for detailed examination. When (and if) the bill is reported out of committee, it receives a third reading and vote, and if it passes this hurdle the bill goes to the other House of Parliament for a repetition of the legislative process there. Bills must pass both houses in identical form before they can be assented to by the governor-general.

Debate in the House of Commons is among the most colorful of any legislative body in the world, and the daily Question Period in the House—when members of Parliament from both sides of the House, Government and Opposition, can address questions to all members of the Cabinet—can be extraordinarily lively and tense. Unlike the British prime minister, who responds to questions only twice a week for fifteen minutes at a time, the Canadian prime minister must be prepared to respond to questions *every* day of the week during Question Period. These questions are designed to elicit information from the Government, bring issues to the attention of the Government, and embarrass the Government, and the prime minister and other members of the cabinet must be prepared to answer a very wide range of inquiries.

Thus, as in other parliamentary systems we disscused earlier in this text, while the Canadian executive branch of government *leads* the legislative branch (in that the leaders of the executive branch are also the leaders of the largest party in the legislative branch), the executive is also *of* the legislative branch, and thereby responsible to it.

ELECTIONS AND PARTIES

Members of the House of Commons are elected by plurality voting in single-member districts. As we have seen is the case elsewhere, there is a relationship between electoral systems and party systems (that is, certain electoral systems may promote or retard the growth of political parties). The Canadian electoral system has had a good deal of impact upon the Canadian party system, and both deserve some comment here.

The Canadian party system is literally a multiparty system, but actually could be called a "two-party-plus" system.[47] One political scientist has argued that the present electoral system in Canada may have negative consequences for elections because of the manner in which it influences the contemporary party system.[48] Specifically, he has suggested that in ten of the fifteen elections through 1968 the electoral system either did not produce a majority government or produced such a majority that the opposition was left ineffective. Although his work only went through 1968, the consequences of elections that he described prior to that time have continued to exist in recent years.

The results from the federal election of 1993 clearly demonstrate the importance of *electoral concentration* of vote. Parties that received electoral support which was sufficiently concentrated won substantial numbers of seats in specific regions of the country—such as the Reform party in the west (winning 18 percent of the seats with almost 19 percent of the votes, mostly in the west), or the *Bloc Québecois* in Quebec (winning 18 percent of the seats with almost 14 percent of the votes, all in Quebec).

On the other hand, the Progressive Conservative party, which had controlled 153 seats in the Parliament elected in 1988, won *only two* seats in the election, despite winning 16 percent of the vote. Thus the *Bloc Québecois* won 13.5 percent of the vote and received fifty-four seats; the Progressive Conservative party won 16 percent of the vote and received *only two* seats, and the Reform party won 18.7 percent of the vote and received fifty-two seats!

The data in Table 13.1 show an overrepresentation for the larger party (receiving 19 percent more seats than it "deserved") and an underrepresentation for the smaller parties in legislative seats (the Conservatives received over 15 percent

TABLE 13.1
The Canadian General Election of 1993: Distribution of Votes

		PARTY					
Province	**Liberal**	**Progressive Conservative**	**New Democratic**	**Bloc Québecois**	**Reform**	**Other**	**Total**
Alberta							
Percent of votes	25.0	14.6	4.1	0	52.1	4.3	100.1[b]
Seats won	4	0	0	0	22	0	26
Percent of seats won	15.4	0	0	0	84.6	0	100
"Imbalance"[a]	−9.6	−14.6	−4.1	0	+32.5	−4.3	
British Columbia							
Percent of votes	28.1	13.4	15.6	0	36.3	6.6	100
Seats won	6	0	2	0	24	0	32
Percent of seats won	18.8	0	6.2	0	75.0	0	100
"Imbalance"[a]	−9.3	−13.4	−9.4	0	+38.7	−6.6	
Manitoba							
Percent of votes	45.0	11.9	16.6	0	22.4	4.2	100.1[b]
Seats won	13	0	0	0	1	0	14
Percent of seats won	92.9	0	0	0	7.1	0	100
"Imbalance"[a]	+47.9	−11.9	−16.6	0	−15.3	−4.2	
New Brunswick							
Percent of votes	56.0	28.0	4.9	0	8.5	2.7	100.1[b]
Seats won	9	1	0	0	0	0	10
Percent of seats won	90	10	0	0	0	0	100
"Imbalance"[a]	+34.0	−18.0	−4.9	0	−8.5	−2.7	
Newfoundland							
Percent of votes	67.5	26.5	3.6	0	1.0	1.5	100.1[b]
Seats won	7	0	0	0	0	0	7
Percent of seats won	100.0	0	0	0	0	0	100
"Imbalance"[a]	+32.5	−26.5	−3.6	0	−1.0	−1.5	
Northwest Territory							
Percent of votes	65.4	16.3	7.7	0	8.4	2.3	100.1[b]
Seats won	2	0	0	0	0	0	2
Percent of seats won	100	0	0	0	0	0	100
"Imbalance"[a]	+34.6	−16.3	−7.7	0	−8.4	−2.3	
Nova Scotia							
Percent of votes	52.0	23.5	6.8	0	13.3	4.5	100.1[b]
Seats won	11	0	0	0	0	0	11
Percent of seats won	100	0	0	0	0	0	100
"Imbalance"[a]	+48.0	−23.5	−6.8	0	−13.3	−4.5	
Ontario							
Percent of votes	52.8	17.7	6.0	0	20.1	3.4	100
Seats won	98	0	0	0	1	0	99
Percent of seats won	99.0	0	0	0	1.0	0	100
"Imbalance"[a]	+46.2	−17.7	−6.0	0	−19.1	−3.4	

TABLE 13.1 *(continued)*

Province	Liberal	Progressive Conservative	New Democratic	Bloc Québecois	Reform	Other	Total
	PARTY						
Prince Edward Island							
Percent of votes	60.2	31.9	5.2	0	1.0	1.7	100
Seats won	4	0	0	0	0	0	4
Percent of seats won	100	0	0	0	0	0	100
"Imbalance"[a]	+39.8	−31.9	−5.2	0	−1.0	−1.7	
Quebec							
Percent of votes	33.0	13.6	1.5	49.2	0	2.7	100
Seats won	19	1	0	54	0	1	75
Percent of seats won	25.3	1.3	0	72	0	1.3	99.9[b]
"Imbalance"[a]	−7.7	−12.3	−1.5	+22.8	0	−1.4	
Saskatchewan							
Percent of votes	32.1	11.3	26.6	0	27.3	2.7	100
Seats won	5	0	5	0	4	0	14
Percent of seats won	35.7	0	35.7	0	28.6	0	100
"Imbalance"[a]	+3.6	−11.3	+9.1	0	+1.3	−2.7	
Yukon							
Percent of votes	23.2	17.8	43.4	0	13.1	2.5	100
Seats won	0	0	1	0	0	0	1
Percent of seats won	0	0	100	0	0	0	100
"Imbalance"[a]	−23.2	−17.8	+56.6	0	−13.1	−2.5	
Percent of Overall Vote	41.2	16.0	6.9	13.5	18.7	3.7	100
Number of Seats Before 1993 Election	(79)	(153)	(43)	(8)	(1)	(1)	285[a]
Number of Seats Won in 1993	178	2	8	54	52	1	295
Percent of Seats	60.3	0.7	2.7	18.3	17.6	0.3	99.9[b]
Imbalance[a]	+19.1	−15.3	−4.2	+4.8	−1.1	−3.4	−0.1[b]

[a] "Imbalance" refers to the difference between the percent of the vote received and the percent of seats in the legislature won by a party.

[b] Does not equal 100 percent because of rounding error.

[c] Ten seats were vacant at the time of the election in 1993.

Sources: The New York Times, October 29, 1993, p. A7; Robert Jackson and Doreen Jackson, *Politics in Canada*, 3rd ed. (Scarborough, Ontario: Prentice Hall of Canada, 1994).

less than they "deserved"). There is no doubt that electoral concentration has a significant impact.

Third and fourth parties have played an important role in Canadian politics in the past, regardless of their strength in the federal House of Commons, both because of their ideologies and because they often control political office at the *provincial* level. The interesting question being asked following the 1993 federal election was whether the Progressive Conservatives and the New Democrats, formerly political parties with national support networks, could "come back" and restore their political strength in the future.

As Mallory has argued, third parties can afford to experiment with new ideas, and can play the necessary role of innovator in the party system.[49] They may also be valuable in that they may attract to the political system people who are not attracted by the major parties. The roles of the Reform party (especially) in the province of Alberta and the *Bloc Québecois* in the province of Quebec demonstrate that a firm basis on the provincial level can be enough to catapult a party to national significance. Although the electoral system has tended to unduly support some parties and weaken others in terms of representation in Commons, these parties have managed to survive and to make themselves heard in Parliament and across the nation, and have thereby performed a function for the political system as a whole.[50]

The implication of the state of the Canadian electoral system is obvious: The system makes it difficult for smaller parties to exist and function, much as proportional representation systems make it easy for smaller parties to exist and function. In systems with proportional representation, a party need only have 1 percent of the national vote in order to be represented in the legislature. In Canada, on the other hand, a party must have a plurality of votes in a single district.

This makes it more difficult to win a seat; not only must the party have a certain level of support, but the support must be sufficiently concentrated in order to have the party win even a single seat and be represented by even one person in Parliament. This will have an effect not only upon the ease with which a party can reach majority status in Parliament, but also upon recruitment to Parliament: Fewer party organizations are able to take part in legislative behavior.

The formal structure of parties in Canada is different from party structures in Britain, partially because of the differences suggested between unitary and federal governmental systems. Figure 13.1 is a general diagram showing the relationships between and among different parts of national party organizations in the Canadian political system.

The federal nature of the Canadian political system has been reflected in the party system, in which provincial party organizations were not run directly by the national party organizations. The relative independence of the provincial party organizations has left these parties in the position of being able to criticize policies of the national party organizations if they see fit to do so. This allows sectionalism to have some voice within a national party organization, something with both positive and negative consequences.[51]

With the virtual obliteration of the Progressive Conservatives as a national political party in the 1993 election, going from 153 seats in the House of Commons to two seats in the House, only one political party remains as a significant entity on both the national and the provincial level—the Liberal party. The two other parties of significant size in the House of Commons—the *Bloc Québecois* and the Reform party—are both very regionally concentrated, the *Bloc* in Quebec and the Reform party in the west. It is unclear the degree to which a national organization can continue to exist for the Conservatives, or the degree to which truly national organizations will develop for either the *Bloc* or the Reform party.

Traditionally, the national and provincial executives of political parties have met at least annually; their role in the party policy-making process has been some-

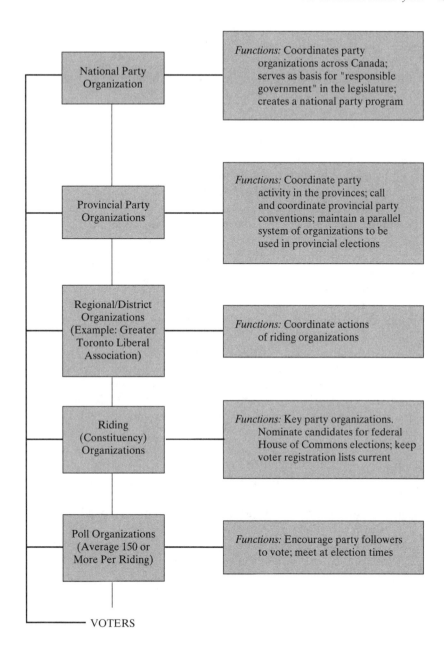

FIGURE 13.1   Hierarchy of Canadian Political Party Organizations

Source: Material derived from R.M. Dawson and Norman Ward, *The Government of Canada* (Toronto: University of Toronto Press, 1977), pp. 438–468.

what ambiguous. Van Loon and Whittington have suggested that "the feeling persists, especially in the caucus, that the executive exists to administer the party machinery, and the caucus to determine party policy."[52] Thus, some tension has existed within the respective party organizations as to who, in fact, should have influence upon the policy-making decisions that must be made.

Party organization in the Parliament is most evident in the party caucus. There, policy questions are discussed, although these discussions vary in liveliness depending upon whether the given party is in or out of power. There is some difference of opinion over the role of the caucus in party policy formation. Some have suggested that in the Opposition party the caucus is quite lively, while in the Government party there is likely to be more formal distinction between frontbench and backbench positions, and the backbenchers are likely to have less input into the policy-deciding process.[53] Others have argued that Government backbenchers do, in fact, have a great deal of influence in their party's caucus.[54]

Another link that the Canadian parties have with the public is that of the party convention.[55] Party conventions may have one of several purposes. Among other reasons, they may be used to increase party morale, to help formulate party policy, or to choose new leadership. Conventions vary in frequency. The New Democratic party holds a regular convention every two years to discuss its leadership and the issues it believes are most important to its political future.[56] The Liberal and Progressive Conservative parties are supposed to hold conventions every two to four years, or so their platforms indicate. However, if the party is functioning well, or if there is little public desire for such a participatory event, the party is likely to postpone the convention until such demands occur.[57] On the other hand, conventions may be called *early* to respond to special party needs or electoral weaknesses of party leaders.

For example, in June 1983 the National Conservative party held a special leadership convention, called because of a lack of confidence on the part of many Conservative leaders in the party's leader (and former prime minister), Joe Clark.[58] Clark was, in fact, defeated on the fourth ballot of the leadership convention; and Quebec businessman Brian Mulroney was chosen to head the Conservative party and, should the Conservatives win a majority in the House of Commons in the future, to be prime minister. The Conservatives won a majority of seats in the House of Commons in the 1983 election, and Mulroney became prime minister and remained so until the summer of 1993, when he retired from politics.

Given the results of the election of 1993 it was inevitable that both the Progressive Conservatives and the New Democrats would seek new national leadership. The Conservatives fell from 153 seats in the 1988 parliament to two seats in the 1993 parliament, and the New Democrats fell from forty-three seats in the 1988 parliament to eight seats in the 1993 parliament. Both Kim Campbell, the Progressive Conservative leader (and prime minister of Canada for less than six months), and Audrey McLaughlin, the leader of the New Democrats, were well aware that electoral results of this nature lead to only one outcome—new party leadership.

SUMMARY

We began this chapter with the statement that although the Canadian political system could be seen to have a great many similarities to the British political system, it would be seen in the course of the chapter that many significant structural and behavioral differences exist between the two nations. This has been shown to be the case.

The federal nature of the Canadian political system has many significant ramifications for the practice of Canadian politics. Canadian federalism is quite different from other federal power relationships, such as those in Germany, Australia, or the United States; provinces have a great deal of power in Canada and the Dominion government is weaker in relation to the provinces than are many other federal national governments in relation to the governments of their component parts.

Beyond this, the special binational character of the Canadian national identity, and the particular conflicts that exist in Canadian society as a result of English-French tensions, have added a dimension to Canadian political debates that simply does not exist in other systems. Questions dealing with the special role of Quebec in the Canadian federal system, the "special status" of Quebec in the Canadian constitutional system, and the future role of a French Canadian nation within Canada are all unique challenges to political stability in a future Canadian polity.

We observed several structural factors that are different in Canada than they are elsewhere. A written constitution with an entrenched bill of rights and an active system of judicial review clearly separate Canada from the British system of government, which served as the original model for Canadian politics.

A number of legislative distinctions exist, too. The ability of the backbencher to introduce legislation without the formal permission of his or her party whip is of no little significance in terms of the autonomy of individual legislators. Similarly, rules governing debate, the introduction of motions, and so on, are all more flexible and permissive in Canada than they are in many other parliamentary systems. The system of committees, and other recent changes in parliamentary procedure designed to give individual legislators a more significant role in the legislative process, clearly set Canada apart from other Westminster-model parliamentary systems.

One of the most significant structural characteristics observed in the Canadian political system is the electoral system itself. The existence of single-member districts with a multiparty system is unusual, and the system has been shown to have a bias when electoral results are examined.

Although Canada began as a British territory, and in its early years developed a political and constitutional system "similar in principle" to that of the United Kingdom, we have seen that there are a number of respects in which Canada is significantly different from Britain. The political institutions and corresponding political behaviors that have evolved over the last 128 years have demonstrated that Canada is, indeed, a mature, independent nation; while Canada may have started out as a "child" in the British "family," modelling governmental institutions and political practices after the practice of the British "adults," over time institutions and behaviors have developed that demonstrate a uniquely Canadian way of addressing political challenges and problems.

Notes

1. In 1965 Minister of Justice Guy Favreau indicated in a review of practices of amending the constitution of Canada that although an enactment by the British is necessary to amend the BNA Act, such action is taken only upon formal request from Canada. No Act of the British Parliament affecting Canada is, therefore, passed unless it is requested and consented to by Canada. Conversely, every amendment requested by Canada in the past has been enacted. See Guy Favreau, *The Amendment of the Constitution of Canada* (Ottawa: Queen's Printer, 1965), p. 44.

2. Robert Jackson and Michael Atkinson, *The Canadian Legislative System* (Toronto: Macmillan, 1974), p. 76.

3. Richard Van Loon and Michael Whittington, *The Canadian Political System* (Toronto: McGraw-Hill, 1971), p. 111.

4. Ibid., p. 100.

5. Robert Dawson, *The Government of Canada* (Toronto: University of Toronto Press, 1954), p. 63.

6. The history leading up to the new constitution was long and arduous, and hotly debated. For discussion of the process, as well as the significance of the new document, see Gregory Mahler, *New Dimensions of Canadian Federalism: Canada in Comparative Perspective* (Rutherford, N.J.: Fairleigh Dickinson University Press, 1987), chap. 3: "Canadian Federalism and Constitutional Amendment and Reform in Canada," pp. 57–83.

7. There has been an explosion of literature on the Canadian Constitution in the last few years as a result of the revision and "patriation" of the Constitution. See, for instance, Michael Behiels, ed., *The Meech Lake Primer: Conflicting Views of the 1987 Constitutional Accord* (Ottawa: University of Ottawa Press, 1989), Raymond Breton, *Why Meech Failed: Lessons for Canadian Constitutionmaking* (Toronto: C.D. Howe Institute, 1992), Duncan Cameron and Miriam Smith, eds., *Constitutional Politics: The Canadian Forum Book on the Federal Constitutional Proposals, 1991–1992* (Toronto: J. Lorimer, 1992), or Peter Russell, *Constitutional Odyssey: Can Canadians Become a Sovereign People?* (Toronto: University of Toronto Press, 1993).

8. One of the best studies of this area is that by David Bell, *The Roots of Disunity: A Study of Canadian Political Culture* (Toronto: Oxford University Press, 1992). Another study that demonstrates the range of Canadian ethnic roots is that by Allan Kornberg, *Politics and Culture in Canada* (Ann Arbor: Center for Political Studies, University of Michigan, 1992). The major cultural cleavage in Canada, of course, one to which we shall return later in this chapter, is that between English Canada and French Canada, the latter primarily in Quebec. On this, see Kenneth McRoberts, *English Canada and Quebec: Avoiding the Issue* (North York, Ont.: York University Press, 1991).

9. Allan Kornberg, *Canadian Legislative Behavior* (New York: Holt, Rinehart, and Winston, 1967), p. 17. The provinces are still very significant players in the Canadian political system, far more important, in fact, than are states in the United States. One of the best studies of the role of provinces in the policy-making process, despite the fact that it is over twenty years old, is that by Richard Simeon, *Federal-Provincial Diplomacy: The Making of Recent Policy in Canada* (Toronto: University of Toronto Press, 1972). More recent studies would include the following: William Chandler and Christian Zollner, eds., *Challenges to Federalism: Policy-Making in Canada and the Federal Republic of Germany* (Kingston, Ont.: Queen's University, 1989), Bruce Hodgins, ed., *Federalism in Canada and Australia: Historical Perspectives, 1920–1988* (Peterborough, Ont.: Trent University, 1989), or Richard Simeon, *State, Society, and the Development of Canadian Federalism* (Toronto: University of Toronto Press, 1990).

10. See William Ormsby, *The Emergence of the Federal Concept in Canada: 1839–1845* (Toronto: University of Toronto Press, 1969), J.R. Mallory, "The Five Faces of Federalism," pp. 19–30 in J. Peter Meekison, ed., *Canadian Federalism: Myth or Reality* (Toronto: Methuen, 1977), or Garth Stevenson, *Unfulfilled Union: Canadian Federalism and National Unity* (Toronto: Macmillan of Canada, 1979), pp. 29–48.

11. Steven Muller, "Federalism and the Party System in Canada," in A. Wildavsky, ed., *American Federalism in Perspective* (Boston: Little, Brown, 1967), p. 147. One of the best studies of the role of the Judicial Committee in the shaping of Canada's Constitution is that by G.P. Browne, *The Judicial Committee and the British North America Act* (Toronto: University of Toronto Press, 1967). A more recent volume is that by Christopher Manfredi, *Judicial Power and the Charter: Canada and the Paradox of Liberal Constitutionalism* (Toronto: McClelland and Stewart, 1992).

12. A.R.M. Lower, *Evolving Canadian Federalism* (Durham, N.C.: Duke University Press, 1958). A very good study is that by Ivan Bernier and André Lajoie, *The Supreme Court of Canada as an Instrument of Political Change* (Toronto: University of Toronto Press, 1986). A more focused study is that by Edward McWhinney, *Canada and the Constitution, 1979–1982* (Toronto: University of Toronto Press, 1982).

13. See Simeon, *Federal-Provincial Diplomacy,* for one of the best studies of this issue. More recent studies on fiscal federalism would include the following: J. C. Strick, *Canadian Public Finance* (Toronto: Holt, Rinehart and Winston, 1978), A. Breton and A. Scott, *The Economic Constitution of Federal States* (Toronto: University of Toronto Press, 1978), Mark R. Krasnick, *Fiscal Federalism* (Toronto: University of Toronto Press, 1986), or Allan MacEachen, *Federal-Provincial Fiscal Arrangements in the Eighties* (Ottawa: Department of Finance, Canada, 1981).

14. See Edwin Black, *Divided Loyalties: Canadian Concepts of Federalism* (Montreal: McGill-Queen's University Press, 1975), especially pp. 1–21. Peter Aucoin's study, *The Centralization-Decentralization Conundrum: Organization and Management in the Canadian Government* (Toronto: University of Toronto Press, 1988), is a very good examination of the subject, as is the much shorter essay by Howard Cody, "The Evolution of Federal-Provincial Relations in Canada," *American Review of Canadian Studies* 7:1 (1977): 55–83.

15. For example, see Gilles Lalande, *In Defense of Federalism: A View from Quebec* (Toronto: McClelland and Stewart, 1978).

16. Allan Kornberg et al., "Federalism and Fragmentation: Political Support in Canada," *Journal of Politics* 41 (1979), p. 891. See also the more recent study by Allan Kornberg, William Mishler, and Harold Clarke, *Representative Democracy in the Canadian Provinces* (Scarborough, Ont.: Prentice Hall Canada, 1982).

17. William Mathie, "Political Community and the Canadian Experience: Reflections on Nationalism, Federalism, and Unity," *Canadian Journal of Political Science* 12 (1979): 19. It has already been observed that in many respects the "central" problem of federalism in Canada has to do with the question of Quebec and its relation with the federal government, a topic to which we shall return later in this chapter.

18. Again, see the very good essay by Cody, "The Evolution of Federal-Provincial Relations in Canada," for a discussion of this history.

19. Alan Cairns, "The Other Crisis of Canadian Federalism," *Canadian Public Administration* 22 (1979): 176–177.

20. Ibid., p. 175.

21. See Dominique Clift, *Quebec Nationalism in Crisis* (Montreal: McGill-Queen's University Press, 1982), for a very good discussion of nationalism in Quebec. Another excellent resource in this area is that by John Dickinson and Brian Young, *A Short History of Quebec,* 2nd ed. (Toronto: Copp Clark Pittman, 1993).

22. See Stanley Ryerson, *French Canada: A Study in Canadian Democracy* (Toronto: Progress Books, 1980).

23. This is a very interesting dimension of Canadian history, and is covered very nicely in Edgar McInnis's volume, *Canada: A Political and Social History* (Toronto: Holt, Rinehart and Winston of Canada, 1969). A very good discussion of "the constraints of history" in Quebec can be found in the volume by Guy Lachapelle, Gérald Bernier, Daniel Salée, and Luc Bernier, *The Quebec Democracy: Structures, Processes, and Policies* (Montreal: McGraw-Hill Ryerson, 1993).

24. See A. Brichant, *Option Canada: The Economic Implications of Separatism for the Province of Quebec* (Montreal: The Canada Committee, 1968), David Cameron, *Nationalism, Self-Determination and the Quebec Question* (Toronto: Macmillan of Canada, 1974), or Herbert Quinn, *The Union Nationale: Quebec Nationalism from Duplessis to Levesque* (Toronto: University of Toronto Press, 1979).

25. Two very good general discussions of these issues include André Bernard, *What Does Quebec Want?* (Toronto: James Lorimer, 1978), and Richard Basham, *Crisis in Blanc and White: Urbanization and Ethnic Identity in French Canada* (Cambridge, Mass.: Schenkman Publishing, 1978).

26. Rand Dyck, *Provincial Politics in Canada* (Scarborough, Ont.: Prentice Hall Canada, 1991), p. 215.

27. One of the classic works of this period was by Pierre Vallières, titled *White Niggers of America* (Toronto: McClelland and Stewart, 1971). See, for discussion of the evolution of Quebec society, Michael Behiels, *Prelude to Quebec's Quiet Revolution: Liberalism Versus Neo-Nationalism, 1945–1960* (Kingston: McGill-Queen's University Press, 1985), and Georges Mathews, *The Quiet Resolution: Quebec's Challenge to Canada* (Toronto: Summerhill Press, 1990).

28. This is clearly explained in Black, *Divided Loyalties.*

29. Discussion of the "Meech Lake" agreement, named after the site at which initial agreement was reached, has been the subject of a massive literature in recent years. See, among others, Andrew Cohen, *A Deal Undone: The Making and Breaking of the Meech Lake Accord* (Vancouver: Douglas and McIntyre, 1990), Bruce Carson, *The Meech Lake Accord: Linguistic Duality and the Distinct Society* (Ottawa: Library of Parliament, Research Branch, 1989), Lorne Ingle, ed., *Meech Lake Reconsidered* (Hull, Que.: Voyageur Publishing, 1989), or Pierre Trudeau, *Pierre Trudeau Speaks Out on Meech Lake* (Toronto: General Paperbacks, 1990).

30. This would be a grant in which the federal government might say, to take an example from the field of education, "We know that you have the authority to develop a network of community colleges and we do not, but if you will develop a network of colleges according to our specifications, we'll pay for the overwhelming percent of the cost of the development." While many of the provincial governments have accepted these types of offers—on the grounds that they're getting something (such as a network of community colleges) for a significantly lower cost than otherwise might be the case—Quebec has opposed these offers on the principle that the federal government shouldn't be involved at all in issues over which provinces have jurisdiction. See Simeon, *Federal Provincial Diplomacy;* see also Daniel Drache and Roberto Perin, eds., *Negotiating with a Sovereign Quebec* (Toronto: J. Lorimer, 1992), and Donald Rowat, ed., *Cases on Canadian Policy-Making* (Ottawa: Carleton University, 1987).

31. See William Coleman, *The Independence Movement in Quebec, 1945–1980* (Toronto: University of Toronto Press, 1984), John Fitzmaurice, *Quebec and Canada: Past, Present, and Future* (New York: St. Martin's Press, 1985), or William Shaw and Lionel Albert, *Partition: The Price of Quebec's Independence* (Montreal: Thornhill Publishers, 1980), for examples of this literature.

32. A good description of the evolution of this power in Canada can be found in James Mallory, *The Structure of Canadian Government* (Toronto: Macmillan, 1971), pp. 11–21. See also Robert Jackson and Doreen Jackson, *Politics in Canada: Culture, Institutions, Behaviour and Public Policy*, 2nd ed. (Scarborough, Ont.: Prentice Hall Canada, 1990), p. 281.

33. Jackson and Atkinson, *The Canadian Legislative System*, p. 53.

34. Allan Kornberg and William Mishler, *Influence in Parliament: Canada* (Durham, N.C.: Duke University Press, 1976), p. 34.

35. Ibid., pp. 35–36. Recent work on the power of the prime minister would include Gordon Donaldson, *Eighteen Men: The Prime Ministers of Canada* (Toronto: Doubleday, 1985), Ron Graham, *One-Eyed Kings: Promise and Illusion in Canadian Politics* (Toronto: Collins, 1986), Leslie Pal and David Taras, eds., *Prime Ministers and Premiers* (Scarborough, Ont.: Prentice Hall Canada, 1988), and R. Malcolm Punnett, *The Prime Minister in Canadian Government and Politics* (Toronto: Macmillan of Canada, 1977).

36. For discussions of the cabinet and its formation, see Robert Dawson and W.F. Dawson, *Democratic Government in Canada* (Toronto: University of Toronto Press, 1971), pp. 46–54.

37. Jackson and Atkinson, *The Canadian Legislative System*, p. 38.

38. In addition to sources mentioned in Note 24, the "classic" study in this area is that by Thomas Hockin, *Power: The Prime Minister and Political Leadership in Canada*, 2nd ed. (Scarborough, Ont.: Prentice Hall Canada, 1977).

39. Kornberg, *Canadian Legislative Behavior*, p. 19.

40. See F.A. Kunz, *The Modern Senate of Canada* (Toronto: University of Toronto Press, 1965).

41. There is a substantial literature on Senate reform. A good recent effort is that by Jonathan Lemco, "Senate Reform: A Fruitless Endeavour," *Journal of Commonwealth and Comparative Politics* 24:3 (1986): 269–277. See also Randall White, *Voice of Region: The Long Journey to Senate Reform in Canada* (Toronto: Dundurn Press, 1990), and "Report of the Joint Committee on the Reform of the Canadian Senate," *Parliamentarian* 65:3 (1984): 204–207.

42. A very good review essay of recent scholarship on the Canadian Parliament can be found in the piece by Michael Atkinson and Paul Thomas, "Studying the Canadian Parliament," *Legislative Studies Quarterly* 18:3 (1993): 423–451.

43. Kornberg, *Canadian Legislative Behavior*, p. 13.

44. Ibid., p. 131.

45. Jackson and Jackson, *Politics in Canada*, p. 330.

46. See the essay by James McGrath, "Reflections on Reform," *Parliamentarian* 67:1 (1986): 5–8.

47. Leon Epstein wrote the classic article in this area, "A Comparative Study of Canadian Parties," *American Political Science Review* 58 (1964): 46–59. More recent studies have included Alain Gagnon and A. Brian Tanguay, eds., *Canadian Parties in Transition: Discourse, Organization, and Representation* (Toronto: Nelson, 1989), William Christian, *Political Parties and Ideologies in Canada* (Toronto: McGraw-Hill Ryerson, 1989), George Perlin, ed., *Party Democracy in Canada: The Role of National Party Conventions* (Scarborough, Ont.: Prentice Hall Canada, 1988), and especially Hugh Thorburn, ed., *Party Politics in Canada*, 5th ed. (Scarborough, Ont.: Prentice Hall Canada, 1985).

48. Alan Cairns, "The Electoral and the Party System in Canada," *Canadian Journal of Political Science* 1 (1968): 61–75. See also Kenneth Carty, ed., *Canadian Political Party Systems: A Reader* (Peterborough, Ont.: Broadview Press, 1992), and Harold D. Clarke, ed., *Absent Mandate: Interpreting Change in Canadian Elections* (Toronto: Gage Educational Publishing, 1991).

49. Mallory, *The Structure of Canadian Government*, p. 202.

50. For excellent descriptions of third parties in Canada, see Leo Zakuta, *A Protest Movement Becalmed* (Toronto: University of Toronto Press, 1964), Walter Young, *The Anatomy of a Party: The National CCF, 1932–1961* (Toronto: University of Toronto Press, 1969), Michael B. Stein, *The Dynamics of Right-Wing Protest: A Political Analysis of the Social Credit in Quebec* (Toronto: University of Toronto Press, 1973); and Maurice Pinard, *The Rise of a Third Party: A Study of Crisis Politics* (Englewood Cliffs, N.J.: Prentice Hall, 1971). More recent studies of third parties include Desmond Morton, *The New Democrats 1961–1986: The Politics of Change* (Toronto: Copp Clark Pitman Ltd., 1986), and Nelson Wiseman, *Social Democracy in Manitoba: A History of the CCF/NDP* (Winnipeg: University of Manitoba Press, 1984).

51. See Ronald Kerr, *Western Canadian Politics: The Radical Tradition* (Edmonton: West Institute for Western Canadian Studies, 1981), Donald Blake, *Two Political Worlds: Parties and Voting in British Columbia* (Vancouver: University of British Columbia Press, 1985), Harold Clarke, *Partisan Inconsistency and Partisan Change in a Federal State: The Case of Canada* (Toronto: University of Toronto Press, 1987), or Peter Aucoin, ed., *Party Government and Regional Representation in Canada*, vol. 36, Royal Commission on the Economic Union and Development Prospects for Canada (Toronto: University of Toronto Press, 1985).

52. Van Loon and Whittington, *The Canadian Political System*, p. 243.

53. Ibid., p. 244.

54. Kornberg and Mishler, *Influence in Parliament*, p. 180.

55. See George Perlin, ed., *Party Democracy in Canada: The Politics of National Party Conventions* (Scarborough, Ont.: Prentice Hall Canada, 1988).

56. See John Richards, Robert Cairns, and Larry Pratt, eds., *Social Democracy Without Illusions: Renewal of the Canadian Left* (Toronto: McClelland and Stewart, 1991).

57. These are discussed in Perlin, *Party Democracy in Canada*.

58. A very good study of the brief period of leadership of Joe Clark can be found in Warner Troyer, *200 Days: Joe Clark in Power: The Anatomy of the Rise and Fall of the 21st Government* (Toronto: Personal Library Publisher, 1980).

14

The Russian Political System

The study of politics in Russia, as well as Russia's political heritage, requires a deviation from the normal pattern of the area studies chapters preceding this one. Our fundamental premise in this volume has been that if we study the basic constitutional structures of a political regime we will develop some understanding of how the regime operates. Thus in many instances we have paid relatively little attention, comparatively speaking, to social issues, political parties, ideologies, and interest groups in each of our "country portraits."

This is not to suggest that the detailed study of political parties in Britain, for example, would not contribute a great deal to our understanding of the operation of the British political system. It does. What we have suggested, however, is that it is *possible* to understand how the British political system generally operates without a detailed examination of the Labour and Conservative parties. Similarly, it is possible to become *acquainted* (and remember, our "country portraits" do not claim to be comprehensive, but are simply designed as introductions) with the other political systems we have examined without detailed knowledge of their respective political parties.

This is all said by way of introduction to the chapter on the Russian political system because Russia poses an exception to the general patterns described above. While it is true that we can understand the essential pattern of operation of these other political systems by confining our examination to what might be called "constitutional political structures," a similar examination of the Russian political system might give us an unrealistic or inadequate image of the pattern of political operations there. The Russian political system, while it has an extensive history, is a very new system in many important respects; we must appreciate its newness, and the circumstances from which it emerged, if we are to understand its operation.

Accordingly, after an examination of the Russian political heritage, we will turn our attention to a tentative examination of the new constitution and the system of constitutional political structures in the new political system that is called Russia. We must recall that Russia does not have a democratic history upon which to draw at moments of stress, and it does not have numerous democratic precedents to use as examples during moments of political crisis. Thus, while we may describe a number of (relatively new) political institutions, only time will tell us the degree to which they will either endure or be effective.

THE COUNTRY THAT IS CALLED RUSSIA

For many years the name "Russia" was used interchangeably with "the Union of Soviet Socialist Republics," the USSR, despite the fact that such a usage was incorrect. Russia was *part of* the USSR, but not *the same as* the USSR. The USSR was the largest country in the world, making up nearly one-sixth of the earth's land mass—"more than twice the size of the United States, almost as big as the United States, Canada, and Mexico put together ... only slightly smaller than the whole continent of Africa."[1] (This kind of comparison was slightly misleading, however, because a careful study of the Soviet map would have shown that a significant portion of the USSR was "not conducive to protracted habitation for sizeable populations."[2])

The Russian Political Heritage

Russia has existed for more than eleven centuries, under a variety of names and a variety of rulers. Under the Soviet regime many suggested that there were a number of historical factors in the Soviet political heritage that had proven to be significant in influencing Soviet development in a non-Western direction;[3] clearly, the same thing can be said about Russia. Patterns of behavior, such as the "persistent tradition of absolutism in government, the recurrent use of revolutionary violence to solve political problems, and the lack of experience with democratic institutions and constitutional procedures,"[4] all contributed to a political tradition in the Soviet Union—and now Russia—that was distinctly different from that shared by most Western (democratic) nations. (See Table 14.1.)

One major pattern in the Russian past was the history of revolutions, which led to the Revolution of 1917.[5] Among the earliest acts that can be called revolutions in Russian history was a shake-up in government led by Ivan the Terrible in 1564. Ivan was rebelling not against the government (he was tsar at the time!) but against the nobles in his regime, claiming that they were evil and traitorous. He agreed to maintain the throne only under the condition that he be given control of a secret police network called the Oprichnina, which he used to destroy the power of the no-

TABLE 14.1
Some Important Landmarks in Russian History

Year	Event
1237–40	Mongol (Tatar) conquest of Russia begins 200 years of Mongol rule ("The Tatar Yoke").
1480	Ivan III frees Muscovy from Mongol rule.
1712	Peter the Great moves capital of Russia to Saint Petersburg (now Leningrad) for a "window to the West".
1861	Emancipation of the serfs by Alexander II.
1905	Revolution forces Nicholas II to grant token reform, including establishment of a parliament (the Duma).
1917	March Revolution overthrows monarchy and establishes moderate socialist government; November Revolution brings Lenin's Bolsheviks to power.
1917–21	War Communism.
1921–28	New Economic Policy.
1924–38	Death of Lenin in 1924 leads to a struggle for power. Stalin emerges on top and then ruthlessly consolidates his control.
1953	Death of Stalin.
1957	Consolidation of power by Khruschev.
1964	Khruschev ousted; replaced by Brezhnev and Kosygin.
1982	Brezhnev dies; succeeded by Andropov.
1984	Andropov dies; succeeded by Chernenko.
1985	Chernenko dies; succeeded by Gorbachev; Gorbachev elected to new presidency of Soviet Union.
1991	Boris Yeltsin elected president of Russia (June); attempted *coup d'état*/overthrow of Gorbachev (August 19); Gorbachev resigns from Communist Party (August 24); Commonwealth of Independent States treaty signed (December 21); breakup of USSR; Gorbachev resigns as USSR president (December 25).

Source: Adapted from David Roth and Frank Wilson, *The Comparative Study of Politics* (Englewood Cliffs, N.J.: Prentice Hall, 1980), p. 24; see also *Vital Speeches*, *The New York Times*, and *The Los Angeles Times*.

bles by arresting them, exiling them, and taking over their estates. Ivan's actions served to neutralize any threat that the nobility had posed to the power of the tsar.

The revolt of December 1825, known as the Decembrist Uprising, was an attempt by the tsar's guards to overthrow the tsar (Nicholas I, 1825–1855) and do away with the restrictive, autocratic government of Russia. Partially because of the uncertainty of the revolutionaries, who could not agree on the kind of regime that they wanted to replace the tsar, the revolt was suppressed and the tsar increased governmental repression.

The oppressiveness of the tsar, however, did not check the spread of revolutionary ideas. Although the tsar freed the serfs in 1861 as a gesture to placate public unrest, revolutionary fervor continued to spread. Political organization was begun by a revolutionary intelligentsia, primarily organized in the Narodnik movement. The Narodniki were originally intellectually based—drawn from student and intellectual groups—but later the movement drew from wider circles. The movement had as its goal the promotion of a socialist society, maintaining that the traditional Russian village was socialist in orientation. The Narodniki did not view Western-style industrialization as a positive goal for Russian society, and they argued that "once the aristocratic system and the feudal order were destroyed, Russia would spontaneously be recognized as a vast association of agrarian cooperative communities."[6]

The first Marxist organization in Russia, called the Emancipation of Labor, was founded in 1883 by a group led by George Plekhanov. Between 1883 and 1894 this kind of group was formed in most major Russian cities, including one formed in St. Petersburg in 1895 and led by Lenin. Both Stalin (whose real name was Joseph Dzhugashvili) and Trotsky (whose real name was Leon Bronstein) became active in politics during this time. In 1898 the first Russian Social Democratic party convention was held in Minsk, its goal being to consolidate various factions of Marxists.

The second Russian Social Democratic party convention was held in 1903, meeting first in Brussels (because it was not permitted in Russia), then moving to London. In London the party divided into two factions over the issue of organization. Some party members wanted a European-style Social Democratic party. Lenin argued against that form of party, saying that the tsar's secret police would not permit such an open party to operate freely. He argued in favor of a restricted, tightly organized party of dedicated revolutionaries. The party split into two factions over this question on a 33–18 vote.[7] Lenin was leader of the majority faction, called the Bolsheviks. The labels Bolshevik (majority) and Menshevik (minority) stuck to the two factions of the party, and the two factions of the Russian Social Democratic party were thereafter known as the Bolsheviks and the Mensheviks.

At this time Lenin presented his proposals, which he had introduced in his earlier publication *What Is to Be Done?* (published in 1902). In that work he called for a new kind of nonelectoral party organization, designed not so much to compete for power in elections, but "to seize power on behalf of the working class and to establish a `dictatorship of the proletariat'."[8]

At the turn of the twentieth century, Russia was again near revolution. Strikes and industrial unrest spread throughout the country as a result of yet another economic crisis. On January 9, 1905 ("Bloody Sunday"), soldiers fired on a procession of workers bringing a list of grievances to Tsar Nicholas II, killing hundreds and beginning a revolt. Workers' councils, called *soviets*, were formed in many cities to direct strike activities. Leon Trotsky, a leader of the St. Petersburg soviet, issued a call for constitutional reforms, free elections, a parliament, and freedom for political parties to form.

The tsar managed to put down the revolt, but acceded to many of the requests as an effort to promote the stability of his regime. In the October Manifesto, he promised a national parliament (the Duma), a constitution, free elections, and protection of civil liberties. After 1905 Russia was a much more liberal and less oppressive society than it had been previously, although the tsar was still the most significant political actor because of his power of absolute veto over the Duma and his power to dismiss the Duma at will.[9]

The year 1917 saw new revolution in Russia. Russia's performance in World War I, coupled with continued poor economic growth and increased governmental repressiveness, led to more rebellions. The tsar was overthrown in March 1917, and the Duma became the Provisional Government; it granted amnesty to most of the Bolshevik leaders who had been exiled (like Lenin) or sent to Siberia (like Stalin) by the tsar, and allowed them to return to the political scene. From the beginning of the Revolution, the workers' councils, the soviets, played central roles in the co-ordination of revolutionary activity. The Petrograd (the new name for St. Petersburg) soviet, in fact, rivalled the Provisional Government (the Duma) as a source of leadership.

In April 1917, Lenin returned to Russia and issued his "April Theses," calling for the overthrow of the Provisional Government and the transformation of the "bourgeois democratic revolution" into a revolution sponsored by the "proletarian class". The Provisional Government, headed by Alexander Kerensky, opposed Lenin's policies, but in the end could not stand up to the Bolshevik organization. On the night of November 6–7, 1917, all members of the Provisional Government were arrested by the Red Guard, on Lenin's orders. Lenin announced that the former government was dissolved, and that the Petrograd soviet, headed by its Central Executive Committee, was now in control. The new government was headed by a Council of Peoples' Commissars, led by Lenin as Chairman, Stalin as Commissar of Nationalities, and Trotsky as Commissar of Foreign Affairs.

From 1917 through 1991 the Soviet Union existed as a Marxist-Leninist political system, moving through a number of different leaders, through varying degrees of authoritarian government, and through varying degrees of aggressiveness about spreading the doctrine of Marxism-Leninism to other political systems.[10] With the coming to power of Mikhail Gorbachev in 1985, a new era began.[11] This included a gradual relaxation of the degree to which the Communist party of the Soviet Union ran the government and, equally important, included a corresponding increase in human rights tolerated by the central government as well as a corresponding diminution in the amount of control Moscow insisted on having over the fifteen "independent republics" of the Soviet Union.[12]

In November 1989 the wall dividing Germany's East and West Berlin was opened, and shortly thereafter physically came down.[13] Eventually, in 1990, East and West Germany were reunified. This reunification, combined with other effects of the centrifugal forces of nationalism, had a critical impact upon the Soviet Union and its satellite governments in Eastern Europe. In 1991, under Mikhail Gorbachev, discussions were undertaken about a restructuring of the Soviet Union into a new confederation, giving more power to the individual republics. This led, as we shall further discuss shortly, to the creation of the Commonwealth of Independent States and the death of the Union of Soviet Socialist Republics. It was, indeed, a "new world order."[14]

The Devolution of the Soviet Union

The USSR was composed of fifteen union republics—hence the name Union of Soviet Socialist Republics—in a highly heterogeneous political system. (See Table 14.2.) The Soviet nation consisted:

> of more than a hundred large and small ethnic groups with their own distinct cultural heritages. Many, but not all, ethnic groups [had] their own territories within

TABLE 14.2
The Composition of the USSR

Name of Union Republic	Date Created	Capital	Area (in square miles)	1986 Estimated Population (in millions)
Russian SSR	November 1917	Moscow	6,592,800	144.1
Ukrainian SSR	December 1917	Kiev	233,100	50.0
Belorussian SSR	January 1919	Minsk	80,200	10.0
Uzbekian SSR	October 1924	Tashkent	172,700	18.5
Kazakhian SSR	December 1936	Alma-Ata	1,049,200	16.0
Georgian SSR	February 1921	Tbilisi	26,911	5.2
Azerbaidzhanian SSR	April 1920	Baku	33,400	6.7
Lithuanian SSR	July 1940	Bilnius	26,173	3.6
Moldavian SSR	August 1940	Kishinev	13,012	4.1
Latvian SSR	July 1940	Riga	24,695	2.6
Kirgizian SSR	December 1936	Frunze	76,642	4.1
Tadzhikian SSR	October 1929	Dushambe	54,019	4.6
Armenian SSR	November 1920	Erevan	11,306	3.4
Turkmenian SSR	October 1924	Ashkabad	188,417	3.3
Estonian SSR	July 1940	Tallin	17,413	1.5

Source: Mark S. Hoffman, ed., *The World Almanac and Book of Facts, 1989* (New York: World Almanac, 1989), p. 726.

the USSR. These territories were designated, in descending order of importance, as "Union Republics" [15] "autonomous republics" [11], "autonomous regions" [8], and "autonomous areas" [10].[15]

In the late 1980s the heterogeneous nature of the Soviet Union became the cause of tension—and open violence—in Soviet politics. The "nationality question"[16] was the cause of many deaths in 1989 as various ethnic groups protested that they were not receiving adequate attention from Moscow.[17] The goals of these ethnic groups were often territorial, but occasionally involved unhappiness with religious, political, or economic policies. According to the U.S. State Department, about thirty-five borders within the Soviet Union were being disputed between different national groups in the Soviet Union in early 1989, including conflicts in Armenia, Azerbaijan, Kazakhstan, Uzbekistan, Lithuania, and Georgia, to name just a few.[18]

The largest single geographic component of the USSR was the Russian Soviet Federative Socialist Republic (RSFSR), making up over three-fourths of the USSR. The fourteen other union republics apart from Russia were all called "Soviet Socialist Republics" (SSRs): Armenian SSR, Azerbaidzhanian SSR, Belorussian SSR, Estonian SSR, Georgian SSR, Latvian SSR, Lithuanian SSR, Kazakhian SSR, Kirghizian SSR, Moldavian SSR, Tadzhikian SSR, Turkmenian SSR, Ukrainian SSR, and Uzbekian SSR.[19]

Both the 1936 Soviet constitution and the 1977 Soviet constitution suggested that the USSR was a federal political system. The federal relationship, as it was described earlier in this text, proved to be more imaginary than real, however. In reality, the Soviet Union was a very centralized unitary system with a number of component units that had no real powers of their own, and thus could not be called "federal" in any meaningful sense of the term.

Soviet federalism was developed by Lenin and Stalin as a vehicle for controlling many of the "independent republics" that had been included in the Russian Empire. In the Revolution of 1917 the Bolsheviks had promised self-determination to the various national minorities; military conquest did not appear to them to be a preferential strategy, if they had any choice. By making the new state a "federation" it was possible to at least maintain the impression that the member units retained some autonomy, albeit token autonomy.[20]

The constitution of 1924 contained a number of clauses reflecting the "federal" nature of the regime. In addition to the usual powers granted federal governments (found in federal regimes of the day, including Canada, Germany, the United States, and Australia), such as the power to coin money, to have an army, and the like, the Soviet constitution gave the federal government a great number of economic planning powers, central to Marxist ideology. The constitution had no bill of rights and no electoral laws; it left these areas of concern, as well as the areas of civil and criminal law, to the member republics.[21] In practice, however, things didn't work out this way.

It is interesting to note that the 1977 constitution, in an early draft, suggested doing away with the Soviet federation and creating a unitary state. The plan was turned down, and deleted from the final draft of the constitution. The 1977 constitution referred to the USSR as a "unitary, federal, and multinational state, formed on the basis of the principle of socialist federalism and as a result of the free self-determination of nations and the voluntary union of equal Soviet Socialist Republics."[22]

The Soviet federal structure was partially reflected in the constitutional structure of the government in one of the two houses of the Soviet legislature, the Supreme Soviet. Under the 1988 amendment to the constitution, 750 members of the Supreme Soviet were to be elected on the basis of governmental units, with each of the country's republics having the same representation in the legislature; thus Estonia's 1.5 million citizens had the same number of representatives as Ukraine's 50 million citizens.[23]

As we noted above, by 1991 the gradually increasing spirit of nationalism that had begun to reassert its presence in a variety of the "independent" republics was too strong to ignore any longer. The Union of Soviet Socialist Republics was dissolved,[24] and a new structure of association, the Commonwealth of Independent States, emerged to replace the USSR as a vehicle for the association of a number of truly independent republics, all of which had been union republics within the USSR.[25]

Not all of the former components of the USSR chose to join the Commonwealth of Independent States; Estonia, Latvia, and Lithuania, the Baltic republics of the USSR, were not interested in prolonging a formal association with the other states. In 1991 the other states had been willing is to stay within the USSR and to create a looser confederation, still calling the association the Union of Soviet Socialist Republics. Following an attempted overthrow of the government in 1991 by ultraconservative forces opposed to these changes,[26] however, and following the resignation of President Gorbachev from the Communist party,[27] the other republics decided that *more* independence from Moscow, rather than less, was the better course to follow in the future.

IDEOLOGY

The political regime that was referred to as the USSR had an ideological foundation officially referred to as "Marxism-Leninism."[28] This Marxism-Leninism was

> officially regarded in the Soviet Union as an exact science, a "correct grasp" of which makes possible a scientific understanding of the past, present and future of the human race.[29]

Ultimately, Marxism-Leninism was based upon the *Communist Manifesto* (written in 1848) and subsequent writings of its authors, Karl Marx and Friedrich Engels. More directly, however, political ideology in the Soviet Union could be explained as Marxism interpreted and applied by Soviet leaders of the day, including Lenin, Stalin, Khrushchev, and Brezhnev.[30] Each of these leaders in turn interpreted and revised Marx's ideas so that the particular version of Marxism would support the regime of the day and provide a rationalization for the policies of the government in power.[31]

The perspectives of Marx were, in fact, different from those of Lenin, Stalin, Khrushchev, Brezhnev, or even Gorbachev. Marx was a theorist, dealing with philosophies and ideas. Lenin and his followers were pragmatists—political actors—interested in the philosophy suggested by Marx but faced with the challenge of putting the theories into concrete form, of operationalizing the ideology.

As the economic, social, and political characteristics of the Soviet Union changed, Marx's ideas had to be revised to fit the times. Lenin, for example, revised Marxian theory to justify its relevance to the conditions of the Soviet Union during the period between 1917 and 1924.

Lenin's major modifications of Marxism were three: First, he insisted upon a military-like organization of his political party, against the contemporary trend of social democratic parties in Europe. His argument was that "in a nondemocratic country a Marxist party built on democratic principles was doomed to failure." Second, he advocated promoting an alliance between the weak Russian proletariat (the factory and industrial workers) and the poor majority of peasants, partially to help compensate for the fact that the proletariat was not as large as it was envisioned to be in Marx's theory. Third, he justified a "proletarian revolution" in Russia when, in fact, agrarian Russia was hardly the industrialized society that Marx had in mind when he was writing his treatises.[32]

Lenin died in January 1924. Following his death there was a power struggle to see who would be the next leader. The two major contestants were Joseph Stalin and Leon Trotsky. Stalin's position emerged as the stronger of the two; as secretary-general of the Communist party of the Soviet Union, he had been able to build a strong base of power.

In 1936 Stalin had a new constitution written that he proclaimed to be the most democratic in the world. He created a new parliament, and a bill of rights (although we should note that it did not effectively protect individual rights from governmental abuses), and at the same time he centralized power to guarantee that no one would be able to challenge his control. After securing his hold on power, Stalin claimed that the Marxist revolution was completed within the USSR.[33] Stalin, accordingly, turned his attention away from the revolution within the state, to revolution in other states. Stalin felt that the Soviet system could assist Marxist revolutions in other parts of the world, after it had developed into a militarily powerful regime.

In terms of major modifications of Marxism (or of "Marxism-Leninism-Stalinism," as he preferred to call it), Stalin's contributions were neither as many nor as significant as those of Lenin. He did make some contributions to the Soviet polity, however, including the creation of the structure of the five-year plan to direct the development of the Soviet state[34] and the introduction of the concept of "enemy of the people" into Soviet ideology.[35]

Nikita Khrushchev emerged as Soviet leader in 1957. In a manner similar to Lenin and Stalin, Khrushchev was said by students of Marxism to have contributed several major theoretical modifications to the Marxism-Leninism-Stalinism of his day.[36]

Less than ten years later, while Chairman and First Secretary Khrushchev was vacationing, he was "deposed" by a team headed by Leonid Brezhnev and Alexi Kosygin in October 1964. The post-Khrushchev leadership, primarily Brezhnev, undertook somewhat of a retrenchment following the ouster of Khrushchev. The liberalization by Khrushchev of restrictions in the areas of arts, literature, and education was again tightened; the Soviet Union's apparent relaxation of its control over its satellites also was reversed with the 1968 crushing of the Czechoslovakian uprising.[37]

Following the death of Leonid Brezhnev in November 1982, the future direction of Soviet ideology was uncertain. Yuri Andropov, former head of the KGB (the State Security Committee) and Politburo member, was selected to take over as secretary-general of the Communist party. His period of leadership was brief and did not contribute anything in the way of ideological significance, primarily because of his age and illness. When Andropov died in 1984, he was replaced by Konstantin Chernenko, another senior party leader, who also died in office after a very brief period of leadership. The accession to office of Mikhail Gorbachev in 1985 suggested the promise of significant change, but in 1985 *no* observer of the Soviet system would have imagined the degree of change that would come within the next seven years.

THE RUSSIAN CONSTITUTION

For the person studying American politics, the U.S. Constitution is a highly significant document. On the other hand, studies of Soviet politics traditionally did not spend a great deal of time or attention explaining the Soviet constitution, because it was *not* a meaningful or significant document in the Soviet political regime. To the contrary, if a student were to carefully study the Soviet constitution he or she would undoubtedly have found that it made an understanding of the Soviet polity more difficult, rather than easier, to grasp.

The Russian constitutional system in 1994 is one that is developing a number of democratic political structures. This development, however, is often slow and frequently painful. As we will see later in this chapter, a pluralistic system of political parties is in the process of developing in Russia today, and debate over what *should be* the new constitutional institutions of the regime is very intense and visible in the public arena, even to the point of leading to public violence.

Indeed, part of the violence in Russia in mid-1993—including what the leaders of Parliament referred to as a *coup d'état* by President Boris Yeltsin, and what Yeltsin referred to as *unconstitutional behavior* by the leaders of Parliament—was caused precisely because *both* sides of the debate were firmly committed to what they called *constitutional government*; they simply couldn't agree on what *kind* of constitution Russia ought to have.[38]

Thus, we should note that it is very clear that the new generation of Russian leaders considers their constitutional institutions to be very important, even if they cannot agree on precisely what those institutions should be. We will examine recent evolutions of these institutions later in this chapter.

One problem that has made the development of constitutional consensus more difficult in Russia is that there has been no tradition of stable constitutional government in Russia or the Soviet Union. As was noted earlier, before the dissolution of the Soviet Union it was believed that "the constitutional structure of the Soviet Union has always been an elaborate facade behind which one-party rule and totalitarianism have occupied the political scene. . . . The Statute of the Communist party is a more important document than the Constitution of the USSR."[39] Yet, it is clear that the *existence* of a constitution must have been important to the Bolsheviks, and to their political successors: The Soviet Union had a number of constitutions, and political leaders would not have undertaken the effort to create the constitutions if they did not feel that the exercise would be worth their while. Indeed, as recently as the fall of 1988 the Soviet government devoted significant time and effort to the process of constitutional reform.

Since the Revolution of 1917 there have been six constitutional eras in the USSR and Russia. First, on July 10, 1918, a new constitution was put into force in Russia. This was followed by the second era, with the arrival of the first constitution of the USSR in January 1924. In 1935 a third era came about when a constitutional commission was appointed and instructed to draft a new constitution for the USSR, to replace its original 1924 constitution. The new constitution was approved late in 1936.

After Stalin's death, movements were launched to create a new constitution, but progress was slow. In 1962 Khrushchev began efforts to draft a new constitution, but his ouster in 1964 stalled the project. Although Brezhnev became Chairman of the Constitutional Commission, the project was not one of high priority for Brezhnev at the time. A fourth constitutional era came when "without the usual advance clues, there came the abrupt announcement in May 1977 that the new Draft Constitution would soon be published for nationwide discussion."[40]

Under Mikhail Gorbachev a new constitutional balance of power, a fifth era, was brought about in 1988 and 1989 with a new Supreme Soviet and Soviet presidency, which will be described below. With the resignation of President Gorbachev[41] and the dissolution of the Soviet Union in 1991, a new constitutional era began for Russia. It was still evolving in September 1993, when some argued that a civil war was narrowly averted involving a conflict between Boris Yeltsin and the more conservative Russian Parliament.

In November 1993 President Yeltsin announced that a new constitution for Russia would be placed before the Russian voters on December 12, 1993, at the same time as they would be asked to vote for members of the new parliament. Early reports indicated that the new constitution would give the president the right, under limited conditions, to issue decrees having the force of law; to dissolve parliament; to declare a state of emergency; and to temporarily curb civil rights. It would also give Russians a number of unprecedented guarantees of personal freedoms and entrench a number of reforms of Communist-era economic policies.

In the December 1993 election the new constitution was approved by a significant margin, but Yeltsin's party did not win a majority in the new parliament. While many debated whether this was a result of the unpopularity of his economic policies, his ineffective campaigning before the election, or a personal rejection of Yeltsin himself, the outcome was a state of uncertainty. Although Yeltsin vowed to press on with his economic and political reforms, it appeared that his policies would have as much difficulty in the new parliament as they had experienced in the old parliament.

The question can be asked, "Why did Soviet leaders continue the `constitutional ruse,' as it could be called, having constitutions that were primarily of symbolic significance?" The answer appears to be that the Soviets had an ambivalent attitude toward constitutions. On one hand, in terms of Marxist ideology, they saw both the state and its structures, such as a constitution, as evils. On the other hand, they were willing to recognize constitutions as *necessary* evils—necessary for providing external and internal legitimacy, and for helping to run the regime in the "transitional period" during which time the state "evolves" from capitalism to socialism to communism.

Even though Lenin and his fellow revolutionary leaders were in the middle of a significant domestic battle with other Soviet political leaders, they still believed that it was important to have a constitutional framework for their new government.[42] The role of the constitution in the USSR was to give "legal expression to the basic ideological norms of Soviet doctrine."[43]

STRUCTURES OF THE GOVERNMENT

The Congress of People's Deputies

The idea for the Congress of People's Deputies was first suggested by Mikhail Gorbachev in the late fall of 1988 as part of a package of reforms for the Soviet Union's government. One observer noted that Gorbachev had become:

increasingly frustrated and angry at the resistance being mounted to his reforms by Party and state bureaucrats. He holds these officials to blame for the economic stagnation and moral decline from which his country suffers, and accuses them of stifling the initiative of the population.[44]

The Congress of People's Deputies, the first elections for which were held in March 1989, was intended to be a more active legislature than had been the case with the Supreme Soviet in the past; its members would be elected from competitive elections, and it would elect from among its 2,250 members 542 members of a new, much more active, and more powerful Supreme Soviet.

The exact role of the new Congress of People's Deputies was still being negotiated at its first meeting in June 1989. Among the agreements reached at that time were these:

1) The Congress would convene twice a year instead of once, as originally proposed by Gorbachev;

2) Deputies of the (2,250-member) Congress who were not elected to the (542-member) Supreme Soviet or its commissions or committees could participate in the sessions and have access to the information and documents made available to the Supreme Soviet; and

3) The Congress would retain the "right to cancel or change any document, any legislative act, and any decision taken by the Supreme Soviet."[45]

The Supreme Soviet

Prior to the constitutional amendment proposed by Mikhail Gorbachev in late 1988, the Supreme Soviet was a very weak (essentially rubber-stamp) legislative body that approved whatever legislation was placed before it by Communist party officials, despite the fact that it was described (in Chapter 15 of the Constitution) as "the supreme body of state power in the USSR . . . empowered to resolve all questions placed within the jurisdiction of the USSR by this constitution."[46]

The Supreme Soviet was a bicameral body, composed of the Soviet of the Union and the Soviet of Nationalities, members of which were all elected at the same time for four-year terms. Members of the Soviet of the Union were elected on the basis of population. Members of the Soviet of Nationalities represented the "federal" nature of the political system, with each union republic having thirty-two seats, each autonomous republic having eleven seats, each autonomous region having five seats, and each national area having one seat. The two houses of the Supreme Soviet had over 1,500 representatives.

As noted earlier, in 1988 Mikhail Gorbachev proposed a fundamental change in the institution, "asking the Supreme Soviet to abolish itself,"[47] and to create a new institution in its place, the new Congress of People's Deputies. As part of his package of proposals, Gorbachev proposed that the Congress would elect from among its own members a *new* Supreme Soviet, one that would "act as a full-time legislature for the nearly eight months it will be in session."[48] It would meet for two sessions each year—one in the spring and one in the fall, each lasting three or four months.[49] On paper, at least, the new Supreme Soviet was to be much more active, and important, than its predecessor had been.[50]

At the same time that new institutions were being created at the level of the USSR government, new institutions were proposed and created for the Russian government, too. Institutions of the Russian Republic were essentially parallel to those of the Soviet Union, with a Russian Federation Supreme Soviet made up of a Council of the Republic and a Council of Nationalities. The executive branch was to be led by a president, assisted by a government (a chairman and a number of ministers) drawn from the Supreme Soviet. In essence the Russian government was very much a French-model government, led by a strong president.[51]

In the fall of 1993, when Yeltsin won his "battle for supremacy between the executive and legislative branches" and called for new legislative elections, he also ordered replacement of all of the regional and territorial legislatures. He demanded that they "submit to new elections and face a drastic reduction in their size. . . . The new councils, to be called assemblies or dumas, a term used in czarist Russia, will be made up of 15 to 50 full-time legislators. They are to replace the existing councils, called soviets, whose membership in some regions exceeds 300."[52] As we noted earlier, although new elections took place across Russia, Yeltsin did not win the popular mandate that he had sought, placing the precise status of his own personal power in question.

The New Presidency

Until the 1989 changes in the power of the Supreme Soviet, one of its most important structures was the Presidium (its full title was the Presidium of the Supreme Soviet of the USSR). It had thirty-nine members, including a chairman, a first vice-chairman, fifteen vice-chairmen (one from each union republic Supreme Soviet), a secretary, and twenty-one members. Members of the Presidium were elected by the USSR Supreme Soviet, "at a joint meeting of its chambers," from among its members in both houses. The Presidium was referred to as "the continuously functioning agency of the USSR Supreme Soviet, accountable to the latter for all its activity, and exercising . . . the functions of supreme body of state power of the USSR in intervals between sessions of the Supreme Soviet."[53]

Thus, although the legislative function may have rested *de jure* with the 1,517-member Supreme Soviet, it was possible to say that this function was *usually* exercised by the Presidium's chairman and a few assistants in the name of the Presidium, carrying out "most of the legislative functions of the government."[54] The chairman of the Presidium was the most visible of the thirty-nine members, however, and he usually acted in the name of the complete body. Until 1989 the chairman of the Presidium was often referred to by Western media as the president of the USSR.

In October 1988 Andrei Gromyko was forced to retire from the position of chairman of the Presidium, and was replaced by Mikhail Gorbachev.[55] As part of Gorbachev's package of reforms for the Supreme Soviet, he suggested the creation of a new position of an executive president, called the chairman of the USSR Supreme

Soviet, who would be elected by the Congress of People's Deputies.[56] Gorbachev "made no secret of his intention to become the first holder of the new, extremely powerful post of executive president."[57] On May 23, 1989, Gorbachev was nominated in the newly created Congress of People's Deputies for the new position, and on May 26 he was elected president by 96 percent of the deputies voting.[58]

The Russian presidency was created at the same time, and Boris Yeltsin was elected president of Russia on June 12, 1991.[59] As we noted above, much of his effort in his first two years in office was spent fighting with the Russian parliament, many members of which were remnants from the days of Communist control of the institutions of the Soviet Union. Following his battle with the Parliament in the fall of 1993, Yeltsin was confident that the elections in December 1993 would produce a new constitution with increased power for the president, and a parliament more sympathetic to his economic and political goals. The constitution was approved; the sympathetic parliament did not come into being.

Elections in Russia

The Soviet regime had an elaborate electoral system, but one in which "meaningful" elections did not take place; elections served to legitimize the Communist party of the Soviet Union and to further entrench the Communist party's grasp on power. Under the new electoral system in 1989, elections became far more open, and competitive, than they had been in the past.

Under this system the Congress of People's Deputies was directly elected by the people, and consisted of three types of deputies, two-thirds to be elected by the public. First, 750 deputies were elected from "territorial election districts" with an equal numbers of voters in each district. A second group of 750 deputies was elected on the basis of governmental units, with each of the USSR republics having an equal number of representatives. A third group of 750 deputies—not selected in public elections— was allocated to "public and professional organizations." This was "one of the innovations introduced by Gorbachev at the All-Union Party Conference in June 1988, in connection with the creation of the Congress."[60] Of these 750 seats, 425 were "reserved for the Communist Party and for a cluster of semi-independent public organizations that are either affiliated with the Party or dominated by it."[61]

There was real electoral competition for seats for the Congress. By the end of February 1989, 2,895 candidates had been nominated for the 1,500 seats that were to be elected by the general public, and 880 candidates were nominated for the 750 seats allotted to the "public organizations." In 1,116 (of the 1,500) electoral constituencies, voters had a choice of two or more candidates; in 384 constituencies, there was only one candidate.[62] District caucuses met to decide on candidates in the electoral competitions. "Voters' caucuses were made up of electors committed to various candidates. . . . Often these meetings were stormy marathons, but in some cases the authorities manipulated them to make sure the local machine candidates ran unopposed."[63]

At the first meeting of the Congress of People's Deputies at the end of May 1989, its members elected from among their numbers a 542-member Supreme Soviet, which held its first meeting in the first week of June. Over time, this Soviet did, in fact, turn out to be more powerful and active than its predecessor. In fact, one consequence of Gorbachev's reforms was that the new Soviet and Gorbachev regularly struggled for power.

As was noted above, following the dissolution of the USSR, institutions that had been less than national institutions under the USSR system (such as the Russian legislature) became national institutions. While Yeltsin was elected in June 1991 as a symbol of a "new" approach to political power, the Russian Parliament with which he had to interact was a holdover from earlier years, and was still dominated by more conservative deputies—and often deputies sympathetic to now-rejected Communist goals and ideals.

This was, in fact, one of the sources of tension leading up to President Yeltsin "firing" the Russian Parliament in September 1993 and calling for new elections. Yeltsin argued that the Parliament did not represent the "democratic" mood of the republic, and a substantial proportion of the deputies, in fact, represented the rejected Communist forces of the old order. Only a new election, he argued, could provide the Russian people with a truly representative parliament.

Unfortunately for Yeltsin, the results of the election did not provide the solution to political conflict in Russia that he had hoped for. Not only did his party not receive a majority in the new parliament, but a new political leader, Vladimir Zhirinovsky—leader of an ultranationalist, reactionary party, "quick to blame foreigners, intellectuals, or unappreciative betters" for problems in Russia—was thrust into a position of political leadership.[64] Zhirinovsky blamed Yeltsin for the nation's problems, made speeches that reminded observers more of the Cold War than of more recent Russian history, and claimed a substantial share of power for himself and his party. The future of Russian democracy was again placed into question.

THE RUSSIAN CONSTITUTIONAL COURT

The Constitutional Court of the Russian Federation has been described as "the first independent court to be established in Russia since the Bolshevik Revolution."[65] The Court was established in October 1991 by the Fourth Russian Congress of People's Deputies. While the law that created the Court indicated that the Court was "prohibited from considering political questions," it has been frequently caught in the middle of explicitly political quarrels between President Yeltsin and the Russian Parliament.

In fact, although the Court initially tried to walk a very narrow line and offend neither the Parliament nor the president, its decisions favored the Parliament significantly more frequently than they did the president.

> Yeltsin's supporters thereupon began to accuse the court and its chairman, Zorkin, of being biased in favor of the congress and against the president. In a recent interview, however, Zorkin tried to justify his stance by saying that the court could not help overruling Yeltsin's decrees more often than acts of the parliament, because the latter did not infringe the constitution as gravely as the president did.[66]

RUSSIAN POLITICAL PARTIES

In the "old" Soviet system, when one thought of political parties one thought only of the Communist party of the Soviet Union (CPSU). The CPSU was *virtually* a governing organization in the USSR, and was "by far the most important political institution in that country."[67] The party, however, was more than generally "a leading and directing force." It "justified its own existence in terms of its understanding of the ideology" of the Soviet Union.[68] While the role of the CPSU changed relatively quickly from one of absolute dominance to one of being outlawed,[69] the structure of the political party has come to play a much more realistic role in Russian politics.

In recent years, a number of significant political parties and movements have come into existence (some more democratically oriented than others),[70] as indicated in Table 14.3. Some of these parties, such as the Republican Party of the Russian Federation (RFRP), have roots in earlier democratic movements. The RFRP was "a spin-off of the former Democratic Platform of the Communist Party of the Soviet Union, which broke away from the Communist Party of the Soviet Union (CPSU) itself at the Twenty-eighth CPSU Congress."[71] On the other hand, other parties are direct descendants of the CPSU itself. The Union of Communist Parties was "once the ruling and only party of the USSR . . . [and] reorganized itself into the UCP and held its Twenty-ninth Congress in March 1993. The congress was attended by more than 400 delegates from eleven republics of the former Soviet Union."[72]

POLITICAL SUCCESSION, RUSSIAN STYLE

The issue of the succession of leadership in the Soviet Union and Russia illustrates the problem that we mentioned earlier about a lack of established democratic traditions and commitment to peaceful democratic transitions from one leader to another.[73]

Leonid Brezhnev was able to arrange the ouster of Nikita Khrushchev

TABLE 14.3
Some Contemporary Political Parties and Movements in Russia

Democratic Organizations	Centrist Organizations	Communist Organizations
Democratic Russia Movement	Civic Union	Communist Party of the Russian Federation
Russian Movement for Democratic Reform	Democratic Party of Russia	Socialist Party of Working People
Democratic Choice	People's Party of Free Russia	Union of Communist Parties
Republican Party of the Russian Federation	New Generation–New Policy Movement	Russian Communist Workers' Party
Russian Party of Free Labor	All-Russian Union Renewal	All-Union Communist Party of Bolsheviks

Source: Based upon data presented in *Radio Free Europe/Radio Liberty Research Report* 2:20 (May 14, 1993): 21–22.

through political alliances in central Communist Party structures; in 1977 he expanded his base of power by acquiring the position of chairman of the Presidium of the Supreme Soviet in addition to his position as general secretary of the Communist party. The leaders who followed Brezhnev to the post of party General Secretary, Yuri Andropov and Konstantin Chernenko, were both old party functionaries, and because of their ages (79 and 82 years, respectively) and accompanying illness, their opportunities to lead and to suggest significant policy innovations were few.

Many sovietologists were keenly interested in what would happen in the process of succession of Brezhnev. Some thought it would introduce conflict and instability, some thought it would simply maintain the status quo, and some thought that it would open up major avenues for reform in Soviet politics. In fact, scholars have begun to conclude that the most accurate characterization would be a combination of the second and third outcomes.

> Not only did Brezhnev's death not precipitate a political cataclysm or usurpation of party authority, but equilibrium was preserved through the death and replacement of two short-lived successors, Yuri Andropov and Konstantin Chernenko. The transition has not ground out a replica of the Brezhnev regime, either. Brezhnev's style and important parts of his program have been disowned by new leaders, starting with Andropov and then, after a lull under Chernenko, more forcefully by Mikhail Gorbachev.[74]

Andropov's ill health made him a weak leader, and he placed a special emphasis on what was called "collective leadership" during his brief time in office. He was not able to create a new cabinet to reflect his own preferences, but was forced to permit the existing members of the Politburo, the party secretariat, and most top government functionaries to retain their positions. This was to no small degree because he "owed his election as general secretary primarily to [Defense Minister Marshal] Ustinov and [Foreign Minister Alexi] Gromyko."

> Because of the power political situation, [Andropov] was equally dependent on an alliance with Chernenko, who had been the losing candidate in the election, and with Prime Minister Tikhonov and Grishin, head of the large Moscow party organization. Both were supporters of Chernenko. Andropov also had to show consideration for that part of the "Brezhnev faction,". . . who had voted for him.[75]

When Chernenko succeeded to the general secretary position, he was able to arrange for himself to be elected chairman of the Presidium of the Supreme Soviet relatively quickly, in June 1983. As with Andropov, Chernenko's health very quickly limited his ability to exercise the potential power of his office. At this time Mikhail Gorbachev rose to the position of second secretary of the Central Committee, and frequently substituted for the chairman when Chernenko's health forced him to take lengthy breaks from activity.

When Mikhail Gorbachev assumed the USSR's top position in the spring of 1985, some suggested that his assumption of power might "well prove to be a major turning point in Soviet history."[76] Others asked if he would "make a difference" in the way the Soviet regime functioned.[77] As we have already noted, he introduced a number of very significant structural changes in his first few years in office, even though he continued to face strong resistance from the entrenched bureaucracy to his call for "a qualitatively new state of society, and that in the broadest sense of the word."[78]

THE RUSSIAN SYSTEM IN PERSPECTIVE

The Russian system provides an interesting case study, both in its own right and in a comparative perspective. Russia is actively evolving from one period and style of politics to another. We can see that the changes from *Soviet* institutions and political behavior to *Russian* institutions and behavior have been, and will continue to be, both dramatic and traumatic. Indeed, no one knows at this point whether Russia's recent experiences with democracy will, in fact, endure.

The Russian case is an illustration of a society without a history of democratic institutions and political behavior attempting to establish democratic institutions and behavior. Many Russian leaders claim to want a Western-style parliamentary democracy; this will not come without a long period of tension and effort on the part of the Russian people.

In short, the Russian system is quite different from other political systems we have met over the course of our studies. Nations in flux, as we see in the case of Russia, are nations with significant *potential*, but ones that have to worry about the potential for violence and self-destruction as well as the potential for accomplishment. The *single most important* lesson we should draw from our studies is that we cannot walk into any new political study with the assumption that all politics operate in the same fashion as they do in the United States. In this manner, we can see the values of cross-national political inquiry. Our new perspectives provide us with a better ability to make our own observations in the future and to draw our own conclusions as we continue our studies.

Notes

1. Vadim Medish, *The Soviet Union* (Englewood Cliffs, N.J.: Prentice Hall, 1981), p. 1.
2. John S. Reshetar, *The Soviet Polity* (New York: Harper and Row, 1978), p. 21.
3. Adam Ulam, *A History of Soviet Russia* (New York: Praeger, 1976), is a good reference in this area.
4. Gwendolen M. Carter, *The Government of the Soviet Union* (New York: Harcourt, Brace, Jovanovich, 1972), p. 14.
5. This section is based upon a much longer section written by Vernon V. Aspaturian, "Soviet Politics," in Roy C. Macridis, *Modern Political Systems: Europe* (Englewood Cliffs, N.J.: Prentice Hall, 1978), pp. 335–340. See also the very good discussion of Russia's revolutionary heritage in Gordon B. Smith, *Soviet Politics: Continuity and Contradiction* (New York: St. Martin's Press, 1988).
6. Aspaturian, "Soviet Politics," p. 336.
7. Michael G. Roskin, *Countries and Concepts* (Englewood Cliffs, N.J.: Prentice Hall, 1982), p. 219.
8. Aspaturian, "Soviet Politics," p. 338.
9. Adam B. Ulam, *The Russian Political System* (New York: Random House, 1974), p. 27.

10. A very good general history is that by Donald Treadgold, *Twentieth-Century Russia* (Boulder, Colo.: Westview Press, 1989). A more specialized study is by Robert V. Daniels, ed., *Documentary History of Communism in Russia: From Lenin to Gorbachev* (Hanover, N.H.: University Press of New England, 1993).

11. A good history looking at the relative impact of Mikhail Gorbachev in historical context is by Peter Martin and Colin Lankester, *From Romanov to Gorbachev: Russia in the 20th Century* (London: Stanley Thornes, 1989).

12. See Valerie Bunce, "Domestic Reform and International Change: The Gorbachev Reforms in Historical Perspective," *International Organization* 47:1 (1993): 107–138, Nicholas Werth, "In the Years of Perestroika," *Dissent* 39:4 (1992): 498–510, and Christopher Young, "The Strategy of Political Liberalization: A Comparative View of Gorbachev's Reforms," *World Politics* 45:1 (1992): 47–65.

13. See John Bligh, Jr., "The Fall Plus One," *Business America*, December 3, 1990, p. 3.

14. In September 1990 President Bush discussed the Persian Gulf crisis and international relations in a speech entitled "Toward a New World Order" (*U.S. Department of State Dispatch*, September 17, 1990, vol. 1, no. 3, p. 91). More recently, and related to the Soviet Union, in May 1991 Bush spoke of "The Possibility of New World Order, Unlocking the Promise of Freedom" (*Vital Speeches*, May 15, 1991, vol. 57, no. 15, p. 450).

15. Medish, *The Soviet Union*, pp. 29–30.

16. Ronald Grigor Suny, "The Nationality Question," in Janet Podell and Steven Anzovin, eds., *The Soviet Union* (New York: H. W. Wilson, 1988), p. 136.

17. Indeed, "in his closing speech to the first session of the new Congress of People's Deputies, Mikhail Gorbachev commented that no single issue had been so widely discussed by the Congress as that of interethnic relations." *Radio Liberty: Report on the USSR* 1:24 (June 16, 1989): 21.

18. Celestine Bohlen, "The Soviets and the Enmities Within," *The New York Times*, April 16, 1989, p. E1.

19. Description of the non-Russian nationalities may be found in some detail in Reshetar, *The Soviet Polity*, pp. 10–18.

20. Ulam, *The Russian Political System*, p. 69.

21. John N. Hazard, *The Soviet System of Government* (Chicago: University of Chicago Press, 1980), pp. 98–99.

22. Robert Sharlet, *The New Soviet Constitution of 1977* (Brunswick, Ohio: King's Court Communications, 1978) p. 97.

23. Felicity Barringer, "Soviets Draft Plans for Government Change," *The New York Times*, October 22, 1988, p. A3.

24. Adam Ulam's essay, "Looking at the Past: The Unraveling of the Soviet Union," *Current History* 91:567 (1992): 339–347, is very good in this regard.

25. "Commonwealth of Independent States Treaty Signed," *The New York Times*, December 23, 1991, p. A10. On the C.I.S., see James Riordan, *Russia and the Commonwealth of Independent States* (Morristown, N.J.: Silver Burdett Press, 1992), Ryszard Piotrowicz, "The CIS: Acronym as Anachronism," *Coexistence* 29:4 (1992): 377–388, and Alexei Pushkov, "The Commonwealth of Independent States: Still Alive Though Not Kicking," *NATO Review* 40:3 (1992): 13–18.

26. "Soviet Coup Started," *The Los Angeles Times*, August 30, 1991, p. A1. See also A.S. Durgo, ed., *Russia Changes: The Events of August 1991 and the Russian Constitution* (Commack, N.Y.: Nova Science Publishers, Inc., 1992), Richard Sakwa, "The Revolution of 1991 in Russia: Interpretations of the Moscow Coup," *Coexistence* 29:4 (1992): 335–376, Victoria Bonnell, Ann Cooper, and Gregory Freidin, eds., *Russia at the Barricades: Eyewitness Accounts of the August 1991 Coup* (Armonk, N.Y.: M.E. Sharpe, 1993).

27. "Gorbachev Resigns from C.P.S.U.," *The New York Times*, August 25, 1991, p. A1.

28. A very good collection on ideology in the Soviet Union is in Steven White and Alex Pravda, eds., *Ideology and Soviet Politics* (New York: St. Martin's Press, 1988).

29. Hugh Seton-Watson, "The Historical Roots," in Curtis Keeble, ed., *The Soviet State: The Domestic Roots of Soviet Foreign Policy* (Boulder, Colo.: Westview Press, 1985), p. 9.

30. Marxism is a highly elaborate theoretical framework, far beyond our level of analysis here in any detail. See Gustav Wetter, *Soviet Ideology* (New York: Praeger, 1962), for a very good introduction to the ideas of Marxism as interpreted in the Soviet Union.

31. Sam C. Sarkesian and James Buck, *Comparative Politics* (Sherman Oaks, Calif.: Alfred Publishing Co., 1979), pp. 97–98.

32. Medish, *The Soviet Union*, pp. 67–68.

33. Sarkesian and Buck, *Comparative Politics*, p. 101.

34. Aspaturian, "Soviet Politics," p. 356.

35. Ibid.

36. Ibid., p. 358.

37. Carter, *The Government of the Soviet Union*, p. 13. See also Donald R. Kelley, "Developments in Ideology," in Donald R. Kelley, ed., *Soviet Politics in the Brezhnev Era* (New York: Praeger, 1980), pp. 182–199.

38. See Steven Erlanger's article, "Now Yeltsin Must Govern: Struggle with Hard-Liners Over for Now, Talk Is of 'A Second Russian Revolution'," *The New York Times*, October 10, 1993, p. A1.

39. Ulam, *The Russian Political System*, p. 59.

40. Sharlet, *The New Soviet Constitution of 1977*, pp. 4–6.

41. "Resignation of President Mikhail Gorbachev," *Vital Speeches* 58:7 (January 15, 1992): 194.

42. Reshetar, *The Soviet Polity*, p. 172.

43. Aspaturian, "Soviet Politics," p. 401. See also Sharlet, *The New Soviet Constitution of 1977*, pp. 73–132.

44. Elizabeth Teague, "Gorbachev's First Four Years," *Radio Liberty: Report on the USSR* 1:9 (March 3, 1989): 3–4.

45. See Dawn Mann, "The Opening of the Congress," *Radio Liberty: Report on the USSR* 1:23 (June 9, 1989): 1–2.

46. Sharlet, *The New Soviet Constitution of 1977*, p. 108.

47. Paul Quinn-Judge, "Gorbachev Dominance Displayed in Parliament," *The Christian Science Monitor*, December 1, 1988, p. 1.

48. David Remnick, "New Soviet Congress Tackles Procedure," *The Washington Post*, May 27, 1989, p. A15.

49. Bill Keller, "A Guide to the Election Process," *The New York Times*, March 26, 1989, p. E3.

50. Dawn Mann and Julia Wishnevsky, "Composition of Congress of People's Deputies," *Radio Liberty, Report on the USSR* 1:18 (May 5, 1989): 6.

51. See *Radio Free Europe/Radio Liberty Research Report* 2:20 (May 14, 1992): 112–119.

52. Celestine Bohlen, "Yeltsin Orders Replacement of Legislatures of Regions," *The New York Times*, October 9, 1993, p. A9.

53. Sharlet, *The New Soviet Constitution of 1977*, p. 112.

54. D. Richard Little, *Governing the Soviet Union* (New York: Longman, 1989), p. 157.

55. Paul Quinn-Judge, "New Parliament: How Different?" *The Christian Science Monitor*, March 24, 1989, p. 2.

56. Vera Tolz, "The USSR This Week," *Radio Liberty: Report on the USSR* 1:1 (January 6, 1989): 26.

57. Teague, "Gorbachev's First Four Years," p. 4.

58. See Michael Parks, "Party Picks Gorbachev as Nominee for President at People's Congress," *The Los Angeles Times*, May 23, 1989, p. A8, and Michael Parks, "New Russian Congress Elects Gorbachev to Presidency," *The Los Angeles Times*, May 26, 1989, p. A1.

59. See "Yeltsin Elected President," *U.S. News and World Report* 110:21 (June 17, 1991): 36–38.

60. There was an official list of "public organizations" published that indicated how many "mandates" (deputies) each of the officially recognized "organizations" could have. Some examples from the list of thirty-six organizations: The Communist party received 100 seats, KOMSOMOL received 75, the All-Union Central Trade-Union Council received 100, the USSR Union of Architects received 10, the USSR Union of Designers received 5, the Union

of Red Cross and Red Crescent Societies received 10, the Soviet Peace Fund received 7, Public Sports Organizations received 3, and the All-Union Voluntary Temperance Society received 1. Dawn Mann, "Elections to the Congress of People's Deputies Nearly Over," *Radio Liberty: Report on the USSR* 1:15 (April 14, 1989): 8–9.

61. Victor Yasmann, "Quotas of Seats in Congress of People's Deputies for Public and Professional Organizations," *Radio Liberty Report on the USSR* 1:4 (January 27, 1989): 9.

62. Bill Keller, "Soviets Savor Vote in Freest Election Since '17 Revolution," *The New York Times*, March 27, 1989, p. A1.

63. "A Guide to the Election Process," *The New York Times*, March 26, 1989, p. E3.

64. See "Muscovite with Bravado," *The New York Times*, December 14, 1993, p. A1.

65. This section is based upon a more detailed discussion in *Radio Free Europe/Radio Liberty Research Report* 2:20 (May 14, 1992): 14.

66. Ibid.

67. Ronald Hill and Peter Frank, *The Soviet Communist Party* (London: Allen & Unwin, 1981), p. 1. See also Sharlet, *The New Soviet Constitution of 1977*, p. 12.

68. Hill and Frank, *The Soviet Communist Party*, p. 4.

69. See Rita DiLeo, "The Soviet Communist Party, 1988–1991: From Power to Ostracism," *Coexistence* 29:4 (1992): 321–334.

70. See the essay by Roy Medvedev, "After the Communist Collapse: New Political Tendencies in Russia," *Dissent* 39:4 (Fall 1992): 489–498. For other recent works on Russian parties, see Vladimir Pribylovskii, *Dictionary of Political Parties and Organizations in Russia* (Berkeley, Calif.: Center for Strategic and International Studies, 1992), or Alexander Dallin, ed., *Political Parties in Russia* (Los Angeles: University of California Press, 1993).

71. "The Political Spectrum," *Russian Life* (Spring 1993): 10.

72. Ibid., p. 11.

73. Much of the material in the next few paragraphs is based upon much more extensive analysis in Boris Meissner, "Implications of Leadership and Social Change for Soviet Policies," in Kinya Niiseki, ed., *The Soviet Union in Transition* (Boulder, Colo.: Westview Press, 1987), pp. 50–56.

74. Timothy Colton, *The Dilemma of Reform in the Soviet Union* (New York: Council on Foreign Relations, 1986), pp. 68–69.

75. Meissner, "Leadership," p. 52.

76. Herbert J. Ellison, "Gorbachev and Reform: An Introduction," in Lawrence W. Lerner and Donald W. Treadgold, eds., *Gorbachev and the Soviet Future* (Boulder, Colo.: Westview Press, 1988), p. 1.

77. There is an absolutely massive literature on Gorbachev, only a few years into his occupancy of the leadership position. See, among others, Ilya Zemtsov and John Farrar, *Gorbachev: The Man and the System* (New Brunswick, N.J.: Transaction Publishers, 1989), Seweryn Bialer, ed., *Politics, Society, and Nationality Inside Gorbachev's Russia* (Boulder, Colo.: Westview Press, 1989), or R.F. Miller, J.H. Miller, and T.H. Rigby, eds., *Gorbachev at the Helm: A New Era in Soviet Politics?* (London: Croom Helm, 1987).

78. Robert C. Tucker, *Political Culture and Leadership in Soviet Russia: From Lenin to Gorbachev* (New York: W.W. Norton, 1987), p. 148. For discussion of Gorbachev's policies, see Hiroshi Kimura, "'Gorbachevism'—Simply Old Wine in a New Bottle?" in Niiseki, ed., *The Soviet Union in Transition*, pp. 29–31. See also Archie Brown, "The Russian Political Scene: The Era of Gorbachev?" in Lerner and Treadgold, *Gorbachev and the Soviet Future*, p. 21, and T.H. Rigby, "The Gorbachev Era Launched," in Miller, Miller, and Rigby, *Gorbachev at the Helm*, pp. 235–236.

15

The Mexican Political System

Mexico represents many different—as well as interesting and important—variations from other nations we have already examined in this text. It is our first Latin American nation. It is the first nation included in the second part of this volume that is presidential, not parliamentary, in its basic political structures. It is also the first nation included in the second part of this text that belongs to the "developing," rather than "developed," group of nations as we described them in Chapter 3. These differences—among others—guarantee that in this chapter we shall note several differences in both political structure and political behavior from those we have observed in other chapters.

THE MEXICAN POLITICAL HERITAGE

Although Mexico has not had a revolution since early in this century (1910–1921), this fact alone should not be taken to suggest that there have been no issues of controversy in Mexican politics since that time, or that there has not been any significant political instability in domestic politics there. Such is not the case. Indeed:

> [T]he Mexican political culture is a fragmented one in which the violence of internecine struggle has appeared again and again in the absence of consensus on fundamentals as to the way government should operate—its relationship to citizens, their relationship to government, and the overall goals toward which policy should

be directed, that is, the basic purposes of government. All these matters have been much disputed, leaving in various sectors of society residues of commitment to values regarding proper uses of governmental power and reasons for existence of government which are at variance with major characteristics of the present system.[1]

Mexico has, even in very recent years, experienced some very tense moments in the political arena. In 1968 several hundred students were killed in Mexico City while demonstrating against the government; massive land expropriation was undertaken in 1976; and an economic crisis happened in 1982. Indeed, many claimed that the 1988 presidential election was "stolen" by the forces of President Carlos Salinas de Gortari when it was clear that the candidate of the Institutional Revolutionary party (PRI) might actually lose a presidential election for the first time in modern history.[2]

More recently, violence that broke out in the south of Mexico in January 1994 was of deep concern to the central government. The insurrection was more significant than any had thought likely to arise from concerns about social issues—specifically dealing with land reform—and President Salinas de Gortari had to send the army against the group of insurgents that called themselves "Zapatistas" when they seized their state's second largest city, San Cristobal de las Casas, and three other sizable towns.[3] President Salinas promised amnesty for the rebel leaders, and government action on the issues related to poverty and land reform, but all of Mexico was shaken that such a level of violence took place. We shall return to further discussion of some of these issues later in this chapter.

In the early 1970s Mexico seemed to have turned the corner and to have entered an era of rapid development and increasing prosperity. Mexico's oil industry was rapidly expanding and became the fourth largest in the world.[4] Today, however, primarily as a result of the decline in world oil prices, Mexico's economy is in a shambles, and domestic politics have reflected the economic tensions in society. As one scholar has noted, "Mexico's famed political stability has not been destroyed by the country's current economic crisis. But that stability can no longer be taken for granted."[5]

Mexico's political history falls into several broad eras.[6] Prior to the year 1521 Mexico was ruled by a series of Indian empires. Between 1521 and 1810, Mexico was under Spanish colonial power. Mexico first revolted against the Spanish on September 16, 1810; the struggle took until 1821 before a stable independent government was installed. Between 1821 and 1877 there were a number of emperors, dictators, and presidents in power, and Mexico lost Texas (1836) and later (from 1846 to 1848) what today are California, Nevada, Utah, most of Arizona and New Mexico, and parts of Wyoming and Colorado, to the United States.

In 1855 the Indian leader Benito Juárez began to introduce political reforms in Mexico, but his stay in power was short-lived; between 1861 and 1867 Mexico fell under European rule. In 1867 Juárez again took power as president, and he executed Maximilian of Austria, who had become emperor of Mexico in 1864.

From 1876 to 1911 Mexican politics were dominated by the long and dictatorial presidency of Porfirio Diaz (1876–1880 and 1884–1911). The Diaz regime led to the social revolution of 1910-1921,[7] and the revolution is regarded by most Mexicans as the beginning of modern Mexican politics.

> The commonly accepted and most convenient symbol for the beginning of Mexico's modernization process is the Mexican Revolution of 1910, although the pressures of both economic and political change had been building up for some time before. Since that date, considering the number and complexity of the problems involved, Mexico has progressed amazingly in its evolution toward modernity.[8]

POLITICAL STABILITY

Over the last several decades, Mexico's stability has been the single most visible characteristic separating it from other Latin American nations. It has continued to operate under the same general political structures for over fifty years, and it is the only major Latin American political system not to have had a military coup since the end of World War II. In another exception to the general Latin American pattern, every Mexican president elected since the presidential election of 1934 has served out his full six-year term and participated in a peaceful transition of power rather than having his power seized by a *coup* or *junta* of one kind or another.

"Stability" as we have used the term here does not mean that Mexican society has not suffered any social tensions, however.[9] In March of 1994 this level of instability included for the first time in modern history the assassination of a presidential candidate (a point which we shall further develop later in this chapter). In this context, "stability" is used in a more restrictive sense to indicate the continuity of major political structures. One important example of this relative stability is the relation between the Mexican military and the civilian government. Where military coups are common in Central and South America, such is not the case in Mexico.

> In the 1980s, the pace of military presence quickened as Mexico faced new experiences and challenges, many of them facilitating the political emergence of men in uniform. . . . Indications pointed to more influence in the future. Conversely, equally convincing indicators argued for the continued superiority of Mexico's civilian authority. In the final analysis, the emerging scenario may produce a change in the degree of military influence, but it is not destined to significantly alter ongoing civil dominance.[10]

Among the many very important aspects of Mexican culture that have contributed to this pattern of stability is the process of political socialization in Mexico. The socialization process is important to scholars "interested in learning about the complex influences affecting the builders of a nation emerging from a violent twentieth-century revolution."[11]

It has been suggested that Mexico's socialization patterns have been transformed in recent years, resulting in significant changes in the socialization process.[12] These changes include an expansion of mass education—today nearly one-third of school-aged Mexican children are in school. Until recently "the elite has generally been able to protect itself in privileged sanctuaries,"[13] but an increasingly educated mass population is beginning to want to change that relationship.[14] In the long run, "the positive impacts of educational changes on political stability are more direct and predictable than the negative consequences."[15] Student groups see increasing educational opportunities not only as avenues for advancement but also as means to further develop governmental expertise and legitimacy.

For those who were adolescents in the early years of the twentieth century, the revolution was an event of overwhelming significance; for the "postrevolutionary generation" the most important characteristic of the environment in which they were reared was "the prevalence of violence and instability."[16] Thus, a stable contemporary regime is an important factor in the lives of most Mexican political elites today.

THE MEXICAN CONSTITUTION

Mexico's contemporary political system was born in revolution. The new constitution, amending the constitution of 1857, was announced in February 1917 and has been the constitution of Mexico since then. Three characteristics reflected in the constitution can be identified as being typical of themes running throughout Mexican politics: representative democracy, presidential dictatorship, and corporatism.[17]

Mexico's leadership in 1917 believed in the virtues of classical liberalism and established a constitution based upon *representative democracy*. It guaranteed equal rights for all citizens; provided for separation of powers in the legislative, executive, and judicial branches of government; and established representative government based upon the ultimate sovereignty of the people. It also produced a centralized federal government that had significant political powers; for example, the constitution permitted the government to nationalize the petroleum industry in 1938 and allowed it to restrict foreign ownership of land in Mexico.[18]

While some aspects of the constitution clearly appear to be based upon fundamental principles of representative democracy, others are not. Indeed, some observers have suggested that Mexico today has virtually a *presidential dictatorship*. The president has the right to issue executive decrees, which have the force of law; despite the notion of "separation of powers," the president is permitted to introduce proposals in the legislature on his own authority (something that the American president, for example, is not permitted to do). This gives him a direct legislative power, in addition to his executive power. The president also has the power to appoint and remove judges, which gives him clear judicial power as well. Thus the president's power:

> is such that it absorbs and is complementary to the powers of the other two branches of government. In addition, the sovereignty of the states is found to be extremely limited by the Federation and subject to the discretionary powers of the president. The result is the establishment of a constitutional dictatorship of the presidential variety.[19]

The third theme of Mexican politics is that of *corporatism*, which we defined earlier in this book as implying a "close interaction of groups and government," where "organizations are integrated in the government decision-making process." As the government's financial planning has come under increased pressures in recent years, tensions have begun to develop in the government-business relationship, and the government has anxiously sought ways to smooth over the sources of tension. Indeed, one observer recently noted that "the period since 1982 has been characterized by the private sector's search for guarantees of its interests within the Mexican political system."[20]

Mexican labor law recognizes classes in society, and the Courts of Conciliation and Arbitration are given authority to resolve conflicts between labor and owners. There are many governmental boards and commissions that provide industrial and interest groups with a role in policy making.[21] These commissions can be referred to as "corporate" because through appointment of leaders of different social and economic groups to membership on the boards, these groups are, indeed, integrated in the government decision-making process.[22]

MEXICAN FEDERALISM

Mexico is a federal political system, including thirty-one states and one federal district, each of which has some policy jurisdiction. As we shall note shortly, however, the Mexican states do not have the degree of power in relation to Mexico City that the German Länder or the Canadian provinces have in relation to their respective national capitals, for example. Each state has its own constitution and has the right to pass its own laws, within some clearly defined parameters. Each state elects its own governor, who holds office for a term of six years. The state legislatures have three-year terms of office.[23]

It should be noted that despite the preeminence of the federal president in the political system, governors are significant political actors in Mexican politics, and charges of electoral fraud have been regularly levelled in gubernatorial elections as well as elections for the presidency and Congress. In the 1991 elections, which included elections for the Chamber of Deputies, half of the Senate, and governors of six of the thirty-one states, there were significant charges of fraud in two gubernatorial contests. In one, in the state of Guanajuanto, the candidate for the Institutional Revolutionary party (PRI) was initially declared the winner, despite charges of seventeen different types of irregularities in the voting.[24] Eventually, the victorious PRI candidate, Raymond Aquirre, announced that "he would not take up the governorship" because of public opinion in favor of the candidate of the National Action party (PAN), Vicente Fox. Many observers suggested that President Carlos Salinas de Gortari had "asked" Aguirre to step down in order to relieve pressure on the PRI and to give more legitimacy to PRI victories elsewhere.[25]

The overwhelming power of the president in the Mexican political system— a subject to which we shall return shortly—has done a great deal to weaken Mexican federalism. The president exercises control over state government, much as he exercises control over other branches of the federal government, through both constitutional and traditional justifications.

[T]he President is the ultimate power in state politics. He has authority to intervene to replace personnel of state governments with those who promise greater service in satisfying his policy needs. Under Article 76 of the Constitution, the President, acting through the Senate and the Ministry of Interior, is able to declare that the constitutional powers of a state have disappeared and appoint a provisional governor pending new state elections.[26]

Most frequently, however, the major source of presidential power, rather than coming exclusively from legal or constitutional structures, emanates from practical sources, such as the president's control (through legislation) of grant programs, federal financial aid to the states, and similar sources.

In recent years there has been an increasing policy of administrative decentralization in Mexico. This has been suggested by many to be especially necessary given recent "hyperurbanization" in Mexico—the rush of so many rural residents to the urban area surrounding Mexico City. The Mexican government has become aware that educational, cultural, and health resources simply must be made available far more broadly geographically in contemporary Mexico; if not, some experts say, the rush to move to the urban areas will continue.[27]

Mexico's approach to federalism is, as we noted, far more centralized than that which we observed in Germany or Canada. Indeed, "the central government bureaucracy, dominated by the presidency, is the main source of public policy."[28] Thus, apart from the observation that states and state governments exist, our attention can remained focused on the *national* level of government if we are seeking an understanding of how political institutions and political behavior operate in Mexico.

THE PRESIDENCY

Simón Bolivar (1783–1830), a South American revolutionary leader, once observed that the new republics of the Americas needed kings who could be referred to as presidents, and added that, in Mexico at least, these kings were kings for six-year periods.[29] The Mexican president is elected by direct popular vote in elections and can hold office for a single six-year term, after which time the individual can never be reelected. He must be at least 35 years of age, and must be a native-born Mexican who is the son of native-born Mexicans.[30] He cannot be a clergyman of a religious group. If he has been in either the military or the cabinet (which all recent presidents have been), he must have retired from that position at least six months prior to the election. The president is, very clearly, the single most powerful individual in Mexican politics.[31]

Power

Much of the president's power comes from his constitutional role in government, and students of Mexican politics have suggested that the president "encounters no effective restraint *within* government."[32] In that role he has very wide power to appoint and remove government officials (much broader fiscal powers than, say, the American president), the capacity to initiate and veto legislation, and the power to control the military. (Since the revolution, the military has been reorganized, and today it is restricted in its power to influence policy.)[33] Although legislators in Mexico have the power to introduce legislation, legislation is overwhelmingly introduced by the president.

> In addition to the President's vast field of action with regard to the initiation of legislation and his work to secure its passage, there is also a presidential veto power which never comes into play in practice because the legislature does not amend bills without prior consultation with the executive, thus eliminating the necessity of employing a veto. The veto remains, however, as a legal means at his disposal.[34]

Nomination and Selection

The presidential election of 1988 was the first presidential election in modern Mexican history in which the outcome was truly in doubt, although by the time the votes were all counted (and, opposition leaders charged, rigged) the PRI candidate again won.[35] This fact notwithstanding, however, the modern practice of presidential selection in Mexico has more often focused upon *intra*party competition (within the framework of the PRI itself) than upon *inter*party competition (with other political parties).

The usual practice within the PRI in recent presidential elections has been to have the incumbent president hand-pick his successor, invariably from among those individuals who have been active in his cabinet. As noted above, the constitution requires that a cabinet officer seeking the presidency must resign from office at least six months before the presidential elections, but this has not provided any difficulties for recent candidates. There are some personal and socioeconomic characteristics that are apparently valued by presidents when selecting their successors, including physical appearance, a neutral position in relation to organized religion, a middle-class background, a large state as place of origin, and a wife who "has a moderate interest in public affairs."[36] (For a list of recent presidents of Mexico, see Table 15.1.)

When an incumbent president nears the final year of his six-year term of office, pressures begin to be exerted on him to "name" his successor. Incumbents have tried to resist this pressure for as long as possible, however, because once an incumbent names the "heir apparent," he loses much of his own political power and will

TABLE 15.1
Some Recent Mexican Presidents

Gustavo Diaz Ordaz	1964–1970
Luis Echeverria Alvarez	1970–1976
José Lopez Portillo	1976–1982
Miguel de la Madrid Hurtado	1982–1988
Carlos Salinas de Gortari	1988–1994

not be able to accomplish as much as he previously could.[37] One scholar, in fact, has identified nine different stages in the process of the selection of a new president:

1. President consults with advisors and colleagues as to acceptability of possible nominees.
2. The President announces his choice.
3. Power-seekers and political leaders in the PRI praise the candidate-designate.
4. Candidate is officially nominated at the PRI rally.
5. The campaign takes place.
6. The election takes place.
7. The winning candidate officially accepts the election results.
8. The new president selects his advisors.
9. The new president selects an advantageous time to announce his appointments.[38]

Once the outgoing president "nominates" his successor—who in recent elections had been a member of the cabinet and thus immediately resigned from the cabinet—the nominee of the PRI is expected to travel all over the country, campaigning for office and meeting leaders of interest groups, local leaders, business leaders, community politicians, and so on. In fact, he is improving his knowledge of local problems at the same time that he is increasing his own visibility in the eyes of the electorate. Past experience has shown that even the most isolated of Mexican villages will be visited—if not by the candidate himself then by one of his campaign workers—over the course of the campaign. Indeed it was during a "fact-finding" visit to Tijuana that Luis Donaldo Colosio Murrieta, the hand-picked successor to President Carlos Salinas de Gortari was assassinated in March of 1994. Colosio was travelling around Mexico, meeting people, and hearing their comments, when he was killed, leaving a vacuum in the top Mexican leadership and requiring the selection of a new designated leader of the P.R.I. and presumptive winner of the presidential election.

Some have questioned why Mexico should even go through this ritual if the results of the election are certain. There are at least two reasons why the national campaign is useful, even if it contains no surprises. First, the act of campaigning itself helps to create support for the regime, and thereby affords the government greater legitimacy than it might otherwise have without a campaign. Second, the presidential campaign can make a significant difference to candidates for the Senate and the Chamber of Deputies who are running for office, either on the same side as the presidential candidate or on an opposition ticket.

THE CONGRESS

The Mexican Congress is bicameral, and consists of a Chamber of Deputies and a Senate. The Congress is very clearly inferior to the president in the structures of governmental power, and its consent to presidential legislative proposals can be counted upon.

As long as the official party carries out its functions of liaison and political communication effectively, and as long as the President successfully balances interest conflicts with regard to special goals of the various organizations, there is every reason to expect that legal approval for the acts of the President can be obtained from the Congress without question.[39]

In fact, recent scholarship has indicated that presidential proposals have been approved unanimously 80 to 95 percent of the time in recent years, and are normally opposed by less than 5 percent of the members of the Congress.[40]

The Senate

Senators are elected for six-year terms, with two senators elected from each of the thirty-one states and two elected from the federal district. The Senate elected in the elections of July 7, 1988, was made up of sixty senators of the PRI and four senators of the National Democratic Front (later known as the PRD). In the off-year elections of 1991, in which thirty-two seats of the Senate were up for election, the PAN candidate for Senate from Baja California was elected—the first PAN Senate victory in its forty-eight-year history; all of the other thirty-one races were won by PRI candidates.[41] (See Table 15.2.) The Senate today is "frankly regarded in Mexico as a rubber stamp for presidential policy."[42] Senators are elected by direct popular vote, with one-half of the Senate being elected every three years.

The Chamber of Deputies

The 500 deputies are elected for three-year terms according to a system of single-member-district voting and "partial proportional representation," under which 200 of the 500 seats in the Chamber are elected by proportional representation, while the other 300 seats are elected from single-member districts.

The 300 single-member-district seats are based upon population, but the constitution guarantees each state at least two deputies. Although each state's *number* of seats is based upon the state's total population as a share of the national population, there is no constitutional provision that forces the states to divide their quota of seats into equally populated districts. Indeed, as Table 15.3 shows, there was quite

TABLE 15.2
Mexican Senate Membership, 1991

Party	Senators Elected in 1988	Senators Elected in 1991	Total
National Action Party (PAN)	—	1	1
Institutional Revolutionary Party (PRI)	30	31	61
Party of the Democratic Revolution (PRD)*	2	—	2
Total	32	32	64

* In 1988, the PRD was known as the National Democratic Front.

Source: Data provided by the Embassy of Mexico, Washington, D.C., November 22, 1993.

TABLE 15.3
Population of Mexican Electoral Districts, 1985

Number of Voters in District	Number of Districts
Over 250,000	1
200,000–249,999	3
150,000–199,999	33
100,000–149,999	186
50,000–99,999	74
Under 50,000	3
Total	300

Source: John Bailey, *Governing Mexico: The Statecraft of Crisis Management* (New York: St. Martin's Press, 1988), p. 151.

a significant variation in population among the 300 electoral districts in the federal election of 1985.

Comprehensive electoral reform was introduced in 1977; it raised the number of deputies from about 200 (the exact number depended upon how many minority party deputies were elected)[43] to 400, and this reform became effective with the 1979–1980 legislative session. For the 1988 election the total number of seats was raised to 500; the number of seats remained 500 for the 1991 election. Of these seats, 300 were elected by a single-member-district, majority-vote system, with those districts based upon population as in electoral systems we have seen in Britain, Canada, or Germany. (See Table 15.4).

Mexico's electoral system strengthens the voice of the opposition parties in the Chamber of Deputies. Without a specific structure saving seats for minority parties, the PRI would hold 96 percent of the seats in the Chamber of Deputies and the PAN the remaining 4 percent. One hundred fifty of the 500 seats in the Chamber are "reserved" for minority parties and are divided among the states to be distributed by a complex proportional representation system.

If a party wins fewer than sixty of the district-based seats, and if that party has entered candidates in at least one-third of the 300 district-based electoral contests throughout the entire nation, then it is entitled to a share (determined by a specific formula, provided that the party received at least 1.5 percent of the total vote) of the 200 at-large proportional seats; all of the opposition parties together are guaranteed at least 150 of these 200 at-large proportional seats.

Thus, 30 percent of the seats in the Chamber of Deputies are guaranteed to opposition parties, *as well as* those seats they can win in the 300 district-based electoral races. This means that although the power of the Chamber of Deputies is limited, the opposition is *guaranteed* a presence there.[44] Several smaller parties have benefited from the at-large proportional seats.[45]

THE BUREAUCRACY

By the mid-1970s, the Mexican federal public sector included 1,075 agencies with nearly 3.4 million employees—nearly 17 percent of the country's total work force.[46]

TABLE 15.4

The 1991 Election for the Mexican Chamber of Deputies

	Percent of Votes	Number of Seats by Direct Election	Number of Seats by Proportional Allotment	Total Number of Seats (Percent)
National Action Party (PAN)	17.7%	10	79	89 (17.8%)
Institutional Revolutionary Party (PRI)	61.4	290	30	320 (64.0)
Popular Socialist Party (PPS)	1.8	0	12	12 (2.4)
Party of the Democratic Revolution (PRD)	8.3	0	41	41 (8.2)
Cardenista Front for National Renewal (PFCRN)	4.4	0	23	23 (4.6)
True Party for the Mexican Revolution (PARM)	2.1	0	15	15 (3.0)
Mexican Democratic Party (PDM)	1.1	0	0	0
Revolutionary Workers' Party (PRT)	0.6	0	0	0
Mexican Ecological Party (PEM)	1.4	0	0	0
Labor Party (PT)	1.1	0	0	0
Total	99.9%*	300	200	500 (100%)

* Does not add to 100% because of rounding.

Source: Data provided by the Embassy of Mexico, Washington, D.C., November 22, 1993.

The administration of President de la Madrid sought to decentralize some of this bureaucracy, emphasizing regional programs and the increased participation of state and local governments in programs, especially those dealing with health care and education.[47]

We noted in Chapter 3 that there are many quasi-governmental organizations in Mexico that complement the federal and state governments' efforts to enact policy. A recent study listed 123 decentralized agencies, 292 public enterprises, 187 commissions, and 160 development trusts, as well as 18 regular ministries and departments of state making up the federal bureaucratic infrastructure.[48] A critic of the degree of direct government involvement in private business recently wrote that:

> The State participates in, among other things, six firms which manufacture stoves, refrigerators, and other domestic appliances, seven which manufacture cardboard boxes, paper bags, announcement cards, and paper forms; it manufactures, sells, and distributes desk supplies; it owns a soft drink bottling plant, a dish factory, a bicycle manufacturing plant, six textile mills, an airline, fifteen holding companies whose social objectives range from the administration of buildings to the construction of hotels, buildings, homes, warehouses, factories, developments, and urban

housing units; it runs a factory which produces balanced animal feed, a television channel, eighteen firms dedicated to theater administration, a casino, three wood-working shops, a firm which makes synthetic rubber, another which makes door-locks, and a luxury housing development in the Federal District.[49]

As we shall discuss below, one political party—the Institutional Revolutionary party (PRI)—dominates federal politics, and in a similar way it dominates bureaucratic politics as well. Although the federal government has sought to decentralize the bureaucracy somewhat in recent years, it is still the case that massive bureaucracy affects the ability of the central government to enact policy, especially in central industrial areas such as oil, petroleum exploration and distribution (PEMEX), steel (SIDERMEX), fertilizers (FERTIMEX), and food purchasing, processing, and distribution (CONASUPO).[50]

POLITICAL PARTIES AND ELECTIONS

A strong relationship exists between the dominant political party and the state in Mexico, but there remains a clear difference between the two. The primary function of the dominant party is to mobilize support and to legitimize the state. "That is, the party's single most important task is to legitimize and to provide an ideological base of support for the state rather than to press the demands of its formal constituency on the state."[51]

Although Mexico is often thought of as a one-party nation because of the history of the dominance of the PRI, such is not literally the case; a number of opposition parties operate in the Mexican political arena. Although only three parties won seats to the Chamber of Deputies in 1988, the National Democratic Front took the place of seven smaller parties in the 1985 Congress.[52] There are many opposition groups in society, made up of peasants, students,[53] and workers.[54]

In the state and local elections of 1983 the major opposition party, the National Action party (PAN), won in a record number of state capitals and major cities. This led many to ask what the future held for the dominant party, namely the PRI. To a large degree the problems of the PRI lie in its clear identification with the Mexican status quo, the party that has been in power for decades in Mexican politics; recent leaders have called for significant reform in the PRI.[55] Although opposition parties have been able to win occasional gubernatorial and Senate races in recent years, the PRI is clearly the dominant party in Mexico today.

The PRI has been the major party in Mexico for over fifty years.[56] It is so well entrenched and central to the operation of the government that it "serves as a subordinate extension of the presidency and central government bureaucracy."[57] The PRI has three major factions—an agrarian faction, a labor faction, and a "popular" faction—and is governed by a national party congress called the National Assembly. The National Assembly is directed by the National Executive Committee, which is selected from among members of the Assembly. Each of the three factions of the PRI vies for power on the Executive Committee, and although these three factions are ostensibly all on the same side in an election, there is often great competition between and among them for formal party leadership positions.

The PRI continues to play a very important role in Mexican politics. It provides a "channel of information to the presidency that complements those of the military and civilian bureaucracies"; it organizes political support for presidential policies; it mobilizes interest groups; it "contributes to socialization of both elite and popular strata"; it controls thousands of elective and appointive jobs across the nation and helps to recruit candidates for those positions; it is important in the organization of and participation in elections; and finally, it is crucial in the succession process of the presidency.[58] The PRI has been referred to as a "semi-authoritarian" organization; that is, one that "enjoys genuine popular support, even though it resorts to electoral fraud when such is deemed required."[59]

The topic of fraud is one that is frequently associated with the PRI and elections at all levels—presidential, congressional, and state.[60] The clear perception—despite denials from PRI officials—is that the PRI is perfectly willing to do whatever it takes to win elections, even if that means vote fraud. As noted above, in the 1993 gubernatorial elections in the state of Guanajuanto, independent Mexican observers

> said they had detected 17 types of irregularities in the voting. They included stuffing or stealing of ballot boxes, police intimidation at polling places, and multiple voting by PRI supporters.[61]

While federal electoral officials initially called these charges "highly exaggerated," within a two-week period the PRI victor had announced that he would not assume the governorship because of political pressure being exerted by an outraged public.

The National Democratic Front (FDN) was a new competing party in the 1988 election. Its roots, however, were not new, but included the Mexican Communist party (PCM),[62] which changed its name to the Unified Socialist Party of Mexico (PSUM) in 1981 when it joined with several smaller parties in a left-of-center coalition. The PSUM was able to provide the PRI with some serious competition at the state level of politics, although it was not very effective in federal elections until 1988.[63] The FDN is regarded by many as not a true party, but rather an electoral coalition whose roots include not only the Communist PCM or PSUM but also a healthy non-Communist tradition. The FDN competed as the PRD, the Party of the Democratic Revolution, in 1991.

The major right-of-center parties include the Mexican Democratic party (PDM) and the National Action party (PAN). Both parties have been more successful in elections since reforms in 1977 created at-large proportional representation in the Chamber of Deputies, and they have offered the PRI some serious competition at the state level of politics. The PDM has been considered "the most conservative party with registration in Mexico,"[64] and has its strongest political support in the countryside.

The PAN is considered the major party of the "political right" in Mexico today.[65] The major difference between the PAN and the PRI included the PAN's greater criticism of the United States, and the PAN's desire to "restore to the church the rights of religious education and political participation which were taken away from it by the Constitution of 1917."[66]

The role of opposition parties has increased in Mexico over time. In recent years:

> Mexico's leadership tinkered with the electoral process as a way of encouraging political opposition and legitimizing their own rule. Their adjustments to the electoral process came about . . . because some government leaders believed the time had arrived for a more pluralistic system.[67]

These changes allowed more members of the opposition parties to win election to the Chamber of Deputies, the lower branch of the legislature, which in Mexico is not a very powerful check on the president's power. Thus, the president and the PRI were able to increase their perceived legitimacy by encouraging the opposition parties, without giving up any real political power at all.[68]

Even though the PRI has won nearly every federal election held since 1929—including all presidential races, all state gubernatorial races, and virtually all Senate races—the Mexican electoral arena contains real electoral competition.[69] As we have just indicated, there *are* opposition parties in Mexican politics, and these parties take their roles seriously.[70] Some recent observers have noted that elections in Mexico are not meaningless and have suggested that "the single-party nature of the Mexican regime is passing."[71] The reforms of 1977 and 1988, alluded to earlier, were designed to increase political participation and to stimulate electoral competition. By one measure the reforms were effective; since they were enacted, in fact, opposition to the PRI has increased.

> However, the PRI has mobilized even greater numbers of voters to support the continued rule of the current ruling elite and has shown an ability to still use its old techniques of electoral fraud if necessary to win an important race. Thus, even though the opposition's voice has strengthened, the regime's base has been refortified, at least for now.[72]

POLITICAL DEVELOPMENT AND ECONOMICS

Two distinct problem areas confront the Mexican government today. Both of these problems, it can be asserted, are a function of the economic crisis primarily brought about by the fall of the price of oil.[73] One of these concerns urban migration, and the unique set of problems facing Mexico City today. The massive pattern of migration from rural Mexico to the capital city is putting intolerable demands upon the infrastructure of Mexico City and has already had significant effects upon the quality of life there, something to which we shall return momentarily. The second problem has an international dimension, and concerns the implications of the massive (and illegal) flow of Mexican population across its northern border with the United States.

Mexico City has suffered the same problems of urban migration as have the major cities of many developing nations. The crises of poverty and high unemployment often serve to push significant populations from rural areas to the urban capital area in search of jobs and better living conditions. To show the magnitude of this population movement to urban areas, in 1910, 28.7 percent of Mexico's population lived in an urban setting. This figure had increased to 33.5 percent by 1930, 42.6 percent by 1950, 58.6 percent by 1970, and was estimated to be over 65 percent in 1980.[74] According to a 1993 World Bank study, this figure had increased to 73 percent by 1991; 45 percent of Mexico's total population lived in cities of 1 million or more population.[75] Ironically, the migrants usually find neither jobs nor better living conditions; rather, these migrations contribute to greater unemployment and worse living conditions.

> Mexico City has grown faster, and with less coordinated planning, than any other city in the world. After World War II, its population stood at two million; by 1960 it had climbed to five million; and by 1970, nine million. Today [1986] its population exceeds seventeen million, making it the world's second largest city, after Tokyo.[76]

Mexico City represents the worst of this general problem. In 1990, 25 percent of Mexico's entire population lived in Mexico City.[77] Mexico City is "an environmental disaster" in a variety of respects. Over 2 million of its residents have no running water, sometimes living more than three city blocks from the nearest faucet. Over 3 million of its inhabitants have no sewage facilities. The city produces over 14,000 tons of garbage *every day*, but can process only 8,000 tons. Breathing the polluted air of Mexico City (caused by 3 million cars, 7,000 buses, and over 13,000 factories) has been likened to smoking two packs of cigarettes a day, and the combination of chemical and biological poisons has been estimated to kill over 30,000 children annually through respiratory and gastrointestinal disease. "Overall," one study has noted, "pollution may account for the deaths of nearly 100,000 people a year."[78]

It is this type of situation that has contributed to the desire of many Mexicans to leave their homeland and head north to a country where, they have heard, there are jobs for those who want them and a better life for those who are willing to work for it. About half of Mexico's population of 70 million people are under 21 years of age and have "little or no chance for employment."[79] The Mexican-American border is nearly 2,000 miles long, and issues such as smuggling, illegal immigration,[80] and the border's ecology (including air and water pollution) have proven to be a source of irritation in Mexican-American relations.[81]

The North American Free Trade Agreement (NAFTA), ratified in November 1993, was designed to do something about the border problem. NAFTA, negotiated by the governments of Mexico, the United States, and Canada, was designed to lower tariffs among the three nations and to generally improve trade opportunities among the three North American neighbors. One result of NAFTA, it was argued, would be increased job opportunities in Mexico, with higher salaries.

American critics of NAFTA argued that while it might benefit Mexico, it would result in a significant loss of American jobs. They also held that it would have a generally negative effect upon the continental environment because Mexican environmental standards were much lower than American standards. Businesses, they said, would move from the United States to Mexico to find cheaper labor and less stringent environmental regulations.

Supporters of NAFTA countered that Mexico had promised to strengthen its environmental regulations so that there would be no "belt" of environmental disasters along the Mexican-American border. They also argued that while some U.S. jobs might be lost to Mexicans, the corresponding increase in U.S. jobs because of the expanded market open to Americans would more than make up for the loss.

It will be several years before the net effects of NAFTA are clear. In the meantime, leaders on both sides of the Mexican-American border hope that the illegal population flow will decrease as a result of NAFTA and the economic growth that (it is hoped) will develop on the Mexican side of the border.

Both of these problems were to some degree a function of Mexican economic stagnation. As one scholar noted, "the causes of Mexico's deepest crisis in modern times are clearly economic."[82] The fall in the price of oil, which contributed to and exacerbated an extremely low economic growth rate (0.2 percent) and a massive foreign debt problem (over $100 billion),[83] and an inflation rate of almost 100 percent[84] (made even worse by natural disasters such as an earthquake in September 1985), have left Mexico reeling and have left Mexicans unsure of the future of their nation.

Mexico's problems became really serious (as we suggested in Chapter 3 could be the case in countries that base their economic development upon a single "crop") as a result of the fall in the world price of oil.[85] Mexico did a great deal of borrowing through the late 1970s to finance its economic growth, agreeing to pay as much as a 17 percent interest rate on its loans because it was counting upon a continuation of the very high price of oil. The policy seemed reasonable, given the vast expansion of the Mexican petroleum industry; exports of 200,000 barrels daily in 1977 expanding to 1.5 million barrels in 1982. Because the Mexican government built its budgets on an anticipated oil price of nearly $36 per barrel, when oil fell to nearly $30 a barrel the country came under tremendous financial stress. It failed to make scheduled payments on its loans in 1982.[86] As the price of oil has fallen lower, to below $20 a barrel today, Mexico's situation has appeared increasingly grim.[87]

The 1993 World Bank report indicated that while Mexico's external debt was $57.4 billion in 1980, by 1991 it had increased to $101.7 billion. This 1991 debt was equal to 36.9 percent of Mexico's GNP, a staggering debt burden.[88]

The prognosis for the near future for Mexico—as for many developing nations[89]—does not look good. The issues of poverty, equity, and growth have taken on a very politicized character in Mexico,[90] which today is "a country of poor people living in the midst of an elite becoming rich at their expense. Wherever one turns, there is evidence of official policies and institutions that are heightening the differences among classes." The richest 5 percent of families in 1986 had an average income thirty-six times greater than that of the poorest 10 percent of families; the poorest half of the population receives less than 20 percent of total personal income, while the richest 10 percent of the population receives almost half of Mexico's total income.[91] The 1993 World Bank study indicated that the richest 20 percent of the

Mexican population accounted for 56 percent of all Mexican income or consumption.[92]

> Everywhere urban Mexicans feel they are being strangled as the quality of life worsens. They are extorted by urban transit systems and by the police, medical care is either inadequate or nonexistent, in many proletarian suburbs the running water works only from one to three o'clock in the morning while in the wealthy communities like Pedregal in Mexico City it runs all the time.[93]

The combination of a continued high birth rate, the burden of its external debts, and a continuation of a low world price for oil will not contribute to Mexico rapidly "turning its economy around." In fact, "the country which for so long enjoyed life in the fast lane will have to throttle back its expectations and accustom itself to live in the slow lane instead."[94] Questions related to human survival, to having enough to eat, and to the government's role in improving the quality of life for most Mexicans will not go away in the near future, and those questions will affect the future of Mexican politics.[95]

REVOLUTION AND INSTITUTIONALIZATION

We have seen—albeit briefly—in this chapter that Mexico provides us with the opportunity to view a different type of political system from others we have met in this volume, in many respects a significantly different system. The state of Mexico was born in revolution and social upheaval, and for nearly seventy years it has been endeavoring to establish the kinds of social and political institutions that would ensure domestic stability and social harmony.

To a substantial degree, especially if we compare Mexico with her neighbors to the south, the endeavors have been successful if for no other reason than that Mexico has not experienced the regular military *coups d'état* experienced so often by so many Latin American nations. Indeed, as we noted earlier, there has been no revolution in Mexico since the 1910–1921 social dislocation.

We must be less laudatory in other respects, however. The Mexican political system apparently borders on being an authoritarian one, whether or not we say that the president is an "elective king." Clearly the president dominates the political landscape, essentially pre-empting the power of the judicial and the legislative branches of government. This power is far greater than that given the British prime minister through the convention of party discipline. The vast number of allegations of electoral corruption and voter fraud seem to indicate that although all presidential transitions for the last fifty years have been peaceful ones, there is no fundamental commitment on the part of political elites to accept the will of the majority.

Moreover, Mexico is still suffering many of the problems faced by other nations in the developing world. Economic problems, distributional problems, and technological problems have meant that the general quality of life in Mexico has not been able to improve as much as Mexico's leaders might have liked. Some of these problems, such as the drop in the price of oil, are beyond the ability of the Mexican government to control. Other problems, such as the birth rate or the lack of an effective distribution of health and education resources, can be influenced by government policy, but only very slowly. Still other problems, such as shortcomings of governmental infrastructure or voter fraud or corruption in government, can be dealt with more quickly, but the government has yet to do so.

Some have argued that it is *the system itself* that is the real problem in Mexico. The relative stability of Mexico until recent times was based upon real reforms (particularly reforms in land ownership) that occurred as a result of the revolution, and that were considered during the period from 1934 to 1940 when Lázaro Cárdenas was president. The PRI, it has been argued, dominated the Mexican political arena for so long precisely because it embodied those reforms. As those reforms have begun to become inadequate in recent years, problems of stability (and stagnation and corruption) have resulted.[96]

The PRI system, like many "corporatist" systems of Latin America, generates greater inequalities as a major output of the system itself. The system is simply not geared to produce more equitable outcomes, nor to produce a more equal and just society. If the system is unable to produce greater equity, it is argued, it is because of the system itself, not solely because of the lack of resources in the society or the general level of development of Mexico.[97]

Notes

1. L. Vincent Padgett, *The Mexican Political System* (Boston: Houghton Mifflin, 1976), p. 10.

2. There was very widespread coverage of these charges in the foreign press. See, to take just a few examples, Marjorie Miller, "Indications of Mexico Election Fraud Mount," *The Los Angeles Times*, July 15, 1988, p. 10, Larry Rohter, "Mexicans Protest Delay in Results of the Elections," *The New York Times*, July 11, 1988, p. A1, Alan Riding, "'Alchemy' Taints Voting in Mexico's Countryside," *The New York Times*, July 14, 1988, p. A1, or Larry Rohter, "Mexican Opposition Parties Move to Overturn Vote Tally," *The New York Times*, August 15, 1988, p. A5.

3. See Tim Golden, "In Remote Mexican Village, Roots of Rebellion Are Bared," *The New York Times*, January 17, 1994, p. A1.

4. Robert Long, "Preface," in Robert E. Long, ed., *Mexico* (New York: H.W. Wilson, 1986), p. 5.

5. Jorge Castaneda, "Mexico at the Brink," *Foreign Affairs* 64 (1985–1986): 287.

6. A good historical overview can be found in Kenneth Johnson, *Mexican Democracy: A Critical View* (New York: Praeger, 1984). Chap. 2 is titled "The Aztec Legacy and Independence," and chap. 3 is titled "Emerging Nationhood and the Great Revolution." A different—class-oriented—approach is offered by James D. Cockcroft, *Mexico: Class Formation, Capital Accumulation, and the State* (New York: Monthly Review Press, 1983). A very good general history is that of Michael Meyer and William Sherman, *The Course of Mexican History* (New York: Oxford University Press, 1987).

7. A good discussion of the revolution can be found in Judith Adler Hellman, *Mexico in Crisis* (New York: Holmes and Meier, 1983), pp. 3–31.

8. Robert E. Scott, "Mexico: The Established Revolution," in Lucian W. Pye and Sidney Verba, eds., *Political Culture and Political Development* (Princeton, N.J.: Princeton University Press, 1965), p. 332. A very good description of the "modern" period can be found in Juan Felipe Leal, "The Mexican State, 1915–1973: A Historical Interpretation," in Nora Hamilton and Timothy F. Harding, eds., *Modern Mexico: State, Economy, and Social Conflict* (Beverly Hills, Calif.: Sage Publications, 1986), pp. 21–42.

9. A good discussion of this use of the term "stability" can be found in Daniel Levy and Gabriel Szekely, *Mexico: Paradoxes of Stability and Change*, 2nd ed. (Boulder, Colo.: Westview, 1987), Johnson, *Mexican Democracy*, and Miguel Centano, *Democracy Within Reason: Technocratic Revolution in Mexico* (University Park, Pa.: Pennsylvania State University Press, 1994).

10. Edward J. Williams, "The Evolution of the Mexican Military and Its Implications for Civil-Military Relations," in Roderic Camp, *Mexico's Political Stability: The Next Five Years* (Boulder, Colo.: Westview Press, 1986), p. 143. For more on this subject, see David Ronfeldt, ed., *The Modern Mexican Military: A Reassessment* (La Jolla: Center for U.S.-Mexican Studies, University of California, San Diego, 1984).

11. Roderic Camp, *The Making of a Government: Political Leaders in Modern Mexico* (Tucson: University of Arizona Press, 1984), p. 1.

12. Daniel C. Levy, "The Political Consequences of Changing Socialization Patterns," in Camp, *Mexico's Political Stability*, p. 19.

13. Levy, "Political Consequences," p. 21.

14. This theme is discussed in Joe Foweraker and Ann Craig, eds., *Popular Movements and Political Change in Mexico* (Boulder, Colo.: Lynne Rienner, 1990).

15. Levy, "Political Consequences," p. 25.

16. Camp, *The Making of a Government*, pp. 39–40. Camp discusses a wide range of variables significant in the process of political socialization in Mexico, including the role of parents, friends, and events as socializers; the social influence of the school environment; the impact of books and teachers; and the value systems of contemporary Mexican leaders.

17. Much of the discussion in the few paragraphs that follow is derived from much more extensive discussion in Leal, "The Mexican State," pp. 29–32.

18. John Bailey, "The Impact of Major Groups on Policy-Making Trends in Government-Business Relations in Mexico," in Camp, *Mexico's Political Stability*, p. 125.

19. Leal, "The Mexican State," p. 30.

20. John Bailey, *Governing Mexico: The Statecraft of Crisis Management* (New York: St. Martin's Press, 1988), p. 139.

21. See Daniel Morales-Gomez and Carlos Torres, *The State, Corporatist Politics, and Educational Policy Making in Mexico* (Westport, Conn.: Greenwood Press, 1990).

22. See Dan La Botz, *The Crisis of Mexican Labor* (Westport, Conn.: Greenwood Press, 1988).

23. See Nettie Benson, *The Provincial Deputation in Mexico: Harbinger of Provincial Autonomy, Independence, and Federalism* (Austin: University of Texas Press, 1992).

24. See *Facts on File* 51:2648 (August 22, 1991): 636.

25. *Facts on File* 51:2650 (September 5, 1991): 667.

26. Padgett, *The Mexican Political System*, p. 204.

27. William Glade, "Distributional and Sectoral Problems in the New Economic Policy," in Camp, *Mexico's Political Stability*, p. 95.

28. Bailey, "The Impact of Major Groups," p. 126.

29. Johnson, *Mexican Democracy*, p. 116.

30. The use of "he" here is intentional: The constitution requires that the individual chosen as president of Mexico must be male.

31. Recent works on the Mexican presidency include George Philip, *The Presidency in Mexican Politics* (New York: St. Martin's Press, 1991), and Samuel Schmidt, *The Deterioration of the Mexican Presidency: The Years of Luis Echeverria* (Tucson: University of Arizona Press, 1991).

32. Bailey, *Governing Mexico*, p. 32. Emphasis his.

33. Susan Eckstein, *The Impact of Revolution: A Comparative Analysis of Mexico and Bolivia* (Beverly Hills, Calif.: Sage Publications, 1976), p. 25.

34. Padgett, *The Mexican Political System*, p. 199.

35. Again, in addition to sources cited above, examples of these articles covering the presidential and congressional elections would include Alan Riding, "When the Bubble Burst for the Mexican Rulers," *The New York Times*, July 9, 1988, p. A5, Larry Rohter, "Electoral Panel Prolongs Delay in Mexico Tally," *The New York Times*, July 9, 1988, p. A1, and Larry Rohter, "Still Setback Seen for Ruling Party in Mexican Voting," *The New York Times*, July 8,

1988, p. A1. A good general study is that by Edgar Butler and Jorge Bustamante, eds., *Succesion Presidencial: The Nineteen Eighty-Eight Mexican Presidential Election* (Boulder, Colo.: Westview Press, 1990).

36. Padgett, *The Mexican Political System*, pp. 188–189.

37. Johnson, *Mexican Democracy*, pp. 123–124.

38. Frank Brandenburg, *The Making of Modern Mexico* (Englewood Cliffs, N.J.: Prentice Hall, 1964), pp. 145–150.

39. Padgett, *The Mexican Political System*, p. 200.

40. Merilee Serrill Grindle, *Bureaucrats, Politicians, and Peasants in Mexico: A Case Study in Public Policy* (Berkeley: University of California Press, 1977), p. 7.

41. See *Facts on File* 51:2648 (August 22, 1991): 635–636.

42. Hellman, *Mexico in Crisis*, p. 127.

43. Under the system enacted in 1963, deputies were chosen by a combination of winner-take-all and proportional representation. "Under this system, opposition parties were granted five seats in the Chamber of Deputies if they received at least 2.5 percent of the national vote and up to fifteen additional (twenty in all) deputies, one for each additional 0.5 percent of the national vote. In 1973 the threshold for representation in the Chamber was lowered from 2.5 to 1.5 percent and the maximum number of seats available to an opposition party under this `party deputy' system was increased to twenty-five. This greatly improved the opposition's opportunities to win seats in the Chamber but also decreased the PRI's need to allow the opposition to win some district elections as a means of indicating the competitiveness of the political and electoral systems." Joseph Klesner, "Changing Patterns of Electoral Participation and Official Party Support in Mexico," in Judith Gentleman, ed., *Mexican Politics in Transition* (Boulder, Colo.: Westview Press, 1987), p. 99.

44. Roderic Camp, "Potential Strengths of the Political Opposition and What It Means to the PRI," in Camp, *Mexico's Political Stability*, p. 187.

45. Johnson, *Mexican Democracy*, p. 12.

46. Bailey, *Governing Mexico*, p. 62.

47. Discussion of this can be found in some detail in Bailey, *Governing Mexico*, pp. 83–88.

48. Grindle, *Bureaucrats, Politicians, and Peasants*, p. 3.

49. Juan José Hinojosa, "El Estado: Empresario por distracción," *Excelsior* (Mexico City), December 4, 1974, p. 6, as cited in Grindle, *Bureaucrats, Politicians, and Peasants*, p. 4.

50. Bailey, *Governing Mexico*, p. 61.

51. Daniel Levy and Gabriel Székely, *Mexico: Paradoxes of Stability and Change* (Boulder, Colo.: Westview Press, 1983), p. 56.

52. In the Chamber of Deputies elected July 7, 1985, the distribution of seats was as follows:

	Direct Election	Proportional Allotment
Institutional Revolutionary Party	289	
National Action Party	9	32
Authentic Party of the Mexican Revolution	2	7
Mexican Democratic Party		12
Unified Socialist Party of Mexico		12
Workers' Socialist Party		12
Popular Socialist Party		11
Revolutionary Workers' Party		6
Mexican Workers' Party		6
Total	300	98

Source: Arthur S. Banks, ed., *Political Handbook of the World* (Binghamton, N.Y.: CSA Publications, 1988), p. 388.

53. A very good description of the 1968 student movement can be found in chap. 6, "The Student Movement of 1968: A Case Study," in Hellman, *Mexico in Crisis*, pp. 173–186.

54. See Evelyn P. Stevens, "'The Opposition' in Mexico: Always a Bridesmaid, Never Yet the Bride," in Gentleman, *Mexican Politics in Transition*, pp. 217–226.

55. Wayne A. Cornelius, "Political Liberalization in an Authoritarian Regime: Mexico, 1976–1985," in Gentleman, *Mexican Politics in Transition*, pp. 32–36. See also John Bailey, "Can the PRI Be Reformed? Decentralized Candidate Selection," in Gentleman, *Mexican Politics in Transition* pp. 63–92, and Norman E. Cox, "Changes in the Mexican Political System," in George Philip, ed., *Politics in Mexico* (London: Croom Helm, 1985), pp. 15–53.

56. When the party was first organized in 1929 its name was the National Revolutionary Party; in 1938 it became the Mexican Revolutionary Party. In 1946 the name was changed for the third, and last, time to the PRI. A good discussion of the development of the PRI can be found in Hellman, *Mexico in Crisis*, pp. 33–57, chap. 2: "A Ruling Party Is Formed." See also Dale Story, *Mexico's Ruling Party: Stability and Authority* (Westport, Conn.: Greenwood Publishing, 1986).

57. John Bailey, "What Explains the Decline of the PRI and Will It Continue?" in Camp, *Mexico's Political Stability*, p. 159.

58. Bailey, "The PRI," p. 163.

59. Bailey, "The PRI," p. 179, n. 1. On authoritarianism in Mexico, see Kevin Middlebrook, *Political Liberalization in an Authoritarian Regime* (San Diego: Center for U.S.-Mexican Studies, 1985).

60. See "It's Our Ruling Party, and We'll Cry If We Want To," *The New York Times*, March 14, 1993, p. E2, or Andrew Reding, "Mexico: Are Its Elections Fair? Corruption Is Still the Norm," *Journal of Commerce* 391 (January 31, 1992): 4a. A broader description of the problem can be found in Stephen Morris, *Corruption and Politics in Contemporary Mexico* (Tuscaloosa, Ala.: University of Alabama Press, 1991).

61. *Facts on File* 51:2648 (August 22, 1991): 636.

62. Students interested in Marxism and communism in Mexico should consult Barry Carr, *Marxism and Communism in Twentieth-Century Mexico* (Lincoln: University of Nebraska Press, 1992).

63. See Barry Carr, "The PSUM: The Unification Process on the Mexican Left, 1981–1985," in Gentleman, *Mexican Politics in Transition* pp. 281–304.

64. Klesner, "Changing Patterns," p. 101.

65. See Dale Story, "The PAN, the Private Sector, and the Future of the Mexican Opposition," in Gentleman, *Mexican Politics in Transition* pp. 261–273.

66. Johnson, *Mexican Democracy*, p. 145.

67. Camp, "Potential Strengths," p. 186.

68. A very good discussion of this liberalization can be found in Cornelius, "Political Liberalization," pp. 15–40. In this chapter Cornelius seeks to understand "the impulse toward liberalization in a 57-year-old hegemonic party regime, in which the ruling Institutional Revolutionary Party (PRI) has never lost—or been forced to surrender—a single nationally important office." (p. 15)

69. A good general study was that by Arturo Alvarado, *Electoral Patterns and Perspectives in Mexico* (San Diego: Center for U.S.-Mexican Studies, 1987).

70. See Carolos Gil, ed., *Hope and Frustration: Interviews with Leaders of Mexico's Political Opposition* (Wilmington, Del.: Scholarly Resources, 1992), or Miguel Cenieno, *Mexico in the Nineteen-Nineties: Government and Opposition Speak Out* (San Diego: Center for U.S.-Mexican Studies, 1991).

71. Klesner, "Changing Patterns," p. 95.

72. Klesner, "Changing Patterns," p. 98. Much more discussion of the problem of electoral fraud can be found in Silvia Gómez Tagle, "Democracy and Power in Mexico: The Meaning of Conflict in the 1979, 1982, and 1985 Federal Elections," in Gentleman, *Mexican Politics in Transition*, pp. 153–180.

73. A good discussion of this problem can be found in Judith Teichman, *Policymaking in Mexico: From Boom to Crisis* (London: Routledge, Chapman, and Hall, 1988).

74. Hellman, *Mexico in Crisis*, p. 115.

75. World Bank, *World Development Report, 1993* (New York: Oxford University Press, 1993), p. 299.

76. Robert Long, "Urban Migration: The Dilemma of Mexico City," in Long, *Mexico*, p. 98.

77. World Bank, *World Development Report*, p. 299.

78. Otto Friedrich, "A Proud Capital's Distress," in Long, *Mexico*, p. 100.

79. Johnson, *Mexican Democracy*, p. 19.

80. By one estimate in 1980 more than 3 million Mexicans were in the United States illegally. Johnson, *Mexican Democracy*, p. 20. See Johnson's chap. 7, "Mexican Migration to the United States," pp. 209–229.

81. Edward Williams, "The Implications of the Border for Mexican Policy and Mexican-United States Relations," in Camp, *Mexico's Political Stability*, pp. 211–233.

82. Castaneda, "Mexico at the Brink," p. 287 A good analysis of the problem can be found in William Chislett, "The Causes of Mexico's Financial Crisis and the Lessons to Be Learned: Economic Policy, 1970–1983," in Philip, *Politics in Mexico*, pp. 1–14.

83. *The New York Times*, July 8, 1989, p. A15.

84. Jerry R. Ladman, "The Roots of the Crisis," in Jerry R. Ladman, ed., *Mexico: A Country in Crisis* (El Paso: University of Texas Press, 1986), p. 3.

85. A good review of policy discussion in Mexico after the fall of the price of oil can be found in Judith Gentleman, "Mexico After the Oil Boom: PRI Management of the Political Impact of National Disillusionment," in Gentleman, *Mexican Politics in Transition*, pp. 41–61.

86. John S. De Mott, "Mexico Tightens Its Belt," in Long, *Mexico*, pp. 42–43. Much of the trouble Mexico had at this time has been attributed, as well, to a great scandal within the PEMEX management. See, for some detailed discussion of "The Great PEMEX Scandal," Johnson, *Mexican Democracy*, pp. 185–196. Discussion of long-term implications of this can be found in Miguel S. Wionczek, "Mexico's External Debt Revisited: The 1985 Rescheduling Debt Arrangement: Lessons for Latin America," in *The Debt Crisis in Latin America* (Stockholm: Institute of Latin American Studies, 1986), pp. 81–106.

87. See Susan Purcell, *Debt and the Restructuring of Mexico* (New York: Council on Foreign Relations, 1988).

88. World Bank, *World Development Report*, p. 279.

89. And we should note here that the kinds of problems faced by Mexico are characteristic of problems faced by *many* other developing nations and Latin American nations. See, for an example of discussion of this problem, *The Debt Crisis in Latin America*, or Economic Commission for Latin America and the Caribbean, *External Debt in Latin America: Adjustment Policies and Renegotiation* (Boulder, Colo.: Lynne Rienner, 1985).

90. Angus Maddison, *The Political Economy of Poverty, Equity, and Growth: Brazil and Mexico* (New York: Oxford University Press, 1992).

91. David Barkin, "Mexico's Albatross: The U.S. Economy," in Hamilton and Harding, *Modern Mexico*, p. 107.

92. World Bank, *World Development Report*, p. 297.

93. Johnson, *Mexican Democracy*, p. 9.

94. William P. Glade, "How Will Economic Recovery Be Managed?" in Camp, *Mexico's Political Stability*, p. 48.

95. Jonathan Fox, *The Politics of Food in Mexico: State Power and Social Mobilization* (New York: Oxford University Press, 1993).

96. This problem is discussed in Jaime E. Rodriguez, ed., *The Revolutionary Process in Mexico* (Berkeley: University of California Press, 1990).

97. A much more detailed discussion of this general problem can be found in Wayne Cornelius and Judith Gentleman, eds., *Mexico's Alternative Political Futures* (San Diego: Center for U.S.-Mexican Studies, 1989).

16

The Nigerian Political System

INTRODUCTION

Our final "case study" of this volume, Nigeria, is another deviation from the pattern we have established, not only because it is the first African nation we have met, but also—and more important—because Nigeria is the first nation that we will have examined in this text that does not have a firm tradition of being governed by civilian government. In the case of Mexico we saw a nation that is a *developing* nation, but one that has been more or less politically *stable* since the period of Mexican revolution from 1910 to 1921.

Nigeria has been far less stable than Mexico, and in this respect represents a pattern that can be seen across the African continent, in which protracted political stability has not yet been achieved. Since independence in 1960, Nigeria has seen civil war, several coups, a prolonged state of emergency, and two relatively brief periods of civilian rule. One of the long-term periods of military rule—for almost fourteen years beginning in 1966—was begun in the name of democracy and with the articulated goal of saving the Nigerian federation. Many today wonder whether stable democratic government is even possible in the Nigerian political culture.

We will begin this chapter with a brief discussion of Nigerian political history. Here we will become familiar with the major sources of conflict in Nigeria's contemporary political setting and the ways in which these sources have interacted, again and again, with the political culture to lead to political violence. We will also discuss the likelihood of Nigeria's breaking out of this "cycle of violence" in the near future.

Following this historical discussion, we will undertake a brief examination of the context of African politics more generally. We will see the extent to which Nigeria's pattern of political instability is fairly typical of political instability in other African settings, and we will briefly discuss some of the reasons for this instability. Then we will (again, briefly) examine the way that other nations have responded to this instability and worked to become more stable.

We then will turn our attention to the kind of examination that we have undertaken in the preceding "country studies" chapters of this volume, briefly examining Nigerian political institutions (when civilian political institutions have been permitted to exist), the role of political parties and elections in Nigeria, and the evolution of Nigeria's commitment to constitutionalism.

NIGERIA'S POLITICAL HISTORY

The territory that is labelled "Nigeria" on today's political map has changed substantially over time. It is the largest of the West African coastal states, and has the highest population in Africa, estimated at over 99 million in mid-1991.[1] There are a number of cultural and ethnic strains in Nigeria, with the three largest ethnic groups being the Hausa, the Yoruba, and the Ibo (sometimes spelled "Igbo") peoples. We shall return to a discussion of the pattern of competition and violence between and among these groups later in this chapter.

By 1861, Lagos, the port city and Nigeria's capital, and much of what today is Nigeria became part of British territorial possessions in West Africa, which at the time also included modern-day Sierra Leone and Ghana, then called the Gold Coast. British colonial dominion over areas of West Africa increased over time, including what we today call Benin and Niger as well as other territories.

In 1914 the areas referred to as Northern Nigeria and Southern Nigeria were unified, although they were administered separately. In 1920, portions of (formerly German) Cameroon became British mandatory territory as a result of action by the League of Nations following World War I; this territory was administered as part of Nigeria for the next four decades. Various nationalist movements first began to appear in the 1920s; their leaders were agreed in their opposition to continued British administration of Nigeria, but were unable to agree on what form of government should ultimately replace the British colonial system.

Much of this lack of agreement was influenced, if not driven, by ethnic cleavages in society, running primarily along the tribal lines indicated above. These cleavages led to two different types of nationalism emerging in Nigeria at the time: a kind of "modern" nationalism that focused on the creation of a single nation-state to take the place of the British colonial institutions, and a more "traditional" nationalism, which focused on the creation of a number of different nation-states based upon traditional ethnic lines. Each of the three major ethnic groups in Nigeria—the Hausa-Fulani (in the north), the Ibo (in the east), and the Yoruba (in the west)—has historically dominated one region of the country.[2] This domination has led to mutual recrimination, suspicion, and political violence over the years.

British administration of Nigeria during this period was unremarkable in colonial terms;[3] Nigeria was one territory among many in the British Empire, and British political institutions and political behaviors were "transplanted" from Westminster to Nigeria in the same manner that they were "transplanted" to India, Palestine, and Singapore.

History has shown, however, that transplanting political institutions doesn't always work very effectively. Indeed, following the unsuccessful 1983 election that led to the demise of the Second Republic, one student of Nigeria's political institutions wrote that:

> . . . there was nothing automatic, and certainly nothing simple, about Africa's adoption of democracy in the form . . . that has worked well in certain of the Western developed countries.
> It is clear that Nigeria's colonial experience was much less conducive to the growth and health of systems of competitive electoral democracy than was assumed, naively, by the "institution transfer" idea. Nigeria's heritage from sixty years of British colonial rule was not democracy, but the administrative state—benignly autocratic, perhaps, but still autocratic.[4]

By 1954 a new constitution had been introduced in Nigeria, including the British-style parliamentary system of government with the principles of ministerial responsibility.[5] Nigeria was given a federal structure, with Northern, Southern, Eastern, and Western regions having some autonomy;[6] this federal structure had the consequence of making Nigeria's constitutional structures "necessarily more complex."[7] In 1957 the Western and Eastern regions became formally self-governing in regional affairs within a federal structure, and a Federal Executive Council was created to prepare Nigeria for independence. In 1959 the Northern region became self-governing in regional affairs, and national parliamentary elections were held.

The development of a federal political structure was significant for Nigeria's political future; it meant that each of the regions of Nigeria, as has been pointed out, was able to retain some degree of autonomy and identity. This served to weaken many of the forces that were leading to the development of a *national* political identity.[8] As will be shown later in this chapter, one of the traditional problems frustrating Nigerian national integration has been the notion of a *tribal* or *ethnic* identity. A federal political structure permitted these subnational forces to survive; this was characteristic of the British "traditional desire to federate colonial territories, making possible interstate divisions into intrastate divisions."[9]

Nigeria became independent on October 1, 1960, but remained a member of the British Commonwealth.[10] Abubakar Tafawa Balewa was the first democratically elected prime minister. As soon as independence was achieved, ethnic and regional tensions (which were related, since ethnic groups were concentrated in different regions of the country) grew and distrust increased between the slowly developing north and the more advanced south. Northerners were concerned that the (Southern) Ibo were running the country and dominating policy decisions; Southerners were concerned that the (Northern) Hausa and Yoruba were ignoring their needs and concerns.

The next year, in February 1961, a plebiscite was held in neighboring Cameroon. The Northern region of Cameroon voted to merge with Nigeria's Northern region; Southern Cameroon voted to join a federal union with the former territory of French Cameroon. In May 1962 riots caused the federal government to declare a state of emergency in the Western region of Nigeria.

In October 1963 Nigeria amended its constitution to become a republic. That is, Nigeria was no longer officially a monarchy (headed by a queen who was also queen of the United Kingdom), but instead was to be headed by an elected president. Although the formal, structural position of head of state was changed, Nigeria chose to remain within the Commonwealth. Nnamdi Azikiwe was installed as the first president of Nigeria.

In December 1964 and January 1965 parliamentary elections were held in Nigeria, the first since independence. Abubakar Tafawa Balewa's party, the Nigerian National Alliance, won a majority in the parliament, and Balewa formed a new government.[11]

Later that year, however, violence resurfaced in Western Nigeria. In January 1966 a *coup d'état* took place; it was "mainly but not exclusively"[12] led by Ibo political leaders. President Balewa and the premiers of both the Western and Northern regions of Nigeria were assassinated. A Federal Military Government (FMG), led by Major General Johnson Aguiyi Ironsi, was created to restore order, and all political parties were banned. The FMG promised to prepare the country for a return to civilian rule at an unspecified point in the future. Later that year another *coup* took place, this time led by Northern troops. In this *coup* Ironsi was killed, as were a number of Ibo officers. Lieutenant Colonel Yakubu Gowon was named as head of the FMG.

Because the First Republic lasted only five years, from 1961 to 1966, it did not accomplish a great deal in terms of institutionalizing democracy in Nigeria.

> So completely had [the republic] failed in that brief period that the *coup* ending it was greeted with every indication of relief and even jubilation, particularly among the highly-educated public who had become disgusted with "democratic" misrule. Suspension of the instruments of legitimation seemed to enjoy the widest possible legitimacy.[13]

Between 1966 and 1976 four different *coups d'état* and a major civil war took place. This lack of success with democratic structures and resulting violent political behavior was cyclical: One bad experience made it more difficult for a democratic government to "take hold" subsequently, and military regimes succeeded one another when they became dissatisfied with the way society and the economy were developing. The first democratic government lasted barely five years before it was replaced by a military regime; the second democratic regime (from 1979 to 1983) was no more successful.

In 1967 a meeting was held in Ghana to try to break the cycle of violence and murder in Nigeria, and to find some way to save the Nigerian federal government. In March of that year the FMG decreed that all executive and legislative power would reside in a Supreme Military Council, headed by (now) Major General Gowon. Two months later Eastern Nigeria voted to secede from Nigeria, and proclaimed its establishment as the independent Republic of Biafra.

For almost three years, from July 1967 to January 1970, civil war raged in Nigeria, and thousands were killed. An unconditional cease-fire was agreed to by the Biafran leaders in January 12, 1970. Estimates of casualties (including deaths by starvation during the thirty-month war) ranged from 1 to 2 million.

At the end of the war the Biafrans were accepted back into Nigeria under an amnesty program, and the FMG worked to integrate the various regions of the country, both economically and socially. A national development plan was begun, which was intended to promote *national* rather than *regional* thinking. This development program was primarily funded by oil revenues, and based upon these resources many believed that Nigeria could overcome the experiences of its past and look forward to a stable and progressive future.

In October 1970, Major General Gowon announced that the first civilian elections of a Second Republic would take place in 1976, but he wanted a new constitution and a new census completed before then. In 1974 he announced a change of mind, and postponed elections and a return to civilian rule indefinitely. In July 1975, Gowon was overthrown in a bloodless coup. Gowon was replaced by General Murtala Ramat Muhammed, who announced that civilian government would be restored in October 1979. However, Muhammed was assassinated in a *coup* attempt in February 1976; Lieutenant General Olusegun Obasanjo was chosen by military leaders to be head of the FMG, and he promised to see to it that civilian government would be restored in 1979.

The ensuing two years saw substantial progress in the return to normalcy in Nigeria. In March 1976 the FMG issued a decree establishing a nineteen-state federation, with a new federal capital in Abuja. In October 1977 a Constituent Assembly was convened to work on a new draft constitution, based on an American-style presidential system.

In July and August of 1979 civilian elections did, in fact, take place. On October 1, 1979, Alhaji Shehu Shagari was inaugurated as president of Nigeria, and civilian rule was reestablished. Shagari's National Party of Nigeria—with a substantial Northern base—defeated a number of other political parties in a close election, but fell short of receiving a majority in the national legislature. This resulted in a political alliance being formed between Shagari and the Ibo leader Nnamdi Azikiwe, the president of Nigeria during the First Republic.

The elections of 1979 "seemed to go off reasonably well," especially in light of Nigeria's political history for the ten years preceding the elections.

> Most important was the fact that at least a conditional victory was scored over [vote] "rigging." All five elections [an election for the national Senate on July 7, an election for the national House of Representatives on July 14, an election for state assemblies on July 21, an election for state governors on July 28, and an election for the federal president on August 11] were conducted on schedule and in an orderly

manner, and there was general agreement that, in the main, they had been free and fair.[14]

Even though the elections had been relatively "free and fair," they had not been able to overcome the regional and ethnic tensions so characteristic of Nigerian politics. The problem was that the "big three" parties in the elections each received the overwhelming proportion of their votes from their own specific regions of the nation. The Unity Party of Nigeria (UPN) received 78 percent of its votes from four primarily Yoruba states. The Nigerian People's Party (NPP) received 71 percent of its votes from two Ibo states. The People's Redemption Party received 79 percent of its votes from two states in the far north. Regionalism and ethnic loyalties survived and thrived.[15]

Many suggested that although the 1979 elections were a qualified success, the *real* test of democratic commitment in Nigeria would come during the next election, in 1983. After all, the 1979 elections had been set up by the Federal Military Government, so there was every reason to expect that if the FMG were truly committed to the reestablishment of civilian government, the elections would be (more or less) efficiently run and equitably administered. What would happen when the first *civilian government* administered its first elections was another thing entirely. "In 1983 it would be the political authority itself that would ultimately be responsible for the integrity of the electoral system."[16]

Unfortunately for Nigeria, in 1980 the world economic recession began, and one consequence of this recession was a drop in the price of oil. As we noted in Chapter 3, when nations are too dependent upon a single "crop" or industry or resource, their economies are very vulnerable. This vulnerability had disastrous consequences for Nigeria; the price of oil fell 43 percent by the end of 1983, and the public's confidence in the ability of the civilian government to run the economy took a comparable plunge.[17]

This drop in public confidence was reflected in the 1983 election campaigns, which experienced far more violence than the 1979 election. While the elections took place without incident and as scheduled in August and September of 1983, "the level of rigging and falsification was quite obviously higher than in 1979. In fact, the campaigns themselves centered largely on charges and counter-charges of plans for rigging, while political violence resulted in numerous deaths."[18] When the election results were announced, the Nigerian People's Party—the party that had been in power—had won.

Between September 1983 and December 1983, some significant events took place: A number of decisions in the nation's courts confirmed that there *had* been corruption and vote fraud in the elections, and an economic crisis was becoming increasingly intense. Although the newly reelected Shagari government began to develop economic policy initiatives for responding to the economic crisis, including constructing what was perceived as "a harsh austerity budget for 1984," it was too late to stop alternative forces. On December 31, 1983, a military *coup* reestablished military rule.

Interestingly, despite the participation by so many in the democratic electoral processes just four months earlier, scarcely a voice was raised against the suspension of the Second Republic. To the contrary, there was every evidence of public rejoicing at the overthrow of the Shagari regime. And there was evidence as well of *anger* directed against the corruption, violence, and mismanagement that was now said to have been the essence of Second Republic "democracy."[19]

Between 1983 and 1993 a variety of military regimes controlled the Nigerian state. The 1983 *coup* had "effectively invalidated"[20] the 1983 summer election, and led to another decade of military rule. As noted above, it was ironic that "far from being regarded as unnecessary, premature, or even undemocratic, the coup of 31 December 1983 met with the broadest and most enthusiastic support."[21]

In June 1993 a new anti-sedition law was passed after retired General Olusegun Obasanjo criticized President Ibrahim Babangida in a published interview. Babangida had cancelled the promised presidential election in November 1992, and Obasanjo had criticized him, announcing that such action was detrimental to the nation.[22]

On June 12, 1993, Nigeria held its first presidential election since 1983, but immediately after the election took place the military government of President Babangida froze the release of the results of the election "until fraud charges could be investigated."[23] He also "rescinded his promise to surrender power to a civilian government on August 27." This was the fourth time in three years that Babangida had backed away from a promise to relinquish power. This act, in fact, "appeared to confirm the suspicion of human rights activists that Babangida had never intended to permit civilian rule. Many observers suggested that the entire electoral process had been a well-orchestrated sham."[24]

On June 26, 1993, Babangida announced that new presidential elections would take place soon, but gave no date for the elections. He also promised that a civilian government "would be in place" by August 27, as he had indicated earlier. He announced that he had cancelled the results of the June election because it had come to his attention that the two candidates "had spent more than $60 million buying votes."[25]

Much to the surprise of many who believed that Babangida never intended to step down, General Babangida resigned from office on August 26, 1993, after serving eight years as military dictator of Nigeria.[26] The leader of the new, non-elected Interim Administration was Ernest Shonekan, a major Nigerian industrialist; the bulk of the membership of the new administration was made up of supporters of Babangida.

In his first address as leader, Shonekan promised to schedule new elections for Nigeria by March 1994.[27] On November 17, 1993, however, Defense Minister General Sani Abacha forced Shonekan from office and declared himself to be Nigeria's new ruler. "Immediately after taking command, Abacha began to dismantle democratic institutions, constructed over eight years, that had been a sign of Nigeria's progress toward implementing a civilian government."[28] Democratic reforms in Nigeria, at least for the present, were again frustrated.

FEDERALISM AND NATIONAL INTEGRATION

One of the key characteristics of the Nigerian political system with implications for political unification and political stability has been that Nigeria has been a *federal* political structure. As was suggested earlier, many of the federal political institutions that were created in Nigeria, even prior to independence, have had the effect of slowing down, or even completely blocking, the process of national integration discussed in the first chapter of this volume.

From 1906 to 1912, Nigeria was made up of two regions, a Northern region and a Southern region. In 1912 these were combined by Sir Frederick Lugard and re-divided into three regions; Lugard became governor general of Nigeria, and appointed a lieutenant governor for each of the three regions, the north, the west, and the east. After independence in 1960 a fourth region was established, a "midwestern" region.

> Nigeria inherited a federal structure when it achieved independence in 1960. Britain had dealt with the heterogeneity of the population of this large colony by dividing it into three regions corresponding to the three major ethnic groups—the Hausa, Yoruba, and Ibgo—which were joined under a federal constitution. But the way the country was divided transgressed a basic principle of successful federation, namely, that the component units of the federation should be approximately equal in power, so that no one unit can dominate another unit or subject the federal government to its own control. The northern region, which was dominated by the Hausa, was much larger than the other two regions combined. . . . The successive military *coups* of 1966 and the civil war that followed had much to do with the defective constitutional structure. . . ."[29]

Problems in Nigeria have traditionally corresponded to regional identity. The Nigerian civil war in 1967 resulted when "the easterners tried to set up their region as an independent state on the basis of the regional boundaries drawn by the British."[30] The creation of a new state of Biafra in what had been the eastern region of Nigeria[31] was a result of an effort "on the part of mainly Igbo-speaking people to set up an independent state, or, in other words, to transform an ethnic group into a nation."[32]

AFRICAN POLITICAL PATTERNS

Africa is a vast region, and making general observations about politics in such a varied continent involves serious risks. With over fifty independent states, Africa has a staggering range of political institutions, political histories, political cultures, and political customs.

> To lump these states together and talk about "African politics" is somewhat misleading because there are important differences between them. There is, for example, a wide cultural gap between the North African states and the Black African states south of the Sahara. The geographic and demographic differences are often striking, as witnessed by the huge Sudan and Zaire on the one hand, and the tiny Rwanda, Burundi and Swaziland on the other; within West Africa, oil-rich Nigeria—

four times the size of Britain and with a population exceeding 100 million—contrasts sharply with the Gambia, which, with an area of just over four thousand square miles and a population of approximately 900,000, was once (in pre-independence days) described as "an eel wriggling its way through a slab of French territory."[33]

Our purpose here is not to even attempt a comprehensive "continental" examination. Rather, here we seek to identify just a few of the major "themes" or patterns of behavior that we can see as being significant in Africa, and especially West Africa, which will provide a context within which we can appreciate political developments in Nigeria.

We can identify, in fact, some patterns that *most* African states have in common.[34] Most African states were colonies of other (European) powers, and achieved independence from their colonial powers after 1960. Most states are still working to develop "a new identity as nation-states." Most states are very poor, very rural, and very vulnerable to the world economy. Most states have a very heterogeneous political culture, as a result of the number and variety of traditional tribal units within their borders.

Contrary to what many think, elections and democratic politics *do* have a significant history in the African setting. "Elections have long been a conspicuous element of the political landscape of independent Africa. . . . Africans were elected to legislative councils in the 1920s in Ghana, Kenya, Nigeria, Sierra Leone, and Zambia."[35] In recent times, however, the "conventional wisdom" about the success and significance of elections in Africa has become more and more negative and pessimistic.

> Elections in much of contemporary Africa were widely regarded as irrelevant or a sham. There was growing evidence of elections which did not reflect democratic values; that those responsible followed neither the electoral procedures set out in the institutions bequeathed at independence nor other requirements of free and fair competition. Some concluded that the misuse and abuse of electoral institutions demonstrated that the process was ill-suited to Africa.[36]

One recent study of West African politics was subtitled "Seeking Unity in Diversity,"[37] and this, in brief, tells the trials of most African nations. With the exception of Liberia, all of the states of West Africa, and most of the states of the rest of Africa, were the creation of colonial powers that divided the continent up during the late nineteenth century.

It is clear that the various colonial powers that ruled Africa into the twentieth century—including Italy, France, Germany, Portugal, and the United Kingdom, among others—were concerned about the development of these nations as suppliers of goods and services; national integration was not a high priority on their political agendas. Thus, railroads and highways were designed to run from the hinterlands of the nations to the coast so that raw materials could be shipped to the colonial power; but transportation *within* the African state, from one interior location to another interior location, might have remained very difficult.

In addition to a lack of development of those infrastructures that could have promoted a sense of national integration, the borders of the African states were themselves entirely artificial creations. As Figure 16.1 illustrates, the *primary* units of loyalty in Africa, tribal units, have never corresponded to what we today look upon as "national borders." French or British or German colonial officers may have decided to draw a national border between what today is Nigeria and what today is Cameroon, but as far as the people living in those regions were concerned, some of the soon-to-be-Nigerians had more in common with soon-to-be-Cameroonois than they did with other soon-to-be-Nigerians. This made it very difficult to develop any sense of what it meant to be a "Nigerian" for much of the population in that region.

In recent years we have seen prolonged and bloody civil wars in many nations in West Africa. Where actual warfare hasn't broken out, we have seen situations of essentially authoritarian government that has been clear in its intention to remain in power, whatever the cost. The cost of these wars, of course, in addition to the thousands and thousands of lives that have been lost, has been a lack of economic and political development. It has been hard enough for developing nations to make progress in their economic development when they have been able to focus all of their resources and efforts on the process of development itself. When their resources and efforts have been diverted to fighting to remain in power, or to drive someone else out of power, the nations have lost momentum in the development process; some are almost hopelessly behind in the quest for political stability and economic progress. We will very briefly look at three nations for examples of these types of problems, and others, to develop an appreciation for the situation faced by Nigeria today.[38]

Liberia today barely exists as a "real" nation, after three years of an extremely destructive civil war that has left few of the nation's roads, industries, or national political, cultural, social, educational, or economic institutions intact. Electricity is frequently unavailable; travel from one area of the country to another is often impossible because roads and bridges have been destroyed, and different armies control different parts of the nation. The only factor responsible for a lack of fighting at the end of 1993 was that the country was occupied by a Western African army made up of soldiers from a number of West African states. Although elections for a new government were scheduled to take place early in 1994, many political leaders there were skeptical about the future of Liberia, and feared that only the winning candidate in the 1994 election (if it takes place) would accept the outcomes of the election; new fighting would begin as soon as the results of the election were announced.

In the *Côte d'Ivoire*—what used to be called the Ivory Coast—the first president, Felix Houphouët-Boigny, ruled with a firm hand from the time of independence in 1960 through 1993. Only recently has any real pro-democracy movement become active, resulting in the existence today of several opposition political parties and a handful of members of opposition parties in the national legislature there for the first time since independence. Despite the fact that the Côte d'Ivoire has been among West Africa's more stable and prosperous states over the last three decades, many observers were concerned about what would happen when Houphouët-Boigny finally retired from politics, or died in office. Then, they argued, would come the real test of whether the Côte d'Ivoire has been successful in the type of political de-

FIGURE 16.1   Nigeria in The Ethnic Mosaic of Africa. The map of
Africa looks very different when lines are drawn along tribal boundaries.
Copyright© 1988 by the New York Times Company. Reprinted by permission.

velopment and integration of democratic values that we discussed in the first chapter of this text.

On December 7, 1993, Houphouët-Boigny died, and the moment of truth had arrived. Henri Bedie, Speaker of the Parliament, was constitutionally next in line to be President of the Côte d'Ivoire. Premier Alassane Ouattara claimed power, but the Supreme Court of the Côte d'Ivoire ruled that Bedie should succeed Houphouët-Boigny and serve out the remainder of his term. A potential tense situation was calmed the next day when France's President, François Mitterand, gave his official condolences to Bedie, not Ouattara. Since France still has considerable influence in the Côte d'Ivoire, Mitterand's gesture bestowed a legitimacy upon Bedie that served to stifle, for the time being at least, any claims to power by Ouattara.[39]

Although *Kenya* today is the most industrialized country in East Africa, it still has many problems to resolve. Since becoming independent in 1963 under the leadership of Jomo Kenyatta, Kenya made tremendous strides in industrial and economic development, although many suggested that it was making significantly less progress in political and democratic development. "Under Kenyatta, Kenya became a de facto one-party state. The principal opposition party, the Kenya People's Union (KPU), was ultimately suppressed and its leadership harassed and jailed."[40]

After Kenyatta died in 1978, Daniel arap Moi became president, a position he retains to this day. The political climate under Moi has become more and more closed and repressive in recent years. In 1982 an attempted *coup* resulted in many deaths and serious political censorship and repression.

> In the aftermath of the *coup* attempt all parties other than KANU [Kenya African National Union] were formally outlawed. Moi followed up this step by declaring, in 1986, that KANU was above the government, the Parliament, and the judiciary. Press restrictions, detentions, and blatant acts of intimidation, including public death threats toward sitting parliamentary members, have since become common.[41]

Although pro-democracy movements have become increasingly vocal in recent years, many are still concerned about the state of democracy in Kenya and the likelihood of continued political stability there.

In December 1992 Moi was reelected president with 37 percent of the vote (the rest of the vote was divided among a number of alternative candidates); he was sworn in as Kenya's newest president on January 4, 1993.[42] On January 27, one day after the swearing-in of the new Parliament—in which Moi's Kenya African National Union party controlled 97 of 202 seats—Moi suspended Parliament.[43] This was the first parliament to have elected opposition members since the early 1960s, and its suspension led to substantial criticism of Moi and much fear that the future of democracy in Kenya did not appear positive.

POLITICAL INSTITUTIONS OF NIGERIA

Nigeria's civilian constitution provides for three independent branches of government; when Nigeria has had a civilian government, the government has been composed of an executive branch, a legislative branch, and a judicial branch.[44] During civilian rule, the popularly elected president headed a cabinet having at least one minister from each of the nineteen states. A bicameral National Assembly existed, composed of a 95-member Senate (five senators per state) and a 449-member House of Representatives. States' powers were defined in the Constitution, and each had a directly elected governor and a unicameral House of Assembly.

Nigeria's judicial system was based upon British common law, but modi-fied by Nigeria's judicial history. The judicial system resembled that of the United States, with a federal Supreme Court, Courts of Appeals, and a Federal High Court. The Supreme Court had original jurisdiction in cases involving constitutional ques-tions. State judicial systems, reflecting the federal nature of the regime, were made up of state high courts, magistrates' courts, and customary and area (Moslem) courts.

Clearly the most significant political institution in Nigeria has been a struc-ture external to the presidency, the legislature, and the judiciary: the military. The general topic of civil-military relations has been of crucial importance in Nigeria,[45] and the appeal of military governments in Nigeria has echoed the advantages usu-ally claimed for (and by) the military:

> Probably General Gowon reflected the mood of the country when later he stated "the country acquiesced in the installation of a Military Regime only because it de-sired that order and discipline should be restored in the conduct of the affairs of this country, that swift reforms will be introduced to produce just and honest govern-ment." The *coup d'état* was just the culmination of a long process of institutional con-flict resulting from the clash of political cultures. To many Nigerians, democracy did not die with the *coup*, on the contrary it gave opportunity to make a fresh start to-wards the realization of democratic values.[46]

The experience of the military *coup*, of course, is not unique to Nigeria. Moreover, the experience of the military *coup* is not even an especially uncommon event in African history. Why are military *coups* so common? Three reasons are of-ten cited to explain their frequency. First, "the army can stage a *coup* because, hav-ing control of the weaponry, it has the capacity for organized violence." The weapons exist, and the army controls the weapons. Second, a chain of command exists in the military by which an individual can organize and carry out a *coup*. Third, military leaders are often in a position to criticize corruption and poor administration that they see in the government.[47]

> In coming under military rule, Nigeria joined a new mainstream of African political experience. In the next decade, more than a hundred *coups* or attempted *coups* oc-curred in the African countries. By 1978 more than half of the countries on the con-tinent . . . had experienced military rule. As in so many other cases, military rule in Nigeria stretched on and on. Intramilitary coups were experiences . . . providing the change of regime that had never been produced by the First Republic electoral in-stitutions. . . . In Nigerian thought, civilian democratic rule is always suspended, not abolished. It is striking that no military government so far has asserted a right to rule that is more than custodial, conditional, and temporary. . . ."[48]

Another major factor leading to military *coups* relates to a characteristic that we have already mentioned here. Put simply, "popular explanations of [*coups*] rely heavily on what is seen as the *bête noire* of many African states—tribalism."[49]

POLITICAL PARTIES AND POLITICAL BEHAVIOR

We should begin a discussion of political parties in Nigeria by examining the generic functions of political parties in Africa. What roles do parties play in African democracies? Several different roles and functions have been identified in the literature, including an integrative function, an educative function, a legitimizing function, a policy function, and a communication function, among others.[50]

The *integrative* function of parties can be crucial in the development of new political systems. Citizens of Nigeria need to start to think of themselves as Nigerians, rather than as Ibos, Hausas, Yorubas, or members of other ethnic groups. The institution of the political party could, if truly integrative national parties existed, help in this regard by showing Nigerians from all ethnic groups and from all regions that they do, in fact, have a great deal in common.

Unfortunately, as we have already noted, the political parties that exist are overwhelmingly dominated by specific ethnic groups, and are identified as such. Thus, when the Nigerian People's Party receives 71 percent of its votes from two overwhelmingly Ibo states, there is a very limited amount that it can do to promote national integration. This is an example of an instance in which political parties *could* make a contribution to national integration, but thus far in Nigeria's history have failed to do so.

The *educative* function of political parties contributes a great deal in established democracies. By raising issues of importance to the regime during and between election campaigns, and by participating in debates and discussion of these issues, parties help to educate the public both as to those concerns of which the public should be aware and as to the possible responses to those concerns.

During the three election campaigns in modern Nigerian political history (in 1961, 1979, and 1983), the political parties did, indeed, participate actively in this manner. This type of public debate and discussion has been absent in recent years, and many Nigerians say that this is one of the aspects of electoral democracy that has been most missed under military rule.[51]

The *legitimizing* function is one that is very important for new nations. Political parties can contribute to feelings of the public that the government is behaving in a reasonable manner, that the government deserves to exist, and that they should obey the rules of the government. A lack of legitimacy can be very significant for a government, especially a new government, because it makes the likelihood of some kind of *coup* far greater than it would be if the government were perceived as being legitimate.

This type of situation is typified by the reactions to the *coups* of 1966 and 1983. We illustrated for both of these *coups* that even though there was widespread participation in the democratic election process, many Nigerians felt that the government was not legitimate and was not behaving in the way that a legitimate government would behave. Consequently, they not only permitted military *coups*, but actually appeared pleased when the *coups* took place.

Parties can be important in the creation of *policy*, too. They are, after all, the primary means of organization of the national legislature. They serve as vehicles by which new policy ideas are introduced in the government, whether in the executive branch, in the legislative branch, or often in the bureaucracy, and they can make a significant contribution to the policy-making process overall.

Because Nigeria has experienced democratic government for only about one-third of its independent existence, political parties have not had much of an opportunity to be effective in the policy arena. Just as the government party was beginning to introduce some effective policy options to address the economic crisis of 1983, the military took over the reins of the civilian government and, of course, banned political party action during the period of military rule.

Thus this dimension of political party activity, too, is one of potential as far as Nigeria is concerned. Only with a prolonged period of party government will political parties be able to make a significant contribution to the Nigerian policy process.

Finally, political parties have traditionally played a significant role in the process of political *communication*. Although direct, official channels of representation exist in democratic governments, and individuals will contact their representatives in government directly, it is axiomatic that political parties can serve as a very effective alternative channel of communication that enables citizens to let the government know their demands.

This function was especially important in Nigeria for the parties that were out of power. Many Ibo citizens felt that they could not talk with government officials unless those officials were also Ibo. By using the structure of the Nigerian People's Party, which was itself overwhelmingly Ibo in nature, these citizens could communicate their views to the government and make requests of the government that they felt might not otherwise be possible. This, in turn, helped to promote the image of the government as legitimate, and contributed to the other functions parties perform, including national integration and education.

Prior to Nigeria's independence, political parties played an active, if somewhat limited, function in the development of national integration, political education, and political legitimation of the nationalist ideal.[52] A substantial number of political parties participated in the 1979 elections.[53] The National Party of Nigeria, a conservative party, won the 1979 presidential election, and entered into a ruling coalition with the Nigerian People's Party. The main opposition was made up of the (liberal) United Party of Nigeria and two smaller parties, the Great Nigeria People's Party and the (socialist) People's Redemption Party. In 1979 state elections, the National Party of Nigeria won in seven states, the Unity Party of Nigeria in five, the Nigerian People's Party in three, the Great Nigeria People's Party in two, and the People's Redemption Party in one.[54]

Conclusions: The Future of Nigerian Politics

We suggested at the outset of this chapter that Nigeria has faced a number of challenges to its development, most especially a crisis of national legitimacy caused by ethnic and tribal identities frustrating the development of a sense of national identity. In this respect, Nigeria is typical of many developing nations, and it is consistent with challenges to political development and political modernization that were discussed in the very early chapters of this text.

When we look to Nigeria's future, what we see is *potential*. As we noted earlier in this chapter, Nigeria is familiar with democratic political institutions: Free and fair elections have existed in Nigeria; open electoral campaigns have taken place; responsible government has existed.

The problem has been, as we noted has been the case in many other African states besides Nigeria, that because Nigerians have not had very much experience with democratic government, the national frustration level is relatively low. There is not much currency of political goodwill in the "bank" of public opinion, and when crises have come about—either political crises or economic crises—the government of the day has not had a very large "savings account" of public support from which to draw resources. This has, of course, resulted in the military stepping in and taking over the reins of government during both the First and Second Republics.

The trick in Nigeria will be to develop a *national commitment* to democratic "rules of the game" that will endure. The public—including military leaders—must be committed to democratic institutions in order to make those institutions work effectively. If the public finds it acceptable that as soon as a democratically elected government is unable to deal with political and economic crises it can legitimately be replaced by the military, then the future for democratic government in Nigeria looks bleak.

Can this type of commitment ever be developed? The answer is "Yes, but . . ." It can be developed, but it will require a true commitment *by the military* and *by the national political elite* to not give up on the government at the first sign of an inability to resolve a crisis. There must be a commitment to give the government time, and to continue to give the government the public's support, to enable the government to try various policy alternatives. There must be a commitment that if the government is unable to be effective in dealing with whatever problems arise, then the government will be replaced, but *only by democratic and constitutional* means. This commitment has not yet been demonstrated in Nigeria.

The problems faced by Nigeria are not, of course, unique to Nigeria. Similar challenges, and military *coups*, have been characteristic of a number of countries in Africa (and Asia and Latin America, for that matter). While many suggest that the future looks dim, others have suggested that there *is* hope for democracy in Africa (and, by extension, in Nigeria),[55] but only time will tell.

Notes

1. World Bank, *World Development Report, 1993* (New York: Oxford University Press, 1993), p. 238.
2. Leslie Rubin and Brian Weinstein, *Introduction to African Politics: A Continental Approach* (New York: Praeger, 1974), pp. 170–171.

3. Walter Crocker, *Nigeria: A Critique of British Colonial Administration* (Freeport, N.Y.: Books for Libraries Press, 1971). This is a reprint of a book first published in 1936, which contains a number of firsthand observations about the nature of British colonial government in Nigeria. A more contemporary discussion of these issues can be found in Kwamena Bentsi-Enchill, "Developments in Former British West Africa," in David P. Currie, ed., *Federalism and the New Nations of Africa* (Chicago: University of Chicago Press, 1964), pp. 75–100. See also William Tordoff, *Government and Politics in Africa* (Bloomington: Indiana University Press, 1993), pp. 24–41.

4. Paul A. Beckett, "Elections and Democracy in Nigeria," in Fred M. Hayward, ed., *Elections in Independent Africa* (Boulder, Colo.: Westview Press, 1987), pp. 110–111.

5. A very good description of Nigerian constitutional development can be found in Kalu Ezera, *Constitutional Developments in Nigeria* (Cambridge: Cambridge University Press, 1960). Discussion of early political structures in Nigeria, prior to 1962, can be found in Eme O. Awa, *Federal Government in Nigeria* (Los Angeles: University of California Press, 1964), pp. 113–253.

6. Good discussion of Nigerian federalism can be found in Uma O. Eleazu, *Federalism and Nation-Building: The Nigerian Experience, 1954–1964* (Elms Court: Arthur Stockwell, Ltd., 1977).

7. Tordoff, *Government and Politics in Africa*, p. 58.

8. Even local political institutions played a significant role in this process. See Awa, *Federal Government in Nigeria*, pp. 273–314.

9. Rubin and Weinstein, *Introduction to African Politics*, p. 54.

10. Much of the pre-independence historical discussion that follows is derived from a much longer and more detailed discussion in Henry Bretton, *Power and Stability in Nigeria: The Politics of Decolonization* (New York: Praeger, 1962). Later material follows William Miles, *Elections in Nigeria: A Grassroots Perspective* (Boulder, Colo.: Lynne Rienner, 1988).

11. Very good discussion of the First Republic can be found in William D. Graf, *The Nigerian State: Political Economy, State, Class, and Political System in the Post-Colonial Era* (London: James Currey, 1988), pp. 25–40.

12. Rubin and Weinstein, *Introduction to African Politics*, pp. 170–171.

13. Beckett, "Elections and Democracy in Nigeria," pp. 89–90.

14. Ibid., p. 101.

15. Ibid., p. 102.

16. Ibid., p. 104.

17. Ibid., pp. 104–106.

18. Ibid., p. 106.

19. Ibid., pp. 106–107.

20. Miles, *Elections in Nigeria*, p. 11.

21. Beckett, "Elections and Democracy in Nigeria," p. 89.

22. *Facts on File* 53:2741 (June 10, 1993), p. 438.

23. *Facts on File* 53:2742 (June 17, 1993), p. 452.

24. *Facts on File* 53:2743 (June 24, 1993), p. 478.

25. *Facts on File* 53:2744 (July 1, 1993), p. 495.

26. Ibid.

27. *Facts on File* 53:2753 (September 2, 1993), p. 658.

28. *Facts on File* 53:2765 (November 25, 1993), p. 887.

29. Rubin and Weinstein, *Introduction to African Politics*, p. 254.

30. Ibid., p. 54.

31. A good background of the Nigerian civil war can be found in Sir Rex Niven, *The War of Nigerian Unity* (Totowa, N.J.: Rowman and Littlefield, 1970).

32. Rubin and Weinstein, *Introduction to African Politics*, pp. 170–171.

33. Tordoff, *Government and Politics in Africa*, p. 1.

34. This paragraph is based upon a much longer section in Tordoff, *Government and Politics in Africa*, pp. 1–3.

35. Fred Hayward, "Introduction," in Hayward, *Elections in Independent Africa*, p. 1.

36. Ibid.

37. *Global Studies: Africa* (Guilford, Conn.: Dushkin Publishing, 1991), p. 17.

38. A very good general discussion of African politics can be found in Rubin and Weinstein, *Introduction to African Politics.*

39. *Facts on File* 53:2768 (December 16, 1993), p. 941.

40. *Global Studies: Africa,* p. 107.

41. Ibid.

42. *Facts on File* 53:2721 (January 21, 1993), p. 39.

43. *Facts on File* 53:2730 (March 25, 1993), p. 219.

44. A discussion of Nigeria's early political structures and the "export model" of Westminster government that came to Nigeria can be found in Bretton, *Power and Stability in Nigeria,* p. 19.

45. See, for discussion of this theme, Tordoff, *Government and Politics in Africa,* pp. 157–160, 165; and Graf, *The Nigerian State,* pp. 41–52 and 149–173.

46. Eleazu, *Federalism and Nation-Building,* pp. 5–7.

47. Tordoff, *Government and Politics in Africa,* pp. 166–167.

48. Beckett, "Elections and Democracy in Nigeria," pp. 89–90.

49. Eleazu, *Federalism and Nation-Building,* p. 7.

50. There is substantial discussion of all of these functions, and others, in Tordoff, *Government and Politics in Africa,* pp. 91–120. See also chapters on Tanzania, Kenya, and Zaire in Hayward, *Elections in Independent Africa.*

51. Beckett, "Elections and Democracy in Nigeria," pp. 94–98.

52. For a discussion of early political parties in Nigeria, prior to 1962, see Awa, *Federal Government in Nigeria.*

53. See Oyeleye Oyediran, "Political Parties: Formation and Candidate Selection," pp. 43–66 in Oyeleye Oyediran, ed., *The Nigerian 1979 Elections* (Lagos: Macmillan Nigeria, 1981). See also Henry Bienen, *Political Conflict and Economic Change in Nigeria* (London: Frank Cass, 1985), pp. 133–180, for further discussion of the 1979 Nigerian elections.

54. Discussion of political parties in the 1979 election can be found in Ladun Anise, "Political Parties and Election Manifestoes," in Oyediran, *The Nigerian 1979 Elections,* pp. 67–92.

55. Harry Goulbourne, "Conclusion: The Future of Democracy in Africa," pp. 229–242 in Robin Cohen and Harry Goulbourne, eds., *Democracy and Socialism in Africa* (Boulder, Colo.: Westview Press, 1991).

Index

A

Act of Settlement (1701), and British Constitution, 26, 183
Act of Union with Ireland (1800, British), 183
Act of Union with Scotland (1707, British), 183
Administration, public, 118–19
  decisions as source of law, 132
  structures, Japan, 268–69
Africa:
  colonialism, 357–59
  crisis of penetration, 18
  political patterns, 356–60
Age, and candidacy in elections, 151
Agents of political socialization, 163–65
Aggregate level data, 9
Agriculture, as a problem of development, 63
Akihito, Emperor, 263
Algeria, Revolution in (1958), 210–11
Almond, Gabriel:
  constitutions, 35
  political culture, 14–15
  political socialization, 164
  structural-functionalism, 14
Amendment clause of constitution, 29, 131
American Revolution, and ideology, 36, 174
Analysis, levels of, 9

Analytic political systems, 11–12
Anarchism, 39
Andropov, Yuri:
  Marxism, 314
  Soviet succession, 321–23
Anglo-American law, 129
Aquinas, Thomas, and idea of law, 127
Arafat, Yassir, 175
Argentina:
  federal government, 31
  judicial review in, 136
Aristotle:
  constitutions, 40–41
  definition of politics, 1
  political culture, 15
  political socialization, 162
Armenia, in Soviet Union, 311
Article 16, French Constitution, 215
Asia:
  decentralization, 55
  economic resources, 49
Asian Cooperation, and economic nationalism, 53
Australia:
  bicameralism, 74
  court structures in, 134
  electoral system of, 150
  executive titles in, 105
  federal government, 31
  judicial review in, 136

M

N